# THE
# ENGLISH POEMS OF
# JOHN MILTON

*From the edition of*
### H. C. BEECHING

*Together with an Introduction by*
### CHARLES WILLIAMS
*and*
*A Reader's Guide to Milton*
*compiled by*
### WALTER SKEAT, M.A.

GEOFFREY CUMBERLEGE
OXFORD UNIVERSITY PRESS
LONDON NEW YORK TORONTO

## JOHN MILTON

Born, Bread Street, London    9 December 1608
Died, Bunhill Fields, London    10 November 1674

*This edition of the English Poems of John Milton
was first published in* The World's Classics *in* 1913
*and reprinted in* 1921, 1923, 1926, 1929, 1932 *and*
1936. *In* 1940 *a new edition was published with an
Introduction by Charles Williams and 'A Reader's
Guide to Milton', compiled by Walter Skeat;
reprinted in* 1942, *entirely reset in* 1946, *and
reprinted in* 1948.

PRINTED IN GREAT BRITAIN

# CONTENTS

MISCELLANEOUS POEMS—*continued*

# INTRODUCTION

WE have been fortunate enough to live at a time when the reputation of John Milton has been seriously attacked. The result of this attack, which has come from various sources otherwise not noticeably sympathetic with each other, has been to distract the orthodox defenders of Milton, and to compel the reconsideration everywhere of his power as a poet. This reconsideration of poetic glory has now reached everyone but Shakespeare—and, it seems, the metaphysicals and W. B. Yeats. All these, it is true, are united by one general tendency—the tendency to suggest, by one means or another, 'the feeling intellect' of which Wordsworth spoke. It has been because of his supposed lack of that intellect that Milton has been chiefly repudiated. He has been supposed to be a heavy and, if resounding, yet, one might say, a comatose poet. He has been called, personally, a bad man. Mr. Middleton Murry has said so in so many words: 'On the moral and spiritual side I find it easy enough to place him; he is, simply, a bad man of a very particular kind.' But Mr. Murry went on to profess himself puzzled: 'The difficulty is . . . that a poet so evidently great in some valid sense of the word, should have so little intimate meaning for us. We cannot make him real. He does not, either in his great effects or his little ones, trouble our depths.'[1]

The success of such an attack—I do not suggest that that particular demonstration was confined to Mr. Murry; I quote him because those sentences form a convenient and compact epigram of the Opposition—lay chiefly in two things: (i) the lack of power in the orthodox party; (ii) the chance that Mr. Eliot had, about the same time, defined certain weaknesses in Milton. The orthodox Chairs of Literature, it must be admitted, had for long professed the traditional view of an august, solemn, proud, and (on the whole) unintelligent and uninteresting Milton. Professor Oliver Elton had already committed

---

[1] *Studies in Keats*, second edition.

himself to the hint that Milton's subject could not concern us. 'What is made of the central myth? Does it in Milton's hands embody some enduring truth that speaks to the imagination? I doubt it.'[1] The great academic teachers confined themselves to analyses of his diction and his rhythm. Remote from us (they, in fact, declared) was his pre-empted Eden; the pride of his Satan was his own pride, and he approved it. They argued over his Arianism or his Calvinism. They confined his instrument to the organ. They denied him cheerfulness and laughter (he who, it is said, used to sing while he had the gout!). They gloomed over him, as (they supposed) he, in his arrogant self-respect, gloomed over the world.

In the midst of this monotonous and uncritical praise, there emerged the calm voice of Mr. Eliot commenting on their subject—already admitted by them to be, to all intents and purposes, poetically alien from us. The present writer, disagreeing firmly with the effect of Mr. Eliot and indeed with some of Mr. Eliot, may admit his gratitude to Mr. Eliot for one or two critical statements. But 'the corrupt following' of Mr. Eliot went to lengths which Mr. Eliot (so far as I know) never suggested. Some writer—I have forgotten whom and I certainly will not look him up—said that Mr. Eliot had 'destroyed Milton in a parenthesis'. In fact, it might be permissible to say that no critic of Milton ought to be uninformed of Mr. Eliot's article, 'A Note on the Verse of John Milton'.[2] I shall not discuss it here, because, frankly, I wish to discuss Milton; it is why other distinguished critics must also be ignored.

The general opposition resolved itself into four statements: (i) that Milton was a bad man; (ii) that Milton was, especially, a proud man and was continually writing approvingly about his own pride (Blake's incorrect epigram—that Milton 'was of the devil's party without knowing it'—was generally used here); (iii) that Milton's verse is hard, sonorous, and insensitive; (iv) that Milton's subject was remote and uninteresting. This being almost exactly what the orthodox party had been, for centuries, saying with admiration, they were quite helpless when

---

[1] *The English Muse.*          [2] *Essays and Studies,* 1937.

they found it said with contempt. The solemn rituals in praise of Milton were suddenly profaned by a change of accent, but the choruses had not altered; what then were the pious worshippers to do?

There had been, of course, another possibility all along; it may be put very briefly by saying that Milton was not a fool. The peculiar ignorance of Christian doctrine which distinguished most of the academic Chairs and of the unacademic journalists who had been hymning Milton had not prevented them from arguing about the subtle theological point of the Nature of the Divine Son in *Paradise Lost*. The peculiar opposition to high speculations on the nature of chastity felt in both academic and unacademic circles had prevented any serious appreciation of that great miracle of the transmutation of the flesh proposed in *Comus*. And the peculiar ignorance of morals also felt everywhere had enabled both circles to assume that Milton might be proud and that yet he might not at the same time believe that pride was wrong and foolish. It was never thought that, if he sinned, he might repent, and that his repentance might be written as high in his poetry as, after another manner, Dante's in his. Finally, it was not supposed, in either of those circles, that Satan could be supposed to be Satan, and therefore a tempter; that Christ (in *Paradise Regained*) could be supposed to hold human culture a poor thing in comparison with the salvation of the soul; or that Samson, in the last great poem, could in fact reach a point of humility at which he could bring himself occasionally to protest like Job against the apparent dealings of God with the soul.

I have said nothing here against the explicit denial to Milton of any drama or of any humanity. Those denials, as well as the others, had been consecrated by custom and a false *pietas*. Yet there was no need for them. The great and sensitive poetry of that august genius had escaped his admirers. 'Milton', said Landor, 'wrote English like a learned language'; no one had thought it worth while to learn it as a living language. All *Paradise Lost* was supposed to be an image of pride; and yet much of *Paradise Lost* can be felt to revolve, laughingly and harmoniously, round the solemn and helpless image of pride. To discuss this in full would need a volume. All that can be done here is to dwell on a few chief points in the discussion of *Paradise Lost*, with one or two comments on the other poems. And we may begin with *Comus*.

*Comus* is a kind of philosophical ballet. Comus himself is, no doubt, a black enchanter, but he talks the most beautiful poetry, and he does not seriously interrupt the dance of the three young creatures opposed to him, with their heavenly attendant: there is a particular evasion of violence (when Comus is 'driven in'). But what is this ritual ballet about? It is about an attempted outrage on a Mystery. The mystery which Comus desires to profane is the Mystery of Chastity. It is no use trying to deal with *Comus* and omitting chastity; *Hamlet* without the Prince would be an exciting melodrama compared to the result of that other eviction. Chastity (not only, though perhaps chiefly, that particular form of it which is Virginity; it will be observed that Sabrina, the chaste goddess, is particularly favourable to herds and shepherd life) is the means, in *Comus*, by which all evils are defeated, the flesh is transmuted, and a very high and particular Joy ensured. It may be true that we ourselves do not believe that to be so, but our disbelief is largely as habitual as our admiration of *Comus*. That is why it has been possible to admire *Comus* without any serious realization of the mystery of chastity, in spite of John Milton.

> To him that dares
> Arm his profane tongue with contemptuous words
> Against the Sun-clad power of Chastity,
> Fain would I something say, yet to what end? . . .

And that, as one may say, is that. Comus is a fool in these matters, and

> worthy that thou should'st not know
> More happiness than is thy present lot.

But the Lady and her brothers and the Attendant Spirit and Sabrina do know. They know that Chastity is the guardian and protector of fruitfulness, that Temperance is the means of intense Joy. In their eyes Comus, by refusing to admit the general principle of things and to be obedient to it, is foolishly and sinfully limiting the nature of Joy. He prefers drunkenness to the taste of wine and promiscuousness to sensitiveness. He knows nothing about that other power which can make the flesh itself immortal; he prefers to sit about in sepulchres. Let him, cries the whole lovely dance.

Obedience then and Joy are the knowledge, in their degree, of those three Youths of *Comus*. And *Paradise Lost*, following long after, did not forget its prelude. It dealt with the same subject, but differently. Obedience, in the longer poem, is no longer that of a particular devotion to a particular law; it is the proper order of the universe in relation to a universal law, the law of self-abnegation in love. This, like chastity, is a mystery, but a mystery so simple that only the two sublimely innocent figures of Adam and Eve—beautiful, august, pure, and lucid—are able to express it; they, and the glowing fires of the celestial hierarchy; they, and beyond them the passionate deity of the Divine Son. It is not only a law—something that ought to be obeyed—but a fact—something that obeys and is obeyed. There remains, nevertheless, the possibility of disobedience to the law, of revolt against the fact. That disobedience depends on choice; and it is that choice on which the poem concentrates.

*Comus* had not gone so far. There is challenge there but no analysis of choice. Indeed, that is a problem which has been very rarely attacked in English verse. Generally the poets have confined themselves, sooner or later, to showing the decision; and certainly the actual motion of the will in its pure essence is inconceivable by the human imagination. Even Shakespeare, in *Macbeth*, when he reached that point, disguised it; Macbeth is half-determined; he asks if he will be safe; and when he is assured of safety he finds that he is wholly determined. But the actual decision is not there. Twice in *Paradise Lost* Milton attempted that problem: the first effort is contracted into Satan's speech on Niphates (iv. 32–113); the second is expanded into Eve's temptation, which begins with her dream (v. 8–135) and ends with the sensual degradation of her and Adam, so that the two of them, in another sense than *Comus* had foreseen, are 'lingering and sitting by a new-made grave'. Her temptation certainly is greater than that of her younger sister, the Lady, though it depends on the same method of flattery. To be praised and lured aside by such lines as 'love-darting eyes or tresses like the morn' is well enough; but Eve needs a lordlier and more subtle, even a more metaphysical, attraction:

> Wonder not, sovran Mistress, if perchance
> Thou canst, who art sole Wonder.

This flattery is, however, of the same kind as Satan has previously, one may say, offered to himself; and, in a lesser degree, to the angels whom he persuades to follow him, in that speech (v. 769–799) which is the nearest thing in English poetry to Antony's speech in *Julius Caesar*, though Milton's lines are perhaps even more highly wrought, as they had to be, the speech being shorter. Every word echoes another; each accent is calculated— 'magnific titles . . . merely titular', and so on. The aim in all three instances is the same; it is the awakening, in Satan, in Eve, in the angels, of a sense of proper dignity, of self-admiration, of rights withheld, of injured merit. This, it is asserted, Milton himself felt about himself. Perhaps; but if he did, then he certainly also thought it foolish and wrong. We need not fall back on any exterior evidence for that nor on any exposition of Christian morals; the evidence is in the poem itself. Satan thinks himself impaired, and what is the result? 'deep malice thence conceiving and disdain'. He is full of injured merit; what is the result? 'high disdain'. He is the full example of the self-loving spirit, and his effort throughout the poem is to lure everyone, Eve, Adam, the angels, into that same state of self-love. His description of himself in the first two books is truthful enough—

> that fixt mind
> And high disdain from sense of injured merit
> That with the mightiest raised me to contend. . . .

But it is also ironical. Certainly Satan has this sense; only this sense has landed him in hell—and in inaccuracy.

Hell is always inaccurate. He goes on to say of the Omnipotence that he and his followers 'shook his throne': it is only afterwards that we discover that this is entirely untrue. Milton knew as well as we do that Omnipotence cannot be shaken; therefore the drama lies not in that foolish effort but in the terror of the obstinacy that provoked it, and in the result; not in the fight but in the fall. The irrepressible laughter of heaven at the solemn antics of 'injured merit', of the 'self impair'd', breaks out. Love laughs at anti-love.

> 'Nearly it now concerns us to be sure
> Of our Omnipotence' . . .
> To whom the Son, with calm aspect and clear
> Lightning divine, ineffable, serene,
> Made answer: 'Mighty Father, thou thy foes
> Justly hast in derision.'

In fact, the rebel angels only get as far through heaven as they do because God precisely suspends their real impairment—

> What sin hath impaired, which yet hath wrought
> Insensibly, for I suspend their doom.

So much for Milton's approval of the self-loving spirit. He thought pride, egotism, and a proper sense of one's own rights the greatest of all temptations; he was, no doubt, like most people, subject to it. And he thought it led straight to inaccuracy and malice, and finally to idiocy and hell. Milton may sometimes have liked to think of himself as proud, but it is extraordinarily unlikely that he liked to think of himself as malicious and idiotic. Yet it is those two qualities he attributes to Satan as a result of his energy of self-love. When Satan sees Eve:

> Her graceful Innocence, her every air
> Of gesture or least action overawed
> His malice . . .
> That space the Evil one abstracted stood
> From his own evil, and for the time remained
> Stupidly good.

It is not, however, Eve alone who is the image of some state of being opposite to Satan's. It is all the rest of the poem, but especially it is the Divine Son. Precisely as the mark of Satan and the rebel angels is that they will not consent to be derived from anyone else; he will have it that he was like Topsy and grew by himself; so the mark of the Son, of the angels, of Adam, of Eve, is that they derive, and take delight in deriving, from someone else. Their joy is in that derivation-in-love. The Divine Son carries it into the highest state—

> this I my glory account,
> My exaltation and my whole delight,
> That thou in me well pleased declar'st thy will
> Fulfilled, which to fulfil is all my bliss.

So Eve, in a state of passionate and pure love, to Adam:

> My author and disposer, what thou bid'st
> Unargued I obey.

Milton had his own views on the relation between the sexes, which (like almost any other views of the relation between the sexes) were probably wrong. But this last quotation does not spring from that only; it springs from the essential fact of things; which is everywhere this derivation-in-love. The Son is the Image of that, as Satan is the Image of personal clamour for personal independence. The casting-out of the rebel angels from heaven is the result of the conflict between the two Images—in so far as there can be any conflict between the state which is in utter union with Omnipotence and the state which is only in union with itself—if that, and the Niphates speech suggests that it is not even that. The obstinate figure of Satan does but throw up the intertwined beauty and lightness of the universe beyond him, the universe (and more than the universe) which understands, enjoys, and maintains, its continuous derivation, lordship, and obedience.

In this sense, therefore, the poem is concerned with a contrast and a conflict between two states of being. But those states are not only mythological; they are human and contemporary, and thus the poem has a great deal of interest for us. The overthrow of the rebel angels is the overthrow, spiritually, of all in whom that deriving and nourishing Love is dead. The very blaze of eyes from the chariot in which the Divine Son rides is the spectacle of a living and stupendous universe rolling on the 'exhausted' rebels. There needs no battle; the exposition of the Divine Nature is enough.

> Sole Victor, from the expulsion of his foes,
> Messias his triumphal chariot turned.

It is we who are involved, one way or the other: it is not only to Adam that the Archangel's word is addressed— 'Remember, and fear to transgress'.[1]

*Paradise Lost* then is chiefly concerned with the choice between these two states of being, with the temptations which provoke men and women to that sense of 'injured merit', as Eve and Satan are provoked, and with the terrible result of indulging that sense. It is true that John Milton was not a man for compromise. When Adam, in the fullness of his passion for Eve, really does abandon heaven and his knowledge of God for her, Milton denounced his act. But it was, after all, Milton who imagined his passion so intensely as to make us almost wish that it could be approved. There and elsewhere *Paradise Lost* is full of the senses—even Shakespeare hardly made the human hand more moving. This would perhaps be more obvious if we were more attentive to the tenderness of some of the verse. It is no doubt as a result of the long tradition of the organ-music of Milton that the shyness of some of his verse passes unnoticed. The famous prayer to 'justify the ways of God to man' is a prayer of humility. This is seen by considering the lines that lead up to it. Milton, invoking the Holy Spirit, says:

> Thou from the first
> Wast present, and with mighty wings outspread
> Dovelike sat'st brooding on the vast abyss,
> And mad'st it pregnant: what in me is dark
> Illumine . . . .

And so on. Now the point is that 'Dovelike' and 'pregnant' are words which cannot be sonorous and tre-

---

[1] 'The self-loving man', wrote Pascal about the same time as Milton wrote *Paradise Lost*, 'conceives a mortal enmity against that truth which reproves him. . . . He would annihilate it, but, unable to destroy it in its essence, he destroys it as far as possible in his own knowledge and in that of others.'—'Warring in heaven against heaven's *matchless* king'; *matchless* is the whole point.

mendous; it would make nonsense of them emotionally. The passage is daring in its hope, but shyly and modestly daring, palpitating with its own wonder at its own audacity. Milton may have been proud on earth (and repented of it), but he was not proud in his approach to heaven.

There is another word, at the other end of the poem, which is another example of a certain misreading. The renewed and repentant passion of Eve for Adam expresses itself.

> In me is no delay; with thee to go
> Is to stay here, without thee here to stay
> Is to go hence unwilling; thou to me
> Art all things under heaven, all places thou,
> Who for my wilful crime art banished hence.

This again is derivation (she from him and he from her), and the knowledge of derivation. After which outbreak of human love, the lines sink again into a shy softness of hope.

> This further consolation yet secure
> I carry hence; though all by me is lost,
> Such favour I unworthy am vouchsafed,
> By me the promised Seed shall all restore.

'The promised Seed' is, of course, Christ. But Milton did not choose to use any such august title. He preferred, there, the word Seed, and the literal meaning is not to be forgotten in the metaphorical. The metaphorical refers back to the glorious, devoted, self-abandoned figure—glorious because self-abandoned—which has again and again been deliberately contrasted with Satan throughout the poem; I need name only the pause in heaven and the pause in hell (ii. 417–29; iii. 217–26), the two progresses through Chaos (ii. 871–1033; vii. 192–221; and the Chaos is not only exterior; it is also the interior chaos of the human soul); and, of course, the conflict in heaven. But the literal meaning of 'Seed' is of the new, tiny, important thing, the actuality of the promise, the almost invisible activity upon which all depends. So small, so intimate, so definite, is the word that the line becomes breathless with it and with the hope of it. That breathless audacity of purpose towards the beginning of the poem is answered

by a breathless audacity of expectation towards the end.
And at the very end humanity has its turn in the hand
again, the hand which has meant so much at certain
crises of the poem: at the separation, as if symbolically,
of a derived love from its source—

> So saying, from her husband's hand her hand
> Soft she withdrew;

and in the sin (the derived love working against its human
and Divine sources):

> So saying, her rash hand in evil hour
> Forth reaching to the fruit, she plucked, she ate;

and so now in the rejoined union of that penitence and
humility which Milton knew so well:

> They hand in hand with wandering steps and slow
> Through Eden took their solitary way.

There are no linked lovers in our streets who are not more
beautiful and more unfortunate because of those last
lines; no reunion, of such a kind, which is not more sad
and more full of hope. And then it is said that Milton
is inhuman. The whole of our visibility, metaphysical,
psychological, actual, has been increased by him.

It is the word 'solitary', however, which looks forward to the last two poems—to *Paradise Regained* and
to *Samson*. The first is completely different from *Paradise
Lost*. The verse is, on the whole, less infinitely sensitive
than that of the earlier poem; it is already changing to
something else. There are few personages; in the earlier
there had been many. They are brooding rather than
active. And whereas in *Paradise Lost* everything had
been exposed from the beginning, now the chief thing is
hidden. The centre had previously been a spectacle;
now it is a secret. The Blessed Virgin is in a state of
expectation:

> his absence now
> Thus long to some great purpose he observes.

Christ himself waits:

> to what intent
> I learn not yet, perhaps I need not know.
> For what concerns my knowledge God reveals

The urgency is in Satan, but even he is here haunted by the unknown: 'who this is we must learn.'

It is the discovery of this nature, which Satan does not know, and which Christ only half-knows, that is the theme of the poem. Christ's answers to Satan's efforts to find out are, in a sense, riddles, for they are given half in his own terms and half in Satan's. Food; glory; kingdoms; earthly wisdom—these are the temptations; through all of them, in Milton's phrase,

> the Son of God
> Went on and stayed not.

He goes on—or in ('into himself descended'). It is precisely into his Nature that the argument plunges to seek its discovery, but the moral trials are hardly enough; at the end Milton used something else. He came to the mysterious 'standing'; moral temptation is lost in what lies behind it. 'Stand or cast thyself down': be whatever you are. But the answer is still a riddle; it has precisely the lightness, almost the happiness, certainly the heavenly mockery which is always the answer to the hellish sneer. Satan is as hopelessly foolish as ever, and Jesus speaks to him, in the technique of this poem, as the Divine Son had spoken of him to the Father in the *Paradise Lost*:

> To whom the Son with calm aspect and clear
> Lightning divine, ineffable, serene,
> Made answer.

> To whom thus Jesus: Also it is written
> Tempt not the Lord thy God; he said and stood.
> But Satan, smitten with amazement, fell.

He and his had been in the same case before—

> They astonished all resistance lost,
> All courage; down their idle weapons dropped . . .
> Exhausted, spiritless, afflicted, fallen.

'So, strook with dread and anguish, fell the Fiend.' Heaven is always unexpected to the self-loving spirit; he can never understand whence it derives, for he has himself renounced all derivation, as do those who follow him. It was this great and fundamental fact of human existence which Milton very well understood; it was this which his genius exerted all his tenderness and all his sublimity to express; it was this which is the cause of the continual laughter of *Paradise Lost*, and it was because of this that Milton invoked that Spirit which Itself derives from the co-equal Two.

It is not possible in the remaining space to discuss *Samson*. The verse again has changed, and I doubt if we have yet properly learnt its style. 'A little onward lend thy guiding hand'—to what? To the 'acquist Of true experience from this great event'. What then is our true experience from the poem? Much every way; perhaps not the least is the sense of the union of Necessity and Freewill. That had been discussed in *Paradise Lost*, as an accompaniment to the spectacle and analysis of man choosing. But there the actual stress had been a little on the choice; here it is a little on 'dire Necessity'. Here 'the cherub Contemplation' is allowed even fuller view. The persons, if they do not exactly accuse God, at least indicate to God the unanswered questions. There is no humility in refraining from asking the questions; the humility consists in believing that there may be an answer. Both asking and believing are desirable, and both are here. In the earlier poems the sense of a full comprehension had been chiefly felt in the Figure of the Divine Son —and therefore either in heaven or (if among men) then prophesied for the future. But in *Samson* there is more than a hint that the great satisfaction of all distresses is already there. It is perhaps not by a poetic accident that here and there in the poem Milton wrote like Shakespeare; in other places, like himself with a new song. The modest and appealing courage of the opening of *Paradise Lost*—'and justify the ways of God to man'— becomes an angelic beauty of victory—

> Just are the ways of God,
> And justifiable to men,
> Unless there be who think not God at all.
> If any be, they walk obscure,
> For of such doctrine never was there school
> But the heart of the fool,
> And no man therein doctor but himself.

That is precisely Satan—and men and women. But 'Nothing is here for tears' is here no Stoic maxim, but something beyond—something 'comely and reviving'.

The phrase would cover most of Milton. So far from being granite, his verse is a continual spring of beauty, of goodness, of tenderness, of humility. The one thing he always denounced as sin and (equally) as folly was the self-closed 'independent' spirit, the spirit that thinks itself of 'merit', especially 'of injured merit'. It does not seem a moral entirely without relevance to us. All things derive in love—and beyond all things, in the only self-adequate Existence, there is the root of that fact, as of all. It is known in God; the Father speaks—

> and on his Son with rays direct
> Shone full; he all his Father manifest
> Ineffably into his face received,
> And thus the Filial Godhead answering spake.

'Filial . . . answering.' Milton has been too long deprived of half his genius. He did his best to make clear what he was saying. But then, as his admirer John Dryden wrote:

> Dim as the borrowed beams of moon and stars
> To lonely, weary, wandering travellers
> Is Reason to the soul.

> CHARLES WILLIAMS.

# MISCELLANEOUS POEMS

## ON THE MORNING OF CHRIST'S NATIVITY

*Composed* 1629

### I

This is the month, and this the happy morn,
Wherein the Son of Heaven's eternal King,
Of wedded Maid and Virgin Mother born,
Our great redemption from above did bring;
For so the holy sages once did sing,
　　That He our deadly forfeit should release,
And with His Father work us a perpetual peace.

### II

That glorious Form, that Light unsufferable,
And that far-beaming blaze of Majesty,
Wherewith He wont at Heaven's high council-table　　10
To sit the midst of Trinal Unity,
He laid aside; and here with us to be
　　Forsook the courts of everlasting day,
And chose with us a darksome house of mortal clay.

### III

Say, Heavenly Muse, shall not thy sacred vein
Afford a present to the Infant God?
Hast thou no verse, no hymn, or solemn strain,
To welcome Him to this His new abode,
Now while the Heaven, by the Sun's team untrod,　　20
　　Hath took no print of the approaching light,
And all the spangled host keep watch in squadrons
　　bright?

### IV

See how from far upon the eastern road
The star-led wizards haste with odours sweet!
O run, prevent them with thy humble ode,
And lay it lowly at His blessed feet;
Have thou the honour first thy Lord to greet,
    And join thy voice unto the angel quire,
From out His secret altar touched with hallowed fire.

### THE HYMN

#### I

It was the winter wild,
While the Heaven-born Child                                  30
    All meanly wrapt in the rude manger lies;
Nature in awe to Him
Had doffed her gaudy trim,
    With her great Master so to sympathize:
It was no season then for her
To wanton with the sun her lusty paramour.

#### II

Only with speeches fair
She woos the gentle air
    To hide her guilty front with innocent snow,
And on her naked shame,                                      40
Pollute with sinful blame,
    The saintly veil of maiden white to throw,
Confounded, that her Maker's eyes
Should look so near upon her foul deformities.

#### III

But He, her fears to cease,
Sent down the meek-eyed Peace;
    She crowned with olive green came softly sliding
Down through the turning sphere,
His ready harbinger,
    With turtle wing the amorous clouds dividing,         50
And waving wide her myrtle wand,
She strikes a universal peace through sea and land.

IV

No war or battle's sound
Was heard the world around,
　　The idle spear and shield were high up-hung:
The hooked chariot stood
Unstained with hostile blood,
　　The trumpet spake not to the armed throng,
And kings sat still with awful eye,
As if they surely knew their sovran Lord was by.　　60


V

But peaceful was the night
Wherein the Prince of Light
　　His reign of peace upon the earth began:
The winds with wonder whist,
Smoothly the waters kissed,
　　Whispering new joys to the mild Ocean,
Who now hath quite forgot to rave,
While birds of calm sit brooding on the charmed wave.


VI

The stars with deep amaze
Stand fixed in steadfast gaze,　　　　　　　70
　　Bending one way their precious influence,
And will not take their flight,
For all the morning light,
　　Or Lucifer that often warned them thence;
But in their glimmering orbs did glow,
Until their Lord Himself bespake, and bid them go.


VII

And though the shady gloom
Had given day her room,
　　The sun himself withheld his wonted speed,
And hid his head for shame,　　　　　　80
As his inferior flame
　　The new-enlightened world no more should need;
He saw a greater Sun appear
Than his bright throne or burning axle-tree could bear.

### VIII

The shepherds on the lawn,
Or ere the point of dawn,
  Sat simply chatting in a rustic row;
Full little thought they then
That the mighty Pan
  Was kindly come to live with them below;          90
Perhaps their loves or else their sheep,
Was all that did their silly thoughts so busy keep.

### IX

When such music sweet
Their hearts and ears did greet,
  As never was by mortal finger strook,
Divinely warbled voice
Answering the stringed noise,
  As all their souls in blissful rapture took:
The air such pleasure loth to lose,
With thousand echoes still prolongs each heavenly
    close.          100

### X

Nature that heard such sound
Beneath the hollow round
  Of Cynthia's seat, the airy region thrilling,
Now was almost won
To think her part was done,
  And that her reign had here its last fulfilling;
She knew such harmony alone
Could hold all Heaven and Earth in happier union.

### XI

At last surrounds their sight
A globe of circular light,          110
  That with long beams the shame-faced night arrayed,
The helmed cherubim
And sworded seraphim
  Are seen in glittering ranks with wings displayed,
Harping in loud and solemn quire,
With unexpressive notes to Heaven's new-born Heir.

### XII

Such music (as 'tis said)
Before was never made,
  But when of old the sons of morning sung,
While the Creator great          120
His constellations set,
  And the well-balanced world on hinges hung,
And cast the dark foundations deep,
And bid the welt'ring waves their oozy channel keep.

### XIII

Ring out, ye crystal spheres,
Once bless our human ears
  (If ye have power to touch our senses so),
And let your silver chime
Move in melodious time,
  And let the base of Heaven's deep organ blow;     130
And with your ninefold harmony
Make up full consort to th' angelic symphony.

### XIV

For if such holy song
Enwrap our fancy long,
  Time will run back and fetch the age of gold,
And speckled vanity
Will sicken soon, and die,
  And lep'rous sin will melt from earthly mould,
And Hell itself will pass away          139
And leave her dolorous mansions to the peering day.

### XV

Yea, Truth and Justice then
Will down return to men,
  Orbed in a rainbow; and, like glories wearing,
Mercy will sit between,
Throned in celestial sheen,
  With radiant feet the tissued clouds down-steering,
And Heaven, as at some festival,
Will open wide the gates of her high palace-hall.

### XVI

But wisest Fate says No,
This must not yet be so,                                    150
   The Babe lies yet in smiling infancy,
That on the bitter cross
Must redeem our loss,
   So both Himself and us to glorify:
Yet first to those ychained in sleep,
The wakeful trump of doom must thunder through the
   deep,

### XVII

With such a horrid clang
As on Mount Sinai rang,
   While the red fire and smould'ring clouds out-brake:
The aged Earth aghast                                      160
With terror of that blast
   Shall from the surface to the centre shake;
When at the world's last session,
The dreadful Judge in middle air shall spread His
   throne.

### XVIII

And then at last our bliss
Full and perfect is,
   But now begins; for from this happy day
Th' old Dragon under-ground
In straiter limits bound,
   Not half so far casts his usurped sway,                170
And, wroth to see his kingdom fail,
Swinges the scaly horror of his folded tail.

### XIX

The oracles are dumb,
No voice or hideous hum
   Runs through the arched roof in words deceiving.
Apollo from his shrine
Can no more divine,
   With hollow shriek the steep of Delphos leaving.
No nightly trance or breathed spell                        179
Inspires the pale-eyed priest from the prophetic cell.

### XX

The lonely mountains o'er,
And the resounding shore,
   A voice of weeping heard, and loud lament;
From haunted spring and dale,
Edged with poplar pale,
   The parting Genius is with sighing sent,
With flower-inwoven tresses torn
The nymphs in twilight shade of tangled thickets mourn.

### XXI

In consecrated earth,
And on the holy hearth,       190
   The Lars and Lemures moan with midnight plaint;
In urns and altars round,
A drear and dying sound
   Affrights the Flamens at their service quaint;
And the chill marble seems to sweat,
While each peculiar power forgoes his wonted seat.

### XXII

Peor and Baalim
Forsake their temples dim,
   With that twice-battered god of Palestine;
And mooned Ashtaroth,       200
Heaven's queen and mother both,
   Now sits not girt with tapers' holy shrine;
The Libyc Hammon shrinks his horn,
In vain the Tyrian maids their wounded Thammuz mourn.

### XXIII

And sullen Moloch fled,
Hath left in shadows dread
   His burning idol all of blackest hue;
In vain with cymbals' ring
They call the grisly king,
   In dismal dance about the furnace blue;    210
The brutish gods of Nile as fast,
Isis and Orus, and the dog Anubis, haste.

### XXIV

Nor is Osiris seen
In Memphian grove or green,
   Trampling the unshowered grass with lowings loud:
Nor can he be at rest
Within his sacred chest,
   Nought but profoundest Hell can be his shroud,
In vain with timbrelled anthems dark
The sable-stoled sorcerers bear his worshipped ark.     220

### XXV

He feels from Juda's land
The dreaded Infant's hand,
   The rays of Bethlehem blind his dusky eyn;
Nor all the gods beside,
Longer dare abide,
   Not Typhon huge ending in snaky twine:
Our Babe, to show His Godhead true,
Can in His swaddling bands control the damned crew.

### XXVI

So when the sun in bed,
Curtained with cloudy red,                               230
   Pillows his chin upon an orient wave,
The flocking shadows pale
Troop to th' infernal jail,
   Each fettered ghost slips to his several grave,
And the yellow-skirted fays
Fly after the night-steeds, leaving their moon-loved maze.

### XXVII

But see, the Virgin blest
Hath laid her Babe to rest:
   Time is our tedious song should here have ending,
Heaven's youngest teemed star,                          240
Hath fixed her polished car,
   Her sleeping Lord with handmaid lamp attending:
And all about the courtly stable,
Bright-harnessed angels sit in order serviceable.

## A PARAPHRASE ON PSALM CXIV

*This and the following Psalm were done by the
Author at fifteen years old*

WHEN the blest seed of Terah's faithful son,
After long toil their liberty had won,
And passed from Pharian fields to Canaan land,
Led by the strength of the Almighty's hand,
Jehovah's wonders were in Israel shown,
His praise and glory was in Israel known.
That saw the troubled sea, and shivering fled,
And sought to hide his froth-becurled head
Low in the earth; Jordan's clear streams recoil,
As a faint host that hath received the foil.          10
The high, huge-bellied mountains skip like rams
Amongst their ewes, the little hills like lambs.
Why fled the ocean? And why skipped the mountains?
Why turned Jordan toward his crystal fountains?
Shake earth, and at the presence be aghast
Of Him that ever was, and ay shall last,
That glassy floods from rugged rocks can crush,
And make soft rills from fiery flint-stones gush.


## PSALM CXXXVI

LET us with a gladsome mind
Praise the Lord, for He is kind,
   For His mercies ay endure,
   Ever faithful, ever sure.

Let us blaze His name abroad,
For of gods He is the God;
   For, &c.

O let us His praises tell,
Who doth the wrathful tyrants quell;          10
   For, &c.

Who with His miracles doth make
Amazed Heaven and Earth to shake;
   For, &c.

Who by His wisdom did create
The painted Heavens so full of state;
   For, &c.           20

Who did the solid Earth ordain
To rise above the watery plain;
   For, &c.

Who by His all-commanding might
Did fill the new-made world with light;
   For, &c.

And caused the golden-tressed sun
All the day long his course to run;      30
   For, &c.

The horned moon to shine by night
Amongst her spangled sisters bright.
   For, &c.

He with His thunder-clasping hand
Smote the first-born of Egypt land;
   For, &c.           40

And, in despite of Pharaoh fell,
He brought from thence His Israel.
   For, &c.

The ruddy waves He cleft in twain
Of the Erythræan main.
   For, &c.

The floods stood still like walls of glass,
While the Hebrew bands did pass;      50
   For, &c.

But full soon they did devour
The tawny king with all his power.
   For, &c.

His chosen people He did bless
In the wasteful wilderness.
   For, &c.                                    60

In bloody battle He brought down
Kings of prowess and renown.
   For, &c.

He foiled bold Seon and his host,
That ruled the Amorrean coast;
   For, &c.

And large-limbed Og He did subdue,
With all his over-hardy crew;                    70
   For, &c.

And to His servant Israel,
He gave their land therein to dwell.
   For, &c.

He hath with a piteous eye
Beheld us in our misery;                         80
   For, &c.

And freed us from the slavery
Of the invading enemy.
   For, &c.

All living creatures He doth feed,
And with full hand supplies their need.
   For, &c.

Let us therefore warble forth
His mighty majesty and worth;                    90
   For, &c.

That His mansion hath on high
Above the reach of mortal eye.
   For His mercies ay endure,
   Ever faithful, ever sure.

## THE PASSION

### I

ERE-WHILE of music and ethereal mirth,
Wherewith the stage of air and earth did ring,
And joyous news of Heavenly Infant's birth,
My muse with angels did divide to sing;
But headlong joy is ever on the wing,
　　In wintry solstice like the shortened light,
Soon swallowed up in dark and long out-living night.

### II

For now to sorrow must I tune my song,
And set my harp to notes of saddest woe,
Which on our dearest Lord did seize ere long,　　10
Dangers, and snares, and wrongs, and worse than so,
Which He for us did freely undergo;
　　Most perfect hero, tried in heaviest plight
Of labours huge and hard, too hard for human wight.

### III

He sovran Priest, stooping His regal head,
That dropped with odorous oil down His fair eyes,
Poor fleshly tabernacle entered,
His starry front low-roofed beneath the skies;
O what a mask was there, what a disguise!
　　Yet more; the stroke of death He must abide,　　20
Then lies Him meekly down fast by His brethren's side.

### IV

These latest scenes confine my roving verse,
To this horizon is my Phoebus bound,
His godlike acts, and His temptations fierce,
And former sufferings otherwhere are found;
Loud o'er the rest Cremona's trump doth sound;
　　Me softer airs befit, and softer strings
Of lute or viol still, more apt for mournful things.

### V

Befriend me, Night, best patroness of grief,
Over the pole thy thickest mantle throw,                    30
And work my flattered fancy to belief,
That Heaven and Earth are coloured with my woe;
My sorrows are too dark for day to know:
    The leaves should all be black whereon I write,
And letters, where my tears have washed, a wannish white.

### VI

See, see the chariot and those rushing wheels
That whirled the prophet up at Chebar flood:
My spirit some transporting cherub feels,
To bear me where the towers of Salem stood,
Once glorious towers, now sunk in guiltless blood;    40
    There doth my soul in holy vision sit,
In pensive trance, and anguish, and ecstatic fit.

### VII

Mine eye hath found that sad sepulchral rock
That was the casket of Heaven's richest store,
And here though grief my feeble hands uplock,
Yet on the softened quarry would I score
My plaining verse as lively as before;
    For sure so well instructed are my tears,
That they would fitly fall in ordered characters.

### VIII

Or should I thence hurried on viewless wing,    50
Take up a weeping on the mountains wild,
The gentle neighbourhood of grove and spring
Would soon unbosom all their echoes mild,
And I (for grief is easily beguiled)
    Might think th' infection of my sorrows loud
Had got a race of mourners on some pregnant cloud.

*This subject, the author finding to be above the years he had
    when he wrote it, and nothing satisfied with what was begun,
    left it unfinished.*

## ON TIME

Fly, envious Time, till thou run out thy race,
Call on the lazy, leaden-stepping hours,
Whose speed is but the heavy plummet's pace,
And glut thyself with what thy womb devours,
Which is no more than what is false and vain,
And merely mortal dross;
So little is our loss,
So little is thy gain.
For when as each thing bad thou hast entombed,
And last of all thy greedy self consumed,                    10
Then long Eternity shall greet our bliss
With an individual kiss,
And joy shall overtake us as a flood;
When every thing that is sincerely good
And perfectly divine,
With Truth, and Peace, and Love shall ever shine
About the supreme throne
Of Him, t'whose happy-making sight alone
When once our heavenly-guided soul shall climb,
Then, all this earthy grossness quit,                        20
Attired with stars we shall for ever sit
   Triumphing over Death, and Chance, and thee, O Time.


## UPON THE CIRCUMCISION

Ye flaming powers and winged Warriors bright,
That erst with music and triumphant song,
First heard by happy watchful shepherds' ear,
So sweetly sung your joy the clouds along
Through the soft silence of the list'ning night;
Now mourn; and if sad share with us to bear
Your fiery essence can distil no tear,
Burn in your sighs, and borrow
Seas wept from our deep sorrow.
He who with all Heaven's heraldry whilere                    10

Entered the world, now bleeds to give us ease;
Alas, how soon our sin
  Sore doth begin
    His infancy to seize!

O more exceeding love, or law more just?
Just law indeed, but more exceeding love!
For we by rightful doom remediless
Were lost in death, till He that dwelt above
High-throned in secret bliss, for us, frail dust,
Emptied His glory, even to nakedness,    20
And that great cov'nant which we still transgress
Entirely satisfied,
And the full wrath beside
Of vengeful Justice bore for our excess,
And seals obedience first with wounding smart
This day; but O ere long
Huge pangs and strong
    Will pierce more near His heart!

# AT A SOLEMN MUSIC

Blest pair of Sirens, pledges of Heaven's joy,
Sphere-born harmonious sisters, Voice and Verse,
Wed your divine sounds; and mixed power employ
Dead things with inbreathed sense able to pierce,
And to our high-raised phantasy present
That undisturbed song of pure consent,
Ay sung before the sapphire-coloured throne
To Him that sits thereon,
With saintly shout and solemn jubilee;
Where the bright seraphim in burning row    10
Their loud uplifted angel-trumpets blow,
And the cherubic host in thousand quires
Touch their immortal harps of golden wires,
With those just spirits that wear victorious palms,
Hymns devout and holy psalms
Singing everlastingly;
That we on earth with undiscording voice
May rightly answer that melodious noise:

As once we did, till disproportioned sin
Jarred against nature's chime, and with harsh din    20
Broke the fair music that all creatures made
To their great Lord; whose love their motion swayed
In perfect diapason, whilst they stood
In first obedience and their state of good.
O may we soon again renew that song,
And keep in tune with Heaven, till God ere long
To His celestial consort us unite,
To live with Him, and sing in endless morn of light.


## AN EPITAPH ON THE MARCHIONESS
## OF WINCHESTER

THIS rich marble doth inter
The honoured wife of Winchester,
A viscount's daughter, an earl's heir,
Besides what her virtues fair
Added to her noble birth
More than she could own from earth.
Summers three times eight save one
She had told; alas too soon,
After so short time of breath,
To house with darkness and with death.    10
Yet had the number of her days
Been as complete as was her praise;
Nature and fate had had no strife
In giving limit to her life.
Her high birth and her graces sweet
Quickly found a lover meet;
The virgin quire for her request
The god that sits at marriage-feast;
He at their invoking came
But with a scarce well-lighted flame,    20
And in his garland, as he stood,
Ye might discern a cypress bud.
Once had the early matrons run
To greet her of a lovely son,
And now with second hope she goes,
And calls Lucina to her throes;

But whether by mischance or blame
Atropos for Lucina came;
And with remorseless cruelty,
Spoiled at once both fruit and tree:                    30
The hapless babe before his birth
Had burial, yet not laid in earth,
And the languished mother's womb
Was not long a living tomb.
So have I seen some tender slip
Saved with care from winter's nip,
The pride of her carnation train,
Plucked up by some unheedy swain,
Who only thought to crop the flower
New shot up from vernal shower;                    40
But the fair blossom hangs the head
Sideways, as on a dying bed,
And those pearls of dew she wears
Prove to be presaging tears
Which the sad morn had let fall
On her hast'ning funeral.
Gentle lady, may thy grave
Peace and quiet ever have;
After this thy travail sore
Sweet rest seize thee evermore,                    50
That to give the world increase
Short'ned hast thy own life's lease;
Here, besides the sorrowing
That thy noble house doth bring,
Here be tears of perfect moan
Wept for thee in Helicon,
And some flowers, and some bays,
For thy hearse to strew the ways,
Sent thee from the banks of Came,
Devoted to thy virtuous name;                    60
Whilst thou, bright saint, high sit'st in glory,
Next her much like to thee in story,
That fair Syrian shepherdess,
Who after years of barrenness,
The highly favoured Joseph bore
To him that served for her before,
And at her next birth, much like thee,

Through pangs fled to felicity,
Far within the bosom bright
Of blazing Majesty and Light,
There with thee, new welcome saint,          70
Like fortunes may her soul acquaint,
With thee there clad in radiant sheen,
No marchioness, but now a queen.


## SONG ON MAY MORNING

Now the bright morning-star, day's harbinger,
Comes dancing from the east, and leads with her
The flowery May, who from her green lap throws
The yellow cowslip and the pale primrose.
   Hail, bounteous May, that dost inspire,
   Mirth and youth and warm desire,
   Woods and groves are of thy dressing,
   Hill and dale doth boast thy blessing.
Thus we salute thee with our early song,
And welcome thee, and wish thee long.          10


## ON SHAKESPEARE. 1630

What needs my Shakespeare for his honoured bones,
The labour of an age in piled stones,
Or that his hallowed relics should be hid
Under a star-ypointing pyramid?
Dear son of memory, great heir of fame,
What need'st thou such weak witness of thy name?
Thou in our wonder and astonishment
Hast built thyself a live-long monument.
For whilst to th' shame of slow-endeavouring art,
Thy easy numbers flow, and that each heart          10
Hath from the leaves of thy unvalued book
Those Delphic lines with deep impression took;
Then thou, our fancy of itself bereaving,
Dost make us marble with too much conceiving;
And so sepulchered in such pomp dost lie,
That kings for such a tomb would wish to die.

## ON THE UNIVERSITY CARRIER

#### WHO SICKENED IN THE TIME OF HIS VACANCY, BEING FORBID TO GO TO LONDON BY REASON OF THE PLAGUE

HERE lies old Hobson, Death hath broke his girt,
And here, alas, hath laid him in the dirt;
Or else, the ways being foul, twenty to one
He's here stuck in a slough and overthrown.
'Twas such a shifter, that if truth were known,
Death was half glad when he had got him down;
For he had any time this ten years full
Dodged with him betwixt Cambridge and The Bull.
And surely Death could never have prevailed
Had not his weekly course of carriage failed;          10
But lately, finding him so long at home,
And thinking now his journey's end was come,
And that he had ta'en up his latest inn,
In the kind office of a chamberlin
Showed him his room where he must lodge that night,
Pulled off his boots, and took away the light.
If any ask for him, it shall be said,
'Hobson has supped, and 's newly gone to bed.'

## ANOTHER ON THE SAME

HERE lieth one who did most truly prove
That he could never die while he could move;
So hung his destiny, never to rot
While he might still jog on and keep his trot;
Made of sphere-metal, never to decay
Until his revolution was at stay.
Time numbers motion, yet (without a crime
'Gainst old truth) motion numbered out his time;
And, like an engine moved with wheel and weight,
His principles being ceased, he ended straight.          10
Rest, that gives all men life, gave him his death,
And too much breathing put him out of breath;

Nor were it contradiction to affirm
Too long vacation hastened on his term.
Merely to drive the time away he sickened,
Fainted, and died, nor would with ale be quickened.
'Nay,' quoth he, on his swooning bed outstretched,
'If I may not carry, sure I'll ne'er be fetched,
But vow, though the cross doctors all stood hearers,
For one carrier put down to make six bearers.'                    20
Ease was his chief disease; and, to judge right,
He died for heaviness that his cart went light.
His leisure told him that his time was come,
And lack of load made his life burdensome,
That even to his last breath (there be that say't),
As he were pressed to death, he cried, 'More weight!'
But, had his doings lasted as they were,
He had been an immortal carrier.
Obedient to the moon he spent his date
In course reciprocal, and had his fate                           30
Linked to the mutual flowing of the seas;
Yet (strange to think) his wain was his increase.
His letters are delivered all and gone;
Only remains this superscription.


# L'ALLEGRO

HENCE, loathed Melancholy,
    Of Cerberus and blackest Midnight born
In Stygian cave forlorn
    'Mongst horrid shapes, and shrieks, and sights unholy!
Find out some uncouth cell,
    Where brooding Darkness spreads his jealous wings,
    And the night-raven sings;
    There, under ebon shades and low-browed rocks,
As ragged as thy locks,
    In dark Cimmerian desert ever dwell.                         10
But come, thou Goddess fair and free,
In heaven yclept Euphrosyne,
And by men heart-easing Mirth;
Whom lovely Venus, at a birth,

With two sister Graces more,
To ivy-crowned Bacchus bore:
Or whether (as some sager sing)
The frolic wind that breathes the spring,
Zephyr, with Aurora playing,                    20
As he met her once a-Maying,
There, on beds of violets blue,
And fresh-blown roses washed in dew,
Filled her with thee, a daughter fair,
So buxom, blithe, and debonair.
   Haste thee, Nymph, and bring with thee
Jest, and youthful Jollity,
Quips and Cranks and wanton Wiles,
Nods and Becks and wreathed Smiles,
Such as hang on Hebe's cheek,
And love to live in dimple sleek;               30
Sport that wrinkled Care derides,
And Laughter holding both his sides.
Come, and trip it, as you go,
On the light fantastic toe;
And in thy right hand lead with thee
The mountain-nymph, sweet Liberty;
And, if I give thee honour due,
Mirth, admit me of thy crew,
To live with her, and live with thee,
In unreproved pleasures free;                   40
To hear the lark begin his flight,
And, singing, startle the dull night,
From his watch-tower in the skies,
Till the dappled dawn doth rise;
Then to come, in spite of sorrow,
And at my window bid good morrow,
Through the sweet-briar or the vine,
Or the twisted eglantine;
While the cock, with lively din,
Scatters the rear of darkness thin;             50
And to the stack, or the barn door,
Stoutly struts his dames before:
Oft list'ning how the hounds and horn
Cheerly rouse the slumb'ring morn,
From the side of some hoar hill,

Through the high wood echoing shrill:
Sometime walking, not unseen,
By hedgerow elms, on hillocks green,
Right against the eastern gate
Where the great Sun begins his state,                    60
Robed in flames and amber light,
The clouds in thousand liveries dight;
While the ploughman, near at hand,
Whistles o'er the furrowed land,
And the milkmaid singeth blithe,
And the mower whets his scythe,
And every shepherd tells his tale
Under the hawthorn in the dale.
Straight mine eye hath caught new pleasures,
Whilst the landskip round it measures:                    70
Russet lawns, and fallows grey,
Where the nibbling flocks do stray;
Mountains on whose barren breast
The labouring clouds do often rest;
Meadows trim with daisies pied;
Shallow brooks, and rivers wide;
Towers and battlements it sees
Bosomed high in tufted trees,
Where perhaps some beauty lies,
The cynosure of neighbouring eyes.                        80
Hard by a cottage chimney smokes
From betwixt two aged oaks,
Where Corydon and Thyrsis met
Are at their savoury dinner set
Of herbs and other country messes,
Which the neat-handed Phillis dresses;
And then in haste her bower she leaves,
With Thestylis to bind the sheaves;
Or, if the earlier season lead,
To the tanned haycock in the mead.                        90
Sometimes, with secure delight,
The upland hamlets will invite,
When the merry bells ring round,
And the jocund rebecks sound
To many a youth and many a maid
Dancing in the chequered shade,

And young and old come forth to play
On a sunshine holiday,
Till the livelong daylight fail:
Then to the spicy nut-brown ale,                    100
With stories told of many a feat,
How Faëry Mab the junkets eat.
She was pinched and pulled, she said;
And by the Friars' lantern led,
Tells how the drudging goblin sweat
To earn his cream-bowl duly set,
When in one night, ere glimpse of morn,
His shadowy flail hath threshed the corn
That ten day-labourers could not end;
Then lies him down the lubber fiend,                    110
And, stretched out all the chimney's length,
Basks at the fire his hairy strength,
And crop-full out of doors he flings,
Ere the first cock his matin rings.
Thus done the tales, to bed they creep,
By whispering winds soon lulled asleep.
Towered cities please us then,
And the busy hum of men,
Where throngs of knights and barons bold,
In weeds of peace, high triumphs hold,                    120
With store of ladies, whose bright eyes
Rain influence, and judge the prize
Of wit or arms, while both contend
To win her grace whom all commend.
There let Hymen oft appear
In saffron robe, with taper clear,
And pomp, and feast, and revelry,
With mask and antique pageantry;
Such sights as youthful poets dream
On summer eves by haunted stream.                    130
Then to the well-trod stage anon,
If Jonson's learned sock be on,
Or sweetest Shakespeare, Fancy's child,
Warble his native wood-notes wild.
    And ever, against eating cares,
Lap me in soft Lydian airs,
Married to immortal verse,

Such as the meeting soul may pierce,
In notes with many a winding bout
Of linked sweetness long drawn out          140
With wanton heed and giddy cunning,
The melting voice through mazes running,
Untwisting all the chains that tie
The hidden soul of harmony;
That Orpheus' self may heave his head
From golden slumber on a bed
Of heaped Elysian flowers, and hear
Such strains as would have won the ear
Of Pluto to have quite set free
His half-regained Eurydice.                  150
   These delights if thou canst give,
Mirth, with thee I mean to live.


# IL PENSEROSO

HENCE, vain deluding Joys,
   The brood of Folly without father bred!
How little you bested,
   Or fill the fixed mind with all your toys!
Dwell in some idle brain,
   And fancies fond with gaudy shapes possess,
As thick and numberless
   As the gay motes that people the sunbeams,
Or likest hovering dreams,
   The fickle pensioners of Morpheus' train.   10
But, hail! thou Goddess sage and holy,
Hail, divinest Melancholy!
Whose saintly visage is too bright
To hit the sense of human sight,
And therefore to our weaker view
O'erlaid with black, staid Wisdom's hue;
Black, but such as in esteem
Prince Memnon's sister might beseem,
Or that starred Ethiop queen that strove
To set her beauty's praise above           20

The Sea-Nymphs, and their powers offended.
Yet thou art higher far descended:
Thee bright-haired Vesta long of yore
To solitary Saturn bore;
His daughter she; in Saturn's reign
Such mixture was not held a stain.
Oft in glimmering bowers and glades
He met her, and in secret shades
Of woody Ida's inmost grove,
Whilst yet there was no fear of Jove.                30
Come, pensive Nun, devout and pure,
Sober, steadfast, and demure,
All in a robe of darkest grain,
Flowing with majestic train,
And sable stole of cypress lawn
Over thy decent shoulders drawn.
Come, but keep thy wonted state,
With even step, and musing gait,
And looks commercing with the skies,
Thy rapt soul sitting in thine eyes:                40
There, held in holy passion still,
Forget thyself to marble, till
With a sad leaden downward cast
Thou fix them on the earth as fast.
And join with thee calm Peace and Quiet,
Spare Fast, that oft with gods doth diet,
And hears the Muses in a ring
Ay round about Jove's altar sing;
And add to these retired Leisure,
That in trim gardens takes his pleasure;            50
But, first and chiefest, with thee bring
Him that yon soars on golden wing,
Guiding the fiery-wheeled throne,
The Cherub Contemplation;
And the mute Silence hist along,
'Less Philomel will deign a song,
In her sweetest, saddest plight,
Smoothing the rugged brow of Night,
While Cynthia checks her dragon yoke
Gently o'er th' accustomed oak.                     60
Sweet bird, that shunn'st the noise of folly,

Most musical, most melancholy!
Thee, chauntress, oft the woods among
I woo, to hear thy even-song;
And, missing thee, I walk unseen
On the dry smooth-shaven green,
To behold the wand'ring moon,
Riding near her highest noon,
Like one that had been led astray
Through the heaven's wide pathless way,    70
And oft, as if her head she bowed,
Stooping through a fleecy cloud.
Oft, on a plat of rising ground,
I hear the far-off curfew sound,
Over some wide-watered shore,
Swinging slow with sullen roar;
Or, if the air will not permit,
Some still removed place will fit,
Where glowing embers through the room
Teach light to counterfeit a gloom,    80
Far from all resort of mirth,
Save the cricket on the hearth,
Or the bellman's drowsy charm
To bless the doors from nightly harm.
Or let my lamp, at midnight hour,
Be seen in some high lonely tower,
Where I may oft outwatch the Bear,
With thrice great Hermes, or unsphere
The spirit of Plato, to unfold
What worlds or what vast regions hold    90
The immortal mind that hath forsook
Her mansion in this fleshly nook;
And of those demons that are found
In fire, air, flood, or underground,
Whose power hath a true consent
With planet or with element.
Sometime let gorgeous Tragedy
In sceptred pall come sweeping by,
Presenting Thebes, or Pelops' line,
Or the tale of Troy divine,    100
Or what (though rare) of later age
Ennobled hath the buskined stage.

But, O sad Virgin! that thy power
Might raise Musaeus from his bower;
Or bid the soul of Orpheus sing
Such notes as, warbled to the string,
Drew iron tears down Pluto's cheek,
And made Hell grant what love did seek;
Or call up him that left half-told
The story of Cambuscan bold,        110
Of Camball, and of Algarsife,
And who had Canace to wife,
That owned the virtuous ring and glass,
And of the wondrous horse of brass
On which the Tartar king did ride;
And if aught else great bards beside
In sage and solemn tunes have sung,
Of tourneys, and of trophies hung,
Of forests, and enchantments drear,
Where more is meant than meets the ear.    120
  Thus, Night, oft see me in thy pale career,
Till civil-suited Morn appear,
Not tricked and frounced, as she was wont
With the Attic boy to hunt,
But kerchieft in a comely cloud,
While rocking winds are piping loud,
Or ushered with a shower still,
When the gust hath blown his fill,
Ending on the rustling leaves,
With minute-drops from off the eaves.    130
And, when the sun begins to fling
His flaring beams, me, Goddess, bring
To arched walks of twilight groves,
And shadows brown, that Sylvan loves,
Of pine, or monumental oak,
Where the rude axe with heaved stroke
Was never heard the nymphs to daunt,
Or fright them from their hallowed haunt.
There, in close covert, by some brook,
Where no profaner eye may look,    140
Hide me from day's garish eye,
While the bee with honied thigh,
That at her flowery work doth sing,

And the waters murmuring,
With such consort as they keep,
Entice the dewy-feathered Sleep.
And let some strange mysterious dream
Wave at his wings, in airy stream
Of lively portraiture displayed,
Softly on my eyelids laid;             150
And, as I wake, sweet music breathe
Above, about, or underneath,
Sent by some Spirit to mortals good,
Or th' unseen Genius of the wood.
   But let my due feet never fail
To walk the studious cloister's pale,
And love the high embowed roof,
With antique pillars massy-proof,
And storied windows richly dight,
Casting a dim religious light.           160
There let the pealing organ blow,
To the full-voiced quire below,
In service high and anthems clear,
As may with sweetness, through mine ear,
Dissolve me into ecstasies,
And bring all Heaven before mine eyes.
And may at last my weary age
Find out the peaceful hermitage,
The hairy gown and mossy cell,
Where I may sit and rightly spell       170
Of every star that heaven doth shew,
And every herb that sips the dew,
Till old experience do attain
To something like prophetic strain.
   These pleasures, Melancholy, give;
And I with thee will choose to live.

## SONNETS

### TO THE NIGHTINGALE

O NIGHTINGALE that on yon bloomy spray
    Warbl'st at eve, when all the woods are still,
    Thou with fresh hope the lover's heart dost fill,
    While the jolly hours lead on propitious May.
Thy liquid notes that close the eye of day,
    First heard before the shallow cuckoo's bill,
    Portend success in love. O, if Jove's will
Have linked that amorous power to thy soft lay,
Now timely sing, ere the rude bird of hate
    Foretell my hopeless doom, in some grove nigh;    10
    As thou from year to year hast sung too late
For my relief, yet hadst no reason why.
    Whether the Muse or Love call thee his mate,
    Both them I serve, and of their train am I.

### ON BEING ARRIVED AT TWENTY-THREE YEARS OF AGE

How soon hath Time, the subtle thief of youth,
    Stolen on his wing my three-and-twentieth year!
    My hasting days fly on with full career,
    But my late spring no bud or blossom shew'th.
Perhaps my semblance might deceive the truth
    That I to manhood am arrived so near;
    And inward ripeness doth much less appear,
    That some more timely-happy spirits indu'th.
Yet, be it less or more, or soon or slow,
    It shall be still in strictest measure even    10
    To that same lot, however mean or high,
Toward which Time leads me, and the will of Heaven.
    All is, if I have grace to use it so,
    As ever in my great Task-Master's eye.

## WHEN THE ASSAULT WAS INTENDED TO THE CITY

Captain or Colonel, or Knight in Arms,
  Whose chance on these defenceless doors may seize,
  If deed of honour did thee ever please,
  Guard them, and him within protect from harms.
He can requite thee; for he knows the charms
  That call fame on such gentle acts as these,
  And he can spread thy name o'er lands and seas,
  Whatever clime the sun's bright circle warms.
Lift not thy spear against the Muses' bower:
  The great Emathian conqueror bid spare      10
  The house of Pindarus, when temple and tower
Went to the ground; and the repeated air
  Of sad Electra's poet had the power
  To save th' Athenian walls from ruin bare.

## TO A VIRTUOUS YOUNG LADY

Lady, that in the prime of earliest youth
  Wisely hath shunned the broad way and the green,
  And with those few art eminently seen
  That labour up the hill of heavenly Truth;
The better part with Mary and with Ruth
  Chosen thou hast; and they that overween,
  And at thy growing virtues fret their spleen,
  No anger find in thee, but pity and ruth.
Thy care is fixed, and zealously attends
  To fill thy odorous lamp with deeds of light,      10
  And hope that reaps not shame. Therefore be sure
Thou, when the Bridegroom with his feastful friends
  Passes to bliss at the mid-hour of night,
  Hast gained thy entrance, Virgin wise and pure.

## TO THE LADY MARGARET LEY

DAUGHTER to that good Earl, once President
  Of England's Council and her Treasury,
  Who lived in both unstained with gold or fee,
  And left them both, more in himself content,
Till the sad breaking of that Parliament
  Broke him, as that dishonest victory
  At Chæronea, fatal to liberty,
  Killed with report that old man eloquent.
Though later born than to have known the days
  Wherein your father flourished, yet by you,          10
  Madam, methinks I see him living yet:
So well your words his noble virtues praise,
  That all both judge you to relate them true
  And to possess them, honoured Margaret.


## ARCADES

*Part of an Entertainment presented to the Countess
  Dowager of Derby at Harefield by some Noble Persons
  of her Family; who appear on the Scene in pastoral habit,
  moving toward the seat of state, with this song:*

### I. *Song*

LOOK, Nymphs, and Shepherds, look!
What sudden blaze of majesty
Is that which we from hence descry,
Too divine to be mistook?
    This, this is she
To whom our vows and wishes bend:
Here our solemn search hath end.

Fame, that her high worth to raise
Seemed erst so lavish and profuse,
We may justly now accuse          10
Of detraction from her praise:
    Less than half we find expressed;
    Envy bid conceal the rest.

Mark what radiant state she spreads,
In circle round her shining throne.
Shooting her beams like silver threads:
This, this is she alone,
    Sitting like a goddess bright
    In the centre of her light.


Might she the wise Latona be,          20
Or the towered Cybele,
Mother of a hundred gods?
Juno dares not give her odds:
    Who had thought this clime had held
    A deity so unparalleled?


*As they come forward, the* GENIUS OF THE WOOD *appears,
and, turning toward them, speaks.*

  *Gen.* Stay, gentle Swains, for, though in this disguise,
I see bright honour sparkle through your eyes;
Of famous Arcady ye are, and sprung
Of that renowned flood, so often sung,
Divine Alpheus, who, by secret sluice,      30
Stole under seas to meet his Arethuse;
And ye, the breathing roses of the wood,
Fair silver-buskined Nymphs, as great and good.
I know this quest of yours and free intent
Was all in honour and devotion meant
To the great mistress of yon princely shrine,
Whom with low reverence I adore as mine,
And with all helpful service will comply
To further this night's glad solemnity,
And lead ye where ye may more near behold    40
What shallow-searching Fame hath left untold;
Which I full oft, amidst these shades alone,
Have sat to wonder at, and gaze upon.
For know, by lot from Jove, I am the Power
Of this fair wood, and live in oaken bower,
To nurse the saplings tall, and curl the grove
With ringlets quaint and wanton windings wove;
And all my plants I save from nightly ill

Of noisome winds and blasting vapours chill;
And from the boughs brush off the evil dew, 50
And heal the harms of thwarting thunder blue,
Or what the cross dire-looking planet smites,
Or hurtful worm with cankered venom bites.
When evening grey doth rise, I fetch my round
Over the mount, and all this hallowed ground;
And early, ere the odorous breath of morn
Awakes the slumbering leaves, or tasselled horn
Shakes the high thicket, haste I all about,
Number my ranks, and visit every sprout
With puissant words and murmurs made to bless. 60
But else, in deep of night, when drowsiness
Hath locked up mortal sense, then listen I
To the celestial Sirens' harmony,
That sit upon the nine infolded spheres,
And sing to those that hold the vital shears,
And turn the adamantine spindle round
On which the fate of gods and men is wound.
Such sweet compulsion doth in music lie,
To lull the daughters of Necessity,
And keep unsteady Nature to her law, 70
And the low world in measured motion draw
After the heavenly tune, which none can hear
Of human mould with gross unpurged ear.
And yet such music worthiest were to blaze
The peerless height of her immortal praise
Whose lustre leads us, and for her most fit,
If my inferior hand or voice could hit
Inimitable sounds. Yet, as we go,
Whate'er the skill of lesser gods can show
I will assay, her worth to celebrate, 80
And so attend ye toward her glittering state;
Where ye may all, that are of noble stem,
Approach, and kiss her sacred vesture's hem.

## II. *Song*

O'er the smooth enamelled green,
Where no print of step hath been,
Follow me, as I sing
And touch the warbled string:

Under the shady roof
Of branching elm star-proof
    Follow me.                                    90
I will bring you where she sits,
Clad in splendour as befits
    Her deity.
    Such a rural Queen
    All Arcadia hath not seen.

### III. *Song*

Nymphs and Shepherds, dance no more
    By sandy Ladon's lilied banks;
On old Lycæus, or Cyllene hoar,
    Trip no more in twilight ranks;
Though Erymanth your loss deplore,            100
    A better soil shall give ye thanks.
From the stony Mænalus
Bring your flocks, and live with us;
Here ye shall have greater grace,
To serve the Lady of this place.
Though Syrinx your Pan's mistress were,
Yet Syrinx well might wait on her.
    Such a rural Queen
    All Arcadia hath not seen.

# LYCIDAS

*In this Monody the Author bewails a learned Friend,
unfortunately drowned in his passage from Chester on
the Irish Seas, 1637; and, by occasion, foretells the ruin
of our corrupted Clergy, then in their height.*

YET once more, O ye laurels, and once more,
Ye myrtles brown, with ivy never sere,
I come to pluck your berries harsh and crude,
And with forced fingers rude
Shatter your leaves before the mellowing year.
Bitter constraint and sad occasion dear
Compels me to disturb your season due;
For Lycidas is dead, dead ere his prime,

Young Lycidas, and hath not left his peer.
Who would not sing for Lycidas? he knew                    10
Himself to sing, and build the lofty rhyme.
He must not float upon his watery bier
Unwept, and welter to the parching wind,
Without the meed of some melodious tear.
    Begin, then, Sisters of the sacred well
That from beneath the seat of Jove doth spring;
Begin, and somewhat loudly sweep the string.
Hence with denial vain and coy excuse:
So may some gentle Muse
With lucky words favour my destined urn,                    20
And as he passes turn,
And bid fair peace be to my sable shroud!
For we were nursed upon the self-same hill,
Fed the same flock, by fountain, shade, and rill;
Together both, ere the high lawns appeared
Under the opening eyelids of the Morn,
We drove a-field, and both together heard
What time the grey-fly winds her sultry horn,
Batt'ning our flocks with the fresh dews of night,
Oft till the star that rose at evening bright                    30
Toward heaven's descent had sloped his westering
    wheel.
Meanwhile the rural ditties were not mute,
Tempered to th' oaten flute;
Rough Satyrs danced, and Fauns with cloven heel
From the glad sound would not be absent long;
And old Damætas loved to hear our song.
    But, oh! the heavy change, now thou art gone,
Now thou art gone, and never must return!
Thee, Shepherd, thee the woods, and desert caves,
With wild thyme and the gadding vine o'ergrown,                    40
And all their echoes, mourn.
The willows, and the hazel copses green,
Shall now no more be seen,
Fanning their joyous leaves to thy soft lays.
As killing as the canker to the rose,
Or taint-worm to the weanling herds that graze,
Or frost to flowers, that their gay wardrobe wear,
When first the white-thorn blows;

Such, Lycidas, thy loss to shepherd's ear.
    Where were ye, Nymphs, when the remorseless deep 50
Closed o'er the head of your loved Lycidas?
For neither were ye playing on the steep,
Where your old bards, the famous Druids, lie,
Nor on the shaggy top of Mona high,
Nor yet where Deva spreads her wizard stream.
Ay me! I fondly dream
Had ye been there, . . . for what could that have done?
What could the Muse herself that Orpheus bore,
The Muse herself, for her enchanting son,
Whom universal nature did lament,            60
When, by the rout that made the hideous roar,
His gory visage down the stream was sent,
Down the swift Hebrus to the Lesbian shore?
    Alas! what boots it with incessant care
To tend the homely, slighted, shepherd's trade,
And strictly meditate the thankless Muse?
Were it not better done, as others use,
To sport with Amaryllis in the shade,
Or with the tangles of Neæra's hair?
Fame is the spur that the clear spirit doth raise    70
(That last infirmity of noble mind)
To scorn delights, and live laborious days;
But the fair guerdon when we hope to find,
And think to burst out into sudden blaze,
Comes the blind Fury with th' abhorred shears,
And slits the thin-spun life. 'But not the praise,'
Phœbus replied, and touched my trembling ears:
'Fame is no plant that grows on mortal soil,
Nor in the glistering foil
Set off to the world, nor in broad rumour lies,    80
But lives and spreads aloft by those pure eyes
And perfect witness of all-judging Jove;
As he pronounces lastly on each deed,
Of so much fame in heaven expect thy meed.'
    O fountain Arethuse, and thou honoured flood,
Smooth-sliding Mincius, crowned with vocal reeds,
That strain I heard was of a higher mood.
But now my oat proceeds,
And listens to the Herald of the Sea

That came in Neptune's plea. 90
He asked the waves, and asked the felon winds,
What hard mishap hath doomed this gentle swain?
And questioned every gust of rugged wings
That blows from off each beaked promontory.
They knew not of his story;
And sage Hippotades their answer brings;
That not a blast was from his dungeon strayed,
The air was calm, and on the level brine
Sleek Panope with all her sisters played.
It was that fatal and perfidious bark, 100
Built in th' eclipse, and rigged with curses dark,
That sunk so low that sacred head of thine.
  Next, Camus, reverend sire, went footing slow,
His mantle hairy, and his bonnet sedge,
Inwrought with figures dim, and on the edge
Like to that sanguine flower inscribed with woe.
'Ah! who hath reft,' quoth he, 'my dearest pledge?'
Last came, and last did go,
The Pilot of the Galilean Lake;
Two massy keys he bore of metals twain 110
(The golden opes, the iron shuts amain).
He shook his mitred locks, and stern bespake:—
'How well could I have spared for thee, young swain,
Enow of such as, for their bellies' sake,
Creep, and intrude, and climb into the fold!
Of other care they little reck'ning make
Than how to scramble at the shearers' feast,
And shove away the worthy bidden guest.
Blind mouths! that scarce themselves know how to hold
A sheep-hook, or have learned aught else the least 120
That to the faithful herdman's art belongs!
What recks it them? What need they? They are sped;
And, when they list, their lean and flashy songs
Grate on their scrannel pipes of wretched straw;
The hungry sheep look up, and are not fed,
But, swoln with wind and the rank mist they draw,
Rot inwardly, and foul contagion spread:
Besides what the grim wolf with privy paw
Daily devours apace, and nothing said.
But that two-handed engine at the door 130

Stands ready to smite once, and smite no more.'
   Return, Alpheus, the dread voice is past
That shrunk thy streams; return, Sicilian Muse,
And call the vales, and bid them hither cast
Their bells and flowrets of a thousand hues.
Ye valleys low, where the mild whispers use
Of shades, and wanton winds, and gushing brooks,
On whose fresh lap the swart star sparely looks,
Throw hither all your quaint enamelled eyes,
That on the green turf suck the honied showers,   140
And purple all the ground with vernal flowers.
Bring the rathe primrose that forsaken dies,
The tufted crow-toe, and pale jessamine,
The white pink, and the pansy freaked with jet,
The glowing violet,
The musk-rose, and the well-attired woodbine,
With cowslips wan that hang the pensive head,
And every flower that sad embroidery wears:
Bid amaranthus all his beauty shed,
And daffadillies fill their cups with tears,   150
To strew the laureate hearse where Lycid lies.
For so, to interpose a little ease,
Let our frail thoughts dally with false surmise.
Ay me! whilst thee the shores and sounding seas
Wash far away, where'er thy bones are hurled;
Whether beyond the stormy Hebrides,
Where thou perhaps under the whelming tide
Visit'st the bottom of the monstrous world;
Or whether thou, to our moist vows denied,
Sleep'st by the fable of Bellerus old,   160
Where the great Vision of the guarded mount
Looks toward Namancos, and Bayona's hold.
Look homeward, Angel, now, and melt with ruth:
And, O ye dolphins, waft the hapless youth.
   Weep no more, woeful shepherds, weep no more,
For Lycidas, your sorrow, is not dead,
Sunk though he be beneath the wat'ry floor.
So sinks the day-star in the ocean bed,
And yet anon repairs his drooping head,
And tricks his beams, and with new-spangled ore   170
Flames in the forehead of the morning sky:

So Lycidas sunk low, but mounted high,
Through the dear might of Him that walked the waves;
Where, other groves and other streams along,
With nectar pure his oozy locks he laves,
And hears the unexpressive nuptial song,
In the blest kingdoms meek of joy and love.
There entertain him all the Saints above,
In solemn troops, and sweet societies,
That sing, and singing in their glory move,                 180
And wipe the tears for ever from his eyes.
Now, Lycidas, the shepherds weep no more;
Henceforth thou art the Genius of the shore,
In thy large recompense, and shalt be good
To all that wander in that perilous flood.
  Thus sang the uncouth swain to th' oaks and rills,
While the still morn went out with sandals grey:
He touched the tender stops of various quills,
With eager thought warbling his Doric lay:
And now the sun had stretched out all the hills,            190
And now was dropt into the western bay;
At last he rose, and twitched his mantle blue:
To-morrow to fresh woods, and pastures new.

# COMUS

## A MASK

*To the Right Honourable John, Lord Viscount Brackley,*
*son and heir-apparent to the Earl of Bridgewater, &c.*

MY LORD,
    This Poem, which received its first occasion of birth from yourself and others of your noble family, and much honour from your own person in the performance, now returns again to make a final dedication of itself to you. Although not openly acknowledged by the Author, yet it is a legitimate offspring, so lovely, and so much desired, that the often copying of it hath tired my pen to give my several friends satisfaction, and brought me to a necessity of producing it to the public view; and now to offer it up, in all rightful devotion, to those fair hopes and rare endowments of your much-promising youth, which give a full assurance, to all that know you, of a future excellence. Live, sweet Lord, to be the honour of your name; and receive this as your own from the hands of him who hath by many favours been long obliged to your most honoured parents, and, as in this representation your attendant Thyrsis, so now in all real expression

Your faithful and most humble Servant,<br>H. LAWES.

*The Copy of a Letter written by Sir Henry Wotton to the*
*Author upon the following Poem.*

From the College, this 13 of April, 1638.

SIR,
    It was a special favour when you lately bestowed upon me here the first taste of your acquaintance, though no longer than to make me know that I wanted more time to value it and to enjoy it rightly; and, in truth, if I could then have imagined your farther stay in these parts, which I understood afterwards by Mr. H., I would have been bold, in our vulgar phrase, to mend my draught (for you left me with an extreme thirst), and to have begged your conversation again, jointly with your said learned friend, at a poor meal or two, that we might have banded together some good authors of the ancient time; among which I observed you to have been familiar.
    Since your going, you have charged me with new

obligations, both for a very kind letter from you dated the 6th of this month, and for a dainty piece of entertainment which came therewith. Wherein I should much commend the tragical part, if the lyrical did not ravish me with a certain Doric delicacy in your Songs and Odes, whereunto I must plainly confess to have seen yet nothing parallel in our language: *Ipsa mollities*. But I must not omit to tell you that I now only owe you thanks for intimating unto me (how modestly soever) the true artificer. For the work itself I had viewed some good while before with singular delight; having received it from our common friend Mr. R., in the very close of the late R.'s Poems, printed at Oxford: whereunto it was added (as I now suppose) that the accessory might help out the principal, according to the art of stationers, and to leave the reader *con la bocca dolce*.

Now, Sir, concerning your travels; wherein I may challenge a little more privilege of discourse with you. I suppose you will not blanch Paris in your way; therefore I have been bold to trouble you with a few lines to Mr. M. B., whom you shall easily find attending the young Lord S. as his governor; and you may surely receive from him good directions for the shaping of your farther journey into Italy where he did reside, by my choice, some time for the King, after mine own recess from Venice.

I should think that your best line will be through the whole length of France to Marseilles, and thence by sea to Genoa; whence the passage into Tuscany is as diurnal as a Gravesend barge. I hasten, as you do, to Florence or Siena, the rather to tell you a short story, from the interest you have given me in your safety.

At Siena I was tabled in the house of one Alberto Scipioni, an old Roman courtier in dangerous times; having been steward to the Duca di Pagliano, who with all his family were strangled, save this only man that escaped by foresight of the tempest. With him I had often much chat of those affairs, into which he took pleasure to look back from his native harbour; and, at my departure toward Rome (which had been the centre of his experience), I had won confidence enough to beg his advice how I might carry myself securely there without offence of others or of mine own conscience. 'Signor Arrigo mio,' says he, '*I pensieri stretti ed il viso sciolto* will go safely over the whole world.' Of which Delphian oracle (for so I have found it) your judgement doth need no commentary; and therefore, Sir, I will commit you, with it, to the best of all securities, God's dear love, remaining

Your friend, as much at command<br>as any of longer date,<br>HENRY WOTTON.

*Postscript.*

Sir: I have expressly sent this my footboy to prevent your departure without some acknowledgement from me of the receipt of your obliging letter; having myself through some business, I know not how, neglected the ordinary conveyance. In any part where I shall understand you fixed, I shall be glad, and diligent to entertain you with home-novelties, even for some fomentation of our friendship, too soon interrupted in the cradle.

## THE PERSONS

The ATTENDANT SPIRIT, afterwards in the habit of THYRSIS.
COMUS, with his Crew.
THE LADY.
FIRST BROTHER.
SECOND BROTHER.
SABRINA, the Nymph.

The Chief Persons which presented were:—

    The Lord Brackley;
    Mr. Thomas Egerton, his Brother;
    The Lady Alice Egerton.

# A MASK

## PRESENTED AT LUDLOW CASTLE, 1634, &c.

*The first Scene discovers a wild wood.*

*The* ATTENDANT SPIRIT *descends or enters.*

BEFORE the starry threshold of Jove's court
My mansion is, where those immortal shapes
Of bright aerial spirits live insphered
In regions mild of calm and serene air,
Above the smoke and stir of this dim spot
Which men call Earth, and, with low-thoughted care,
Confined and pestered in this pinfold here,
Strive to keep up a frail and feverish being,
Unmindful of the crown that Virtue gives,
After this mortal change, to her true servants     10
Amongst the enthron'd gods on sainted seats.
Yet some there be that by due steps aspire
To lay their just hands on that golden key
That opes the palace of eternity.
To such my errand is; and, but for such,
I would not soil these pure ambrosial weeds
With the rank vapours of this sin-worn mould.
    But to my task. Neptune, besides the sway
Of every salt flood and each ebbing stream,
Took in by lot 'twixt high and nether Jove     20
Imperial rule of all the sea-girt isles
That, like to rich and various gems, inlay
The unadorned bosom of the deep;
Which he, to grace his tributary gods,
By course commits to several government,
And gives them leave to wear their sapphire crowns
And wield their little tridents. But this Isle,
The greatest and the best of all the main,
He quarters to his blue-haired deities;

And all this tract that fronts the falling sun          30
A noble Peer of mickle trust and power
Has in his charge, with tempered awe to guide
An old and haughty nation, proud in arms:
Where his fair offspring, nursed in princely lore,
Are coming to attend their father's state,
And new-entrusted sceptre. But their way
Lies through the perplex'd paths of this drear wood,
The nodding horror of whose shady brows
Threats the forlorn and wand'ring passenger;
And here their tender age might suffer peril,          40
But that, by quick command from sovran Jove,
I was despatched for their defence and guard.
And listen why; for I will tell you now
What never yet was heard in tale or song,
From old or modern bard, in hall or bower.
     Bacchus, that first from out the purple grape
Crushed the sweet poison of misused wine,
After the Tuscan mariners transformed,
Coasting the Tyrrhene shore, as the winds listed,
On Circe's island fell. (Who knows not Circe,          50
The daughter of the Sun, whose charmed cup
Whoever tasted lost his upright shape,
And downward fell into a grovelling swine?)
This Nymph, that gazed upon his clust'ring locks,
With ivy berries wreathed, and his blithe youth,
Had by him, ere he parted thence, a son
Much like his father, but his mother more,
Whom therefore she brought up, and Comus named:
Who, ripe and frolic of his full-grown age,
Roving the Celtic and Iberian fields,          60
At last betakes him to this ominous wood,
And, in thick shelter of black shades imbowered,
Excels his mother at her mighty art;
Off'ring to every weary traveller
His orient liquor in a crystal glass,
To quench the drouth of Phœbus; which as they taste
(For most do taste through fond intemperate thirst),
Soon as the potion works, their human count'nance,
Th' express resemblance of the gods, is changed
Into some brutish form of wolf or bear,          70

Or ounce or tiger, hog, or bearded goat,
All other parts remaining as they were.
And they, so perfect is their misery,
Not once perceive their foul disfigurement,
But boast themselves more comely than before,
And all their friends and native home forget,
To roll with pleasure in a sensual sty.
Therefore, when any favoured of high Jove
Chances to pass through this adventurous glade,
Swift as the sparkle of a glancing star          80
I shoot from heaven, to give him safe convoy,
As now I do. But first I must put off
These my sky-robes, spun out of Iris' woof,
And take the weeds and likeness of a swain
That to the service of this house belongs,
Who, with his soft pipe and smooth-dittied song,
Well knows to still the wild winds when they roar,
And hush the waving woods; nor of less faith,
And in this office of his mountain watch
Likeliest, and nearest to the present aid          90
Of this occasion. But I hear the tread
Of hateful steps; I must be viewless now.

COMUS *enters, with a charming-rod in one hand, his glass in*
   *the other: with him a rout of monsters, headed like*
   *sundry sorts of wild beasts, but otherwise like men and*
   *women, their apparel glistering. They come in making*
   *a riotous and unruly noise, with torches in their hands.*

   *Comus.* The star that bids the shepherd fold
Now the top of heaven doth hold;
And the gilded car of day
His glowing axle doth allay
In the steep Atlantic stream:
And the slope sun his upward beam
Shoots against the dusky pole,
Pacing toward the other goal          100
Of his chamber in the east.
Meanwhile, welcome joy and feast,
Midnight shout and revelry,
Tipsy dance and jollity.

Braid your locks with rosy twine,
Dropping odours, dropping wine.
Rigour now is gone to bed;
And Advice with scrupulous head,
Strict Age, and sour Severity,
With their grave saws, in slumber lie.                    110
We, that are of purer fire,
Imitate the starry quire,
Who, in their nightly watchful spheres,
Lead in swift round the months and years.
The sounds and seas, with all their finny drove,
Now to the moon in wavering morrice move;
And on the tawny sands and shelves
Trip the pert fairies and the dapper elves.
By dimpled brook and fountain-brim,
The wood-nymphs, decked with daisies trim,                120
Their merry wakes and pastimes keep:
What hath night to do with sleep?
Night hath better sweets to prove:
Venus now wakes, and wakens Love.
Come, let us our rites begin;
'Tis only daylight that makes sin,
Which these dun shades will ne'er report.
Hail, goddess of nocturnal sport,
Dark-veiled Cotytto, t' whom the secret flame
Of midnight torches burns! mysterious dame,              130
That ne'er art called but when the dragon womb
Of Stygian darkness spets her thickest gloom,
And makes one blot of all the air!
Stay thy cloudy ebon chair,
Wherein thou rid'st with Hecat', and befriend
Us thy vowed priests, till utmost end
Of all thy dues be done, and none left out;
Ere the blabbing eastern scout,
The nice Morn on th' Indian steep,
From her cabined loophole peep,                          140
And to the tell-tale Sun descry
Our concealed solemnity.
Come, knit hands, and beat the ground
In a light fantastic round.

*The Measure.*

Break off, break off! I feel the different pace
Of some chaste footing near about this ground.
Run to your shrouds within these brakes and trees;
Our number may affright.  Some virgin sure
(For so I can distinguish by mine art)
Benighted in these woods!  Now to my charms,                150
And to my wily trains: I shall ere long
Be well stocked with as fair a herd as grazed
About my mother Circe.  Thus I hurl
My dazzling spells into the spongy air,
Of power to cheat the eye with blear illusion,
And give it false presentments, lest the place
And my quaint habits breed astonishment,
And put the damsel to suspicious flight;
Which must not be, for that 's against my course.
I, under fair pretence of friendly ends,                      160
And well-placed words of glozing courtesy,
Baited with reasons not unplausible,
Wind me into the easy-hearted man,
And hug him into snares.  When once her eye
Hath met the virtue of this magic dust
I shall appear some harmless villager,
Whom thrift keeps up about his country gear.
But here she comes; I fairly step aside
And hearken, if I may, her business here.                     169

*The* LADY *enters.*

*Lady.*  This way the noise was, if mine ear be true,
My best guide now.  Methought it was the sound
Of riot and ill-managed merriment,
Such as the jocund flute or gamesome pipe
Stirs up among the loose unlettered hinds,
When, for their teeming flocks and granges full,
In wanton dance they praise the bounteous Pan,
And thank the gods amiss.  I should be loth
To meet the rudeness and swilled insolence
Of such late wassailers; yet, oh! where else
Shall I inform my unacquainted feet                            180
In the blind mazes of this tangled wood?
My brothers, when they saw me wearied out
With this long way, resolving here to lodge

Under the spreading favour of these pines,
Stepped, as they said, to the next thicket-side
To bring me berries, or such cooling fruit
As the kind hospitable woods provide.
They left me then when the grey-hooded Even,
Like a sad votarist in palmer's weed,
Rose from the hindmost wheels of Phœbus' wain.     190
But where they are, and why they came not back,
Is now the labour of my thoughts.  'Tis likeliest
They had engaged their wand'ring steps too far;
And envious darkness, ere they could return,
Had stole them from me. Else, O thievish Night,
Why shouldst thou, but for some felonious end,
In thy dark lantern thus close up the stars
That Nature hung in heaven, and filled their lamps
With everlasting oil, to give due light
To the misled and lonely traveller?              200
This is the place, as well as I may guess,
Whence even now the tumult of loud mirth
Was rife, and perfect in my list'ning ear;
Yet nought but single darkness do I find.
What might this be? A thousand fantasies
Begin to throng into my memory,
Of calling shapes, and beck'ning shadows dire,
And airy tongues that syllable men's names
On sands and shores and desert wildernesses.
These thoughts may startle well, but not astound  210
The virtuous mind, that ever walks attended
By a strong siding champion, Conscience.
O welcome, pure-eyed Faith, white-handed Hope,
Thou hovering angel girt with golden wings,
And thou unblemished form of Chastity!
I see ye visibly, and now believe
That He, the Supreme Good, t' whom all things ill
Are but as slavish officers of vengeance,
Would send a glistering guardian, if need were,
To keep my life and honour unassailed.           220
Was I deceived, or did a sable cloud
Turn forth her silver lining on the night?
I did not err: there does a sable cloud
Turn forth her silver lining on the night,

And casts a gleam over this tufted grove.
I cannot hallo to my brothers, but
Such noise as I can make to be heard farthest
I'll venture; for my new-enlivened spirits
Prompt me, and they perhaps are not far off.

### Song.

Sweet Echo, sweetest nymph, that liv'st unseen          230
  Within thy airy shell
  By slow Meander's margent green,
And in the violet-embroidered vale
  Where the love-lorn nightingale
Nightly to thee her sad song mourneth well:
  Canst thou not tell me of a gentle pair
   That likest thy Narcissus are?
    O if thou have
   Hid them in some flowery cave,
    Tell me but where,                     240
  Sweet Queen of Parley, Daughter of the Sphere!
  So may'st thou be translated to the skies,
And give resounding grace to all Heaven's harmonies!

*Comus.* Can any mortal mixture of earth's mould
Breathe such divine enchanting ravishment?
Sure something holy lodges in that breast,
And with these raptures moves the vocal air
To testify his hidden residence.
How sweetly did they float upon the wings
Of silence, through the empty-vaulted night,          250
At every fall smoothing the raven down
Of darkness till it smiled! I have oft heard
My mother Circe with the Sirens three,
Amidst the flowery-kirtled Naiades,
Culling their potent herbs and baleful drugs,
Who, as they sung, would take the prisoned soul,
And lap it in Elysium: Scylla wept,
And chid her barking waves into attention,
And fell Charybdis murmured soft applause.
Yet they in pleasing slumber lulled the sense,          260
And in sweet madness robbed it of itself;
But such a sacred and home-felt delight,

Such sober certainty of waking bliss,
I never heard till now. I'll speak to her,
And she shall be my queen.—Hail, foreign wonder!
Whom certain these rough shades did never breed,
Unless the goddess that in rural shrine
Dwell'st here with Pan or Sylvan, by blest song
Forbidding every bleak unkindly fog
To touch the prosperous growth of this tall wood.    270

   *Lady*.  Nay, gentle shepherd, ill is lost that praise
That is addressed to unattending ears.
Not any boast of skill, but extreme shift
How to regain my severed company,
Compelled me to awake the courteous Echo
To give me answer from her mossy couch.

   *Comus*.  What chance, good Lady, hath bereft you
    thus?

   *Lady*.  Dim darkness and this leafy labyrinth.

   *Comus*.  Could that divide you from near-ushering
    guides?

   *Lady*.  They left me weary on a grassy turf.    280

   *Comus*.  By falsehood, or discourtesy, or why?

   *Lady*.  To seek i' the valley some cool friendly spring.

   *Comus*.  And left your fair side all unguarded, Lady?

   *Lady*.  They were but twain, and purposed quick
    return.

   *Comus*.  Perhaps forestalling night prevented them.

   *Lady*.  How easy my misfortune is to hit!

   *Comus*.  Imports their loss, beside the present need?

   *Lady*.  No less than if I should my brothers lose.

   *Comus*.  Were they of manly prime, or youthful bloom?

   *Lady*.  As smooth as Hebe's their unrazored lips.    290

   *Comus*.  Two such I saw, what time the laboured
    ox
In his loose traces from the furrow came,
And the swinked hedger at his supper sat.
I saw them under a green mantling vine,
That crawls along the side of yon small hill,
Plucking ripe clusters from the tender shoots;
Their port was more than human, as they stood.
I took it for a faëry vision
Of some gay creatures of the element,

That in the colours of the rainbow live,                    300
And play i' the plighted clouds. I was awe-struck,
And, as I passed, I worshipped. If those you seek,
It were a journey like the path to Heaven
To help you find them.
    *Lady.*            Gentle villager,
What readiest way would bring me to that place?
    *Comus.* Due west it rises from this shrubby point.
    *Lady.* To find out that, good shepherd, I suppose,
In such a scant allowance of star-light,
Would overtask the best land-pilot's art,
Without the sure guess of well-practised feet.                    310
    *Comus.* I know each lane, and every alley green,
Dingle, or bushy dell, of this wild wood,
And every bosky bourn from side to side,
My daily walks and ancient neighbourhood;
And, if your stray attendance be yet lodged,
Or shroud within these limits, I shall know
Ere morrow wake, or the low-roosted lark
From her thatched pallet rouse. If otherwise,
I can conduct you, Lady, to a low
But loyal cottage, where you may be safe                    320
Till further quest.
    *Lady.*          Shepherd, I take thy word,
And trust thy honest-offered courtesy,
Which oft is sooner found in lowly sheds,
With smoky rafters, than in tap'stry halls
And courts of princes, where it first was named,
And yet is most pretended. In a place
Less warranted than this, or less secure,
I cannot be, that I should fear to change it.
Eye me, blest Providence, and square my trial                    329
To my proportioned strength! Shepherd, lead on. . . .

### The TWO BROTHERS.

    *Eld. Bro.* Unmuffle, ye faint stars; and thou, fair moon,
That wont'st to love the traveller's benison,
Stoop thy pale visage through an amber cloud,
And disinherit Chaos, that reigns here
In double night of darkness and of shades;

Or, if your influence be quite dammed up
With black usurping mists, some gentle taper,
Though a rush-candle from the wicker hole
Of some clay habitation, visit us
With thy long levelled rule of streaming light,        340
And thou shalt be our star of Arcady,
Or Tyrian Cynosure.

   *Sec. Bro.*   Or, if our eyes
Be barred that happiness, might we but hear
The folded flocks penned in their wattled cotes,
Or sound of pastoral reed with oaten stops,
Or whistle from the lodge, or village cock
Count the night-watches to his feathery dames,
'Twould be some solace yet, some little cheering,
In this close dungeon of innumerous boughs.
But, oh, that hapless virgin, our lost sister!        350
Where may she wander now, whither betake her
From the chill dew, amongst rude burs and thistles?
Perhaps some cold bank is her bolster now,
Or 'gainst the rugged bark of some broad elm
Leans her unpillowed head, fraught with sad fears.
What if in wild amazement and affright,
Or, while we speak, within the direful grasp
Of savage hunger, or of savage heat!

  *Eld. Bro.* Peace, brother: be not over-exquisite
To cast the fashion of uncertain evils;        360
For, grant they be so, while they rest unknown,
What need a man forestall his date of grief,
And run to meet what he would most avoid?
Or, if they be but false alarms of fear,
How bitter is such self-delusion!
I do not think my sister so to seek,
Or so unprincipled in virtue's book,
And the sweet peace that goodness bosoms ever,
As that the single want of light and noise
(Not being in danger, as I trust she is not)        370
Could stir the constant mood of her calm thoughts,
And put them into misbecoming plight.
Virtue could see to do what Virtue would
By her own radiant light, though sun and moon
Were in the flat sea sunk. And Wisdom's self

Oft seeks to sweet retired solitude,
Where, with her best nurse, Contemplation,
She plumes her feathers, and lets grow her wings,
That, in the various bustle of resort,
Were all to-ruffled, and sometimes impaired.          380
He that has light within his own clear breast
May sit i' the centre, and enjoy bright day:
But he that hides a dark soul and foul thoughts,
Benighted walks under the midday sun;
Himself is his own dungeon.

    *Sec. Bro.*            'Tis most true
That musing Meditation most affects
The pensive secrecy of desert cell,
Far from the cheerful haunt of men and herds,
And sits as safe as in a senate-house;
For who would rob a hermit of his weeds.              390
His few books, or his beads, or maple dish,
Or do his grey hairs any violence?
But Beauty, like the fair Hesperian tree
Laden with blooming gold, had need the guard
Of dragon-watch with unenchanted eye,
To save her blossoms, and defend her fruit,
From the rash hand of bold Incontinence.
You may as well spread out the unsunn'd heaps
Of miser's treasure by an outlaw's den,
And tell me it is safe, as bid me hope               400
Danger will wink on Opportunity,
And let a single helpless maiden pass
Uninjured in this wild surrounding waste.
Of night or loneliness it recks me not;
I fear the dread events that dog them both,
Lest some ill greeting touch attempt the person
Of our unowned sister.

    *Eld. Bro.*        I do not, brother,
Infer as if I thought my sister's state
Secure without all doubt or controversy;
Yet, where an equal poise of hope and fear           410
Does arbitrate th' event, my nature is
That I incline to hope rather than fear,
And gladly banish squint suspicion.
My sister is not so defenceless left

As you imagine; she has a hidden strength,
Which you remember not.
    *Sec. Bro.*          What hidden strength,
Unless the strength of Heaven, if you mean that?
    *Eld. Bro.*  I mean that too, but yet a hidden
      strength,
Which, if Heaven gave it, may be termed her own;
'Tis chastity, my brother, chastity:               420
She that has that, is clad in complete steel,
And, like a quivered nymph with arrows keen,
May trace huge forests, and unharboured heaths,
Infamous hills, and sandy perilous wilds;
Where, through the sacred rays of chastity,
No savage fierce, bandit, or mountaineer,
Will dare to soil her virgin purity.
Yea, there where very desolation dwells,
By grots and caverns shagged with horrid shades,
She may pass on with unblenched majesty,      430
Be it not done in pride, or in presumption.
Some say no evil thing that walks by night
In fog or fire, by lake or moorish fen,
Blue meagre hag, or stubborn unlaid ghost,
That breaks his magic chains at curfew time,
No goblin or swart faëry of the mine,
Hath hurtful power o'er true virginity.
Do ye believe me yet, or shall I call
Antiquity from the old schools of Greece
To testify the arms of chastity?              440
Hence had the huntress Dian her dread bow,
Fair silver-shafted queen for ever chaste,
Wherewith she tamed the brinded lioness
And spotted mountain pard, but set at nought
The frivolous bolt of Cupid; gods and men
Feared her stern frown, and she was queen o' the
    woods.
What was that snaky-headed Gorgon shield
That wise Minerva wore, unconquered virgin,
Wherewith she freezed her foes to congealed stone,
But rigid looks of chaste austerity,          450
And noble grace that dashed brute violence
With sudden adoration and blank awe?

So dear to Heaven is saintly chastity,
That when a soul is found sincerely so,
A thousand liveried angels lackey her,
Driving far off each thing of sin and guilt,
And in clear dream and solemn vision
Tell her of things that no gross ear can hear;
Till oft converse with heavenly habitants
Begin to cast a beam on th' outward shape,                460
The unpolluted temple of the mind,
And turns it by degrees to the soul's essence,
Till all be made immortal.  But when lust
By unchaste looks, loose gestures, and foul talk,
But most by lewd and lavish act of sin,
Lets in defilement to the inward parts,
The soul grows clotted by contagion,
Imbodies, and imbrutes, till she quite lose
The divine property of her first being.
Such are those thick and gloomy shadows damp      470
Oft seen in charnel-vaults and sepulchres,
Lingering and sitting by a new-made grave,
As loth to leave the body that it loved,
And linked itself by carnal sensualty
To a degenerate and degraded state.
    *Sec. Bro.* How charming is divine Philosophy!
Not harsh and crabbed, as dull fools suppose,
But musical as is Apollo's lute,
And a perpetual feast of nectared sweets,
Where no crude surfeit reigns.
    *Eld. Bro.*             List! list! I hear      480
Some far-off hallo break the silent air.
    *Sec. Bro.* Methought so too; what should it be?
    *Eld. Bro.*                For certain,
Either some one like us night-foundered here,
Or else some neighbour woodman, or, at worst,
Some roving robber calling to his fellows.
    *Sec. Bro.* Heaven keep my sister! Again, again
    and near!
Best draw, and stand upon our guard.
    *Eld. Bro.*                I'll hallo.
If he be friendly, he comes well: if not,
Defence is a good cause, and Heaven be for us!

*The* ATTENDANT SPIRIT, *habited like a Shepherd.*

That hallo I should know. What are you? speak.        490
Come not too near; you fall on iron stakes else.
   *Spir.* What voice is that? my young Lord? speak
    again.
   *Sec. Bro.* O brother, 'tis my father's shepherd, sure.
   *Eld. Bro.* Thyrsis! whose artful strains have oft
    delayed
The huddling brook to hear his madrigal,
And sweetened every musk-rose of the dale.
How cam'st thou here, good swain? hath any ram
Slipped from the fold, or young kid lost his dam,
Or straggling wether the pent flock forsook?
How couldst thou find this dark sequestered nook?   500
   *Spir.* O my loved master's heir, and his next joy,
I came not here on such a trivial toy
As a strayed ewe, or to pursue the stealth
Of pilfering wolf; not all the fleecy wealth
That doth enrich these downs is worth a thought
To this my errand, and the care it brought.
But, oh! my virgin Lady, where is she?
How chance she is not in your company?
   *Eld. Bro.* To tell thee sadly, Shepherd, without
    blame
Or our neglect, we lost her as we came.            510
   *Spir.* Ay me unhappy! then my fears are true.
   *Eld. Bro.* What fears, good Thyrsis? Prithee briefly
    shew.
   *Spir.* I'll tell ye. 'Tis not vain or fabulous,
(Though so esteemed by shallow ignorance)
What the sage poets, taught by th' heavenly Muse,
Storied of old in high immortal verse
Of dire Chimeras and enchanted isles,
And rifted rocks whose entrance leads to Hell;
For such there be, but unbelief is blind.
   Within the navel of this hideous wood,           520
Immured in cypress shades, a sorcerer dwells,
Of Bacchus and of Circe born, great Comus,
Deep skilled in all his mother's witcheries,
And here to every thirsty wanderer

By sly enticement gives his baneful cup,
With many murmurs mixed, whose pleasing poison
The visage quite transforms of him that drinks,
And the inglorious likeness of a beast
Fixes instead, unmoulding reason's mintage,
Charactered in the face. This have I learnt          530
Tending my flocks hard by i' th' hilly crofts
That brow this bottom glade; whence night by night
He and his monstrous rout are heard to howl
Like stabled wolves, or tigers at their prey,
Doing abhorred rites to Hecate
In their obscured haunts of inmost bowers.
Yet have they many baits and guileful spells
To inveigle and invite th' unwary sense
Of them that pass unweeting by the way.
This evening late, by then the chewing flocks          540
Had ta'en their supper on the savoury herb
Of knot-grass dew-besprent, and were in fold,
I sat me down to watch upon a bank
With ivy canopied, and interwove
With flaunting honeysuckle, and began,
Wrapt in a pleasing fit of melancholy,
To meditate my rural minstrelsy,
Till Fancy had her fill. But ere a close
The wonted roar was up amidst the woods,
And filled the air with barbarous dissonance;          550
At which I ceased, and listened them a while,
Till an unusual stop of sudden silence
Gave respite to the drowsy frighted steeds
That draw the litter of close-curtained Sleep.
At last a soft and solemn-breathing sound
Rose like a steam of rich distill'd perfumes,
And stole upon the air, that even Silence
Was took ere she was ware, and wished she might
Deny her nature, and be never more
Still to be so displaced. I was all ear,          560
And took in strains that might create a soul
Under the ribs of Death. But, oh! ere long
Too well I did perceive it was the voice
Of my most honoured Lady, your dear sister.
Amazed I stood, harrowed with grief and fear;

And 'O poor hapless nightingale,' thought I,
'How sweet thou sing'st, how near the deadly snare!'
Then down the lawns I ran with headlong haste,
Through paths and turnings often trod by day,
Till, guided by mine ear, I found the place          570
Where that damned wizard, hid in sly disguise,
(For so by certain signs I knew,) had met
Already, ere my best speed could prevent,
The aidless innocent Lady, his wished prey;
Who gently asked if he had seen such two,
Supposing him some neighbour villager.
Longer I durst not stay, but soon I guessed
Ye were the two she meant; with that I sprung
Into swift flight, till I had found you here;
But further know I not.
    *Sec. Bro.*        O night and shades,     580
How are ye joined with hell in triple knot
Against th' unarmed weakness of one virgin,
Alone and helpless! Is this the confidence
You gave me, brother?
    *Eld. Bro.*        Yes, and keep it still;
Lean on it safely; not a period
Shall be unsaid for me. Against the threats
Of malice or of sorcery, or that power
Which erring men call Chance, this I hold firm:
Virtue may be assailed, but never hurt,
Surprised by unjust force, but not enthralled:     590
Yea, even that which Mischief meant most harm
Shall in the happy trial prove most glory.
But evil on itself shall back recoil,
And mix no more with goodness, when at last,
Gathered like scum, and settled to itself,
It shall be in eternal restless change
Self-fed and self-consum'd. If this fail,
The pillared firmament is rottenness,
And earth's base built on stubble.    But come, let's on!
Against th' opposing will and arm of Heaven        600
May never this just sword be lifted up;
But, for that damned magician, let him be girt
With all the grisly legions that troop
Under the sooty flag of Acheron,

Harpies and Hydras, or all the monstrous forms
'Twixt Africa and Ind, I'll find him out,
And force him to restore his purchase back,
Or drag him by the curls to a foul death,
Cursed as his life.
    *Spir.*          Alas! good venturous youth, 610
I love thy courage yet, and bold emprise;
But here thy sword can do thee little stead.
Far other arms and other weapons must
Be those that quell the might of hellish charms.
He with his bare wand can unthread thy joints,
And crumble all thy sinews.
    *Eld. Bro.*       Why prithee, Shepherd,
How durst thou then thyself approach so near
As to make this relation?
    *Spir.*          Care and utmost shifts
How to secure the Lady from surprisal
Brought to my mind a certain shepherd lad
Of small regard to see to, yet well skilled 620
In every virtuous plant and healing herb
That spreads her verdant leaf to the morning ray.
He loved me well, and oft would beg me sing;
Which when I did, he on the tender grass
Would sit, and hearken even to ecstasy;
And in requital ope his leathern scrip,
And show me simples of a thousand names,
Telling their strange and vigorous faculties.
Amongst the rest a small unsightly root,
But of divine effect, he culled me out. 630
The leaf was darkish, and had prickles on it,
But in another country, as he said,
Bore a bright golden flower, but not in this soil:
Unknown, and like esteemed, and the dull swain
Treads on it daily with his clouted shoon;
And yet more med'cinal is it than that moly
That Hermes once to wise Ulysses gave;
He called it hæmony, and gave it me,
And bade me keep it as of sovran use
'Gainst all enchantments, mildew blast, or damp, 640
Or ghastly Furies' apparition.
I pursed it up, but little reck'ning made,

Till now that this extremity compelled,
But now I find it true; for by this means
I knew the foul enchanter, though disguised,
Entered the very lime-twigs of his spells,
And yet came off.  If you have this about you
(As I will give you when we go) you may
Boldly assault the necromancer's hall;
Where if he be, with dauntless hardihood          650
And brandished blade rush on him, break his glass,
And shed the luscious liquor on the ground,
But seize his wand; though he and his curst crew
Fierce sign of battle make, and menace high,
Or, like the sons of Vulcan, vomit smoke,
Yet will they soon retire, if he but shrink.

    *Eld. Bro.*  Thyrsis, lead on apace; I'll follow thee:
And some good angel bear a shield before us!


*The Scene changes to a stately palace, set out with all*
    *manner of deliciousness; soft music, tables spread with*
    *all dainties.* COMUS *appears with his rabble, and the*
    LADY *set in an enchanted chair: to whom he offers his*
    *glass; which she puts by, and goes about to rise.*

    *Comus.*  Nay, Lady, sit.  If I but wave this wand,
Your nerves are all chained up in alabaster,          660
And you a statue, or as Daphne was
Root-bound, that fled Apollo.
    *Lady.*                              Fool, do not boast.
Thou canst not touch the freedom of my mind
With all thy charms, although this corporal rind
Thou hast immanacled while Heaven sees good.
    *Comus.*  Why are you vexed, Lady? why do you frown?
Here dwell no frowns, nor anger; from these gates
Sorrow flies far.  See, here be all the pleasures
That fancy can beget on youthful thoughts,
When the fresh blood grows lively, and returns          670
Brisk as the April buds in primrose season.
And first behold this cordial julep here,
That flames and dances in his crystal bounds,
With spirits of balm and fragant syrups mixed.
Not that Nepenthes which the wife of Thone

In Egypt gave to Jove-born Helena,
Is of such power to stir up joy as this,
To life so friendly, or so cool to thirst.
Why should you be so cruel to yourself,
And to those dainty limbs, which Nature lent    680
For gentle usage and soft delicacy?
But you invert the cov'nants of her trust,
And harshly deal, like an ill borrower,
With that which you received on other terms;
Scorning the unexempt condition
By which all mortal frailty must subsist,
Refreshment after toil, ease after pain,
That have been tired all day without repast,
And timely rest have wanted; but, fair virgin,
This will restore all soon.
   *Lady.*    'Twill not, false traitor!   690
'Twill not restore the truth and honesty
That thou hast banished from thy tongue with lies.
Was this the cottage and the safe abode
Thou told'st me of? What grim aspects are these,
These ugly-headed monsters? Mercy guard me!
Hence with thy brewed enchantments, foul deceiver!
Hast thou betrayed my credulous innocence
With vizored falsehood and base forgery?
And wouldst thou seek again to trap me here
With liquorish baits, fit to ensnare a brute?   700
Were it a draught for Juno when she banquets,
I would not taste thy treasonous offer; none
But such as are good men can give good things;
And that which is not good, is not delicious
To a well-governed and wise appetite.
   *Comus.* O foolishness of men! that lend their ears
To those budge doctors of the Stoic fur,
And fetch their precepts from the Cynic tub,
Praising the lean and sallow Abstinence!
Wherefore did Nature pour her bounties forth   710
With such a full and unwithdrawing hand,
Covering the earth with odours, fruits, and flocks,
Thronging the seas with spawn innumerable,
But all to please and sate the curious taste?
And set to work millions of spinning worms,

That in their green shops weave the smooth-haired silk,
To deck her sons; and, that no corner might
Be vacant of her plenty, in her own loins
She hutched th' all-worshipped ore and precious gems
To store her children with. If all the world          720
Should, in a pet of temperance, feed on pulse,
Drink the clear stream, and nothing wear but frieze,
Th' All-giver would be unthanked, would be unpraised,
Not half his riches known, and yet despised;
And we should serve him as a grudging master,
As a penurious niggard of his wealth,
And live like Nature's bastards, not her sons,
Who would be quite surcharged with her own weight,
And strangled with her waste fertility:
Th' earth cumbered, and the wing'd air darked with
          plumes.                                      730
The herds would over-multitude their lords,
The sea o'erfraught would swell, and th' unsought
          diamonds·
Would so emblaze the forehead of the deep,
And so bestud with stars, that they below
Would grow inured to light, and come at last
To gaze upon the sun with shameless brows.
List, Lady; be not coy, and be not cozened
With that same vaunted name, Virginity.
Beauty is Nature's coin; must not be hoarded,
But must be current; and the good thereof          740
Consists in mutual and partaken bliss,
Unsavoury in th' enjoyment of itself.
If you let slip time, like a neglected rose
It withers on the stalk with languished head.
Beauty is Nature's brag, and must be shown
In courts, at feasts, and high solemnities,
Where most may wonder at the workmanship;
It is for homely features to keep home;
They had their names thence: coarse complexions
And cheeks of sorry grain will serve to ply          750
The sampler, and to tease the huswife's wool.
What need a vermeil-tinctured lip for that,
Love-darting eyes, or tresses like the morn?
There was another meaning in these gifts;

Think what, and be advised; you are but young yet.

*Lady*.  I had not thought to have unlocked my lips
In this unhallowed air, but that this juggler
Would think to charm my judgement, as mine eyes,
Obtruding false rules pranked in reason's garb.
I hate when vice can bolt her arguments          760
And virtue has no tongue to check her pride.
Impostor! do not charge most innocent Nature,
As if she would her children should be riotous
With her abundance.  She, good cateress,
Means her provision only to the good,
That live according to her sober laws,
And holy dictate of spare Temperance.
If every just man that now pines with want
Had but a moderate and beseeming share
Of that which lewdly-pampered Luxury          770
Now heaps upon some few with vast excess,
Nature's full blessings would be well-dispensed
In unsuperfluous even proportion,
And she no whit encumbered with her store;
And then the Giver would be better thanked,
His praise due paid: for swinish gluttony
Ne'er looks to Heaven amidst his gorgeous feast,
But with besotted base ingratitude
Crams, and blasphemes his Feeder.  Shall I go on?
Or have I said enough?  To him that dares        780
Arm his profane tongue with contemptuous words
Against the sun-clad power of chastity
Fain would I something say;—yet to what end?
Thou hast nor ear, nor soul, to apprehend
The sublime notion and high mystery
That must be uttered to unfold the sage
And serious doctrine of Virginity;
And thou art worthy that thou shouldst not know
More happiness than this thy present lot.
Enjoy your dear wit, and gay rhetoric,          790
That hath so well been taught her dazzling fence;
Thou art not fit to hear thyself convinced.
Yet, should I try, the uncontrolled worth
Of this pure cause would kindle my rapt spirits

To such a flame of sacred vehemence
That dumb things would be moved to sympathize,
And the brute Earth would lend her nerves, and
    shake,
Till all thy magic structures, reared so high,
Were shattered into heaps o'er thy false head.
    *Comus.* She fables not. I feel that I do fear      800
Her words set off by some superior power;
And though not mortal, yet a cold shuddering dew
Dips me all o'er, as when the wrath of Jove
Speaks thunder and the chains of Erebus
To some of Saturn's crew. I must dissemble,
And try her yet more strongly.—Come, no more!
This is mere moral babble, and direct
Against the canon laws of our foundation.
I must not suffer this; yet 'tis but the lees
And settlings of a melancholy blood.      810
But this will cure all straight; one sip of this
Will bathe the drooping spirits in delight
Beyond the bliss of dreams. Be wise, and taste.


*The* BROTHERS *rush in with swords drawn, wrest his glass
    out of his hand, and break it against the ground: his
    rout make sign of resistance, but are all driven in. The*
    ATTENDANT SPIRIT *comes in.*

    *Spir.* What! have you let the false enchanter scape?
O ye mistook; ye should have snatched his wand,
And bound him fast. Without his rod reversed,
And backward mutters of dissevering power,
We cannot free the Lady that sits here
In stony fetters fixed and motionless.
Yet stay, be not disturbed; now I bethink me,      820
Some other means I have which may be used,
Which once of Melibœus old I learnt,
The soothest shepherd that e'er piped on plains.
    There is a gentle Nymph not far from hence,
That with moist curb sways the smooth Severn stream:
Sabrina is her name, a virgin pure;
Whilom she was the daughter of Locrine,
That had the sceptre from his father Brute.

She, guiltless damsel, flying the mad pursuit
Of her enraged stepdame Guendolen,                 830
Commended her fair innocence to the flood
That stayed her flight with his cross-flowing course.
The water-nymphs, that in the bottom played,
Held up their pearled wrists, and took her in,
Bearing her straight to aged Nereus' hall;
Who, piteous of her woes, reared her lank head,
And gave her to his daughters to imbathe
In nectared lavers strewed with asphodel,
And through the porch and inlet of each sense
Dropped in ambrosial oils, till she revived,        840
And underwent a quick immortal change,
Made Goddess of the river; still she retains
Her maiden gentleness, and oft at eve
Visits the herds along the twilight meadows,
Helping all urchin blasts, and ill-luck signs
That the shrewd meddling elf delights to make,
Which she with precious vialed liquors heals.
For which the shepherds, at their festivals,
Carol her goodness loud in rustic lays,
And throw sweet garland wreaths into her stream     850
Of pansies, pinks, and gaudy daffodils.
And, as the old swain said, she can unlock
The clasping charm, and thaw the numbing spell,
If she be right invoked in warbled song;
For maidenhood she loves, and will be swift
To aid a virgin, such as was herself,
In hard-besetting need. This will I try,
And add the power of some adjuring verse.

*Song.*

Sabrina fair,
    Listen where thou art sitting                  860
Under the glassy, cool, translucent wave,
    In twisted braids of lilies knitting
The loose train of thy amber-dropping hair;
    Listen for dear honour's sake,
    Goddess of the silver lake,
        Listen and save!

Listen, and appear to us,
In name of great Oceanus,
By the earth-shaking Neptune's mace,
And Tethys' grave majestic pace;               870
By hoary Nereus' wrinkled look,
And the Carpathian wizard's hook;
By scaly Triton's winding shell,
And old soothsaying Glaucus' spell;
By Leucothea's lovely hands,
And her son that rules the strands;
By Thetis' tinsel-slippered feet,
And the songs of Sirens sweet;
By dead Parthenope's dear tomb,
And fair Ligea's golden comb,                  880
Wherewith she sits on diamond rocks
Sleeking her soft alluring locks;
By all the nymphs that nightly dance
Upon thy streams with wily glance;
Rise, rise, and heave thy rosy head
From thy coral-paven bed,
And bridle in thy headlong wave,
Till thou our summons answered have.

                    Listen and save!


SABRINA *rises, attended by Water-nymphs, and sings.*

By the rushy-fringed bank,                     890
Where grows the willow and the osier dank,
    My sliding chariot stays,
Thick set with agate, and the azurn sheen
Of turkis blue, and emerald green,
      That in the channel strays:
Whilst from off the waters fleet
Thus I set my printless feet
O'er the cowslip's velvet head,
    That bends not as I tread.
Gentle swain, at thy request                   900
      I am here!
    *Spir.* Goddess dear,
We implore thy powerful hand
To undo the charmed band

Of true virgin here distressed
Through the force and through the wile
Of unblessed enchanter vile.
　　*Sabr.* Shepherd, 'tis my office best
To help ensnared chastity.
Brightest Lady, look on me.　　　　　　　910
Thus I sprinkle on thy breast
Drops that from my fountain pure,
I have kept of precious cure,
Thrice upon thy finger's tip,
Thrice upon thy rubied lip:
Next this marble venomed seat,
Smeared with gums of glutinous heat,
I touch with chaste palms moist and cold;
Now the spell hath lost his hold;
And I must haste ere morning hour　　　920
To wait in Amphitrite's bower.

SABRINA *descends, and the* LADY *rises out of her seat.*
　　*Spir.* Virgin, daughter of Locrine,
Sprung of old Anchises' line,
May thy brimmed waves for this
Their full tribute never miss
From a thousand petty rills,
That tumble down the snowy hills;
Summer drouth or singed air
Never scorch thy tresses fair,
Nor wet October's torrent flood　　　930
Thy molten crystal fill with mud;
May thy billows roll ashore
The beryl, and the golden ore;
May thy lofty head be crowned
With many a tower and terrace round,
And here and there thy banks upon
With groves of myrrh and cinnamon.
　　Come, Lady; while Heaven lends us grace,
Let us fly this cursed place,
Lest the sorcerer us entice　　　　　　940
With some other new device.
Not a waste or needless sound
Till we come to holier ground.

I shall be your faithful guide
Through this gloomy covert wide;
And not many furlongs thence
Is your Father's residence,
Where this night are met in state
Many a friend to gratulate
His wish'd presence, and beside         950
All the swains that there abide
With jigs and rural dance resort.
We shall catch them at their sport,
And our sudden coming there
Will double all their mirth and cheer.
Come, let us haste; the stars grow high,
But Night sits monarch yet in the mid sky.

*The Scene changes, presenting Ludlow Town, and the President's Castle: then come in Country Dancers: after them the* ATTENDANT SPIRIT, *with the two* BROTHERS *and the* LADY.

### Song.

*Spir.*  Back, shepherds, back! Enough your play,
Till next sunshine holiday.
Here be, without duck or nod,         960
Other trippings to be trod
Of lighter toes, and such court guise
As Mercury did first devise
With the mincing Dryades
On the lawns, and on the leas.

*This second Song presents them to their Father and Mother.*

Noble Lord and Lady bright,
I have brought ye new delight;
Here behold so goodly grown
Three fair branches of your own.
Heaven hath timely tried their youth,         970
Their faith, their patience, and their truth,
And sent them here through hard assays
With a crown of deathless praise,
To triumph in victorious dance
O'er sensual Folly and Intemperance.

*The dances ended, the* SPIRIT *epiloguizes.*

*Spir.* To the ocean now I fly,
And those happy climes that lie
Where day never shuts his eye,
Up in the broad fields of the sky.
There I suck the liquid air,                    980
All amidst the gardens fair
Of Hesperus, and his daughters three
That sing about the golden tree.
Along the crisped shades and bowers
Revels the spruce and jocund Spring;
The Graces and the rosy-bosomed Hours
Thither all their bounties bring,
That there eternal Summer dwells;
And west winds with musky wing
About the cedarn alleys fling                    990
Nard, and cassia's balmy smells.
Iris there with humid bow
Waters the odorous banks, that blow
Flowers of more mingled hue
Than her purfled scarf can shew,
And drenches with Elysian dew
(List, mortals, if your ears be true)
Beds of hyacinth and roses,
Where young Adonis oft reposes,
Waxing well of his deep wound,                    1000
In slumber soft, and on the ground
Sadly sits th' Assyrian queen.
But far above, in spangled sheen,
Celestial Cupid, her famed son, advanced
Holds his dear Psyche, sweet entranced
After her wandering labours long,
Till free consent the gods among
Make her his eternal bride;
And from her fair unspotted side
Two blissful twins are to be born,                    1010
Youth and Joy; so Jove hath sworn.
But now my task is smoothly done,
I can fly, or I can run
Quickly to the green earth's end,
Where the bowed welkin slow doth bend:

And from thence can soar as soon
To the corners of the moon.
   Mortals, that would follow me,
Love Virtue; she alone is free.
She can teach ye how to climb       1020
Higher than the sphery chime;
Or, if Virtue feeble were,
Heaven itself would stoop to her

# POEMS ADDED IN THE 1673 EDITION

*Anno aetatis* 17

## ON THE DEATH OF A FAIR INFANT DYING OF A COUGH

### I

O FAIREST flower, no sooner blown but blasted,
Soft silken primrose fading timelessly,
Summer's chief honour, if thou hadst outlasted
Bleak Winter's force that made thy blossom dry;
For he, being amorous on that lovely dye
   That did thy cheek envermeil, thought to kiss,
But killed, alas! and then bewailed his fatal bliss.

### II

For since grim Aquilo, his charioteer,
By boist'rous rape th' Athenian damsel got,
He thought it touched his deity full near,     10
If likewise he some fair one wedded not;
Thereby to wipe away th' infamous blot
   Of long uncoupled bed and childless eld,
Which 'mongst the wanton gods a foul reproach was held.

### III

So, mounting up in icy-pearled car,
Through middle empire of the freezing air
He wandered long, till thee he spied from far;
There ended was his quest, there ceased his care.
Down he descended from his snow-soft chair,
   But, all unwares, with his cold-kind embrace,     20
Unhoused thy virgin soul from her fair biding-place.

### IV

Yet art thou not inglorious in thy fate;
For so Apollo, with unweeting hand,
Whilom did slay his dearly-loved mate,
Young Hyacinth, born on Eurotas' strand,
Young Hyacinth, the pride of Spartan land;
   But then transformed him to a purple flower:
Alack, that so to change thee Winter had no power!

### V

Yet can I not persuade me thou art dead,
Or that thy corse corrupts in earth's dark womb,   30
Or that thy beauties lie in wormy bed
Hid from the world in a low-delved tomb;
Could Heaven, for pity, thee so strictly doom?
   Oh no! for something in thy face did shine
Above mortality, that showed thou wast divine.

### VI

Resolve me, then, O soul most surely blest
(If so it be that thou these plaints dost hear)!
Tell me, bright Spirit, where'er thou hoverest,
Whether above that high first-moving sphere,
Or in the Elysian fields (if such there were),   40
   O say me true if thou wert mortal wight,
And why from us so quickly thou didst take thy flight.

### VII

Wert thou some star, which from the ruined roof
Of shaked Olympus by mischance didst fall;
Which careful Jove in nature's true behoof
Took up, and in fit place did reinstall?
Or did of late Earth's sons besiege the wall
   Of sheeny Heaven, and thou some goddess fled
Amongst us here below to hide thy nectared head?

### VIII

Or wert thou that just Maid who once before   50
Forsook the hated earth, oh! tell me sooth,
And cam'st again to visit us once more?

Or wert thou [Mercy] that sweet smiling Youth?
Or that crowned Matron, sage white-robed Truth?
  Or any other of that heavenly brood
Let down in cloudy throne to do the world some good?

### IX

Or wert thou of the golden-winged host,
Who, having clad thyself in human weed,
To earth from thy prefixed seat didst post,
And after short abode fly back with speed,               60
As if to show what creatures Heaven doth breed;
  Thereby to set the hearts of men on fire
To scorn the sordid world, and unto Heaven aspire?

### X

But oh! why didst thou not stay here below
To bless us with thy Heaven-loved innocence,
To slake his wrath whom sin hath made our foe,
To turn swift-rushing black perdition hence,
Or drive away the slaughtering pestilence,
  To stand 'twixt us and our deserved smart?
But thou canst best perform that office where thou art.

### XI

Then thou, the mother of so sweet a child,            71
Her false imagined loss cease to lament,
And wisely learn to curb thy sorrows wild;
Think what a present thou to God hast sent,
And render him with patience what he lent:
  This if thou do, he will an offspring give
That till the world's last end shall make thy name to live.

*Anno aetatis* 19

## AT A VACATION EXERCISE IN THE
## COLLEGE, PART LATIN PART ENGLISH

*The Latin Speeches ended, the English thus began:—*

HAIL, native language, that by sinews weak
Didst move my first endeavouring tongue to speak,
And mad'st imperfect words with childish trips,
Half unpronounced, slide through my infant lips,
Driving dumb Silence from the portal door,
Where he had mutely sat two years before:
Here I salute thee, and thy pardon ask
That now I use thee in my latter task:
Small loss it is that thence can come unto thee,
I know my tongue but little grace can do thee.          10
Thou need'st not be ambitious to be first,
Believe me, I have thither packed the worst:
And, if it happen as I did forecast,
The daintiest dishes shall be served up last.
I pray thee then deny me not thy aid
For this same small neglect that I have made;
But haste thee straight to do me once a pleasure,
And from thy wardrobe bring thy chiefest treasure;
Not those new-fangled toys, and trimming slight
Which takes our late fantastics with delight;          20
But cull those richest robes and gay'st attire,
Which deepest spirits and choicest wits desire.
I have some naked thoughts that rove about,
And loudly knock to have their passage out,
And, weary of their place, do only stay
Till thou hast decked them in thy best array;
That so they may, without suspect or fears,
Fly swiftly to this fair assembly's ears.
Yet I had rather, if I were to choose,
Thy service in some graver subject use,          30
Such as may make thee search thy coffers round,
Before thou clothe my fancy in fit sound:

Such where the deep transported mind may soar
Above the wheeling poles, and at Heaven's door
Look in, and see each blissful deity
How he before the thunderous throne doth lie,
Listening to what unshorn Apollo sings
To the touch of golden wires, while Hebe brings
Immortal nectar to her kingly sire;
Then, passing through the spheres of watchful fire,    40
And misty regions of wide air next under,
And hills of snow and lofts of piled thunder,
May tell at length how green-eyed Neptune raves,
In Heaven's defiance mustering all his waves;
Then sing of secret things that came to pass
When beldam Nature in her cradle was;
And last of kings and queens and heroes old,
Such as the wise Demodocus once told
In solemn songs at king Alcinous' feast,
While sad Ulysses' soul and all the rest    50
Are held, with his melodious harmony,
In willing chains and sweet captivity.
But fie, my wandering Muse, how thou dost stray!
Expectance calls thee now another way.
Thou know'st it must be now thy only bent
To keep in compass of thy predicament.
Then quick about thy purposed business come,
That to the next I may resign my room.

*Then* ENS *is represented as Father of the Predicaments, his ten Sons; whereof the eldest stood for* SUBSTANCE *with his Canons; which* ENS, *thus speaking, explains:*—

Good luck befriend thee, Son; for at thy birth
The faëry ladies danced upon the hearth.    60
Thy drowsy nurse hath sworn she did them spy
Come tripping to the room where thou didst lie,
And, sweetly singing round about thy bed,
Strew all their blessings on thy sleeping head.
She heard them give thee this, that thou shouldst still
From eyes of mortals walk invisible.
Yet there is something that doth force my fear;
For once it was my dismal hap to hear

A Sibyl old, bow-bent with crooked age,
That far events full wisely could presage,          70
And, in Time's long and dark prospective-glass,
Foresaw what future days should bring to pass.
  'Your son', said she '(nor can you it prevent),
Shall subject be to many an Accident.
O'er all his brethren he shall reign as king;
Yet every one shall make him underling,
And those that cannot live from him asunder
Ungratefully shall strive to keep him under.
In worth and excellence he shall outgo them,
Yet, being above them, he shall be below them;          80
From others he shall stand in need of nothing,
Yet on his brothers shall depend for clothing,
To find a foe it shall not be his hap,
And peace shall lull him in her flow'ry lap;
Yet shall he live in strife, and at his door
Devouring war shall never cease to roar;
Yea, it shall be his natural property
To harbour those that are at enmity.'
What power, what force, what mighty spell, if not
Your learned hands, can loose this Gordian knot?          90

*The next,* QUANTITY *and* QUALITY, *spake in prose: then*
          RELATION *was called by his name.*

Rivers, arise: whether thou be the son
Of utmost Tweed, or Ouse, or gulfy Dun,
Or Trent, who, like some earth-born giant, spreads
His thirty arms along the indented meads,
Or sullen Mole, that runneth underneath,
Or Severn swift, guilty of maiden's death,
Or rocky Avon, or of sedgy Lea,
Or coaly Tyne, or ancient hallowed Dee,
Or Humber loud, that keeps the Scythian's name,
Or Medway smooth, or royal-towered Thame.          100

          *The rest was prose.*

# THE FIFTH ODE OF HORACE

## Lib. I

*Quis multa gracilis te puer in rosa*

*Rendered almost word for word, without rhyme, according
to the Latin measure, as near as the language will
permit.*

WHAT slender youth, bedewed with liquid odours,
Courts thee on roses in some pleasant cave,
    Pyrrha? For whom bind'st thou
    In wreaths thy golden hair,
Plain in thy neatness? Oh, how oft shall he
On faith and changed gods complain, and seas
    Rough with black winds and storms
    Unwonted shall admire!
Who now enjoys thee credulous, all gold;
Who always vacant, always amiable,          10
    Hopes thee, of flattering gales
    Unmindful. Hapless they
To whom thou untried seem'st fair! Me, in my vowed
Picture, the sacred wall declares t' have hung
    My dank and dropping weeds
    To the stern God of Sea.

*[The Latin text follows.]*

# SONNETS

## ON THE DETRACTION WHICH FOLLOWED UPON MY WRITING CERTAIN TREATISES

A BOOK was writ of late called *Tetrachordon*,
  And wov'n close, both matter, form, and style;
  The subject new: it walked the town awhile,
  Numb'ring good intellects; now seldom pored on.
Cries the stall-reader, 'Bless us! what a word on
  A title-page is this!'; and some in file
  Stand spelling false, while one might walk to Mile-
  End Green. Why is it harder, sirs, than *Gordon*,
*Colkitto*, or *Macdonnel*, or *Galasp*?                          9
  Those rugged names to our like mouths grow sleek
  That would have made Quintilian stare and gasp.
Thy age, like ours, O soul of Sir John Cheek,
  Hated not learning worse than toad or asp,
  When thou taught'st Cambridge and King Edward
    Greek.

## ON THE SAME

I DID but prompt the age to quit their clogs
  By the known rules of ancient liberty,
  When straight a barbarous noise environs me
  Of owls and cuckoos, asses, apes, and dogs;
As when those hinds that were transformed to frogs
  Railed at Latona's twin-born progeny,
  Which after held the Sun and Moon in fee.
  But this is got by casting pearl to hogs,
That bawl for freedom in their senseless mood,
  And still revolt when Truth would set them free.     10
  Licence they mean when they cry Liberty;
For who loves that must first be wise and good:
  But from that mark how far they rove we see,
  For all this waste of wealth, and loss of blood.

## TO MR. H. LAWES ON HIS AIRS

HARRY, whose tuneful and well-measured song
  First taught our English music how to span
  Words with just note and accent, not to scan
  With Midas' ears, committing short and long:
Thy worth and skill exempts thee from the throng,
  With praise enough for Envy to look wan;
  To after age thou shalt be writ the man
  That with smooth air couldst humour best our tongue.
Thou honour'st Verse, and Verse must lend her wing
  To honour thee, the priest of Phoebus' quire,     10
  That tun'st their happiest lines in hymn or story.
Dante shall give Fame leave to set thee higher
  Than his Casella, whom he wooed to sing,
  Met in the milder shades of Purgatory.

## ON THE RELIGIOUS MEMORY OF MRS. CATHE-
### RINE THOMSON, MY CHRISTIAN FRIEND,
### DECEASED DECEMBER 16, 1646

WHEN Faith and Love, which parted from thee never,
  Had ripened thy just soul to dwell with God,
  Meekly thou didst resign this earthy load
  Of Death, called Life, which us from Life doth sever.
Thy works, and alms, and all thy good endeavour,
  Stayed not behind, nor in the grave were trod;
  But, as Faith pointed with her golden rod,
  Followed thee up to joy and bliss for ever.
Love led them on; and Faith, who knew them best
  Thy handmaids, clad them o'er with purple beams
  And azure wings, that up they flew so drest,     11
And spake the truth of thee on glorious themes
  Before the Judge; who thenceforth bid thee rest,
  And drink thy fill of pure immortal streams.

## ON THE LATE MASSACRE IN PIEDMONT

AVENGE, O Lord, thy slaughtered saints, whose bones
  Lie scattered on the Alpine mountains cold;
  Even them who kept thy truth so pure of old,
  When all our fathers worshipped stocks and stones,
Forget not: in thy book record their groans
  Who were thy sheep, and in their ancient fold
  Slain by the bloody Piedmontese, that rolled
  Mother with infant down the rocks. Their moans
The vales redoubled to the hills, and they
  To Heaven. Their martyred blood and ashes sow
  O'er all th' Italian fields, where still doth sway          11
The triple Tyrant; that from these may grow
  A hundredfold, who, having learnt thy way,
  Early may fly the Babylonian woe.

## ON HIS BLINDNESS

WHEN I consider how my light is spent,
  Ere half my days in this dark world and wide,
  And that one talent which is death to hide
  Lodged with me useless, though my soul more bent
To serve therewith my Maker, and present
  My true account, lest He returning chide;
  'Doth God exact day-labour, light denied?'
  I fondly ask: but Patience, to prevent
That murmur, soon replies, 'God doth not need
  Either man's work or his own gifts. Who best          10
  Bear his mild yoke, they serve him best: his state
Is kingly: thousands at his bidding speed,
  And post o'er land and ocean without rest;
  They also serve who only stand and wait.'

## TO MR. LAWRENCE

LAWRENCE, of virtuous father virtuous son,
  Now that the fields are dank, and ways are mire,
  Where shall we sometimes meet, and by the fire
  Help waste a sullen day, what may be won
From the hard season gaining?  Time will run
  On smoother, till Favonius reinspire
  The frozen earth, and clothe in fresh attire
  The lily and rose, that neither sowed nor spun.
What neat repast shall feast us, light and choice,
  Of Attic taste, with wine, whence we may rise      10
  To hear the lute well touched, or artful voice
Warble immortal notes and Tuscan air?
  He who of those delights can judge, and spare
  To interpose them oft, is not unwise.

## TO CYRIACK SKINNER

CYRIACK, whose grandsire on the royal bench
  Of British Themis, with no mean applause,
  Pronounced, and in his volumes taught our laws,
  Which others at their bar so often wrench;
To-day deep thoughts resolve with me to drench
  In mirth, that after no repenting draws;
  Let Euclid rest, and Archimedes pause,
  And what the Swede intend, and what the French.
To measure life learn thou betimes, and know
  Toward solid good what leads the nearest way;      10
  For other things mild Heaven a time ordains,
And disapproves that care, though wise in show,
  That with superfluous burden loads the day,
  And, when God sends a cheerful hour, refrains.

## ON HIS DECEASED WIFE

METHOUGHT I saw my late espoused saint
   Brought to me like Alcestis from the grave,
   Whom Jove's great son to her glad husband gave,
   Rescued from Death by force, though pale and faint.
Mine, as whom washed from spot of childbed taint
   Purification in the Old Law did save,
   And such as yet once more I trust to have
   Full sight of her in Heaven without restraint,
Came vested all in white, pure as her mind.
   Her face was veiled; yet to my fancied sight       10
   Love, sweetness, goodness, in her person shined
So clear as in no face with more delight.
   But, O! as to embrace me she inclined,
   I waked, she fled, and day brought back my night.

## ON THE NEW FORCERS OF CONSCIENCE
## UNDER THE LONG PARLIAMENT

BECAUSE you have thrown off your Prelate Lord,
   And with stiff vows renounced his Liturgy,
   To seize the widowed whore Plurality
   From them whose sin ye envied, not abhorred,
Dare ye for this adjure the civil sword
   To force our consciences that Christ set free,
   And ride us with a classic hierarchy,
   Taught ye by mere A. S. and Rutherford?
Men whose life, learning, faith, and pure intent,
   Would have been held in high esteem with Paul,       10
   Must now be named and printed heretics
By shallow Edwards and Scotch What-d'ye-call!
   But we do hope to find out all your tricks,
   Your plots and packing, worse than those of Trent,
                     That so the Parliament
May with their wholesome and preventive shears
Clip your phylacteries, though baulk your ears,
                     And succour our just fears,
When they shall read this clearly in your charge:
New *Presbyter* is but old *Priest* writ large.       20

## ON THE LORD GENERAL FAIRFAX, AT THE SIEGE OF COLCHESTER

FAIRFAX, whose name in arms through Europe rings,
    Filling each mouth with envy or with praise,
    And all her jealous monarchs with amaze,
    And rumours loud, that daunt remotest kings,
Thy firm unshaken virtue ever brings
    Victory home, though new rebellions raise
    Their Hydra heads, and the false North displays
    Her broken league to imp their serpent wings.
O yet a nobler task awaits thy hand
    (For what can war but endless war still breed?),    10
    Till truth and right from violence be freed,
And public faith cleared from the shameful brand
    Of public fraud. In vain doth Valour bleed,
    While Avarice and Rapine share the land.

## TO THE LORD GENERAL CROMWELL, MAY 1652

*On the proposals of certain ministers at the Committee
for Propagation of the Gospel*

CROMWELL, our chief of men, who through a cloud
    Not of war only, but detractions rude,
    Guided by faith and matchless fortitude,
    To peace and truth thy glorious way hast ploughed,
And on the neck of crowned Fortune proud
    Hast reared God's trophies, and his work pursued;
    While Darwen stream, with blood of Scots imbrued,
    And Dunbar field, resounds thy praises loud,
And Worcester's laureate wreath: yet much remains
    To conquer still; Peace hath her victories    10
    No less renowned than War: new foes arise,
Threatening to bind our souls with secular chains.
    Help us to save free conscience from the paw
    Of hireling wolves, whose Gospel is their maw.

## TO SIR HENRY VANE THE YOUNGER

VANE, young in years, but in sage counsel old,
    Than whom a better senator ne'er held
    The helm of Rome, when gowns, not arms, repelled
    The fierce Epirot and the African bold,
Whether to settle peace, or to unfold
    The drift of hollow states, hard to be spelled;
    Then to advise how war may best, upheld,
    Move by her two main nerves, iron and gold,
In all her equipage; besides, to know
    Both spiritual power and civil, what each means,    10
    What severs each, thou hast learned, which few have
        done.
The bounds of either sword to thee we owe:
    Therefore on thy firm hand Religion leans
    In peace, and reck'ns thee her eldest son.

## TO MR. CYRIACK SKINNER UPON HIS
### BLINDNESS

CYRIACK, this three years' day these eyes, though clear
    To outward view of blemish or of spot,
    Bereft of light, their seeing have forgot;
    Nor to their idle orbs doth sight appear
Of sun, or moon, or star, throughout the year,
    Or man, or woman. Yet I argue not
    Against Heaven's hand or will, nor bate a jot
    Of heart or hope; but still bear up and steer
Right onward. What supports me, dost thou ask?
    The conscience, friend, to have lost them overplied    10
    In Liberty's defence, my noble task,
Of which all Europe talks from side to side.
    This thought might lead me through the world's vain
        mask
    Content, though blind, had I no better guide.

## PSALM I

*Done into verse, 1653*

BLESS'D is the man who hath not walked astray
In counsel of the wicked, and i' the way
Of sinners hath not stood, and in the seat
Of scorners hath not sat; but in the great
Jehovah's Law is ever his delight,
And in his law he studies day and night.
He shall be as a tree which planted grows
By wat'ry streams, and in his season knows
To yield his fruit; and his leaf shall not fall;
And what he takes in hand shall prosper all.          10
Not so the wicked; but, as chaff which fanned
The wind drives, so the wicked shall not stand
In judgement, or abide their trial then,
Nor sinners in th' assembly of just men.
For the Lord knows th' upright way of the just,
And the way of bad men to ruin must.

## PSALM II

*Done August 8, 1653.—Terzetti*

WHY do the Gentiles tumult, and the nations
　　Muse a vain thing, the kings of th' earth upstand
　　With power, and princes in their congregations
Lay deep their plots together through each land
　　Against the Lord and his Messiah dear?
'Let us break off,' say they, 'by strength of hand,
　　Their bonds, and cast from us, no more to wear,
　　Their twisted cords.' He who in Heaven doth dwell
　　Shall laugh; the Lord shall scoff them, then severe
Speak to them in his wrath, and in his fell          10
　　And fierce ire trouble them. 'But I', saith he,
　　'Anointed have my King (though ye rebel)
On Sion my holy hill.' A firm decree
　　I will declare: the Lord to me hath said,
　　'Thou art my Son; I have begotten thee
This day; ask of me, and the grant is made.
　　As thy possession I on thee bestow
　　Th' heathen, and, as thy conquest to be swayed,

Earth's utmost bounds: them shalt thou bring full low
  With iron sceptre bruised, and them disperse    20
  Like to a potter's vessel shivered so.'
And now be wise at length, ye kings averse;
  Be taught, ye judges of the earth; with fear
  Jehovah serve, and let your joy converse
With trembling; kiss the Son, lest he appear
  In anger, and ye perish in the way,
  If once his wrath take fire, like fuel sere.
Happy all those who have in him their stay.


## PSALM III

*August 9, 1653*

*When he fled from Absalom*

Lord, how many are my foes!
  How many those
That in arms against me rise!
  Many are they
That of my life distrustfully thus say,
'No help for him in God there lies.'
But thou, Lord, art my shield, my glory;
  Thee, through my story,
Th' exalter of my head I count:
  Aloud I cried    10
Unto Jehovah; he full soon replied,
And heard me from his holy mount.
I lay and slept; I waked again:
  For my sustain
Was the Lord. Of many millions
  The populous rout
I fear not, though encamping round about,
They pitch against me their pavilions.
Rise, Lord; save me, my God! for thou
  Hast smote ere now    20
On the cheek-bone all my foes,
  Of men abhorred
Hast broke the teeth. This help was from the Lord;
Thy blessing on thy people flows.

# PSALM IV

### *August* 10, 1653

ANSWER me when I call,
God of my righteousness;
In straits and in distress
Thou didst me disenthrall
And set at large: now spare,
Now pity me, and hear my earnest prayer.
    Great ones, how long will ye
My glory have in scorn?
How long be thus forborne
Still to love vanity?           10
To love, to seek, to prize
Things false and vain, and nothing else but lies?
    Yet know the Lord hath chose,
Chose to himself apart,
The good and meek of heart
(For whom to choose he knows);
Jehovah from on high
Will hear my voice what time to him I cry.
    Be awed, and do not sin;
Speak to your hearts alone         20
Upon your beds, each one,
And be at peace within.
Offer the offerings just
Of righteousness, and in Jehovah trust.
    Many there be that say
'Who yet will show us good?'
Talking like this world's brood;
But, Lord, thus let me pray:
On us lift up the light,
Lift up the favour, of thy count'nance bright.    30
    Into my heart more joy
And gladness thou hast put
Than when a year of glut
Their stores doth over-cloy,
And from their plenteous grounds
With vast increase their corn and wine abounds.

In peace at once will I
   Both lay me down and sleep;
For thou alone dost keep
   Me safe where'er I lie:
      As in a rocky cell                                    40
Thou, Lord, alone in safety mak'st me dwell.


## PSALM V

### *August* 12, 1653

JEHOVAH, to my words give ear,
   My meditation weigh;
The voice of my complaining hear,
My King and God, for unto thee I pray.
   Jehovah, thou my early voice
      Shalt in the morning hear;
   I' the morning I to thee with choice
Will rank my prayers, and watch till thou appear.
   For thou art not a God that takes
      In wickedness delight;                                10
   Evil with thee no biding makes;
Fools or mad men stand not within thy sight.
   All workers of iniquity
      Thou hat'st; and them unblest
   Thou wilt destroy that speak a lie;
The bloody and guileful man God doth detest.
   But I will in thy mercies dear,
      Thy numerous mercies, go
   Into thy house; I, in thy fear,
Will towards thy holy temple worship low.                  20
   Lord, lead me in thy righteousness,
      Lead me, because of those
   That do observe if I transgress;
Set thy ways right before, where my step goes.
   For in his faltering mouth unstable
      No word is firm or sooth
   Their inside, troubles miserable;
An open grave their throat, their tongue they smooth.
   God, find them guilty; let them fall
      By their own counsels quelled;                        30
   Push them in their rebellions all

Still on; for against thee they have rebelled.
  Then all who trust in thee shall bring
    Their joy, while thou from blame
  Defend'st them: they shall ever sing,
And shall triumph in thee, who love thy name.
  For thou, Jehovah, wilt be found
    To bless the just man still:
  As with a shield thou wilt surround
Him with thy lasting favour and goodwill.    40

# PSALM VI

### *August* 13, 1653

LORD, in thine anger do not reprehend me,
  Nor in thy hot displeasure me correct;
  Pity me, Lord, for I am much deject,
Am very weak and faint; heal and amend me:
For all my bones, that even with anguish ache,
  Are troubled; yea, my soul is troubled sore;
  And thou, O Lord, how long? Turn, Lord; restore
My soul; oh, save me, for thy goodness' sake!
For in death no remembrance is of thee;
  Who in the grave can celebrate thy praise?    10
  Wearied I am with sighing out my days;
Nightly my couch I make a kind of sea;
My bed I water with my tears; mine eye
  Through grief consumes, is waxen old and dark
  I' the midst of all mine enemies that mark.
Depart, all ye that work iniquity,
Depart from me; for the voice of my weeping
  The Lord hath heard; the Lord hath heard my prayer;
  My supplication with acceptance fair
The Lord will own, and have me in his keeping.    20
Mine enemies shall all be blank, and dashed
  With much confusion; then grow red with shame,
  They shall return in haste the way they came,
And in a moment shall be quite abashed.

## PSALM VII

*August* 14, 1653

*Upon the words of Chush the Benjamite against him*

LORD, my God, to thee I fly;
Save me, and secure me under
Thy protection while I cry;
Lest, as a lion (and no wonder),
He haste to tear my soul asunder,
Tearing and no rescue nigh.

Lord, my God, if I have thought
Or done this; if wickedness
Be in my hands; if I have wrought
Ill to him that meant me peace;                    10
Or to him have rendered less,
And not freed my foe for naught:

Let th' enemy pursue my soul,
And overtake it; let him tread
My life down to the earth, and roll
In the dust my glory dead,
In the dust, and there outspread
Lodge it with dishonour foul.

Rise, Jehovah, in thine ire;
Rouse thyself amidst the rage                      20
Of my foes that urge like fire;
And wake for me, their fury assuage;
Judgement here thou didst engage
And command, which I desire.

So th' assemblies of each nation
Will surround thee, seeking right:
Thence to thy glorious habitation
Return on high, and in their sight.
Jehovah judgeth most upright
All people from the world's foundation.             30

Judge me, Lord; be judge in this
According to my righteousness,
And the innocence which is
Upon me: cause at length to cease
Of evil men the wickedness,
And their power that do amiss.


But the just establish fast,
Since thou art the just God that tries
Hearts and reins. On God is cast
My defence, and in him lies;                    40
In him who, both just and wise,
Saves th' upright of heart at last.


God is a just judge and severe,
And God is every day offended;
If th' unjust will not forbear,
His sword he whets; his bow hath bended
Already, and for him intended
The tools of death that waits him near.


(His arrows purposely made he
For them that persecute.) Behold                50
He travails big with vanity;
Trouble he hath conceived of old
As in a womb, and from that mould
Hath at length brought forth a lie.


He digg'd a pit, and delved it deep,
And fell into the pit he made:
His mischief, that due course doth keep,
Turns on his head; and his ill trade
Of violence will undelayed
Fall on his crown with ruin steep.              60


Then will I Jehovah's praise
According to his justice raise,
And sing the Name and Deity
Of Jehovah the Most High.

## PSALM VIII

*August* 14, 1653

O JEHOVAH our Lord, how wondrous great
   And glorious is thy name through all the earth!
So as above the heavens thy praise to set,
   Out of the tender mouths of latest birth,

Out of the mouths of babes and sucklings thou
   Hast founded strength, because of all thy foes,
To stint th' enemy, and slack th' avenger's brow,
   That bends his rage thy providence to oppose.

When I behold thy heavens, thy fingers' art,
   The moon and stars, which thou so bright hast set   10
In the pure firmament, then saith my heart,
   O what is man that thou rememb'rest yet

And think'st upon him; or of man begot
   That him thou visit'st, and of him art found?
Scarce to be less than gods thou mad'st his lot;
   With honour and with state thou hast him crowned.

O'er the works of thy hand thou mad'st him lord;
   Thou hast put all under his lordly feet,
All flocks and herds, by thy commanding word,
   All beasts that in the field or forest meet,   20

Fowl of the heavens, and fish that through the wet
   Sea-paths in shoals do slide, and know no dearth.
O Jehovah our Lord, how wondrous great
   And glorious is thy name through all the earth!

*April, 1648.—J.M.*

*Nine of the Psalms done into Metre; wherein all, but what is in a different character, are the very words of the Text, translated from the original.*

### PSALM LXXX

1 THOU Shepherd that dost Israel *keep,*
    Give ear *in time of need,*
Who leadest like a flock of sheep
    *Thy loved* Joseph's seed,
That sitt'st between the Cherubs *bright,*
    *Between their wings outspread*
Shine forth, *and from thy cloud give light,*
    *And on our foes thy dread.*
2 In Ephraim's view and Benjamin's,
    And in Manasseh's sight,                    10
Awake[1] thy strength, come, and *be seen*
    *To save us by thy might.*
3 Turn us again; *thy grace divine*
    *To us,* O God, *vouchsafe;*
Cause thou thy face on us to shine,
    And then we shall be safe.
4 Lord God of Hosts, how long wilt thou,
    How long wilt thou declare,
Thy[2] smoking wrath, *and angry brow,*
    Against thy people's prayer?              20
5 Thou feed'st them with the bread of tears;
    Their bread with tears they eat;
And mak'st them largely[3] drink the tears
    *Wherewith their cheeks are wet.*
6 A strife thou mak'st us *and a prey*
    To every neighbour foe;
Among themselves they[4] laugh, they[4] play,
    And[4] flouts at us they throw.
7 Return us, *and thy grace divine,*

*Gnorera.*    [2] *Gnashanta.*    *Shalish.*    *Jilgnagu.*

O God of Hosts, *vouchsafe;*    30
Cause thou thy face on us to shine,
 And then we shall be safe.

8 A Vine from Egypt thou hast brought,
 *Thy free love made it thine,*
And drov'st out nations *proud and haut,*
 To plant this *lovely* Vine.

9 Thou didst prepare for it a place,
 And root it deep and fast,
That it *began to grow apace,*
 *And* filled the land *at last.*    40

10 With her *green* shade *that* covered *all,*
 The hills were *overspread,*
Her boughs as *high as* cedars tall
 *Advanced their lofty head.*

11 Her branches *on the western side*
 Down to the sea she sent,
And *upward* to that river *wide*
 Her other branches *went.*

12 Why hast thou laid her hedges low,
 And broken down her fence,    50
That all may pluck her, as they go,
 *With rudest violence?*

13 The *tusked* boar out of the wood
 Upturns it by the roots;
Wild beasts there browse, and make their food,
 *Her grapes and tender shoots.*

14 Return now, God of Hosts; look down
 From Heaven, thy seat divine;
Behold *us, but without a frown,*
 And visit this *thy* Vine.    60

15 Visit this Vine, which thy right hand
 Hath set, and planted *long,*
And the young branch, that for thyself
 Thou hast made firm and strong.

16 But now it is consumed with fire,
 And cut *with axes* down;
They perish at thy dreadful ire,
 At thy rebuke and frown.

17 Upon the Man of thy right hand
 Let thy *good* hand be *laid;*    70

Upon the Son of Man, whom Thou
  Strong for thyself hast made.
18 So shall we not go back from thee
  *To ways of sin and shame,*
Quicken us thou; then *gladly* we
  Shall call upon thy Name.
Return us, *and thy grace divine,*
  Lord God of Hosts, *vouchsafe,*
Cause thou thy face on us to shine,
  And then we shall be safe.                   80

## PSALM LXXXI

1 To God our strength sing loud *and clear:*
  Sing loud to God *our King;*
To Jacob's God, *that all may hear,*
  Loud acclamations ring.
2 Prepare a hymn, prepare a song;
  The timbrel hither bring;
The *cheerful* psalt'ry bring along,
  And harp *with* pleasant *string.*
3 Blow, *as is wont,* in the new moon,
  With trumpets' *lofty sound,*                10
Th' appointed time, the day whereon
  Our solemn feast *comes round.*
4 This was a statute *given of old*
  For Israel *to observe,*
A law of Jacob's God *to hold,*
  *From whence they might not swerve.*
5 This he a testimony ordained
  In Joseph, *not to change,*
When as he passed through Egypt land;
  The tongue I heard was strange.              20
6 From burden, *and from slavish toil,*
  I set his shoulder free;
His hands from pots, *and miry soil,*
  Delivered were *by me.*
7 When trouble did thee sore assail,
  *On me then* didst thou call,
And I to free thee *did not fail,*
  *And led thee out of thrall.*

I answered thee in[1] thunder deep,
  With clouds encompassed round;     30
I tried thee at the water *steep*
  Of Meriba *renowned.*

8 Hear, O my people, *hearken well:*
   I testify to thee,
 *Thou ancient flock of* Israel,
   If thou wilt list to me:

9 Throughout the land of thy abode
   No alien God shall be,
 Nor shalt thou to a foreign god
   In honour bend thy knee.     40

10 I am the Lord thy God, which brought
   Thee out of Egypt land;
 Ask large enough, and I, *besought,*
   Will grant thy full demand.

11 And yet my people would not *hear,*
   *Nor* hearken to my voice;
 And Israel, *whom I loved so dear,*
   Misliked me for his choice.

12 Then did I leave them to their will,
   And to their wand'ring mind;     50
 Their own conceits they followed still,
   Their own devices blind.

13 Oh that my people would *be wise,*
   *To* serve me *all their days!*
 And oh that Israel would *advise*
   *To* walk my *righteous* ways!

14 Then would I soon bring down their foes,
   *That now so proudly rise,*
 And turn my hand against *all those*
   *That are* their enemies.     60

15 Who hate the Lord should *then be fain*
   *To* bow to him and bend;
 But *they, his people, should remain;*
   Their time should have no end.

16 And he would feed them *from the shock*
   With flour of finest wheat,
 And satisfy them from the rock
   With honey *for their meat.*

        [1] *Be Sether ragnam.*

## PSALM LXXXII

1 GOD in the [1] great [1] assembly stands
   *Of kings and lordly states*
   Among the gods [2] on both his hands
   He judges and debates.

2 How long will ye [3] pervert the right
   With [3] judgement false and wrong,
   Favouring the wicked *by your might,*
   *Who thence grow bold and strong?*

3 [4] Regard the [4] weak and fatherless;
   [4] Despatch the [4] poor man's cause;                    10
   And [5] raise the man in deep distress
   By [5] just and equal laws.

4 Defend the poor and desolate,
   And rescue from the hands
   Of wicked men the low estate
   Of him *that help demands.*

5 They know not, nor will understand;
   In darkness they walk on;
   The earth's foundations all are [6] moved,
   And [6] out of order gone.                                20

6 I said that ye were gods, yea, all
   The sons of God most high;

7 But ye shall die like men, and fall
   As other princes *die.*

8 Rise, God; [7] judge thou the earth *in might;*
   This *wicked* earth [7] redress;
   For thou art he who shalt by right
   The nations all possess.


## PSALM LXXXIII

1 BE not thou silent *now at length;*
   O God, hold not thy peace:
   Sit not thou still, O God of *strength;*
   *We cry and do not cease.*

---

[1] *Bagnadath-el.*      [2] *Bekerev.*      [3] *Tishphetu gnavel.*
[4] *Shiphtu-dal.*       [5] *Hatzdiku.*      [6] *Jimmotu.*
[7] *Shiphta.*

E

2 For lo! thy *furious* foes *now* [1] swell,
    And [1] storm outrageously;
And they that hate thee, *proud and fell,*
    Exalt their heads full high.

3 Against thy people they [2] contrive
    [3] Their plots and counsels deep;        10
    [4] Them to ensnare they chiefly **strive**
    [5] Whom thou dost hide and keep.

4 'Come, let us cut them off,' say they,
    'Till they no nation be;
That Israel's name for ever may
    Be lost in memory.'

5 For they consult [6] with all their might,
    And all as one in mind
Themselves against thee they unite,
    And in firm union bind.        20

6 The tents of Edom, and the brood
    Of *scornful* Ishmael,
Moab, with them of Hagar's blood,
    *That in the desert dwell,*

7 Gebal and Ammon *there conspire,*
    And *hateful* Amalek,
The Philistines, and they of Tyre,
    *Whose bounds the sea doth check.*

8 With them *great* Ashur also bands,
    *And doth confirm the knot;*        30
*All these have lent their armed hands*
    To aid the sons of Lot.

9 Do to them as to Midian *bold,*
    *That wasted all the coast;*
To Sisera, and as *is told*
    *Thou didst* to Jabin's *host,*
When at the brook of Kishon *old*
    *They were repulsed and slain,*

10 At Endor quite cut off, and rolled
    As dung upon the plain.        40

11 As Zeb and Oreb evil sped,
    So let their princes speed,

---

[1] *Jehemajun.*        [2] *Jagnarimu.*        [3] *Sod.*
[4] *Jithjagnatsu gnal.*        [5] *Tsephuneca.*        [6] *Lev jachdau.*

As Zeba and Zalmunna *bled*,
  So let their princes *bleed*.
12 *For they amidst their pride* have said,
    'By right now shall we seize
God's houses, and *will now invade*
    [1] Their stately palaces.'
13 My God, oh make them as a wheel;
    *No quiet let them find;*      50
Giddy and *restless* let *them* reel,
    Like stubble from the wind.
14 As, *when* an *aged* wood takes fire
    *Which on a sudden strays,*
The *greedy* flame runs higher and higher,
    Till all the mountains blaze;
15 So with thy whirlwind them pursue,
    And with thy tempest chase;
16 [2]And till they [2] yield thee honour due,
    Lord, fill with shame their face.      60
17 Ashamed and troubled let them be,
    Troubled and shamed for ever,
Ever confounded, and so die
    With shame, *and 'scape it never.*
18 Then shall they know that thou, whose name
    Jehovah is, alone
Art the Most High, *and thou the same*
    O'er all the earth *art One.*


## PSALM LXXXIV

1 How lovely are thy dwellings fair!
    O Lord of Hosts, how dear
The *pleasant* tabernacles are
    *Where thou dost dwell so near!*
2 My soul doth long and almost die
    Thy courts, O Lord, to see;
My heart and flesh aloud do cry,
    O living God, for thee.

---

[1] *Neoth Elohim bears both.*
[2] *They seek thy Name.* Heb,

3 There even the sparrow, *freed from wrong*,
   Hath found a house of *rest;*          10
The swallow there, to lay her young,
   Hath built her *brooding* nest;
Even *by* thy altars, Lord of Hosts,
   *They find their safe abode;*
*And home they fly from round the coasts*
   *Toward thee*, my King, my God.
4 Happy, who in thy house reside,
   Where thee they ever praise!
5 Happy, whose strength in thee doth bide,
   And in their hearts thy ways!         20
6 They pass through Baca's *thirsty* vale,
   *That dry and barren ground*,
As through a fruitful wat'ry dale
   Where springs and showers abound.
7 They journey on from strength to strength
   *With joy and gladsome cheer*,
*Till* all before *our* God *at length*
   In Sion do appear.
8 Lord God of Hosts, hear *now* my prayer,
   O Jacob's God, give ear:         30
9 Thou, God, our shield, look on the face
   Of thy anointed *dear*.
10 For one day in thy courts *to be*
   Is better *and more blest*
Than *in the joys of vanity*
   A thousand days *at best*.
I in the temple of my God
   Had rather keep a door
Than dwell in tents *and rich abode*
   With sin *for evermore*.         40
11 For God the Lord, both sun and shield,
   Gives grace and glory *bright;*
No good from them shall be withheld
   Whose ways are just and right.
12 Lord *God* of Hosts *that reign'st on high*,
   That man is *truly* blest
Who *only* on thee doth rely
   And in thee only rest.

## PSALM LXXXV

1 THY land to favour graciously
  Thou hast not, Lord, been slack;
Thou hast from *hard* captivity
  Returned Jacob back.
2 Th' iniquity thou didst forgive
  *That wrought* thy people woe,
And all their sin *that did thee grieve*
  Hast hid *where none shall know.*
3 Thine anger all thou hadst removed,
  And *calmly* didst return                           10
From thy [1] fierce wrath, which we had proved
  Far worse than fire to burn.
4 God of our saving health and peace,
  Turn us, and us restore;
Thine indignation cause to cease
  Toward us, *and chide no more.*
5 Wilt thou be angry without end,
  For ever angry thus?
Wilt thou thy frowning ire extend
  From age to age on us?                              20
6 Wilt thou not [2] turn and *hear our voice,*
  And us again [2] revive,
That so thy people may rejoice,
  By thee preserved alive?
7 Cause us to see thy goodness, Lord,
  To us thy mercy shew;
Thy saving health to us afford,
  *And life in us renew.*
8 *And now* what God the Lord will speak
  I will *go straight and* hear,                      30
For to his people he speaks peace,
  And to his saints *full dear;*
To his dear saints he will speak peace;
  But let them never more
Return to folly, *but surcease*
  *To trespass as before.*

Heb. *The burning heat of thy wrath.*
[1] Heb. *Turn to quicken us.*

9 Surely to such as do him fear
   Salvation is at hand,
And glory shall *ere long appear*
   *To* dwell within our land.     40

10 Mercy and Truth, *that long were missed,*
   Now *joyfully* are met;
*Sweet* Peace and Righteousness have kissed,
   *And hand in hand are set.*

11 Truth from the earth *like to a flower*
   Shall bud and blossom *then;*
And Justice from her heavenly bower
   Look down *on mortal men.*

12 The Lord will also then bestow
   Whatever thing is good;     50
Our land shall forth in plenty throw
   Her fruits *to be our food.*

13 Before him Righteousness shall go,
   *His royal harbinger:*
Then [1] will he come, and not be slow;
   His footsteps cannot err.


## PSALM LXXXVI

1 THY *gracious* ear, O Lord, incline;
   O hear me, *I thee pray;*
For I am poor, and almost pine
   With need *and sad decay.*

2 Preserve my soul, for [2] I have trod
   Thy ways, and love the just;
Save thou thy servant, O my God,
   Who *still* in thee doth trust.

3 Pity me, Lord, for daily thee
   I call; 4 O, make rejoice     10
Thy servant's soul! for, Lord, to thee
   I lift my soul *and voice.*

5 For thou art good; thou, Lord, art prone
   To pardon; thou to all

---

[1] Heb. *He will set his steps to the way.*
[2] Heb. *I am good, loving, a doer of good and holy things.*

Art full of mercy, thou *alone*,
    To them that on thee call.
6 Unto my supplication, Lord,
    Give ear, and to the cry
Of my *incessant* prayers afford
    Thy hearing graciously.        20
7 I in the day of my distress
    Will call on thee *for aid;*
For thou wilt *grant* me *free access,*
    *And* answer *what I prayed.*
8 Like thee among the gods is none,
    O Lord; nor any works
*Of all that other gods have done*
    Like to thy *glorious* works.
9 The nations all whom thou hast made
    Shall come, *and all shall frame*    30
To bow them low before thee, Lord,
    And glorify thy name.
10 For great thou art, and wonders great
    By thy strong hand are done;
Thou *in thy everlasting seat*
    Remainest God alone.
11 Teach me, O Lord, thy way *most right;*
    I in thy truth will bide;
To fear thy name my heart unite;
    *So shall it never slide.*    40
12 Thee will I praise, O Lord my God,
    *Thee honour and adore*
With my whole heart, and blaze abroad
    Thy name for evermore.
13 For great thy mercy is toward me,
    And thou hast freed my soul,
Ev'n from the lowest hell set free,
    *From deepest darkness foul.*
14 O God, the proud against me rise,
    And violent men are met    50
To seek my life, and in their eyes
    No fear of thee have set.
15 But thou, Lord, art the God most mild,
    Readiest thy grace to shew,
Slow to be angry, and *art styled*

Most merciful, most true.
16 Oh turn to me *thy face at length*,
   And me have mercy on;
Unto thy servant give thy strength,
   And save thy handmaid's son.                    60
17 Some sign of good to me afford,
   And let my foes *then see*,
And be ashamed, because thou, Lord,
   Dost help and comfort me.


## PSALM LXXXVII

1 AMONG the holy mountains *high*
   Is his foundation fast;
   *There seated in his sanctuary,*
   *His temple there is placed.*
2 Sion's *fair* gates the Lord loves more
   Than all the dwellings *fair*
   Of Jacob's *land, though there be store,*
   *And all within his care.*
3 City of God, most glorious things
   Of thee *abroad* are spoke.                    10
4 I mention Egypt, *where proud kings*
   *Did our forefathers yoke;*
   I mention Babel to my friends,
   Philistia *full of scorn,*
   And Tyre, with Ethiop's *utmost ends;*
   Lo! this man there was born.
5 But *twice that praise shall in our ear*
   Be said of Sion *last:*
   This and this man was born in her;
   High God shall fix her fast.                    20
6 The Lord shall write it in a scroll,
   That ne'er shall be out-worn,
   When he the nations doth enrol
   That this man there was born.
7 Both they who sing and they who dance
   *With sacred songs are there;*
   In thee *fresh brooks and soft streams glance,*
   *And* all my fountains *clear.*

## PSALM LXXXVIII

1 LORD GOD, that dost me save and keep,
   All day to thee I cry,
And all night long before thee *weep*,
   Before thee *prostrate lie.*
2 Into thy presence let my prayer,
   *With sighs devout, ascend;*
And to my cries, that *ceaseless are,*
   Thine ear with favour bend.
3 For, cloyed with woes and trouble store,
   Surcharged my soul doth lie;     10
My life, *at death's uncheerful door,*
   Unto the grave draws nigh.
4 Reckoned I am with them that pass
   Down to the *dismal pit;*
I am a [1] man, but weak, alas!
   And for that name unfit.
5 From life discharged and parted quite
   Among the dead *to sleep,*
And like the slain *in bloody fight*
   That in the grave lie *deep;*     20
Whom thou rememberest no more,
   Dost never more regard:
Them, from thy hand delivered o'er,
   *Death's hideous house hath barred.*
6 Thou, in the lowest pit *profound,*
   Hast set me *all forlorn,*
Where thickest darkness *hovers round,*
   In horrid deeps *to mourn.*
7 Thy wrath, *from which no shelter saves,*
   Full sore doth press on me;     30
  [2] Thou break'st upon me all thy waves,
    [2] And all thy waves break me.
8 Thou dost my friends from me estrange,
   And mak'st me odious,
Me to them odious, *for they change,*
   And I here pent up thus.

[1] Heb. *A man without manly strength.*
[2] *The* Heb. *bears both.*

9  Through sorrow and affliction great
   Mine eye grows dim and dead;
  Lord, all the day I thee entreat,
   My hands to thee I spread.        40

10  Wilt thou do wonders on the dead?
   Shall the deceased arise
  And praise thee *from their loathsome bed*
   *With pale and hollow eyes?*

11  Shall they thy loving-kindness tell
   On whom the grave *hath hold?*
  Or they *who* in perdition *dwell*
   Thy faithfulness *unfold?*

12  In darkness can thy mighty *hand*
   *Or* wondrous acts be known?       50
  Thy justice in the *gloomy* land
   Of *dark* oblivion?

13  But I to thee, O Lord, do cry
   *Ere yet my life be spent;*
  And *up to thee* my prayer *doth hie*
   Each morn, and thee prevent.

14  Why wilt thou, Lord, my soul forsake
   And hide thy face from me,

15  That am already bruised, and [1] shake
   With terror sent from thee;      60
  Bruised and afflicted, and *so low*
   As ready to expire,
  While I thy terrors undergo,
   Astonished with thine ire?

16  Thy fierce wrath over me doth flow,
   Thy threat'nings cut me through:

17  All day they round about me go,
   Like waves they me pursue.

18  Lover and friend thou hast removed,
   And severed from me far:      70
  They *fly me now* whom I have loved,
   And as in darkness are.

Heb. *Prae Concussione.*

## A COLLECTION OF PASSAGES TRANSLATED
## IN THE PROSE WRITINGS

[From *Of Reformation in England*, 1641]

AH, Constantine, of how much ill was cause,
Not thy conversion, but those rich domains
That the first wealthy Pope received of thee!

[DANTE, *Inferno*, xix. 115.]

FOUNDED in chaste and humble poverty,
'Gainst them that raised thee dost thou lift thy horn,
Impudent whore? where hast thou placed thy hope?
In thy adulterers, or thy ill-got wealth?
Another Constantine comes not in haste.

[PETRARCH, *Sonnet* 107.]

AND to be short, at last his guide him brings
Into a goodly valley, where he sees
A mighty mass of things strangely confused,
Things that on earth were lost or were abused.

Then passed he to a flowery mountain green,
Which once smelt sweet, now stinks as odiously:
This was that gift (if you the truth will have)
That Constantine to good Sylvestro gave.

[ARIOSTO, *Orl. Fur.* xxxiv. 72, 79.]

[From *Reason of Church Government*, 1641]

WHEN I die, let the Earth be rolled in flames.

[From *Apology for Smectymnuus*, 1642]

LAUGHING to teach the truth
What hinders? as some teachers give to boys
Junkets and knacks, that they may learn apace.

[HORACE, *Sat.* i. 1. 24.]

JESTING decides great things
Stronglier, and better oft than earnest can.

[HORACE, *Sat.* i. 10. 14.]

'TIS you that say it, not I. You do the deeds,
And your ungodly deeds find me the words.

[SOPHOCLES, *Electra*, 624.]

[From *Areopagitica*, 1644]

THIS is true Liberty, when freeborn men,
Having to advise the public, may speak free:
Which he who can and will deserves high praise:
Who neither can nor will may hold his peace.
What can be juster in a state than this?

[EURIPIDES, *Supplices*, 438.]

[From *Tetrachordon*, 1645]

WHOM do we count a good man? Whom but he
Who keeps the laws and statutes of the senate,
Who judges in great suits and controversies,
Whose witness and opinion wins the cause?
But his own house, and the whole neighbourhood,
Sees his foul inside through his whited skin.

[HORACE, *Epist.* i. 16. 40.]

[From *The Tenure of Kings and Magistrates*, 1649]

THERE can be slain
No sacrifice to God more acceptable
Than an unjust and wicked king.

[SENECA, *Her. Fur.* 922.]

[From *History of Britain*, 1670]

BRUTUS *thus addresses* Diana *in the country of* Leogecia.

GODDESS of Shades, and Huntress, who at will
Walk'st on the rolling sphere, and through the deep,
On thy third reign, the Earth, look now, and tell
What land, what seat of rest thou bidd'st me seek,
What certain seat, where I may worship thee
For ay, with temples vowed, and virgin quires.

*To whom, sleeping before the altar,* Diana *in a Vision
that night thus answered.*

BRUTUS, far to the west, in th' ocean wide,
Beyond the realm of Gaul, a land there lies,
Sea-girt it lies, where giants dwelt of old;
Now void, it fits thy people.  Thither bend
Thy course; there shalt thou find a lasting seat;
There to thy sons another Troy shall rise,
And kings be born of thee, whose dreaded might
Shall awe the world, and conquer nations bold.

PARADISE LOST

# THE PRINTER TO THE READER

COURTEOUS Reader, there was no Argument at first intended to the book, but for the satisfaction of many that have desired it, I have procured it, and withal a reason of that which stumbled many others, why the poem rimes not.

S. SIMMONS.

## THE VERSE

THE measure is English heroic verse without rime, as that of Homer in Greek, and of Virgil in Latin—rime being no necessary adjunct or true ornament of poem or good verse, in longer works especially, but the invention of a barbarous age, to set off wretched matter and lame metre; graced indeed since by the use of some famous modern poets, carried away by custom, but much to their own vexation, hindrance, and constraint to express many things otherwise, and for the most part worse, than else they would have expressed them. Not without cause, therefore, some both Italian and Spanish poets of prime note have rejected rime both in longer and shorter works, as have also long since our best English tragedies, as a thing of itself, to all judicious ears, trivial and of no true musical delight; which consists only in apt numbers, fit quantity of syllables, and the sense variously drawn out from one verse into another, not in the jingling sound of like endings—a fault avoided by the learned ancients both in poetry and all good oratory. This neglect then of rime so little is to be taken for a defect, though it may seem so perhaps to vulgar readers, that it rather is to be esteemed an example set—the first in English—of ancient liberty recovered to heroic poem from the troublesome and modern bondage of riming.

# PARADISE LOST

## BOOK I

### THE ARGUMENT

*This First Book proposes, first in brief, the whole subject,—
Man's disobedience, and the loss thereupon of Paradise,
wherein he was placed; then touches the prime cause of his
fall—the Serpent, or rather Satan in the Serpent; who, revolting from God, and drawing to his side many legions of Angels,
was, by the command of God, driven out of Heaven, with all
his crew, into the great Deep. Which action passed over, the
Poem hastens into the midst of things; presenting Satan, with
his Angels, now fallen into Hell—described here not in the
Centre (for heaven and earth may be supposed as yet not made,
certainly not yet accursed), but in a place of utter darkness,
fitliest called Chaos. Here Satan, with his Angels lying on the
burning lake, thunderstruck and astonished, after a certain
space recovers, as from confusion; calls up him who, next in
order and dignity, lay by him: they confer of their miserable
fall. Satan awakens all his legions, who lay till then in the
same manner confounded. They rise: their numbers; array of
battle; their chief leaders named, according to the idols known
afterwards in Canaan and the countries adjoining. To these
Satan directs his speech; comforts them with hope yet of
regaining Heaven; but tells them, lastly, of a new world and
new kind of creature to be created, according to an ancient
prophecy, or report, in Heaven—for that Angels were long
before this visible creation was the opinion of many ancient
Fathers. To find out the truth of this prophecy, and what to
determine thereon, he refers to a full council. What his
associates thence attempt. Pandemonium, the palace of Satan,
rises, suddenly built out of the Deep; the infernal Peers there
sit in council.*

OF Man's first disobedience, and the fruit
Of that forbidden tree, whose mortal taste
Brought death into the World, and all our woe,
With loss of Eden, till one greater Man
Restore us, and regain the blissful seat,
Sing, Heavenly Muse, that on the secret top
Of Oreb, or of Sinai, didst inspire
That shepherd who first taught the chosen seed
In the beginning how the heavens and earth
Rose out of Chaos: or, if Sion hill                              10
Delight thee more, and Siloa's brook that flowed
Fast by the oracle of God, I thence
Invoke thy aid to my adventurous song,
That with no middle flight intends to soar
Above th' Aonian mount, while it pursues
Things unattempted yet in prose or rime.
And chiefly Thou, O Spirit, that dost prefer
Before all temples th' upright heart and pure,
Instruct me, for Thou know'st; Thou from the first
Wast present, and, with mighty wings outspread,               20
Dove-like sat'st brooding on the vast Abyss,
And mad'st it pregnant: what in me is dark
Illumine, what is low raise and support;
That, to the height of this great argument,
I may assert Eternal Providence,
And justify the ways of God to men.
    Say first—for Heaven hides nothing from thy view,
Nor the deep tract of Hell—say first what cause
Moved our grand Parents, in that happy state,
Favoured of Heaven so highly, to fall off                       30
From their Creator, and transgress his will
For one restraint, lords of the world besides?
Who first seduced them to that foul revolt?
Th' infernal Serpent; he it was whose guile,
Stirred up with envy and revenge, deceived
The mother of mankind, what time his pride
Had cast him out from Heaven, with all his host
Of rebel Angels, by whose aid, aspiring
To set himself in glory above his peers,
He trusted to have equalled the Most High,                      40
If he opposed; and, with ambitious aim

Against the throne and monarchy of God,
Raised impious war in Heaven and battle proud,
With vain attempt.  Him th' Almighty Power
Hurled headlong flaming from the ethereal sky,
With hideous ruin and combustion, down
To bottomless perdition, there to dwell
In adamantine chains and penal fire,
Who durst defy th' Omnipotent to arms.
Nine times the space that measures day and night      50
To mortal men, he, with his horrid crew,
Lay vanquished, rolling in the fiery gulf,
Confounded, though immortal; but his doom
Reserved him to more wrath; for now the thought
Both of lost happiness and lasting pain
Torments him: round he throws his baleful eyes,
That witnessed huge affliction and dismay,
Mixed with obdurate pride and steadfast hate:
At once, as far as Angel's ken, he views
The dismal situation waste and wild;                  60
A dungeon horrible, on all sides round,
As one great furnace flamed; yet from those flames
No light, but rather darkness visible
Served only to discover sights of woe,
Regions of sorrow, doleful shades, where peace
And rest can never dwell, hope never comes
That comes to all, but torture without end
Still urges, and a fiery deluge, fed
With ever-burning sulphur unconsumed.
Such place Eternal Justice had prepared               70
For those rebellious; here their prison ordained
In utter darkness, and their portion set,
As far removed from God and light of Heaven
As from the centre thrice to th' utmost pole.
Oh, how unlike the place from whence they fell!
There the companions of his fall, o'erwhelmed
With floods and whirlwinds of tempestuous fire,
He soon discerns; and, weltering by his side,
One next himself in power, and next in crime,
Long after known in Palestine, and named             80
Beëlzebub.  To whom th' Arch-Enemy,
And thence in Heaven called Satan, with bold words

Breaking the horrid silence, thus began:—
  'If thou beest he—but oh, how fall'n! how changed
From him who, in the happy realms of light,
Clothed with transcendent brightness, didst outshine
Myriads, though bright!—if he whom mutual league,
United thoughts and counsels, equal hope
And hazard in the glorious enterprise,
Joined with me once, now misery hath joined          90
In equal ruin: into what pit thou seest
From what height fallen: so much the stronger proved
He with his thunder: and till then who knew
The force of those dire arms? Yet not for those,
Nor what the potent Victor in his rage
Can else inflict, do I repent, or change,
Though changed in outward lustre, that fixed mind,
And high disdain from sense of injured merit,
That with the Mightiest raised me to contend,
And to the fierce contention brought along          100
Innumerable force of Spirits armed,
That durst dislike his reign, and, me preferring,
His utmost power with adverse power opposed
In dubious battle on the plains of Heaven,
And shook his throne. What though the field be lost?
All is not lost—the unconquerable will,
And study of revenge, immortal hate,
And courage never to submit or yield:
And what is else not to be overcome.
That glory never shall his wrath or might          110
Extort from me. To bow and sue for grace
With suppliant knee, and deify his power
Who, from the terror of this arm, so late
Doubted his empire—that were low indeed;
That were an ignominy and shame beneath
This downfall; since by fate the strength of Gods,
And this empyreal substance, cannot fail;
Since, through experience of this great event,
In arms not worse, in foresight much advanced,
We may with more successful hope resolve          120
To wage by force or guile eternal war
Irreconcilable, to our grand Foe,
Who now triumphs, and in th' excess of joy

Sole reigning holds the tyranny of Heaven.'
     So spake th' apostate Angel, though in pain,
Vaunting aloud, but racked with deep despair;
And him thus answered soon his bold compeer:—
     'O Prince, O Chief of many throned Powers
That led th' embattled Seraphim to war
Under thy conduct, and, in dreadful deeds          130
Fearless, endangered Heaven's perpetual King,
And put to proof his high supremacy,
Whether upheld by strength, or chance, or fate!
Too well I see and rue the dire event
That, with sad overthrow and foul defeat,
Hath lost us Heaven, and all this mighty host
In horrible destruction laid thus low,
As far as Gods and Heavenly Essences
Can perish: for the mind and spirit remains
Invincible, and vigour soon returns,          140
Though all our glory extinct, and happy state
Here swallowed up in endless misery.
But what if he our Conqueror (whom I now
Of force believe almighty, since no less
Than such could have o'erpowered such force as ours)
Have left us this our spirit and strength entire,
Strongly to suffer and support our pains,
That we may so suffice his vengeful ire,
Or do him mightier service as his thralls
By right of war, whate'er his business be,          150
Here in the heart of Hell to work in fire,
Or do his errands in the gloomy Deep?
What can it then avail though yet we feel
Strength undiminished, or eternal being
To undergo eternal punishment?'
     Whereto with speedy words th' Arch-Fiend replied:—
     'Fall'n Cherub, to be weak is miserable,
Doing or suffering: but of this be sure—
To do aught good never will be our task,
But ever to do ill our sole delight,          160
As being the contrary to his high will
Whom we resist.  If then his providence
Out of our evil seek to bring forth good,
Our labour must be to pervert that end,

And out of good still to find means of evil;
Which oft-times may succeed so as perhaps
Shall grieve him, if I fail not, and disturb
His inmost counsels from their destined aim.
But see! the angry Victor hath recalled
His ministers of vengeance and pursuit                          170
Back to the gates of Heaven: the sulphurous hail,
Shot after us in storm, o'erblown hath laid
The fiery surge that from the precipice
Of Heaven received us falling; and the thunder,
Winged with red lightning and impetuous rage,
Perhaps hath spent his shafts, and ceases now
To bellow through the vast and boundless Deep.
Let us not slip th' occasion, whether scorn
Or satiate fury yield it from our Foe.
Seest thou yon dreary plain, forlorn and wild,                  180
The seat of desolation, void of light,
Save what the glimmering of these livid flames
Casts pale and dreadful? Thither let us tend
From off the tossing of these fiery waves;
There rest, if any rest can harbour there;
And, reassembling our afflicted powers,
Consult how we may henceforth most offend
Our Enemy, our own loss how repair,
How overcome this dire calamity,
What reinforcement we may gain from hope,                       190
If not, what resolution from despair.'
    Thus Satan, talking to his nearest mate,
With head uplift above the wave, and eyes
That sparkling blazed; his other parts besides
Prone on the flood, extended long and large,
Lay floating many a rood, in bulk as huge
As whom the fables name of monstrous size,
Titanian or Earth-born, that warred on Jove,
Briareos or Typhon, whom the den
By ancient Tarsus held, or that sea-beast                       200
Leviathan, which God of all his works
Created hugest that swim th' ocean-stream.
Him, haply slumbering on the Norway foam,
The pilot of some small night-foundered skiff,
Deeming some island, oft, as seamen tell,

With fixed anchor in his scaly rind,
Moors by his side under the lee, while night
Invests the sea, and wished morn delays.
So stretched out huge in length the Arch-Fiend lay,
Chained on the burning lake; nor ever thence          210
Had risen, or heaved his head, but that the will
And high permission of all-ruling Heaven
Left him at large to his own dark designs,
That with reiterated crimes he might
Heap on himself damnation, while he sought
Evil to others, and enraged might see
How all his malice served but to bring forth
Infinite goodness, grace, and mercy, shown
On Man by him seduced; but on himself
Treble confusion, wrath, and vengeance poured.        220
Forthwith upright he rears from off the pool
His mighty stature; on each hand the flames,
Driven backward, slope their pointing spires, and, rolled
In billows, leave i' the midst a horrid vale.
Then with expanded wings he steers his flight
Aloft, incumbent on the dusky air,
That felt unusual weight; till on dry land
He lights; if it were land that ever burned
With solid, as the lake with liquid fire,
And such appeared in hue as when the force           230
Of subterranean wind transports a hill
Torn from Pelorus, or the shattered side
Of thundering Aetna, whose combustible
And fuelled entrails, thence conceiving fire,
Sublimed with mineral fury, aid the winds,
And leave a singed bottom all involved
With stench and smoke; such resting found the sole
Of unblest feet.  Him followed his next mate;
Both glorying to have 'scaped the Stygian flood
As gods, and by their own recovered strength,        240
Not by the sufferance of Supernal Power.
   'Is this the region, this the soil, the clime,'
Said then the lost Archangel, 'this the seat
That we must change for Heaven?—this mournful
     gloom
For that celestial light?  Be it so, since he

Who now is sovran can dispose and bid
What shall be right: farthest from him is best,
Whom reason hath equalled, force hath made supreme
Above his equals.  Farewell, happy fields,
Where joy for ever dwells!  Hail, horrors! hail,          250
Infernal World! and thou, profoundest Hell,
Receive thy new possessor—one who brings
A mind not to be changed by place or time.
The mind is its own place, and in itself
Can make a Heaven of Hell, a Hell of Heaven.
What matter where, if I be still the same,
And what I should be, all but less than he
Whom thunder hath made greater?  Here at least
We shall be free; th' Almighty hath not built
Here for his envy, will not drive us hence:          260
Here we may reign secure; and, in my choice,
To reign is worth ambition, though in Hell:
Better to reign in Hell than serve in Heaven.
But wherefore let we then our faithful friends,
Th' associates and co-partners of our loss,
Lie thus astonished on th' oblivious pool,
And call them not to share with us their part
In this unhappy mansion, or once more
With rallied arms to try what may be yet
Regained in Heaven, or what more lost in Hell?'          270
    So Satan spake; and him Beëlzebub
Thus answered:—'Leader of those armies bright
Which, but th' Omnipotent, none could have foiled,
If once they hear that voice, their liveliest pledge
Of hope in fears and dangers, heard so oft
In worst extremes, and on the perilous edge
Of battle, when it raged, in all assaults
Their surest signal, they will soon resume
New courage and revive, though now they lie
Grovelling and prostrate on yon lake of fire,          280
As we erewhile, astounded and amazed;
No wonder, fall'n such a pernicious height!'
    He scarce had ceased when the superior Fiend
Was moving toward the shore; his ponderous shield,
Ethereal temper, massy, large, and round,
Behind him cast.  The broad circumference

Hung on his shoulders like the moon, whose orb
Through optic glass the Tuscan artist views
At evening, from the top of Fesolè,
Or in Valdarno, to descry new lands,       290
Rivers, or mountains, in her spotty globe.
His spear, to equal which the tallest pine
Hewn on Norwegian hills, to be the mast
Of some great ammiral, were but a wand,
He walked with, to support uneasy steps
Over the burning marle, not like those steps
On Heaven's azure; and the torrid clime
Smote on him sore besides, vaulted with fire.
Nathless he so endured, till on the beach
Of that inflamed sea he stood, and called       300
His legions, Angel forms, who lay entranced
Thick as autumnal leaves that strow the brooks
In Vallombrosa, where th' Etrurian shades
High over-arched embower; or scattered sedge
Afloat, when with fierce winds Orion armed
Hath vexed the Red-Sea coast, whose waves o'erthrew
Busiris and his Memphian chivalry,
While with perfidious hatred they pursued
The sojourners of Goshen, who beheld
From the safe shore their floating carcases       310
And broken chariot-wheels. So thick bestrown,
Abject and lost, lay these, covering the flood,
Under amazement of their hideous change.
He called so loud that all the hollow deep
Of Hell resounded:—'Princes, Potentates,
Warriors, the Flower of Heaven, once yours, now lost,
If such astonishment as this can seize
Eternal Spirits! or have ye chosen this place
After the toil of battle to repose
Your wearied virtue, for the ease you find       320
To slumber here, as in the vales of Heaven?
Or in this abject posture have ye sworn
To adore the Conqueror? who now beholds
Cherub and Seraph rolling in the flood
With scattered arms and ensigns, till anon
His swift pursuers from Heaven-gates discern
Th' advantage, and, descending, tread us down

Thus drooping, or with linked thunderbolts
Transfix us to the bottom of this gulf?—
Awake, arise, or be for ever fallen!'                      330
    They heard, and were abashed, and up they sprung
Upon the wing; as when men wont to watch
On duty, sleeping found by whom they dread,
Rouse and bestir themselves ere well awake.
Nor did they not perceive the evil plight
In which they were, or the fierce pains not feel,
Yet to their General's voice they soon obeyed
Innumerable.  As when the potent rod
Of Amram's son, in Egypt's evil day,
Waved round the coast, up-called a pitchy cloud      340
Of locusts, warping on the eastern wind,
That o'er the realm of impious Pharaoh hung
Like Night, and darkened all the land of Nile;
So numberless were those bad Angels seen
Hovering on wing under the cope of Hell,
'Twixt upper, nether, and surrounding fires;
Till, as a signal given, th' uplifted spear
Of their great Sultan waving to direct
Their course, in even balance down they light
On the firm brimstone, and fill all the plain:      350
A multitude like which the populous North
Poured never from her frozen loins to pass
Rhene or the Danaw, when her barbarous sons
Came like a deluge on the South, and spread
Beneath Gibraltar to the Libyan sands.
Forthwith, from every squadron and each band,
The heads and leaders thither haste where stood
Their great Commander; godlike Shapes, and Forms
Excelling human; princely Dignities;
And Powers that erst in Heaven sat on thrones,      360
Though of their names in Heavenly records now
Be no memorial, blotted out and rased
By their rebellion from the Books of Life.
Nor had they yet among the sons of Eve
Got them new names, till, wandering o'er the earth,
Through God's high sufferance for the trial of man,
By falsities and lies the greatest part
Of mankind they corrupted to forsake

God their Creator, and th' invisible
Glory of him that made them to transform        370
Oft to the image of a brute, adorned
With gay religions full of pomp and gold,
And devils to adore for deities:
Then were they known to men by various names,
And various idols through the heathen world.
Say, Muse, their names then known, who first, who
     last,
Roused from the slumber on that fiery couch,
At their great Emperor's call, as next in worth
Came singly where he stood on the bare strand,
While the promiscuous crowd stood yet aloof.        380
The chief were those who, from the pit of Hell
Roaming to seek their prey on Earth, durst fix
Their seats, long after, next the seat of God,
Their altars by his altar, gods adored
Among the nations round, and durst abide
Jehovah thund'ring out of Sion, throned
Between the Cherubim; yea, often placed
Within his sanctuary itself their shrines,
Abominations; and with cursed things
His holy rites and solemn feasts profaned,        390
And with their darkness durst affront his light.
First, Moloch, horrid king, besmeared with blood
Of human sacrifice, and parents' tears;
Though, for the noise of drums and timbrels loud,
Their children's cries unheard that passed through fire
To his grim idol.  Him the Ammonite
Worshipped in Rabba and her watery plain,
In Argob and in Basan, to the stream
Of utmost Arnon.  Nor content with such
Audacious neighbourhood, the wisest heart        400
Of Solomon he led by fraud to build
His temple right against the temple of God
On that opprobrious hill, and made his grove
The pleasant valley of Hinnom, Tophet thence
And black Gehenna called, the type of Hell.
Next Chemos, th' obscene dread of Moab's sons,
From Aroer to Nebo and the wild
Of southmost Abarim; in Hesebon

And Horonaim, Seon's realm, beyond
The flow'ry dale of Sibma, clad with vines,                410
And Elealè to th' Asphaltic Pool:
Peor his other name, when he enticed
Israel in Sittim, on their march from Nile,
To do him wanton rites, which cost them woe.
Yet thence his lustful orgies he enlarged
Even to that hill of scandal, by the grove
Of Moloch homicide, lust hard by hate,
Till good Josiah drove them thence to Hell.
With these came they who, from the bordering flood
Of old Euphrates to the brook that parts              420
Egypt from Syrian ground, had general names
Of Baalim and Ashtaroth—those male,
These feminine. For Spirits, when they please,
Can either sex assume, or both; so soft
And uncompounded is their essence pure,
Not tied or manacled with joint or limb,
Nor founded on the brittle strength of bones,
Like cumbrous flesh; but, in what shape they choose,
Dilated or condensed, bright or obscure,
Can execute their aery purposes,                      430
And works of love or enmity fulfil.
For those the race of Israel oft forsook
Their Living Strength, and unfrequented left
His righteous altar, bowing lowly down
To bestial gods; for which their heads, as low
Bowed down in battle, sunk before the spear
Of despicable foes. With these in troop
Came Astoreth, whom the Phœnicians called
Astarte, queen of heaven, with crescent horns;
To whose bright image nightly by the moon             440
Sidonian virgins paid their vows and songs;
In Sion also not unsung, where stood
Her temple on th' offensive mountain, built
By that uxorious king whose heart, though large,
Beguiled by fair idolatresses, fell
To idols foul. Thammuz came next behind,
Whose annual wound in Lebanon allured
The Syrian damsels to lament his fate
In amorous ditties all a summer's day,

While smooth Adonis from his native rock              450
Ran purple to the sea, supposed with blood
Of Thammuz yearly wounded: the love-tale
Infected Sion's daughters with like heat,
Whose wanton passions in the sacred porch
Ezekiel saw, when, by the vision led,
His eye surveyed the dark idolatries
Of alienated Judah.  Next came one
Who mourned in earnest, when the captive ark
Maimed his brute image, head and hands lopped off,
In his own temple, on the grunsel-edge,              460
Where he fell flat and shamed his worshippers:
Dagon his name, sea-monster, upward man
And downward fish; yet had his temple high
Reared in Azotus, dreaded through the coast
Of Palestine, in Gath and Ascalon,
And Accaron and Gaza's frontier bounds.
Him followed Rimmon, whose delightful seat
Was fair Damascus, on the fertile banks
Of Abbana and Pharphar, lucid streams.
He also against the house of God was bold:           470
A leper once he lost, and gained a king—
Ahaz, his sottish conqueror, whom he drew
God's altar to disparage and displace
For one of Syrian mode, whereon to burn
His odious offerings, and adore the gods
Whom he had vanquished.  After these appeared
A crew who, under names of old renown—
Osiris, Isis, Orus, and their train—
With monstrous shapes and sorceries abused
Fanatic Egypt and her priests, to seek              480
Their wandering gods disguised in brutish forms
Rather than human.  Nor did Israel 'scape
Th' infection, when their borrowed gold composed
The calf in Oreb; and the rebel king
Doubled that sin in Bethel and in Dan,
Lik'ning his Maker to the grazed ox,
Jehovah, who, in one night, when he passed
From Egypt marching, equalled with one stroke
Both her first-born and all her bleating gods.
Belial came last: than whom a Spirit more lewd       490

Fell not from Heaven, or more gross to love
Vice for itself.  To him no temple stood
Or altar smoked; yet who more oft than he
In temples and at altars, when the priest
Turns atheist, as did Eli's sons, who filled
With lust and violence the house of God?
In courts and palaces he also reigns,
And in luxurious cities, where the noise
Of riot ascends above their loftiest towers,
And injury and outrage; and when night          500
Darkens the streets, then wander forth the sons
Of Belial, flown with insolence and wine.
Witness the streets of Sodom, and that night
In Gibeah, when the hospitable door
Exposed a matron, to prevent worse rape.
These were the prime in order and in might:
The rest were long to tell, though far renowned,
Th' Ionian gods—of Javan's issue held
Gods, yet confessed later than Heaven and Earth,
Their boasted parents;—Titan, Heaven's first-born,  510
With his enormous brood, and birthright seized
By younger Saturn: he from mightier Jove,
His own and Rhea's son, like measure found;
So Jove usurping reigned.  These, first in Crete
And Ida known, thence on the snowy top
Of cold Olympus ruled the middle air,
Their highest heaven; or on the Delphian cliff,
Or in Dodona, and through all the bounds
Of Doric land; or who with Saturn old
Fled over Adria to th' Hesperian fields,          520
And o'er the Celtic roamed the utmost Isles.
   All these and more came flocking; but with looks
Downcast and damp; yet such wherein appeared
Obscure some glimpse of joy to have found their Chief
Not in despair, to have found themselves not lost
In loss itself; which on his count'nance cast
Like doubtful hue: but he, his wonted pride
Soon recollecting, with high words, that bore
Semblance of worth, not substance, gently raised
Their fainted courage, and dispelled their fears:  530
Then straight commands that, at the warlike sound

Of trumpets loud and clarions, be upreared
His mighty standard. That proud honour claimed
Azazel as his right, a Cherub tall:
Who forthwith from the glittering staff unfurled
Th' imperial ensign; which, full high advanced,
Shone like a meteor streaming to the wind,
With gems and golden lustre rich emblazed,
Seraphic arms and trophies; all the while
Sonorous metal blowing martial sounds:                    540
At which the universal host up-sent
A shout that tore Hell's concave, and beyond
Frighted the reign of Chaos and old Night.
All in a moment through the gloom were seen
Ten thousand banners rise into the air,
With orient colours waving: with them rose
A forest huge of spears; and thronging helms
Appeared, and serried shields in thick array
Of depth immeasurable. Anon they move
In perfect phalanx to the Dorian mood                    550
Of flutes and soft recorders—such as raised
To height of noblest temper heroes old
Arming to battle, and instead of rage
Deliberate valour breathed, firm, and unmoved
With dread of death to flight or foul retreat;
Nor wanting power to mitigate and suage
With solemn touches troubled thoughts, and chase
Anguish and doubt and fear and sorrow and pain
From mortal or immortal minds. Thus they,
Breathing united force with fixed thought,                    560
Moved on in silence to soft pipes that charmed
Their painful steps o'er the burnt soil. And now
Advanced in view they stand, a horrid front
Of dreadful length and dazzling arms, in guise
Of warriors old, with ordered spear and shield,
Awaiting what command their mighty Chief
Had to impose. He through the armed files
Darts his experienced eye, and soon traverse
The whole battalion views—their order due,
Their visages and statures as of gods;                    570
Their number last he sums. And now his heart
Distends with pride, and, hardening in his strength,

Glories: for never, since created Man,
Met such embodied force as, named with these,
Could merit more than that small infantry
Warred on by cranes—though all the giant brood
Of Phlegra with th' heroic race were joined
That fought at Thebes and Ilium, on each side
Mix'd with auxiliar gods; and what resounds
In fable or romance of Uther's son,                        580
Begirt with British and Armoric knights;
And all who since, baptized or infidel,
Jousted in Aspramont, or Montalban,
Damasco, or Marocco, or Trebisond,
Or whom Biserta sent from Afric shore
When Charlemain with all his peerage fell
By Fontarabbia. Thus far these beyond
Compare of mortal prowess, yet observed
Their dread Commander: he, above the rest
In shape and gesture proudly eminent,                      590
Stood like a tower: his form had yet not lost
All her original brightness, nor appeared
Less than Archangel ruined, and the excess
Of glory obscured: as when the sun new-risen
Looks through the horizontal misty air
Shorn of his beams, or, from behind the moon,
In dim eclipse, disastrous twilight sheds
On half the nations, and with fear of change
Perplexes monarchs. Darkened so, yet shone
Above them all th' Archangel: but his face               600
Deep scars of thunder had intrenched, and care
Sat on his faded cheek, but under brows
Of dauntless courage, and considerate pride
Waiting revenge: cruel his eye, but cast
Signs of remorse and passion, to behold
The fellows of his crime, the followers rather
(Far other once beheld in bliss), condemned
For ever now to have their lot in pain—
Millions of Spirits for his fault amerced
Of Heaven, and from eternal splendours flung             610
For his revolt—yet faithful how they stood,
Their glory withered; as, when Heaven's fire
Hath scathed the forest oaks or mountain pines,

With singed top their stately growth, though bare,
Stands on the blasted heath. He now prepared
To speak; whereat their doubled ranks they bend
From wing to wing, and half enclose him round
With all his peers: attention held them mute.
Thrice he assayed, and thrice, in spite of scorn,
Tears, such as Angels weep, burst forth: at last          620
Words interwove with sighs found out their way:—
    'O myriads of immortal Spirits! O Powers
Matchless, but with th' Almighty!—and that strife
Was not inglorious, though th' event was dire,
As this place testifies, and this dire change,
Hateful to utter. But what power of mind,
Foreseeing or presaging, from the depth
Of knowledge past or present, could have feared
How such united force of gods, how such
As stood like these, could ever know repulse?             630
For who can yet believe, though after loss,
That all these puissant legions, whose exile
Hath emptied Heaven, shall fail to reascend,
Self-raised, and repossess their native seat?
For me, be witness all the host of Heaven,
If counsels different, or danger shunned
By me, have lost our hopes. But he who reigns
Monarch in Heaven till then as one secure
Sat on his throne, upheld by old repute,
Consent or custom, and his regal state                    640
Put forth at full, but still his strength concealed—
Which tempted our attempt, and wrought our fall.
Henceforth his might we know, and know our own,
So as not either to provoke, or dread
New war, provoked: our better part remains
To work in close design, by fraud or guile,
What force effected not; that he no less
At length from us may find, who overcomes
By force hath overcome but half his foe.
Space may produce new Worlds; whereof so rife              650
There went a fame in Heaven that he ere long
Intended to create, and therein plant
A generation whom his choice regard
Should favour equal to the Sons of Heaven.

Thither, if but to pry, shall be perhaps
Our first eruption—thither, or elsewhere;
For this infernal pit shall never hold
Celestial Spirits in bondage, nor th' Abyss
Long under darkness cover.  But these thoughts
Full counsel must mature.  Peace is despaired;          660
For who can think submission?  War then, war
Open or understood, must be resolved.'

　　He spake; and, to confirm his words, out-flew
Millions of flaming swords, drawn from the thighs
Of mighty Cherubim; the sudden blaze
Far round illumined Hell.  Highly they raged
Against the Highest, and fierce with grasped arms
Clashed on their sounding shields the din of war,
Hurling defiance toward the vault of Heaven.

　　There stood a hill not far, whose grisly top          670
Belched fire and rolling smoke; the rest entire
Shone with a glossy scurf—undoubted sign
That in his womb was hid metallic ore,
The work of sulphur.  Thither, winged with speed,
A numerous brigade hastened: as when bands
Of pioneers, with spade and pickaxe armed,
Forerun the royal camp, to trench a field,
Or cast a rampart.  Mammon led them on,
Mammon, the least erected Spirit that fell
From Heaven; for even in Heaven his looks and thoughts
Were always downward bent, admiring more          681
The riches of Heaven's pavement, trodden gold,
Than aught divine or holy else enjoyed
In vision beatific; by him first
Men also, and by his suggestion taught,
Ransacked the centre, and with impious hands
Rifled the bowels of their mother Earth
For treasures better hid.  Soon had his crew
Opened into the hill a spacious wound,
And digged out ribs of gold.  Let none admire          690
That riches grow in Hell; that soil may best
Deserve the precious bane.  And here let those
Who boast in mortal things, and wondering tell
Of Babel, and the works of Memphian kings,
Learn how their greatest monuments of fame,

And strength, and art, are easily outdone
By Spirits reprobate, and in an hour
What in an age they, with incessant toil
And hands innumerable, scarce perform.
Nigh on the plain, in many cells prepared,  700
That underneath had veins of liquid fire
Sluiced from the lake, a second multitude
With wondrous art founded the massy ore,
Severing each kind, and scummed the bullion-dross:
A third as soon had formed within the ground
A various mould, and from the boiling cells
By strange conveyance filled each hollow nook;
As in an organ, from one blast of wind,
To many a row of pipes the sound-board breathes.
Anon out of the earth a fabric huge  710
Rose like an exhalation, with the sound
Of dulcet symphonies and voices sweet,
Built like a temple, where pilasters round
Were set, and Doric pillars overlaid
With golden architrave; nor did there want
Cornice or frieze, with bossy sculptures graven:
The roof was fretted gold. Not Babylon
Nor great Alcairo such magnificence
Equalled in all their glories, to enshrine
Belus or Serapis their gods, or seat  720
Their kings, when Egypt with Assyria strove
In wealth and luxury. The ascending pile
Stood fixed her stately height; and straight the doors
Opening their brazen folds, discover, wide
Within, her ample spaces o'er the smooth
And level pavement: from the arched roof,
Pendent by subtle magic, many a row
Of starry lamps and blazing cressets, fed
With naphtha and asphaltus, yielded light
As from a sky. The hasty multitude  730
Admiring entered; and the work some praise,
And some the architect: his hand was known
In Heaven by many a towered structure high,
Where sceptred Angels held their residence,
And sat as Princes, whom the supreme King
Exalted to such power, and gave to rule,

Each in his hierarchy, the Orders bright.
Nor was his name unheard or unadored
In ancient Greece; and in Ausonian land
Men called him Mulciber; and how he fell          740
From Heaven they fabled, thrown by angry Jove
Sheer o'er the crystal battlements: from morn
To noon he fell, from noon to dewy eve,
A summer's day, and with the setting sun
Dropped from the zenith, like a falling star,
On Lemnos, th' Aegaean isle. Thus they relate,
Erring; for he with this rebellious rout
Fell long before; nor aught availed him now
To have built in Heaven high towers; nor did he scape
By all his engines, but was headlong sent,          750
With his industrious crew, to build in Hell.
    Meanwhile the winged Heralds, by command
Of sovran power, with awful ceremony
And trumpet's sound, throughout the host proclaim
A solemn council forthwith to be held
At Pandemonium, the high capital
Of Satan and his peers. Their summons called
From every band and squared regiment
By place or choice the worthiest: they anon
With hundreds and with thousands trooping came          760
Attended: all access was thronged; the gates
And porches wide, but chief the spacious hall
(Though like a covered field, where champions bold
Wont ride in armed, and at the Soldan's chair
Defied the best of Paynim chivalry
To mortal combat, or career with lance)
Thick swarmed, both on the ground and in the air,
Brushed with the hiss of rustling wings. As bees
In spring-time, when the Sun with Taurus rides,
Pour forth their populous youth about the hive          770
In clusters; they among fresh dews and flowers
Fly to and fro, or on the smoothed plank,
The suburb of their straw-built citadel,
New rubbed with balm, expatiate, and confer
Their state-affairs: so thick the aery crowd
Swarmed and were straitened; till, the signal given,
Behold a wonder! they but now who seemed

In bigness to surpass Earth's giant sons,
Now less than smallest dwarfs, in narrow room
Throng numberless—like that pygmean race          780
Beyond the Indian mount; or faëry elves,
Whose midnight revels, by a forest-side
Or fountain, some belated peasant sees,
Or dreams he sees, while overhead the Moon
Sits arbitress, and nearer to the Earth
Wheels her pale course: they, on their mirth and dance
Intent, with jocund music charm his ear;
At once with joy and fear his heart rebounds.
Thus incorporeal Spirits to smallest forms
Reduced their shapes immense, and were at large,   790
Though without number still, amidst the hall
Of that infernal court. But far within,
And in their own dimensions like themselves,
The great Seraphic Lords and Cherubim
In close recess and secret conclave sat,
A thousand demi-gods on golden seats,
Frequent and full. After short silence then,
And summons read, the great consult began.

*The End of the First Book.*

# PARADISE LOST

## BOOK II

### THE ARGUMENT

*The consultation begun, Satan debates whether another battle
be to be hazarded for the recovery of Heaven: some advise it,
others dissuade. A third proposal is preferred, mentioned
before by Satan, to search the truth of that prophecy or tradition in Heaven concerning another world, and another kind of
creature, equal, or not much inferior, to themselves, about this
time to be created. Their doubt who shall be sent on this
difficult search: Satan, their chief, undertakes alone the
voyage; is honoured and applauded. The council thus ended,
the rest betake them several ways and to several employments,
as their inclinations lead them, to entertain the time till Satan
return. He passes on his journey to Hell-gates; finds them
shut, and who sat there to guard them; by whom at length they
are opened, and discover to him the great gulf between Hell
and Heaven; with what difficulty he passes through, directed
by Chaos, the Power of that place, to the sight of this new
World which he sought.*

HIGH on a throne of royal state, which far
Outshone the wealth of Ormus and of Ind,
Or where the gorgeous East with richest hand
Showers on her kings barbaric pearl and gold,
Satan exalted sat, by merit raised
To that bad eminence; and, from despair
Thus high uplifted beyond hope, aspires
Beyond thus high, insatiate to pursue
Vain war with Heaven; and, by success untaught,
His proud imaginations thus displayed:—                    10
   'Powers and Dominions, Deities of Heaven!—
For, since no deep within her gulf can hold
Immortal vigour, though oppressed and fall'n,
I give not Heaven for lost: from this descent

Celestial Virtues rising will appear
More glorious and more dread than from no fall,
And trust themselves to fear no second fate!—
Me though just right, and the fixed laws of Heaven,
Did first create your leader, next, free choice,
With what besides, in council or in fight,                    20
Hath been achieved of merit, yet this loss,
Thus far at least recovered, hath much more
Established in a safe, unenvied throne,
Yielded with full consent.  The happier state
In Heaven, which follows dignity, might draw
Envy from each inferior; but who here
Will envy whom the highest place exposes
Foremost to stand against the Thunderer's aim
Your bulwark, and condemns to greatest share
Of endless pain?  Where there is, then, no good        30
For which to strive, no strife can grow up there
From faction: for none sure will claim in Hell
Precedence; none, whose portion is so small
Of present pain, that with ambitious mind
Will covet more!  With this advantage, then,
To union, and firm faith, and firm accord,
More than can be in Heaven, we now return
To claim our just inheritance of old,
Surer to prosper than prosperity
Could have assured us; and by what best way,        40
Whether of open war or covert guile,
We now debate; who can advise, may speak.'
    He ceased; and next him Moloch, sceptred king,
Stood up—the strongest and the fiercest Spirit
That fought in Heaven, now fiercer by despair.
His trust was with th' Eternal to be deemed
Equal in strength, and rather than be less
Cared not to be at all; with that care lost
Went all his fear: of God, or Hell, or worse,
He recked not, and these words thereafter spake:—   50
    'My sentence is for open war.  Of wiles,
More unexpert, I boast not: them let those
Contrive who need, or when they need; not now,
For, while they sit contriving, shall the rest—
Millions that stand in arms, and longing wait

The signal to ascend—sit lingering here,
Heaven's fugitives, and for their dwelling-place
Accept this dark opprobrious den of shame,
The prison of his tyranny who reigns
By our delay? No! let us rather choose,                    60
Armed with Hell-flames and fury, all at once
O'er Heaven's high towers to force resistless way,
Turning our tortures into horrid arms
Against the Torturer; when, to meet the noise
Of his almighty engine, he shall hear
Infernal thunder, and, for lightning, see
Black fire and horror shot with equal rage
Among his Angels, and his throne itself
Mixed with Tartarean sulphur and strange fire,
His own invented torments. But perhaps                    70
The way seems difficult, and steep to scale
With upright wing against a higher foe!
Let such bethink them, if the sleepy drench
Of that forgetful lake benumb not still,
That in our proper motion we ascend
Up to our native seat; descent and fall
To us is adverse. Who but felt of late,
When the fierce foe hung on our broken rear
Insulting, and pursued us through the Deep,
With what compulsion and laborious flight                    80
We sunk thus low? Th' ascent is easy, then;
Th' event is feared! Should we again provoke
Our stronger, some worse way his wrath may find
To our destruction, if there be in Hell
Fear to be worse destroyed! What can be worse
Than to dwell here, driven out from bliss, condemned
In this abhorred deep to utter woe;
Where pain of unextinguishable fire
Must exercise us without hope of end
The vassals of his anger, when the scourge                    90
Inexorably, and the torturing hour,
Calls us to penance? More destroyed than thus,
We should be quite abolished, and expire.
What fear we then? what doubt we to incense
His utmost ire? which, to the height enraged,
Will either quite consume us, and reduce

To nothing this essential—happier far
Than miserable to have eternal being!—
Or, if our substance be indeed divine,
And cannot cease to be, we are at worst       100
On this side nothing; and by proof we feel
Our power sufficient to disturb his Heaven,
And with perpetual inroads to alarm,
Though inaccessible, his fatal throne:
Which, if not victory, is yet revenge.'

    He ended frowning, and his look denounced
Desperate revenge, and battle dangerous
To less than gods. On th' other side up rose
Belial, in act more graceful and humane;
A fairer person lost not Heaven; he seemed       110
For dignity composed, and high exploit.
But all was false and hollow; though his tongue
Dropped manna, and could make the worse appear
The better reason, to perplex and dash
Maturest counsels: for his thoughts were low;
To vice industrious, but to nobler deeds
Timorous and slothful: yet he pleased the ear,
And with persuasive accent thus began:—

    'I should be much for open war, O Peers,
As not behind in hate, if what was urged       120
Main reason to persuade immediate war
Did not dissuade me most, and seem to cast
Ominous conjecture on the whole success;
When he who most excels in fact of arms,
In what he counsels and in what excels
Mistrustful, grounds his courage on despair
And utter dissolution, as the scope
Of all his aim, after some dire revenge.
First, what revenge? The towers of Heaven are filled
With armed watch, that render all access       130
Impregnable: oft on the bordering Deep
Encamp their legions, or with obscure wing
Scout far and wide into the realm of Night,
Scorning surprise. Or could we break our way
By force, and at our heels all Hell should rise
With blackest insurrection, to confound
Heaven's purest light, yet our great Enemy,

All incorruptible, would on his throne
Sit unpolluted, and th' ethereal mould,
Incapable of stain, would soon expel          140
Her mischief, and purge off the baser fire,
Victorious. Thus repulsed, our final hope
Is flat despair: we must exasperate
Th' Almighty Victor to spend all his rage;
And that must end us; that must be our cure—
To be no more; sad cure; for who would lose,
Though full of pain, this intellectual being,
Those thoughts that wander through eternity,
To perish rather, swallowed up and lost
In the wide womb of uncreated Night,          150
Devoid of sense and motion? And who knows,
Let this be good, whether our angry Foe
Can give it, or will ever? How he can
Is doubtful; that he never will is sure.
Will he, so wise, let loose at once his ire,
Belike through impotence or unaware,
To give his enemies their wish, and end
Them in his anger whom his anger saves
To punish endless? "Wherefore cease we, then?"
Say they who counsel war; "we are decreed,          160
Reserved, and destined to eternal woe;
Whatever doing, what can we suffer more,
What can we suffer worse?" Is this, then, worst—
Thus sitting, thus consulting, thus in arms?
What when we fled amain, pursued and struck
With Heaven's afflicting thunder, and besought
The Deep to shelter us? this Hell then seemed
A refuge from those wounds. Or when we lay
Chained on the burning lake? that sure was worse.
What if the breath that kindled those grim fires,          170
Awaked, should blow them into sevenfold rage,
And plunge us in the flames; or from above
Should intermitted vengeance arm again
His red right hand to plague us? What if all
Her stores were opened, and this firmament
Of Hell should spout her cataracts of fire,
Impendent horrors, threat'ning hideous fall
One day upon our heads; while we perhaps,

Designing or exhorting glorious war,
Caught in a fiery tempest, shall be hurled,          180
Each on his rock transfixed, the sport and prey
Of racking whirlwinds, or for ever sunk
Under yon boiling ocean, wrapt in chains,
There to converse with everlasting groans,
Unrespited, unpitied, unreprieved,
Ages of hopeless end? This would be worse.
War, therefore, open or concealed, alike
My voice dissuades; for what can force or guile
With him, or who deceive his mind, whose eye
Views all things at one view? He from Heaven's
          height          190
All these our motions vain sees and derides,
Not more almighty to resist our might
Than wise to frustrate all our plots and wiles.
Shall we, then, live thus vile—the race of Heaven
Thus trampled, thus expelled, to suffer here
Chains and these torments? Better these than worse,
By my advice; since fate inevitable
Subdues us, and omnipotent decree,
The Victor's will. To suffer, as to do,
Our strength is equal; nor the law unjust          200
That so ordains: this was at first resolved,
If we were wise, against so great a foe
Contending, and so doubtful what might fall.
I laugh when those who at the spear are bold
And vent'rous, if that fail them, shrink, and fear
What yet they know must follow—to endure
Exile, or ignominy, or bonds, or pain,
The sentence of their conqueror. This is now
Our doom; which if we can sustain and bear,
Our Supreme Foe in time may much remit          210
His anger, and perhaps, thus far removed,
Not mind us not offending, satisfied
With what is punished; whence these raging fires
Will slacken, if his breath stir not their flames.
Our purer essence then will overcome
Their noxious vapour; or, inured, not feel;
Or, changed at length, and to the place conformed
In temper and in nature, will receive

Familiar the fierce heat, and void of pain;
This horror will grow mild, this darkness light;　　220
Besides what hope the never-ending flight
Of future days may bring, what chance, what change
Worth waiting—since our present lot appears
For happy though but ill, for ill not worst,
If we procure not to ourselves more woe.'
　　Thus Belial, with words clothed in reason's garb,
Counselled ignoble ease and peaceful sloth,
Not peace; and after him thus Mammon spake—
　　'Either to disenthrone the King of Heaven
We war, if war be best, or to regain　　230
Our own right lost. Him to unthrone we then
May hope, when everlasting Fate shall yield
To fickle Chance, and Chaos judge the strife.
The former vain to hope argues as vain
The latter; for what place can be for us
Within Heaven's bound, unless Heaven's Lord Supreme
We overpower? Suppose he should relent,
And publish grace to all, on promise made
Of new subjection; with what eyes could we
Stand in his presence humble, and receive　　240
Strict laws imposed, to celebrate his throne
With warbled hymns, and to his Godhead sing
Forced Halleluiahs, while he lordly sits
Our envied sovran, and his altar breathes
Ambrosial odours and ambrosial flowers,
Our servile offerings? This must be our task
In Heaven, this our delight. How wearisome
Eternity so spent in worship paid
To whom we hate! Let us not then pursue,
By force impossible, by leave obtained　　250
Unacceptable, though in Heaven, our state
Of splendid vassalage; but rather seek
Our own good from ourselves, and from our own
Live to ourselves, though in this vast recess,
Free and to none accountable, preferring
Hard liberty before the easy yoke
Of servile pomp. Our greatness will appear
Then most conspicuous when great things of small,
Useful of hurtful, prosperous of adverse,

We can create, and in what place soe'er                          260
Thrive under evil, and work ease out of pain
Through labour and endurance. This deep world
Of darkness do we dread? How oft amidst
Thick clouds and dark doth Heaven's all-ruling Sire
Choose to reside, his glory unobscured,
And with the majesty of darkness round
Covers his throne, from whence deep thunders roar,
Mustering their rage, and Heaven resembles Hell!
As he our darkness, cannot we his light
Imitate when we please? This desert soil                         270
Wants not her hidden lustre, gems and gold;
Nor want we skill or art from whence to raise
Magnificence; and what can Heaven show more?
Our torments also may, in length of time,
Become our elements, these piercing fires
As soft as now severe, our temper changed
Into their temper; which must needs remove
The sensible of pain. All things invite
To peaceful counsels, and the settled state
Of order, how in safety best we may                              280
Compose our present evils, with regard
Of what we are and where, dismissing quite
All thoughts of war. Ye have what I advise.'
      He scarce had finished, when such murmur filled
Th' assembly as when hollow rocks retain
The sound of blustering winds, which all night long
Had roused the sea, now with hoarse cadence lull
Seafaring men o'erwatched, whose bark by chance,
Or pinnace, anchors in a craggy bay
After the tempest. Such applause was heard                       290
As Mammon ended, and his sentence pleased,
Advising peace: for such another field
They dreaded worse than Hell; so much the fear
Of thunder and the sword of Michael
Wrought still within them; and no less desire
To found this nether empire, which might rise,
By policy and long process of time,
In emulation opposite to Heaven.
Which when Beëlzebub perceived—than whom,
Satan except, none higher sat—with grave                         300

Aspect he rose, and in his rising seemed
A pillar of state; deep on his front engraven
Deliberation sat, and public care;
And princely counsel in his face yet shone,
Majestic, though in ruin: sage he stood,
With Atlantean shoulders, fit to bear
The weight of mightiest monarchies; his look
Drew audience and attention still as night
Or summer's noontide air, while thus he spake:—
　'Thrones and Imperial Powers, Offspring of Heaven,
Ethereal Virtues! or these titles now          311
Must we renounce, and, changing style, be called
Princes of Hell? for so the popular vote
Inclines, here to continue, and build up here
A growing empire; doubtless; while we dream,
And know not that the King of Heaven hath doomed
This place our dungeon, not our safe retreat
Beyond his potent arm, to live exempt
From Heaven's high jurisdiction, in new league
Banded against his throne, but to remain          320
In strictest bondage, though thus far removed,
Under th' inevitable curb, reserved
His captive multitude. For he, be sure,
In height or depth, still first and last will reign
Sole king, and of his kingdom lose no part
By our revolt, but over Hell extend
His empire, and with iron sceptre rule
Us here, as with his golden those in Heaven.
What sit we then projecting peace and war?
War hath determined us and foiled with loss          330
Irreparable; terms of peace yet none
Vouchsafed or sought; for what peace will be given
To us enslaved, but custody severe,
And stripes, and arbitrary punishment
Inflicted? and what peace can we return,
But, to our power, hostility and hate,
Untamed reluctance, and revenge, though slow,
Yet ever plotting how the Conqueror least
May reap his conquest, and may least rejoice
In doing what we most in suffering feel?          340
Nor will occasion want, nor shall we need

With dangerous expedition to invade
Heaven, whose high walls fear no assault or siege,
Or ambush from the Deep. What if we find
Some easier enterprise? There is a place
(If ancient and prophetic fame in Heaven
Err not)—another World, the happy seat
Of some new race, called Man, about this time
To be created like to us, though less
In power and excellence, but favoured more          350
Of him who rules above; so was his will
Pronounced among the gods, and by an oath
That shook Heaven's whole circumference confirmed.
Thither let us bend all our thoughts, to learn
What creatures there inhabit, of what mould
Or substance, how endued, and what their power,
And where their weakness, how attempted best,
By force or subtlety. Though Heaven be shut,
And Heaven's high Arbitrator sit secure
In his own strength, this place may lie exposed,     360
The utmost border of his kingdom, left
To their defence who hold it: here, perhaps,
Some advantageous act may be achieved
By sudden onset—either with Hell-fire
To waste his whole creation, or possess
All as our own, and drive, as we were driven,
The puny habitants; or, if not drive,
Seduce them to our party, that their God
May prove their foe, and with repenting hand
Abolish his own works. This would surpass          370
Common revenge, and interrupt his joy
In our confusion, and our joy upraise
In his disturbance; when his darling sons,
Hurled headlong to partake with us, shall curse
Their frail originals, and faded bliss—
Faded so soon! Advise if this be worth
Attempting, or to sit in darkness here
Hatching vain empires.' Thus Beëlzebub
Pleaded his devilish counsel—first devised
By Satan, and in part proposed: for whence          380
But from the author of all ill could spring
So deep a malice, to confound the race

Of mankind in one root, and Earth with Hell
To mingle and involve, done all to spite
The great Creator?  But their spite still serves
His glory to augment.  The bold design
Pleased highly those Infernal States, and joy
Sparkled in all their eyes: with full assent
They vote: whereat his speech he thus renews:—
   'Well have ye judged, well ended long debate,   390
Synod of Gods, and, like to what ye are,
Great things resolved, which from the lowest deep
Will once more lift us up, in spite of fate,
Nearer our ancient seat—perhaps in view
Of those bright confines, whence, with neighbouring
    arms,
And opportune excursion, we may chance
Re-enter Heaven; or else in some mild zone
Dwell, not unvisited of Heaven's fair light
Secure, and at the brightening orient beam
Purge off this gloom: the soft delicious air,   400
To heal the scar of these corrosive fires,
Shall breathe her balm.  But, first, whom shall we send
In search of this new world?  whom shall we find
Sufficient? who shall tempt with wand'ring feet
The dark, unbottomed, infinite abyss,
And through the palpable obscure find out
His uncouth way, or spread his aery flight,
Upborne with indefatigable wings
Over the vast abrupt, ere he arrive
The happy isle?  What strength, what art, can then   410
Suffice, or what evasion bear him safe
Through the strict senteries and stations thick
Of Angels watching round?  Here he had need
All circumspection: and we now no less
Choice in our suffrage; for on whom we send
The weight of all, and our last hope, relies.'
   This said, he sat; and expectation held
His look suspense, awaiting who appeared
To second, or oppose, or undertake
The perilous attempt.  But all sat mute,   420
Pondering the danger with deep thoughts; and each
In other's count'nance read his own dismay,

Astonished. None among the choice and prime
Of those Heaven-warring champions could be found
So hardy as to proffer or accept,
Alone, the dreadful voyage; till, at last,
Satan, whom now transcendent glory raised
Above his fellows, with monarchal pride
Conscious of highest worth, unmoved thus spake:—
  'O Progeny of Heaven! Empyreal Thrones!        430
With reason hath deep silence and demur
Seized us, though undismayed: long is the way
And hard that out of Hell leads up to light;
Our prison strong, this huge convex of fire,
Outrageous to devour, immures us round
Ninefold; and gates of burning adamant,
Barred over us, prohibit all egress.
These passed, if any pass, the void profound
Of unessential Night receives him next,
Wide-gaping, and with utter loss of being        440
Threatens him, plunged in that abortive gulf.
If thence he scape, into whatever world,
Or unknown region, what remains him less
Than unknown dangers, and as hard escape?
But I should ill become this throne, O Peers,
And this imperial sovranty, adorned
With splendour, armed with power, if aught proposed
And judged of public moment in the shape
Of difficulty or danger could deter
Me from attempting. Wherefore do I assume        450
These royalties, and not refuse to reign,
Refusing to accept as great a share
Of hazard as of honour, due alike
To him who reigns, and so much to him due
Of hazard more as he above the rest
High honoured sits? Go, therefore, mighty Powers,
Terror of Heaven, though fallen; intend at home,
While here shall be our home, what best may ease
The present misery, and render Hell
More tolerable; if there be cure or charm        460
To respite, or deceive, or slack the pain
Of this ill mansion: intermit no watch
Against a wakeful foe, while I abroad

Through all the coasts of dark destruction seek
Deliverance for us all: this enterprise
None shall partake with me.' Thus saying, rose
The Monarch, and prevented all reply;
Prudent, lest, from his resolution raised,
Others among the chief might offer now,
Certain to be refused, what erst they feared,        470
And, so refused, might in opinion stand
His rivals, winning cheap the high repute
Which he through hazard huge must earn.  But they
Dreaded not more th' adventure than his voice
Forbidding; and at once with him they rose.
Their rising all at once was as the sound
Of thunder heard remote.  Towards him they bend
With awful reverence prone, and as a God
Extol him equal to the Highest in Heaven.
Nor failed they to express how much they praised        480
That for the general safety he despised
His own: for neither do the Spirits damned
Lose all their virtue; lest bad men should boast
Their specious deeds on earth, which glory excites,
Or close ambition varnished o'er with zeal.
Thus they their doubtful consultations dark
Ended, rejoicing in their matchless chief:
As when from mountain-tops the dusky clouds
Ascending, while the north wind sleeps, o'erspread
Heaven's cheerful face, the louring element        490
Scowls o'er the darkened landscape snow, or shower,
If chance the radiant sun, with farewell sweet,
Extend his evening beam, the fields revive,
The birds their notes renew, and bleating herds
Attest their joy, that hill and valley rings.
O shame to men! Devil with devil damned
Firm concord holds; men only disagree
Of creatures rational, though under hope
Of heavenly grace, and, God proclaiming peace,
Yet live in hatred, enmity, and strife        500
Among themselves, and levy cruel wars,
Wasting the earth, each other to destroy:
As if (which might induce us to accord)
Man had not hellish foes enough besides,

That day and night for his destruction wait!
   The Stygian council thus dissolved; and forth
In order came the grand Infernal Peers:
Midst came their mighty Paramount, and seemed
Alone th' antagonist of Heaven, nor less
Than Hell's dread Emperor, with pomp supreme,    510
And god-like imitated state: him round
A globe of fiery Seraphim enclosed
With bright emblazonry, and horrent arms.
Then of their session ended they bid cry
With trumpet's regal sound the great result:
Toward the four winds four speedy Cherubim
Put to their mouths the sounding alchemy
By herald's voice explained; the hollow abyss
Heard far and wide, and all the host of Hell
With deafening shout returned them loud acclaim.   520
Thence more at ease their minds, and somewhat raised
By false presumptuous hope, the ranged Powers
Disband, and, wandering, each his several way
Pursues, as inclination or sad choice
Leads him perplexed, where he may likeliest find
Truce to his restless thoughts, and entertain
The irksome hours, till his great chief return.
Part on the plain, or in the air sublime,
Upon the wing or in swift race contend,
As at th' Olympian games or Pythian fields;   530
Part curb their fiery steeds, or shun the goal
With rapid wheels, or fronted brigades form:
As when, to warn proud cities, war appears
Waged in the troubled sky, and armies rush
To battle in the clouds; before each van
Prick forth the aery knights, and couch their spears,
Till thickest legions close; with feats of arms
From either end of heaven the welkin burns.
Others, with vast Typhoean rage, more fell,
Rend up both rocks and hills, and ride the air   540
In whirlwind; Hell scarce holds the wild uproar;—
As when Alcides, from Oechalia crowned
With conquest, felt th' envenomed robe, and tore
Through pain up by the roots Thessalian pines,
And Lichas from the top of Oeta threw

Into th' Euboic sea.  Others, more mild,
Retreated in a silent valley, sing
With notes angelical to many a harp
Their own heroic deeds, and hapless fall
By doom of battle, and complain that Fate          550
Free Virtue should enthrall to Force or Chance.
Their song was partial; but the harmony
(What could it less when Spirits immortal sing?)
Suspended Hell, and took with ravishment
The thronging audience.  In discourse more sweet
(For Eloquence the Soul, Song charms the Sense)
Others apart sat on a hill retired,
In thoughts more elevate, and reasoned high
Of Providence, Foreknowledge, Will, and Fate—
Fixed fate, free will, foreknowledge absolute—          560
And found no end, in wandering mazes lost.
Of good and evil much they argued then,
Of happiness and final misery,
Passion and apathy, and glory and shame:
Vain wisdom all, and false philosophy!—
Yet, with a pleasing sorcery, could charm
Pain for a while or anguish, and excite
Fallacious hope, or arm th' obdured breast
With stubborn patience as with triple steel.
Another part, in squadrons and gross bands,          570
On bold adventure to discover wide
That dismal world, if any clime perhaps
Might yield them easier habitation, bend
Four ways their flying march, along the banks
Of four infernal rivers, that disgorge
Into the burning lake their baleful streams—
Abhorred Styx, the flood of deadly hate;
Sad Acheron of sorrow, black and deep;
Cocytus, named of lamentation loud
Heard on the rueful stream; fierce Phlegethon,          580
Whose waves of torrent fire inflame with rage.
Far off from these, a slow and silent stream,
Lethe, the river of oblivion, rolls
Her wat'ry labyrinth, whereof who drinks
Forthwith his former state and being forgets,
Forgets both joy and grief, pleasure and pain.

Beyond this flood a frozen continent
Lies dark and wild, beat with perpetual storms
Of whirlwind and dire hail, which on firm land
Thaws not, but gathers heap, and ruin seems          590
Of ancient pile; all else deep snow and ice,
A gulf profound as that Serbonian bog
Betwixt Damiata and Mount Casius old,
Where armies whole have sunk: the parching air
Burns frore, and cold performs th' effect of fire.
Thither, by harpy-footed Furies haled,
At certain revolutions all the damned
Are brought; and feel by turns the bitter change
Of fierce extremes, extremes by change more fierce,
From beds of raging fire to starve in ice          600
Their soft ethereal warmth, and there to pine
Immovable, infixed, and frozen round
Periods of time,—thence hurried back to fire.
They ferry over this Lethean sound
Both to and fro, their sorrow to augment,
And wish and struggle, as they pass, to reach
The tempting stream, with one small drop to lose
In sweet forgetfulness all pain and woe,
All in one moment, and so near the brink;
But Fate withstands, and, to oppose th' attempt,          610
Medusa with Gorgonian terror guards
The ford, and of itself the water flies
All taste of living wight, as once it fled
The lip of Tantalus. Thus roving on
In confused march forlorn, th' adventurous bands,
With shudd'ring horror pale, and eyes aghast,
Viewed first their lamentable lot, and found
No rest. Through many a dark and dreary vale
They passed, and many a region dolorous,
O'er many a frozen, many a fiery Alp,          620
Rocks, caves, lakes, fens, bogs, dens, and shades of
          death—
A universe of death, which God by curse
Created evil, for evil only good;
Where all life dies, death lives, and Nature breeds,
Perverse, all monstrous, all prodigious things,
Abominable, unutterable, and worse

Than fables yet have feigned or fear conceived,
Gorgons, and Hydras, and Chimaeras dire.
 Meanwhile the Adversary of God and Man,
Satan, with thoughts inflamed of highest design,   630
Puts on swift wings, and toward the gates of Hell
Explores his solitary flight: sometimes
He scours the right hand coast, sometimes the left:
Now shaves with level wing the deep, then soars
Up to the fiery concave towering high.
As when far off at sea a fleet descried
Hangs in the clouds, by equinoctial winds
Close sailing from Bengala, or the isles
Of Ternate and Tidore, whence merchants bring
Their spicy drugs; they on the trading flood,   640
Through the wide Ethiopian to the Cape,
Ply stemming nightly toward the pole: so seemed
Far off the flying Fiend.  At last appear
Hell-bounds, high reaching to the horrid roof,
And thrice threefold the gates; three folds were brass,
Three iron, three of adamantine rock,
Impenetrable, impaled with circling fire
Yet unconsumed.  Before the gates there sat
On either side a formidable Shape;
The one seemed woman to the waist, and fair,   650
But ended foul in many a scaly fold,
Voluminous and vast, a serpent armed
With mortal sting.  About her middle round
A cry of Hell-hounds never-ceasing barked
With wide Cerberean mouths full loud, and rung
A hideous peal; yet, when they list, would creep,
If aught disturbed their noise, into her womb,
And kennel there; yet there still barked and howled
Within unseen.  Far less abhorred than these
Vexed Scylla, bathing in the sea that parts   660
Calabria from the hoarse Trinacrian shore;
Nor uglier follow the night-hag, when, called
In secret, riding through the air she comes,
Lured with the smell of infant blood, to dance
With Lapland witches, while the labouring moon
Eclipses at their charms.  The other Shape—
If shape it might be called that shape had none

Distinguishable in member, joint, or limb;
Or substance might be called that shadow seemed,
For each seemed either—black it stood as Night,          670
Fierce as ten Furies, terrible as Hell,
And shook a dreadful dart: what seemed his head
The likeness of a kingly crown had on.
Satan was now at hand, and from his seat
The monster moving onward came as fast
With horrid strides; Hell trembled as he strode.
Th' undaunted Fiend what this might be admired—
Admired, not feared; God and his Son except,
Created thing naught valued he nor shunned;
And with disdainful look thus first began:—          680
    'Whence and what art thou, execrable Shape,
That dar'st, though grim and terrible, advance
Thy miscreated front athwart my way
To yonder gates? Through them I mean to pass,
That be assured, without leave asked of thee.
Retire; or taste thy folly, and learn by proof,
Hell-born, not to contend with Spirits of Heaven.'
    To whom the Goblin, full of wrath, replied:—
'Art thou that Traitor-Angel, art thou he,
Who first broke peace in Heaven and faith, till then          690
Unbroken, and in proud rebellious arms
Drew after him the third part of Heaven's sons,
Conjured against the Highest—for which both thou
And they, outcast from God, are here condemned
To waste eternal days in woe and pain?
And reck'n'st thou thyself with Spirits of Heaven,
Hell-doomed, and breath'st defiance here and scorn
Where I reign king, and, to enrage thee more,
Thy king and lord? Back to thy punishment,
False fugitive; and to thy speed add wings,          700
Lest with a whip of scorpions I pursue
Thy ling'ring, or with one stroke of this dart
Strange horror seize thee, and pangs unfelt before.'
    So spake the grisly Terror, and in shape,
So speaking and so threat'ning, grew tenfold
More dreadful and deform. On th' other side,
Incensed with indignation, Satan stood
Unterrified, and like a comet burned.

That fires the length of Ophiuchus huge
In th' arctic sky, and from his horrid hair     710
Shakes pestilence and war. Each at the head
Levelled his deadly aim; their fatal hands
No second stroke intend; and such a frown
Each cast at th' other as when two black clouds,
With Heaven's artillery fraught, come rattling on
Over the Caspian, then stand front to front
Hovering a space, till winds the signal blow
To join their dark encounter in mid-air:
So frowned the mighty combatants, that Hell
Grew darker at their frown; so matched they stood;   720
For never but once more was either like
To meet so great a foe: and now great deeds
Had been achieved, whereof all Hell had rung,
Had not the snaky Sorceress that sat
Fast by Hell-gate and kept the fatal key
Risen, and with hideous outcry rushed between.
   'O father, what intends thy hand,' she cried,
'Against thy only son? What fury, O son,
Possesses thee to bend that mortal dart
Against thy father's head? and know'st for whom?   730
For him who sits above, and laughs the while
At thee, ordained his drudge to execute
Whate'er his wrath, which he calls justice, bids—
His wrath, which one day will destroy ye both!'
   She spake, and at her words the hellish Pest
Forebore: then these to her Satan returned:—
   'So strange thy outcry, and thy words so strange
Thou interposest, that my sudden hand,
Prevented, spares to tell thee yet by deeds
What it intends, till first I know of thee   740
What thing thou art, thus double-formed, and why,
In this infernal vale first met, thou call'st
Me father, and that phantasm call'st my son.
I know thee not, nor ever saw till now
Sight more detestable than him and thee.'
   T' whom thus the Portress of Hell-gate replied:—
'Hast thou forgot me, then, and do I seem
Now in thine eye so foul?—once deemed so fair
In Heaven, when at th' assembly, and in sight

Of all the Seraphim with thee combined                    750
In bold conspiracy against Heaven's King,
All on a sudden miserable pain
Surprised thee, dim thine eyes, and dizzy swum
In darkness, while thy head flames thick and fast
Threw forth, till on the left side opening wide,
Likest to thee in shape and count'nance bright,
Then shining heavenly fair, a goddess armed,
Out of thy head I sprung. Amazement seized
All th' host of Heaven; back they recoiled afraid
At first, and called me *Sin*, and for a sign       760
Portentous held me; but, familiar grown,
I pleased, and with attractive graces won
The most averse—thee chiefly, who, full oft
Thyself in me thy perfect image viewing,
Becam'st enamoured; and such joy thou took'st
With me in secret that my womb conceived
A growing burden. Meanwhile war arose
And fields were fought in Heaven: wherein remained
(For what could else?) to our Almighty Foe
Clear victory; to our part loss and rout             770
Through all the Empyrean. Down they fell,
Driven headlong from the pitch of Heaven, down
Into this deep; and in the general fall
I also: at which time this powerful key
Into my hand was given, with charge to keep
These gates for ever shut, which none can pass
Without my opening. Pensive here I sat
Alone; but long I sat not, till my womb,
Pregnant by thee, and now excessive grown,
Prodigious motion felt and rueful throes.            780
At last this odious offspring whom thou seest,
Thine own begotten, breaking violent way,
Tore through my entrails, that, with fear and pain
Distorted, all my nether shape thus grew
Transformed: but he my inbred enemy
Forth issued, brandishing his fatal dart,
Made to destroy. I fled, and cried out *Death!*
Hell trembled at the hideous name, and sighed
From all her caves, and back resounded *Death!*
I fled; but he pursued (though more, it seems,       790

Inflamed with lust than rage), and, swifter far,
Me overtook, his mother, all dismayed,
And, in embraces forcible and foul
Engend'ring with me, of that rape begot
These yelling monsters, that with ceaseless cry
Surround me, as thou saw'st, hourly conceived
And hourly born, with sorrow infinite
To me: for, when they list, into the womb
That bred them they return, and howl, and gnaw
My bowels, their repast; then, bursting forth    800
Afresh, with conscious terrors vex me round,
That rest or intermission none I find.
Before mine eyes in opposition sits
Grim Death, my son and foe, who sets them on,
And me, his parent, would full soon devour
For want of other prey, but that he knows
His end with mine involved, and knows that I
Should prove a bitter morsel, and his bane,
Whenever that shall be: so Fate pronounced.
But thou, O father, I forewarn thee, shun    810
His deadly arrow; neither vainly hope
To be invulnerable in those bright arms,
Though tempered heavenly; for that mortal dint,
Save he who reigns above, none can resist.'
    She finished; and the subtle Fiend his lore
Soon learned, now milder, and thus answered smooth:—
    'Dear daughter—since thou claim'st me for thy sire,
And my fair son here show'st me, the dear pledge
Of dalliance had with thee in Heaven, and joys
Then sweet, now sad to mention, through dire change
Befall'n us unforeseen, unthought-of, know    821
I come no enemy, but to set free
From out this dark and dismal house of pain
Both him and thee, and all the heavenly host
Of Spirits that, in our just pretences armed,
Fell with us from on high. From them I go
This uncouth errand sole, and one for all
Myself expose, with lonely steps to tread
Th' unfounded deep, and through the void immense
To search, with wand'ring quest, a place foretold    830
Should be—and, by concurring signs, ere now

Created vast and round—a place of bliss
In the purlieus of Heaven; and therein placed
A race of upstart creatures, to supply
Perhaps our vacant room, though more removed,
Lest Heaven, surcharged with potent multitude,
Might hap to move new broils. Be this, or aught
Than this more secret, now designed, I haste
To know; and, this once known, shall soon return,
And bring ye to the place where thou and Death          840
Shall dwell at ease, and up and down unseen
Wing silently the buxom air, embalmed
With odours. There ye shall be fed and filled
Immeasurably; all things shall be your prey.'
He ceased; for both seemed highly pleased, and Death
Grinned horrible a ghastly smile, to hear
His famine should be filled, and blessed his maw
Destined to that good hour. No less rejoiced
His mother bad, and thus bespake her sire:—
'The key of this infernal Pit, by due                    850
And by command of Heaven's all-powerful King
I keep, by him forbidden to unlock
These adamantine gates; against all force
Death ready stands to interpose his dart,
Fearless to be o'ermatched by living might.
But what owe I to his commands above,
Who hates me, and hath hither thrust me down
Into this gloom of Tartarus profound,
To sit in hateful office here confined,
Inhabitant of Heaven and heavenly-born,                  860
Here in perpetual agony and pain,
With terrors and with clamours compassed round
Of mine own brood, that on my bowels feed?
Thou art my father, thou my author, thou
My being gav'st me; whom should I obey
But thee? whom follow? thou wilt bring me soon
To that new world of light and bliss, among
The gods who live at ease, where I shall reign
At thy right hand voluptuous, as beseems
Thy daughter and thy darling, without end.'              870
    Thus saying, from her side the fatal key,
Sad instrument of all our woe, she took;

And, towards the gate rolling her bestial train,
Forthwith the huge portcullis high up drew,
Which, but herself, not all the Stygian Powers
Could once have moved; then in the key-hole turns
Th' intricate wards, and every bolt and bar
Of massy iron or solid rock with ease
Unfastens. On a sudden open fly,
With impetuous recoil and jarring sound,          880
Th' infernal doors, and on their hinges grate
Harsh thunder, that the lowest bottom shook
Of Erebus. She opened; but to shut
Excelled her power: the gates wide open stood,
That with extended wings a bannered host,
Under spread ensigns marching, might pass through
With horse and chariots ranked in loose array;
So wide they stood, and like a furnace-mouth
Cast forth redounding smoke and ruddy flame.
Before their eyes in sudden view appear          890
The secrets of the hoary deep, a dark
Illimitable ocean, without bound,
Without dimension; where length, breadth, and height,
And time, and place, are lost; where eldest Night
And Chaos, ancestors of Nature, hold
Eternal anarchy, amidst the noise
Of endless wars, and by confusion stand.
For Hot, Cold, Moist, and Dry, four champions fierce,
Strive here for mastery, and to battle bring
Their embryon atoms: they around the flag          900
Of each his faction, in their several clans,
Light-armed or heavy, sharp, smooth, swift, or slow,
Swarm populous, unnumbered as the sands
Of Barca or Cyrene's torrid soil,
Levied to side with warring winds, and poise
Their lighter wings. To whom these most adhere
He rules a moment: Chaos umpire sits,
And by decision more embroils the fray
By which he reigns: next him, high arbiter,
Chance governs all. Into this wild abyss,          910
The womb of Nature, and perhaps her grave,
Of neither sea, nor shore, nor air, nor fire,
But all these in their pregnant causes mixed

Confusedly, and which thus must ever fight,
Unless th' Almighty Maker them ordain
His dark materials to create more worlds—
Into this wild abyss the wary Fiend
Stood on the brink of Hell and looked a while,
Pondering his voyage; for no narrow frith
He had to cross.  Nor was his ear less pealed          920
With noises loud and ruinous (to compare
Great things with small) than when Bellona storms
With all her battering engines bent to rase
Some capital city; or less than if this frame
Of Heaven were falling, and these elements
In mutiny had from her axle torn
The steadfast Earth.  At last his sail-broad vans
He spreads for flight, and, in the surging smoke
Uplifted, spurns the ground; thence many a league,
As in a cloudy chair, ascending rides                  930
Audacious; but, that seat soon failing, meets
A vast vacuity.  All unawares,
Fluttering his pennons vain, plumb-down he drops
Ten thousand fathom deep, and to this hour
Down had been falling, had not, by ill chance,
The strong rebuff of some tumultuous cloud,
Instinct with fire and nitre, hurried him
As many miles aloft: that fury stayed,
Quenched in a boggy Syrtis, neither sea,
Nor good dry land: nigh foundered, on he fares,        940
Treading the crude consistence, half on foot,
Half flying; behoves him now both oar and sail.
As when a gryphon through the wilderness
With winged course, o'er hill or moory dale,
Pursues the Arimaspian, who by stealth
Had from his wakeful custody purloined
The guarded gold; so eagerly the Fiend
O'er bog or steep, through strait, rough, dense, or rare,
With head, hands, wings, or feet, pursues his way,
And swims, or sinks, or wades, or creeps, or flies.    950
At length a universal hubbub wild
Of stunning sounds, and voices all confused,
Borne through the hollow dark, assaults his ear
With loudest vehemence: thither he plies,

Undaunted, to meet there whatever Power
Or Spirit of the nethermost abyss
Might in that noise reside, of whom to ask
Which way the nearest coast of darkness lies
Bordering on light; when straight behold the throne
Of Chaos, and his dark pavilion spread                    960
Wide on the wasteful deep; with him enthroned
Sat sable-vested Night, eldest of things,
The consort of his reign; and by them stood
Orcus and Ades, and the dreaded name
Of Demogorgon; Rumour next, and Chance,
And Tumult, and Confusion, all embroiled,
And Discord with a thousand various mouths.
    T' whom Satan, turning boldly, thus:—'Ye Powers
And Spirits of this nethermost abyss,
Chaos and ancient Night, I come no spy                    970
With purpose to explore or to disturb
The secrets of your realm; but, by constraint
Wandering this darksome desert, as my way
Lies through your spacious empire up to light,
Alone and without guide, half lost, I seek
What readiest path leads where your gloomy bounds
Confine with Heaven; or, if some other place,
From your dominion won, th' Ethereal King
Possesses lately, thither to arrive
I travel this profound.  Direct my course:                980
Directed, no mean recompense it brings
To your behoof, if I that region lost,
All usurpation thence expelled, reduce
To her original darkness and your sway
(Which is my present journey), and once more
Erect the standard there of ancient Night;
Yours be th' advantage all, mine the revenge!'
    Thus Satan; and him thus the Anarch old,
With falt'ring speech and visage incomposed,
Answered:—'I know thee, stranger, who thou art—          990
That mighty leading Angel, who of late
Made head against Heaven's King, though overthrown.
I saw and heard; for such a numerous host
Fled not in silence through the frighted deep,
With ruin upon ruin, rout on rout,

Confusion worse confounded; and Heaven-gates
Poured out by millions her victorious bands,
Pursuing. I upon my frontiers here
Keep residence; if all I can will serve
That little which is left so to defend,                          1000
Encroached on still through our intestine broils
Weakening the sceptre of old Night: first, Hell,
Your dungeon, stretching far and wide beneath;
Now lately Heaven and Earth, another world
Hung o'er my realm, linked in a golden chain
To that side Heaven from whence your legions fell!
If that way be your walk, you have not far;
So much the nearer danger. Go, and speed;
Havoc, and spoil, and ruin, are my gain.'
    He ceased; and Satan stayed not to reply,                    1010
But, glad that now his sea should find a shore,
With fresh alacrity and force renewed
Springs upward, like a pyramid of fire,
Into the wild expanse, and through the shock
Of fighting elements, on all sides round
Environed, wins his way; harder beset
And more endangered than when Argo passed
Through Bosporus betwixt the justling rocks,
Or when Ulysses on the larboard shunned
Charybdis, and by th' other whirlpool steered.                  1020
So he with difficulty and labour hard
Moved on, with difficulty and labour he;
But, he once passed, soon after, when Man fell,
Strange alteration! Sin and Death amain,
Following his track (such was the will of Heaven),
Paved after him a broad and beaten way
Over the dark abyss, whose boiling gulf
Tamely endured a bridge of wondrous length,
From Hell continued, reaching th' utmost orb
Of this frail world; by which the Spirits perverse              1030
With easy intercourse pass to and fro
To tempt or punish mortals, except whom
God and good Angels guard by special grace.
    But now at last the sacred influence
Of light appears, and from the walls of Heaven
Shoots far into the bosom of dim Night

A glimmering dawn.  Here Nature first begins
Her farthest verge, and Chaos to retire,
As from her outmost works, a broken foe,
With tumult less and with less hostile din,                    1040
That Satan with less toil, and now with ease.
Wafts on the calmer wave by dubious light,
And, like a weather-beaten vessel, holds
Gladly the port, though shrouds and tackle torn;
Or in the emptier waste, resembling air,
Weighs his spread wings, at leisure to behold
Far off th' empyreal Heaven, extended wide
In circuit, undetermined square or round,
With opal towers and battlements adorned
Of living sapphire, once his native seat;                      1050
And, fast by, hanging in a golden chain,
This pendent World, in bigness as a star
Of smallest magnitude close by the moon.
Thither, full fraught with mischievous revenge
Accursed, and in a cursed hour, he hies.


*The End of the Second Book.*

# PARADISE LOST

## BOOK III

### THE ARGUMENT

*God, sitting on his throne, sees Satan flying towards this World, then newly created; shows him to the Son, who sat at his right hand; foretells the success of Satan in perverting mankind; clears his own justice and wisdom from all imputation, having created Man free and able enough to have withstood his Tempter; yet declares his purpose of grace towards him, in regard he fell not of his own malice, as did Satan, but by him seduced. The Son of God renders praises to his Father for the manifestation of his gracious purpose towards Man; but God again declares that grace cannot be extended towards Man without the satisfaction of Divine Justice; Man hath offended the majesty of God by aspiring to Godhead, and therefore, with all his progeny, devoted to death, must die, unless some one can be found sufficient to answer for his offence, and undergo his punishment. The Son of God freely offers himself a ransom for Man: the Father accepts him, ordains his incarnation, pronounces his exaltation above all names in Heaven and Earth; commands all the Angels to adore him: they obey, and, hymning to their harps in full quire, celebrate the Father and the Son. Meanwhile, Satan alights upon the bare convex of this World's outermost orb; where wandering he first finds a place since called the Limbo of Vanity; what persons and things fly up thither: thence comes to the gate of Heaven, described ascending by stairs, and the waters above the firmament that flow about it. His passage thence to the orb of the Sun: he finds there Uriel, the regent of that orb, but first changes himself into the shape of a meaner Angel, and, pretending a zealous desire to behold the new Creation, and Man whom God had placed here, inquires of him the place of his habitation, and is directed: alights first on Mount Niphates.*

HAIL, holy Light, offspring of Heaven first-born!
Or of th' Eternal coeternal beam
May I express thee unblamed? since God is light,
And never but in unapproached light
Dwelt from eternity, dwelt then in thee,
Bright effluence of bright essence increate!
Or hear'st thou rather pure ethereal stream,
Whose fountain who shall tell? before the Sun,
Before the Heavens, thou wert, and at the voice
Of God, as with a mantle, didst invest                    10
The rising world of waters dark and deep,
Won from the void and formless Infinite!
Thee I revisit now with bolder wing,
Escaped the Stygian Pool, though long detained
In that obscure sojourn, while in my flight,
Through utter and through middle darkness borne,
With other notes than to th' Orphean lyre
I sung of Chaos and eternal Night,
Taught by the Heavenly Muse to venture down
The dark descent, and up to reascend,                     20
Though hard and rare: thee I revisit safe,
And feel thy sovran vital lamp; but thou
Revisit'st not these eyes, that roll in vain
To find thy piercing ray, and find no dawn;
So thick a drop serene hath quenched their orbs,
Or dim suffusion veiled. Yet not the more
Cease I to wander where the Muses haunt
Clear spring, or shady grove, or sunny hill,
Smit with the love of sacred song; but chief
Thee, Sion, and the flowery brooks beneath,               30
That wash thy hallowed feet, and warbling flow,
Nightly I visit: nor sometimes forget
Those other two equalled with me in fate,
So were I equalled with them in renown,
Blind Thamyris and blind Maeonides,
And Tiresias and Phineus, prophets old:
Then feed on thoughts that voluntary move
Harmonious numbers; as the wakeful bird
Sings darkling, and, in shadiest covert hid,
Tunes her nocturnal note. Thus with the year             40
Seasons return; but not to me returns

Day, or the sweet approach of even or morn,
Or sight of vernal bloom, or summer's rose,
Or flocks, or herds, or human face divine;
But cloud instead and ever-during dark
Surrounds me, from the cheerful ways of men
Cut off, and, for the book of knowledge fair,
Presented with a universal blank
Of Nature's works, to me expunged and rased,
And wisdom at one entrance quite shut out.                    50
So much the rather thou, Celestial Light,
Shine inward, and the mind through all her powers
Irradiate; there plant eyes; all mist from thence
Purge and disperse, that I may see and tell
Of things invisible to mortal sight.
    Now had the Almighty Father from above,
From the pure empyrean where he sits
High throned above all height, bent down his eye,
His own works and their works at once to view:
About him all the Sanctities of Heaven                        60
Stood thick as stars, and from his sight received
Beatitude past utterance; on his right
The radiant image of his glory sat,
His only Son; on Earth he first beheld
Our two first parents, yet the only two
Of mankind, in the happy garden placed,
Reaping immortal fruits of joy and love,
Uninterrupted joy, unrivalled love,
In blissful solitude; he then surveyed
Hell and the gulf between, and Satan there                    70
Coasting the wall of Heaven on this side Night,
In the dun air sublime, and ready now
To stoop, with wearied wings and willing feet,
On the bare outside of this World, that seemed
Firm land imbosomed without firmament,
Uncertain which, in ocean or in air.
Him God beholding from his prospect high,
Wherein past, present, future, he beholds,
Thus to his only Son foreseeing spake:—
    'Only-begotten Son, seest thou what rage                  80
Transports our Adversary? whom no bounds
Prescribed, no bars of Hell, nor all the chains

Heaped on him there, nor yet the main abyss
Wide interrupt, can hold; so bent he seems
On desperate revenge, that shall redound
Upon his own rebellious head.  And now,
Through all restraint broke loose, he wings his way
Not far off Heaven, in the precincts of light,
Directly towards the new-created World,
And Man there placed, with purpose to assay          90
If him by force he can destroy, or worse,
By some false guile pervert: and shall pervert;
For Man will hearken to his glozing lies,
And easily transgress the sole command,
Sole pledge of his obedience: so will fall
He and his faithless progeny.  Whose fault?
Whose but his own?  Ingrate, he had of me
All he could have; I made him just and right,
Sufficient to have stood, though free to fall.
Such I created all th' Ethereal Powers               100
And Spirits, both them who stood and them who failed;
Freely they stood who stood, and fell who fell.
Not free, what proof could they have given sincere
Of true allegiance, constant faith, or love,
Where only what they needs must do appeared,
Not what they would?  What praise could they receive,
What pleasure I, from such obedience paid,
When Will and Reason (Reason also is Choice),
Useless and vain, of freedom both despoiled,
Made passive both, had served Necessity,            110
Not me?  They, therefore, as to right belonged,
So were created, nor can justly accuse
Their Maker, or their making, or their fate,
As if Predestination overruled
Their will, disposed by absolute decree
Or high foreknowledge; they themselves decreed
Their own revolt, not I: if I foreknew,
Foreknowledge had no influence on their fault,
Which had no less proved certain unforeknown.
So without least impulse or shadow of fate,         120
Or aught by me immutably foreseen,
They trespass, authors to themselves in all,
Both what they judge and what they choose; for so

I formed them free, and free they must remain
Till they enthrall themselves: I else must change
Their nature, and revoke the high decree
Unchangeable, eternal, which ordained
Their freedom; they themselves ordained their fall.
The first sort by their own suggestion fell,
Self-tempted, self-depraved; Man falls, deceived　　130
By the other first: Man, therefore, shall find grace;
The other, none: in mercy and justice both,
Through Heaven and Earth, so shall my glory excel;
But mercy, first and last, shall brightest shine.'
　　Thus while God spake, ambrosial fragrance filled
All Heaven, and in the blessed Spirits elect
Sense of new joy ineffable diffused.
Beyond compare the Son of God was seen
Most glorious; in him all his Father shone
Substantially expressed; and in his face　　140
Divine compassion visibly appeared,
Love without end, and without measure grace;
Which uttering, thus he to his Father spake:—
　　'O Father, gracious was that word which closed
Thy sovran sentence, that Man should find grace;
For which both Heaven and Earth shall high extol
Thy praises, with th' innumerable sound
Of hymns and sacred songs, wherewith thy throne
Encompassed shall resound thee ever blest.
For should Man finally be lost—should Man,　　150
Thy creature late so loved, thy youngest son,
Fall circumvented thus by fraud, though joined
With his own folly? That be from thee far,
That far be from thee, Father, who art judge
Of all things made, and judgest only right!
Or shall the Adversary thus obtain
His end, and frustrate thine? shall he fulfil
His malice, and thy goodness bring to naught,
Or proud return, though to his heavier doom,
Yet with revenge accomplished, and to Hell　　160
Draw after him the whole race of mankind,
By him corrupted? Or wilt thou thyself
Abolish thy creation, and unmake,
For him, what for thy glory thou hast made?—

So should thy goodness and thy greatness both
Be questioned and blasphemed without defence.'
    To whom the great Creator thus replied:—
'O Son, in whom my soul hath chief delight,
Son of my bosom, Son who art alone
My word, my wisdom, and effectual might,       170
All hast thou spoken as my thoughts are, all
As my eternal purpose hath decreed.
Man shall not quite be lost, but saved who will;
Yet not of will in him, but grace in me
Freely vouchsafed. Once more I will renew
His lapsed powers, though forfeit, and enthralled
By sin to foul exorbitant desires:
Upheld by me, yet once more he shall stand
On even ground against his mortal foe—
By me upheld, that he may know how frail       180
His fallen condition is, and to me owe
All his deliv'rance, and to none but me.
Some I have chosen of peculiar grace,
Elect above the rest; so is my will:
The rest shall hear me call, and oft be warned
Their sinful state, and to appease betimes
Th' incensed Deity, while offered grace
Invites; for I will clear their senses dark
What may suffice, and soften stony hearts
To pray, repent, and bring obedience due.       190
To prayer, repentance, and obedience due,
Though but endeavoured with sincere intent,
Mine ear shall not be slow, mine eye not shut.
And I will place within them as a guide
My umpire Conscience; whom if they will hear,
Light after light well used they shall attain,
And to the end persisting safe arrive.
This my long sufferance, and my day of grace,
They who neglect and scorn shall never taste;
But hard be hardened, blind be blinded more,       200
That they may stumble on, and deeper fall;
And none but such from mercy I exclude.——
But yet all is not done. Man disobeying,
Disloyal, breaks his fealty, and sins
Against the high supremacy of Heaven,

Affecting Godhead, and, so losing all,
To expiate his treason hath naught left,
But, to destruction sacred and devote,
He with his whole posterity must die;—
Die he or Justice must; unless for him                    210
Some other, able, and as willing, pay
The rigid satisfaction, death for death.
Say, Heavenly Powers, where shall we find such love?
Which of ye will be mortal, to redeem
Man's mortal crime, and just, th' unjust to save?
Dwells in all Heaven charity so dear?'
    He asked, but all the Heavenly Quire stood mute,
And silence was in Heaven: on Man's behalf
Patron or intercessor none appeared,
Much less that durst upon his own head draw            220
The deadly forfeiture, and ransom set.
And now without redemption all mankind
Must have been lost, adjudged to Death and Hell
By doom severe, had not the Son of God,
In whom the fulness dwells of love divine,
His dearest mediation thus renewed:—
    'Father, thy word is passed, Man shall find grace;
And shall Grace not find means, that finds her way,
The speediest of thy winged messengers,
To visit all thy creatures, and to all                    230
Comes unprevented, unimplored, unsought?
Happy for Man, so coming! He her aid
Can never seek, once dead in sins and lost—
Atonement for himself, or offering meet,
Indebted and undone, hath none to bring.
Behold me, then: me for him, life for life,
I offer; on me let thine anger fall;
Account me Man: I for his sake will leave
Thy bosom, and this glory next to thee
Freely put off, and for him lastly die                    240
Well pleased; on me let Death wreak all his rage.
Under his gloomy power I shall not long
Lie vanquished. Thou hast given me to possess
Life in myself for ever; by thee I live;
Though now to Death I yield, and am his due,
All that of me can die, yet, that debt paid,

Thou wilt not leave me in the loathsome grave
His prey, nor suffer my unspotted soul
For ever with corruption there to dwell;
But I shall rise victorious, and subdue          250
My vanquisher, spoiled of his vaunted spoil.
Death his death's wound shall then receive, and stoop
Inglorious, of his mortal sting disarmed;
I through the ample air in triumph high
Shall lead Hell captive maugre Hell, and show
The powers of darkness bound. Thou, at the sight
Pleased, out of Heaven shalt look down and smile,
While, by thee raised, I ruin all my foes—
Death last, and with his carcase glut the grave;
Then, with the multitude of my redeemed,          260
Shall enter Heaven, long absent, and return,
Father, to see thy face, wherein no cloud
Of anger shall remain, but peace assured
And reconcilement: wrath shall be no more
Thenceforth, but in thy presence joy entire.'

　　His words here ended; but his meek aspect
Silent yet spake, and breathed immortal love
To mortal men, above which only shone
Filial obedience: as a sacrifice
Glad to be offered, he attends the will          270
Of his great Father. Admiration seized
All Heaven, what this might mean, and whither tend,
Wondering; but soon th' Almighty thus replied:—
　　'O thou in Heaven and Earth the only peace
Found out for mankind under wrath, O thou
My sole complacence! well thou know'st how dear
To me are all my works; nor Man the least,
Though last created, that for him I spare
Thee from my bosom and right hand, to save,
By losing thee a while, the whole race lost!          280
Thou, therefore, whom thou only canst redeem,
Their nature also to thy nature join;
And be thyself Man among men on Earth,
Made flesh, when time shall be, of virgin seed,
By wondrous birth; be thou in Adam's room
The head of all mankind, though Adam's son.
As in him perish all men, so in thee,

As from a second root, shall be restored
As many as are restored; without thee, none.
His crime makes guilty all his sons; thy merit,                    290
Imputed, shall absolve them who renounce
Their own both righteous and unrighteous deeds,
And live in thee transplanted, and from thee
Receive new life. So Man, as is most just,
Shall satisfy for Man, be judged and die
And dying rise, and, rising, with him raise
His brethren, ransomed with his own dear life.
So Heavenly love shall outdo hellish hate,
Giving to death, and dying to redeem,
So dearly to redeem what hellish hate                    300
So easily destroyed, and still destroys
In those who, when they may, accept not grace.
Nor shalt thou, by descending to assume
Man's nature, lessen or degrade thine own.
Because thou hast, though throned in highest bliss
Equal to God, and equally enjoying
God-like fruition, quitted all to save
A world from utter loss, and hast been found
By merit more than birthright Son of God—
Found worthiest to be so by being good,                    310
Far more than great or high; because in thee
Love hath abounded more than glory abounds;
Therefore thy humiliation shall exalt
With thee thy manhood also to this throne:
Here shalt thou sit incarnate, here shalt reign
Both God and Man, Son both of God and Man,
Anointed universal King. All power
I give thee; reign for ever, and assume
Thy merits; under thee, as Head Supreme,
Thrones, Princedoms, Powers, Dominions, I reduce:                    320
All knees to thee shall bow of them that bide
In Heaven, or Earth, or, under Earth, in Hell.
When thou, attended gloriously from Heaven,
Shalt in the sky appear, and from thee send
The summoning Archangels to proclaim
Thy dread tribunal, forthwith from all winds
The living, and forthwith the cited dead
Of all past ages, to the general doom

Shall hasten; such a peal shall rouse their sleep.
Then, all thy Saints assembled, thou shalt judge          330
Bad men and Angels; they arraigned shall sink
Beneath thy sentence; Hell, her numbers full,
Thenceforth shall be for ever shut.  Meanwhile
The World shall burn, and from her ashes spring
New Heaven and Earth, wherein the just shall dwell,
And, after all their tribulations long,
See golden days, fruitful of golden deeds,
With Joy and Love triumphing, and fair Truth.
Then thou thy regal sceptre shalt lay by;
For regal sceptre then no more shall need;          340
God shall be all in all.  But all ye Gods,
Adore him who, to compass all this, dies;
Adore the Son, and honour him as me.'
    No sooner had th' Almighty ceased, but all
The multitude of Angels, with a shout
Loud as from numbers without number, sweet
As from blest voices, uttering joy, Heaven rung
With jubilee, and loud hosannas filled
Th' eternal regions.  Lowly reverent
Towards either throne they bow, and to the ground          350
With solemn adoration down they cast
Their crowns, inwove with amarant and gold,—
Immortal amarant, a flower which once
In Paradise, fast by the Tree of Life,
Began to bloom; but soon for Man's offence
To Heaven removed, where first it grew, there grows,
And flowers aloft, shading the Fount of Life,
And where the River of Bliss through midst of Heaven
Rolls o'er Elysian flowers her amber stream!
With these, that never fade, the Spirits elect          360
Bind their resplendent locks, inwreathed with beams.
Now in loose garlands thick thrown off, the bright
Pavement, that like a sea of jasper shone,
Impurpled with celestial roses smiled.
Then, crowned again, their golden harps they took—
Harps ever tuned, that glittering by their side
Like quivers hung; and with preamble sweet
Of charming symphony they introduce
Their sacred song, and waken raptures high:

No voice exempt, no voice but well could join          370
Melodious part; such concord is in Heaven.
   Thee, Father, first they sung, Omnipotent,
Immutable, Immortal, Infinite,
Eternal King; thee, Author of all being,
Fountain of Light, thyself invisible
Amidst the glorious brightness where thou sitt'st
Throned inaccessible, but when thou shad'st
The full blaze of thy beams, and through a cloud
Drawn round about thee like a radiant shrine,
Dark with excessive bright thy skirts appear,          380
Yet dazzle Heaven, that brightest Seraphim
Approach not, but with both wings veil their eyes.
Thee next they sang, of all creation first,
Begotten Son, Divine Similitude,
In whose conspicuous count'nance, without cloud
Made visible, th' Almighty Father shines,
Whom else no creature can behold: on thee
Impressed the effulgence of his glory abides;
Transfused on thee his ample Spirit rests.
He Heaven of Heavens, and all the Powers therein,     390
By thee created; and by thee threw down
Th' aspiring Dominations: thou that day
Thy Father's dreadful thunder didst not spare,
Nor stop thy flaming chariot-wheels, that shook
Heaven's everlasting frame, while o'er the necks
Thou drov'st of warring Angels disarrayed.
Back from pursuit, thy Powers with loud acclaim
Thee only extolled, Son of thy Father's might,
To execute fierce vengeance on his foes.
Not so on Man: him, through their malice fallen,      400
Father of mercy and grace, thou didst not doom
So strictly, but much more to pity incline.
No sooner did thy dear and only Son
Perceive thee purposed not to doom frail Man
So strictly, but much more to pity inclined;
He, to appease thy wrath, and end the strife
Of mercy and justice in thy face discerned,
Regardless of the bliss wherein he sat
Second to thee, offered himself to die
For Man's offence. O unexampled love!                  410

Love nowhere to be found less than Divine!
Hail, Son of God, Saviour of men! Thy name
Shall be the copious matter of my song
Henceforth, and never shall my harp thy praise
Forget, nor from thy Father's praise disjoin!

    Thus they in Heaven, above the starry sphere,
Their happy hours in joy and hymning spent.
Meanwhile, upon the firm opacous globe
Of this round World, whose first convex divides
The luminous inferior orbs, enclosed                                    420
From Chaos and th' inroad of Darkness old,
Satan alighted walks. A globe far off
It seemed; now seems a boundless continent,
Dark, waste, and wild, under the frown of Night
Starless exposed, and ever-threatening storms
Of Chaos blustering round, inclement sky,
Save on that side which from the wall of Heaven,
Though distant far, some small reflection gains
Of glimmering air less vexed with tempest loud:
Here walked the Fiend at large in spacious field.                       430
As when a vulture, on Imaus bred,
Whose snowy ridge the roving Tartar bounds,
Dislodging from a region scarce of prey
To gorge the flesh of lambs or yeanling kids
On hills where flocks are fed, flies toward the springs
Of Ganges or Hydaspes, Indian streams,
But in his way lights on the barren plains
Of Sericana, where Chineses drive
With sails and wind their cany waggons light;
So, on this windy sea of land, the Fiend                                440
Walked up and down alone, bent on his prey:
Alone, for other creature in this place,
Living or lifeless, to be found was none;—
None yet; but store hereafter from the Earth
Up hither like aerial vapours flew
Of all things transitory and vain, when sin
With vanity had filled the works of men:
Both all things vain, and all who in vain things
Built their fond hopes of glory or lasting fame,
Or happiness in this or th' other life;                                 450
All who have their reward on earth, the fruits

Of painful superstition and blind zeal,
Naught seeking but the praise of men, here find
Fit retribution, empty as their deeds;
All th' unaccomplished works of Nature's hand,
Abortive, monstrous, or unkindly mixed,
Dissolved on Earth, fleet hither, and in vain,
Till final dissolution, wander here—
Not in the neighbouring Moon, as some have dreamed:
Those argent fields more likely habitants,          460
Translated Saints, or middle Spirits hold,
Betwixt th' angelical and human kind:
Hither, of ill-joined sons and daughters born,
First from the ancient world those Giants came,
With many a vain exploit, though then renowned:
The builders next of Babel on the plain
Of Sennaar, and still with vain design
New Babels, had they wherewithal, would build:
Others came single; he who, to be deemed
A god, leaped fondly into Aetna flames,          470
Empedocles; and he who, to enjoy
Plato's Elysium, leaped into the sea,
Cleombrotus; and many more, too long,
Embryos and idiots, eremites and friars,
White, black, and grey, with all their trumpery.
Here pilgrims roam, that strayed so far to seek
In Golgotha him dead who lives in Heaven;
And they who, to be sure of Paradise,
Dying put on the weeds of Dominic,
Or in Franciscan think to pass disguised.          480
They pass the planets seven, and pass the fixed,
And that crystalline sphere whose balance weighs
The trepidation talked, and that first moved;
And now Saint Peter at Heaven's wicket seems
To wait them with his keys, and now at foot
Of Heaven's ascent they lift their feet, when, lo!
A violent cross-wind from either coast
Blows them transverse, ten thousand leagues awry,
Into the devious air: then might ye see
Cowls, hoods, and habits, with their wearers, tossed   490
And fluttered into rags; then reliques, beads,
Indulgences, dispenses, pardons, bulls,

The sport of winds: all these, upwhirled aloft,
Fly o'er the backside of the World far off
Into a Limbo large and broad, since called
The Paradise of Fools; to few unknown
Long after, now unpeopled and untrod.
All this dark globe the Fiend found as he passed;
And long he wandered, till at last a gleam
Of dawning light turned thitherward in haste            500
His travelled steps.  Far distant he descries,
Ascending by degrees magnificent
Up to the wall of Heaven, a structure high;
At top whereof, but far more rich, appeared
The work as of a kingly palace-gate,
With frontispiece of diamond and gold
Embellished; thick with sparkling orient gems
The portal shone, inimitable on Earth
By model, or by shading pencil drawn.
The stairs were such as whereon Jacob saw            510
Angels ascending and descending, bands
Of guardians bright, when he from Esau fled
To Padan-Aram, in the field of Luz
Dreaming by night under the open sky,
And waking cried, *This is the gate of Heaven.*
Each stair mysteriously was meant, nor stood
There always, but drawn up to Heaven sometimes
Viewless; and underneath a bright sea flowed
Of jasper, or of liquid pearl, whereon
Who after came from Earth sailing arrived            520
Wafted by Angels, or flew o'er the lake
Rapt in a chariot drawn by fiery steeds.
The stairs were then let down, whether to dare
The Fiend by easy ascent, or aggravate
His sad exclusion from the doors of bliss:
Direct against which opened from beneath,
Just o'er the blissful seat of Paradise,
A passage down to th' Earth, a passage wide,
Wider by far than that of after-times
Over Mount Sion, and, though that were large,            530
Over the Promised Land to God so dear,
By which, to visit oft those happy tribes,
On high behests his Angels to and fro

Passed frequent, and his eye with choice regard
From Paneas, the fount of Jordan's flood,
To Beërsaba, where the Holy Land
Borders on Egypt and the Arabian shore.
So wide the opening seemed, where bounds were set
To darkness, such as bound the ocean wave.
Satan from hence, now on the lower stair,                    540
That scaled by steps of gold to Heaven-gate,
Looks down with wonder at the sudden view
Of all this World at once.  As when a scout,
Through dark and desert ways with peril gone
All night, at last by break of cheerful dawn
Obtains the brow of some high-climbing hill,
Which to his eye discovers unaware
The goodly prospect of some foreign land
First seen, or some renowned metropolis
With glistering spires and pinnacles adorned,             550
Which now the rising sun gilds with his beams;
Such wonder seized, though after Heaven seen,
The Spirit malign, but much more envy seized,
At sight of all this World beheld so fair.
Round he surveys (and well might, where he stood
So high above the circling canopy
Of Night's extended shade) from eastern point
Of Libra to the fleecy star that bears
Andromeda far off Atlantic seas
Beyond th' horizon; then from pole to pole              560
He views in breadth,—and, without longer pause,
Down right into the World's first region throws
His flight precipitant, and winds with ease
Through the pure marble air his oblique way
Amongst innumerable stars, that shone
Stars distant, but nigh-hand seemed other worlds;
Or other worlds they seemed, or happy isles,
Like those Hesperian Gardens famed of old,
Fortunate fields, and groves, and flowery vales;
Thrice happy isles! but who dwelt happy there           570
He stayed not to inquire: above them all
The golden Sun, in splendour likest Heaven,
Allured his eye.  Thither his course he bends,
Through the calm firmament (but up or down,

By centre or eccentric, hard to tell,
Or longitude) where the great luminary,
Aloof the vulgar constellations thick,
That from his lordly eye keep distance due,
Dispenses light from far.  They, as they move
Their starry dance in numbers that compute          580
Days, months, and years, towards his all-cheering lamp
Turn swift their various motions, or are turned
By his magnetic beam, that gently warms
The Universe, and to each inward part
With gentle penetration, though unseen,
Shoots invisible virtue even to the deep;
So wondrously was set his station bright.
There lands the Fiend, a spot like which perhaps
Astronomer in the Sun's lucent orb
Through his glazed optic tube yet never saw.          590
The place he found beyond expression bright,
Compared with aught on Earth, metal or stone—
Not all parts like, but all alike informed
With radiant light, as glowing iron with fire.
If metal, part seemed gold, part silver clear;
If stone, carbuncle most or chrysolite,
Ruby or topaz, to the twelve that shone
In Aaron's breastplate, and a stone besides,
Imagined rather oft than elsewhere seen—
That stone, or like to that, which here below          600
Philosophers in vain so long have sought;
In vain, though by their powerful art they bind
Volatile Hermes, and call up unbound
In various shapes old Proteus from the sea,
Drained through a limbec to his native form.
What wonder then if fields and regions here
Breathe forth elixir pure, and rivers run
Potable gold, when, with one virtuous touch,
Th' arch-chemic Sun, so far from us remote,
Produces, with terrestrial humour mixed,          610
Here in the dark so many precious things
Of colour glorious and effect so rare?
Here matter new to gaze the Devil met
Undazzled.  Far and wide his eye commands:
For sight no obstacle found here, nor shade,

But all sunshine, as when his beams at noon
Culminate from th' equator, as they now
Shot upward still direct, whence no way round
Shadow from body opaque can fall; and the air,
Nowhere so clear, sharpened his visual ray                    620
To objects distant far, whereby he soon
Saw within ken a glorious Angel stand,
The same whom John saw also in the Sun.
His back was turned, but not his brightness hid:
Of beaming sunny rays a golden tiar
Circled his head, nor less his locks behind
Illustrious on his shoulders fledge with wings
Lay waving round: on some great charge employed
He seemed, or fixed in cogitation deep.
Glad was the Spirit impure, as now in hope                    630
To find who might direct his wandering flight
To Paradise, the happy seat of Man,
His journey's end, and our beginning woe.
But first he casts to change his proper shape,
Which else might work him danger or delay:
And now a stripling Cherub he appears,
Not of the prime, yet such as in his face
Youth smiled celestial, and to every limb
Suitable grace diffused; so well he feigned.
Under a coronet his flowing hair                              640
In curls on either cheek played; wings he wore
Of many a coloured plume sprinkled with gold,
His habit fit for speed succinct, and held
Before his decent steps a silver wand.
He drew not nigh unheard; the Angel bright,
Ere he drew nigh, his radiant visage turned,
Admonished by his ear, and straight was known
Th' Archangel Uriel—one of the seven
Who in God's presence, nearest to his throne,
Stand ready at command, and are his eyes                      650
That run through all the Heavens, or down to th' Earth
Bear his swift errands over moist and dry,
O'er sea and land: him Satan thus accosts:—
    'Uriel! for thou of those seven Spirits that stand
In sight of God's high throne, gloriously bright,
The first art wont his great authentic will

Interpreter through highest Heaven to bring,
Where all his Sons thy embassy attend,
And here art likeliest by supreme decree
Like honour to obtain, and as his eye      660
To visit oft this new Creation round—
Unspeakable desire to see and know
All these his wondrous works, but chiefly Man,
His chief delight and favour, him for whom
All these his works so wondrous he ordained,
Hath brought me from the quires of Cherubim
Alone thus wandering. Brightest Seraph, tell
In which of all these shining orbs hath Man
His fixed seat—or fixed seat hath none,
But all these shining orbs his choice to dwell—      670
That I may find him, and with secret gaze
Or open admiration him behold
On whom the great Creator hath bestowed
Worlds, and on whom hath all these graces poured;
That both in him and all things, as is meet,
The Universal Maker we may praise;
Who justly hath driven out his rebel foes
To deepest Hell, and, to repair that loss,
Created this new happy race of Men
To serve him better: wise are all his ways!'      680
     So spake the false dissembler unperceived;
For neither man nor angel can discern
Hypocrisy—the only evil that walks
Invisible, except to God alone,
By his permissive will, through Heaven and Earth;
And oft, though Wisdom wake, Suspicion sleeps
At Wisdom's gate, and to Simplicity
Resigns her charge, while Goodness thinks no ill
Where no ill seems: which now for once beguiled
Uriel, though Regent of the Sun, and held      690
The sharpest-sighted Spirit of all in Heaven;
Who to the fraudulent impostor foul,
In his uprightness, answer thus returned:—
     'Fair Angel, thy desire, which tends to know
The works of God, thereby to glorify
The great Work-master, leads to no excess
That reaches blame, but rather merits praise

The more it seems excess, that led thee hither
From thy empyreal mansion thus alone,
To witness with thine eyes what some perhaps,          700
Contented with report, hear only in Heaven:
For wonderful indeed are all his works,
Pleasant to know, and worthiest to be all
Had in remembrance always with delight!
But what created mind can comprehend
Their number, or the wisdom infinite
That brought them forth, but hid their causes deep?
I saw when, at his word, the formless mass,
This World's material mould, came to a heap:
Confusion heard his voice, and wild Uproar          710
Stood ruled, stood vast Infinitude confined;
Till, at his second bidding, Darkness fled,
Light shone, and order from disorder sprung.
Swift to their several quarters hasted then
The cumbrous elements, Earth, Flood, Air, Fire;
And this ethereal quintessence of Heaven
Flew upward, spirited with various forms,
That rolled orbicular, and turned to stars
Numberless, as thou seest, and how they move:
Each had his place appointed, each his course;          720
The rest in circuit walls this Universe.
Look downward on that globe, whose hither side
With light from hence, though but reflected, shines:
That place is Earth, the seat of Man; that light
His day, which else, as th' other hemisphere,
Night would invade; but there the neighbouring Moon
(So call that opposite fair star) her aid
Timely interposes, and, her monthly round
Still ending, still renewing, through mid-heaven,
With borrowed light her countenance triform          730
Hence fills and empties to enlighten the Earth,
And in her pale dominion checks the night.
That spot to which I point is Paradise,
Adam's abode; those lofty shades his bower.
Thy way thou canst not miss; me mine requires.'
    Thus said, he turned; and Satan, bowing low,
As to superior Spirits is wont in Heaven,
Where honour due and reverence none neglects

Took leave, and toward the coast of Earth beneath,
Down from the ecliptic, sped with hoped success,        740
Throws his steep flight in many an aery wheel,
Nor stayed, till on Niphates' top he lights.


*The End of the Third Book.*

# PARADISE LOST

## BOOK IV

### THE ARGUMENT

*Satan, now in prospect of Eden, and nigh the place where he
must now attempt the bold enterprise which he undertook alone
against God and Man, falls into many doubts with himself, and
many passions, fear, envy, and despair; but at length confirms
himself in evil; journeys on to Paradise; whose outward prospect
and situation is described; overleaps the bounds; sits, in the
shape of a cormorant, on the Tree of Life, as highest in the
Garden, to look about him. The Garden described; Satan's
first sight of Adam and Eve; his wonder at their excellent form
and happy state, but with resolution to work their fall; over-
hears their discourse; thence gathers that the Tree of Knowledge was forbidden them to eat of under penalty of death, and
thereon intends to found his temptation by seducing them to
transgress; then leaves them a while, to know further of their
state by some other means. Meanwhile Uriel, descending on
a sunbeam, warns Gabriel, who had in charge the gate of
Paradise, that some evil Spirit had escaped the Deep, and
passed at noon by his Sphere, in the shape of a good Angel,
down to Paradise, discovered after by his furious gestures in
the mount. Gabriel promises to find him out ere morning.
Night coming on, Adam and Eve discourse of going to their
rest: their bower described; their evening worship. Gabriel,
drawing forth his bands of night-watch to walk the round of
Paradise, appoints two strong Angels to Adam's bower, lest
the evil Spirit should be there doing some harm to Adam or Eve
sleeping: there they find him at the ear of Eve, tempting her in
a dream, and bring him, though unwilling, to Gabriel: by whom
questioned, he scornfully answers; prepares resistance; but,
hindered by a sign from Heaven, flies out of Paradise.*

O FOR that warning voice, which he who saw
Th' Apocalypse heard cry in Heaven aloud,
Then when the dragon, put to second rout,
Came furious down to be revenged on men,

*Woe to the inhabitants on Earth!* that now,
While time was, our first parents had been warned
The coming of their secret foe, and scaped,
Haply so scaped, his mortal snare! For now
Satan, now first inflamed with rage, came down,
The tempter, ere th' accuser, of mankind,                    10
To wreak on innocent frail Man his loss
Of that first battle, and his flight to Hell:
Yet not rejoicing in his speed, though bold
Far off and fearless, nor with cause to boast,
Begins his dire attempt; which, nigh the birth
Now rolling, boils in his tumultuous breast
And like a devilish engine back recoils
Upon himself; horror and doubt distract
His troubled thoughts, and from the bottom stir
The Hell within him; for within him Hell            20
He brings, and round about him, nor from Hell
One step, no more than from himself, can fly
By change of place. Now conscience wakes despair
That slumbered; wakes the bitter memory
Of what he was, what is, and what must be
Worse; of worse deeds worse sufferings must ensue.
Sometimes towards Eden, which now in his view,
Lay pleasant, his grieved look he fixes sad:
Sometimes towards Heaven and the full-blazing Sun,
Which now sat high in his meridian tower;            30
Then, much revolving, thus in sighs began:—
    'O thou that, with surpassing glory crowned,
Look'st from thy sole dominion like the god
Of this new World—at whose sight all the stars
Hide their diminished heads—to thee I call,
But with no friendly voice, and add thy name,
O Sun, to tell thee how I hate thy beams,
That bring to my remembrance from what state
I fell, how glorious once above thy sphere,
Till pride and worse ambition threw me down,            40
Warring in Heaven against Heaven's matchless King:
Ah wherefore? He deserved no such return
From me, whom he created what I was
In that bright eminence, and with his good
Upbraided none; nor was his service hard.

What could be less than to afford him praise,
The easiest recompense, and pay him thanks,
How due! Yet all his good proved ill in me,
And wrought but malice; lifted up so high,
I 'sdained subjection, and thought one step higher    50
Would set me highest, and in a moment quit
The debt immense of endless gratitude,
So burdensome, still paying, still to owe;
Forgetful what from him I still received;
And understood not that a grateful mind
By owing owes not, but still pays, at once
Indebted and discharged; what burden then?
Oh, had his powerful destiny ordained
Me some inferior Angel, I had stood
Then happy; no unbounded hope had raised    60
Ambition. Yet why not? some other Power
As great might have aspired, and me, though mean,
Drawn to his part; but other Powers as great
Fell not, but stand unshaken, from within
Or from without, to all temptations armed!
Hadst thou the same free will and power to stand?
Thou hadst. Whom hast thou then, or what, to accuse,
But Heaven's free love dealt equally to all?
Be then his love accursed, since, love or hate,
To me alike it deals eternal woe.    70
Nay, curs'd be thou; since against his thy will
Chose freely what it now so justly rues.
Me miserable! which way shall I fly
Infinite wrath and infinite despair?
Which way I fly is Hell; myself am Hell;
And, in the lowest deep, a lower deep
Still threat'ning to devour me opens wide,
To which the Hell I suffer seems a Heaven.
O, then, at last relent! is there no place
Left for repentance, none for pardon left?    80
None left but by submission; and that word
Disdain forbids me, and my dread of shame
Among the Spirits beneath, whom I seduced
With other promises and other vaunts
Than to submit, boasting I could subdue
Th' Omnipotent. Ay me! they little know

How dearly I abide that boast so vain,
Under what torments inwardly I groan:
While they adore me on the throne of Hell,
With diadem and sceptre high advanced,                                90
The lower still I fall, only supreme
In misery: such joy ambition finds!
But say I could repent, and could obtain,
By act of grace, my former state; how soon
Would height recall high thoughts, how soon unsay
What feigned submission swore! Ease would recant
Vows made in pain, as violent and void;
For never can true reconcilement grow
Where wounds of deadly hate have pierced so deep:
Which would but lead me to a worse relapse                            100
And heavier fall; so should I purchase dear
Short intermission, bought with double smart.
This knows my Punisher; therefore as far
From granting he, as I from begging, peace.
All hope excluded thus, behold, instead
Of us, outcast, exiled, his new delight,
Mankind, created, and for him this World!
So farewell hope, and with hope, farewell fear,
Farewell remorse! All good to me is lost;
Evil, be thou my Good: by thee at least                               110
Divided empire with Heaven's King I hold,
By thee, and more than half perhaps will reign;
As Man ere long, and this new World, shall know.'
   Thus while he spake, each passion dimmed his face,
Thrice changed with pale ire, envy, and despair;
Which marred his borrowed visage, and betrayed
Him counterfeit, if any eye beheld:
For Heavenly minds from such distempers foul
Are ever clear. Whereof he soon aware
Each perturbation smoothed with outward calm,                         120
Artificer of fraud; and was the first
That practised falsehood under saintly show,
Deep malice to conceal, couched with revenge:
Yet not enough had practised to deceive
Uriel, once warned; whose eye pursued him down
The way he went, and on th' Assyrian mount
Saw him disfigured, more than could befall

Spirit of happy sort: his gestures fierce
He marked and mad demeanour, then alone,
As he supposed, all unobserved, unseen.     130
So on he fares, and to the border comes
Of Eden, where delicious Paradise,
Now nearer, crowns with her enclosure green,
As with a rural mound, the champaign head
Of a steep wilderness, whose hairy sides
With thicket overgrown, grotesque and wild,
Access denied; and overhead up-grew
Insuperable height of loftiest shade,
Cedar, and pine, and fir, and branching palm,
A sylvan scene, and, as the ranks ascend     140
Shade above shade, a woody theatre
Of stateliest view. Yet higher than their tops
The verdurous wall of Paradise up-sprung;
Which to our general sire gave prospect large
Into his nether empire neighbouring round.
And higher than that wall a circling row
Of goodliest trees, loaden with fairest fruit,
Blossoms and fruits at once of golden hue,
Appeared, with gay enamelled colours mixed;
On which the sun more glad impressed his beams     150
Than in fair evening cloud, or humid bow,
When God hath showered the earth: so lovely seemed
That landscape; and of pure, now purer air
Meets his approach, and to the heart inspires
Vernal delight and joy, able to drive
All sadness but despair. Now gentle gales,
Fanning their odoriferous wings, dispense
Native perfumes, and whisper whence they stole
Those balmy spoils. As when to them who sail
Beyond the Cape of Hope, and now are past     160
Mozambic, off at sea north-east winds blow
Sabean odours from the spicy shore
Of Araby the Blest, with such delay
Well pleased they slack their course, and many a league
Cheered with the grateful smell old Ocean smiles;
So entertained those odorous sweets the Fiend
Who came their bane, though with them better pleased
Than Asmodëus with the fishy fume

That drove him, though enamoured, from the spouse
Of Tobit's son, and with a vengeance sent                    170
From Media post to Egypt, there fast bound.
      Now to th' ascent of that steep sávage hill
Satan had journeyed on, pensive and slow;
But further way found none; so thick entwined,
As one continued brake, the undergrowth
Of shrubs and tangling bushes had perplexed
All path of man or beast that passed that way.
One gate there only was, and that looked east
On th' other side: which when th' Arch-felon saw,
Due entrance he disdained, and, in contempt,                 180
At one slight bound high overleaped all bound
Of hill or highest wall, and sheer within
Lights on his feet. As when a prowling wolf,
Whom hunger drives to seek new haunt for prey,
Watching where shepherds pen their flocks at eve,
In hurdled cotes amid the field secure,
Leaps o'er the fence with ease into the fold;
Or as a thief, bent to unhoard the cash
Of some rich burgher, whose substantial doors,
Cross-barred and bolted fast, fear no assault,               190
In at the window climbs, or o'er the tiles;
So clomb this first grand Thief into God's fold:
So since into his Church lewd hirelings climb.
Thence up he flew, and on the Tree of Life,
The middle tree and highest there that grew,
Sat like a cormorant; yet not true life
Thereby regained, but sat devising death
To them who lived; nor on the virtue thought
Of that life-giving plant, but only used
For prospect what, well used, had been the pledge            200
Of immortality. So little knows
Any, but God alone, to value right
The good before him, but perverts best things
To worst abuse, or to their meanest use.
Beneath him, with new wonder, now he views,
To all delight of human sense exposed,
In narrow room Nature's whole wealth; yea, more!—
A Heaven on Earth: for blissful Paradise
Of God the garden was, by him in the east

Of Eden planted; Eden stretched her line      210
From Auran eastward to the royal towers
Of great Seleucia, built by Grecian kings,
Or where the sons of Eden long before
Dwelt in Telassar. In this pleasant soil
His far more pleasant garden God ordained.
Out of the fertile ground he caused to grow
All trees of noblest kind for sight, smell, taste;
And all amid them stood the Tree of Life,
High eminent, blooming ambrosial fruit
Of vegetable gold; and, next to life,      220
Our death, the Tree of Knowledge, grew fast by—
Knowledge of good, bought dear by knowing ill.
Southward through Eden went a river large,
Nor changed his course, but through the shaggy hill
Passed underneath ingulfed; for God had thrown
That mountain, as his garden-mould, high raised
Upon the rapid current, which through veins
Of porous earth with kindly thirst updrawn
Rose a fresh fountain, and with many a rill
Watered the garden; thence united fell      230
Down the steep glade, and met the nether flood,
Which from his darksome passage now appears,
And now, divided into four main streams,
Runs diverse, wandering many a famous realm
And country whereof here needs no account;
But rather to tell how, if Art could tell
How, from that sapphire fount the crisped brooks,
Rolling on orient pearl and sands of gold,
With mazy error under pendent shades
Ran nectar, visiting each plant, and fed      240
Flowers worthy of Paradise, which not nice Art
In beds and curious knots, but Nature boon
Poured forth profuse on hill, and dale, and plain,
Both where the morning sun first warmly smote
The open field, and where the unpierc'd shade
Embrowned the noontide bowers. Thus was this place,
A happy rural seat of various view:
Groves whose rich trees wept odorous gums and balm;
Others whose fruit, burnished with golden rind,
Hung amiable—Hesperian fables true,      250

If true, here only—and of delicious taste.
Betwixt them lawns, or level downs, and flocks
Grazing the tender herb, were interposed,
Or palmy hillock; or the flowery lap
Of some irriguous valley spread her store,
Flowers of all hue, and without thorn the rose.
Another side, umbrageous grots and caves
Of cool recess, o'er which the mantling vine
Lays forth her purple grape, and gently creeps
Luxuriant; meanwhile murmuring waters fall          20
Down the slope hills, dispersed, or in a lake,
That to the fringed bank with myrtle crowned
Her crystal mirror holds, unite their streams.
The birds their quire apply; airs, vernal airs,
Breathing the smell of field and grove, attune
The trembling leaves, while universal Pan,
Knit with the Graces and the Hours in dance,
Led on th' eternal Spring. Not that fair field
Of Enna, where Proserpin gathering flowers,
Herself a fairer flower, by gloomy Dis          27
Was gathered—which cost Ceres all that pain
To seek her through the world—nor that sweet grove
Of Daphne, by Orontes and th' inspired
Castalian spring, might with this Paradise
Of Eden strive; nor that Nyseian isle,
Girt with the river Triton, where old Cham,
Whom Gentiles Ammon call, and Libyan Jove,
Hid Amalthea, and her florid son,
Young Bacchus, from his stepdame Rhea's eye;
Nor, where Abassin kings their issue guard,          28
Mount Amara (though this by some supposed
True Paradise) under the Ethiop line
By Nilus' head, enclosed with shining rock,
A whole day's journey high, but wide remote
From this Assyrian garden, where the Fiend
Saw undelighted all delight, all kind
Of living creatures, new to sight and strange.
Two of far nobler shape, erect and tall,
God-like erect, with native honour clad
In naked majesty, seemed lords of all,          29
And worthy seemed; for in their looks divine

The image of their glorious Maker shone,
Truth, wisdom, sanctitude severe and pure—
Severe, but in true filial freedom placed;
Whence true authority in men: though both
Not equal, as their sex not equal seemed;
For contemplation he and valour formed,
For softness she and sweet attractive grace;
He for God only, she for God in him.
His fair large front and eye sublime declared          300
Absolute rule; and hyacinthine locks
Round from his parted forelock manly hung
Clustering, but not beneath his shoulders broad:
She, as a veil down to the slender waist,
Her unadorned golden tresses wore
Dishevelled, but in wanton ringlets waved
As the vine curls her tendrils, which implied
Subjection, but required with gentle sway,
And by her yielded, by him best received,
Yielded with coy submission, modest pride,              310
And sweet, reluctant, amorous delay.
Nor those mysterious parts were then concealed;
Then was not guilty shame: dishonest Shame
Of Nature's works, Honour dishonourable,
Sin-bred, how have ye troubled all mankind
With shows instead, mere shows of seeming pure,
And banished from man's life his happiest life
Simplicity and spotless innocence!
So passed they naked on, nor shunned the sight
Of God or Angel; for they thought no ill;                320
So hand in hand they passed, the loveliest pair
That ever since in love's embraces met—
Adam, the goodliest man of men since born
His sons; the fairest of her daughters Eve.
Under a tuft of shade that on a green
Stood whispering soft, by a fresh fountain-side,
They sat them down; and, after no more toil
Of their sweet gard'ning labour than sufficed
To recommend cool Zephyr, and made ease
More easy, wholesome thirst and appetite                 330
More grateful, to their supper-fruits they fell—
Nectarine fruits, which the compliant boughs

Yielded them, sidelong as they sat recline
On the soft downy bank damasked with flowers.
The savoury pulp they chew, and in the rind,
Still as they thirsted, scoop the brimming stream;
Nor gentle purpose, nor endearing smiles
Wanted, nor youthful dalliance, as beseems
Fair couple linked in happy nuptial league,
Alone as they.  About them frisking played          340
All beasts of th' earth, since wild, and of all chase
In wood or wilderness, forest or den;
Sporting the lion ramped, and in his paw
Dandled the kid; bears, tigers, ounces, pards,
Gambolled before them; th' unwieldy elephant,
To make them mirth, used all his might, and wreathed
His lithe proboscis; close the serpent sly,
Insinuating, wove with Gordian twine
His braided train, and of his fatal guile
Gave proof unheeded.  Others on the grass          350
Couched, and, now filled with pasture, gazing sat,
Or bedward ruminating; for the sun,
Declined, was hasting now with prone career
To th' Ocean Isles, and in th' ascending scale
Of Heaven the stars that usher evening rose;
When Satan still in gaze, as first he stood,
Scarce thus at length failed speech recovered sad:—
    'O Hell! what do mine eyes with grief behold?
Into our room of bliss thus high advanced
Creatures of other mould—Earth-born perhaps,          360
Not Spirits, yet to Heavenly Spirits bright
Little inferior—whom my thoughts pursue
With wonder, and could love; so lively shines
In them divine resemblance, and such grace
The hand that formed them on their shape hath poured.
Ah! gentle pair, ye little think how nigh
Your change approaches, when all these delights
Will vanish, and deliver ye to woe—
More woe, the more your taste is now of joy:
Happy, but for so happy ill secured          370
Long to continue, and this high seat, your Heaven,
Ill fenced for Heaven to keep out such a foe
As now is entered; yet no purposed foe

To you, whom I could pity thus forlorn,
Though I unpitied.  League with you I seek,
And mutual amity, so strait, so close,
That I with you must dwell, or you with me,
Henceforth.  My dwelling, haply, may not please,
Like this fair Paradise, your sense; yet such
Accept your Maker's work; he gave it me,            380
Which I as freely give.  Hell shall unfold,
To entertain you two, her widest gates,
And send forth all her kings; there will be room,
Not like these narrow limits, to receive
Your numerous offspring; if no better place,
Thank him who puts me, loath, to this revenge
On you, who wrong me not, for him who wronged.
And, should I at your harmless innocence
Melt, as I do, yet public reason just,
Honour and empire with revenge enlarged            390
By conquering this new world, compels me now
To do what else, though damned, I should abhor.'
   So spake the Fiend, and with necessity,
The tyrant's plea, excused his devilish deeds.
Then from his lofty stand on that high tree
Down he alights among the sportful herd
Of those four-footed kinds, himself now one,
Now other, as their shape served best his end
Nearer to view his prey, and, unespied,
To mark what of their state he more might learn     400
By word or action marked.  About them round
A lion now he stalks with fiery glare;
Then as a tiger, who by chance hath spied
In some purlieu two gentle fawns at play,
Straight couches close; then, rising, changes oft
His couchant watch, as one who chose his ground,
Whence rushing he might surest seize them both
Gripped in each paw: when Adam, first of men,
To first of women, Eve, thus moving speech,
Turned him all ear to hear new utterance flow:—     410
   'Sole partner and sole part of all these joys,
Dearer thyself than all, needs must the Power
That made us, and for us this ample World,
Be infinitely good, and of his good

As liberal and free as infinite;
That raised us from the dust, and placed us here
In all this happiness, who at his hand
Have nothing merited, nor can perform
Aught whereof he hath need; he who requires
From us no other service than to keep                        42?
This one, this easy charge, of all the trees
In Paradise that bear delicious fruit
So various, not to taste that only Tree
Of Knowledge, planted by the Tree of Life;
So near grows Death to Life, whate'er Death is—
Some dreadful thing no doubt; for well thou know'st
God hath pronounced it Death to taste that Tree:
The only sign of our obedience left
Among so many signs of power and rule
Conferred upon us, and dominion given                       43?
Over all other creatures that possess
Earth, Air, and Sea. Then let us not think hard
One easy prohibition, who enjoy
Free leave so large to all things else, and choice
Unlimited of manifold delights;
But let us ever praise him, and extol
His bounty, following our delightful task,
To prune these growing plants, and tend these flowers;
Which, were it toilsome, yet with thee were sweet.'
    To whom thus Eve replied:—'O thou for whom            44?
And from whom I was formed flesh of thy flesh,
And without whom am to no end, my guide
And head! what thou hast said is just and right.
For we to him, indeed, all praises owe,
And daily thanks—I chiefly, who enjoy
So far the happier lot, enjoying thee
Pre-eminent by so much odds, while thou
Like consort to thyself canst nowhere find.
That day I oft remember, when from sleep
I first awaked, and found myself reposed,                    450
Under a shade, on flowers, much wondering where
And what I was, whence thither brought, and how.
Not distant far from thence a murmuring sound
Of waters issued from a cave, and spread
Into a liquid plain; then stood unmoved,

Pure as th' expanse of Heaven. I thither went
With unexperienced thought, and laid me down
On the green bank, to look into the clear
Smooth lake, that to me seemed another sky.
As I bent down to look, just opposite,      460
A shape within the wat'ry gleam appeared,
Bending to look on me. I started back,
It started back; but pleased I soon returned,
Pleased it returned as soon with answering looks
Of sympathy and love. There I had fixed
Mine eyes till now, and pined with vain desire,
Had not a voice thus warned me: "What thou seest,
What there thou seest, fair creature, is thyself;
With thee it came and goes: but follow me,
And I will bring thee where no shadow stays      470
Thy coming, and thy soft embraces—he
Whose image thou art; him thou shalt enjoy
Inseparably thine; to him shalt bear
Multitudes like thyself, and thence be called
Mother of human race." What could I do,
But follow straight, invisibly thus led?
Till I espied thee, fair, indeed, and tall,
Under a platan; yet methought less fair,
Less winning soft, less amiably mild,
Than that smooth wat'ry image. Back I turned;      480
Thou, following, cried'st aloud, "Return, fair Eve;
Whom fliest thou? Whom thus fliest, of him thou art,
His flesh, his bone; to give thee being I lent
Out of my side to thee, nearest my heart,
Substantial life, to have thee by my side
Henceforth an individual solace dear:
Part of my soul I seek thee, and thee claim
My other half." With that thy gentle hand
Seized mine: I yielded, and from that time see
How beauty is excelled by manly grace      490
And wisdom, which alone is truly fair.'
     So spake our general mother, and, with eyes
Of conjugal attraction unreproved,
And meek surrender, half-embracing leaned
On our first father; half her swelling breast
Naked met his, under the flowing gold

Of her loose tresses hid.  He, in delight
Both of her beauty and submissive charms,
Smiled with superior love, as Jupiter
On Juno smiles when he impregns the clouds          500
That shed May flowers, and pressed her matron lip
With kisses pure.  Aside the Devil turned
For envy; yet with jealous leer malign
Eyed them askance, and to himself thus 'plained:—
    'Sight hateful, sight tormenting!  Thus these two,
Imparadised in one another's arms,
The happier Eden, shall enjoy their fill
Of bliss on bliss; while I to Hell am thrust,
Where neither joy nor love, but fierce desire,
Among our other torments not the least,          510
Still unfulfilled, with pain of longing pines!
Yet let me not forget what I have gained
From their own mouths.  All is not theirs, it seems;
One fatal tree there stands, of Knowledge called,
Forbidden them to taste.  Knowledge forbidden?
Suspicious, reasonless!  Why should their Lord
Envy them that?  Can it be sin to know?
Can it be death?  And do they only stand
By ignorance?  Is that their happy state,
The proof of their obedience and their faith?          520
O fair foundation laid whereon to build
Their ruin!  Hence I will excite their minds
With more desire to know, and to reject
Envious commands, invented with design
To keep them low, whom knowledge might exalt
Equal with gods.  Aspiring to be such,
They taste and die: what likelier can ensue?
But first with narrow search I must walk round
This garden, and no corner leave unspied;
A chance but chance may lead where I may meet          530
Some wandering Spirit of Heaven, by fountain-side,
Or in thick shade retired, from him to draw
What further would be learned.  Live while ye may,
Yet happy pair; enjoy, till I return,
Short pleasures; for long woes are to succeed!
    So saying, his proud step he scornful turned,
But with sly circumspection, and began

Through wood, through waste, o'er hill, o'er dale, his
    roam.
Meanwhile in utmost longitude, where Heaven
With Earth and Ocean meets, the setting Sun      540
Slowly descended, and with right aspect
Against the eastern gate of Paradise
Levelled his evening rays. It was a rock
Of alabaster, piled up to the clouds,
Conspicuous far, winding with one ascent
Accessible from Earth, one entrance high;
The rest was craggy cliff, that overhung
Still as it rose, impossible to climb.
Betwixt these rocky pillars Gabriel sat,
Chief of th' angelic guards, awaiting night;     550
About him exercised heroic games
Th' unarmed youth of Heaven; but nigh at hand
Celestial armoury, shields, helms, and spears,
Hung high, with diamond flaming and with gold.
Thither came Uriel, gliding through the even
On a sunbeam, swift as a shooting star
In autumn thwarts the night, when vapours fired
Impress the air, and shows the mariner
From what point of his compass to beware
Impetuous winds. He thus began in haste:—    560
  'Gabriel, to thee thy course by lot hath given
Charge and strict watch that to this happy place
No evil thing approach or enter in.
This day at height of noon came to my sphere
A Spirit, zealous, as he seemed, to know
More of the Almighty's works, and chiefly Man,
God's latest image. I described his way
Bent all on speed, and marked his aery gait,
But in the mount that lies from Eden north,
Where he first lighted, soon discerned his looks    570
Alien from Heaven, with passions foul obscured.
Mine eye pursued him still, but under shade
Lost sight of him. One of the banished crew,
I fear, hath ventured from the deep, to raise
New troubles; him thy care must be to find.'
  To whom the winged Warrior thus returned:—
'Uriel, no wonder if thy perfect sight,

Amid the Sun's bright circle where thou sitt'st,
See far and wide.  In at this gate none pass
The vigilance here placed, but such as come        580
Well known from Heaven; and since meridian hour
No creature thence.  If Spirit of other sort,
So minded, have o'erleaped these earthly bounds
On purpose, hard thou know'st it to exclude
Spiritual substance with corporeal bar.
But if within the circuit of these walks,
In whatsoever shape, he lurk of whom
Thou tell'st, by morrow dawning I shall know.'
    So promised he; and Uriel to his charge
Returned on that bright beam, whose point now raised
Bore him slope downward to the Sun, now fall'n        591
Beneath th' Azores; whither the prime orb,
Incredible how swift, had thither rolled
Diurnal, or this less volubil Earth,
By shorter flight to th' east, had left him there
Arraying with reflected purple and gold
The clouds that on his western throne attend.
Now came still Evening on, and Twilight grey
Had in her sober livery all things clad;
Silence accompanied; for beast and bird,        600
They to their grassy couch, these to their nests
Were slunk, all but the wakeful nightingale;
She all night long her amorous descant sung:
Silence was pleased: now glowed the firmament
With living sapphires; Hesperus, that led
The starry host, rode brightest, till the Moon,
Rising in clouded majesty, at length
Apparent queen, unveiled her peerless light,
And o'er the dark her silver mantle threw;
    When Adam thus to Eve:—'Fair consort, th' hour        610
Of night, and all things now retired to rest,
Mind us of like repose; since God hath set
Labour and rest, as day and night, to men
Successive, and the timely dew of sleep,
Now falling with soft slumberous weight, inclines
Our eyelids.  Other creatures all day long
Rove idle, unemployed, and less need rest;
Man hath his daily work of body or mind

Appointed, which declares his dignity,
And the regard of Heaven on all his ways;                    620
While other animals unactive range,
And of their doings God takes no account.
To-morrow, ere fresh morning streak the east
With first approach of light, we must be risen,
And at our pleasant labour, to reform
Yon flowery arbours, yonder alleys green,
Our walks at noon, with branches overgrown,
That mock our scant manuring and require
More hands than ours to lop their wanton growth.
Those blossoms also, and those dropping gums,                    630
That lie bestrewn, unsightly and unsmooth,
Ask riddance, if we mean to tread with ease.
Meanwhile, as Nature wills, Night bids us rest.'
　　To whom thus Eve, with perfect beauty adorned:—
'My author and disposer, what thou bidd'st
Unargued I obey; so God ordains:
God is thy law, thou mine: to know no more
Is woman's happiest knowledge, and her praise.
With thee conversing, I forget all time,
All seasons, and their change; all please alike.                    640
Sweet is the breath of Morn, her rising sweet,
With charm of earliest birds; pleasant the Sun,
When first on this delightful land he spreads
His orient beams, on herb, tree, fruit, and flower,
Glist'ring with dew; fragrant the fertile Earth
After soft showers; and sweet the coming-on
Of grateful Evening mild; then silent Night,
With this her solemn bird, and this fair Moon,
And these the gems of Heaven, her starry train:
But neither breath of Morn, when she ascends                    650
With charm of earliest birds; nor rising Sun
On this delightful land; nor herb, fruit, flower,
Glist'ring with dew; nor fragrance after showers;
Nor grateful Evening mild; nor silent Night,
With this her solemn bird; nor walk by moon,
Or glittering starlight, without thee is sweet.
But wherefore all night long shine these? for whom
This glorious sight, when sleep hath shut all eyes?'
　　To whom our general ancestor replied:—

'Daughter of God and Man, accomplished Eve,　660
Those have their course to finish round the Earth
By morrow evening, and from land to land
In order, though to nations yet unborn,
Minist'ring light prepared, they set and rise;
Lest total darkness should by night regain
Her old possession, and extinguish life
In nature and all things; which these soft fires
Not only enlighten, but with kindly heat
Of various influence foment and warm,
Temper or nourish, or in part shed down　670
Their stellar virtue on all kinds that grow
On Earth, made hereby apter to receive
Perfection from the Sun's more potent ray.
These, then, though unbeheld in deep of night,
Shine not in vain. Nor think, though men were none,
That Heaven would want spectators, God want praise.
Millions of spiritual creatures walk the Earth
Unseen, both when we wake, and when we sleep:
All these with ceaseless praise his works behold
Both day and night. How often, from the steep　680
Of echoing hill or thicket, have we heard
Celestial voices to the midnight air,
Sole, or responsive each to other's note,
Singing their great Creator! Oft in bands
While they keep watch, or nightly rounding walk,
With heavenly touch of instrumental sounds
In full harmonic number joined, their songs
Divide the night, and lift our thoughts to Heaven.'
　Thus talking, hand in hand alone they passed
On to their blissful bower. It was a place　690
Chosen by the sovran Planter, when he framed
All things to Man's delightful use; the roof
Of thickest covert was inwoven shade,
Laurel and myrtle, and what higher grew
Of firm and fragrant leaf; on either side
Acanthus, and each odorous bushy shrub,
Fenced up the verdant wall; each beauteous flower,
Iris all hues, roses, and jessamine,
Reared high their flourished heads between, and wrought
Mosaic; under foot the violet,　700

Crocus, and hyacinth, with rich inlay
Broidered the ground, more coloured than with stone
Of costliest emblem: other creature here,
Beast, bird, insect, or worm, durst enter none;
Such was their awe of Man.  In shadier bower
More sacred and sequestered, though but feigned,
Pan or Sylvanus never slept, nor Nymph,
Nor Faunus haunted.  Here, in close recess,
With flowers, garlands, and sweet-smelling herbs,
Espoused Eve decked first her nuptial bed,　　　710
And heavenly choirs the hymenaean sung,
What day the genial Angel to our sire
Brought her, in naked beauty more adorned,
More lovely, than Pandora, whom the gods
Endowed with all their gifts; and, O! too like
In sad event, when, to the unwiser son
Of Japhet brought by Hermes, she ensnared
Mankind with her fair looks, to be avenged
On him who had stole Jove's authentic fire.
　　Thus at their shady lodge arrived, both stood,　　　720
Both turned, and under open sky adored
The God that made both Sky, Air, Earth, and Heaven,
Which they beheld, the Moon's resplendent globe,
And starry Pole:—'Thou also mad'st the Night,
Maker Omnipotent; and thou the Day,
Which we, in our appointed work employed,
Have finished, happy in our mutual help
And mutual love, the crown of all our bliss
Ordained by thee; and this delicious place,
For us too large, where thy abundance wants　　　730
Partakers, and uncropped falls to the ground.
But thou hast promised from us two a race
To fill the Earth, who shall with us extol
Thy goodness infinite, both when we wake,
And when we seek, as now, thy gift of sleep.'
　　This said unanimous, and other rites
Observing none, but adoration pure,
Which God likes best, into their inmost bower
Handed they went; and, eased the putting-off
These troublesome disguises which we wear,　　　740
Straight side by side were laid; nor turned, I ween,

Adam from his fair spouse, nor Eve the rites
Mysterious of connubial love refused:
Whatever hypocrites austerely talk
Of purity, and place, and innocence,
Defaming as impure what God declares
Pure, and commands to some, leaves free to all.
Our Maker bids increase; who bids abstain
But our destroyer, foe to God and Man?
Hail, wedded Love, mysterious law, true source          750
Of human offspring, sole propriety
In Paradise of all things common else!
By thee adulterous lust was driven from men
Among the bestial herds to range; by thee,
Founded in reason, loyal, just, and pure,
Relations dear, and all the charities
Of father, son, and brother, first were known.
Far be it that I should write thee sin or blame,
Or think thee unbefitting holiest place,
Perpetual fountain of domestic sweets,          760
Whose bed is undefiled and chaste pronounced,
Present, or past, as saints and patriarchs used.
Here Love his golden shafts employs, here lights
His constant lamp, and waves his purple wings,
Reigns here and revels; not in the bought smile
Of harlots, loveless, joyless, unendeared,
Casual fruition; nor in court amours,
Mixed dance, or wanton mask, or midnight ball,
Or serenade, which the starved lover sings
To his proud fair, best quitted with disdain.          770
These, lulled by nightingales, embracing slept,
And on their naked limbs the flowery roof
Showered roses, which the morn repaired. Sleep on,
Blest pair! and, O! yet happiest, if ye seek
No happier state, and know to know no more!
    Now had Night measured with her shadowy cone
Halfway up-hill this vast sublunar vault,
And from their ivory port the Cherubim
Forth issuing, at th' accustomed hour, stood armed
To their night-watches in warlike parade;          780
When Gabriel to his next in power thus spake:—
    'Uzziel, half these draw off, and coast the south

With strictest watch; these other wheel the north;
Our circuit meets full west.' As flame they part,
Half wheeling to the shield, half to the spear.
From these, two strong and subtle Spirits he called
That near him stood, and gave them thus in charge:—
    'Ithuriel and Zephon, with winged speed
Search through this Garden; leave unsearched no nook;
But chiefly where those two fair creatures lodge,     790
Now laid perhaps asleep, secure of harm.
This evening from the Sun's decline arrived
Who tells of some infernal Spirit seen
Hitherward bent (who could have thought?), escaped
The bars of Hell, on errand bad, no doubt:
Such, where ye find, seize fast, and hither bring.'
    So saying, on he led his radiant files,
Dazzling the Moon; these to the bower direct
In search of whom they sought. Him there they found
Squat like a toad, close at the ear of Eve,     800
Assaying by his devilish art to reach
The organs of her fancy, and with them forge
Illusions as he list, phantasms and dreams;
Or if, inspiring venom, he might taint
Th' animal spirits, that from pure blood arise
Like gentle breaths from rivers pure, thence raise,
At least distempered, discontented thoughts,
Vain hopes, vain aims, inordinate desires,
Blown up with high conceits engendering pride.
Him thus intent Ithuriel with his spear     810
Touched lightly; for no falsehood can endure
Touch of celestial temper, but returns
Of force to its own likeness. Up he starts,
Discovered and surprised. As, when a spark
Lights on a heap of nitrous powder, laid
Fit for the tun, some magazine to store
Against a rumoured war, the smutty grain,
With sudden blaze diffused, inflames the air;
So started up, in his own shape, the Fiend.
Back stepped those two fair Angels, half amazed     820
So sudden to behold the grisly King;
Yet thus, unmoved with fear, accost him soon:—
    'Which of those rebel Spirits adjudged to Hell

Com'st thou, escaped thy prison? and, transformed,
Why satt'st thou like an enemy in wait,
Here watching at the head of these that sleep?'
   'Know ye not, then,' said Satan, filled with scorn,
'Know ye not me? Ye knew me once no mate
For you, there sitting where ye durst not soar!
Not to know me argues yourselves unknown,        830
The lowest of your throng; or, if ye know,
Why ask ye, and superfluous begin
Your message, like to end as much in vain?'
To whom thus Zephon, answering scorn with scorn:—
'Think not, revolted Spirit, thy shape the same,
Or undiminished brightness, to be known
As when thou stood'st in Heaven upright and pure.
That glory then, when thou no more wast good,
Departed from thee; and thou resemblest now
Thy sin and place of doom obscure and foul.      840
But come; for thou, be sure, shalt give account
To him who sent us, whose charge is to keep
This place inviolable, and these from harm.'
   So spake the Cherub; and his grave rebuke,
Severe in youthful beauty, added grace
Invincible. Abashed the Devil stood,
And felt how awful goodness is, and saw
Virtue in her shape how lovely—saw, and pined
His loss; but chiefly to find here observed
His lustre visibly impaired; yet seemed      850
Undaunted. 'If I must contend,' said he,
'Best with the best—the sender, not the sent;
Or all at once: more glory will be won,
Or less be lost.' 'Thy fear,' said Zephon bold,
'Will save us trial what the least can do
Single against the wicked, and thence weak.'
   The Fiend replied not, overcome with rage;
But, like a proud steed reined, went haughty on,
Champing his iron curb. To strive or fly
He held it vain; awe from above had quelled      860
His heart, not else dismayed. Now drew they nigh
The western point, where those half-rounding guards
Just met, and, closing, stood in squadron joined,
Awaiting next command. To whom their chief,

Gabriel, from the front thus called aloud:—
'O friends, I hear the tread of nimble feet
Hasting this way, and now by glimpse discern
Ithuriel and Zephon through the shade;
And with them comes a third, of regal port,
But faded splendour wan, who by his gait        870
And fierce demeanour seems the Prince of Hell—
Not likely to part hence without contest.
Stand firm, for in his look defiance lours.'

    He scarce had ended, when those two approached,
And brief related whom they brought, where found,
How busied, in what form and posture couched.

    To whom, with stern regard, thus Gabriel spake:—
'Why hast thou, Satan, broke the bounds prescribed
To thy transgressions, and disturbed the charge
Of others, who approve not to transgress        880
By thy example, but have power and right
To question thy bold entrance on this place;
Employed, it seems, to violate sleep, and those
Whose dwelling God hath planted here in bliss?'

    To whom thus Satan, with contemptuous brow:—
'Gabriel, thou hadst in Heaven the esteem of wise;
And such I held thee; but this question asked
Puts me in doubt. Lives there who loves his pain?
Who would not, finding way, break loose from Hell,
Though thither doomed? Thou wouldst thyself, no
        doubt,                                  890
And boldly venture to whatever place
Farthest from pain, where thou mightst hope to change
Torment with ease, and soonest recompense
Dole with delight; which in this place I sought:
To thee no reason, who know'st only good,
But evil hast not tried. And wilt object
His will who bound us? Let him surer bar
His iron gates, if he intends our stay
In that dark durance. Thus much what was asked:
The rest is true; they found me where they say;   900
But that implies not violence or harm.'

    Thus he in scorn. The warlike Angel moved,
Disdainfully half smiling, thus replied:—
'O loss of one in Heaven to judge of wise,

Since Satan fell, whom folly overthrew,
And now returns him from his prison scaped,
Gravely in doubt whether to hold them wise
Or not, who ask what boldness brought him hither
Unlicensed from his bounds in Hell prescribed!
So wise he judges it to fly from pain,                              910
However, and to scape his punishment!
So judge thou still, presumptuous, till the wrath,
Which thou incurr'st by flying, meet thy flight
Sevenfold, and scourge that wisdom back to Hell,
Which taught thee yet no better that no pain
Can equal anger infinite provoked.
But wherefore thou alone? Wherefore with thee
Came not all Hell broke loose? Is pain to them
Less pain, less to be fled? or thou than they
Less hardy to endure? Courageous chief,                            920
The first in flight from pain, hadst thou alleged
To thy deserted host this cause of flight,
Thou surely hadst not come sole fugitive.'

    To which the Fiend thus answered, frowning stern:—
'Not that I less endure, or shrink from pain,
Insulting Angel! well thou know'st I stood
Thy fiercest, when in battle to thy aid
The blasting volleyed thunder made all speed
And seconded thy else not dreaded spear.
But still thy words at random, as before,                          930
Argue thy inexperience what behoves,
From hard assays and ill successes past,
A faithful leader—not to hazard all
Through ways of danger by himself untried.
I, therefore, I alone, first undertook
To wing the desolate abyss, and spy
This new-created World, whereof in Hell
Fame is not silent, here in hope to find
Better abode, and my afflicted Powers
To settle here on Earth, or in mid Air;                            940
Though for possession put to try once more
What thou and thy gay legions dare against;
Whose easier business were to serve their Lord
High up in Heaven, with songs to hymn his throne,
And practised distances to cringe, not fight.'

To whom the Warrior-Angel soon replied:—
'To say and straight unsay, pretending first
Wise to fly pain, professing next the spy,
Argues no leader, but a liar traced,
Satan; and couldst thou "faithful" add? O name, 950
O sacred name of faithfulness profaned!
Faithful to whom? to thy rebellious crew?
Army of fiends, fit body to fit head!
Was this your discipline and faith engaged,
Your military obedience, to dissolve
Allegiance to th' acknowledged Power Supreme?
And thou, sly hypocrite, who now wouldst seem
Patron of liberty, who more than thou
Once fawned, and cringed, and servilely adored
Heaven's awful Monarch? wherefore, but in hope 960
To dispossess him, and thyself to reign?
But mark what I areed thee now: Avaunt!
Fly thither whence thou fledd'st. If from this hour
Within these hallowed limits thou appear,
Back to th' Infernal Pit I drag thee chained,
And seal thee so as henceforth not to scorn
The facile gates of Hell too slightly barred.'
    So threatened he; but Satan to no threats
Gave heed, but waxing more in rage, replied:—
    'Then, when I am thy captive, talk of chains, 970
Proud limitary Cherub! but ere then
Far heavier load thyself expect to feel
From my prevailing arm, though Heaven's King
Ride on thy wings, and thou with thy compeers,
Used to the yoke, draw'st his triumphant wheels
In progress through the road of Heaven star-paved.'
    While thus he spake, th' angelic squadron bright
Turned fiery red, sharpning in mooned horns
Their phalanx, and began to hem him round
With ported spears, as thick as when a field 980
Of Ceres, ripe for harvest waving, bends
Her bearded grove of ears which way the wind
Sways them; the careful ploughman doubting stands,
Lest on the threshing-floor his hopeful sheaves
Prove chaff. On th' other side, Satan, alarmed,
Collecting all his might, dilated stood,

Like Tenerife or Atlas unremoved:
His stature reached the sky, and on his crest
Sat Horror plumed; nor wanted in his grasp
What seemed both spear and shield. Now dreadful
          deeds                                              990
Might have ensued; nor only Paradise,
In this commotion, but the starry cope
Of Heaven perhaps, or all the elements
At least, had gone to wrack, disturbed and torn
With violence of this conflict, had not soon
Th' Eternal, to prevent such horrid fray,
Hung forth in Heaven his golden scales, yet seen
Betwixt Astraea and the Scorpion sign,
Wherein all things created first he weighed,
The pendulous round Earth with balanced air          1000
In counterpoise, now ponders all events,
Battles and realms. In these he put two weights,
The sequel each of parting and of fight:
The latter quick up flew, and kicked the beam;
Which Gabriel spying thus bespake the Fiend:—
     'Satan, I know thy strength, and thou know'st mine,
Neither our own, but given; what folly then
To boast what arms can do! since thine no more
Than Heaven permits, nor mine, though doubled now
To trample thee as mire. For proof look up,          1010
And read thy lot in yon celestial sign,
Where thou art weighed, and shown how light, how weak,
If thou resist.' The Fiend looked up, and knew
His mounted scale aloft; nor more; but fled
Murmuring; and with him fled the shades of Night.


     *The End of the Fourth Book.*

# PARADISE LOST

## BOOK V

### THE ARGUMENT

*Morning approached, Eve relates to Adam her troublesome dream; he likes it not, yet comforts her; they come forth to their day labours: their morning hymn at the door of their bower. God, to render Man inexcusable, sends Raphael to admonish him of his obedience, of his free estate, of his enemy near at hand, who he is, and why his enemy, and whatever else may avail Adam to know. Raphael comes down to Paradise; his appearance described; his coming discerned by Adam afar off, sitting at the door of his bower; he goes out to meet him, brings him to his lodge, entertains him with the choicest fruits of Paradise, got together by Eve; their discourse at table. Raphael performs his message, minds Adam of his state and of his enemy; relates, at Adam's request, who that enemy is, and how he came to be so, beginning from his first revolt in Heaven, and the occasion thereof; how he drew his legions after him to the parts of the North, and there incited them to rebel with him, persuading all but only Abdiel, a seraph, who in argument dissuades and opposes him, then forsakes him.*

Now Morn, her rosy steps in th' eastern clime
Advancing, sowed the earth with orient pearl,
When Adam waked, so customed; for his sleep
Was aery light, from pure digestion bred,
And temperate vapours bland, which th' only sound
Of leaves and fuming rills, Aurora's fan,
Lightly dispersed, and the shrill matin song
Of birds on every bough. So much the more
His wonder was to find unwakened Eve,
With tresses discomposed, and glowing cheek,          10
As through unquiet rest. He, on his side
Leaning half raised, with looks of cordial love
Hung over her enamoured, and beheld

Beauty which, whether waking or asleep,
Shot forth peculiar graces; then, with voice
Mild as when Zephyrus on Flora breathes,
Her hand soft touching, whispered thus:—'Awake,
My fairest, my espoused, my latest found,
Heaven's last, best gift, my ever-new delight!
Awake! the morning shines, and the fresh field            20
Calls us; we lose the prime, to mark how spring
Our tended plants, how blows the citron grove,
What drops the myrrh, and what the balmy reed,
How Nature paints her colours, how the bee
Sits on the bloom extracting liquid sweet.'
    Such whispering waked her, but with startled eye
On Adam; whom embracing, thus she spake:—
    'O sole in whom my thoughts find all repose,
My glory, my perfection! glad I see
Thy face, and morn returned; for I this night            30
(Such night till this I never passed) have dreamed,
If dreamed, not, as I oft am wont, of thee,
Works of day past, or morrow's next design;
But of offence and trouble, which my mind
Knew never till this irksome night. Methought
Close at mine ear one called me forth to walk
With gentle voice; I thought it thine: it said,
"Why sleep'st thou, Eve? now is the pleasant time,
The cool, the silent, save where silence yields
To the night-warbling bird, that now awake            40
Tunes sweetest his love-laboured song; now reigns
Full-orbed the moon, and, with more pleasing light,
Shadowy sets off the face of things—in vain,
If none regard. Heaven wakes with all his eyes;
Whom to behold but thee, Nature's desire,
In whose sight all things joy, with ravishment
Attracted by thy beauty still to gaze?"
I rose as at thy call, but found thee not:
To find thee I directed then my walk;
And on, methought, alone I passed through ways            50
That brought me on a sudden to the tree
Of interdicted Knowledge. Fair it seemed,
Much fairer to my fancy than by day;
And, as I wondering looked, beside it stood

One shaped and winged like one of those from Heaven
By us oft seen: his dewy locks distilled
Ambrosia. On that tree he also gazed;
And, "O fair plant," said he, "with fruit surcharged,
Deigns none to ease thy load, and taste thy sweet,
Nor God, nor Man? Is knowledge so despised?          60
Or envy, or what reserve forbids to taste?
Forbid who will, none shall from me withhold
Longer thy offered good, why else set here?"
This said, he paused not, but with vent'rous arm
He plucked, he tasted. Me damp horror chilled
At such bold words vouched with a deed so bold;
But he thus, overjoyed: "O fruit divine,
Sweet of thyself, but much more sweet thus cropped,
Forbidden here, it seems, as only fit
For gods, yet able to make gods of men!              70
And why not gods of men, since good, the more
Communicated, more abundant grows,
The author not impaired, but honoured more?
Here, happy creature, fair angelic Eve!
Partake thou also: happy though thou art,
Happier thou may'st be, worthier canst not be.
Taste this, and be henceforth among the gods
Thyself a goddess; not to Earth confined,
But sometimes in the Air, as we; sometimes
Ascend to Heaven, by merit thine, and see           80
What life the gods live there, and such live thou."
So saying, he drew nigh, and to me held,
Even to my mouth, of that same fruit held part
Which he had plucked: the pleasant savoury smell
So quickened appetite that I, methought,
Could not but taste. Forthwith up to the clouds
With him I flew, and underneath beheld
The Earth outstretched immense, a prospect wide
And various: wondering at my flight and change
To this high exaltation, suddenly                   90
My guide was gone, and I, methought, sunk down,
And fell asleep; but O, how glad I waked
To find this but a dream!' Thus Eve her night
Related, and thus Adam answered sad:—

  'Best image of myself, and dearer half,

The trouble of thy thoughts this night in sleep
Affects me equally; nor can I like
This uncouth dream—of evil sprung, I fear;
Yet evil whence?  In thee can harbour none,
Created pure.  But know that in the soul                    100
Are many lesser faculties, that serve
Reason as chief.  Among these Fancy next
Her office holds; of all external things,
Which the five watchful senses represent,
She forms imaginations, aery shapes,
Which Reason, joining or disjoining, frames
All what we affirm or what deny, and call
Our knowledge or opinion; then retires
Into her private cell when Nature rests.
Oft, in her absence, mimic Fancy wakes                      110
To imitate her; but, misjoining shapes,
Wild work produces oft, and most in dreams,
Ill matching words and deeds long past or late.
Some such resemblances, methinks, I find
Of our last evening's talk in this thy dream,
But with addition strange.  Yet be not sad:
Evil into the mind of God or Man
May come and go, so unapproved, and leave
No spot or blame behind; which gives me hope
That what in sleep thou didst abhor to dream              120
Waking thou never wilt consent to do.
Be not disheartened, then, nor cloud those looks,
That wont to be more cheerful and serene
Than when fair Morning first smiles on the world;
And let us to our fresh employments rise
Among the groves, the fountains, and the flowers,
That open now their choicest bosomed smells,
Reserved from night, and kept for thee in store.'
   So cheered he his fair spouse; and she was cheered,
But silently a gentle tear let fall                         130
From either eye, and wiped them with her hair:
Two other precious drops that ready stood,
Each in their crystal sluice, he, ere they fell,
Kissed as the gracious signs of sweet remorse
And pious awe, that feared to have offended.
   So all was cleared, and to the field they haste.

But first, from under shady arborous roof,
Soon as they forth were come to open sight
Of day-spring, and the Sun—who, scarce uprisen,
With wheels yet hovering o'er the ocean brim,    140
Shot parallel to the Earth his dewy ray,
Discovering in wide landscape all the east
Of Paradise and Eden's happy plains—
Lowly they bowed, adoring, and began
Their orisons, each morning duly paid
In various style; for neither various style
Nor holy rapture wanted they to praise
Their Maker, in fit strains pronounced, or sung
Unmeditated; such prompt eloquence
Flowed from their lips, in prose or numerous verse,  150
More tuneable than needed lute or harp
To add more sweetness: and they thus began:—
   'These are thy glorious works, Parent of good,
Almighty! thine this universal frame,
Thus wondrous fair: thyself how wondrous then!
Unspeakable! who sitt'st above these heavens
To us invisible, or dimly seen
In these thy lowest works; yet these declare
Thy goodness beyond thought, and power divine.
Speak, ye who best can tell, ye sons of Light,  160
Angels—for ye behold him, and with songs
And choral symphonies, day without night,
Circle his throne rejoicing—ye in Heaven;
On Earth join, all ye creatures, to extol
Him first, him last, him midst, and without end.
Fairest of Stars, last in the train of Night,
If better thou belong not to the Dawn,
Sure pledge of day, that crown'st the smiling morn
With thy bright circlet, praise him in thy sphere
While day arises, that sweet hour of prime.  170
Thou Sun, of this great World both eye and soul,
Acknowledge him thy greater; sound his praise
In thy eternal course, both when thou climb'st
And when high noon hast gained, and when thou fall'st.
Moon, that now meet'st the orient Sun, now fliest,
With the fixed Stars, fixed in their orb that flies;
And ye five other wandering Fires, that move

In mystic dance, not without song, resound
His praise who out of Darkness called up Light.
Air, and ye Elements, the eldest birth                          180
Of Nature's womb, that in quaternion run
Perpetual circle, multiform, and mix
And nourish all things, let your ceaseless change
Vary to our great Maker still new praise.
Ye Mists and Exhalations, that now rise
From hill or steaming lake, dusky or grey,
Till the sun paint your fleecy skirts with gold,
In honour to the World's great Author rise;
Whether to deck with clouds the uncoloured sky,
Or wet the thirsty earth with falling showers,                  190
Rising or falling, still advance his praise.
His praise, ye Winds, that from four quarters blow,
Breathe soft or loud; and wave your tops, ye Pines,
With every Plant, in sign of worship wave.
Fountains, and ye, that warble, as ye flow,
Melodious murmurs, warbling tune his praise.
Join voices, all ye living Souls; ye Birds,
That, singing, up to Heaven-gate ascend,
Bear on your wings and in your notes his praise.
Ye that in waters glide, and ye that walk                       200
The earth, and stately tread, or lowly creep,
Witness if I be silent, morn or even,
To hill or valley, fountain, or fresh shade,
Made vocal by my song, and taught his praise.
Hail, universal Lord! Be bounteous still
To give us only good; and, if the night
Have gathered aught of evil, or concealed,
Disperse it, as now light dispels the dark.'
    So prayed they innocent, and to their thoughts
Firm peace recovered soon, and wonted calm.                     210
On to their morning's rural work they haste,
Among sweet dews and flowers, where any row
Of fruit-trees, over-woody, reached too far
Their pampered boughs, and needed hands to check
Fruitless embraces: or they led the vine
To wed her elm; she, spoused, about him twines
Her marriageable arms, and with her brings
Her dower, th' adopted clusters, to adorn

His barren leaves.  Them thus employed beheld
With pity Heaven's high King, and to him called     220
Raphael, the sociable Spirit, that deigned
To travel with Tobias, and secured
His marriage with the seven-times-wedded maid.

'Raphael,' said he, 'thou hear'st what stir on Earth
Satan, from Hell 'scaped through the darksome gulf,
Hath raised in Paradise, and how disturbed
This night the human pair; how he designs
In them at once to ruin all mankind.
Go, therefore; half this day, as friend with friend
Converse with Adam, in what bower or shade     230
Thou find'st him from the heat of noon retired
To respite his day-labour with repast
Or with repose; and such discourse bring on
As may advise him of his happy state—
Happiness in his power left free to will,
Left to his own free will, his will though free
Yet mutable.  Whence warn him to beware
He swerve not, too secure: tell him withal
His danger, and from whom; what enemy,
Late fallen himself from Heaven, is plotting now     240
The fall of others from like state of bliss.
By violence? no, for that shall be withstood;
But by deceit and lies.  This let him know,
Lest, wilfully transgressing, he pretend
Surprisal, unadmonished, unforewarned.'

So spake th' Eternal Father, and fulfilled
All justice.  Nor delayed the winged Saint
After his charge received; but from among
Thousand celestial Ardours, where he stood
Veiled with his gorgeous wings, upspringing light,     250
Flew through the midst of Heaven.  Th' angelic quires,
On each hand parting, to his speed gave way
Through all th' empyreal road, till, at the gate
Of Heaven arrived, the gate self-opened wide,
On golden hinges turning, as by work
Divine the sovran Architect had framed.
From hence—no cloud or, to obstruct his sight,
Star interposed, however small—he sees,
Not unconform to other shining globes,

Earth, and the Garden of God, with cedars crowned  260
Above all hills; as when by night the glass
Of Galileo, less assured, observes
Imagined lands and regions in the Moon;
Or pilot from amidst the Cyclades
Delos or Samos first appearing kens,
A cloudy spot. Down thither prone in flight
He speeds, and through the vast ethereal sky
Sails between worlds and worlds, with steady wing
Now on the polar winds; then with quick fan
Winnows the buxom air, till, within soar        270
Of towering eagles, to all the fowls he seems
A phœnix, gazed by all, as that sole bird,
When, to enshrine his relics in the Sun's
Bright temple, to Egyptian Thebes he flies.
At once on th' eastern cliff of Paradise
He lights, and to his proper shape returns,
A Seraph winged. Six wings he wore, to shade
His lineaments divine: the pair that clad
Each shoulder broad came mantling o'er his breast
With regal ornament; the middle pair        280
Girt like a starry zone his waist, and round
Skirted his loins and thighs with downy gold
And colours dipped in Heaven; the third his feet
Shadowed from either heel with feathered mail,
Sky-tinctured grain. Like Maia's son he stood,
And shook his plumes, that heavenly fragrance filled
The circuit wide. Straight knew him all the bands
Of Angels under watch, and to his state
And to his message high in honour rise;
For on some message high they guessed him bound.
Their glittering tents he passed, and now is come        291
Into the blissful field, through groves of myrrh,
And flowering odours, cassia, nard, and balm,
A wilderness of sweets; for Nature here
Wantoned as in her prime, and played at will
Her virgin fancies, pouring forth more sweet,
Wild above rule or art, enormous bliss.
Him, through the spicy forest onward come,
Adam discerned, as in the door he sat
Of his cool bower, while now the mounted Sun        300

Shot down direct his fervid rays, to warm
Earth's inmost womb, more warmth than Adam needs;
And Eve, within, due at her hour, prepared
For dinner savoury fruits, of taste to please
True appetite, and not disrelish thirst
Of nectarous draughts between, from milky stream,
Berry or grape: to whom thus Adam called:—
   'Haste hither, Eve, and, worth thy sight, behold
Eastward among those trees what glorious Shape
Comes this way moving; seems another morn          310
Risen on mid-noon.  Some great behest from Heaven
To us perhaps he brings, and will vouchsafe
This day to be our guest.  But go with speed,
And what thy stores contain bring forth, and pour
Abundance, fit to honour and receive
Our heavenly stranger; well we may afford
Our givers their own gifts, and large bestow
From large bestowed, where Nature multiplies
Her fertile growth, and by disburd'ning grows
More fruitful; which instructs us not to spare.'   320
   To whom thus Eve:—'Adam, Earth's hallowed mould,
Of God inspired, small store will serve where store,
All seasons, ripe for use hangs on the stalk;
Save what, by frugal storing, firmness gains
To nourish, and superfluous moist consumes.
But I will haste, and from each bough and brake,
Each plant and juiciest gourd, will pluck such choice
To entertain our Angel-guest as he,
Beholding, shall confess that here on Earth
God hath dispensed his bounties as in Heaven.'     330
   So saying, with dispatchful looks in haste
She turns, on hospitable thoughts intent
What choice to choose for delicacy best,
What order so contrived as not to mix
Tastes, not well joined, inelegant, but bring
Taste after taste upheld with kindliest change:
Bestirs her then, and from each tender stalk
Whatever Earth, all-bearing mother, yields
In India East or West, or middle shore
In Pontus or the Punic coast, or where            340
Alcinous reigned, fruit of all kinds, in coat

Rough or smooth rind, or bearded husk, or shell,
She gathers, tribute large, and on the board
Heaps with unsparing hand.  For drink the grape
She crushes, inoffensive must, and meaths
From many a berry, and from sweet kernels pressed
She tempers dulcet creams—nor these to hold
Wants her fit vessels pure; then strews the ground
With rose and odours from the shrub unfumed.
  Meanwhile our primitive great Sire, to meet           350
His godlike guest, walks forth, without more train
Accompanied than with his own complete
Perfections; in himself was all his state,
More solemn than the tedious pomp that waits
On princes, when their rich retinue long
Of horses led and grooms besmeared with gold
Dazzles the crowd and sets them all agape.
Nearer his presence, Adam, though not awed,
Yet with submiss approach and reverence meek,
As to a superior nature, bowing low,                    360
Thus said:—'Native of Heaven (for other place
None can than Heaven such glorious shape contain),
Since, by descending from the thrones above,
Those happy places thou hast deigned a while
To want, and honour these, vouchsafe with us,
Two only, who yet by sovran gift possess
This spacious ground, in yonder shady bower
To rest, and what the garden choicest bears
To sit and taste, till this meridian heat
Be over, and the sun more cool decline.'               370
  Whom thus the angelic Virtue answered mild:—
'Adam, I therefore came; nor art thou such
Created, or such place hast here to dwell,
As may not oft invite, though Spirits of Heaven,
To visit thee. Lead on, then, where thy bower
O'ershades; for these mid-hours, till evening rise,
I have at will.' So to the sylvan lodge
They came, that like Pomona's arbour smiled
With flowerets decked and fragrant smells. But Eve,
Undecked, save with herself, more lovely fair           380
Than wood-nymph, or the fairest goddess feigned
Of three that in Mount Ida naked strove,

Stood to entertain her guest from Heaven; no veil
She needed, virtue-proof; no thought infirm
Altered her cheek. On whom the Angel 'Hail!'
Bestowed—the holy salutation used
Long after to blest Mary, second Eve:—
'Hail! Mother of mankind, whose fruitful womb
Shall fill the world more numerous with thy sons
Than with these various fruits the trees of God            390
Have heaped this table!' Raised of grassy turf
Their table was, and mossy seats had round,
And on her ample square, from side to side,
All Autumn piled, though Spring and Autumn here
Danced hand in hand. A while discourse they hold;
No fear lest dinner cool; when thus began
Our Author:—'Heavenly stranger, please to taste
These bounties, which our Nourisher, from whom
All perfect good, unmeasured out, descends,
To us for food and for delight hath caused            400
The Earth to yield: unsavoury food, perhaps,
To spiritual natures; only this I know,
That one Celestial Father gives to all.'
    To whom the Angel:—'Therefore, what he gives
(Whose praise be ever sung) to Man, in part
Spiritual, may of purest Spirits be found
No ingrateful food: and food alike those pure
Intelligential substances require
As doth your rational; and both contain
Within them every lower faculty            410
Of sense, whereby they hear, see, smell, touch, taste,
Tasting concoct, digest, assimilate,
And corporeal to incorporeal turn.
For know, whatever was created needs
To be sustained and fed. Of elements
The grosser feeds the purer: Earth the Sea;
Earth and the Sea feed Air; the Air those Fires
Ethereal, and, as lowest, first the Moon;
Whence in her visage round those spots, unpurged
Vapours not yet into her substance turned.            420
Nor doth the Moon no nourishment exhale
From her moist continent to higher orbs.
The Sun, that light imparts to all, receives

From all his alimental recompense
In humid exhalations, and at even
Sups with the Ocean.  Though in Heaven the trees
Of life ambrosial fruitage bear, and vines
Yield nectar—though from off the boughs each morn
We brush mellifluous dews, and find the ground
Covered with pearly grain—yet God hath here          430
Varied his bounty so with new delights
As may compare with Heaven; and to taste
Think not I shall be nice.'  So down they sat,
And to their viands fell; nor seemingly
The Angel, nor in mist—the common gloss
Of theologians—but with keen dispatch
Of real hunger, and concoctive heat
To transubstantiate: what redounds transpires
Through Spirits with ease; nor wonder, if by fire
Of sooty coal the empiric alchemist                  440
Can turn, or holds it possible to turn,
Metals of drossiest ore to perfect gold,
As from the mine.  Meanwhile at table Eve
Ministered naked, and their flowing cups
With pleasant liquors crowned.  O innocence
Deserving Paradise!  If ever, then,
Then had the Sons of God excuse to have been
Enamoured at that sight.  But in those hearts
Love unlibidinous reigned, nor jealousy
Was understood, the injured lover's hell.            450
    Thus when with meats and drinks they had sufficed,
Not burdened nature, sudden mind arose
In Adam not to let th' occasion pass,
Given him by this great conference, to know
Of things above his world, and of their being
Who dwell in Heaven, whose excellence he saw
Transcend his own so far, whose radiant forms,
Divine effulgence, whose high power so far
Exceeded human; and his wary speech
Thus to th' empyreal minister he framed:—            460
    'Inhabitant with God, now know I well
Thy favour, in this honour done to Man;
Under whose lowly roof thou hast vouchsafed
To enter, and these earthly fruits to taste,

Food not of Angels, yet accepted so
As that more willingly thou couldst not seem
At Heaven's high feasts to have fed: yet what compare!'
    To whom the winged Hierarch replied:—
'O Adam, one Almighty is, from whom
All things proceed, and up to him return,          470
If not depraved from good, created all
Such to perfection; one first matter all,
Endued with various forms, various degrees
Of substance, and, in things that live, of life;
But more refined, more spirituous and pure,
As nearer to him placed or nearer tending
Each in their several active spheres assigned,
Till body up to spirit work, in bounds
Proportioned to each kind. So from the root
Springs lighter the green stalk, from thence the leaves
More aery, last the bright consummate flower    481
Spirits odorous breathes: flowers and their fruit,
Man's nourishment, by gradual scale sublimed,
To vital spirits aspire, to animal,
To intellectual; give both life and sense,
Fancy and understanding; whence the Soul
Reason receives, and Reason is her being,
Discursive, or intuitive: discourse
Is oftest yours, the latter most is ours,
Differing but in degree, of kind the same.    490
Wonder not, then, what God for you saw good
If I refuse not, but convert, as you,
To proper substance. Time may come when Men
With Angels may participate, and find
No inconvenient diet, nor too light fare;
And from these corporal nutriments, perhaps,
Your bodies may at last turn all to spirit,
Improved by tract of time, and winged ascend
Ethereal, as we, or may at choice
Here or in heavenly paradises dwell,    500
If ye be found obedient, and retain
Unalterably firm his love entire
Whose progeny you are. Meanwhile enjoy
Your fill what happiness this happy state
Can comprehend, incapable of more.'

To whom the Patriarch of Mankind replied:—
'O favourable Spirit, propitious guest,
Well hast thou taught the way that might direct
Our knowledge, and the scale of Nature set
From centre to circumference, whereon,                    510
In contemplation of created things,
By steps we may ascend to God.  But say,
What meant that caution joined, *If ye be found
Obedient?*  Can we want obedience, then,
To him, or possibly his love desert,
Who formed us from the dust, and placed us here
Full to the utmost measure of what bliss
Human desires can seek or apprehend?'

To whom the Angel:—'Son of Heaven and Earth,
Attend!  That thou art happy, owe to God;              520
That thou continuest such, owe to thyself,
That is, to thy obedience; therein stand.
This was that caution given thee; be advised.
God made thee perfect, not immutable;
And good he made thee; but to persevere
He left it in thy power, ordained thy will
By nature free, not over-ruled by fate
Inextricable, or strict necessity.
Our voluntary service he requires,
Not our necessitated.  Such with him              530
Finds no acceptance, nor can find; for how
Can hearts not free be tried whether they serve
Willing or no, who will but what they must
By destiny, and can no other choose?
Myself, and all th' Angelic Host, that stand
In sight of God enthroned, our happy state
Hold, as you yours, while our obedience holds.
On other surety none: freely we serve,
Because we freely love, as in our will
To love or not; in this we stand or fall:              540
And some are fall'n, to disobedience fall'n,
And so from Heaven to deepest Hell.  O fall
From what high state of bliss into what woe!'

To whom our great Progenitor:—'Thy words
Attentive, and with more delighted ear,
Divine instructor, I have heard, than when

Cherubic songs by night from neighbouring hills
Aerial music send.  Nor knew I not
To be, both will and deed, created free.
Yet that we never shall forget to love　　　550
Our Maker, and obey him whose command
Single is yet so just, my constant thoughts
Assured me, and still assure; though what thou tell'st
Hath passed in Heaven some doubt within me move,
But more desire to hear, if thou consent,
The full relation, which must needs be strange,
Worthy of sacred silence to be heard.
And we have yet large day, for scarce the Sun
Hath finished half his journey, and scarce begins
His other half in the great zone of Heaven.'　　　560
　　Thus Adam made request; and Raphael,
After short pause assenting, thus began:—
　　'High matter thou enjoin'st me, O prime of Men—
Sad task and hard; for how shall I relate
To human sense th' invisible exploits
Of warring Spirits? how, without remorse,
The ruin of so many, glorious once
And perfect while they stood? how, last, unfold
The secrets of another world, perhaps
Not lawful to reveal?  Yet for thy good　　　570
This is dispensed; and what surmounts the reach
Of human sense I shall delineate so,
By likening spiritual to corporal forms,
As may express them best—though what if Earth
Be but the shadow of Heaven, and things therein
Each to other like, more than on Earth is thought?
　　'As yet this World was not, and Chaos wild
Reigned where these Heavens now roll, where Earth now
　　　rests
Upon her centre poised, when on a day
(For Time, though in Eternity, applied　　　580
To motion, measures all things durable
By present, past, and future), on such day
As Heaven's great year brings forth, th' empyreal host
Of Angels, by imperial summons called,
Innumerable before th' Almighty's throne
Forthwith from all the ends of Heaven appeared

Under their hierarchs in orders bright.
Ten thousand thousand ensigns high advanced,
Standards and gonfalons, 'twixt van and rear,
Stream in the air, and for distinction serve          590
Of hierarchies, of orders, and degrees;
Or in their glittering tissues bear emblazed
Holy memorials, acts of zeal and love
Recorded eminent.  Thus when in orbs
Of circuit inexpressible they stood,
Orb within orb, the Father Infinite,
By whom in bliss embosomed sat the Son,
Amidst as from a flaming mount, whose top
Brightness had made invisible, thus spake:—
      ' "Hear, all ye Angels, Progeny of Light,          600
Thrones, Dominations, Princedoms, Virtues, Powers,
Hear my decree, which unrevoked shall stand!
This day I have begot whom I declare
My only Son, and on this holy hill
Him have anointed, whom ye now behold
At my right hand.  Your head I him appoint,
And by myself have sworn to him shall bow
All knees in Heaven, and shall confess him Lord.
Under his great vicegerent reign abide,
United as one individual soul,          610
For ever happy.  Him who disobeys
Me disobeys, breaks union, and, that day,
Cast out from God and blessed vision, falls
Into utter darkness, deep engulfed, his place
Ordained without redemption, without end."
      'So spake th' Omnipotent, and with his words
All seemed well pleased; all seemed, but were not all.
That day, as other solemn days, they spent
In song and dance about the sacred hill—
Mystical dance, which yonder starry sphere          620
Of planets and of fixed in all her wheels
Resembles nearest; mazes intricate,
Eccentric, intervolved, yet regular
Then most when most irregular they seem;
And in their motions harmony divine
So smoothes her charming tones that God's own ear
Listens delighted.  Evening now approached

(For we have also our evening and our morn—
We ours for change delectable, not need),
Forthwith from dance to sweet repast they turn          630
Desirous: all in circles as they stood,
Tables are set, and on a sudden piled
With Angels' food; and rubied nectar flows:
In pearl, in diamond, and massy gold,
Fruit of delicious vines, the growth of Heaven.
On flowers reposed, and with fresh flowerets crowned,
They eat, they drink, and in communion sweet
Quaff immortality and joy, secure
Of surfeit where full measure only bounds
Excess, before th' all-bounteous King, who showered
With copious hand, rejoicing in their joy.          641
Now when ambrosial Night, with clouds exhaled
From that high mount of God whence light and shade
Spring both, the face of brightest Heaven had changed
To grateful twilight (for Night comes not there
In darker veil), and roseate dews disposed
All but th' unsleeping eyes of God to rest,
Wide over all the plain, and wider far
Than all this globous Earth in plain outspread
(Such are the courts of God), th' Angelic throng,          650
Dispersed in bands and files, their camp extend
By living streams among the trees of life—
Pavilions numberless and sudden reared,
Celestial tabernacles, where they slept,
Fanned with cool winds; save those who, in their course,
Melodious hymns about the sovran throne
Alternate all night long.  But not so waked
Satan—so call him now; his former name
Is heard no more in Heaven: he, of the first,
If not the first Archangel, great in power,          660
In favour, and pre-eminence, yet fraught
With envy against the Son of God, that day
Honoured by his great Father, and proclaimed
Messiah, King Anointed, could not bear,
Through pride, that sight, and thought himself impaired.
Deep malice thence conceiving and disdain,
Soon as midnight brought on the dusky hour
Friendliest to sleep and silence, he resolved

With all his legions to dislodge, and leave
Unworshipped, unobeyed, the Throne supreme,                    670
Contemptuous, and, his next subordinate
Awakening, thus to him in secret spake:—
   ' "Sleep'st thou, companion dear? what sleep can close
Thy eyelids? and rememb'rest what decree
Of yesterday, so late hath passed the lips
Of Heaven's Almighty? Thou to me thy thoughts
Wast wont, I mine to thee was wont, to impart;
Both waking we were one; how then can now
Thy sleep dissent? New laws thou seest imposed;
New laws from him who reigns new minds may raise
In us who serve—new counsels, to debate                        681
What doubtful may ensue. More in this place
To utter is not safe. Assemble thou
Of all those myriads which we lead the chief;
Tell them that, by command, ere yet dim Night
Her shadowy cloud withdraws, I am to haste,
And all who under me their banners wave,
Homeward with flying march where we possess
The quarters of the North, there to prepare
Fit entertainment to receive our King,                         690
The great Messiah, and his new commands,
Who speedily through all the hierarchies
Intends to pass triumphant, and give laws.'
  'So spake the false Archangel, and infused
Bad influence into th' unwary breast
Of his associate: he together calls,
Or several one by one, the regent Powers,
Under him regent; tells, as he was taught,
That, the Most High commanding, now ere Night,
Now ere dim Night had disencumbered Heaven,                    700
The great hierarchal standard was to move;
Tells the suggested cause, and casts between
Ambiguous words and jealousies, to sound
Or taint integrity. But all obeyed
The wonted signal and superior voice
Of their great Potentate; for great indeed
His name, and high was his degree in Heaven:
His count'nance, as the morning-star that guides
The starry flock, allured them, and with lies

Drew after him the third part of Heaven's host.    710
Meanwhile, th' Eternal Eye, whose sight discerns
Abstrusest thoughts, from forth his holy mount,
And from within the golden lamps that burn
Nightly before him, saw without their light
Rebellion rising—saw in whom, how spread
Among the Sons of Morn, what multitudes
Were banded to oppose his high decree;
And, smiling, to his only Son thus said:—

  ' "Son, thou in whom my glory I behold
In full resplendence, Heir of all my might,    720
Nearly it now concerns us to be sure
Of our omnipotence, and with what arms
We mean to hold what anciently we claim
Of deity or empire: such a foe
Is rising, who intends to erect his throne
Equal to ours, throughout the spacious North:
Nor so content, hath in his thought to try
In battle what our power is or our right.
Let us advise, and to this hazard draw
With speed what force is left, and all employ    730
In our defence, lest unawares we lose
This our high place, our sanctuary, our hill."

  'To whom the Son, with calm aspect and clear
Light'ning divine, ineffable, serene,
Made answer:—"Mighty Father, thou thy foes
Justly hast in derision, and secure
Laugh'st at their vain designs and tumults vain—
Matter to me of glory, whom their hate
Illustrates, when they see all regal power
Given me to quell their pride, and in event    740
Know whether I be dextrous to subdue
Thy rebels, or be found the worst in Heaven."

  'So spake the Son; but Satan with his Powers
Far was advanced on winged speed, an host
Innumerable as the stars of night,
Or stars of morning, dewdrops which the sun
Impearls on every leaf and every flower.
Regions they passed, the mighty regencies
Of Seraphim and Potentates and Thrones
In their triple degrees—regions to which    750

All thy dominion, Adam, is no more
Than what this garden is to all the earth
And all the sea, from one entire globose
Stretched into longitude; which having passed,
At length into the limits of the North
They came, and Satan to his royal seat
High on a hill, far-blazing, as a mount
Raised on a mount, with pyramids and towers
From diamond quarries hewn and rocks of gold—
The palace of great Lucifer (so call                    760
That structure, in the dialect of men
Interpreted) which, not long after, he,
Affecting all equality with God,
In imitation of that mount whereon
Messiah was declared in sight of Heaven,
The Mountain of the Congregation called;
For thither he assembled all his train,
Pretending so commanded to consult
About the great reception of their King
Thither to come, and with calumnious art                 770
Of counterfeited truth thus held their ears:—
    ' "Thrones,   Dominations,   Princedoms,   Virtues,
        Powers—
If these magnific titles yet remain
Not merely titular, since by decree
Another now hath to himself engrossed
All power, and us eclipsed under the name
Of King Anointed; for whom all this haste
Of midnight march, and hurried meeting here,
This only to consult, how we may best,
With what may be devised of honours new,                 780
Receive him coming to receive from us
Knee-tribute yet unpaid, prostration vile!
Too much to one! but double how endured—
To one and to his image now proclaimed?
But what if better counsels might erect
Our minds, and teach us to cast off this yoke?
Will ye submit your necks, and choose to bend
The supple knee? ye will not, if I trust
To know ye right, or if ye know yourselves
Natives and Sons of Heaven possessed before             790

By none, and, if not equal all, yet free,
Equally free; for orders and degrees
Jar not with liberty, but well consist.
Who can in reason, then, or right, assume
Monarchy over such as live by right
His equals—if in power and splendour less,
In freedom equal? or can introduce
Law and edict on us, who without law
Err not? much less for this to be our Lord,
And look for adoration, to th' abuse                 800
Of those imperial titles which assert
Our being ordained to govern, not to serve!"
    'Thus far his bold discourse without control
Had audience, when, among the Seraphim,
Abdiel, than whom none with more zeal adored
The Deity, and divine commands obeyed,
Stood up, and in a flame of zeal severe
The current of his fury thus opposed:—
    ' "O argument blasphemous, false, and proud!
Words which no ear ever to hear in Heaven          810
Expected; least of all from thee, ingrate,
In place thyself so high above thy peers!
Canst thou with impious obloquy condemn
The just decree of God, pronounced and sworn,
That to his only Son, by right endued
With regal sceptre, every soul in Heaven
Shall bend the knee, and in that honour due
Confess him rightful King? Unjust, thou say'st,
Flatly unjust, to bind with laws the free,
And equal over equals to let reign,                 820
One over all with unsucceeded power!
Shalt thou give law to God? shalt thou dispute
With him the points of liberty, who made
Thee what thou art, and formed the Powers of Heaven
Such as he pleased, and circumscribed their being?
Yet, by experience taught, we know how good,
And of our good and of our dignity
How provident, he is—how far from thought
To make us less; bent rather to exalt
Our happy state, under one head more near          830
United. But—to grant it thee unjust

That equal over equals monarch reign—
Thyself, though great and glorious, dost thou count,
Or all angelic nature joined in one,
Equal to him, begotten Son, by whom,
As by his Word, the mighty Father made
All things, even thee, and all the Spirits of Heaven
By him created in their bright degrees,
Crowned them with glory, and to their glory named
Thrones, Dominations, Princedoms, Virtues, Powers?—
Essential Powers; nor by his reign obscured,               841
But more illustrious made; since he, the head,
One of our number thus reduced becomes;
His laws our laws; all honour to him done
Returns our own. Cease, then, this impious rage,
And tempt not these; but hasten to appease
Th' incensed Father and th' incensed Son
While pardon may be found, in time besought."
   'So spake the fervent Angel; but his zeal
None seconded, as out of season judged,                    850
Or singular and rash: whereat rejoiced
Th' Apostate, and, more haughty, thus replied:—
   "'That we were formed, then, say'st thou? and the work
Of secondary hands, by task transferred
From Father to his Son? Strange point and new!
Doctrine which we would know whence learned! Who saw
When this creation was? Remember'st thou
Thy making, while the Maker gave thee being?
We know no time when we were not as now;
Know none before us, self-begot, self-raised              860
By our own quickening power when fatal course
Had circled his full orb, the birth mature
Of this our native Heaven, Ethereal Sons.
Our puissance is our own; our own right hand
Shall teach us highest deeds, by proof to try
Who is our equal: then thou shalt behold
Whether by supplication we intreat
Address, and to begirt the Almighty Throne
Beseeching or besieging. This report,
These tidings, carry to th' anointed King;                 870

And fly, ere evil intercept thy flight."
  'He said; and, as the sound of waters deep,
Hoarse murmur echoed to his words applause
Through the infinite host, nor less for that
The flaming Seraph, fearless, though alone,
Encompassed round with foes, thus answered bold:—
  ' "O alienate from God, O Spirit accursed,
Forsaken of all good! I see thy fall
Determined, and thy hapless crew involved
In this perfidious fraud, contagion spread          880
Both of thy crime and punishment: henceforth
No more be troubled how to quit the yoke
Of God's Messiah: those indulgent laws
Will not now be vouchsafed; other decrees
Against thee are gone forth without recall;
That golden sceptre which thou didst reject
Is now an iron rod to bruise and break
Thy disobedience. Well thou didst advise;
Yet not for thy advice or threats I fly
These wicked tents devoted, lest the wrath          890
Impendent, raging into sudden flame,
Distinguish not: for soon expect to feel
His thunder on thy head, devouring fire.
Then who created thee lamenting learn
When who can uncreate thee thou shalt know."
  'So spake the Seraph Abdiel, faithful found;
Among the faithless, faithful only he;
Among innumerable false unmoved,
Unshaken, unseduced, unterrified,
His loyalty he kept, his love, his zeal;            900
Nor number nor example with him wrought
To swerve from truth, or change his constant mind,
Though single. From amidst them forth he passed,
Long way through hostile scorn, which he sustained
Superior, nor of violence feared aught;
And with retorted scorn his back he turned
On those proud towers, to swift destruction doomed.'

*The End of the Fifth Book.*

# PARADISE LOST

## BOOK VI

### THE ARGUMENT

*Raphael continues to relate how Michael and Gabriel were
sent forth to battle against Satan and his Angels. The first
fight described: Satan and his Powers retire under night. He
calls a council; invents devilish engines, which, in the second
day's fight, put Michael and his Angels to some disorder; but
they at length, pulling up mountains, overwhelmed both the
force and machines of Satan. Yet, the tumult not so ending,
God, on the third day, sends Messiah his Son, for whom he had
reserved the glory of that victory. He, in the power of his
Father, coming to the place, and causing all his legions to
stand still on either side, with his chariot and thunder driving
into the midst of his enemies, pursues them, unable to resist,
towards the wall of Heaven; which opening, they leap down
with horror and confusion into the place of punishment prepared for them in the Deep. Messiah returns with triumph to
his Father.*

'ALL night the dreadless Angel, unpursued,
Through Heaven's wide champaign held his way, till
    Morn,
Waked by the circling Hours, with rosy hand
Unbarred the gates of Light. There is a cave
Within the Mount of God, fast by his throne,
Where Light and Darkness in perpetual round
Lodge and dislodge by turns—which makes through
    Heaven
Grateful vicissitude, like day and night;
Light issues forth, and at the other door
Obsequious Darkness enters, till her hour       10
To veil the heaven, though darkness there might well
Seem twilight here. And now went forth the Morn
Such as in highest heaven, arrayed in gold

Empyreal; from before her vanished Night,
Shot through with orient beams; when all the plain
Covered with thick embattled squadrons bright,
Chariots, and flaming arms, and fiery steeds,
Reflecting blaze on blaze, first met his view.
War he perceived, war in procinct, and found
Already known what he for news had thought          20
To have reported. Gladly then he mixed
Among those friendly Powers, who him received
With joy and acclamations loud, that one,
That of so many myriads fall'n, yet one
Returned not lost. On to the sacred hill
They led him, high applauded, and present
Before the seat supreme; from whence a voice,
From midst a golden cloud, thus mild was heard:—

 ' "Servant of God, well done! Well hast thou fought
The better fight, who single hast maintained          30
Against revolted multitudes the cause
Of truth, in word mightier than they in arms,
And for the testimony of truth hast borne
Universal reproach, far worse to bear
Than violence; for this was all thy care—
To stand approved in sight of God, though worlds
Judged thee perverse. The easier conquest now
Remains thee, aided by this host of friends,
Back on thy foes more glorious to return
Than scorned thou didst depart; and to subdue          40
By force who reason for their law refuse—
Right reason for their law, and for their King
Messiah, who by right of merit reigns.
Go, Michael, of celestial armies prince,
And thou, in military prowess next,
Gabriel; lead forth to battle these my sons
Invincible; lead forth my armed Saints,
By thousands and by millions ranged for fight,
Equal in number to that godless crew
Rebellious. Them with fire and hostile arms          50
Fearless assault; and, to the brow of Heaven
Pursuing, drive them out from God and bliss
Into their place of punishment, the gulf
Of Tartarus, which ready opens wide

His fiery chaos to receive their fall."
　'So spake the Sovran Voice; and clouds began
To darken all the hill, and smoke to roll
In dusky wreaths reluctant flames, the sign
Of wrath awaked; nor with less dread the loud
Ethereal trumpet from on high 'gan blow.                60
At which command the Powers Militant
That stood for Heaven, in mighty quadrate joined
Of union irresistible, moved on
In silence their bright legions to the sound
Of instrumental harmony, that breathed
Heroic ardour to adventurous deeds
Under their godlike leaders, in the cause
Of God and his Messiah. On they move,
Indissolubly firm; nor obvious hill,
Nor straitening vale, nor wood, nor stream, divides     70
Their perfect ranks; for high above the ground
Their march was, and the passive air upbore
Their nimble tread; as when the total kind
Of birds, in orderly array on wing,
Came summoned over Eden to receive
Their names of thee; so over many a tract
Of Heaven they marched, and many a province wide,
Tenfold the length of this terrene. At last,
Far in th' horizon, to the north, appeared
From skirt to skirt a fiery region, stretched          80
In battailous aspect; and, nearer view,
Bristled with upright beams innumerable
Of rigid spears, and helmets thronged, and shields
Various, with boastful argument portrayed,
The banded Powers of Satan hasting on
With furious expedition: for they weened
That self-same day, by fight or by surprise,
To win the Mount of God, and on his throne
To set the envier of his state, the proud
Aspirer: but their thoughts proved fond and vain       90
In the mid-way; though strange to us it seemed
At first that Angel should with Angel war,
And in fierce hosting meet, who wont to meet
So oft in festivals of joy and love
Unanimous as sons of one great Sire,

Hymning th' Eternal Father.  But the shout
Of battle now began, and rushing sound
Of onset ended soon each milder thought.
High in the midst, exalted as a God,
Th' Apostate in his sun-bright chariot sat,                          100
Idol of majesty divine, enclosed
With flaming Cherubim and golden shields;
Then lighted from his gorgeous throne—for now
'Twixt host and host but narrow space was left,
A dreadful interval, and front to front
Presented stood, in terrible array
Of hideous length.  Before the cloudy van,
On the rough edge of battle ere it joined,
Satan, with vast and haughty strides advanced,
Came towering, armed in adamant and gold.                           110
Abdiel that sight endured not, where he stood
Among the mightiest, bent on highest deeds,
And thus his own undaunted heart explores:—

  ' "O Heaven! that such resemblance of the Highest
Should yet remain, where faith and realty
Remain not!  Wherefore should not strength and
    might
There fail where virtue fails, or weakest prove
Where boldest, though to sight unconquerable?
His puissance, trusting in th' Almighty's aid,
I mean to try, whose reason I have tried                            120
Unsound and false; nor is it aught but just
That he who in debate of truth hath won
Should win in arms, in both disputes alike
Victor.  Though brutish that contest and foul,
When reason hath to deal with force, yet so
Most reason is that reason overcome."

  'So pondering, and from his armed peers
Forth-stepping opposite, halfway he met
His daring foe, at this prevention more
Incensed, and thus securely him defied:—                            130

  ' "Proud, art thou met?  Thy hope was to have
    reached
The height of thy aspiring unopposed—
The throne of God unguarded, and his side
Abandoned at the terror of thy power

Or potent tongue. Fool! not to think how vain
Against th' Omnipotent to rise in arms;
Who, out of smallest things, could without end
Have raised incessant armies to defeat
Thy folly; or with solitary hand,
Reaching beyond all limit, at one blow,                        140
Unaided could have finished thee, and whelmed
Thy legions under darkness! But thou seest
All are not of thy train; there be who faith
Prefer, and piety to God, though then
To thee not visible when I alone
Seemed in thy world erroneous to dissent
From all: my sect thou seest; now learn too late
How few sometimes may know when thousands err."
     'Whom the grand Foe, with scornful eye askance,
Thus answered:—"Ill for thee, but in wished hour     150
Of my revenge, first sought for, thou return'st
From flight, seditious Angel, to receive
Thy merited reward, the first assay
Of this right hand provoked, since first that tongue,
Inspired with contradiction, durst oppose
A third part of the gods, in synod met
Their deities to assert: who, while they feel
Vigour divine within them, can allow
Omnipotence to none. But well thou com'st
Before thy fellows, ambitious to win                           160
From me some plume, that thy success may show
Destruction to the rest. This pause between
(Unanswered lest thou boast) to let thee know.—
At first I thought that Liberty and Heaven
To heavenly souls had been all one; but now
I see that most through sloth had rather serve,
Minist'ring Spirits, trained up in feast and song:
Such hast thou armed, the minstrelsy of Heaven—
Servility with freedom to contend,
As both their deeds compared this day shall prove."  170
     'To whom, in brief, thus Abdiel stern replied:—
"Apostate! still thou err'st, nor end wilt find
Of erring, from the path of truth remote.
Unjustly thou deprav'st it with the name
Of servitude, to serve whom God ordains,

Or Nature: God and Nature bid the same,
When he who rules is worthiest, and excels
Them whom he governs. This is servitude—
To serve th' unwise, or him who hath rebelled
Against his worthier, as thine now serve thee,　　　180
Thyself not free, but to thyself enthralled;
Yet lewdly dar'st our minist'ring upbraid.
Reign thou in Hell, thy kingdom; let me serve
In Heaven God ever blest, and his divine
Behests obey, worthiest to be obeyed.
Yet chains in Hell, not realms, expect; meanwhile,
From me returned, as erst thou saidst, from flight,
This greeting on thy impious crest receive."
　'So saying, a noble stroke he lifted high,
Which hung not, but so swift with tempest fell　　190
On the proud crest of Satan that no sight,
Nor motion of swift thought, less could his shield,
Such ruin intercept. Ten paces huge
He back recoiled; the tenth on bended knee
His massy spear upstayed: as if, on earth,
Winds under ground, or waters forcing way,
Sidelong had pushed a mountain from his seat,
Half-sunk with all his pines. Amazement seized
The rebel Thrones, but greater rage, to see
Thus foiled their mightiest; ours joy filled, and shout,
Presage of victory, and fierce desire　　　201
Of battle: whereat Michael bid sound
Th' Archangel trumpet. Through the vast of Heaven
It sounded, and the faithful armies rung
Hosanna to the Highest; nor stood at gaze
The adverse legions, nor less hideous joined
The horrid shock. Now storming fury rose,
And clamour such as heard in Heaven till now
Was never; arms on armour clashing brayed
Horrible discord, and the madding wheels　　　210
Of brazen chariots raged; dire was the noise
Of conflict; overhead the dismal hiss
Of fiery darts in flaming volleys flew,
And, flying, vaulted either host with fire.
So under fiery cope together rushed
Both battles main, with ruinous assault

And inextinguishable rage. All Heaven
Resounded; and, had Earth been then, all Earth
Had to her centre shook. What wonder, when
Millions of fierce encountering Angels fought          220
On either side, the least of whom could wield
These elements, and arm him with the force
Of all their regions? How much more of power
Army against army numberless to raise
Dreadful combustion warring, and disturb,
Though not destroy, their happy native seat;
Had not th' Eternal King Omnipotent
From his strong hold of Heaven high overruled
And limited their might; though numbered such
As each divided legion might have seemed          230
A numerous host; in strength each armed hand
A legion! Led in fight, yet leader seemed
Each warrior single as in chief; expert
When to advance, or stand, or turn the sway
Of battle, open when, and when to close
The ridges of grim war. No thought of flight,
None of retreat, no unbecoming deed
That argued fear; each on himself relied
As only in his arm the moment lay
Of victory. Deeds of eternal fame          240
Were done, but infinite; for wide was spread
That war, and various: sometimes on firm ground
A standing fight; then, soaring on main wing,
Tormented all the air; all air seemed then
Conflicting fire. Long time in even scale
The battle hung; till Satan, who that day
Prodigious power had shown, and met in arms
No equal, ranging through the dire attack
Of fighting Seraphim confused, at length
Saw where the sword of Michael smote, and felled          250
Squadrons at once: with huge two-handed sway
Brandished aloft, the horrid edge came down
Wide-wasting. Such destruction to withstand
He hasted, and opposed the rocky orb
Of tenfold adamant, his ample shield,
A vast circumference. At his approach
The great Archangel from his warlike toil

Surceased, and, glad, as hoping here to end
Intestine war in Heaven, the Arch-foe subdued,
Or captive dragged in chains, with hostile frown          260
And visage all inflamed, first thus began:—

' "Author of Evil, unknown till thy revolt,
Unnamed in Heaven, now plenteous, as thou seest,
These acts of hateful strife—hateful to all,
Though heaviest, by just measure, on thyself
And thy adherents—how hast thou disturbed
Heaven's blessed peace, and into Nature brought
Misery, uncreated till the crime
Of thy rebellion! how hast thou instilled
Thy malice into thousands, once upright          270
And faithful, now proved false! But think not here
To trouble holy rest; Heaven casts thee out
From all her confines; Heaven, the seat of bliss,
Brooks not the works of violence and war.
Hence, then, and Evil go with thee along,
Thy offspring, to the place of Evil, Hell—
Thou and thy wicked crew! there mingle broils!
Ere this avenging sword begin thy doom,
Or some more sudden vengeance, winged from God,
Precipitate thee with augmented pain."          280

'So spake the Prince of Angels; to whom thus
The Adversary:—"Nor think thou with wind
Of airy threats to awe whom yet with deeds
Thou canst not. Hast thou turned the least of these
To flight—or, if to fall, but that they rise
Unvanquished—easier to transact with me
That thou shouldst hope, imperious, and with threats
To chase me hence? Err not that so shall end
The strife which thou call'st evil, but we style
The strife of glory; which we mean to win,          290
Or turn this Heaven itself into the Hell
Thou fablest; here, however, to dwell free,
If not to reign. Meanwhile thy utmost force—
And join him named Almighty to thy aid—
I fly not, but have sought thee far and nigh."

'They ended parle, and both addressed for fight
Unspeakable; for who, though with the tongue
Of Angels, can relate, or to what things

Liken on Earth conspicuous, that may lift
Human imagination to such height                                    300
Of godlike power? for likest gods they seemed,
Stood they or moved, in stature, motion, arms,
Fit to decide the empire of great Heaven.
Now waved their fiery swords, and in the air
Made horrid circles; two broad suns their shields
Blazed opposite, while Expectation stood
In horror; from each hand with speed retired,
Where erst was thickest fight, th' Angelic throng,
And left large field, unsafe within the wind
Of such commotion: such as (to set forth                           310
Great things by small) if, Nature's concord broke,
Among the constellations war were sprung,
Two planets, rushing from aspect malign
Of fiercest opposition, in mid sky
Should combat, and their jarring spheres confound.
Together both, with next to almighty arm
Uplifted imminent, one stroke they aimed
That might determine, and not need repeat,
As not of power, at once; nor odds appeared
In might or swift prevention. But the sword                         320
Of Michael from the armoury of God
Was given him tempered so that neither keen
Nor solid might resist that edge; it met
The sword of Satan, with steep force to smite
Descending, and in half cut sheer; nor stayed,
But, with swift wheel reverse, deep entering, sheared
All his right side. Then Satan first knew pain,
And writhed him to and fro convolved; so sore
The griding sword with discontinuous wound
Passed through him; but th' ethereal substance closed,
Not long divisible; and from the gash                              331
A stream of nectarous humour issuing flowed
Sanguine, such as celestial Spirits may bleed,
And all his armour stained, erewhile so bright.
Forthwith, on all sides, to his aid was run
By Angels many and strong, who interposed
Defence, while others bore him on their shields
Back to his chariot, where it stood retired
From off the files of war: there they him laid

Gnashing for anguish, and despite, and shame                    840
To find himself not matchless, and his pride
Humbled by such rebuke, so far beneath
His confidence to equal God in power.
Yet soon he healed; for Spirits, that live throughout
Vital in every part—not, as frail Man,
In entrails, heart or head, liver or reins—
Cannot but by annihilating die;
Nor in their liquid texture mortal wound
Receive, no more than can the fluid air;
All heart they live, all head, all eye, all ear,                    350
All intellect, all sense; and as they please
They limb themselves, and colour, shape, or size
Assume, as likes them best, condense or rare.
     'Meanwhile, in other parts, like deeds deserved
Memorial, where the might of Gabriel fought,
And with fierce ensigns pierced the deep array
Of Moloch, furious king, who him defied,
And at his chariot-wheels to drag him bound
Threatened, nor from the Holy One of Heaven
Refrained his tongue blasphemous, but anon,                    360
Down cloven to the waist, with shattered arms
And uncouth pain fled bellowing. On each wing
Uriel and Raphaël his vaunting foe,
Though huge and in a rock of diamond armed,
Vanquished Adramelech and Asmadai,
Two potent Thrones, that to be less than Gods
Disdained, but meaner thoughts learned in their flight,
Mangled with ghastly wounds through plate and mail.
Nor stood unmindful Abdiel to annoy
The atheist crew, but with redoubled blow                    370
Ariel, and Arioch, and the violence
Of Ramiel, scorched and blasted, overthrew.
I might relate of thousands, and their names
Eternize here on Earth; but those elect
Angels, contented with their fame in Heaven,
Seek not the praise of men: the other sort,
In might though wondrous and in acts of war,
Nor of renown less eager, yet by doom
Cancelled from Heaven and sacred memory,
Nameless in dark oblivion let them dwell.                    380

For strength from truth divided, and from just,
Illaudable, naught merits but dispraise
And ignominy, yet to glory aspires,
Vain-glorious, and through infamy seeks fame:
Therefore eternal silence be their doom!
    'And now, their mightiest quelled, the battle swerved,
With many an inroad gored; deformed rout
Entered, and foul disorder; all the ground
With shivered armour strown, and on a heap
Chariot and charioteer lay overturned,                    390
And fiery foaming steeds; what stood, recoiled
O'er-wearied, through the faint Satanic host,
Defensive scarce, or with pale fear surprised—
Then first with fear surprised and sense of pain—
Fled ignominious, to such evil brought
By sin of disobedience, till that hour
Not liable to fear, or flight, or pain.
Far otherwise th' inviolable Saints
In cubic phalanx firm advanced entire,
Invulnerable, impenetrably armed;                         400
Such high advantages their innocence
Gave them above their foes—not to have sinned,
Not to have disobeyed; in fight they stood
Unwearied, unobnoxious to be pained
By wound, though from their place by violence moved.
    'Now Night her course began, and, over Heaven
Inducing darkness, grateful truce imposed
And silence on the odious din of war.
Under her cloudy covert both retired,
Victor and vanquished: on the foughten field            410
Michaël and his Angels prevalent
Encamping, placed in guard their watches round,
Cherubic waving fires: on th' other part,
Satan with his rebellious disappeared,
Far in the dark dislodged, and, void of rest,
His potentates to council called by night,
And in the midst thus undismayed began:—
    ' "O now in danger tried, now known in arms
Not to be overpowered, companions dear,
Found worthy not of liberty alone—                       420
Too mean pretence—but, what we more affect,

Honour, dominion, glory, and renown;
Who have sustained one day in doubtful **fight**
(And, if one day, why not eternal days?)
What Heaven's Lord had powerfullest to send
Against us from about his throne, and judged
Sufficient to subdue us to his will,
But proves not so: then fallible, it seems,
Of future we may deem him, though till now
Omniscient thought! True is, less firmly armed,            430
Some disadvantage we endured, and pain—
Till now not known, but, known, as soon contemned;
Since now we find this our empyreal form
Incapable of mortal injury,
Imperishable, and, though pierced with wound,
Soon closing, and by native vigour healed.
Of evil, then, so small as easy think
The remedy: perhaps more valid arms,
Weapons more violent, when next we meet,
May serve to better us and worse our foes,                 440
Or equal what between us made the odds,
In nature none. If other hidden cause
Left them superior, while we can preserve
Unhurt our minds, and understanding sound,
Due search and consultation will disclose."
    'He sat; and in th' assembly next upstood
Nisroch, of Principalities the prime:
As one he stood escaped from cruel fight,
Sore toiled, his riven arms to havoc hewn,
And, cloudy in aspect, thus answering spake:—             450
    ' "Deliverer from new Lords, leader to free
Enjoyment of our right as Gods! yet hard
For Gods, and too unequal work, we find
Against unequal arms to fight in pain,
Against unpained, impassive; from which evil
Ruin must needs ensue. For what avails
Valour or strength, though matchless, quelled with pain,
Which all subdues, and makes remiss the hands
Of mightiest? Sense of pleasure we may well
Spare out of life perhaps, and not repine,                 460
But live content, which is the calmest life;
But pain is perfect misery, the worst

Of evils, and, excessive, overturns
All patience. He who, therefore, can invent
With what more forcible we may offend
Our yet unwounded enemies, or arm
Ourselves with like defence, to me deserves
No less than for deliverance what we owe."
   'Whereto, with look composed, Satan replied:—
"Not uninvented that, which thou aright                    470
Believ'st so main to our success, I bring.
Which of us who beholds the bright surface
Of this ethereous mould whereon we stand—
This continent of spacious Heaven, adorned
With plant, fruit, flower ambrosial, gems and gold—
Whose eye so superficially surveys
These things as not to mind from whence they grow
Deep under ground: materials dark and crude,
Of spiritous and fiery spume, till, touched
With Heaven's ray, and tempered, they shoot forth          480
So beauteous, opening to the ambient light?
These in their dark nativity the Deep
Shall yield us, pregnant with infernal flame;
Which, into hollow engines long and round
Thick-rammed, at th' other bore with touch of fire
Dilated and infuriate, shall send forth
From far, with thundering noise, among our foes
Such implements of mischief as shall dash
To pieces and o'erwhelm whatever stands
Adverse, that they shall fear we have disarmed           490
The Thunderer of his only dreaded bolt.
Nor long shall be our labour; yet ere dawn
Effect shall end our wish. Meanwhile revive,
Abandon fear; to strength and counsel joined
Think nothing hard, much less to be despaired."
   'He ended; and his words their drooping cheer
Enlightened, and their languished hope revived,
Th' invention all admired, and each how he
To be th' inventor missed; so easy it seemed
Once found, which yet unfound most would have
    thought
Impossible! Yet, haply, of thy race,                      500
In future days, if malice should abound,

Some one, intent on mischief, or inspired
With dev'lish machination, might devise
Like instrument to plague the sons of men
For sin, on war and mutual slaughter bent.
Forthwith from council to the work they flew;
None arguing stood; innumerable hands
Were ready; in a moment up they turned
Wide the celestial soil, and saw beneath          510
Th' originals of Nature in their crude
Conception; sulphurous and nitrous foam
They found, they mingled, and with subtle art,
Concocted and adusted, they reduced
To blackest grain, and into store conveyed.
Part hidden veins digged up (nor hath this Earth
Entrails unlike) of mineral and stone,
Whereof to found their engines and their balls
Of missive ruin; part incentive reed
Provide, pernicious with one touch to fire.       520
So all ere day-spring, under conscious Night,
Secret they finished, and in order set,
With silent circumspection, unespied.
    'Now, when fair Morn orient in Heaven appeared,
Up rose the victor Angels, and to arms
The matin trumpet sung. In arms they stood
Of golden panoply, refulgent host,
Soon banded; others from the dawning hills
Looked round, and scouts each coast light-armed scour,
Each quarter, to descry the distant foe,          530
Where lodged, or whither fled, or if for fight,
In motion or in halt. Him soon they met
Under spread ensigns moving nigh, in slow
But firm battalion: back with speediest sail
Zophiel, of Cherubim the swiftest wing,
Came flying, and in mid air aloud thus cried:—
    ' "Arm, Warriors, arm for fight! The foe at hand,
Whom fled we thought, will save us long pursuit
This day; fear not his flight; so thick a cloud
He comes, and settled in his face I see           540
Sad resolution and secure. Let each
His adamantine coat gird well, and each
Fit well his helm, grip fast his orbed shield,

Borne even or high; for this day will pour down
If I conjecture aught, no drizzling shower,
But rattling storm of arrows barbed with fire."
　'So warned he them, aware themselves, and soon
In order, quit of all impediment,
Instant, without disturb, they took alarm,
And onward move embattled: when, behold,                    550
Not distant far, with heavy pace the foe
Approaching gross and huge, in hollow cube
Training his devilish enginry, impaled
On every side with shadowing squadrons deep,
To hide the fraud.  At interview both stood
A while; but suddenly at head appeared
Satan, and thus was heard commanding loud:—
　'"Vanguard, to right and left the front unfold,
That all may see who hate us how we seek
Peace and composure, and with open breast                    560
Stand ready to receive them, if they like
Our overture, and turn not back perverse:
But that I doubt.  However, witness Heaven!
Heaven, witness thou anon! while we discharge
Freely our part.  Ye, who appointed stand,
Do as you have in charge, and briefly touch
What we propound, and loud that all may hear."
　'So scoffing in ambiguous words, he scarce
Had ended, when to right and left the front
Divided, and to either flank retired;                    570
Which to our eyes discovered, new and strange,
A triple-mounted row of pillars laid
On wheels (for like to pillars most they seemed,
Or hollowed bodies made of oak or fir,
With branches lopped, in wood or mountain felled),
Brass, iron, stony mould, had not their mouths
With hideous orifice gaped on us wide,
Portending hollow truce.  At each, behind,
A Seraph stood, and in his hand a reed
Stood waving, tipped with fire; while we, suspense          580
Collected stood within our thoughts amused;
Not long! for sudden all at once their reeds
Put forth, and to a narrow vent applied
With nicest touch.  Immediate in a flame,

But soon obscured with smoke, all Heaven appeared,
From those deep-throated engines belched, whose
    roar
Embowelled with outrageous noise the air,
And all her entrails tore, disgorging foul
Their devilish glut, chained thunderbolts and hail
Of iron globes; which, on the victor host              590
Levelled, with such impetuous fury smote,
That whom they hit none on their feet might stand,
Though standing else as rocks, but down they fell
By thousands, Angel on Archangel rolled,
The sooner for their arms; unarmed, they might
Have easily, as Spirits, evaded swift
By quick contraction or remove; but now
Foul dissipation followed, and forced rout;
Nor served it to relax their serried files.
What should they do? If on they rushed, repulse       600
Repeated, and indecent overthrow
Doubled, would render them yet more despised,
And to their foes a laughter—for in view
Stood ranked of Seraphim another row,
In posture to displode their second tire
Of thunder; back defeated to return
They worse abhorred. Satan beheld their plight,
And to his mates thus in derision called:—

  ' "O friends, why come not on these victors proud?
Erewhile they fierce were coming; and, when we,     610
To entertain them fair with open front
And breast (what could we more?) propounded terms
Of composition, straight they changed their minds,
Flew off, and into strange vagaries fell,
As they would dance, yet for a dance they seemed
Somewhat extravagant and wild; perhaps
For joy of offered peace. But I suppose,
If our proposals once again were heard,
We should compel them to a quick result."

  'To whom thus Belial, in like gamesome mood:—    620
"Leader, the terms we sent were terms of weight,
Of hard contents, and full of force urged home,
Such as we might perceive amused them all,
And stumbled many. Who receives them right

Had need from head to foot well understand;
Not understood, this gift they have besides,
They show us when our foes walk not upright."
    'So they among themselves in pleasant vein
Stood scoffing, heightened in their thoughts beyond
All doubt of victory; Eternal Might                       630
To match with their inventions they presumed
So easy, and of his thunder made a scorn,
And all his host derided, while they stood
A while in trouble.  But they stood not long;
Rage prompted them at length, and found them
        arms
Against such hellish mischief fit to oppose.
Forthwith (behold the excellence, the power,
Which God hath in his mighty Angels placed!)
Their arms away they threw, and to the hills
(For Earth hath this variety from Heaven               640
Of pleasure situate in hill and dale)
Light as the lightning-glimpse they ran, they flew;
From their foundations, loosening to and fro,
They plucked the seated hills, with all their load,
Rocks, waters, woods, and, by the shaggy tops
Uplifting, bore them in their hands.  Amaze,
Be sure, and terror seized the rebel host,
When coming towards them so dread they saw
The bottom of the mountains upward turned,
Till on those cursed engines' triple row                  650
They saw them whelmed, and all their confidence
Under the weight of mountains buried deep;
Themselves invaded next, and on their heads
Main promontories flung, which in the air
Came shadowing, and oppressed whole legions armed.
Their armour helped their harm, crushed in and bruised,
Into their substance pent, which wrought them pain
Implacable, and many a dolorous groan,
Long struggling underneath, ere they could wind
Out of such prison, though Spirits of purest light,   660
Purest at first, now gross by sinning grown.
The rest, in imitation, to like arms
Betook them, and the neighbouring hills uptore;
So hills amid the air encountered hills,

Hurled to and fro with jaculation dire
That underground they fought in dismal shade:
Infernal noise! war seemed a civil game
To this uproar; horrid confusion heaped
Upon confusion rose. And now all Heaven
Had gone to wrack, with ruin overspread,                    670
Had not th' Almighty Father, where he sits
Shrined in his sanctuary of Heaven secure,
Consulting on the sum of things, foreseen
This tumult, and permitted all, advised,
That his great purpose he might so fulfil,
To honour his anointed Son, avenged
Upon his enemies, and to declare
All power on him transferred: whence to his Son,
Th' assessor of his throne, he thus began:—
    '"Effulgence of my glory, Son beloved,                 680
Son in whose face invisible is beheld
Visibly, what by Deity I am,
And in whose hand what by decree I do,
Second Omnipotence! two days are passed,
Two days, as we compute the days of Heaven,
Since Michael and his Powers went forth to tame
These disobedient. Sore hath been their fight,
As likeliest was when two such foes met armed:
For to themselves I left them; and thou know'st
Equal in their creation they were formed,                   690
Save what sin hath impaired—which yet hath wrought
Insensibly, for I suspend their doom:
Whence in perpetual fight they needs must last
Endless, and no solution will be found.
War wearied hath performed what war can do,
And to disordered rage let loose the reins,
With mountains, as with weapons, armed; which
    makes
Wild work in Heaven, and dangerous to the main.
Two days are, therefore, passed; the third is thine:
For thee I have ordained it, and thus far                   700
Have suffered, that the glory may be thine
Of ending this great war, since none but thou
Can end it. Into thee such virtue and grace
Immense I have transfused, that all may know

In Heaven and Hell thy power above compare,
And this perverse commotion governed thus,
To manifest thee worthiest to be Heir
Of all things, to be Heir, and to be King
By sacred unction, thy deserved right.
Go, then, thou Mightiest, in thy Father's might;                710
Ascend my chariot; guide the rapid wheels
That shake Heaven's basis; bring forth all my war;
My bow and thunder, my almighty arms,
Gird on, and sword upon thy puissant thigh;
Pursue these Sons of Darkness, drive them out
From all Heaven's bounds into the utter Deep;
There let them learn, as likes them, to despise
God, and Messiah his anointed King."
    'He said, and on his Son with rays direct
Shone full, he all his Father full expressed                720
Ineffably into his face received;
And thus the Filial Godhead answering spake:—
    ' "O Father, O Supreme of Heavenly Thrones,
First, Highest, Holiest, Best, thou always seek'st
To glorify thy Son; I always thee,
As is most just. This I my glory account,
My exaltation, and my whole delight,
That thou in me, well pleased, declar'st thy will
Fulfilled, which to fulfil is all my bliss.
Sceptre and power, thy giving, I assume,                730
And gladlier shall resign when in the end
Thou shalt be all in all, and I in thee
For ever, and in me all whom thou lov'st.
But whom thou hat'st I hate, and can put on
Thy terrors, as I put thy mildness on,
Image of thee in all things: and shall soon,
Armed with thy might, rid Heaven of these rebelled,
To their prepared ill mansion driven down,
To chains of darkness and th' undying worm,
That from thy just obedience could revolt,                740
Whom to obey is happiness entire.
Then shall thy Saints, unmixed, and from th' impure
Far separate, circling thy holy mount,
Unfeigned halleluiahs to thee sing,
Hymns of high praise, and I among them chief."

'So said, he, o'er his sceptre bowing, rose
From the right hand of Glory where he sat;
And the third sacred morn began to shine,
Dawning through Heaven.  Forth rushed with whirlwind
          sound
The chariot of Paternal Deity,                              750
Flashing thick flames, wheel within wheel indrawn,
Itself instinct with spirit, but convoyed
By four cherubic Shapes.  Four faces each
Had wondrous; as with stars, their bodies all
And wings were set with eyes; with eyes the wheels
Of beryl, and careering fires between;
Over their heads a crystal firmament,
Whereon a sapphire throne, inlaid with pure
Amber and colours of the showery arch.
He, in celestial panoply all armed                          760
Of radiant Urim, work divinely wrought,
Ascended; at his right hand Victory
Sat eagle-winged; beside him hung his bow
And quiver with three-bolted thunder stored;
And from about him fierce effusion rolled
Of smoke and bickering flame and sparkles dire.
Attended with ten thousand thousand Saints
He onward came; far off his coming shone;
And twenty thousand (I their number heard)
Chariots of God, half on each hand, were seen.            770
He on the wings of Cherub rode sublime
On the crystalline sky, in sapphire throned.
Illustrious far and wide, but by his own
First seen, them unexpected joy surprised
When the great ensign of Messiah blazed
Aloft, by Angels borne, his sign in Heaven;
Under whose conduct Michael soon reduced
His army, circumfused on either wing,
Under their Head embodied all in one.
Before him Power Divine his way prepared;                  780
At his command the uprooted hills retired
Each to his place; they heard his voice, and went
Obsequious; Heaven his wonted face renewed,
And with fresh flowerets hill and valley smiled.
This saw his hapless foes, but stood obdured,

And to rebellious fight rallied their Powers,
Insensate, hope conceiving from despair.
In Heavenly Spirits could such perverseness dwell?
But to convince the proud what signs avail,
Or wonders move th' obdurate to relent?          790
They, hardened more by what might most reclaim,
Grieving to see his glory, at the sight
Took envy, and, aspiring to his height,
Stood re-embattled fierce, by force or fraud
Weening to prosper, and at length prevail
Against God and Messiah, or to fall
In universal ruin last; and now
To final battle drew, disdaining flight,
Or faint retreat: when the great Son of God
To all his host on either hand thus spake:—          800
  ' "Stand still in bright array, ye Saints; here stand,
Ye angels armed; this day from battle rest.
Faithful hath been your warfare, and of God
Accepted, fearless in his righteous cause;
And, as ye have received, so have ye done,
Invincibly; but of this cursed crew
The punishment to other hand belongs;
Vengeance is his, or whose he sole appoints.
Number to this day's work is not ordained,
Nor multitude; stand only and behold          810
God's indignation on these godless poured
By me; not you, but me, they have despised,
Yet envied; against me is all their rage,
Because the Father, t' whom in Heaven supreme
Kingdom and power and glory appertains,
Hath honoured me, according to his will.
Therefore to me their doom he hath assigned,
That they may have their wish, to try with me
In battle which the stronger proves, they all,
Or I alone against them; since by strength          820
They measure all, of other excellence
Not emulous, nor care who them excels;
Nor other strife with them do I vouchsafe."
  'So spake the Son, and into terror changed
His count'nance, too severe to be beheld,
And full of wrath bent on his enemies.

At once the Four spread out their starry wings
With dreadful shade contiguous, and the orbs
Of his fierce chariot rolled, as with the sound
Of torrent floods, or of a numerous host.                    830
He on his impious foes right onward drove,
Gloomy as Night. Under his burning wheels
The steadfast empyrean shook throughout,
All but the throne itself of God. Full soon
Among them he arrived, in his right hand
Grasping ten thousand thunders, which he sent
Before him, such as in their souls infixed
Plagues. They, astonished, all resistance lost,
All courage; down their idle weapons dropped;
O'er shields, and helms, and helmed heads he rode      840
Of Thrones and mighty Seraphim prostrate,
That wished the mountains now might be again
Thrown on them, as a shelter from his ire.
Nor less on either side tempestuous fell
His arrows, from the fourfold-visaged Four,
Distinct with eyes, and from the living wheels,
Distinct alike with multitude of eyes;
One spirit in them ruled, and every eye
Glared lightning, and shot forth pernicious fire
Among th' accurs'd, that withered all their strength, 850
And of their wonted vigour left them drained,
Exhausted, spiritless, afflicted, fallen.
Yet half his strength he put not forth, but checked
His thunder in mid-volley; for he meant
Not to destroy, but root them out of Heaven.
The overthrown he raised, and, as a herd
Of goats or timorous flock together thronged,
Drove them before him thunderstruck, pursued
With terrors and with furies to the bounds
And crystal wall of Heaven; which, opening wide,     860
Rolled inward, and a spacious gap disclosed
Into the wasteful Deep. The monstrous sight
Struck them with horror backward; but far worse
Urged them behind: headlong themselves they threw
Down from the verge of Heaven: eternal wrath
Burnt after them to the bottomless pit.
    'Hell heard th' unsufferable noise; Hell saw

Heaven ruining from Heaven, and would have fled
Affrighted; but strict Fate had cast too deep
Her dark foundations, and too fast had bound.        870
Nine days they fell; confounded Chaos roared,
And felt tenfold confusion in their fall
Through his wild anarchy; so huge a rout
Encumbered him with ruin. Hell at last,
Yawning, received them whole, and on them closed—
Hell, their fit habitation, fraught with fire
Unquenchable, the house of woe and pain.
Disburdened Heaven rejoiced, and soon repaired
Her mural breach, returning whence it rolled.
Sole victor, from th' expulsion of his foes        880
Messiah his triumphal chariot turned.
To meet him all his Saints, who silent stood
Eye-witnesses of his almighty acts,
With jubilee advanced; and, as they went,
Shaded with branching palm, each order bright
Sung triumph, and him sung victorious King,
Son, Heir, and Lord, to him dominion given,
Worthiest to reign. He celebrated rode,
Triumphant through mid Heaven, into the courts
And temple of his mighty Father throned        890
On high; who into glory him received,
Where now he sits at the right hand of bliss.
   'Thus, measuring things in Heaven by things on
      Earth,
At thy request, and that thou may'st beware
By what is past, to thee I have revealed
What might have else to human race been hid—
The discord which befell, and war in Heaven
Among th' Angelic Powers, and the deep fall
Of those too high aspiring who rebelled
With Satan: he who envies now thy state,        900
Who now is plotting how he may seduce
Thee also from obedience, that, with him
Bereaved of happiness, thou may'st partake
His punishment, eternal misery;
Which would be all his solace and revenge,
As a despite done against the Most High,
Thee once to gain companion of his woe.

But listen not to his temptations; warn
Thy weaker; let it profit thee to have heard,
By terrible example, the reward                    910
Of disobedience: firm they might have stood,
Yet fell: remember, and fear to transgress.'

*The End of the Sixth Book.*

# PARADISE LOST

## BOOK VII

### THE ARGUMENT

*Raphael, at the request of Adam, relates how and wherefore this world was first created:—that God, after the expelling of Satan and his Angels out of Heaven, declared his pleasure to create another world, and other creatures to dwell therein; sends his Son with glory, and attendance of Angels, to perform the work of creation in six days: the Angels celebrate with hymns the performance thereof, and his reascension into Heaven.*

DESCEND from Heaven, Urania, by that name
If rightly thou art called, whose voice divine
Following, above th' Olympian hill I soar,
Above the flight of Pegasean wing.
The meaning, not the name, I call; for thou
Nor of the Muses nine, nor on the top
Of old Olympus dwell'st; but, heavenly-born,
Before the hills appeared or fountain flowed,
Thou with eternal wisdom didst converse,
Wisdom thy sister, and with her didst play                    10
In presence of th' Almighty Father, pleased
With thy celestial song.  Up led by thee,
Into the Heaven of Heavens I have presumed,
An earthly guest, and drawn empyreal air,
Thy temp'ring.  With like safety guided down,
Return me to my native element;
Lest, from this flying steed unreined (as once
Bellerophon, though from a lower clime)
Dismounted, on th' Aleian field I fall,
Erroneous there to wander and forlorn.                        20
Half yet remains unsung, but narrower bound
Within the visible diurnal sphere.
Standing on Earth, not rapt above the pole,
More safe I sing with mortal voice, unchanged

To hoarse or mute, though fallen on evil days,
On evil days though fallen, and evil tongues;
In darkness, and with dangers compassed round,
And solitude; yet not alone, while thou
Visit'st my slumbers nightly, or when Morn
Purples the East. Still govern thou my song,          30
Urania, and fit audience find, though few.
But drive far off the barbarous dissonance
Of Bacchus and his revellers, the race
Of that wild rout that tore the Thracian bard
In Rhodope, where woods and rocks had ears
To rapture, till the savage clamour drowned
Both harp and voice; nor could the Muse defend
Her son. So fail not thou who thee implores;
For thou art heavenly, she an empty dream.

　　Say, Goddess, what ensued when Raphael,          40
The affable Archangel, had forewarned
Adam, by dire example, to beware
Apostasy, by what befell in Heaven
To those apostates, lest the like befall
In Paradise to Adam or his race,
Charged not to touch the interdicted tree,
If they transgress, and slight that sole command,
So easily obeyed amid the choice
Of all tastes else to please their appetite,
Though wandering. He, with his consorted Eve,          50
The story heard attentive, and was filled
With admiration and deep muse, to hear
Of things so high and strange—things to their thought
So unimaginable as hate in Heaven,
And war so near the peace of God in bliss,
With such confusion; but the evil, soon
Driven back, redounded as a flood on those
From whom it sprung, impossible to mix
With blessedness. Whence Adam soon repealed
The doubts that in his heart arose; and, now          60
Led on, yet sinless, with desire to know
What nearer might concern him—how this World
Of heaven and earth conspicuous first began;
When, and whereof, created; for what cause;
What within Eden, or without, was done

Before his memory—as one whose drought,
Yet scarce allayed, still eyes the current stream,
Whose liquid murmur heard new thirst excites,
Proceeded thus to ask his heavenly guest:—
    'Great things, and full of wonder in our ears,        70
Far differing from this World, thou hast revealed,
Divine interpreter! by favour sent
Down from the empyrean to forewarn
Us timely of what might else have been our loss,
Unknown, which human knowledge could not reach;
For which to the infinitely Good we owe
Immortal thanks, and his admonishment
Receive with solemn purpose to observe
Immutably his sovran will, the end
Of what we are. But, since thou hast vouchsafed        80
Gently, for our instruction, to impart
Things above earthly thought, which yet concerned
Our knowing, as to highest wisdom seemed,
Deign to descend now lower, and relate
What may no less perhaps avail us known—
How first began this Heaven which we behold
Distant so high, with moving fires adorned
Innumerable; and this which yields or fills
All space, the ambient air, wide interfused,
Embracing round this florid Earth; what cause        90
Moved the Creator, in his holy rest
Through all eternity, so late to build
In Chaos, and, the work begun, how soon
Absolved: if unforbid thou may'st unfold
What we not to explore the secrets ask
Of his eternal empire, but the more
To magnify his works the more we know.
And the great light of day yet wants to run
Much of his race, though steep. Suspense in Heaven,
Held by thy voice, thy potent voice, he hears,        100
And longer will delay, to hear thee tell
His generation, and the rising birth
Of Nature from the unapparent deep:
Or, if the Star of Evening and the Moon
Haste to thy audience, Night with her will bring
Silence, and Sleep listening to thee will watch;

Or we can bid his absence till thy song
End, and dismiss thee ere the morning shine.'
  Thus Adam his illustrious guest besought;
And thus the godlike Angel answered mild:—                   110
  'This also thy request, with caution asked,
Obtain; though to recount almighty works
What words or tongue of Seraph can suffice,
Or heart of man suffice to comprehend?
Yet what thou canst attain, which best may serve
To glorify the Maker, and infer
Thee also happier, shall not be withheld
Thy hearing, such commission from above
I have received, to answer thy desire
Of knowledge within bounds; beyond abstain                   120
To ask, nor let thine own inventions hope
Things not revealed, which th' invisible King,
Only omniscient, hath suppressed in night,
To none communicable in Earth or Heaven.
Enough is left besides to search and know;
But Knowledge is as food, and needs no less
Her temperance over appetite, to know
In measure what the mind may well contain;
Oppresses else with surfeit, and soon turns
Wisdom to folly, as nourishment to wind.                     130
  'Know then, that after Lucifer from Heaven
(So call him, brighter once amidst the host
Of Angels than that star the stars among)
Fell with his flaming legions through the Deep
Into his place, and the great Son returned
Victorious with his Saints, th' Omnipotent
Eternal Father from his throne beheld
Their multitude, and to his Son thus spake:—
  ' "At least our envious foe hath failed, who thought
All like himself rebellious; by whose aid                    140
This inaccessible high strength, the seat
Of Deity supreme, us dispossessed,
He trusted to have seized, and into fraud
Drew many whom their place knows here no more.
Yet far the greater part have kept, I see,
Their station; Heaven, yet populous, retains
Number sufficient to possess her realms,

Though wide, and this high temple to frequent
With ministeries due and solemn rites.
But, lest his heart exalt him in the harm    150
Already done, to have dispeopled Heaven—
My damage fondly deemed—I can repair
That detriment, if such it be to lose
Self-lost, and in a moment will create
Another world; out of one man a race
Of men innumerable, there to dwell,
Not here, till, by degrees of merit raised,
They open to themselves at length the way
Up hither, under long obedience tried,
And Earth be changed to Heaven, and Heaven to
    Earth,    160
One kingdom, joy and union without end.
Meanwhile inhabit lax, ye Powers of Heaven;
And thou, my Word, begotten Son, by thee
This I perform; speak thou, and be it done!
My overshadowing Spirit and might with thee
I send along; ride forth, and bid the Deep
Within appointed bounds be heaven and earth;
Boundless the deep, because I am who fill
Infinitude, nor vacuous the space,
Though I, uncircumscribed, myself retire,    170
And put not forth my goodness, which is free
To act or not, Necessity and Chance
Approach not me, and what I will is Fate."
    'So spake th' Almighty; and to what he spake
His Word, the Filial Godhead, gave effect.
Immediate are the acts of God, more swift
Than time or motion, but to human ears
Cannot without process of speech be told,
So told as earthly notion can receive.
Great triumph and rejoicing was in Heaven    180
When such was heard declared the Almighty's will.
Glory they sung to the Most High, goodwill
To future men, and in their dwellings peace—
Glory to him whose just avenging ire
Had driven out th' ungodly from his sight
And th' habitations of the just; to him
Glory and praise whose wisdom had ordained

Good out of evil to create—instead
Of Spirits malign, a better race to bring
Into their vacant room, and thence diffuse          190
His good to worlds and ages infinite.
    'So sang the hierarchies.  Meanwhile the Son
On his great expedition now appeared,
Girt with omnipotence, with radiance crowned
Of majesty divine, sapience and love
Immense; and all his Father in him shone.
About his chariot numberless were poured
Cherub and Seraph, Potentates and Thrones,
And Virtues, winged Spirits, and chariots winged
From the armoury of God, where stand of old          200
Myriads, between two brazen mountains lodged
Against a solemn day, harnessed at hand,
Celestial equipage; and now came forth
Spontaneous, for within them Spirit lived,
Attendant on their Lord.  Heaven opened wide
Her ever-during gates, harmonious sound
On golden hinges moving, to let forth
The King of Glory, in his powerful Word
And Spirit coming to create new worlds.
On heavenly ground they stood, and from the shore     210
They viewed the vast immeasurable abyss,
Outrageous as a sea, dark, wasteful, wild,
Up from the bottom turned by furious winds
And surging waves, as mountains to assault
Heaven's height, and with the centre mix the pole.
    ' "Silence, ye troubled waves, and, thou deep,
        peace!"
Said then th' omnific Word: "your discord end!"
Nor stayed; but, on the wings of Cherubim
Uplifted, in paternal glory rode
Far into Chaos and the World unborn;                  220
For Chaos heard his voice.  Him all his train
Followed in bright procession, to behold
Creation, and the wonders of his might.
Then stayed the fervid wheels, and in his hand
He took the golden compasses, prepared
In God's eternal store, to circumscribe
This Universe, and all created things.

One foot he centred, and the other turned
Round through the vast profundity obscure,
And said, "Thus far extend, thus far thy bounds;          230
This be thy just circumference, O World!"
Thus God the Heaven created, thus the Earth,
Matter unformed and void. Darkness profound
Covered th' abyss; but on the wat'ry calm
His brooding wings the Spirit of God outspread,
And vital virtue infused, and vital warmth,
Throughout the fluid mass, but downward purged
The black, tartareous, cold, infernal dregs,
Adverse to life; then founded, then conglobed
Like things to like, the rest to several place          240
Disparted, and between spun out the air,
And Earth, self-balanced, on her centre hung.
  ' "Let there be light!" said God; and forthwith
      light
Ethereal, first of things, quintessence pure,
Sprung from the deep, and from her native East
To journey through the aery gloom began,
Sphered in a radiant cloud—for yet the Sun
Was not; she in a cloudy tabernacle
Sojourned the while. God saw the light was good;
And light from darkness by the hemisphere          250
Divided: light the Day, and darkness Night,
He named. Thus was the first day even and morn;
Nor passed uncelebrated, nor unsung
By the celestial quires, when orient light
Exhaling first from darkness they beheld,
Birth-day of Heaven and Earth. With joy and shout
The hollow universal orb they filled,
And touched their golden harps, and hymning praised
God and his works; Creator him they sung,
Both when first evening was, and when first morn.          260
  'Again God said, "Let there be firmament
Amid the waters, and let it divide
The waters from the waters!" And God made
The firmament, expanse of liquid, pure,
Transparent, elemental air, diffused
In circuit to the uttermost convex
Of this great round—partition firm and sure,

The waters underneath from those above
Dividing; for as Earth, so he the World
Built on circumfluous waters calm, in wide    270
Crystalline ocean, and the loud misrule
Of Chaos far removed, lest fierce extremes
Contiguous might distemper the whole frame:
And Heaven he named the Firmament. So even
And morning chorus sung the second day.
   'The Earth was formed, but, in the womb as yet
Of waters, embryon immature, involved,
Appeared not; over all the face of Earth
Main ocean flowed, not idle, but, with warm
Prolific humour soft'ning all her globe,    280
Fermented the great mother to conceive,
Satiate with genial moisture; when God said,
"Be gathered now, ye waters under Heaven,
Into one place, and let dry land appear!"
Immediately the mountains huge appear
Emergent, and their broad bare backs upheave
Into the clouds; their tops ascend the sky.
So high as heaved the tumid hills, so low
Down sunk a hollow bottom broad and deep,
Capacious bed of waters: thither they    290
Hasted with glad precipitance, uprolled,
As drops on dust conglobing, from the dry:
Part rise in crystal wall, or ridge direct,
For haste; such flight the great command impressed
On the swift floods. As armies at the call
Of trumpet (for of armies thou hast heard)
Troop to their standard, so the wat'ry throng,
Wave rolling after wave, where way they found—
If steep, with torrent rapture, if through plain,
Soft-ebbing; nor withstood them rock or hill;    300
But they, or underground, or circuit wide
With serpent error wandering, found their way,
And on the washy ooze deep channels wore:
Easy, ere God had bid the ground be dry,
All but within those banks where rivers now
Stream, and perpetual draw their humid train.
The dry land Earth, and the great receptacle
Of congregated waters he called Seas:

And saw that it was good, and said, "Let th' Earth
Put forth the verdant grass, herb yielding seed,          310
And fruit-tree yielding fruit after her kind,
Whose seed is in herself upon the Earth!"
He scarce had said when the bare Earth, till then
Desert and bare, unsightly, unadorned,
Brought forth the tender grass, whose verdure clad
Her universal face with pleasant green;
Then herbs of every leaf, that sudden flowered,
Opening their various colours, and made gay
Her bosom, smelling sweet; and, these scarce blown,
Forth flourished thick the clust'ring vine, forth crept          320
The smelling gourd, up stood the corny reed
Embattled in her field: add the humble shrub,
And bush with frizzled hair implicit: last
Rose, as in dance, the stately trees, and spread
Their branches, hung with copious fruit, or gemmed
Their blossoms: with high woods the hills were
          crowned,
With tufts the valleys and each fountain-side,
With borders long the rivers; that Earth now
Seemed like to Heaven, a seat where gods might dwell,
Or wander with delight, and love to haunt          330
Her sacred shades; though God had yet not rained
Upon the Earth, and man to till the ground
None was, but from the Earth a dewy mist
Went up and watered all the ground, and each
Plant of the field, which ere it was in the Earth
God made, and every herb before it grew
On the green stem.  God saw that it was good;
So even and morn recorded the third day.
     'Again th' Almighty spake, "Let there be lights
High in th' expanse of Heaven, to divide          340
The day from night; and let them be for signs,
For seasons, and for days, and circling years;
And let them be for lights, as I ordain
Their office in the firmament of Heaven,
To give light on the Earth!" and it was so.
And God made two great lights, great for their use
To Man, the greater to have rule by day,
The less by night, altern; and made the Stars,

And set them in the firmament of Heaven
To illuminate the Earth, and rule the day                      350
In their vicissitude, and rule the night,
And light from darkness to divide.  God saw,
Surveying his great work, that it was good:
For, of celestial bodies, first the Sun
A mighty sphere he framed, unlightsome first,
Though of ethereal mould; then formed the Moon
Globose, and every magnitude of Stars,
And sowed with stars the Heaven thick as a field.
Of light by far the greater part he took,
Transplanted from her cloudy shrine, and placed             360
In the Sun's orb, made porous to receive
And drink the liquid light, firm to retain
Her gathered beams, great palace now of light.
Hither, as to their fountain, other stars
Repairing, in their golden urns draw light,
And hence the morning planet gilds her horns;
By tincture or reflection they augment
Their small peculiar, though, from human sight
So far remote, with diminution seen.
First in his east the glorious lamp was seen,               370
Regent of day, and all th' horizon round
Invested with bright rays, jocund to run
His longitude through Heaven's high road; the grey
Dawn, and the Pleiades, before him danced,
Shedding sweet influence.  Less bright the Moon,
But opposite in levelled west, was set
His mirror, with full face borrowing her light
From him; for other light she needed none
In that aspect, and still that distance keeps
Till night; then in the east her turn she shines,          380
Revolved on Heaven's great axle, and her reign
With thousand lesser lights dividual holds,
With thousand thousand stars, that then appeared
Spangling the hemisphere: then first adorned
With their bright luminaries, that set and rose,
Glad evening and glad morn crowned the fourth day.
  'And God said, "Let the waters generate
Reptile with spawn abundant, living soul;
And let Fowl fly above the earth, with wings

Displayed on the open firmament of Heaven!"          390
And God created the great whales, and each
Soul living, each that crept, which plenteously
The waters generated by their kinds,
And every bird of wing after his kind,
And saw that it was good, and blessed them, saying,
"Be fruitful, multiply, and, in the seas,
And lakes, and running streams, the waters fill;
And let the fowl be multiplied on the earth!"
Forthwith the sounds and seas, each creek and bay,
With fry innumerable swarm, and shoals          400
Of fish that, with their fins and shining scales,
Glide under the green wave in schools that oft
Bank the mid-sea. Part, single or with mate,
Graze the sea-weed, their pasture, and through groves
Of coral stray, or, sporting with quick glance,
Show to the sun their waved coats dropped with
     gold,
Or, in their pearly shells at ease, attend
Moist nutriment, or under rocks their food
In jointed armour watch; on smooth the seal
And bended dolphins play: part, huge of bulk,          410
Wallowing unwieldy, enormous in their gait,
Tempest the ocean. There leviathan,
Hugest of living creatures, on the deep
Stretched like a promontory, sleeps or swims,
And seems a moving land, and at his gills
Draws in, and at his trunk spouts out, a sea.
Meanwhile the tepid caves, and fens, and shores,
Their brood as numerous hatch, from the egg that
     soon,
Bursting with kindly rupture, forth disclosed
Their callow young; but feathered soon and fledge,          420
They summed their pens, and, soaring th' air sublime,
With clang despised the ground, under a cloud
In prospect. There the eagle and the stork
On cliffs and cedar-tops their eyries build.
Part loosely wing the region; part, more wise,
In common, ranged in figure, wedge their way,
Intelligent of seasons, and set forth
Their aery caravan, high over seas

Flying, and over lands with mutual wing
Easing their flight: so steers the prudent crane          430
Her annual voyage, borne on winds: the air
Floats as they pass, fanned with unnumbered plumes.
From branch to branch the smaller birds with song
Solaced the woods, and spread their painted wings,
Till even; nor then the solemn nightingale
Ceased warbling, but all night tuned her soft lays.
Others, on silver lakes and rivers, bathed
Their downy breast; the swan, with arched neck
Between her white wings mantling proudly, rows
Her state with oary feet; yet oft they quit          440
The dank, and, rising on stiff pennons, tower
The mid aerial sky. Others on ground
Walked firm—the crested cock, whose clarion sounds
The silent hours, and th' other, whose gay train
Adorns him, coloured with the florid hue
Of rainbows and starry eyes. The waters thus
With Fish replenished, and the air with Fowl,
Evening and morn solemnized the fifth day.
     'The sixth, and of Creation last, arose
With evening harps and matin; when God said,          450
"Let th' Earth bring forth soul living in her kind,
Cattle, and creeping things, and beast of the earth,
Each in their kind!" The Earth obeyed, and, straight
Opening her fertile womb, teemed at a birth
Innumerous living creatures, perfect forms,
Limbed and full grown. Out of the ground up rose,
As from his lair, the wild beast, where he wons
In forest wild, in thicket, brake, or den—
Among the trees in pairs they rose, they walked;
The cattle in the fields and meadows green:          460
Those rare and solitary, these in flocks
Pasturing at once, and in broad herds, up sprung.
The grassy clods now calved; now half appeared
The tawny lion, pawing to get free
His hinder parts—then springs, as broke from bonds,
And rampant shakes his brinded mane; the ounce,
The libbard, and the tiger, as the mole
Rising, the crumbled earth above them threw
In hillocks; the swift stag from underground

Bore up his branching head; scarce from his mould    470
Behemoth, biggest born of earth, upheaved
His vastness; fleeced the flocks and bleating rose,
As plants; ambiguous between sea and land,
The river-horse and scaly crocodile.
At once came forth whatever creeps the ground,
Insect or worm. Those waved their limber fans
For wings, and smallest lineaments exact
In all the liveries decked of summer's pride,
With spots of gold and purple, azure and green;
These as a line their long dimension drew        480
Streaking the ground with sinuous trace: not all
Minims of nature; some of serpent kind,
Wondrous in length and corpulence, involved
Their snaky folds, and added wings. First crept
The parsimonious emmet, provident
Of future, in small room large heart enclosed—
Pattern of just equality perhaps
Hereafter—join'd in her popular tribes
Of commonalty. Swarming next appeared
The female bee, that feeds her husband drone        490
Deliciously, and builds her waxen cells
With honey stored. The rest are numberless,
And thou their natures know'st, and gav'st them names,
Needless to thee repeated; nor unknown
The serpent, subtlest beast of all the field,
Of huge extent sometimes, with brazen eyes
And hairy mane terrific, though to thee
Not noxious, but obedient at thy call.
  'Now Heaven in all her glory shone, and rolled
Her motions, as the great First Mover's hand        500
First wheeled their course; Earth, in her rich attire
Consummate lovely smiled; air, water, earth,
By fowl, fish, beast, was flown, was swum, was walked,
Frequent; and of the sixth day yet remained.
There wanted yet the master-work, the end
Of all yet done—a creature who, not prone
And brute as other creatures, but endued
With sanctity of reason, might erect
His stature, and upright with front serene
Govern the rest, self-knowing, and from thence        510

Magnanimous to correspond with Heaven,
But grateful to acknowledge whence his good
Descends; thither with heart, and voice, and eyes
Directed in devotion, to adore
And worship God Supreme, who made him chief
Of all his works.  Therefore the Omnipotent
Eternal Father (for where is not he
Present?) thus to his Son audibly spake:—
    "Let us make now Man in our image, Man
In our similitude, and let them rule                          520
Over the fish and fowl of sea and air,
Beast of the field, and over all the earth,
And every creeping thing that creeps the ground."
This said, he formed thee, Adam, thee, O Man,
Dust of the ground, and in thy nostrils breathed
The breath of life; in his own image he
Created thee, in the image of God
Express, and thou becam'st a living soul.
Male he created thee, but thy consort
Female, for race; then blessed mankind, and said:—
"Be fruitful, multiply, and fill the Earth;                   531
Subdue it, and throughout dominion hold
Over fish of the sea, and fowl of the air,
And every living thing that moves on the Earth!"
Wherever thus created—for no place
Is yet distinct by name—thence, as thou know'st,
He brought thee into this delicious grove,
This garden, planted with the trees of God,
Delectable both to behold and taste,
And freely all their pleasant fruit for food                  540
Gave thee.  All sorts are here that all th' earth yields,
Variety without end; but of the tree
Which, tasted, works knowledge of good and evil
Thou may'st not; in the day thou eat'st thou diest.
Death is the penalty imposed; beware,
And govern well thy appetite, lest Sin
Surprise thee, and her black attendant, Death.
    'Here finished he, and all that he had made
Viewed, and, behold! all was entirely good.
So even and morn accomplished the sixth day;                  550
Yet not till the Creator, from his work

Desisting, though unwearied, up returned,
Up to the Heaven of Heavens, his high abode,
Thence to behold this new-created World,
Th' addition of his empire, how it showed
In prospect from his throne, how good, how fair,
Answering his great idea.  Up he rode,
Followed with acclamation, and the sound
Symphonious of ten thousand harps, that tuned
Angelic harmonies: the earth, the air                    560
Resounded (thou remember'st, for thou heard'st),
The Heavens and all the constellations rung,
The planets in their stations listening stood
While the bright pomp ascended jubilant.
"Open, ye everlasting gates!" they sung;
"Open, ye Heavens, your living doors! let in
The great Creator, from his work returned
Magnificent, his six days' work, a World!
Open, and henceforth oft; for God will deign
To visit oft the dwellings of just men                    570
Delighted, and with frequent intercourse
Thither will send his winged messengers
On errands of supernal grace."  So sung
The glorious train ascending: he through Heaven,
That opened wide her blazing portals, led
To God's eternal house direct the way—
A broad and ample road, whose dust is gold,
And pavement stars, as stars to thee appear
Seen in the galaxy, that milky way
Which nightly as a circling zone thou seest                    580
Powdered with stars.  And now on Earth the seventh
Evening arose in Eden—for the sun
Was set, and twilight from the east came on,
Forerunning night—when at the holy mount
Of Heaven's high-seated top, th' imperial throne
Of Godhead, fixed for ever firm and sure,
The Filial Power arrived, and sat him down
With his great Father; for he also went
Invisible, yet stayed (such privilege
Hath Omnipresence) and the work ordained,                    590
Author and end of all things, and, from work
Now resting, blessed and hallowed the seventh day,

As resting on that day from all his work;
But not in silence holy kept: the harp
Had work, and rested not; the solemn pipe
And dulcimer, all organs of sweet stop,
All sounds on fret by string or golden wire,
Tempered soft tunings, intermixed with voice
Choral or unison; of incense clouds,  600
Fuming from golden censers, hid the Mount.
Creation and the six days' acts they sung:—
"Great are thy works, Jehovah! infinite
Thy power! what thought can measure thee, or tongue
Relate thee—greater now in thy return
Than from the giant-angels? Thee that day
Thy thunders magnified; but to create
Is greater than created to destroy.
Who can impair thee, mighty King, or bound
Thy empire? Easily the proud attempt  610
Of Spirits apostate, and their counsels vain,
Thou hast repelled, while impiously they thought
Thee to diminish, and from thee withdraw
The number of thy worshippers. Who seeks
To lessen thee, against his purpose, serves
To manifest the more thy might; his evil
Thou usest, and from thence creat'st more good.
Witness this new-made World, another Heaven
From Heaven-gate not far, founded in view
On the clear hyaline, the glassy sea;  620
Of amplitude almost immense, with stars
Numerous, and every star perhaps a world
Of destined habitation—but thou know'st
Their seasons; among these the seat of men,
Earth, with her nether ocean circumfused,
Their pleasant dwelling-place. Thrice happy men,
And sons of men, whom God hath thus advanced,
Created in his image, there to dwell
And worship him, and in reward to rule
Over his works, on earth, in sea, or air,  630
And multiply a race of worshippers
Holy and just! thrice happy, if they know
Their happiness, and persevere upright!"
    'So sung they, and the Empyrean rung

With halleluiahs: thus was Sabbath kept.
And thy request think now fulfilled, that asked
How first this World and face of things began,
And what before thy memory was done
From the beginning, that posterity,
Informed by thee, might know; if else thou seek'st
Aught, not surpassing human measure, say.'　　　640

*The End of the Seventh Book.*

# PARADISE LOST

## BOOK VIII

### THE ARGUMENT

*Adam inquires concerning celestial motions, is doubtfully answered, and exhorted to search rather things more worthy of knowledge. Adam assents, and, still desirous to detain Raphael, relates to him what he remembered since his own creation—his placing in Paradise; his talk with God concerning solitude and fit society; his first meeting and nuptials with Eve. His discourse with the Angel thereupon; who, after admonitions repeated, departs.*

THE Angel ended, and in Adam's ear
So charming left his voice that he a while
Thought him still speaking, still stood fixed to hear;
Then, as new-waked, thus gratefully replied:—
'What thanks sufficient, or what recompense
Equal, have I to render thee, divine
Historian, who thus largely hast allayed
The thirst I had of knowledge, and vouchsafed
This friendly condescension to relate
Things else by me unsearchable—now heard          10
With wonder, but delight, and, as is due,
With glory attributed to the high
Creator? Something yet of doubt remains,
Which only thy solution can resolve.
When I behold this goodly frame, this World,
Of Heaven and Earth consisting, and compute
Their magnitudes—this Earth, a spot, a grain,
An atom, with the firmament compared
And all her numbered stars, that seem to roll
Spaces incomprehensible (for such          20
Their distance argues, and their swift return
Diurnal) merely to officiate light
Round this opacous Earth, this punctual spot,
One day and night; in all their vast survey

Useless besides; reasoning, I oft admire
How Nature, wise and frugal, could commit
Such disproportions, with superfluous hand
So many nobler bodies to create,
Greater so manifold, to this one use,
For aught appears, and on their orbs impose          30
Such restless revolution day by day
Repeated, while the sedentary Earth,
That better might with far less compass move,
Served by more noble than herself, attains
Her end without least motion, and receives,
As tribute, such a sumless journey brought
Of incorporeal speed, her warmth and light:
Speed, to describe whose swiftness number fails.'
    So spake our Sire, and by his count'nance seemed
Entering on studious thoughts abstruse; which Eve          40
Perceiving, where she sat retired in sight,
With lowliness majestic from her seat,
And grace that won who saw to wish her stay,
Rose, and went forth among her fruits and flowers,
To visit how they prospered, bud and bloom,
Her nursery; they at her coming sprung,
And, touched by her fair tendance, gladlier grew.
Yet went she not as not with such discourse
Delighted, or not capable her ear
Of what was high; such pleasure she reserved,          50
Adam relating, she sole auditress;
Her husband the relater she preferred
Before the Angel, and of him to ask
Chose rather; he, she knew, would intermix
Grateful digressions, and solve high dispute
With conjugal caresses: from his lip
Not words alone pleased her. Oh, when meet now
Such pairs, in love and mutual honour joined?
With goddess-like demeanour forth she went,
Not unattended; for on her as queen          60
A pomp of winning Graces waited still,
And from about her shot darts of desire
Into all eyes, to wish her still in sight.
And Raphael now to Adam's doubt proposed
Benevolent and facile thus replied:—

'To ask or search I blame thee not; for Heaven
Is as the Book of God before thee set,
Wherein to read his wondrous works, and learn
His seasons, hours, or days, or months, or years.
This to attain, whether Heaven move or Earth          70
Imports not, if thou reckon right; the rest
From Man or Angel the great Architect
Did wisely to conceal, and not divulge
His secrets, to be scanned by them who ought
Rather admire. Or, if they list to try
Conjecture, he his fabric of the Heavens
Hath left to their disputes—perhaps to move
His laughter at their quaint opinions wide
Hereafter, when they come to model Heaven,
And calculate the stars; how they will wield          80
The mighty frame; how build, unbuild, contrive
To save appearances; how gird the sphere
With centric and eccentric scribbled o'er,
Cycle and epicycle, orb in orb.
Already by thy reasoning this I guess,
Who art to lead thy offspring, and supposest
That bodies bright and greater should not serve
The less not bright, nor Heaven such journeys run,
Earth sitting still, when she alone receives
The benefit: consider, first, that great             90
Or bright infers not excellence: the Earth,
Though, in comparison of Heaven, so small,
Nor glistering, may of solid good contain
More plenty than the Sun that barren shines,
Whose virtue on itself works no effect,
But in the fruitful Earth; there first received,
His beams, unactive else, their vigour find.
Yet not to Earth are those bright luminaries
Officious, but to thee, Earth's habitant.
And, for the Heaven's wide circuit, let it speak     100
The Maker's high magnificence, who built
So spacious, and his line stretched out so far,
That Man may know he dwells not in his own—
An edifice too large for him to fill,
Lodged in a small partition, and the rest
Ordained for uses to his Lord best known.

The swiftness of those circles attribute,
Though numberless, to his omnipotence,
That to corporeal substances could add
Speed almost spiritual. Me thou think'st not slow,   110
Who since the morning-hour set out from Heaven
Where God resides, and ere midday arrived
In Eden, distance inexpressible
By numbers that have name. But this I urge,
Admitting motion in the Heavens, to show
Invalid that which thee to doubt it moved;
Not that I so affirm, though so it seem
To thee who hast thy dwelling here on Earth.
God, to remove his ways from human sense,
Placed Heaven from Earth so far, that earthly sight,   120
If it presume, might err in things too high,
And no advantage gain. What if the Sun
Be centre to the World, and other stars,
By his attractive virtue and their own
Incited, dance about him various rounds?
Their wandering course, now high, now low, then hid,
Progressive, retrograde, or standing still,
In six thou seest; and what if, seventh to these,
The planet Earth, so steadfast though she seem,
Insensibly three different motions move?   130
Which else to several spheres thou must ascribe,
Moved contrary with thwart obliquities,
Or save the Sun his labour, and that swift
Nocturnal and diurnal rhomb supposed,
Invisible else above all stars, the wheel
Of Day and Night; which needs not thy belief,
If Earth, industrious of herself, fetch Day,
Travelling east, and with her part averse
From the Sun's beam meet Night, her other part
Still luminous by his ray. What if that light,   140
Sent from her through the wide transpicuous air,
To the terrestrial Moon be as a star,
Enlightening her by day, as she by night
This Earth—reciprocal, if land be there,
Fields and inhabitants? Her spots thou seest
As clouds, and clouds may rain, and rain produce
Fruits in her softened soil, for some to eat

Allotted there; and other Suns, perhaps,
With their attendant Moons, thou wilt descry,
Communicating male and female light—                    150
Which two great sexes animate the World,
Stored in each orb perhaps with some that live.
For such vast room in Nature unpossessed
By living soul, desert and desolate,
Only to shine, yet scarce to contribute
Each orb a glimpse of light, conveyed so far
Down to this habitable, which returns
Light back to them, is obvious to dispute.
But whether thus these things, or whether not—
Whether the Sun, predominant in heaven,                 160
Rise on the Earth, or Earth rise on the Sun;
He from the east his flaming road begin,
Or she from west her silent course advance
With inoffensive pace that spinning sleeps
On her soft axle, while she paces even,
And bears thee soft with the smooth air along—
Solicit not thy thoughts with matters hid:
Leave them to God above; him serve and fear.
Of other creatures as him pleases best,
Wherever placed, let him dispose; joy thou              170
In what he gives to thee, this Paradise
And thy fair Eve; Heaven is for thee too high
To know what passes there. Be lowly wise;
Think only what concerns thee and thy being;
Dream not of other worlds, what creatures there
Live, in what state, condition, or degree—
Contented that thus far hath been revealed
Not of Earth only, but of highest Heaven.'
     To whom thus Adam, cleared of doubt, replied:—
'How fully hast thou satisfied me, pure                 180
Intelligence of Heaven, Angel serene,
And, freed from intricacies, taught to live
The easiest way, nor with perplexing thoughts
To interrupt the sweet of life, from which
God hath bid dwell far off all anxious cares,
And not molest us, unless we ourselves
Seek them with wandering thoughts, and notions vain!
But apt the mind or fancy is to rove

Unchecked, and of her roving is no end;
Till, warned, or by experience taught, she learn        190
That not to know at large of things remote
From use, obscure and subtle, but to know
That which before us lies in daily life,
Is the prime wisdom: what is more is fume,
Or emptiness, or fond impertinence,
And renders us in things that most concern
Unpractised, unprepared, and still to seek.
Therefore from this high pitch let us descend
A lower flight, and speak of things at hand
Useful; whence, haply, mention may arise        200
Of something not unseasonable to ask,
By sufferance, and thy wonted favour, deigned.
Thee I have heard relating what was done
Ere my remembrance; now hear me relate
My story, which, perhaps, thou hast not heard;
And day is yet not spent; till then thou seest
How subtly to detain thee I devise,
Inviting thee to hear while I relate—
Fond, were it not in hope of thy reply.
For, while I sit with thee, I seem in Heaven;        210
And sweeter thy discourse is to my ear
Than fruits of palm-tree, pleasantest to thirst
And hunger both, from labour, at the hour
Of sweet repast; they satiate, and soon fill,
Though pleasant; but thy words, with grace divine
Imbued, bring to their sweetness no satiety.'
        To whom thus Raphael answered, heavenly meek:—
'Nor are thy lips ungraceful, Sire of Men,
Nor tongue ineloquent; for God on thee
Abundantly his gifts hath also poured,        220
Inward and outward both, his image fair:
Speaking or mute all comeliness and grace
Attends thee, and each word, each motion, forms.
Nor less think we in Heaven of thee on Earth
Than of our fellow-servant, and inquire
Gladly into the ways of God with Man;
For God, we see, hath honoured thee, and set
On Man his equal love.  Say therefore on;
For I that day was absent, as befell,

Bound on a voyage uncouth and obscure,                    230
Far on excursion toward the gates of Hell,
Squared in full legion (such command we had),
To see that none thence issued forth a spy
Or enemy, while God was in his work,
Lest he, incensed at such eruption bold,
Destruction with Creation might have mixed.
Not that they durst without his leave attempt;
But us he sends upon his high behests
For state, as sovran King, and to inure
Our prompt obedience. Fast we found, fast shut,          240
The dismal gates, and barricadoed strong;
But, long ere our approaching, heard within
Noise, other than the sound of dance or song—
Torment, and loud lament, and furious rage.
Glad we returned up to the coasts of Light
Ere Sabbath-evening; so we had in charge.
But thy relation now; for I attend,
Pleased with thy words no less than thou with mine.'
      So spake the godlike Power, and thus our Sire:—
'For Man to tell how human life began                    250
Is hard; for who himself beginning knew?
Desire with thee still longer to converse
Induced me. As new-waked from soundest sleep,
Soft on the flowery herb I found me laid,
In balmy sweat, which with his beams the Sun
Soon dried, and on the reeking moisture fed.
Straight toward Heaven my wondering eyes I turned,
And gazed a while the ample sky, till, raised
By quick instinctive motion, up I sprung,
As thitherward endeavouring, and upright                 260
Stood on my feet. About me round I saw
Hill, dale, and shady woods, and sunny plains,
And liquid lapse of murmuring streams; by these,
Creatures that lived and moved, and walked or flew,
Birds on the branches warbling: all things smiled;
With fragrance and with joy my heart o'erflowed.
Myself I then perused, and limb by limb
Surveyed, and sometimes went, and sometimes ran
With supple joints, as lively vigour led;
But who I was, or where, or from what cause,             270

Knew not. To speak I tried, and forthwith spake;
My tongue obeyed, and readily could name
Whate'er I saw. "Thou Sun," said I, "fair light,
And thou enlightened Earth, so fresh and gay,
Ye hills and dales, ye rivers, woods, and plains,
And ye that live and move, fair creatures, tell,
Tell, if ye saw, how came I thus, how here?
Not of myself; by some great Maker then,
In goodness and in power pre-eminent.
Tell me, how may I know him, how adore,　　　　280
From whom I have that thus I move and live,
And feel that I am happier than I know?"
While thus I called, and strayed I knew not whither,
From where I first drew air, and first beheld
This happy light, when answer none returned,
On a green shady bank, profuse of flowers,
Pensive I sat me down. There gentle sleep
First found me, and with soft oppression seized
My drowsed sense, untroubled, though I thought
I then was passing to my former state　　　　290
Insensible, and forthwith to dissolve:
When suddenly stood at my head a dream,
Whose inward apparition gently moved
My fancy to believe I yet had being,
And lived. One came, methought, of shape divine,
And said, "Thy mansion wants thee, Adam; rise,
First Man, of men innumerable ordained
First father! called by thee, I come thy guide
To the garden of bliss, thy seat prepared."
So saying, by the hand he took me, raised,　　　　300
And over fields and waters, as in air
Smooth sliding without step, last led me up
A woody mountain, whose high top was plain,
A circuit wide, enclosed, with goodliest trees
Planted, with walks, and bowers, that what I saw
Of Earth before scarce pleasant seemed. Each tree
Loaden with fairest fruit, that hung to the eye
Tempting, stirred in me sudden appetite
To pluck and eat; whereat I waked, and found
Before mine eyes all real, as the dream　　　　310
Had lively shadowed. Here had new begun

My wandering, had not he who was my guide
Up hither from among the trees appeared,
Presence Divine. Rejoicing, but with awe,
In adoration at his feet I fell
Submiss. He reared me, and, "Whom thou sought'st
      I am,"
Said mildly, "Author of all this thou seest
Above, or round about thee, or beneath.
This Paradise I give thee; count it thine
To till and keep, and of the fruit to eat:          320
Of every tree that in the garden grows
Eat freely with glad heart; fear here no dearth:
But of the tree whose operation brings
Knowledge of good and ill, which I have set,
The pledge of thy obedience and thy faith,
Amid the garden by the Tree of Life—
Remember what I warn thee—shun to taste,
And shun the bitter consequence: for know,
The day thou eat'st thereof, my sole command
Transgressed, inevitably thou shalt die;            330
From that day mortal, and this happy state
Shalt lose, expelled from hence into a world
Of woe and sorrow." Sternly he pronounced
The rigid interdiction, which resounds
Yet dreadful in mine ear, though in my choice
Not to incur; but soon his clear aspect
Returned, and gracious purpose thus renewed:—
"Not only these fair bounds, but all the Earth
To thee and to thy race I give; as lords
Possess it, and all things that therein live,       340
Or live in sea or air, beast, fish, and fowl.
In sign whereof, each bird and beast behold
After their kinds; I bring them to receive
From thee their names, and pay thee fealty
With low subjection. Understand the same
Of fish within their wat'ry residence,
Not hither summoned, since they cannot change
Their element to draw the thinner air."
As thus he spake, each bird and beast behold
Approaching two and two—these cowering low          350
With blandishment; each bird stooped on his wing.

I named them as they passed, and understood
Their nature; with such knowledge God endued
My sudden apprehension. But in these
I found not what methought I wanted still,
And to the Heavenly Vision thus presumed:—
   '"O, by what name—for thou above all these,
Above mankind, or aught than mankind higher,
Surpassest far my naming—how may I
Adore thee, Author of this Universe,                     360
And all this good to Man, for whose well-being
So amply, and with hands so liberal,
Thou hast provided all things? But with me
I see not who partakes. In solitude
What happiness? who can enjoy alone,
Or, all enjoying, what contentment find?"
Thus I, presumptuous; and the Vision bright,
As with a smile more brightened, thus replied:—
   '"What call'st thou solitude? Is not the earth
With various living creatures, and the air,               370
Replenished, and all these at thy command
To come and play before thee? Know'st thou not
Their language and their ways? They also know,
And reason not contemptibly; with these
Find pastime, and bear rule; thy realm is large."
So spake the Universal Lord, and seemed
So ordering. I, with leave of speech implored,
And humble deprecation, thus replied:—
   '"Let not my words offend thee, Heavenly Power;
My Maker, be propitious while I speak.                    380
Hast thou not made me here thy substitute,
And these inferior far beneath me set?
Among unequals what society
Can sort, what harmony or true delight?
Which must be mutual, in proportion due
Given and received; but, in disparity,
The one intense, the other still remiss,
Cannot well suit with either, but soon prove
Tedious alike. Of fellowship I speak
Such as I seek, fit to participate                        390
All rational delight, wherein the brute
Cannot be human consort. They rejoice

Each with their kind, lion with lioness;
So fitly them in pairs thou hast combined:
Much less can bird with beast, or fish with fowl,
So well converse, nor with the ox the ape;
Worse, then, can man with beast, and least of all."
    'Whereto th' Almighty answered, not displeased:—
"A nice and subtle happiness, I see,
Thou to thyself proposest, in the choice                               400
Of thy associates, Adam, and wilt taste
No pleasure, though in pleasure, solitary.
What think'st thou, then, of me, and this my state?
Seem I to thee sufficiently possessed
Of happiness, or not, who am alone
From all eternity? for none I know
Second to me or like, equal much less.
How have I, then, with whom to hold converse,
Save with the creatures which I made, and those
To me inferior, infinite descents                                      410
Beneath what other creatures are to thee?"
    'He ceased, I lowly answered.—"To attain
The height and depth of thy eternal ways
All human thoughts come short, Supreme of Things!
Thou in thyself art perfect, and in thee
Is no deficience found; not so is Man,
But in degree—the cause of his desire
By conversation with his like to help
Or solace his defects. No need that thou
Should'st propagate, already infinite,                                 420
And through all numbers absolute, though One;
But Man by number is to manifest
His single imperfection, and beget
Like of his like, his image multiplied,
In unity defective, which requires
Collateral love, and dearest amity.
Thou, in thy secrecy although alone,
Best with thyself accompanied, seek'st not
Social communication—yet, so pleased,
Canst raise thy creature to what height thou wilt                      430
Of union or communion, deified;
I, by conversing, cannot these erect
From prone, nor in their ways complacence find."

Thus I emboldened spake, and freedom used
Permissive, and acceptance found, which gained
This answer from the gracious Voice Divine:—
  ' "Thus far to try thee, Adam, I was pleased,
And find thee knowing not of beasts alone,
Which thou hast rightly named, but of thyself—
Expressing well the spirit within thee free,          440
My image, not imparted to the brute;
Whose fellowship, therefore, unmeet for thee,
Good reason was thou freely shouldst dislike,
And be so minded still; I, ere thou spak'st,
Knew it not good for Man to be alone,
And no such company as then thou saw'st
Intended thee—for trial only brought,
To see how thou couldst judge of fit and meet.
What next I bring shall please thee, be assured,
Thy likeness, thy fit help, thy other self,          450
Thy wish exactly to thy heart's desire."
  'He ended, or I heard no more; for now
My earthly, by his heavenly overpowered,
Which it had long stood under, strained to the height
In that celestial colloquy sublime,
As with an object that excels the sense,
Dazzled and spent, sunk down, and sought repair
Of sleep, which instantly fell on me, called
By Nature as in aid, and closed mine eyes.
Mine eyes he closed, but open left the cell         460
Of fancy, my internal sight; by which,
Abstract as in a trance, methought I saw,
Though sleeping, where I lay, and saw the Shape
Still glorious before whom awake I stood;
Who, stooping, opened my left side, and took
From thence a rib, with cordial spirits warm,
And life-blood streaming fresh; wide was the wound,
But suddenly with flesh filled up and healed.
The rib he formed and fashioned with his hands;
Under his forming hands a creature grew,         470
Man-like, but different sex, so lovely fair
That what seemed fair in all the world seemed now
Mean, or in her summed up, in her contained,
And in her looks, which from that time infused

Sweetness into my heart, unfelt before,
And into all things from her air inspired
The spirit of love and amorous delight.
She disappeared, and left me dark; I waked
To find her, or for ever to deplore
Her loss, and other pleasures all abjure:                    480
When out of hope, behold her, not far off,
Such as I saw her in my dream, adorned
With what all Earth or Heaven could bestow
To make her amiable.  On she came,
Led by her Heavenly Maker, though unseen,
And guided by his voice, nor uninformed
Of nuptial sanctity and marriage rites.
Grace was in all her steps, Heaven in her eye,
In every gesture dignity and love.
I, overjoyed, could not forbear aloud:—              490
' "This turn hath made amends; thou hast fulfilled
Thy words, Creator bounteous and benign,
Giver of all things fair—but fairest this
Of all thy gifts!—nor enviest.  I now see
Bone of my bone, flesh of my flesh, my self
Before me; Woman is her name, of Man
Extracted; for this cause he shall forgo
Father and mother, and to his wife adhere;
And they shall be one flesh, one heart, one soul."
    'She heard me thus; and, though divinely brought,
Yet innocence and virgin modesty,                    501
Her virtue, and the conscience of her worth,
That would be wooed, and not unsought be won,
Not obvious, not obtrusive, but retired,
The more desirable—or, to say all,
Nature herself, though pure of sinful thought—
Wrought in her so, that, seeing me, she turned.
I followed her; she what was honour knew,
And with obsequious majesty approved
My pleaded reason.  To the nuptial bower             510
I led her blushing like the Morn; all Heaven,
And happy constellations, on that hour
Shed their selectest influence; the Earth
Gave sign of gratulation, and each hill;
Joyous the birds; fresh gales and gentle airs

Whispered it to the woods, and from their wings
Flung rose, flung odours from the spicy shrub,
Disporting, till the amorous bird of night
Sung spousal, and bid haste the Evening-star
On his hill-top to light the bridal lamp.          520

'Thus I have told thee all my state, and brought
My story to the sum of earthly bliss
Which I enjoy, and must confess to find
In all things else delight indeed, but such
As, used or not, works in the mind no change,
Nor vehement desire—these delicacies
I mean of taste, sight, smell, herbs, fruits, and flowers,
Walks, and the melody of birds: but here,
Far otherwise, transported I behold,
Transported touch; here passion first I felt,          530
Commotion strange, in all enjoyments else
Superior and unmoved, here only weak
Against the charm of beauty's powerful glance.
Or Nature failed in me, and left some part
Not proof enough such object to sustain,
Or, from my side subducting, took perhaps
More than enough—at least on her bestowed
Too much of ornament, in outward show
Elaborate, of inward less exact.
For well I understand in the prime end          540
Of Nature her th' inferior, in the mind
And inward faculties, which most excel;
In outward also her resembling less
His image who made both, and less expressing
The character of that dominion given
O'er other creatures.  Yet when I approach
Her loveliness, so absolute she seems
And in herself complete, so well to know
Her own, that what she wills to do or say
Seems wisest, virtuousest, discreetest, best.          550
All higher knowledge in her presence falls
Degraded; Wisdom in discourse with her
Loses, discount'nanced, and like Folly shows;
Authority and Reason on her wait,
As one intended first, not after made
Occasionally; and, to consummate all,

Greatness of mind and nobleness their seat
Build in her loveliest, and create an awe
About her, as a guard angelic placed.'
    To whom the Angel, with contracted brow:—          560
'Accuse not Nature! she hath done her part;
Do thou but thine! and be not diffident
Of Wisdom; she deserts thee not, if thou
Dismiss not her, when most thou need'st her nigh,
By attributing overmuch to things
Less excellent, as thou thyself perceiv'st.
For what admir'st thou, what transports thee so?
An outside; fair, no doubt, and worthy well
Thy cherishing, thy honouring, and thy love;
Not thy subjection: weigh with her thyself;          570
Then value: oft-times nothing profits more
Than self-esteem, grounded on just and right
Well managed. Of that skill, the more thou know'st,
The more she will acknowledge thee her head,
And to realities yield all her shows—
Made so adorn for thy delight the more,
So awful, that with honour thou may'st love
Thy mate, who sees when thou art seen least wise.
But, if the sense of touch, whereby mankind
Is propagated, seem such dear delight          580
Beyond all other, think the same vouchsafed
To cattle and each beast; which would not be
To them made common and divulged, if aught
Therein enjoyed were worthy to subdue
The soul of Man, or passion in him move.
What higher in her society thou find'st
Attractive, human, rational, love still:
In loving thou dost well; in passion not,
Wherein true love consists not. Love refines
The thoughts, and heart enlarges—hath his seat          590
In Reason, and is judicious, is the scale
By which to heavenly love thou may'st ascend,
Not sunk in carnal pleasure; for which cause
Among the beasts no mate for thee was found.'
    To whom thus, half abashed, Adam replied:
'Neither her outside formed so fair, nor aught
In procreation, common to all kinds

(Though higher of the genial bed by far,
And with mysterious reverence, I deem),
So much delights me as those graceful acts,        600
Those thousand decencies, that daily flow
From all her words and actions, mixed with love
And sweet compliance, which declare unfeigned
Union of mind, or in us both one soul—
Harmony to behold in wedded pair
More grateful than harmonious sound to the ear.
Yet these subject not; I to thee disclose
What inward thence I feel, not therefore foiled,
Who meet with various objects, from the sense
Variously representing; yet, still free,        610
Approve the best, and follow what I approve.
To love thou blam'st me not; for Love, thou say'st,
Leads up to Heaven, is both the way and guide;
Bear with me, then, if lawful what I ask.
Love not the Heavenly Spirits, and how their love
Express they, by looks only, or do they mix
Irradiance, virtual or immediate touch?'
    To whom the Angel, with a smile that glowed
Celestial rosy-red, Love's proper hue,
Answered:—'Let it suffice thee that thou know'st        620
Us happy, and without Love no happiness.
Whatever pure thou in the body enjoy'st
(And pure thou wert created) we enjoy
In eminence, and obstacle find none
Of membrane, joint, or limb, exclusive bars:
Easier than air with air, if Spirits embrace,
Total they mix, union of pure with pure
Desiring, nor restrained conveyance need
As flesh to mix with flesh, or soul with soul.
But I can now no more: the parting Sun        630
Beyond the Earth's green cape and verdant isles
Hesperean sets, my signal to depart.
Be strong, live happy, and love! but first of all
Him whom to love is to obey, and keep
His great command; take heed lest passion sway
Thy judgement to do aught which else free-will
Would not admit; thine and of all thy sons
The weal or woe in thee is placed; beware!

Anger and just rebuke, and judgement given,                    10
That brought into this World a world of woe,
Sin and her shadow Death, and Misery,
Death's harbinger. Sad task! yet argument
Not less but more heroic than the wrath
Of stern Achilles on his foe pursued
Thrice fugitive about Troy wall; or rage
Of Turnus for Lavinia disespoused;
Or Neptune's ire, or Juno's, that so long
Perplexed the Greek and Cytherea's son:
If answerable style I can obtain                    20
Of my celestial patroness, who deigns
Her nightly visitation unimplored,
And dictates to me slumbering, or inspires
Easy my unpremeditated verse;
Since first this subject for heroic song
Pleased me, long choosing and beginning late;
Not sedulous by nature to indite
Wars, hitherto the only argument
Heroic deemed, chief mastery to dissect
With long and tedious havoc fabled knights                    30
In battles feigned (the better fortitude
Of patience and heroic martyrdom
Unsung), or to describe races and games,
Or tilting furniture, emblazoned shields,
Impresses quaint, caparisons and steeds,
Bases and tinsel trappings, gorgeous knights
At joust and tournament; then marshalled feast
Served up in hall with sewers and seneschals:
The skill of artifice or office mean;
Not that which justly gives heroic name                    40
To person or to poem! Me, of these
Nor skilled nor studious, higher argument
Remains, sufficient of itself to raise
That name, unless an age too late, or cold
Climate, or years, damp my intended wing
Depressed; and much they may if all be mine,
Not hers who brings it nightly to my ear.
     The sun was sunk, and after him the star
Of Hesperus, whose office is to bring
Twilight upon the Earth, short arbiter                    50

'Twixt day and night, and now from end to end
Night's hemisphere had veiled the horizon round,
When Satan, who late fled before the threats
Of Gabriel out of Eden, now improved
In meditated fraud and malice, bent
On Man's destruction, maugre what might hap
Of heavier on himself, fearless returned.
By night he fled, and at midnight returned
From compassing the Earth; cautious of day,
Since Uriel, Regent of the Sun, descried        60
His entrance, and forewarned the Cherubim
That kept their watch. Thence full of anguish driven,
The space of seven continued nights he rode
With darkness—thrice the equinoctial line
He circled, four times crossed the car of Night
From pole to pole, traversing each colure—
On the eighth returned, and on the coast averse
From entrance or cherubic watch by stealth
Found unsuspected way. There was a place
(Now not, though Sin, not Time, first wrought the
        change)        70
Where Tigris, at the foot of Paradise,
Into a gulf shot under ground, till part
Rose up a fountain by the Tree of Life.
In with the river sunk, and with it rose
Satan, involved in rising mist; then sought
Where to lie hid. Sea he had searched and land
From Eden over Pontus, and the Pool
Maeotis, up beyond the river Ob;
Downward as far antarctic; and, in length,
West from Orontes to the ocean barred        80
At Darien, thence to the land where flows
Ganges and Indus. Thus the orb he roamed
With narrow search, and with inspection deep
Considered every creature, which of all
Most opportune might serve his wiles, and found
The Serpent subtlest beast of all the field.
Him, after long debate, irresolute
Of thoughts revolved, his final sentence chose
Fit vessel, fittest imp of fraud, in whom
To enter, and his dark suggestions hide        90

From sharpest sight; for in the wily snake,
Whatever sleights, none would suspicious mark,
As from his wit and native subtlety
Proceeding, which, in other beasts observed,
Doubt might beget of diabolic power
Active within beyond the sense of brute.
Thus he resolved, but first from inward grief
His bursting passion into plaints thus poured:—
  'O Earth, how like to Heaven, if not preferred
More justly, seat worthier of gods, as built          100
With second thoughts, reforming what was old!
For what God, after better, worse would build?
Terrestrial Heaven, danced round by other Heavens,
That shine, yet bear their bright officious lamps,
Light above light, for thee alone, as seems,
In thee concentring all their precious beams
Of sacred influence! As God in Heaven
Is centre, yet extends to all, so thou
Centring receiv'st from all those orbs; in thee,
Not in themselves, all their known virtue appears,          110
Productive in herb, plant, and nobler birth
Of creatures animate with gradual life
Of growth, sense, reason, all summed up in Man.
With what delight could I have walked thee round,
If I could joy in aught—sweet interchange
Of hill and valley, rivers, woods, and plains,
Now land, now sea, and shores with forest crowned,
Rocks, dens, and caves! But I in none of these
Find place or refuge; and the more I see
Pleasures about me, so much more I feel          120
Torment within me, as from the hateful siege
Of contraries; all good to me becomes
Bane, and in Heaven much worse would be my state.
But neither here seek I, no, nor in Heaven,
To dwell, unless by mast'ring Heaven's Supreme:
Nor hope to be myself less miserable
By what I seek, but others to make such
As I, though thereby worse to me redound.
For only in destroying I find ease
To my relentless thoughts; and him destroyed,          130
Or won to what may work his utter loss,

For whom all this was made, all this will soon
Follow, as to him linked in weal or woe:
In woe then, that destruction wide may range!
To me shall be the glory sole among
The Infernal Powers, in one day to have marred
What he, Almighty styled, six nights and days
Continued making, and who knows how long
Before had been contriving? though perhaps
Not longer than since I in one night freed          140
From servitude inglorious wellnigh half
Th' angelic name, and thinner left the throng
Of his adorers. He, to be avenged,
And to repair his numbers thus impaired—
Whether such virtue, spent of old, now failed
More Angels to create (if they at least
Are his created), or to spite us more—
Determined to advance into our room
A creature formed of earth, and him endow,
Exalted from so base original,                      150
With heavenly spoils, our spoils. What he decreed
He effected; Man he made, and for him built
Magnificent this World, and Earth his seat,
Him lord pronounced, and, O indignity!
Subjected to his service Angel-wings
And flaming ministers, to watch and tend
Their earthly charge. Of these the vigilance
I dread, and to elude, thus wrapped in mist
Of midnight vapour, glide obscure, and pry
In every bush and brake, where hap may find        160
The Serpent sleeping, in whose mazy folds
To hide me, and the dark intent I bring.
O foul descent! that I, who erst contended
With Gods to sit the highest, am now constrained
Into a beast, and, mixed with bestial slime,
This essence to incarnate and imbrute,
That to the height of deity aspired;
But what will not ambition and revenge
Descend to? Who aspires must down as low
As high he soared, obnoxious, first or last,        170
To basest things. Revenge, at first though sweet,
Bitter ere long back on itself recoils.

Let it; I reck not, so it light well aimed,
Since higher I fall short, on him who next
Provokes my envy, this new favourite
Of Heaven, this man of clay, son of despite,
Whom, us the more to spite, his Maker raised
From dust: spite then with spite is best repaid.'
   So saying, through each thicket, dank or dry,
Like a black mist low-creeping, he held on 180
His midnight search, where soonest he might find
The Serpent. Him fast sleeping soon he found,
In labyrinth of many a round self-rolled,
His head the midst, well stored with subtle wiles:
Not yet in horrid shade or dismal den,
Nor nocent yet, but on the grassy herb,
Fearless, unfeared, he slept. In at his mouth
The Devil entered, and his brutal sense,
In heart or head, possessing soon inspired
With act intelligential; but his sleep 190
Disturbed not, waiting close th' approach of morn.
Now, when as sacred light began to dawn
In Eden on the humid flowers, that breathed
Their morning incense, when all things that breathe
From th' Earth's great altar send up silent praise
To the Creator, and his nostrils fill
With grateful smell, forth came the human pair,
And joined their vocal worship to the quire
Of creatures wanting voice; that done, partake
The season, prime for sweetest scents and airs; 200
Then commune how that day they best may ply
Their growing work—for much their work outgrew
The hands' dispatch of two gardening so wide:
And Eve first to her husband thus began:—
   'Adam, well may we labour still to dress
This garden, still to tend plant, herb, and flower,
Our pleasant task enjoined; but, till more hands
Aid us, the work under our labour grows
Luxurious by restraint: what we by day
Lop overgrown, or prune, or prop, or bind, 210
One night or two with wanton growth derides,
Tending to wild. Thou, therefore, now advise,
Or hear what to my mind first thoughts present.

Let us divide our labours—thou where choice
Leads thee, or where most needs, whether to wind
The woodbine round this arbour, or direct
The clasping ivy where to climb; while I
In yonder spring of roses intermixed
With myrtle find what to redress till noon.
For, while so near each other thus all day               220
Our task we choose, what wonder if so near
Looks intervene and smiles, or object new
Casual discourse draw on, which intermits
Our day's work, brought to little, though begun
Early, and th' hour of supper comes unearned!'
    To whom mild answer Adam thus returned:—
'Sole Eve, associate sole, to me beyond
Compare above all living creatures dear!
Well hast thou motioned, well thy thoughts employed
How we might best fulfil the work which here          230
God hath assigned us, nor of me shalt pass
Unpraised; for nothing lovelier can be found
In woman than to study household good,
And good works in her husband to promote.
Yet not so strictly hath our Lord imposed
Labour as to debar us when we need
Refreshment, whether food, or talk between,
Food of the mind, or this sweet intercourse
Of looks and smiles; for smiles from reason flow,
To brute denied, and are of love the food;           240
Love, not the lowest end of human life.
For not to irksome toil, but to delight,
He made us, and delight to reason joined.
These paths and bowers doubt not but our joint hands
Will keep from wilderness with ease, as wide
As we need walk, till younger hands ere long
Assist us. But, if much converse perhaps
Thee satiate, to short absence I could yield;
For solitude sometimes is best society,
And short retirement urges sweet return.              250
But other doubt possesses me, lest harm
Befall thee, severed from me; for thou know'st
What hath been warned us—what malicious foe,
Envying our happiness, and of his own

Despairing, seeks to work us woe and shame
By sly assault, and somewhere nigh at hand
Watches, no doubt, with greedy hope to find
His wish and best advantage, us asunder,
Hopeless to circumvent us joined, where each
To other speedy aid might lend at need;                    260
Whether his first design be to withdraw
Our fealty from God, or to disturb
Conjugal love—than which perhaps no bliss
Enjoyed by us excites his envy more—
Or this, or worse, leave not the faithful side
That gave thee being, still shades thee and protects.
The wife, where danger or dishonour lurks,
Safest and seemliest by her husband stays,
Who guards her, or with her the worst endures.'

    To whom the virgin majesty of Eve,                 270
As one who loves, and some unkindness meets,
With sweet austere composure thus replied:—
'Offspring of Heaven and Earth, and all Earth's lord!
That such an enemy we have, who seeks
Our ruin, both by thee informed I learn,
And from the parting Angel overheard,
As in a shady nook I stood behind,
Just then returned at shut of evening flowers.
But that thou shouldst my firmness therefore doubt
To God or thee, because we have a foe                      280
May tempt it, I expected not to hear.
His violence thou fear'st not, being such
As we, not capable of death or pain,
Can either not receive, or can repel.
His fraud is, then, thy fear; which plain infers
Thy equal fear that my firm faith and love
Can by his fraud be shaken or seduced:
Thoughts, which how found they harbour in thy breast,
Adam! misthought of her to thee so dear?'
    To whom, with healing words, Adam replied:—       290
'Daughter of God and Man, immortal Eve!
For such thou art, from sin and blame entire,
Not diffident of thee do I dissuade
Thy absence from my sight, but to avoid
Th' attempt itself, intended by our foe.

For he who tempts, though in vain, at least asperses
The tempted with dishonour foul, supposed
Not incorruptible of faith, not proof
Against temptation.  Thou thyself with scorn
And anger wouldst resent the offered wrong,            300
Though ineffectual found; misdeem not, then,
If such affront I labour to avert
From thee alone, which on us both at once
The enemy, though bold, will hardly dare;
Or, daring, first on me th' assault shall light.
Nor thou his malice and false guile contemn;
Subtle he needs must be who could seduce
Angels, nor think superfluous others' aid.
I from the influence of thy looks receive
Access in every virtue—in thy sight            310
More wise, more watchful, stronger, if need were
Of outward strength; while shame, thou looking on,
Shame to be overcome or overreached,
Would utmost vigour raise, and raised unite.
Why shouldst not thou like sense within thee feel
When I am present, and thy trial choose
With me, best witness of thy virtue tried?'
    So spake domestic Adam in his care
And matrimonial love; but Eve, who thought
Less attributed to her faith sincere,            320
Thus her reply with accent sweet renewed:—
    'If this be our condition, thus to dwell
In narrow circuit straitened by a foe,
Subtle or violent, we not endued
Single with like defence wherever met,
How are we happy, still in fear of harm?
But harm precedes not sin: only our foe
Tempting affronts us with his foul esteem
Of our integrity: his foul esteem
Sticks no dishonour on our front, but turns            330
Foul on himself; then wherefore shunned or feared
By us, who rather double honour gain
From his surmise proved false, find peace within,
Favour from Heaven, our witness, from th' event?
And what is faith, love, virtue, unassayed
Alone, without exterior help sustained?

Let us not then suspect our happy state
Left so imperfect by the Maker wise
As not secure to single or combined.
Frail is our happiness, if this be so,                    340
And Eden were no Eden, thus exposed.'
 To whom thus Adam fervently replied:—
'O Woman, best are all things as the will
Of God ordained them; his creating hand
Nothing imperfect or deficient left
Of all that he created—much less Man,
Or aught that might his happy state secure,
Secure from outward force. Within himself
The danger lies, yet lies within his power;
Against his will he can receive no harm.             350
But God left free the Will; for what obeys
Reason is free; and Reason he made right,
But bid her well beware, and still erect,
Lest, by some fair appearing good surprised,
She dictate false, and misinform the Will
To do what God expressly hath forbid.
Not then mistrust, but tender love, enjoins
That I should mind thee oft; and mind thou me.
Firm we subsist, yet possible to swerve,
Since Reason not impossibly may meet              360
Some specious object by the foe suborned,
And fall into deception unaware,
Not keeping strictest watch, as she was warned.
Seek not temptation, then, which to avoid
Were better, and most likely if from me
Thou sever not; trial will come unsought.
Wouldst thou approve thy constancy, approve
First thy obedience; th' other who can know,
Not seeing thee attempted, who attest?
But if thou think trial unsought may find           370
Us both securer than thus warned thou seem'st,
Go; for thy stay, not free, absents thee more.
Go in thy native innocence; rely
On what thou hast of virtue; summon all;
For God towards thee hath done his part: do thine.'
 So spake the Patriarch of Mankind; but Eve
Persisted; yet submiss, though last, replied:—

'With thy permission, then, and thus forewarned,
Chiefly by what thy own last reasoning words
Touched only, that our trial, when least sought,        380
May find us both perhaps far less prepared,
The willinger I go, nor much expect
A foe so proud will first the weaker seek;
So bent, the more shall shame him his repulse.'
    Thus saying, from her husband's hand her hand
Soft she withdrew, and, like a wood-nymph light,
Oread or Dryad, or of Delia's train,
Betook her to the groves, but Delia's self
In gait surpassed and goddess-like deport,
Though not as she with bow and quiver armed,        390
But with such gardening tools as Art, yet rude,
Guiltless of fire had formed, or Angels brought.
To Pales, or Pomona, thus adorned,
Likest she seemed—Pomona when she fled
Vertumnus—or to Ceres in her prime,
Yet virgin of Proserpina from Jove.
Her long with ardent look his eye pursued
Delighted, but desiring more her stay.
Oft he to her his charge of quick return
Repeated; she to him as oft engaged        400
To be returned by noon amid the bower,
And all things in best order to invite
Noontide repast, or afternoon's repose.
O much deceived, much failing, hapless Eve,
Of thy presumed return! event perverse!
Thou never from that hour in Paradise
Found'st either sweet repast or sound repose;
Such ambush, hid among sweet flowers and shades,
Waited, with hellish rancour imminent,
To intercept thy way, or send thee back        410
Despoiled of innocence, of faith, of bliss.
For now, and since first break of dawn, the Fiend,
Mere serpent in appearance, forth was come,
And on his quest where likeliest he might find
The only two of mankind, but in them
The whole included race, his purposed prey.
In bower and field he sought, where any tuft
Of grove or garden-plot more pleasant lay.

Their tendance or plantation for delight;
By fountain or by shady rivulet                          420
He sought them both, but wished his hap might find
Eve separate; he wished, but not with hope
Of what so seldom chanced, when to his wish,
Beyond his hope, Eve separate he spies,
Veiled in a cloud of fragrance, where she stood,
Half-spied, so thick the roses bushing round
About her glowed, oft stooping to support
Each flower of slender stalk, whose head, though gay
Carnation, purple, azure, or specked with gold,
Hung drooping unsustained. Them she upstays          430
Gently with myrtle band, mindless the while
Herself, though fairest unsupported flower,
From her best prop so far, and storm so nigh.
Nearer he drew, and many a walk traversed
Of stateliest covert, cedar, pine, or palm;
Then voluble and bold, now hid, now seen
Among thick-wov'n arborets and flowers
Imbordered on each bank, the hand of Eve:
Spot more delicious than those gardens feigned
Or of revived Adonis, or renowned                       440
Alcinous, host of old Laertes' son,
Or that, not mystic, where the sapient king
Held dalliance with his fair Egyptian spouse.
Much he the place admired, the person more.
As one who, long in populous city pent,
Where houses thick and sewers annoy the air,
Forth issuing on a summer's morn, to breathe
Among the pleasant villages and farms
Adjoined, from each thing met conceives delight,
The smell of grain, or tedded grass, or kine,           450
Or dairy, each rural sight, each rural sound;
If chance with nymph-like step fair virgin pass,
What pleasing seemed, for her now pleases more,
She most, and in her looks sums all delight:
Such pleasure took the Serpent to behold
This flowery plat, the sweet recess of Eve
Thus early, thus alone; her heavenly form
Angelic, but more soft and feminine,
Her graceful innocence, her every air

Of gesture **or least action**, overawed                        460
His malice, and with rapine sweet bereaved
His fierceness of the fierce intent it brought.
That space the Evil One abstracted stood
From his own evil, and for the time remained
Stupidly good, of enmity disarmed,
Of guile, of hate, of envy, of revenge.
But the hot hell that always in him burns,
Though in mid Heaven, soon ended his delight,
And tortures him now more, the more he sees
Of pleasure not for him ordained: then soon            470
Fierce hate he recollects, and all his thoughts
Of mischief, gratulating, thus excites:—
    'Thoughts, whither have ye led me? with what sweet
Compulsion thus transported to forget
What hither brought us? hate, not love, nor hope
Of Paradise for Hell, hope here to taste
Of pleasure, but all pleasure to destroy,
Save what is in destroying; other joy
To me is lost.  Then let me not let pass
Occasion which now smiles: behold alone                480
The Woman, opportune to all attempts;
Her husband, for I view far round, not nigh,
Whose higher intellectual more I shun,
And strength, of courage haughty, and of limb
Heroic built, though of terrestrial mould;
Foe not informidable, exempt from wound,
I not; so much hath Hell debased, and pain
Enfeebled me, to what I was in Heaven.
She fair, divinely fair, fit love for gods,
Not terrible, though terror be in love,                490
And beauty, not approached by stronger hate,
Hate stronger under show of love well feigned,
The way which to her ruin now I tend.'
    So spake the Enemy of Mankind, enclosed
In serpent, inmate bad, and toward Eve
Addressed his way; not with indented wave,
Prone on the ground, as since, but on his rear,
Circular base of rising folds, that towered
Fold above fold, a surging maze; his head
Crested aloft, and carbuncle his eyes;                500

With burnished neck of verdant gold, erect
Amidst his circling spires, that on the grass
Floated redundant. Pleasing was his shape
And lovely; never since of serpent kind
Lovelier—not those that in Illyria changed
Hermione and Cadmus, or the god
In Epidaurus; nor to which transformed
Ammonian Jove, or Capitoline, was seen,
He with Olympias, this with her who bore
Scipio, the height of Rome. With tract oblique          510
At first, as one who sought access but feared
To interrupt, sidelong he works his way.
As when a ship, by skilful steersman wrought
Nigh river's mouth or foreland, where the wind
Veers oft, as oft so steers, and shifts her sail,
So varied he, and of his tortuous train
Curled many a wanton wreath in sight of Eve,
To lure her eye; she, busied, heard the sound
Of rustling leaves, but minded not, as used
To such disport before her through the field          520
From every beast, more duteous at her call
Than at Circean call the herd disguised.
He, bolder now, uncalled before her stood,
But as in gaze admiring. Oft he bowed
His turret crest and sleek enamelled neck,
Fawning, and licked the ground, whereon she trod.
His gentle dumb expression turned at length
The eye of Eve to mark his play; he, glad
Of her attention gained, with serpent-tongue
Organic, or impulse of vocal air,          530
His fraudulent temptation thus began:—
    'Wonder not, sovran mistress (if perhaps
Thou canst who art sole wonder), much less arm
Thy looks, the heaven of mildness, with disdain,
Displeased that I approach thee thus, and gaze
Insatiate, I thus single, nor have feared
Thy awful brow, more awful thus retired.
Fairest resemblance of thy Maker fair,
Thee all things living gaze on, all things thine
By gift, and thy celestial beauty adore,          540
With ravishment beheld—there best beheld

Where universally admired. But here,
In this enclosure wild, these beasts among,
Beholders rude, and shallow to discern
Half what in thee is fair, one man except,
Who sees thee (and what is one?) who shouldst be seen
A Goddess among Gods, adored and served
By Angels numberless, thy daily train?'
　　So glozed the Tempter, and his proem tuned.
Into the heart of Eve his words made way,　　　　　550
Though at the voice much marvelling; at length,
Not unamazed, she thus in answer spake:—
　　'What may this mean? Language of Man pronounced
By tongue of brute, and human sense expressed?
The first at least of these I thought denied
To beasts, whom God on their creation-day
Created mute to all articulate sound;
The latter I demur, for in their looks
Much reason, and in their actions, oft appears.
Thee, Serpent, subtlest beast of all the field　　　560
I knew, but not with human voice endued;
Redouble, then, this miracle, and say,
How cam'st thou speakable of mute, and how
To me so friendly grown above the rest
Of brutal kind that daily are in sight:
Say, for such wonder claims attention due.'
　　To whom the guileful Tempter thus replied:—
'Empress of this fair World, resplendent Eve!
Easy to me it is to tell thee all
What thou command'st, and right thou shouldst be
　　　　obeyed.　　　　　570
I was at first as other beasts that graze
The trodden herb, of abject thoughts and low,
As was my food, nor aught but food discerned
Or sex, and apprehended nothing high;
Till on a day, roving the field, I chanced
A goodly tree far distant to behold,
Loaden with fruit of fairest colours mixed,
Ruddy and gold: I nearer drew to gaze;
When from the boughs a savoury odour blown,
Grateful to appetite, more pleased my sense　　　580
Than smell of sweetest fennel, or the teats

Of ewe or goat dropping with milk at even,
Unsucked of lamb or kid, that tend their play.
To satisfy the sharp desire I had
Of tasting those fair apples, I resolved
Not to defer; hunger and thirst at once,
Powerful persuaders, quickened at the scent
Of that alluring fruit, urged me so keen.
About the mossy trunk I wound me soon;
For, high from ground, the branches would require     590
Thy utmost reach, or Adam's: round the tree
All other beasts that saw, with like desire
Longing and envying stood, but could not reach.
Amid the tree now got, where plenty hung
Tempting so nigh, to pluck and eat my fill
I spared not; for such pleasure till that hour
At feed or fountain never had I found.
Sated at length, ere long I might perceive
Strange alteration in me, to degree
Of reason in my inward powers, and speech     600
Wanted not long, though to this shape retained.
Thenceforth to speculations high or deep
I turned my thoughts, and with capacious mind
Considered all things visible in Heaven,
Or Earth, or Middle, all things fair and good.
But all that fair and good in thy divine
Semblance, and in thy beauty's heavenly ray,
United I beheld—no fair to thine
Equivalent or second; which compelled
Me thus, though importune perhaps, to come     610
And gaze, and worship thee of right declared
Sovran of creatures, universal Dame!'
     So talked the spirited sly Snake; and Eve,
Yet more amazed, unwary thus replied:—
     'Serpent, thy overpraising leaves in doubt
The virtue of that fruit, in thee first proved.
But say, where grows the tree? from hence how far?
For many are the trees of God that grow
In Paradise, and various, yet unknown
To us; in such abundance lies our choice     620
As leaves a greater store of fruit untouched,
Still hanging incorruptible, till men

Grow up to their provision, and more hands
Help to disburden Nature of her birth.'
    To whom the wily Adder, blithe and glad:—
'Empress, the way is ready, and not long—
Beyond a row of myrtles, on a flat,
Fast by a fountain, one small thicket past
Of blowing myrrh and balm; if thou accept
My conduct, I can bring thee thither soon.'      630
    'Lead, then,' said Eve. He, leading, swiftly rolled
In tangles, and made intricate seem straight,
To mischief swift. Hope elevates, and joy
Brightens his crest; as when a wandering fire,
Compact of unctuous vapour, which the night
Condenses, and the cold environs round,
Kindled through agitation to a flame
(Which oft, they say, some evil spirit attends),
Hovering and blazing with delusive light,
Misleads th' amazed night-wanderer from his way    640
To bogs and mires, and oft through pond or pool,
There swallowed up and lost, from succour far:
So glistered the dire Snake, and into fraud
Led Eve, our credulous mother, to the Tree
Of Prohibition, root of all our woe;
Which when she saw, thus to her guide she spake:—
    'Serpent, we might have spared our coming hither,
Fruitless to me, though fruit be here to excess,
The credit of whose virtue rest with thee—
Wondrous, indeed, if cause of such effects!     650
But of this tree we may not taste nor touch;
God so commanded, and left that command
Sole daughter of his voice: the rest, we live
Law to ourselves; our reason is our law.'
    To whom the Tempter guilefully replied:—
'Indeed! Hath God then said that of the fruit
Of all these garden-trees ye shall not eat,
Yet lords declared of all in earth or air?'
    To whom thus Eve, yet sinless:—'Of the fruit
Of each tree in the garden we may eat;    660
But of the fruit of this fair tree, amidst
The garden, God hath said, "Ye shall not eat
Thereof, nor shall ye touch it, lest ye die." '

    She scarce had said, though brief, when now more bold
The Tempter, but with show of zeal and love
To Man, and indignation at his wrong,
New part puts on, and, as to passion moved,
Fluctuates disturbed, yet comely, and in act
Raised, as of some great matter to begin.
As when of old some orator renowned       670
In Athens or free Rome, where eloquence
Flourished, since mute, to some great cause addressed,
Stood in himself collected, while each part,
Motion, each act, won audience ere the tongue
Sometimes in height began, as no delay
Of preface brooking through his zeal of right:
So standing, moving, or to height upgrown,
The Tempter, all impassioned, thus began:—
    'O sacred, wise, and wisdom-giving Plant,
Mother of science! now I feel thy power      680
Within me clear, not only to discern
Things in their causes, but to trace the ways
Of highest agents, deemed however wise.
Queen of this Universe! do not believe
Those rigid threats of death; ye shall not die.
How should ye? by the fruit? it gives you life
To knowledge; by the Threatener? look on me,
Me who have touched and tasted, yet both live,
And life more perfect have attained than Fate
Meant me, by venturing higher than my lot.      690
Shall that be shut to Man which to the beast
Is open? or will God incense his ire
For such a petty trespass, and not praise
Rather your dauntless virtue, whom the pain
Of death denounced, whatever thing Death be,
Deterred not from achieving what might lead
To happier life, knowledge of good and evil?
Of good, how just? of evil—if what is evil
Be real, why not known, since easier shunned?
God, therefore, cannot hurt ye, and be just;      700
Not just, not God; not feared then, nor obeyed:
Your fear itself of death removes the fear.
Why, then, was this forbid? Why but to awe?

Why but to keep ye low and ignorant,
His worshippers? He knows that in the day
Ye eat thereof your eyes, that seem so clear,
Yet are but dim, shall perfectly be then
Opened and cleared, and ye shall be as Gods,
Knowing both good and evil, as they know.
That ye should be as Gods, since I as Man,        710
Internal Man, is but proportion meet;
I, of brute, human; ye, of human, Gods.
So ye shall die perhaps, by putting off
Human, to put on Gods—death to be wished,
Though threatened, which no worse than this can bring!
And what are Gods, that Man may not become
As they, participating godlike food?
The Gods are first, and that advantage use
On our belief, that all from them proceeds.
I question it; for this fair Earth I see,        720
Warmed by the Sun, producing every kind;
Them nothing. If they all things, who enclosed
Knowledge of good and evil in this tree,
That whoso eats thereof forthwith attains
Wisdom without their leave? and wherein lies
Th' offence, that Man should thus attain to know?
What can your knowledge hurt him, or this tree
Impart against his will, if all be his?
Or is it envy? and can envy dwell
In heavenly breasts? These, these and many more        730
Causes import your need of this fair fruit.
Goddess humane, reach, then, and freely taste!'
    He ended; and his words, replete with guile,
Into her heart too easy entrance won:
Fixed on the fruit she gazed, which to behold
Might tempt alone; and in her ears the sound
Yet rung of his persuasive words, impregned
With reason, to her seeming, and with truth.
Meanwhile the hour of noon drew on, and waked
An eager appetite, raised by the smell        740
So savoury of that fruit, which with desire,
Inclinable now grown to touch or taste,
Solicited her longing eye; yet first,
Pausing a while, thus to herself she mused:—

'Great are thy virtues, doubtless, best of fruits,
Though kept from Man, and worthy to be admired,
Whose taste, too long forborne, at first assay
Gave elocution to the mute, and taught
The tongue not made for speech to speak thy praise.
Thy praise he also who forbids thy use　　　　　750
Conceals not from us, naming thee the Tree
Of Knowledge, knowledge both of good and evil;
Forbids us then to taste; but his forbidding
Commends thee more, while it infers the good
By thee communicated, and our want;
For good unknown sure is not had, or, had
And yet unknown, is as not had at all.
In plain, then, what forbids he but to know,
Forbids us good, forbids us to be wise?
Such prohibitions bind not. But, if Death　　　　　760
Bind us with after-bands, what profits then
Our inward freedom? In the day we eat
Of this fair fruit, our doom is we shall die!
How dies the Serpent? He hath eaten, and lives,
And knows, and speaks, and reasons, and discerns,
Irrational till then. For us alone
Was death invented? or to us denied
This intellectual food, for beasts reserved?
For beasts it seems; yet that one beast which first
Hath tasted envies not, but brings with joy　　　　　770
The good befall'n him, author unsuspect,
Friendly to Man, far from deceit or guile.
What fear I, then? rather, what know to fear
Under this ignorance of good and evil,
Of God or Death, of law or penalty?
Here grows the cure of all, this fruit divine,
Fair to the eye, inviting to the taste,
Of virtue to make wise. What hinders, then,
To reach, and feed at once both body and mind?'
　　So saying, her rash hand in evil hour　　　　　780
Forth-reaching to the fruit, she plucked, she eat;
Earth felt the wound, and Nature from her seat,
Sighing through all her works, gave signs of woe
That all was lost. Back to the thicket slunk
The guilty Serpent, and well might, for Eve,

Intent now wholly on her taste, naught else
Regarded; such delight till then, as seemed,
In fruit she never tasted, whether true,
Or fancied so through expectation high
Of knowledge; nor was Godhead from her thought.        790
Greedily she engorged without restraint,
And knew not eating death.  Satiate at length,
And heightened as with wine, jocund and boon,
Thus to herself she pleasingly began:—
    'O sovran, virtuous, precious of all trees
In Paradise! of operation blest
To sapience, hitherto obscured, infamed,
And thy fair fruit let hang, as to no end
Created! but henceforth my early care,
Not without song, each morning, and due praise,        800
Shall tend thee, and the fertile burden ease
Of thy full branches, offered free to all;
Till, dieted by thee, I grow mature
In knowledge, as the Gods who all things know.
Though others envy what they cannot give—
For, had the gift been theirs, it had not here
Thus grown!  Experience, next to thee I owe,
Best guide: not following thee, I had remained
In ignorance; thou open'st Wisdom's way,
And giv'st access, though secret she retire.        810
And I perhaps am secret:  Heaven is high—
High, and remote to see from thence distinct
Each thing on Earth; and other care perhaps
May have diverted from continual watch
Our great Forbidder, safe with all his spies
About him.  But to Adam in what sort
Shall I appear?  Shall I to him make known
As yet my change, and give him to partake
Full happiness with me, or rather not,
But keep the odds of knowledge in my power        820
Without co-partner? so to add what wants
In female sex, the more to draw his love,
And render me more equal, and perhaps—
A thing not undesirable—sometime
Superior; for, inferior, who is free?
This may be well; but what if God have seen,

And death ensue? Then I shall be no more;
And Adam, wedded to another Eve,
Shall live with her enjoying, I extinct!
A death to think! Confirmed, then, I resolve          830
Adam shall share with me in bliss or woe.
So dear I love him that with him all deaths
I could endure, without him live no life.'
   So saying, from the tree her step she turned,
But first low reverence done, as to the Power
That dwelt within, whose presence had infused
Into the plant sciential sap, derived
From nectar, drink of Gods.  Adam the while,
Waiting desirous her return, had wove
Of choicest flowers a garland, to adorn          840
Her tresses, and her rural labours crown,
As reapers oft are wont their harvest-queen.
Great joy he promised to his thoughts, and new
Solace in her return, so long delayed;
Yet oft his heart, divine of something ill,
Misgave him.  He the faltering measure felt,
And forth to meet her went, the way she took
That morn when first they parted; by the Tree
Of Knowledge he must pass; there he her met,
Scarce from the tree returning; in her hand          850
A bough of fairest fruit, that downy smiled,
New gathered, and ambrosial smell diffused.
To him she hasted; in her face Excuse
Came prologue, and apology to prompt,
Which, with bland words at will, she thus addressed:—
   'Hast thou not wondered, Adam, at my stay?
Thee I have missed, and thought it long, deprived
Thy presence—agony of love till now
Not felt, nor shall be twice; for never more
Mean I to try, what rash untried I sought,          860
The pain of absence from thy sight. But strange
Hath been the cause, and wonderful to hear:
This tree is not, as we are told, a tree
Of danger tasted, nor to evil unknown
Opening the way, but of divine effect
To open eyes, and make them Gods who taste;
And hath been tasted such. The Serpent wise,

Or not restrained as we, or not obeying,
Hath eaten of the fruit, and is become,
Not dead, as we are threat'ned, but thenceforth          870
Endued with human voice and human sense,
Reasoning to admiration, and with me
Persuasively hath so prevailed that I
Have also tasted, and have also found
Th' effects to correspond—opener mine eyes,
Dim erst, dilated spirits, ampler heart,
And growing up to Godhead; which for thee
Chiefly I sought, without thee can despise.
For bliss, as thou hast part, to me is bliss;
Tedious, unshared with thee, and odious soon.          880
Thou, therefore, also taste, that equal lot
May join us, equal joy, as equal love;
Lest, thou not tasting, different degree
Disjoin us, and I then too late renounce
Deity for thee, when Fate will not permit.'
    Thus Eve, with count'nance blithe, her story told;
But in her cheek distemper flushing glowed.
On th' other side, Adam, soon as he heard
The fatal trespass done by Eve, amazed,
Astonied stood and blank, while horror chill          890
Ran through his veins, and all his joints relaxed.
From his slack hand the garland wreathed for Eve
Down dropped, and all the faded roses shed.
Speechless he stood and pale, till thus at length
First to himself he inward silence broke:—
    'O fairest of creation, last and best
Of all God's works, creature in whom excelled
Whatever can to sight or thought be formed,
Holy, divine, good, amiable, or sweet!
How art thou lost! how on a sudden lost,          900
Defaced, deflowered, and now to death devote!
Rather, how hast thou yielded to transgress
The strict forbiddance, how to violate
The sacred fruit forbidden? Some cursed fraud
Of enemy hath beguiled thee, yet unknown,
And me with thee hath ruined; for with thee
Certain my resolution is to die.
How can I live without thee? how forgo

Thy sweet converse and love so dearly joined,
To live again in these wild woods forlorn?                    910
Should God create another Eve, and I
Another rib afford, yet loss of thee
Would never from my heart. No, no! I feel
The link of nature draw me: flesh of flesh,
Bone of my bone thou art, and from thy state
Mine never shall be parted, bliss or woe.'

  So having said, as one from sad dismay
Recomforted, and, after thoughts disturbed,
Submitting to what seemed remediless,
Thus in calm mood his words to Eve he turned:—    920

  'Bold deed thou hast presumed, adventurous Eve,
And peril great provoked, who thus hast dared
Had it been only coveting to eye
That sacred fruit, sacred to abstinence,
Much more to taste it, under ban to touch.
But past who can recall, or done undo?
Not God Omnipotent, nor Fate! Yet so
Perhaps thou shalt not die; perhaps the fact
Is not so heinous now—foretasted fruit,
Profan'd first by the Serpent, by him first      930
Made common and unhallowed ere our taste,
Nor yet on him found deadly; he yet lives—
Lives, as thou saidst, and gains to live, as Man,
Higher degree of life: inducement strong
To us, as likely, tasting, to attain
Proportional ascent; which cannot be
But to be Gods, or Angels, demi-gods.
Nor can I think that God, Creator wise,
Though threat'ning, will in earnest so destroy
Us, his prime creatures, dignified so high,     940
Set over all his works; which, in our fall,
For us created, needs with us must fail,
Dependent made. So God shall uncreate,
Be frustrate, do, undo, and labour lose—
Not well conceived of God; who, though his power
Creation could repeat, yet would be loth
Us to abolish, lest the Adversary
Triumph and say: "Fickle their state whom God
Most favours; who can please him long? Me first

He ruined, now Mankind; whom will he next?"—    950
Matter of scorn not to be given the Foe.
However, I with thee have fixed my lot,
Certain to undergo like doom, if death
Consort with thee, death is to me as life;
So forcible within my heart I feel
The bond of Nature draw me to my own;
My own in thee; for what thou art is mine.
Our state cannot be severed; we are one,
One flesh; to lose thee were to lose myself.'

    So Adam; and thus Eve to him replied:—    960
'O glorious trial of exceeding love,
Illustrious evidence, example high!
Engaging me to emulate; but, short
Of thy perfection, how shall I attain,
Adam? from whose dear side I boast me sprung,
And gladly of our union hear thee speak,
One heart, one soul in both; whereof good proof
This day affords, declaring thee resolved,
Rather than death, or aught than death more dread,
Shall separate us, linked in love so dear,    970
To undergo with me one guilt, one crime,
If any be, of tasting this fair fruit;
Whose virtue (for of good still good proceeds,
Direct, or by occasion) hath presented
This happy trial of thy love, which else
So eminently never had been known.
Were it I thought death menaced would ensue
This my attempt, I would sustain alone
The worst, and not persuade thee—rather die
Deserted than oblige thee with a fact    980
Pernicious to thy peace, chiefly assured
Remarkably so late of thy so true,
So faithful, love unequalled. But I feel
Far otherwise th' event—not death, but life
Augmented, opened eyes, new hopes, new joys,
Taste so divine that what of sweet before
Hath touched my sense, flat seems to this and harsh.
On my experience, Adam, freely taste,
And fear of death deliver to the winds.'

    So saying, she embraced him, and for joy    990

Tenderly wept, much won that he his love
Had so ennobled as of choice to incur
Divine displeasure for her sake, or death.
In recompense (for such compliance bad
Such recompense best merits), from the bough
She gave him of that fair enticing fruit
With liberal hand. He scrupled not to eat,
Against his better knowledge, not deceived,
But fondly overcome with female charm.
Earth trembled from her entrails, as again        1000
In pangs, and Nature gave a second groan;
Sky loured, and, muttering thunder, some sad drops
Wept at completing of the mortal sin
Original; while Adam took no thought,
Eating his fill, nor Eve to iterate
Her former trespass feared, the more to soothe
Him with her loved society; that now,
As with new wine intoxicated both,
They swim in mirth, and fancy that they feel
Divinity within them breeding wings        1010
Wherewith to scorn the Earth: but that false fruit
Far other operations first displayed,
Carnal desire inflaming; he on Eve
Began to cast lascivious eyes; she him
As wantonly repaid; in lust they burn,
Till Adam thus 'gan Eve to dalliance move:—
    'Eve, now I see thou art exact of taste
And elegant—of sapience no small part;
Since to each meaning savour we apply,
And palate call judicious. I the praise        1020
Yield thee, so well this day thou hast purveyed.
Much pleasure we have lost, while we abstained
From this delightful fruit, nor known till now
True relish, tasting. If such pleasure be
In things to us forbidden, it might be wished
For this one tree had been forbidden ten.
But come; so well refreshed, now let us play,
As meet is, after such delicious fare;
For never did thy beauty, since the day
I saw thee first and wedded thee, adorned        1030
With all perfections, so inflame my sense

With ardour to enjoy thee, fairer now
Than ever—bounty of this virtuous tree!'
   So said he, and forbore not glance or toy
Of amorous intent, well understood
Of Eve, whose eye darted contagious fire.
Her hand he seized, and to a shady bank,
Thick overhead with verdant roof embowered,
He led her, nothing loth; flowers were the couch,
Pansies, and violets, and asphodel,                    1040
And hyacinth—Earth's freshest, softest lap.
There they their fill of love and love's disport
Took largely, of their mutual guilt the seal,
The solace of their sin, till dewy sleep
Oppressed them, wearied with their amorous play.
Soon as the force of that fallacious fruit,
That with exhilarating vapour bland
About their spirits had played, and inmost powers
Made err, was now exhaled, and grosser sleep,
Bred of unkindly fumes, with conscious dreams    1050
Encumbered, now had left them, up they rose
As from unrest, and, each the other viewing,
Soon found their eyes how opened, and their minds
How darkened.  Innocence, that as a veil
Had shadowed them from knowing ill, was gone;
Just confidence, and native righteousness,
And honour, from about them, naked left
To guilty Shame: he covered, but his robe
Uncovered more.  So rose the Danite strong,
Herculean Samson, from the harlot-lap              1060
Of Philistean Dalilah, and waked
Shorn of his strength; they destitute and bare
Of all their virtue.  Silent, and in face
Confounded, long they sat, as stricken mute;
Till Adam, though not less than Eve abashed,
At length gave utterance to these words constrained:—
   'O Eve, in evil hour thou didst give ear
To that false Worm, of whomsoever taught
To counterfeit Man's voice—true in our fall,
False in our promised rising; since our eyes      1070
Opened we find indeed, and find we know
Both good and evil, good lost and evil got:

Bad fruit of knowledge, if this be to know,
Which leaves us naked thus, of honour void,
Of innocence, of faith, of purity,
Our wonted ornaments now soiled and stained,
And in our faces evident the signs
Of foul concupiscence; whence evil store,
Even shame, the last of evils; of the first
Be sure then. How shall I behold the face          1080
Henceforth of God or Angel, erst with joy
And rapture so oft beheld? Those heavenly shapes
Will dazzle now this earthly with their blaze
Insufferably bright. Oh, might I here
In solitude live savage, in some glade
Obscured, where highest woods, impenetrable
To star or sunlight, spread their umbrage broad,
And brown as evening! Cover me, ye pines!
Ye cedars, with innumerable boughs
Hide me, where I may never see them more!          1090
But let us now, as in bad plight, devise
What best may, for the present, serve to hide
The parts of each from other that seem most
To shame obnoxious, and unseemliest seen—
Some tree, whose broad smooth leaves, together sewed,
And girded on our loins, may cover round
Those middle parts, that this new comer, Shame,
There sit not, and reproach us as unclean.'
    So counselled he, and both together went
Into the thickest wood, there soon they chose      1100
The fig-tree—not that kind for fruit renowned,
But such as at this day, to Indians known,
In Malabar or Deccan spreads her arms
Branching so broad and long that in the ground
The bended twigs take root, and daughters grow
About the mother tree, a pillared shade
High overarched, and echoing walks between:
There oft the Indian herdsman, shunning heat,
Shelters in cool, and tends his pasturing herds
At loop-holes cut through thickest shade. Those leaves
They gathered, broad as Amazonian targe,          1111
And with what skill they had together sewed,
To gird their waist—vain covering, if to hide

Their guilt and dreaded shame!  O how unlike
To that first naked glory!  Such of late
Columbus found th' American, so girt
With feathered cincture, naked else and wild,
Among the trees on isles and woody shores.
Thus fenced, and, as they thought, their shame in part
Covered, but not at rest or ease of mind,                    1120
They sat them down to weep.  Nor only tears
Rained at their eyes, but high winds worse within
Began to rise, high passions—anger, hate,
Mistrust, suspicion, discord—and shook sore
Their inward state of mind, calm region once
And full of peace, now tossed and turbulent:
For Understanding ruled not, and the Will
Heard not her lore, both in subjection now
To sensual Appetite, who, from beneath
Usurping over sovran Reason, claimed                         1130
Superior sway.  From thus distempered breast
Adam, estranged in look and altered style,
Speech intermitted thus to Eve renewed:—
    'Would thou hadst hearkened to my words, and stayed
With me, as I besought thee, when that strange
Desire of wandering, this unhappy morn,
I know not whence possessed thee!  We had then
Remained still happy—not, as now, despoiled
Of all our good, shamed, naked, miserable!
Let none henceforth seek needless cause to approve 1140
The faith they owe; when earnestly they seek
Such proof, conclude they then begin to fail.'
    To whom, soon moved with touch of blame, thus
      Eve:—
'What words have passed thy lips, Adam severe?
Imput'st thou that to my default, or will
Of wandering, as thou call'st it, which who knows
But might as ill have happened thou being by,
Or to thyself perhaps?  Hadst thou been there,
Or here th' attempt, thou couldst not have discerned
Fraud in the Serpent, speaking as he spake;              1150
No ground of enmity between us known
Why he should mean me ill or seek to harm.
Was I to have never parted from thy side?

As good have grown there still, a lifeless rib.
Being as I am, why didst not thou, the head,
Command me absolutely not to go,
Going into such danger, as thou saidst?
Too facile then, thou didst not much gainsay,
Nay, didst permit, approve, and fair dismiss.
Hadst thou been firm and fixed in thy dissent,        1160
Neither had I transgressed, nor thou with me.'
    To whom, then first incensed, Adam replied:—
'Is this the love, is this the recompense
Of mine to thee, ingrateful Eve, expressed
Immutable when thou wert lost, not I—
Who might have lived, and joyed immortal bliss,
Yet willingly chose rather death with thee?
And am I now upbraided as the cause
Of thy transgressing? not enough severe,
It seems, in thy restraint!  What could I more?     1170
I warned thee, I admonished thee, foretold
The danger, and the lurking enemy
That lay in wait; beyond this had been force,
And force upon free will hath here no place.
But confidence then bore thee on, secure
Either to meet no danger, or to find
Matter of glorious trial; and perhaps
I also erred in overmuch admiring
What seemed in thee so perfect that I thought
No evil durst attempt thee, but I rue            1180
That error now, which is become my crime,
And thou th' accuser.  Thus it shall befall
Him who, to worth in women overtrusting,
Lets her will rule: restraint she will not brook;
And, left to herself, if evil thence ensue,
She first his weak indulgence will accuse.'
    Thus they in mutual accusation spent
The fruitless hours, but neither self-condemning;
And of their vain contest appeared no end.

*The End of the Ninth Book.*

# PARADISE LOST

## BOOK X

### THE ARGUMENT

*Man's transgression known, the guardian Angels forsake
Paradise, and return up to Heaven to approve their vigilance,
and are approved; God declaring that the entrance of Satan
could not be by them prevented. He sends his Son to judge
the transgressors; who descends, and gives sentence accordingly; then, in pity, clothes them both, and reascends. Sin and
Death sitting till then at the gates of Hell, by wondrous sympathy feeling the success of Satan in this new World, and the
sin by Man there committed, resolve to sit no longer confined
in Hell, but to follow Satan, their sire, up to the place of Man:
to make the way easier from Hell to this World to and fro,
they pave a broad highway or bridge over Chaos, according
to the track that Satan first made; then, preparing for Earth,
they meet him, proud of his success, returning to Hell; their
mutual gratulation. Satan arrives at Pandemonium; in full
assembly relates with boasting his success against Man; instead of applause is entertained with a general hiss by all his
audience, transformed, with himself also, suddenly into Serpents, according to his doom given in Paradise; then, deluded
with a show of the Forbidden Tree springing up before them,
they, greedily reaching to take of the fruit, chew dust and
bitter ashes. The proceedings of Sin and Death: God foretells
the final victory of his Son over them, and the renewing of all
things; but, for the present, commands his Angels to make
several alterations in the Heavens and Elements. Adam, more
and more perceiving his fallen condition, heavily bewails,
rejects the condolement of Eve; she persists, and at length
appeases him: then, to evade the curse likely to fall on their
offspring, proposes to Adam violent ways; which he approves
not, but, conceiving better hope, puts her in mind of the late
promise made them, that her seed should be revenged on the
Serpent, and exhorts her, with him, to seek peace of the offended
Deity by repentance and supplication.*

MEANWHILE the heinous and despiteful act
Of Satan done in Paradise, and how
He, in the Serpent, had perverted Eve,
Her husband she, to taste the fatal fruit,

Was known in Heaven; for what can scape the eye
Of God all-seeing, or deceive his heart
Omniscient? who, in all things wise and just,
Hindered not Satan to attempt the mind
Of Man, with strength entire and free will armed
Complete to have discovered and repulsed          10
Whatever wiles of foe or seeming friend.
For still they knew, and ought to have still remembered.
The high injunction not to taste that fruit,
Whoever tempted; which they not obeying
Incurred (what could they less?) the penalty,
And, manifold in sin, deserved to fall.
Up into Heaven from Paradise in haste
Th' Angelic guards ascended, mute and sad
For Man; for of his state by this they knew,
Much wondering how the subtle Fiend had stol'n          20
Entrance unseen. Soon as th' unwelcome news
From Earth arrived at Heaven-gate, displeased
All were who heard; dim sadness did not spare
That time celestial visages, yet, mixed
With pity, violated not their bliss.
About the new-arrived, in multitudes,
Th' ethereal people ran, to hear and know
How all befell. They towards the throne supreme,
Accountable, made haste, to make appear,
With righteous plea, their utmost vigilance,          30
And easily approved; when the Most High
Eternal Father, from his secret cloud
Amidst, in thunder uttered thus his voice:—
     'Assembled Angels, and ye Powers returned
From unsuccessful charge, be not dismayed
Nor troubled at these tidings from the Earth
Which your sincerest care could not prevent,
Foretold so lately what would come to pass,
When first this Tempter crossed the gulf from Hell.
I told ye then he should prevail, and speed          40
On his bad errand—Man should be seduced,
And flattered out of all, believing lies
Against his Maker; no decree of mine
Concurring to necessitate his fall,
Or touch with lightest moment of impulse

His free will, to her own inclining left
In even scale.  But fall'n he is; and now
What rests, but that the mortal sentence pass
On his transgression, Death denounced that day?
Which he presumes already vain and void,            50
Because not yet inflicted, as he feared,
By some immediate stroke, but soon shall find
Forbearance no acquittance ere day end.
Justice shall not return, as bounty, scorned.
But whom send I to judge them? whom but thee,
Vicegerent Son?  To thee I have transferred
All judgement, whether in Heaven, or Earth, or Hell.
Easy it may be seen that I intend
Mercy colleague with justice, sending thee,
Man's friend, his Mediator, his designed            60
Both ransom and Redeemer voluntary,
And destined Man himself to judge Man fall'n.'
     So spake the Father; and, unfolding bright
Toward the right hand his glory, on the Son
Blazed forth unclouded deity.  He full
Resplendent all his Father manifest
Expressed, and thus divinely answered mild:—
     'Father Eternal, thine is to decree;
Mine both in Heaven and Earth to do thy will
Supreme, that thou in me, thy Son beloved,            70
May'st ever rest well pleased.  I go to judge
On Earth these thy transgressors; but thou know'st,
Whoever judged, the worst on me must light,
When Time shall be; for so I undertook
Before thee, and, not repenting, this obtain
Of right, that I may mitigate their doom
On me derived.  Yet I shall temper so
Justice with mercy as may illustrate most
Them fully satisfied, and thee appease.
Attendance none shall need, nor train, where none            80
Are to behold the judgement but the judged,
Those two; the third best absent is condemned,
Convict by flight, and rebel to all law;
Conviction to the Serpent none belongs.'
     Thus saying, from his radiant seat he rose
Of high collateral glory.  Him Thrones and Powers,

Princedoms, and Dominations, ministrant,
Accompanied to Heaven-gate, from whence
Eden and all the coast in prospect lay.
Down he descended straight; the speed of Gods    90
Time counts not, though with swiftest minutes winged.
Now was the Sun in western cadence low
From noon, and gentle airs due at their hour
To fan the Earth now waked, and usher in
The evening cool, when he, from wrath more cool,
Came, the mild judge and intercessor both,
To sentence Man: the voice of God they heard
Now walking in the Garden, by soft winds
Brought to their ears, while day declined; they heard,
And from his presence hid themselves among    100
The thickest trees, both man and wife, till God,
Approaching, thus to Adam called aloud:—
  'Where art thou, Adam, wont with joy to meet
My coming, seen far off? I miss thee here,
Not pleased, thus entertained with solitude,
Where obvious duty erewhile appeared unsought.
Or come I less conspicuous, or what change
Absents thee, or what chance detains? Come forth!'
  He came, and with him Eve, more loth, though first
To offend, discount'nanced both, and discomposed;    110
Love was not in their looks, either to God
Or to each other, but apparent guilt,
And shame, and perturbation, and despair,
Anger, and obstinacy, and hate, and guile.
Whence Adam, faltering long, thus answered brief:—
  'I heard thee in the garden, and, of thy voice
Afraid, being naked, hid myself.' To whom
The gracious Judge, without revile, replied:—
  'My voice thou oft hast heard, and hast not feared,
But still rejoiced; how is it now become    120
So dreadful to thee? That thou art naked who
Hath told thee? Hast thou eaten of the tree
Whereof I gave thee charge thou shouldst not eat?'
  To whom thus Adam, sore beset, replied:—
'O Heaven! in evil strait this day I stand
Before my Judge—either to undergo
Myself the total crime, or to accuse

    182             M

My other self, the partner of my life,
Whose failing, while her faith to me remains,
I should conceal, and not expose to blame          130
By my complaint.  But strict necessity
Subdues me, and calamitous constraint,
Lest on my head both sin and punishment,
However insupportable, be all
Devolved; though, should I hold my peace, yet thou
Wouldst easily detect what I conceal.
This Woman, whom thou mad'st to be my help,
And gav'st me as thy perfect gift, so good,
So fit, so acceptable, so divine,
That from her hand I could suspect no ill,          140
And what she did, whatever in itself,
Her doing seemed to justify the deed—
She gave me of the tree, and I did eat.'

　　To whom the Sovran Presence thus replied:—
'Was she thy God, that her thou didst obey
Before his voice? or was she made thy guide,
Superior, or but equal, that to her
Thou didst resign thy manhood, and the place
Wherein God set thee above her, made of thee
And for thee, whose perfection far excelled          150
Hers in all real dignity?  Adorned
She was indeed, and lovely, to attract
Thy love, not thy subjection; and her gifts
Were such as under government well seemed—
Unseemly to bear rule; which was thy part
And person, hadst thou known thyself aright.'

　　So having said, he thus to Eve in few:—
'Say, Woman, what is this which thou hast done?'

　　To whom sad Eve, with shame nigh overwhelmed,
Confessing soon, yet not before her Judge          160
Bold or loquacious, thus abashed replied:—
'The Serpent me beguiled, and I did eat.'

　　Which when the Lord God heard, without delay
To judgement he proceeded on th' accused
Serpent, though brute, unable to transfer
The guilt on him who made him instrument
Of mischief, and polluted from the end
Of his creation—justly then accursed,

As vitiated in nature. More to know
Concerned not Man (since he no further knew),          170
Nor altered his offence; yet God at last
To Satan, first in sin, his doom applied,
Though in mysterious terms, judged as then best:
And on the Serpent thus his curse let fall:—
    'Because thou hast done this, thou art accursed
Above all cattle, each beast of the field;
Upon thy belly grovelling thou shalt go,
And dust shalt eat all the days of thy life.
Between thee and the Woman I will put
Enmity, and between thine and her seed;          180
Her seed shall bruise thy head, thou bruise his heel.'
    So spake this oracle—then verified
When Jesus, son of Mary, second Eve,
Saw Satan fall like lightning down from Heaven,
Prince of the Air; then, rising from his grave,
Spoiled Principalities and Powers, triumphed
In open show, and, with ascension bright,
Captivity led captive through the Air,
The realm itself of Satan, long usurped,
Whom he shall tread at last under our feet,          190
Even he who now foretold his fatal bruise,
And to the Woman thus his sentence turned:—
    'Thy sorrow I will greatly multiply
By thy conception; children thou shalt bring
In sorrow forth, and to thy husband's will
Thine shall submit; he over thee shall rule.'
    On Adam last thus judgement he pronounced:—
'Because thou hast hearkened to the voice of thy wife,
And eaten of the tree concerning which
I charged thee, saying, *Thou shalt not eat thereof*,          200
Curs'd is the ground for thy sake; thou in sorrow
Shalt eat thereof all the days of thy life;
Thorns also and thistles it shall bring thee forth
Unbid; and thou shalt eat th' herb of th' field;
In the sweat of thy face shalt thou eat bread,
Till thou return unto the ground; for thou
Out of the ground wast taken: know thy birth,
For dust thou art, and shalt to dust return.'
    So judged he Man, both Judge and Saviour sent,

And th' instant stroke of death, denounced that day,
Removed far off; then, pitying how they stood          211
Before him naked to the air, that now
Must suffer change, disdained not to begin
Thenceforth the form of servant to assume,
As when he washed his servants' feet, so now,
As father of his family, he clad
Their nakedness with skins of beasts, or slain,
Or, as the snake, with youthful coat repaid;
And thought not much to clothe his enemies.
Nor he their outward only with the skins          220
Of beasts, but inward nakedness, much more
Opprobrious, with his robe of righteousness
Arraying, covered from his Father's sight.
To him with swift ascent he up returned,
Into his blissful bosom reassumed
In glory as of old; to him, appeased,
All, though all-knowing, what had passed with Man
Recounted, mixing intercession sweet.
Meanwhile, ere thus was sinned and judged on Earth,
Within the gates of Hell sat Sin and Death,          230
In counterview within the gates, that now
Stood open wide, belching outrageous flame
Far into Chaos, since the Fiend passed through,
Sin opening; who thus now to Death began:—
     'O Son, why sit we here, each other viewing
Idly, while Satan, our great author, thrives
In other worlds, and happier seat provides
For us, his offspring dear? It cannot be
But that success attends him; if mishap,
Ere this he had returned, with fury driven          240
By his avengers, since no place like this
Can fit his punishment, or their revenge.
Methinks I feel new strength within me rise,
Wings growing, and dominion given me large
Beyond this Deep—whatever draws me on,
Or sympathy, or some connatural force,
Powerful at greatest distance to unite
With secret amity things of like kind
By secretest conveyance. Thou, my shade
Inseparable, must with me along;          250

For Death from Sin no power can separate.
But, lest the difficulty of passing back
Stay his return perhaps over this gulf
Impassable, impervious, let us try
Adventurous work, yet to thy power and mine
Not unagreeable! to found a path
Over this main from Hell to that new World
Where Satan now prevails—a monument
Of merit high to all th' infernal host,
Easing their passage hence, for intercourse     260
Or transmigration, as their lot shall lead.
Nor can I miss the way, so strongly drawn
By this new-felt attraction and instinct.'
    Whom thus the meagre Shadow answered soon:—
'Go whither fate and inclination strong
Leads thee; I shall not lag behind, nor err
The way, thou leading: such a scent I draw
Of carnage, prey innumerable, and taste
The savour of death from all things there that live.
Nor shall I to the work thou enterprisest     270
Be wanting, but afford thee equal aid.'
    So saying, with delight he snuffed the smell
Of mortal change on Earth.  As when a flock
Of ravenous fowl, though many a league remote,
Against the day of battle, to a field
Where armies lie encamped come flying, lured
With scent of living carcases designed
For death the following day in bloody fight:
So scented the grim Feature, and upturned
His nostril wide into the murky air,     280
Sagacious of his quarry from so far.
Then both, from out Hell-gates, into the waste
Wide anarchy of Chaos, damp and dark,
Flew diverse, and, with power (their power was great)
Hovering upon the waters, what they met
Solid or slimy, as in raging sea
Tossed up and down, together crowded drove,
From each side shoaling, towards the mouth of Hell;
As when two polar winds, blowing adverse
Upon the Cronian sea, together drive     290
Mountains of ice, that stop th' imagined way

Beyond Petsora eastward to the rich
Cathaian coast.  The aggregated soil
Death with his mace petrific, cold and dry,
As with a trident smote, and fixed as firm
As Delos, floating once; the rest his look
Bound with Gorgonian rigour not to move,
And with asphaltic slime; broad as the gate,
Deep to the roots of Hell the gathered beach
They fastened, and the mole immense wrought on    300
Over the foaming Deep high-arched, a bridge
Of length prodigious, joining to the wall
Immovable of this now fenceless World,
Forfeit to Death—from hence a passage broad,
Smooth, easy, inoffensive, down to Hell.
So, if great things to small may be compared,
Xerxes, the liberty of Greece to yoke,
From Susa, his Memnonian palace high,
Came to the sea, and, over Hellespont
Bridging his way, Europe with Asia joined,    310
And scourged with many a stroke th' indignant waves.
Now had they brought the work by wondrous art
Pontifical—a ridge of pendent rock
Over the vexed abyss, following the track
Of Satan, to the self-same place where he
First lighted from his wing and landed safe
From out of Chaos—to the outside bare
Of this round World.  With pins of adamant
And chains they made all fast, too fast they made
And durable; and now in little space    320
The confines met of empyreal Heaven
And of this World, and on the left hand Hell,
With long reach interposed; three sev'ral ways
In sight to each of these three places led.
And now their way to Earth they had descried,
To Paradise first tending, when, behold
Satan, in likeness of an Angel bright,
Betwixt the Centaur and the Scorpion steering
His zenith, while the Sun in Aries rose:
Disguised he came; but those his children dear    330
Their parent soon discerned, though in disguise.
He, after Eve seduced, unminded slunk

Into the wood fast by, and, changing shape
To observe the sequel, saw his guileful act
By Eve, though all unweeting, seconded
Upon her husband—saw their shame that sought
Vain covertures; but, when he saw descend
The Son of God to judge them, terrified
He fled, not hoping to escape, but shun
The present—fearing, guilty, what his wrath      310
Might suddenly inflict; that past, returned
By night, and, listening where the hapless pair
Sat in their sad discourse and various plaint,
Thence gathered his own doom, which understood
Not instant, but of future time. With joy
And tidings fraught to Hell he now returned,
And at the brink of Chaos, near the foot
Of this new wondrous pontifice, unhoped
Met who to meet him came, his offspring dear.
Great joy was at their meeting, and at sight      350
Of that stupendious bridge his joy increased.
Long he admiring stood, till Sin, his fair
Enchanting daughter, thus the silence broke:—

    'O Parent, these are thy magnific deeds,
Thy trophies! which thou view'st as not thine own;
Thou art their author and prime architect.
For I no sooner in my heart divined
(My heart, which by a secret harmony
Still moves with thine, joined in connexion sweet)
That thou on Earth hadst prospered, which thy looks
Now also evidence, but straight I felt—      361
Though distant from thee worlds between, yet felt—
That I must after thee with this thy son;
Such fatal consequence unites us three.
Hell could no longer hold us in her bounds,
Nor this unvoyageable gulf obscure
Detain from following thy illustrious track.
Thou hast achieved our liberty, confined
Within Hell-gates till now: thou us empowered
To fortify thus far, and overlay      370
With this portentous bridge the dark abyss.
Thine now is all this World; thy virtue hath won
What thy hands builded not; thy wisdom gained,

With odds, what war hath lost, and fully avenged
Our foil in Heaven.  Here thou shalt monarch reign,
There didst not; there let him still victor sway,
As battle hath adjudged, from this new World
Retiring, by his own doom alienated,
And henceforth monarchy with thee divide
Of all things, parted by th' empyreal bounds,                    380
His quadrature, from thy orbicular World,
Or try thee now more dang'rous to his throne.'
    Whom thus the Prince of Darkness answered glad:—
'Fair daughter, and thou, son and grandchild both,
High proof ye now have given to be the race
Of Satan (for I glory in the name,
Antagonist of Heaven's Almighty King),
Amply have merited of me, of all
Th' Infernal Empire, that so near Heaven's door
Triumphal with triumphal act have met,                           390
Mine with this glorious work, and made one realm
Hell and this World—one realm, one continent
Of easy thoroughfare.  Therefore, while I
Descend through Darkness, on your road with ease,
To my associate Powers, them to acquaint
With these successes, and with them rejoice,
You two this way, among those numerous orbs,
All yours, right down to Paradise descend;
There dwell, and reign in bliss; thence on the Earth
Dominion exercise and in the air,                                400
Chiefly on Man, sole lord of all declared;
Him first make sure your thrall, and lastly kill.
My substitutes I send ye, and create
Plenipotent on Earth, of matchless might
Issuing from me.  On your joint vigour now
My hold of this new kingdom all depends,
Through Sin to Death exposed by my exploit.
If your joint power prevail, th' affairs of Hell
No detriment need fear; go, and be strong.'
    So saying, he dismissed them; they with speed          410
Their course through thickest constellations held,
Spreading their bane; the blasted stars looked wan,
And planets, planet-struck, real eclipse
Then suffered.  Th' other way Satan went down

The causey to Hell-gate; on either side
Disparted Chaos overbuilt exclaimed,
And with rebounding surge the bars assailed
That scorned his indignation.  Through the gate,
Wide open and unguarded, Satan passed,
And all about found desolate; for those                    420
Appointed to sit there had left their charge,
Flown to the upper World; the rest were all
Far to the inland retired, about the walls
Of Pandemonium, city and proud seat
Of Lucifer, so by allusion called
Of that bright star to Satan paragoned.
There kept their watch the legions, while the Grand
In council sat, solicitous what chance
Might intercept their Emperor sent; so he
Departing gave command, and they observed.                    430
As when the Tartar from his Russian foe,
By Astracan, over the snowy plains,
Retires, or Bactrian Sophi, from the horns
Of Turkish crescent, leaves all waste beyond
The realm of Aladule, in his retreat
To Tauris or Casbeen: so these, the late
Heaven-banished host, left desert utmost Hell
Many a dark league, reduced in careful watch
Round their metropolis, and now expecting
Each hour their great Adventurer from the search                    440
Of foreign worlds; he through the midst unmarked,
In show plebeian Angel militant
Of lowest order, passed, and, from the door
Of that Plutonian hall, invisible
Ascended his high throne, which, under state
Of richest texture spread, at th' upper end
Was placed in regal lustre.  Down a while
He sat, and round about him saw, unseen.
At last, as from a cloud, his fulgent head
And shape star-bright appeared, or brighter, clad                    450
With what permissive glory since his fall
Was left him, or false glitter.  All amazed
At that so sudden blaze, the Stygian throng
Bent their aspect, and whom they wished beheld,
Their mighty Chief returned: loud was th' acclaim.

Forth rushed in haste the great consulting Peers,
Raised from their dark Divan, and with like joy
Congratulant approached him, who with hand
Silence, and with these words attention, won:—          459
   'Thrones, Dominations, Princedoms, Virtues, Powers!—
For in possession such, not only of right,
I call ye, and declare ye now, returned,
Successful beyond hope, to lead ye forth
Triumphant out of this infernal pit
Abominable, accursed, the house of woe,
And dungeon of our tyrant! Now possess,
As lords, a spacious World, to our native Heaven
Little inferior, by my adventure hard
With peril great achieved. Long were to tell
What I have done, what suffered, with what pain          470
Voyaged th' unreal, vast, unbounded Deep
Of horrible confusion—over which
By Sin and Death a broad way now is paved,
To expedite your glorious march; but I
Toiled out my uncouth passage, forced to ride
Th' untractable Abyss, plunged in the womb
Of unoriginal Night and Chaos wild,
That, jealous of their secrets, fiercely opposed
My journey strange, with clamorous uproar
Protesting Fate supreme; thence how I found          480
The new-created World, which fame in Heaven
Long had foretold, a fabric wonderful,
Of absolute perfection; therein Man
Placed in a paradise, by our exile
Made happy. Him by fraud I have seduced
From his Creator, and, the more to increase
Your wonder, with an apple! He, thereat
Offended—worth your laughter!—hath given up
Both his beloved Man and all his World
To Sin and Death a prey, and so to us,          490
Without our hazard, labour, or alarm,
To range in, and to dwell, and over Man
To rule, as over all he should have ruled.
True is, me also he hath judged; or rather
Me not, but the brute Serpent, in whose shape
Man I deceived. That which to me belongs

Is enmity, which he will put between
Me and Mankind: I am to bruise his heel;
His seed—when is not set—shall bruise my head:
A world who would not purchase with a bruise,     500
Or much more grievous pain? Ye have th' account
Of my performance; what remains, ye Gods,
But up and enter now into full bliss?'
  So having said, a while he stood, expecting
Their universal shout and high applause
To fill his ear; when, contrary, he hears,
On all sides, from innumerable tongues
A dismal universal hiss, the sound
Of public scorn: he wondered, but not long
Had leisure, wondering at himself now more;     510
His visage drawn he felt to sharp and spare,
His arms clung to his ribs, his legs entwining
Each other, till, supplanted, down he fell,
A monstrous serpent on his belly prone,
Reluctant, but in vain; a greater power
Now ruled him, punished in the shape he sinned,
According to his doom: he would have spoke,
But hiss for hiss returned with forked tongue
To forked tongue; for now were all transformed
Alike, to serpents all, as accessories     520
To his bold riot: dreadful was the din
Of hissing through the hall, thick-swarming now
With complicated monsters, head and tail,
Scorpion, and Asp, and Amphisbæna dire,
Cerastes horned, Hydrus, and Ellops drear,
And Dipsas (not so thick swarmed once the soil
Bedropped with blood of Gorgon, or the isle
Ophiusa); but still greatest he the midst,
Now Dragon grown, larger than whom the Sun
Engendered in the Pythian vale on slime,     530
Huge Python; and his power no less he seemed
Above the rest still to retain; they all
Him followed, issuing forth to th' open field,
Where all yet left of that revolted rout,
Heaven-fallen, in station stood or just array,
Sublime with expectation when to see
In triumph issuing forth their glorious Chief;

They saw, but other sight instead—a crowd
Of ugly serpents: horror on them fell,
And horrid sympathy; for what they saw          540
They felt themselves now changing; down their arms,
Down fell both spear and shield; down they as fast,
And the dire hiss renewed, and the dire form
Catched by contagion, like in punishment
As in their crime. Thus was th' applause they meant
Turned to exploding hiss, triumph to shame
Cast on themselves from their own mouths. There stood
A grove hard by, sprung up with this their change,
His will who reigns above, to aggravate
Their penance, laden with fair fruit, like that          550
Which grew in Paradise, the bait of Eve
Used by the Tempter. On that prospect strange
Their earnest eyes they fixed, imagining
For one forbidden tree a multitude
Now risen, to work them further woe or shame;
Yet, parched with scalding thirst and hunger fierce,
Though to delude them sent, could not abstain,
But on they rolled in heaps, and, up the trees
Climbing, sat thicker than the snaky locks
That curled Megæra. Greedily they plucked          560
The fruitage fair to sight, like that which grew
Near that bituminous lake where Sodom flamed;
This, more delusive, not the touch, but taste
Deceived; they, fondly thinking to allay
Their appetite with gust, instead of fruit
Chewed bitter ashes, which th' offended taste
With spattering noise rejected: oft they assayed,
Hunger and thirst constraining; drugged as oft,
With hatefulest disrelish writhed their jaws
With soot and cinders filled; so oft they fell          570
Into the same illusion, not as Man
Whom they triumphed once lapsed. Thus were they plagued,
And, worn with famine, long and ceaseless hiss,
Till their lost shape, permitted, they resumed—
Yearly enjoined, some say, to undergo
This annual humbling certain numbered days,

To dash their pride, and joy for Man seduced.
However, some tradition they dispersed
Among the heathen of their purchase got,
And fabled how the Serpent, whom they called    580
Ophion, with Eurynome (the wide-
Encroaching Eve perhaps), had first the rule
Of high Olympus, thence by Saturn driven
And Ops, ere yet Dictæan Jove was born.

    Meanwhile in Paradise the hellish pair
Too soon arrived—Sin, there in power before
Once actual, now in body, and to dwell
Habitual habitant; behind her Death,
Close following pace for pace, not mounted yet
On his pale horse; to whom Sin thus began:—    590

    'Second of Satan sprung, all-conquering Death!
What think'st thou of our empire now? though earned
With travail difficult, not better far
Than still at Hell's dark threshold to have sat watch,
Unnamed, undreaded, and thyself half-starved?'

    Whom thus the Sin-born Monster answered soon:—
'To me, who with eternal famine pine,
Alike is Hell, or Paradise, or Heaven—
There best where most with ravin I may meet:
Which here, though plenteous, all too little seems    600
To stuff this maw, this vast unhide-bound corpse.'

    To whom th' incestuous Mother thus replied:—
'Thou, therefore, on these herbs, and fruits, and flowers,
Feed first; on each beast next, and fish, and fowl—
No homely morsels; and whatever thing
The scythe of Time mows down devour unspared;
Till I, in Man residing through the race,
His thoughts, his looks, words, actions, all infect,
And season him thy last and sweetest prey.'

    This said, they both betook them several ways,    610
Both to destroy, or unimmortal make
All kinds, and for destruction to mature
Sooner or later; which th' Almighty seeing,
From his transcendent seat the Saints among,
To those bright Orders uttered thus his voice:—

    'See with what heat these dogs of Hell advance
To waste and havoc yonder World, which I

So fair and good created, and had still
Kept in that state, had not the folly of Man
Let in these wasteful furies, who impute          620
Folly to me (so doth the Prince of Hell
And his adherents), that with so much ease
I suffer them to enter and possess
A place so heavenly, and, conniving, seem
To gratify my scornful enemies,
That laugh, as if transported with some fit
Of passion, I to them had quitted all,
At random yielded up to their misrule;
And know not that I called and drew them thither,
My Hell-hounds, to lick up the draff and filth          630
Which Man's polluting sin with taint hath shed
On what was pure; till, crammed and gorged, nigh
          burst
With sucked and glutted offal, at one sling
Of thy victorious arm, well-pleasing Son,
Both Sin and Death, and yawning Grave, at last
Through Chaos hurled, obstruct the mouth of Hell
For ever, and seal up his ravenous jaws.
Then Heaven and Earth, renewed, shall be made pure
To sanctity that shall receive no stain:
Till then the curse pronounced on both precedes.'          640
    He ended, and the Heavenly audience loud
Sung Halleluiah, as the sound of seas,
Through multitude that sung:—'Just are thy ways,
Righteous are thy decrees on all thy works;
Who can extenuate thee? Next, to the Son,
Destined restorer of Mankind, by whom
New Heaven and Earth shall to the ages rise,
Or down from Heaven descend.' Such was their song,
While the Creator, calling forth by name
His mighty Angels, gave them several charge,          650
As sorted best with present things. The Sun
Had first his precept so to move, so shine,
As might affect the Earth with cold and heat
Scarce tolerable, and from the north to call
Decrepit winter, from the south to bring
Solstitial summer's heat. To the blank Moon
Her office they prescribed; to th' other five

Their planetary motions and aspécts,
In sextile, square, and trine, and opposite,
Of noxious efficacy, and when to join                    660
In synod unbenign; and taught the fixed
Their influence malignant when to shower—
Which of them, rising with the Sun or falling,
Should prove tempestuous. To the winds they set
Their corners, when with bluster to confound
Sea, air, and shore; the thunder when to roll
With terror through the dark aerial hall.
Some say he bid his Angels turn askance
The poles of Earth twice ten degrees and more
From the Sun's axle; they with labour pushed                    670
Oblique the centric Globe: some say the Sun
Was bid turn reins from th' equinoctial road
Like distant breadth to Taurus with the seven
Atlantic Sisters, and the Spartan twins,
Up to the Tropic Crab; thence down amain
By Leo, and the Virgin, and the Scales,
As deep as Capricorn; to bring in change
Of seasons to each clime: else had the spring
Perpetual smiled on Earth with vernant flowers,
Equal in days and nights, except to those                    680
Beyond the polar circles; to them day
Had unbenighted shone, while the low Sun,
To recompense his distance, in their sight
Had rounded still th' horizon, and not known
Or east or west—which had forbid the snow
From cold Estotiland, and south as far
Beneath Magellan. At that tasted fruit,
The Sun, as from Thyestean banquet, turned
His course intended; else how had the world
Inhabited, though sinless, more than now                    690
Avoided pinching cold and scorching heat?
These changes in the heavens, though slow, produced
Like change on sea and land—sidereal blast,
Vapour, and mist, and exhalation hot,
Corrupt and pestilent. Now from the north
Of Norumbega, and the Samoed shore,
Bursting their brazen dungeon, armed with ice,
And snow and hail, and stormy gust and flaw,

Boreas and Cæcias and Argestes loud
And Thrascias rend the woods, and seas upturn;          700
With adverse blast upturns them from the south
Notus, and Afer black with thundrous clouds
From Serraliona; thwart of these, as fierce
Forth rush the Levant and the Ponent winds,
Eurus and Zephyr, with their lateral noise,
Sirocco and Libecchio.  Thus began
Outrage from lifeless things; but Discord first,
Daughter of Sin, among th' irrational
Death introduced through fierce antipathy:
Beast now with beast 'gan war, and fowl with fowl,          710
And fish with fish.  To graze the herb all leaving
Devoured each other; nor stood much in awe
Of Man, but fled him, or with countenance grim
Glared on him passing.  These were from without
The growing miseries; which Adam saw
Already in part, though hid in gloomiest shade,
To sorrow abandoned, but worse felt within,
And, in a troubled sea of passion tossed,
Thus to disburden sought with sad complaint:—
　　'O miserable of happy! is this the end          720
Of this new glorious World, and me so late
The glory of that glory? who now, become
Accursed of blessed, hide me from the face
Of God, whom to behold was then my height
Of happiness; yet well, if here would end
The misery!  I deserved it, and would bear
My own deservings; but this will not serve:
All that I eat or drink, or shall beget,
Is propagated curse.  O voice, once heard
Delightfully, "*Increase and multiply;*"          730
Now death to hear! for what can I increase
Or multiply but curses on my head?
Who of all ages to succeed, but, feeling
The evil on him brought by me, will curse
My head?  "Ill fare our ancestor impure!
For this we may thank Adam!" but his thanks
Shall be the execration.  So, besides
Mine own that bide upon me, all from me
Shall with a fierce reflux on me redound—

On me, as on their natural centre, light                    740
Heavy, though in their place.  O fleeting joys
Of Paradise, dear bought with lasting woes!
Did I request thee, Maker, from my clay
To mould me Man?  Did I solicit thee
From darkness to promote me, or here place
In this delicious garden?  As my will
Concurred not to my being, it were but right
And equal to reduce me to my dust,
Desirous to resign and render back
All I received, unable to perform                            750
Thy terms too hard, by which I was to hold
The good I sought not.  To the loss of that,
Sufficient penalty, why hast thou added
The sense of endless woes?  Inexplicable
Thy justice seems.  Yet, to say truth, too late
I thus contest; then should have been refused
Those terms, whatever, when they were proposed.
Thou didst accept them: wilt thou enjoy the good,
Then cavil the conditions?  And, though God
Made thee without thy leave, what if thy son          760
Prove disobedient, and, reproved, retort,
"Wherefore didst thou beget me?  I sought it not!"
Wouldst thou admit for his contempt of thee
That proud excuse? yet him not thy election,
But natural necessity, begot.
    God made thee of choice his own, and of his own
To serve him; thy reward was of his grace;
Thy punishment, then, justly is at his will.
Be it so, for I submit; his doom is fair,
That dust I am, and shall to dust return.                   770
O welcome hour whenever!  Why delays
His hand to execute what his decree
Fixed on this day?  Why do I overlive?
Why am I mocked with death, and lengthened out
To deathless pain?  How gladly would I meet
Mortality, my sentence, and be earth
Insensible! how glad would lay me down
As in my mother's lap!  There I should rest
And sleep secure; his dreadful voice no more
Would thunder in my ears; no fear of worse               780

To me and to my offspring would torment me
With cruel expectation. Yet one doubt
Pursues me still—lest all I cannot die;
Lest that pure breath of life, the Spirit of Man
Which God inspired, cannot together perish
With this corporeal clod. Then, in the grave,
Or in some other dismal place, who knows
But I shall die a living death? O thought
Horrid, if true! Yet why? It was but breath
Of life that sinned: what dies but what had life          790
And sin? The body properly hath neither.
All of me, then, shall die: let this appease
The doubt, since human reach no further knows.
For, though the Lord of all be infinite,
Is his wrath also? be it, Man is not so,
But mortal doomed. How can he exercise
Wrath without end on Man, whom death must end?
Can he make deathless death? that were to make
Strange contradiction; which to God himself
Impossible is held, as argument                          800
Of weakness, not of power. Will he draw out,
For anger's sake, finite to infinite
In punished Man, to satisfy his rigour,
Satisfied never? that were to extend
His sentence beyond dust and Nature's law;
By which all causes else, according still
To the reception of their matter, act,
Not to th' extent of their own sphere. But say
That death be not one stroke, as I supposed,
Bereaving sense, but endless misery                      810
From this day onward, which I feel begun
Both in me and without me, and so last
To perpetuity——Ay me! that fear
Comes thund'ring back with dreadful revolution
On my defenceless head! Both Death and I
Am found eternal, and incorporate both:
Nor I on my part single; in me all
Posterity stands cursed. Fair patrimony
That I must leave ye, sons! Oh, were I able
To waste it all myself, and leave ye none!              820
So disinherited, how would ye bless

Me, now your curse! Ah, why should all Mankind,
For one man's fault, thus guiltless be condemned,
If guiltless? But from me what can proceed
But all corrupt—both mind and will depraved
Not to do only, but to will the same
With me? How can they, then, acquitted stand
In sight of God? Him, after all disputes,
Forced I absolve. All my evasions vain
And reasonings, though through mazes, lead me still
But to my own conviction: first and last                      831
On me, me only, as the source and spring
Of all corruption, all the blame lights due.
So might the wrath! Fond wish! couldst thou support
That burden, heavier than the Earth to bear—
Than all the world much heavier, though divided
With that bad Woman? Thus, what thou desir'st,
And what thou fear'st, alike destroys all hope
Of refuge, and concludes thee miserable
Beyond all past example and future—                          840
To Satan only like, both crime and doom.
O Conscience! into what abyss of fears
And horrors hast thou driven me; out of which
I find no way, from deep to deeper plunged!'
      Thus Adam to himself lamented loud
Through the still night—not now, as ere Man fell,
Wholesome and cool and mild, but with black air
Accompanied, with damps and dreadful gloom;
Which to his evil conscience represented
All things with double terror. On the ground                 850
Outstretched he lay, on the cold grounds, and oft
Cursed his creation; Death as oft accused
Of tardy execution, since denounced
The day of his offence. 'Why comes not Death,'
Said he, 'with one thrice acceptable stroke
To end me? Shall Truth fail to keep her word,
Justice divine not hasten to be just?
But Death comes not at call; Justice divine
Mends not her slowest pace for prayers or cries.
O woods, O fountains, hillocks, dales, and bowers!           860
With other echo late I taught your shades
To answer, and resound far other song.'

Whom thus afflicted when sad Eve beheld,
Desolate where she sat, approaching nigh,
Soft words to his fierce passion she assayed;
But her, with stern regard, he thus repelled:—
    'Out of my sight, thou serpent! That name best
Befits thee with him leagued, thyself as false
And hateful: nothing wants, but that thy shape
Like his, and colour serpentine, may show          870
Thy inward fraud, to warn all creatures from thee
Henceforth, lest that too heavenly form, pretended
To hellish falsehood, snare them. But for thee
I had persisted happy, had not thy pride
And wand'ring vanity, when least was safe,
Rejected my forewarning, and disdained
Not to be trusted—longing to be seen,
Though by the Devil himself; him overweening
To overreach; but, with the Serpent meeting,
Fooled and beguiled; by him thou, I by thee,         880
To trust thee from my side, imagined wise,
Constant, mature, proof against all assaults,
And understood not all was but a show,
Rather than solid virtue, all but a rib
Crooked by nature—bent, as now appears,
More to the part sinister—from me drawn;
Well if thrown out, as supernumerary
To my just number found! Oh, why did God,
Creator wise, that peopled highest Heaven
With Spirits masculine, create at last             890
This novelty on Earth, this fair defect
Of Nature, and not fill the World at once
With men as Angels, without feminine;
Or find some other way to generate
Mankind? This mischief had not then befall'n,
And more that shall befall—innumerable
Disturbances on Earth through female snares,
And strait conjunction with this sex: for either
He never shall find out fit mate, but such
As some misfortune brings him, or mistake;          900
Or whom he wishes most shall seldom gain,
Through her perverseness, but shall see her gained
By a far worse, or, if she love, withheld

By parents; or his happiest choice too late
Shall meet, already linked and wedlock-bound
To a fell adversary, his hate or shame:
Which infinite calamity shall cause
To human life, and household peace confound.'
   He added not, and from her turned; but Eve,
Not so repulsed, with tears that ceased not flowing,   910
And tresses all disordered, at his feet
Fell humble, and, embracing them, besought
His peace, and thus proceeded in her plaint:—
   'Forsake me not thus, Adam! witness Heaven
What love sincere and reverence in my heart
I bear thee, and unweeting have offended,
Unhappily deceived! Thy suppliant
I beg, and clasp thy knees; bereave me not
Whereon I live, thy gentle looks, thy aid,
Thy counsel in this uttermost distress,   920
My only strength and stay. Forlorn of thee,
Whither shall I betake me, where subsist?
While yet we live, scarce one short hour perhaps,
Between us two let there be peace; both joining,
As joined in injuries, one enmity
Against a foe by doom express assigned us,
That cruel Serpent. On me exercise not
Thy hatred for this misery befall'n—
On me already lost, me than thyself
More miserable. Both have sinned; but thou   930
Against God only; I against God and thee,
And to the place of judgement will return,
There with my cries importune Heaven, that all
The sentence, from thy head removed, may light
On me, sole cause to thee of all this woe,
Me, me only, just object of His ire.'
   She ended, weeping; and her lowly plight,
Immoveable till peace obtained from fault
Acknowledged and deplored, in Adam wrought
Commiseration: soon his heart relented   940
Towards her, his life so late, and sole delight,
Now at his feet submissive in distress—
Creature so fair his reconcilement seeking,
His counsel whom she had displeased, his aid.

As one disarmed, his anger all he lost,
And thus with peaceful words upraised her soon:—
    'Unwary, and too desirous, as before
So now, of what thou know'st not, who desir'st
The punishment all on thyself! Alas!
Bear thine own first, ill able to sustain                    950
His full wrath whose thou feel'st as yet least part,
And my displeasure bear'st so ill. If prayers
Could alter high decrees, I to that place
Would speed before thee, and be louder heard,
That on my head all might be visited,
Thy frailty and infirmer sex forgiven,
To me committed, and by me exposed.
But rise; let us no more contend, nor blame
Each other, blamed enough elsewhere, but strive
In offices of love how we may lighten                    960
Each other's burden in our share of woe;
Since this day's death denounced, if aught I see,
Will prove no sudden, but a slow-paced evil,
A long day's dying, to augment our pain,
And to our seed (O hapless seed!) derived.'
    To whom thus Eve, recovering heart, replied:—
'Adam, by sad experiment I know
How little weight my words with thee can find,
Found so erroneous, thence by just event
Found so unfortunate; nevertheless,                    970
Restored by thee, vile as I am, to place
Of new acceptance, hopeful to regain
Thy love, the sole contentment of my heart,
Living or dying from thee I will not hide
What thoughts in my unquiet breast are risen,
Tending to some relief of our extremes,
Or end, though sharp and sad, yet tolerable,
As in our evils, and of easier choice.
If care of our descent perplex us most,
Which must be born to certain woe, devoured                    980
By Death at last (and miserable it is
To be to others cause of misery,
Our own begotten, and of our loins to bring
Into this cursed world a woeful race,
That, after wretched life, must be at last

Food for so foul a monster), in thy power
It lies, yet ere conception, to prevent
The race unblest, to being yet unbegot.
Childless thou art; childless remain; so Death
Shall be deceived his glut, and with us two          990
Be forced to satisfy his ravenous maw.
But, if thou judge it hard and difficult,
Conversing, looking, loving, to abstain
From love's due rites, nuptial embraces sweet,
And with desire to languish without hope
Before the present object languishing
With like desire—which would be misery
And torment less than none of what we dread—
Then, both our selves and seed at once to free
From what we fear for both, let us make short;      1000
Let us seek Death, or, he not found, supply
With our own hands his office on ourselves.
Why stand we longer shivering under fears
That show no end but death, and have the power,
Of many ways to die the shortest choosing,
Destruction with destruction to destroy?'
      She ended here, or vehement despair
Broke off the rest; so much of death her thoughts
Had entertained as dyed her cheeks with pale.
But Adam, with such counsel nothing swayed,         1010
To better hopes his more attentive mind
Labouring had raised, and thus to Eve replied:—
      'Eve, thy contempt of life and pleasure seems
To argue in thee something more sublime
And excellent than what thy mind contemns:
But self-destruction therefore sought refutes
That excellence thought in thee, and implies
Not thy contempt, but anguish and regret
For loss of life and pleasure overlooved.
Or, if thou covet death, as utmost end             1020
Of misery, so thinking to evade
The penalty pronounced, doubt not but God
Hath wiselier armed his vengeful ire than so
To be forestalled: much more I fear lest death
So snatched will not exempt us from the pain
We are by doom to pay; rather such acts

Of contumacy will provoke the Highest
To make death in us live. Then let us seek
Some safer resolution—which methinks
I have in view, calling to mind with heed                    1030
Part of our sentence, that thy seed shall bruise
The Serpent's head: piteous amends! unless
Be meant, whom I conjecture, our grand foe,
Satan, who in the Serpent hath contrived
Against us this deceit: to crush his head
Would be revenge indeed—which will be lost
By death brought on ourselves, or childless days
Resolved as thou proposest; so our foe
Shall scape his punishment ordained, and we
Instead shall double ours upon our heads.                    1040
No more be mentioned, then, of violence
Against ourselves, and wilful barrenness,
That cuts us off from hope, and savours only
Rancour and pride, impatience and despite,
Reluctance against God and his just yoke
Laid on our necks. Remember with what mild
And gracious temper he both heard and judged,
Without wrath or reviling. We expected
Immediate dissolution, which we thought
Was meant by death that day; when, lo! to thee           1050
Pains only in child-bearing were foretold,
And bringing forth, soon recompensed with joy,
Fruit of thy womb. On me the curse aslope
Glanced on the ground: with labour I must earn
My bread; what harm? Idleness had been worse;
My labour will sustain me; and, lest cold
Or heat should injure us, his timely care
Hath, unbesought, provided, and his hands
Clothed us unworthy, pitying while he judged.
How much more, if we pray him, will his ear                1060
Be open, and his heart to pity incline,
And teach us further by what means to shun
Th' inclement seasons, rain, ice, hail, and snow!
Which now the sky, with various face, begins
To show us in this mountain, while the winds
Blow moist and keen, shattering the graceful locks
Of these fair spreading trees; which bids us seek

Some better shroud, some better warmth to cherish
Our limbs benumbed—ere this diurnal star
Leave cold the night, how we his gathered beams      1070
Reflected may with matter sere foment,
Or by collision of two bodies grind
The air attrite to fire; as late the clouds,
Justling, or pushed with winds, rude in their shock,
Tine the slant lightning, whose thwart flame, driven
        down,
Kindles the gummy bark of fir or pine,
And sends a comfortable heat from far,
Which might supply the sun; such fire to use,
And what may else be remedy or cure
To evils which our own misdeeds have wrought,       1080
He will instruct us praying, and of grace
Beseeching him: so as we need not fear
To pass commodiously this life, sustained
By him with many comforts, till we end
In dust, our final rest and native home.
What better can we do than, to the place
Repairing where he judged us, prostrate fall
Before him reverent, and there confess
Humbly our faults, and pardon beg, with tears
Wat'ring the ground, and with our sighs the air      1090
Frequenting, sent from hearts contrite, in sign
Of sorrow unfeigned and humiliation meek?
Undoubtedly he will relent, and turn
From his displeasure; in whose look serene,
When angry most he seemed and most severe,
What else but favour, grace, and mercy shone?'
    So spake our Father penitent; nor Eve
Felt less remorse: they, forthwith to the place
Repairing where he judged them, prostrate fell
Before him reverent, and both confessed             1100
Humbly their faults, and pardon begged, with tears
Wat'ring the ground, and with their sighs the air
Frequenting, sent from hearts contrite, in sign
Of sorrow unfeigned and humiliation meek.

*The End of the Tenth Book.*

# PARADISE LOST

## BOOK XI

### THE ARGUMENT

*The Son of God presents to his Father the prayers of our first
parents now repenting, and intercedes for them. God accepts
them, but declares that they must no longer abide in Paradise;
sends Michael with a band of Cherubim to dispossess them,
but first to reveal to Adam future things: Michael's coming
down. Adam shows to Eve certain ominous signs: he discerns
Michael's approach; goes out to meet him: the Angel de-
nounces their departure. Eve's lamentation. Adam pleads,
but submits: the Angel leads him up to a high hill; sets before
him in vision what shall happen till the Flood.*

THUS they, in lowliest plight, repentant stood
Praying; for from the mercy-seat above
Prevenient grace descending had removed
The stony from their hearts, and made new flesh
Regenerate grow instead, that sighs now breathed
Unutterable, which the Spirit of prayer
Inspired, and winged for Heaven with speedier flight
Than loudest oratory: yet their port
Not of mean suitors; nor important less
Seemed their petition than when th' ancient pair          10
In fables old, less ancient yet than these,
Deucalion and chaste Pyrrha, to restore
The race of mankind drowned, before the shrine
Of Themis stood devout.  To Heaven their prayers
Flew up, nor missed the way, by envious winds
Blown vagabond or frustrate: in they passed
Dimensionless through heavenly doors; then, clad
With incense, where the golden altar fumed,
By their great Intercessor, came in sight
Before the Father's throne.  Them the glad Son          20
Presenting, thus to intercede began:—
  'See, Father, what firstfruits on Earth are sprung
From thy implanted grace in Man—these sighs

And prayers, which in this golden censer, mixed
With incense, I, thy priest, before thee bring;
Fruits of more pleasing savour, from thy seed
Sown with contrition in his heart, than those
Which, his own hand manuring, all the trees
Of Paradise could have produced, ere fall'n
From innocence. Now, therefore, bend thine ear    30
To supplication; hear his sighs, though mute;
Unskilful with what words to pray, let me
Interpret for him, me his advocate
And propitiation; all his works on me,
Good or not good, ingraft; my merit those
Shall perfect, and for these my death shall pay.
Accept me, and in me from these receive
The smell of peace toward Mankind; let him live,
Before thee reconciled, at least his days
Numbered, though sad, till death, his doom (which I    40
To mitigate thus plead, not to reverse),
To better life shall yield him, where with me
All my redeemed may dwell in joy and bliss,
Made one with me, as I with thee am one.'
   To whom the Father, without cloud, serene:—
'All thy request for Man, accepted Son,
Obtain; all thy request was my decree:
But longer in that Paradise to dwell
The law I gave to Nature him forbids;
Those pure immortal elements, that know    50
No gross, no unharmonious mixture foul,
Eject him, tainted now, and purge him off,
As a distemper gross, to air as gross,
And mortal food, as may dispose him best
For dissolution wrought by sin, that first
Distempered all things, and of incorrupt
Corrupted. I at first with two fair gifts
Created him endowed—with Happiness
And Immortality; that fondly lost,
This other served but to eternize woe,    60
Till I provided Death: so Death becomes
His final remedy, and after life
Tried in sharp tribulation, and refined
By faith and faithful works, to second life,

Waked in the renovation of the just,
Resigns him up with Heaven and Earth renewed.
But let us call to synod all the Blest
Through Heaven's wide bounds; from them I will not hide
My judgements—how with Mankind I proceed,
As how with peccant Angels late they saw,                    70
And in their state, though firm, stood more confirmed.'
        He ended, and the Son gave signal high
To the bright Minister that watched, he blew
His trumpet, heard in Oreb since perhaps
When God descended, and perhaps once more
To sound at general doom. Th' angelic blast
Filled all the regions: from their blissful bowers
Of amarantine shade, fountain or spring,
By the waters of life, where'er they sat
In fellowships of joy, the Sons of Light                     80
Hasted, resorting to the summons high,
And took their seats, till from his throne supreme
Th' Almighty thus pronounced his sovran will:—
        'O Sons, like one of us Man is become
To know both good and evil, since his taste
Of that defended fruit; but let him boast
His knowledge of good lost and evil got,
Happier had it sufficed him to have known
Good by itself and evil not at all.
He sorrows now, repents, and prays contrite—                 90
My motions in him; longer than they move,
His heart I know how variable and vain,
Self-left. Lest, therefore, his now bolder hand
Reach also of the Tree of Life, and eat,
And live for ever, dream at least to live
For ever, to remove him I decree,
And send him from the Garden forth, to till
The ground whence he was taken, fitter soil.
        'Michael, this my behest have thou in charge:
Take to thee from among the Cherubim                         100
Thy choice of flaming warriors, lest the Fiend,
Or in behalf of Man, or to invade
Vacant possession, some new trouble raise;
Haste thee, and from the Paradise of God

Without remorse drive out the sinful pair,
From hallowed ground th' unholy, and denounce
To them, and to their progeny, from thence
Perpetual banishment. Yet, lest they faint
At the sad sentence rigorously urged
(For I behold them softened, and with tears          110
Bewailing their excess), all terror hide.
If patiently thy bidding they obey,
Dismiss them not disconsolate; reveal
To Adam what shall come in future days,
As I shall thee enlighten; intermix
My cov'nant in the Woman's seed renewed.
So send them forth, though sorrowing, yet in peace;
And on the east side of the Garden place,
Where entrance up from Eden easiest climbs,
Cherubic watch, and of a sword the flame          120
Wide-waving, all approach far off to fright,
And guard all passage to the Tree of Life;
Lest Paradise a receptacle prove
To Spirits foul, and all my trees their prey,
With whose stol'n fruit Man once more to delude.'
    He ceased, and th' Archangelic Power prepared
For swift descent; with him the cohort bright
Of watchful Cherubim. Four faces each
Had, like a double Janus; all their shape
Spangled with eyes more numerous than those          130
Of Argus, and more wakeful than to drowse,
Charmed with Arcadian pipe, the pastoral reed
Of Hermes, or his opiate rod. Meanwhile,
To resalute the World with sacred light,
Leucothea waked, and with fresh dews embalmed
The Earth, when Adam and first matron Eve
Had ended now their orisons, and found,
Strength added from above, new hope to spring
Out of despair, joy, but with fear yet linked;
Which thus to Eve his welcome words renewed:—          140
    'Eve, easily may faith admit that all
The good which we enjoy from Heaven descends;
But that from us aught should ascend to Heaven
So prevalent as to concern the mind
Of God high-blest, or to incline his will,

Hard to belief may seem; yet this will prayer,
Or one short sigh of human breath, upborne
Even to the seat of God. For, since I sought
By prayer th' offended Deity to appease,
Kneeled and before him humbled all my heart,   150
Methought I saw him placable and mild,
Bending his ear; persuasion in me grew
That I was heard with favour; peace returned
Home to my breast, and to my memory
His promise that thy seed shall bruise our Foe;
Which, then not minded in dismay, yet now
Assures me that the bitterness of death
Is past, and we shall live. Whence hail to thee!
Eve rightly called, Mother of all Mankind,
Mother of all things living, since by thee   160
Man is to live, and all things live for Man.'
  To whom thus Eve, with sad demeanour meek:—
'Ill-worthy I such title should belong
To me transgressor, who, for thee ordained
A help, became thy snare; to me reproach
Rather belongs, distrust and all dispraise:
But infinite in pardon was my Judge,
That I, who first brought death on all, am graced
The source of life; next favourable thou,
Who highly thus t' entitle me vouchsaf'st,   170
Far other name deserving. But the field
To labour calls us, now with sweat imposed,
Though after sleepless night; for see! the Morn,
All unconcerned with our unrest, begins
Her rosy progress smiling; let us forth,
I never from thy side henceforth to stray,
Where'er our day's work lies, though now enjoined
Laborious, till day droop; while here we dwell,
What can be toilsome in these pleasant walks?
Here let us live, though in fall'n state, content.'  180
  So spake, so wished, much-humbled Eve; but Fate
Subscribed not; Nature first gave signs, impressed
On bird, beast, air—air suddenly eclipsed,
After short blush of morn. Nigh in her sight
The bird of Jove, stooped from his aery tour,
Two birds of gayest plume before him drove;

Down from a hill the beast that reigns in woods,
First hunter then, pursued a gentle brace,
Goodliest of all the forest, hart and hind;
Direct to th' eastern gate was bent their flight.            190
Adam observed, and, with his eye the chase
Pursuing, not unmoved, to Eve thus spake:—

'O Eve, some further change awaits us nigh,
Which Heaven by these mute signs in Nature shows,
Forerunners of his purpose, or to warn
Us, haply too secure of our discharge
From penalty because from death released
Some days: how long, and what till then our life,
Who knows, or more than this, that we are dust,
And thither must return, and be no more?            200
Why else this double object in our sight
Of flight pursued in th' air and o'er the ground
One way the self-same hour? Why in the east
Darkness ere day's mid-course, and morning-light
More orient in yon western cloud, that draws
O'er the blue firmament a radiant white,
And slow descends, with something heavenly fraught?'

He erred not; for by this the heavenly bands
Down from a sky of jasper lighted now            210
In Paradise, and on a hill made halt—
A glorious apparition, had not doubt
And carnal fear that day dimmed Adam's eye.
Not that more glorious when the Angels met
Jacob in Mahanaim, where he saw
The field pavilioned with his guardians bright;
Nor that which on the flaming mount appeared
In Dothan, covered with a camp of fire,
Against the Syrian king, who, to surprise
One man, assassin-like, had levied war,
War unproclaimed. The princely Hierarch            220
In their bright stand there left his Powers to seize
Possession of the Garden; he alone,
To find where Adam sheltered, took his way;
Not unperceived of Adam, who to Eve,
While the great visitant approached, thus spake:—

'Eve, now expect great tidings, which, perhaps,
Of us will soon determine, or impose

New laws to be observed; for I descry,
From yonder blazing cloud that veils the hill,
One of the heavenly host, and, by his gait,                    230
None of the meanest—some great Potentate,
Or of the Thrones above, such majesty
Invests him coming; yet not terrible,
That I should fear, nor sociably mild,
As Raphael, that I should much confide,
But solemn and sublime; whom not to offend,
With reverence I must meet, and thou retire.'
　　He ended; and th' Archangel soon drew nigh,
Not in his shape celestial, but as man
Clad to meet man; over his lucid arms                          240
A military vest of purple flowed,
Livelier than Melibœan, or the grain
Of Sarra, worn by kings and heroes old
In time of truce; Iris had dipped the woof:
His starry helm unbuckled showed him prime
In manhood where youth ended; by his side,
As in a glistering zodiac, hung the sword,
Satan's dire dread, and in his hand the spear.
Adam bowed low; he, kingly, from his state
Inclined not, but his coming thus declared:—                   256
　　'Adam, Heaven's high behest no preface needs:
Sufficient that thy prayers are heard, and Death,
Then due by sentence when thou didst transgress,
Defeated of his seizure many days,
Given thee of grace, wherein thou may'st repent,
And one bad act with many deeds well done
May'st cover: well may then thy Lord, appeased,
Redeem thee quite from Death's rapacious claim;
But longer in this Paradise to dwell
Permits not; to remove thee I am come,                         260
And send thee from the garden forth, to till
The ground whence thou wast taken, fitter soil.'
　　He added not; for Adam, at the news
Heart-struck, with chilling gripe of sorrow stood,
That all his senses bound; Eve, who unseen
Yet all had heard, with audible lament
Discovered soon the place of her retire:—
　　'O unexpected stroke, worse than of Death!

Must I thus leave thee, Paradise? thus leave
Thee, native soil, these happy walks and shades,          270
Fit haunt of Gods? where I had hope to spend,
Quiet, though sad, the respite of that day
That must be mortal to us both?  O flowers,
That never will in other climate grow,
My early visitation, and my last
At even, which I bred up with tender hand
From the first opening bud, and gave ye names,
Who now shall rear ye to the Sun, or rank
Your tribes, and water from th' ambrosial fount?
Thee, lastly, nuptial bower, by me adorned          280
With what to sight or smell was sweet, from thee
How shall I part, and whither wander down
Into a lower world, to this obscure
And wild? how shall we breathe in other air
Less pure, accustomed to immortal fruits?'
    Whom thus the Angel interrupted mild:—
'Lament not, Eve, but patiently resign
What justly thou hast lost; nor set thy heart,
Thus over-fond, on that which is not thine.
Thy going is not lonely; with thee goes          290
Thy husband; him to follow thou art bound;
Where he abides, think there thy native soil.'
    Adam, by this from the cold sudden damp
Recovering, and his scattered spirits returned,
To Michael thus his humble words addressed:—
    'Celestial, whether among the Thrones, or named
Of them the highest—for such of shape may seem
Prince above princes—gently hast thou told
Thy message, which might else in telling wound,
And in performing end us; what besides          300
Of sorrow, and dejection, and despair,
Our frailty can sustain, thy tidings bring—
Departure from this happy place, our sweet
Recess, and only consolation left
Familiar to our eyes; all places else
Inhospitable appear, and desolate,
Nor knowing us, nor known: and if by prayer
Incessant I could hope to change the will
Of him who all things can, I would not cease

To weary him with my assiduous cries;                    310
But prayer against his absolute decree
No more avails than breath against the wind,
Blown stifling back on him that breathes it forth:
Therefore to his great bidding I submit.
This most afflicts me—that, departing hence,
As from his face I shall be hid, deprived
His blessed count'nance; here I could frequent,
With worship, place by place where he vouchsafed
Presence Divine, and to my sons relate,
"On this mount he appeared; under this tree            320
Stood visible; among these pines his voice
I heard; here with him at this fountain talked."
So many grateful altars I would rear
Of grassy turf, and pile up every stone
Of lustre from the brook, in memory
Or monument to ages, and thereon
Offer sweet-smelling gums, and fruits, and flowers.
In yonder nether world where shall I seek
His bright appearances, or footstep trace?
For, though I fled him angry, yet, recalled            330
To life prolonged and promised race, I now
Gladly behold though but his utmost skirts
Of glory, and far off his steps adore.'
    To whom thus Michael, with regard benign:—
'Adam, thou know'st Heaven his, and all the Earth,
Not this rock only; his omnipresence fills
Land, sea, and air, and every kind that lives,
Fomented by his virtual power and warmed.
All th' Earth he gave thee to possess and rule,
No despicable gift; surmise not, then,                 340
His presence to these narrow bounds confined
Of Paradise or Eden: this had been
Perhaps thy capital seat, from whence had spread
All generations, and had hither come,
From all the ends of th' Earth, to celebrate
And reverence thee their great progenitor.
But this pre-eminence thou hast lost, brought down
To dwell on even ground now with thy sons:
Yet doubt not but in valley and in plain
God is as here, and will be found alike                350

Present, and of his presence many a sign
Still following thee, still compassing thee round
With goodness and paternal love, his face
Express, and of his steps the track divine.
Which that thou may'st believe, and be confirmed
Ere thou from hence depart, know I am sent
To show thee what shall come in future days
To thee and to thy offspring; good with bad
Expect to hear, supernal grace contending
With sinfulness of men—thereby to learn                360
True patience, and to temper joy with fear
And pious sorrow, equally inured
By moderation either state to bear,
Prosperous or adverse: so shalt thou lead
Safest thy life, and best prepared endure
Thy mortal passage when it comes.  Ascend
This hill; let Eve (for I have drenched her eyes)
Here sleep below while thou to foresight wak'st,
As once thou slept'st while she to life was formed.'
    To whom thus Adam gratefully replied:—                370
'Ascend; I follow thee, safe guide, the path
Thou lead'st me, and to the hand of Heaven submit,
However chastening—to the evil turn
My obvious breast, arming to overcome
By suffering, and earn rest from labour won,
If so I may attain.'  So both ascend
In the visions of God; it was a hill,
Of Paradise the highest, from whose top
The hemisphere of Earth in clearest ken
Stretched out to amplest reach of prospect lay.                380
Not higher that hill, nor wider looking round,
Whereon for different cause the Tempter set
Our second Adam, in the wilderness,
To show him all Earth's kingdoms and their glory.
His eye might there command wherever stood
City of old or modern fame, the seat
Of mightiest empire, from the destined walls
Of Kambalu, seat of Cathaian Can,
And Samarcand by Oxus, Temir's throne,
To Paquin of Sinæan kings, and thence                390
To Agra and Lahor of Great Mogul,

Down to the golden Chersonese, or where
The Persian in Ecbatan sat, or since
In Ispahan, or where the Russian Tsar
In Moscow, or the Sultan in Bizance,
Turkestan-born; nor could his eye not ken
Th' empire of Negus to his utmost port
Ercoco, and the less maritime kings,
Mombaza, and Quiloa, and Melind,
And Sofala (thought Ophir), to the realm          400
Of Congo, and Angola farthest south;
Or thence from Niger flood to Atlas mount,
The kingdoms of Almansor, Fez and Sus,
Marocco, and Algiers, and Tremisen;
On Europe thence, and where Rome was to sway
The world: in spirit perhaps he also saw
Rich Mexico, the seat of Motezume,
And Cusco in Peru, the richer seat
Of Atabalipa, and yet unspoiled
Guiana, whose great city Geryon's sons          410
Call El Dorado: but to nobler sights
Michael from Adam's eyes the film removed,
Which that false fruit that promised clearer sight
Had bred; then purged with euphrasy and rue
The visual nerve, for he had much to see,
And from the well of life three drops instilled.
So deep the power of these ingredients pierced,
Even to the inmost seat of mental sight,
That Adam, now enforced to close his eyes,
Sunk down, and all his spirits became entranced:          420
But him the gentle Angel by the hand
Soon raised, and his attention thus recalled:—

'Adam, now ope thine eyes, and first behold
Th' effects which thy original crime hath wrought
In some to spring from thee, who never touched
Th' excepted tree, nor with the Snake conspired,
Nor sinned thy sin, yet from that sin derive
Corruption to bring forth more violent deeds.'

His eyes he opened, and beheld a field,
Part arable and tilth, whereon were sheaves          430
New-reaped, the other part sheep-walks and folds;
I' th' midst an altar as the landmark stood,

Rustic, of grassy sward; thither anon
A sweaty reaper from his tillage brought
Firstfruits, the green ear and the yellow sheaf,
Uncull'd, as came to hand; a shepherd next,
More meek, came with the firstlings of his flock,
Choicest and best; then, sacrificing, laid
The inwards and their fat, with incense strewed,
On the cleft wood, and all due rites performed.  440
His off'ring soon propitious fire from Heaven
Consumed with nimble glance and grateful steam:
The other's not, for his was not sincere:
Whereat he inly raged, and, as they talked,
Smote him into the midriff with a stone
That beat out life; he fell, and, deadly pale,
Groaned out his soul, with gushing blood effused.
Much at that sight was Adam in his heart
Dismayed, and thus in haste to th' Angel cried:—
'O Teacher, some great mischief hath befallen  450
To that meek man, who well had sacrificed:
Is piety thus and pure devotion paid?'
T' whom Michael thus, he also moved, replied:—
'These two are brethren, Adam, and to come
Out of thy loins; th' unjust the just hath slain,
For envy that his brother's offering found
From Heaven acceptance; but the bloody fact
Will be avenged, and th' other's faith approved
Lose no reward, though here thou see him die,
Rolling in dust and gore.' To which our Sire:—  460
'Alas, both for the deed and for the cause!
But have I now seen Death? Is this the way
I must return to native dust? O sight
Of terror, foul and ugly to behold,
Horrid to think, how horrible to feel!'
To whom thus Michael:—'Death thou hast seen
In his first shape on Man; but many shapes
Of Death, and many are the ways that lead
To his grim cave—all dismal, yet to sense
More terrible at th' entrance than within.  470
Some, as thou saw'st, by violent stroke shall die,
By fire, flood, famine; by intemperance more
In meats and drinks, which on the Earth shall bring

Diseases dire, of which a monstrous crew
Before thee shall appear, that thou may'st know
What misery th' inabstinence of Eve
Shall bring on men.'  Immediately a place
Before his eyes appeared, sad, noisome, dark;
A lazar-house it seemed, wherein were laid
Numbers of all diseased—all maladies          480
Of ghastly spasm, or racking torture, qualms
Of heart-sick agony; all feverous kinds,
Convulsions, epilepsies, fierce catarrhs,
Intestine stone and ulcer, colic pangs,
Demoniac frenzy, moping melancholy,
And moon-struck madness, pining atrophy,
Marasmus, and wide-wasting pestilence,
Dropsies and asthmas, and joint-racking rheums.
Dire was the tossing, deep the groans; Despair
Tended the sick, busiest from couch to couch;          490
And over them triumphant Death his dart
Shook, but delayed to strike, though oft invoked
With vows, as their chief good and final hope.
Sight so deform what heart of rock could long
Dry-eyed behold?  Adam could not, but wept,
Though not of woman born: compassion quelled
His best of man, and gave him up to tears
A space, till firmer thoughts restrained excess,
And, scarce recovering words, his plaint renewed:—
    'O miserable Mankind, to what fall          500
Degraded, to what wretched state reserved!
Better end here unborn.  Why is life given
To be thus wrested from us? rather why
Obtruded on us thus? who, if we knew
What we receive, would either not accept
Life offered, or soon beg to lay it down,
Glad to be so dismissed in peace.  Can thus
Th' image of God in Man, created once
So goodly and erect, though faulty since,
To such unsightly sufferings be debased          510
Under inhuman pains?  Why should not Man,
Retaining still divine similitude
In part, from such deformities be free,
And for his Maker's image' sake exempt?'

'Their Maker's image,' answered Michael, 'then
Forsook them, when themselves they vilified
To serve ungoverned appetite, and took
His image whom they served—a brutish vice,
Inductive mainly to the sin of Eve.
Therefore so abject is their punishment,  520
Disfiguring not God's likeness, but their own;
Or, if his likeness, by themselves defaced,
While they pervert pure Nature's healthful rules
To loathsome sickness—worthily, since they
God's image did not reverence in themselves.'

'I yield it just,' said Adam, 'and submit.
But is there yet no other way, besides
These painful passages, how we may come
To death, and mix with our connatural dust?'

'There is,' said Michael, 'if thou well observe  530
The rule of *Not too much*, by temperance taught
In what thou eat'st and drink'st, seeking from thence
Due nourishment, not gluttonous delight,
Till many years over thy head return:
So may'st thou live, till, like ripe fruit, thou drop
Into thy mother's lap, or be with ease
Gathered, not harshly plucked, for death mature:
This is old age; but then thou must outlive
Thy youth, thy strength, thy beauty, which will change
To withered, weak, and grey; thy senses then,  540
Obtuse, all taste of pleasure must forgo
To what thou hast; and, for the air of youth,
Hopeful and cheerful, in thy blood will reign
A melancholy damp of cold and dry,
To weigh thy spirits down, and last consume
The balm of life.' To whom our Ancestor:—

'Henceforth I fly not death, nor would prolong
Life much, bent rather how I may be quit,
Fairest and easiest, of this cumbrous charge,
Which I must keep till my appointed day  550
Of rend'ring up, and patiently attend
My dissolution.' Michael replied:—

'Nor love thy life, nor hate; but what thou liv'st
Live well; how long or short permit to Heaven:
And now prepare thee for another sight.'

He looked, and saw a spacious plain, whereon
Were tents of various hue; by some were herds
Of cattle grazing: others whence the sound
Of instruments that made melodious chime
Was heard, of harp and organ; and who moved          560
Their stops and chords was seen: his volant touch,
Instinct through all proportions low and high,
Fled and pursued transverse the resonant fugue.
In other part stood one who, at the forge
Labouring, two massy clods of iron and brass
Had melted (whether found where casual fire
Had wasted woods, on mountain or in vale,
Down to the veins of earth, thence gliding hot
To some cave's mouth, or whether washed by stream
From underground); the liquid ore he drained          570
Into fit moulds prepared; from which he formed
First his own tools, then what might else be wrought
Fusil or graven in metal. After these,
But on the hither side, a different sort
From the high neighbouring hills, which was their seat,
Down to the plain descended: by their guise
Just men they seemed, and all their study bent
To worship God aright, and know his works
Not hid; nor those things last which might preserve
Freedom and peace to men: they on the plain          580
Long had not walked, when from the tents behold
A bevy of fair women, richly gay
In gems and wanton dress; to the harp they sung
Soft amorous ditties, and in dance came on:
The men, though grave, eyed them, and let their eyes
Rove without rein, till, in the amorous net
Fast caught, they liked, and each his liking chose;
And now of love they treat, till th' evening-star,
Love's harbinger, appeared; then, all in heat,
They light the nuptial torch, and bid invoke          590
Hymen, then first to marriage rites invoked:
With feast and music all the tents resound.
Such happy interview, and fair event
Of love and youth not lost, songs, garlands, flowers,
And charming symphonies, attached the heart
Of Adam, soon inclined to admit delight,

The bent of Nature; which he thus expressed:—
　'True opener of mine eyes, prime Angel blest,
Much better seems this vision, and more hope
Of peaceful days portends, than those two past:　　　60c
Those were of hate and death, or pain much worse;
Here Nature seems fulfilled in all her ends.'
　　To whom thus Michael:—'Judge not what is best
By pleasure, though to Nature seeming meet,
Created, as thou art, to nobler end,
Holy and pure, conformity divine.
Those tents thou saw'st so pleasant were the tents
Of wickedness, wherein shall dwell his race
Who slew his brother: studious they appear
Of arts that polish life, inventors rare,　　　610
Unmindful of their Maker, though his Spirit
Taught them; but they his gifts acknowledged none
Yet they a beauteous offspring shall beget;
For that fair female troop thou saw'st, that seemed
Of goddesses, so blithe, so smooth, so gay,
Yet empty of all good wherein consists
Woman's domestic honour and chief praise;
Bred only and completed to the taste
Of lustful appetence, to sing, to dance,
To dress, and troll the tongue, and roll the eye;—　　　620
To these that sober race of men, whose lives
Religious titled them the Sons of God,
Shall yield up all their virtue, all their fame,
Ignobly, to the trains and to the smiles
Of these fair atheists, and now swim in joy
(Erelong to swim at large) and laugh; for which
The world erelong a world of tears must weep.'
　　To whom thus Adam, of short joy bereft:—
'O pity and shame, that they who to live well
Entered so fair should turn aside to tread　　　630
Paths indirect, or in the midway faint!
But still I see the tenor of Man's woe
Holds on the same, from Woman to begin,'
　'From Man's effeminate slackness it begins.'
Said th' Angel, 'who should better hold his place
By wisdom, and superior gifts received.
But now prepare thee for another scene.'

  He looked, and saw wide territory spread
Before him—towns, and rural works between,
Cities of men with lofty gates and towers,                    640
Concourse in arms, fierce faces threat'ning war,
Giants of mighty bone and bold emprise.
Part wield their arms, part curb the foaming steed,
Single, or in array of battle ranged,
Both horse and foot, nor idly must'ring stood.
One way a band select from forage drives
A herd of beeves, fair oxen and fair kine,
From a fat meadow-ground, or fleecy flock,
Ewes and their bleating lambs, over the plain,
Their booty; scarce with life the shepherds fly,             650
But call in aid, which makes a bloody fray;
With cruel tournament the squadrons join;
Where cattle pastured late, now scattered lies
With carcases and arms th' ensanguined field
Deserted: others to a city strong
Lay siege, encamped; by battery, scale, and mine,
Assaulting; others from the wall defend
With dart and jav'lin, stones and sulphurous fire;
On each hand slaughter and gigantic deeds.
In other part the sceptred heralds call                       660
To council in the city-gates: anon
Grey-headed men and grave, with warriors mixed,
Assemble, and harangues are heard; but soon
In factious opposition, till at last
Of middle age one rising, eminent
In wise deport, spake much of right and wrong,
Of justice, of religion, truth, and peace,
And judgement from above: him old and young
Exploded, and had seized with violent hands,
Had not a cloud descending snatched him thence,              670
Unseen amid the throng.  So violence
Proceeded, and oppression, and sword-law,
Through all the plain, and refuge none was found.
Adam was all in tears, and to his guide
Lamenting turned full sad:—'Oh, what are these?
Death's ministers, not men! who thus deal death
Inhumanly to men, and multiply
Ten thousandfold the sin of him who slew

His brother; for of whom such massacre                          680
Make they but of their brethren, men of men?
But who was that just man, whom had not Heaven
Rescued, had in his righteousness been lost?'

    To whom thus Michael:—'These are the product
Of those ill-mated marriages thou saw'st,
Where good with bad were matched; who of themselves
Abhor to join, and, by imprudence mixed,
Produce prodigious births of body or mind.
Such were these giants, men of high renown;
For in those days might only shall be admired,
And valour and heroic virtue called;                            690
To overcome in battle, and subdue
Nations, and bring home spoils with infinite
Manslaughter, shall be held the highest pitch
Of human glory, and, for glory done,
Of triumph to be styled great conquerors,
Patrons of mankind, gods, and sons of gods—
Destroyers rightlier called, and plagues of men.
Thus fame shall be achieved, renown on earth,
And what most merits fame in silence hid.
But he, the seventh from thee, whom thou beheld'st      700
The only righteous in a world perverse,
And therefore hated, therefore so beset
With foes, for daring single to be just
And utter odious truth that God would come
To judge them with his Saints—him the Most High,
Rapt in a balmy cloud, with winged steeds,
Did, as thou saw'st, receive, to walk with God
High in salvation and the climes of bliss,
Exempt from death, to show thee what reward
Awaits the good, the rest what punishment;              710
Which now direct thine eyes and soon behold.'

    He looked, and saw the face of things quite changed.
The brazen throat of war had ceased to roar;
All now was turned to jollity and game,
To luxury and riot, feast and dance,
Marrying or prostituting, as befell,
Rape or adultery, where passing fair
Allured them; thence from cups to civil broils.
At length a reverend sire among them came,

And of their doings great dislike declared,                    720
And testified against their ways; he oft
Frequented their assemblies, whereso met,
Triumphs or festivals, and to them preached
Conversion and repentance, as to souls
In prison under judgements imminent;
But all in vain: which when he saw, he ceased
Contending, and removed his tents far off;
Then, from the mountain hewing timber tall,
Began to build a vessel of huge bulk,
Measured by cubit, length, and breadth, and height,  730
Smeared round with pitch, and in the side a door
Contrived, and of provisions laid in large
For man and beast: when lo! a wonder strange!
Of every beast, and bird, and insect small,
Came sevens and pairs, and entered in, as taught
Their order; last, the sire and his three sons,
With their four wives; and God made fast the door.
Meanwhile the south wind rose, and, with black wings
Wide-hovering, all the clouds together drove
From under heaven; the hills, to their supply,            740
Vapour, and exhalation dusk and moist,
Sent up amain; and now the thickened sky
Like a dark ceiling stood: down rushed the rain
Impetuous, and continued till the earth
No more was seen; the floating vessel swum
Uplifted, and secure with beaked prow
Rode tilting o'er the waves; all dwellings else
Flood overwhelmed, and them with all their pomp
Deep under water rolled; sea covered sea,
Sea without shore; and in their palaces,                    750
Where luxury late reigned, sea-monsters whelped
And stabled: of mankind, so numerous late,
All left in one small bottom swum embarked.
How didst thou grieve then, Adam, to behold
The end of all thy offspring, end so sad,
Depopulation! thee another flood,
Of tears and sorrow a flood, thee also drowned,
And sunk thee as thy sons; till, gently reared
By th' Angel, on thy feet thou stood'st at last,
Though comfortless, as when a father mourns        760

His children, all in view destroyed at once,
And scarce to th' Angel utter'dst thus thy plaint:—
  'O visions ill foreseen! better had I
Lived ignorant of future—so had borne
My part of evil only, each day's lot
Enough to bear; those now that were dispensed
The burden of many ages on me light
At once, by my foreknowledge gaining birth
Abortive, to torment me, ere their being,
With thought that they must be. Let no man seek     770
Henceforth to be foretold what shall befall
Him or his children—evil, he may be sure,
Which neither his foreknowing can prevent,
And he the future evil shall no less
In apprehension than in substance feel,
Grievous to bear. But that care now is past;
Man is not whom to warn; those few escaped
Famine and anguish will at last consume,
Wandering that wat'ry desert: I had hope,
When violence was ceased and war on Earth,     780
All would have then gone well, peace would have
      crowned
With length of happy days the race of Man;
But I was far deceived, for now I see
Peace to corrupt no less than war to waste.
How comes it thus? Unfold, Celestial Guide,
And whether here the race of Man will end.'
    To whom thus Michael:—'Those whom last thou
      saw'st
In triumph and luxurious wealth are they
First seen in acts of prowess eminent
And great exploits, but of true virtue void;     790
Who, having spilt much blood, and done much waste,
Subduing nations, and achieved thereby
Fame in the world, high titles, and rich prey,
Shall change their course to pleasure, ease, and sloth,
Surfeit, and lust, till wantonness and pride
Raise out of friendship hostile deeds in peace.
The conquered, also, and enslaved by war,
Shall, with their freedom lost, all virtue lose,
And fear of God—from whom their piety feigned

In sharp contest of battle found no aid                    800
Against invaders; therefore, cooled in zeal,
Thenceforth shall practise how to live secure,
Worldly or dissolute, on what their lords
Shall leave them to enjoy; for th' Earth shall bear
More than enough, that temperance may be tried.
So all shall turn degenerate, all depraved,
Justice and temperance, truth and faith, forgot;
One man except, the only son of light
In a dark age, against example good,
Against allurement, custom, and a world              810
Offended; fearless of reproach and scorn,
Or violence, he of their wicked ways
Shall them admonish, and before them set
The paths of righteousness, how much more safe
And full of peace, denouncing wrath to come
On their impenitence, and shall return
Of them derided, but of God observed
The one just man alive: by his command
Shall build a wondrous ark, as thou beheld'st,
To save himself and household from amidst            820
A world devote to universal wrack.
No sooner he, with them of man and beast
Select for life, shall in the ark be lodged
And sheltered round, but all the cataracts
Of Heaven set open on the Earth shall pour
Rain day and night; all fountains of the deep,
Broke up, shall heave the ocean to usurp
Beyond all bounds, till inundation rise
Above the highest hills: then shall this Mount
Of Paradise by might of waves be moved               830
Out of his place, pushed by the horned flood,
With all his verdure spoiled, and trees adrift,
Down the great river to the opening Gulf,
And there take root, an island salt and bare,
The haunt of seals, and orcs, and sea-mews' clang
To teach thee that God attributes to place
No sanctity, if none be thither brought
By men who there frequent or therein dwell.
And now what further shall ensue behold.'
   He looked, and saw the ark hull on the flood,     840

Which now abated; for the clouds were fled,
Driven by a keen north wind, that, blowing dry,
Wrinkled the face of deluge, as decayed;
And the clear sun on his wide wat'ry glass
Gazed hot, and of the fresh wave largely drew,
As after thirst; which made their flowing shrink
From standing lake to tripping ebb, that stole
With soft foot towards the deep, who now had stopped
His sluices, as the Heaven his windows shut.
The ark no more now floats, but seems on ground,     850
Fast on the top of some high mountain fixed.
And now the tops of hills as rocks appear;
With clamour thence the rapid currents drive
Towards the retreating sea their furious tide.
Forthwith from out the ark a raven flies,
And, after him, the surer messenger,
A dove, sent forth once and again to spy
Green tree or ground whereon his foot may light;
The second time returning, in his bill
An olive-leaf he brings, pacific sign.               860
Anon dry ground appears, and from his ark
The ancient sire descends, with all his train;
Then, with uplifted hands and eyes devout,
Grateful to Heaven, over his head beholds
A dewy cloud, and in the cloud a bow
Conspicuous with three listed colours gay,
Betok'ning peace from God, and cov'nant new.
Whereat the heart of Adam, erst so sad,
Greatly rejoiced; and thus his joy broke forth:—
  'O thou, who future things canst represent         870
As present, Heavenly Instructor, I revive
At this last sight, assured that Man shall live,
With all the creatures, and their seed preserve.
Far less I now lament for one whole world
Of wicked sons destroyed than I rejoice
For one man found so perfect and so just
That God vouchsafes to raise another world
From him, and all his anger to forget.
But say, what mean those coloured streaks in Heaven,
Distended as the brow of God appeased?               880
Or serve they as a flowery verge to bind

The fluid skirts of that same wat'ry cloud,
Lest it again dissolve and shower the Earth?'
    To whom th' Archangel:—'Dextrously thou aim'st.
So willingly doth God remit his ire:
Though late repenting him of Man depraved,
Grieved at his heart, when, looking down, he saw
The whole Earth filled with violence, and all flesh
Corrupting each their way; yet, those removed,
Such grace shall one just man find in his sight          890
That he relents, not to blot out mankind,
And makes a covenant never to destroy
The Earth again by flood, nor let the sea
Surpass his bounds, nor rain to drown the world
With man therein or beast; but, when he brings
Over the Earth a cloud, will therein set
His triple-coloured bow, whereon to look
And call to mind his cov'nant. Day and night,
Seed-time and harvest, heat and hoary frost,
Shall hold their course, till fire purge all things new,  900
Both Heaven and Earth, wherein the just shall dwell.'

*The End of the Eleventh Book.*

# PARADISE LOST

## BOOK XII

### THE ARGUMENT

*The Angel Michael continues, from the Flood, to relate what shall succeed; then, in the mention of Abraham, comes by degrees to explain who that Seed of the Woman shall be which was promised Adam and Eve in the Fall: his incarnation, death, resurrection, and ascension; the state of the Church till his second coming. Adam, greatly satisfied and recomforted by these relations and promises, descends the hill with Michael; wakens Eve, who all this while had slept, but with gentle dreams composed to quietness of mind and submission. Michael in either hand leads them out of Paradise, the fiery sword waving behind them, and the Cherubim taking their stations to guard the place.*

As one who, in his journey, bates at noon,
Though bent on speed, so here the Archangel paused
Betwixt the world destroyed and world restored,
If Adam aught perhaps might interpose;
Then, with transition sweet, new speech resumes:—
  'Thus thou hast seen one world begin and end,
And Man as from a second stock proceed.
Much thou hast yet to see; but I perceive
Thy mortal sight to fail; objects divine
Must needs impair and weary human sense:                    10
Henceforth what is to come I will relate;
Thou, therefore, give due audience, and attend.
  'This second source of men, while yet but few,
And while the dread of judgement past remains
Fresh in their minds, fearing the Deity,
With some regard to what is just and right
Shall lead their lives, and multiply apace,
Labouring the soil, and reaping plenteous crop,
Corn, wine, and oil; and, from the herd or flock
Oft sacrificing bullock, lamb, or kid,                       20
With large wine-offerings poured, and sacred feast,
Shall spend their days in joy unblamed, and dwell

Long time in peace, by families and tribes,
Under paternal rule, till one shall rise,
Of proud, ambitious heart, who, not content
With fair equality, fraternal state,
Will arrogate dominion undeserved
Over his brethren, and quite dispossess
Concord and law of Nature from the Earth—
Hunting (and men, not beasts, shall be his game)        30
With war and hostile snare such as refuse
Subjection to his empire tyrannous:
A mighty hunter thence he shall be styled
Before the Lord, as in despite of Heaven,
Or from Heaven claiming second sovranty,
And from rebellion shall derive his name,
Though of rebellion others he accuse.
He, with a crew, whom like ambition joins
With him or under him to tyrannize,
Marching from Eden towards the west, shall find        40
The plain wherein a black bituminous gurge
Boils out from under ground, the mouth of Hell.
Of brick, and of that stuff, they cast to build
A city and tower, whose top may reach to Heaven;
And get themselves a name, lest, far dispersed
In foreign lands, their memory be lost—
Regardless whether good or evil fame.
But God, who oft descends to visit men
Unseen, and through their habitations walks,
To mark their doings, them beholding soon,        50
Comes down to see their city, ere the tower
Obstruct Heaven-towers, and in derision sets
Upon their tongues a various spirit, to rase
Quite out their native language, and, instead,
To sow a jangling noise of words unknown:
Forthwith a hideous gabble rises loud
Among the builders; each to other calls,
Not understood—till, hoarse and all in rage,
As mocked they storm; great laughter was in Heaven,
And looking down to see the hubbub strange        60
And hear the din; thus was the building left
Ridiculous, and the work *Confusion* named.'
    Whereto thus Adam, fatherly displeased:—

'O execrable son, so to aspire
Above his brethren, to himself assuming
Authority usurped, from God not given:
He gave us only over beast, fish, fowl,
Dominion absolute; that right we hold
By his donation: but man over men
He made not lord—such title to himself                    70
Reserving, human left from human free.
But this usurper his encroachment proud
Stays not on Man; to God his tower intends
Siege and defiance. Wretched man! what food
Will he convey up thither, to sustain
Himself and his rash army, where thin air
Above the clouds will pine his entrails gross,
And famish him of breath, if not of bread?'
   To whom thus Michael:—'Justly thou abhorr'st
That son, who on the quiet state of men                    80
Such trouble brought, affecting to subdue
Rational liberty; yet know withal,
Since thy original lapse, true liberty
Is lost, which always with right reason dwells
Twinned, and from her hath no dividual being.
Reason in Man obscured, or not obeyed,
Immediately inordinate desires
And upstart passions catch the government
From Reason, and to servitude reduce
Man, till then free. Therefore, since he permits          90
Within himself unworthy powers to reign
Over free reason, God, in judgement just,
Subjects him from without to violent lords,
Who oft as undeservedly enthral
His outward freedom. Tyranny must be,
Though to the tyrant thereby no excuse.
Yet sometimes nations will decline so low
From virtue, which is reason, that no wrong,
But justice, and some fatal curse annexed,
Deprives them of their outward liberty,                   100
Their inward lost: witness th' irreverent son
Of him who built the ark, who, for the shame
Done to his father, heard this heavy curse,
*Servant of servants*, on his vicious race.

Thus will this latter, as the former world,
Still tend from bad to worse, till God at last,
Wearied with their iniquities, withdraw
His presence from among them, and avert
His holy eyes, resolving from thenceforth
To leave them to their own polluted ways,          110
And one peculiar nation to select
From all the rest, of whom to be invoked—
A nation from one faithful man to spring:
Him on this side Euphrates yet residing,
Bred up in idol-worship. Oh, that men
(Canst thou believe?) should be so stupid grown,
While yet the patriarch lived who scaped the Flood,
As to forsake the living God, and fall
To worship their own work in wood and stone
For gods!—yet him God the Most High vouchsafes          120
To call by vision from his father's house,
His kindred, and false gods, into a land
Which he will show him, and from him will raise
A mighty nation, and upon him shower
His benediction so, that in his seed
All nations shall be blessed; he straight obeys;
Not knowing to what land, yet firm believes.
I see him, but thou canst not, with what faith
He leaves his gods, his friends, and native soil,
Ur of Chaldæa, passing now the ford          130
To Haran—after him a cumbrous train
Of herds and flocks, and numerous servitude—
Not wand'ring poor, but trusting all his wealth
With God, who called him, in a land unknown.
Canaan he now attains; I see his tents
Pitched about Shechem, and the neighbouring plain
Of Moreh. There, by promise, he receives
Gift to his progeny of all that land,
From Hamath northward to the Desert south
(Things by their names I call, though yet unnamed),          140
From Hermon east to the great western sea;
Mount Hermon, yonder sea, each place behold
In prospect, as I point them: on the shore,
Mount Carmel; here, the double-founted stream,
Jordan, true limit eastward; but his sons

Shall dwell to Senir, that long ridge of hills.
This ponder, that all nations of the Earth
Shall in his seed be blessed; by that seed
Is meant thy great Deliverer, who shall bruise
The Serpent's head; whereof to thee anon                    150
Plainlier shall be revealed.   This patriarch blessed,
Whom *faithful Abraham* due time shall call,
A son, and of his son a grandchild, leaves,
Like him in faith, in wisdom, and renown.
The grandchild, with twelve sons increased, departs
From Canaan to a land hereafter called
Egypt, divided by the river Nile;
See where it flows, disgorging at seven mouths
Into the sea: to sojourn in that land
He comes, invited by a younger son                          160
In time of dearth, a son whose worthy deeds
Raise him to be the second in that realm
Of Pharaoh: there he dies, and leaves his race
Growing into a nation, and now grown
Suspected to a sequent king, who seeks
To stop their overgrowth, as inmate guests
Too numerous; whence of guests he makes them slaves
Inhospitably, and kills their infant males:
Till, by two brethren (those two brethren call
Moses and Aaron) sent from God to claim                     170
His people from enthralment, they return,
With glory and spoil, back to their promised land.
But first the lawless tyrant, who denies
To know their God, or message to regard,
Must be compelled by signs and judgements dire:
To blood unshed the rivers must be turned;
Frogs, lice, and flies must all his palace fill
With loath'd intrusion, and fill all the land;
His cattle must of rot and murrain die;
Botches and blains must all his flesh emboss,               180
And all his people; thunder mixed with hail,
Hail mixed with fire, must rend th' Egyptian sky,
And wheel on th' earth, devouring where it rolls;
What it devours not, herb, or fruit, or grain,
A darksome cloud of locusts swarming down
Must eat, and on the ground leave nothing green;

Darkness must overshadow all his bounds,
Palpable darkness, and blot out three days;
Last, with one midnight-stroke, all the first-born
Of Egypt must lie dead.  Thus with ten wounds            190
This river-dragon, tamed at length, submits
To let his sojourners depart, and oft
Humbles his stubborn heart, but still as ice
More hardened after thaw; till, in his rage
Pursuing whom he late dismissed, the sea
Swallows him with his host, but them lets pass,
As on dry land, between two crystal walls,
Awed by the rod of Moses so to stand
Divided, till his rescued gain their shore:
Such wondrous power God to his saint will lend,       200
Though present in his Angel, who shall go
Before them in a cloud, and pillar of fire—
By day a cloud, by night a pillar of fire—
To guide them in their journey, and remove
Behind them, while th' obdurate king pursues:
All night he will pursue, but his approach
Darkness defends between till morning-watch;
Then through the fiery pillar, and the cloud,
God looking forth will trouble all his host,
And craze their chariot-wheels: when, by command, 210
Moses once more his potent rod extends
Over the sea; the sea his rod obeys;
On their embattled ranks the waves return,
And overwhelm their war: the race elect
Safe towards Canaan, from the shore, advance
Through the wild Desert—not the readiest way,
Lest, ent'ring on the Canaanite alarmed,
War terrify them inexpert, and fear
Return them back to Egypt, choosing rather
Inglorious life with servitude; for life             220
To noble and ignoble is more sweet
Untrained in arms, where rashness leads not on.
This also shall they gain by their delay
In the wide wilderness: there they shall found
Their government, and their great Senate choose
Through the twelve tribes, to rule by laws ordained.
God, from the Mount of Sinai, whose grey top

Shall tremble, he descending, will himself,
In thunder, lightning, and loud trumpet's sound,
Ordain them laws—part, such as appertain          230
To civil justice; part, religious rites
Of sacrifice, informing them, by types
And shadows, of that destined Seed to bruise
The Serpent, by what means he shall achieve
Mankind's deliverance.  But the voice of God
To mortal ear is dreadful: they beseech
That Moses might report to them his will,
And terror cease; he grants what they besought,
Instructed that to God is no access
Without Mediator, whose high office now          240
Moses in figure bears, to introduce
One greater, of whose day he shall foretell,
And all the Prophets, in their age, the times
Of great Messiah shall sing.  Thus laws and rites
Established, such delight hath God in men
Obedient to his will, that he vouchsafes
Among them to set up his tabernacle—
The Holy One with mortal men to dwell:
By his prescript a sanctuary is framed
Of cedar, overlaid with gold; therein          250
An ark, and in the ark his testimony,
The records of his cov'nant; over these
A mercy-seat of gold, between the wings
Of two bright Cherubim; before him burn
Seven lamps, as in a zodiac representing
The heavenly fires; over the tent a cloud
Shall rest by day, a fiery gleam by night,
Save when they journey; and at length they come,
Conducted by his Angel, to the land
Promised to Abraham and his seed: the rest          260
Were long to tell—how many battles fought,
How many kings destroyed, and kingdoms won;
Or how the sun shall in mid-heaven stand still
A day entire, and night's due course adjourn,
Man's voice commanding, "Sun, in Gibeon stand,
And thou, Moon, in the vale of Ajalon,
Till Israel overcome!"—so call the third
From Abraham, son of Isaac, and from him

His whole descent, who thus shall Canaan win.'
  Here Adam interposed:—'O sent from Heaven,  270
Enlightener of my darkness, gracious things
Thou hast revealed, those chiefly which concern
Just Abraham and his seed: now first I find
Mine eyes true opening, and my heart much eased,
Erewhile perplexed with thoughts what would become
Of me and all mankind; but now I see
His day, in whom all nations shall be blessed—
Favour unmerited by me, who sought
Forbidden knowledge by forbidden means.
This yet I apprehend not—why to those  280
Among whom God will deign to dwell on Earth
So many and so various laws are given;
So many laws argue so many sins
Among them; how can God with such reside?'
  To whom thus Michael:—'Doubt not but that sin
Will reign among them, as of thee begot;
And therefore was law given them, to evince
Their natural pravity, by stirring up
Sin against Law to fight, that, when they see
Law can discover sin, but not remove,  290
Save by those shadowy expiations weak,
The blood of bulls and goats, they may conclude
Some blood more precious must be paid for Man,
Just for unjust, that in such righteousness,
To them by faith imputed, they may find
Justification towards God, and peace
Of conscience, which the law by ceremonies
Cannot appease, nor Man the moral part
Perform, and, not performing, cannot live.
So Law appears imperfect, and but given  300
With purpose to resign them, in full time,
Up to a better cov'nant, disciplined
From shadowy types to truth, from flesh to spirit,
From imposition of strict laws to free
Acceptance of large grace, from servile fear
To filial, works of law to works of faith.
And therefore shall not Moses, though of God
Highly beloved, being but the minister
Of Law, his people into Canaan lead;

But Joshua, whom the Gentiles Jesus call,    310
His name and office bearing who shall quell
The adversary Serpent, and bring back
Through the world's wilderness long-wandered Man
Safe to eternal Paradise of rest.
Meanwhile they, in their earthly Canaan placed,
Long time shall dwell and prosper, but when sins
National interrupt their public peace,
Provoking God to raise them enemies—
From whom as oft he saves them penitent,
By Judges first, then under Kings; of whom    320
The second, both for piety renowned
And puissant deeds, a promise shall receive
Irrevocable, that his regal throne
For ever shall endure; the like shall sing
All Prophecy—that of the royal stock
Of David (so I name this king) shall rise
A son, the Woman's Seed to thee foretold.
Foretold to Abraham as in whom shall trust
All nations, and to kings foretold of kings
The last, for of his reign shall be no end.    330
But first a long succession must ensue;
And his next son, for wealth and wisdom famed,
The clouded ark of God, till then in tents
Wand'ring, shall in a glorious temple enshrine.
Such follow him as shall be registered
Part good, part bad; of bad the longer scroll:
Whose foul idolatries and other faults,
Heaped to the popular sum, will so incense
God, as to leave them, and expose their land,
Their city, his temple, and his holy ark,    340
With all his sacred things, a scorn and prey
To that proud city whose high walls thou saw'st
Left in confusion, Babylon thence called.
There in captivity he lets them dwell
The space of seventy years; then brings them back,
Rem-emb'ring mercy, and his cov'nant sworn
To David, stablished as the days of Heaven.
Returned from Babylon by leave of kings,
Their lords, whom God disposed, the house of God
They first re-edify, and for a while    350

In mean estate live moderate, till, grown
In wealth and multitude, factious they grow.
But first among the priests dissension springs—
Men who attend the altar and should most
Endeavour peace: their strife pollution brings
Upon the temple itself; at last they seize
The sceptre, and regard not David's sons,
Then lose it to a stranger, that the true
Anointed King Messiah might be born
Barred of his right; yet at his birth a star,          360
Unseen before in Heaven, proclaims him come,
And guides the eastern sages, who inquire
His place, to offer incense, myrrh, and gold:
His place of birth a solemn Angel tells
To simple shepherds, keeping watch by night;
They gladly thither haste, and by a quire
Of squadroned Angels hear his carol sung.
A Virgin is his mother, but his sire
The Power of the Most High; he shall ascend
The throne hereditary, and bound his reign          370
With Earth's wide bounds, his glory with the Heavens.'
        He ceased, discerning Adam with such joy
Surcharged as had, like grief, been dewed in tears,
Without the vent of words; which these he breathed:—
    'O prophet of glad tidings, finisher
Of utmost hope! now clear I understand
What oft my steadiest thoughts have searched in vain—
Why our great Expectation should be called
The Seed of Woman. Virgin Mother, hail!
High in the love of Heaven, yet from my loins          380
Thou shalt proceed, and from thy womb the Son
Of God Most High; so God with Man unites.
Needs must the Serpent now his capital bruise
Expect with mortal pain: say where and when
Their fight, what stroke shall bruise the Victor's heel.'
        To whom thus Michael:—'Dream not of their fight
As of a duel, of the local wounds
Of head or heel: not therefore joins the Son
Manhood to Godhead, with more strength to foil
Thy enemy; nor so is overcome          390
Satan, whose fall from Heaven, a deadlier bruise,

Disabled not to give thee thy death's wound;
Which he who comes thy Saviour shall recure,
Not by destroying Satan, but his works
In thee and in thy seed: nor can this be,
But by fulfilling that which thou didst want,
Obedience to the law of God, imposed
On penalty of death, and suffering death,
The penalty to thy transgression due,
And due to theirs which out of thine will grow:          400
So only can high justice rest appaid.
The law of God exact he shall fulfil
Both by obedience and by love, though love
Alone fulfil the Law; thy punishment
He shall endure, by coming in the flesh
To a reproachful life and cursed death,
Proclaiming life to all who shall believe
In his redemption, and that his obedience
Imputed becomes theirs by faith—his merits
To save them, not their own, though legal, works.          410
For this he shall live hated, be blasphemed,
Seized on by force, judged, and to death condemned
A shameful and accurs'd, nailed to the cross
By his own nation, slain for bringing life;
But to the cross he nails thy enemies—
The Law that is against thee, and the sins
Of all mankind, with him there crucified,
Never to hurt them more who rightly trust
In this his satisfaction; so he dies,
But soon revives; Death over him no power          420
Shall long usurp; ere the third dawning light
Return, the stars of morn shall see him rise
Out of his grave, fresh as the dawning light,
Thy ransom paid, which Man from Death redeems—
His death for Man, as many as offered life
Neglect not, and the benefit embrace
By faith not void of works. This godlike act
Annuls thy doom, the death thou shouldst have died,
In sin for ever lost from life; this act
Shall bruise the head of Satan, crush his strength,          430
Defeating Sin and Death, his two main arms,
And fix far deeper in his head their stings

Than temporal death shall bruise the Victor's heel,
Or theirs whom he redeems—a death like sleep,
A gentle wafting to immortal life.
Nor after resurrection shall he stay
Longer on Earth than certain times to appear
To his disciples—men who in his life
Still followed him; to them shall leave in charge
To teach all nations what of him they learned          440
And his salvation, them who shall believe
Baptizing in the profluent stream—the sign
Of washing them from guilt of sin to life
Pure, and in mind prepared, if so befall,
For death like that which the Redeemer died.
All nations they shall teach; for from that day
Not only to the sons of Abraham's loins
Salvation shall be preached, but to the sons
Of Abraham's faith wherever through the world;
So in his seed all nations shall be blessed.          450
Then to the Heaven of Heavens he shall ascend
With victory, triumphing through the air
Over his foes and thine; there shall surprise
The Serpent, Prince of Air, and drag in chains
Through all his realm, and there confounded leave;
Then enter into glory, and resume
His seat at God's right hand, exalted high
Above all names in Heaven; and thence shall come,
When this World's dissolution shall be ripe,
With glory and power, to judge both quick and dead—
To judge th' unfaithful dead, but to reward          461
His faithful, and receive them into bliss,
Whether in Heaven or Earth; for then the Earth
Shall all be Paradise, far happier place
Than this of Eden, and far happier days.'
    So spake th' Archangel Michael; then paused,
As at the World's great period; and our Sire,
Replete with joy and wonder, thus replied:—
'O goodness infinite, goodness immense,
That all this good of evil shall produce,          470
And evil turn to good—more wonderful
Than that by which creation first brought forth
Light out of darkness! Full of doubt I stand,

Whether I should repent me now of sin
By me done and occasioned, or rejoice
Much more that much more good thereof shall spring—
To God more glory, more good-will to men
From God—and over wrath grace shall abound.
But say, if our Deliverer up to Heaven
Must reascend, what will betide the few,                      480
His faithful, left among th' unfaithful herd,
The enemies of truth? Who then shall guide
His people, who defend? Will they not deal
Worse with his followers than with him they dealt?'
    'Be sure they will,' said th' Angel; 'but from Heaven
He to his own a Comforter will send,
The promise of the Father, who shall dwell,
His Spirit, within them, and the law of faith
Working through love upon their hearts shall write,
To guide them in all truth, and also arm                     490
With spiritual armour, able to resist
Satan's assaults, and quench his fiery darts—
What man can do against them, not afraid,
Though to the death; against such cruelties
With inward consolations recompensed,
And oft supported so as shall amaze
Their proudest persecutors: for the Spirit,
Poured first on his Apostles, whom he sends
To evangelize the nations, then on all
Baptized, shall them with wondrous gifts endue              500
To speak all tongues, and do all miracles,
As did their Lord before them. Thus they win
Great numbers of each nation to receive
With joy the tidings brought from Heaven: at length,
Their ministry performed, and race well run,
Their doctrine and their story written left,
They die; but in their room, as they forewarn,
Wolves shall succeed for teachers, grievous wolves,
Who all the sacred mysteries of Heaven
To their own vile advantages shall turn                      510
Of lucre and ambition, and the truth
With superstitions and traditions taint,
Left only in those written records pure,
Though not but by the Spirit understood.

Then shall they seek to avail themselves of names,
Places, and titles, and with these to join
Secular power, though feigning still to act
By spiritual; to themselves appropriating
The Spirit of God, promised alike and given
To all believers; and, from that pretence,                    520
Spiritual laws by carnal power shall force
On every conscience—laws which none shall find
Left them enrolled, or what the Spirit within
Shall on the heart engrave. What will they then
But force the Spirit of Grace itself, and bind
His consort, Liberty? what but unbuild
His living temples, built by faith to stand—
Their own faith, not another's? for, on Earth,
Who against faith and conscience can be heard
Infallible? Yet many will presume:                            530
Whence heavy persecution shall arise
On all who in the worship persevere
Of Spirit and Truth; the rest, far greater part,
Will deem in outward rites and specious forms
Religion satisfied; Truth shall retire
Bestuck with sland'rous darts, and works of Faith
Rarely be found: so shall the World go on,
To good malignant, to bad men benign,
Under her own weight groaning, till the day
Appear of respiration to the just                             540
And vengeance to the wicked, at return
Of him so lately promised to thy aid,
The Woman's Seed—obscurely then foretold,
Now amplier known thy Saviour and thy Lord;
Last in the clouds from Heaven to be revealed
In glory of the Father, to dissolve
Satan with his perverted World; then raise
From the conflagrant mass, purged and refined,
New Heavens, new Earth, Ages of endless date
Founded in righteousness and peace and love,                  550
To bring forth fruits, joy and eternal bliss.'
    He ended; and thus Adam last replied:—
'How soon hath thy prediction, Seer blest,
Measured this transient World, the race of Time,
Till Time stand fixed: beyond is all abyss—

Eternity, whose end no eye can reach.
Greatly instructed I shall hence depart,
Greatly in peace of thought, and have my fill
Of knowledge, what this vessel can contain;
Beyond which was my folly to aspire.                         560
Henceforth I learn that to obey is best,
And love with fear the only God, to walk
As in his presence, ever to observe
His providence, and on him sole depend.
Merciful over all his works, with good
Still overcoming evil, and by small
Accomplishing great things—by things deemed weak
Subverting worldly-strong, and worldly-wise
By simply meek; that suffering for Truth's sake
Is fortitude to highest victory,                            570
And to the faithful death the gate of life—
Taught this by his example whom I now
Acknowledge my Redeemer ever blest.'
    To whom thus also th' Angel last replied:—
'This having learned, thou hast attained the sum
Of wisdom; hope no higher, though all the stars
Thou knew'st by name, and all th' ethereal powers,
All secrets of the deep, all Nature's works,
Or works of God in heaven, air, earth, or sea,
And all the riches of this world enjoy'dst,                 580
And all the rule, one empire. Only add
Deeds to thy knowledge answerable; add faith;
Add virtue, patience, temperance; add love,
By name to come called Charity, the soul
Of all the rest: then wilt thou not be loth
To leave this Paradise, but shalt possess
A Paradise within thee, happier far.
Let us descend now, therefore, from this top
Of speculation; for the hour precise
Exacts our parting hence; and, see! the guards,            590
By me encamped on yonder hill, expect
Their motion, at whose front a flaming sword,
In signal of remove, waves fiercely round.
We may no longer stay: go, waken Eve;
Her also I with gentle dreams have calmed,
Portending good, and all her spirits composed

To meek submission: thou, at season fit,
Let her with thee partake what thou hast heard—
Chiefly what may concern her faith to know,
The great deliverance by her seed to come          600
(For by the Woman's Seed) on all mankind—
That ye may live, which will be many days,
Both in one faith unanimous, though sad
With cause for evils past, yet much more cheered
With meditation on the happy end.'

  He ended, and they both descend the hill;
Descended, Adam to the bower where Eve
Lay sleeping ran before, but found her waked:
And thus with words not sad she him received:—

  'Whence thou return'st and whither went'st I know;
For God is also in sleep, and dreams advise,          611
Which he hath sent propitious, some great good
Presaging, since, with sorrow and heart's distress
Wearied, I fell asleep: but now lead on;
In me is no delay; with thee to go
Is to stay here; without thee here to stay
Is to go hence unwilling; thou to me
Art all things under Heaven, all places thou,
Who for my wilful crime art banished hence.
This further consolation yet secure          620
I carry hence: though all by me is lost,
Such favour I unworthy am vouchsafed,
By me the Promised Seed shall all restore.'

  So spake our mother Eve; and Adam heard
Well pleased, but answered not; for now too nigh
Th' Archangel stood, and from the other hill
To their fixed station, all in bright array
The Cherubim descended, on the ground
Gliding meteorous, as evening mist,
Risen from a river, o'er the marish glides,          630
And gathers ground fast at the labourer's heel
Homeward returning. High in front advanced,
The brandished sword of God before them blazed,
Fierce as a comet, which with torrid heat,
And vapour as the Libyan air adust,
Began to parch that temperate clime; whereat
In either hand the hast'ning Angel caught

Our lingering parents, and to th' eastern gate
Led them direct, and down the cliff as fast
To the subjected plain; then disappeared.                    640
They, looking back, all the eastern side beheld
Of Paradise, so late their happy seat,
Waved over by that flaming brand, the gate
With dreadful faces thronged and fiery arms:
Some natural tears they dropped, but wiped them soon;
The world was all before them, where to choose
Their place of rest, and Providence their guide:
They, hand in hand, with wandering steps and slow,
Through Eden took their solitary way.

*The End.*

# PARADISE REGAINED

## THE FIRST BOOK

I, WHO erewhile the happy Garden sung,
By one man's disobedience lost, now sing
Recovered Paradise to all mankind,
By one man's firm obedience fully tried
Through all temptation, and the Tempter foiled
In all his wiles, defeated and repulsed,
And Eden raised in the waste wilderness.

    Thou Spirit, who led'st this glorious Eremite
Into the desert, his victorious field
Against the spiritual foe, and brought'st him thence    10
By proof th' undoubted Son of God, inspire,
As thou art wont, my prompted song, else mute,
And bear through height or depth of Nature's bounds,
With prosperous wing full summed, to tell of deeds
Above heroic, though in secret done,
And unrecorded left through many an age:
Worthy t' have not remained so long unsung.

    Now had the great Proclaimer, with a voice
More awful than the sound of trumpet, cried
Repentance, and Heaven's kingdom nigh at hand    20
To all baptized. To his great baptism flocked
With awe the regions round, and with them came
From Nazareth the son of Joseph deemed
To the flood Jordan—came as then obscure,
Unmarked, unknown: but him the Baptist soon
Descried, divinely warned, and witness bore
As to his worthier, and would have resigned
To him his heavenly office, nor was long
His witness unconfirmed: on him baptized
Heaven opened, and in likeness of a dove    30
The Spirit descended, while the Father's voice
From Heaven pronounced him his beloved Son.
That heard the Adversary, who, roving still
About the world, at that assembly famed

Would not be last, and, with the voice divine
Nigh thunder-struck, th' exalted man to whom
Such high attest was given a while surveyed
With wonder; then, with envy fraught and rage,
Flies to his place, nor rests, but in mid air
To council summons all his mighty peers,                    40
Within thick clouds and dark tenfold involved,
A gloomy consistory; and them amidst,
With looks aghast and sad, he thus bespake:—
    'O ancient Powers of Air and this wide World
(For much more willingly I mention air,
This our old conquest, than remember Hell,
Our hated habitation), well ye know
How many ages, as the years of men,
This universe we have possessed, and ruled
In manner at our will th' affairs of Earth,                  50
Since Adam and his facile consort Eve
Lost Paradise, deceived by me, though since
With dread attending when that fatal wound
Shall be inflicted by the seed of Eve
Upon my head. Long the decrees of Heaven
Delay, for longest time to him is short;
And now, too soon for us, the circling hours
This dreaded time have compassed, wherein we
Must bide the stroke of that long-threatened wound
(At least, if so we can, and by the head                     60
Broken be not intended all our power
To be infringed, our freedom and our being
In this fair empire won of earth and air)—
For this ill news I bring: the Woman's Seed,
Destined to this, is late of woman born:
His birth to our just fear gave no small cause;
But his growth now to youth's full flower, displaying
All virtue, grace and wisdom to achieve
Things highest, greatest, multiplies my fear.
Before him a great Prophet, to proclaim                      70
His coming, is sent harbinger, who all
Invites, and in the consecrated stream
Pretends to wash off sin, and fit them so
Purified to receive him pure, or rather
To do him honour as their King; all come,

And he himself among them was baptized—
Not thence to be more pure, but to receive
The testimony of Heaven, that who he is
Thenceforth the nations may not doubt.  I saw
The Prophet do him reverence; on him, rising          80
Out of the water, Heaven above the clouds
Unfold her crystal doors; thence on his head
A perfect dove descend (whate'er it meant);
And out of Heaven the sovran voice I heard,
"This is my Son beloved, in him am pleased."
His mother, then, is mortal, but his Sire
He who obtains the monarchy of Heaven;
And what will He not do to advance his Son?
His first-begot we know, and sore have felt,
When his fierce thunder drove us to the Deep;          90
Who this is we must learn, for Man he seems
In all his lineaments, though in his face
The glimpses of his Father's glory shine.
Ye see our danger on the utmost edge
Of hazard, which admits no long debate,
But must with something sudden be opposed
(Not force, but well-couched fraud, well-woven snares),
Ere in the head of nations he appear,
Their king, their leader, and supreme on Earth.
I, when no other durst, sole undertook          100
The dismal expedition to find out
And ruin Adam, and the exploit performed
Successfully: a calmer voyage now
Will waft me; and the way found prosperous once
Induces best to hope of like success.'
     He ended, and his words impression left
Of much amazement to th' infernal crew,
Distracted and surprised with deep dismay
At these sad tidings; but no time was then
For long indulgence to their fears or grief:          110
Unanimous they all commit the care
And management of this main enterprise
To him, their great Dictator, whose attempt
At first against mankind so well had thrived
In Adam's overthrow, and led their march
From Hell's deep-vaulted den to dwell in light,

Regents, and potentates, and kings, yea gods,
Of many a pleasant realm and province wide.
So to the coast of Jordan he directs
His easy steps, girded with snaky wiles,          120
Where he might likeliest find this new-declared,
This man of men, attested Son of God,
Temptation and all guile on him to try—
So to subvert whom he suspected raised
To end his reign on Earth so long enjoyed:
But, contrary, unweeting he fulfilled
The purposed counsel, pre-ordained and fixed,
Of the Most High, who, in full frequence bright
Of Angels, thus to Gabriel smiling spake:—
'Gabriel, this day, by proof, thou shalt behold,      130
Thou and all Angels conversant on Earth
With Man or men's affairs, how I begin
To verify that solemn message late,
On which I sent thee to the Virgin pure
In Galilee, that she should bear a son,
Great in renown, and called the Son of God:
Then told'st her, doubting how these things could be
To her a virgin, that on her should come
The Holy Ghost, and the power of the Highest
O'ershadow her: this Man, born and now upgrown,   140
To show him worthy of his birth divine
And high prediction, henceforth I expose
To Satan; let him tempt, and now assay
His utmost subtlety, because he boasts
And vaunts of his great cunning to the throng
Of his apostasy; he might have learnt
Less overweening, since he failed in Job,
Whose constant perseverance overcame
Whate'er his cruel malice could invent.
He now shall know I can produce a man,            150
Of female seed, far abler to resist
All his solicitations, and at length
All his vast force, and drive him back to Hell—
Winning by conquest what the first man lost
By fallacy surprised. But first I mean
To exercise him in the Wilderness;
There he shall first lay down the rudiments

Of his great warfare, ere I send him forth
To conquer Sin and Death, the two grand foes,
By humiliation and strong sufferance;                       160
His weakness shall o'ercome Satanic strength,
And all the world, and mass of sinful flesh;
That all the Angels and ethereal Powers—
They now, and men hereafter—may discern
From what consummate virtue I have chose
This perfect man, by merit called my Son,
To earn salvation for the sons of men.'
    So spake the Eternal Father, and all Heaven
Admiring stood a space; then into hymns
Burst forth, and in celestial measures moved,              170
Circling the throne and singing, while the hand
Sung with the voice, and this the argument:—
    'Victory and triumph to the Son of God,
Now ent'ring his great duel, not of arms,
But to vanquish by wisdom hellish wiles.
The Father knows the Son; therefore secure
Ventures his filial virtue, though untried,
Against whate'er may tempt, whate'er seduce,
Allure, or terrify, or undermine.
Be frustrate, all ye stratagems of Hell,                   180
And, devilish machinations, come to nought!'
    So they in Heaven their odes and vigils tuned.
Meanwhile the Son of God, who yet some days
Lodged in Bethabara, where John baptized,
Musing and much revolving in his breast
How best the mighty work he might begin
Of Saviour to mankind, and which way first
Publish his godlike office now mature,
One day forth walked alone, the Spirit leading
And his deep thoughts, the better to converse             190
With solitude, till far from track of men,
Thought following thought, and step by step led on,
He entered now the bordering Desert wild,
And, with dark shades and rocks environed round,
His holy meditations thus pursued:—
    'O what a multitude of thoughts at once
Awakened in me swarm, while I consider
What from within I feel myself, and hear

What from without comes often to my ears,
Ill sorting with my present state compared.                        200
When I was yet a child, no childish play
To me was pleasing; all my mind was set
Serious to learn and know, and thence to do,
What might be public good; myself I thought
Born to that end, born to promote all truth,
All righteous things; therefore, above my years,
The Law of God I read, and found it sweet;
Made it my whole delight, and in it grew
To such perfection that, ere yet my age
Had measured twice six years, at our great Feast        210
I went into the Temple, there to hear
The teachers of our Law, and to propose
What might improve my knowledge or their own,
And was admired by all, yet this not all
To which my spirit aspired, victorious deeds
Flamed in my heart, heroic acts, one while
To rescue Israel from the Roman yoke;
Thence to subdue and quell, o'er all the earth,
Brute violence and proud tyrannic power
Till truth were freed, and equity restored:                        220
Yet held it more humane, more heavenly, first
By winning words to conquer willing hearts,
And make persuasion do the work of fear;
At least to try, and teach the erring soul,
Not wilfully misdoing, but unware
Misled; the stubborn only to subdue.
These growing thoughts my mother soon perceiving,
By words at times cast forth, inly rejoiced,
And said to me apart, "High are thy thoughts,
O Son! but nourish them, and let them soar                         230
To what height sacred virtue and true worth
Can raise them, though above example high;
By matchless deeds express thy matchless Sire.
For know, thou art no son of mortal man;
Though men esteem thee low of parentage,
Thy Father is the Eternal King who rules
All Heaven and Earth, Angels and sons of men.
A messenger from God foretold thy birth
Conceived in me a virgin; he foretold

Thou shouldst be great, and sit on David's throne,    240
And of thy kingdom there should be no end.
At thy nativity a glorious quire
Of Angels, in the fields of Bethlehem, sung
To shepherds, watching at their folds by night,
And told them the Messiah now was born,
Where they might see him; and to thee they came,
Directed to the manger where thou lay'st;
For in the inn was left no better room.
A star, not seen before, in Heaven appearing,
Guided the wise men thither from the East,    250
To honour thee with incense, myrrh, and gold;
By whose bright course led on they found the place,
Affirming it thy star, new-graven in heaven,
By which they knew thee King of Israel born.
Just Simeon and prophetic Anna, warned
By vision, found thee in the Temple, and spake,
Before the altar and the vested priest,
Like things of thee to all that present stood."
This having heard, straight I again revolved
The Law and Prophets, searching what was writ    260
Concerning the Messiah, to our scribes
Known partly, and soon found of whom they spake
I am—this chiefly, that my way must lie
Through many a hard assay, even to the death,
Ere I the promised kingdom can attain,
Or work redemption for mankind, whose sins'
Full weight must be transferred upon my head.
Yet, neither thus disheartened or dismayed,
The time prefixed I waited; when behold
The Baptist (of whose birth I oft had heard,    270
Not knew by sight) now come, who was to come
Before Messiah, and his way prepare.
I, as all others, to his baptism came,
Which I believed was from above; but he
Straight knew me, and with loudest voice proclaimed
Me him (for it was shown him so from Heaven)—
Me him whose harbinger he was; and first
Refused on me his baptism to confer,
As much his greater, and was hardly won;
But, as I rose out of the laving stream,    280

Heaven opened her eternal doors, from whence
The Spirit descended on me like a dove;
And last, the sum of all, my Father's voice,
Audibly heard from Heaven, pronounced me his,
Me his beloved Son, in whom alone
He was well pleased: by which I knew the time
Now full, that I no more should live obscure,
But openly begin, as best becomes
The authority which I derived from Heaven.
And now by some strong motion I am led          290
Into this wilderness; to what intent
I learn not yet, perhaps I need not know;
For what concerns my knowledge God reveals.'
    So spake our Morning Star, then in his rise,
And, looking round, on every side beheld
A pathless desert, dusk with horrid shades.
The way he came not having marked, return
Was difficult, by human steps untrod;
And he still on was led, but with such thoughts
Accompanied of things past and to come          300
Lodged in his breast, as well might recommend
Such solitude before choicest society.
Full forty days he passed—whether on hill
Sometimes, anon in shady vale, each night
Under the covert of some ancient oak
Or cedar to defend him from the dew,
Or harboured in one cave, is not revealed;
Nor tasted human food, nor hunger felt,
Till those days ended; hungered then at last
Among wild beasts. They at his sight grew mild,   310
Nor sleeping him nor waking harmed; his walk
The fiery serpent fled and noxious worm;
The lion and fierce tiger glared aloof.
But now an aged man in rural weeds,
Following, as seemed, the quest of some stray ewe,
Or withered sticks to gather, which might serve
Against a winter's day, when winds blow keen,
To warm him wet returned from field at eve,
He saw approach; who first with curious eye       319
Perused him, then with words thus uttered spake:—
    'Sir, what ill chance hath brought thee to this place,

So far from path or road of men, who pass
In troop or caravan? for single none
Durst ever, who returned, and dropped not here
His carcase, pined with hunger and with drouth.
I ask the rather, and the more admire,
For that to me thou seem'st the man whom late
Our new baptizing Prophet at the ford
Of Jordan honoured so, and called thee Son
Of God; I saw and heard, for we sometimes          330
Who dwell this wild, constrained by want, come forth
To town or village nigh (nighest is far),
Where aught we hear, and curious are to hear,
What happens new; fame also finds us out.'
     To whom the Son of God:—'Who brought me hither
Will bring me hence; no other guide I seek.'
     'By miracle he may,' replied the swain;
'What other way I see not; for we here
Live on tough roots and stubs, to thirst inured
More than the camel, and to drink go far—          340
Men to much misery and hardship born.
But, if thou be the Son of God, command
That out of these hard stones be made thee bread;
So shalt thou save thyself, and us relieve
With food, whereof we wretched seldom taste.'
     He ended, and the Son of God replied:—
'Think'st thou such force in bread? Is it not written
(For I discern thee other than thou seem'st),
Man lives not by bread only, but each word
Proceeding from the mouth of God, who fed          350
Our fathers here with manna? In the Mount
Moses was forty days, nor eat nor drank;
And forty days Elijah without food
Wandered this barren waste; the same I now.
Why dost thou, then, suggest to me distrust,
Knowing who I am, as I know who thou art?'
     Whom thus answered th' Arch-Fiend, now undis-
          guised:—
' 'Tis true, I am that Spirit unfortunate
Who, leagued with millions more in rash revolt,
Kept not my happy station, but was driven          360
With them from bliss to the bottomless Deep—

Yet to that hideous place not so confined
By rigour unconniving but that oft,
Leaving my dolorous prison, I enjoy
Large liberty to round this globe of Earth,
Or range in th' air; nor from the Heaven of Heavens
Hath he excluded my resort sometimes.
I came, among the Sons of God, when he
Gave up into my hands Uzzean Job,
To prove him, and illustrate his high worth;        370
And, when to all his Angels he proposed
To draw the proud king Ahab into fraud,
That he might fall in Ramoth, they demurring,
I undertook that office, and the tongues
Of all his flattering prophets glibbed with lies
To his destruction, as I had in charge:
For what he bids I do; though I have lost
Much lustre of my native brightness, lost
To be beloved of God, I have not lost
To love, at least contemplate and admire,        380
What I see excellent in good, or fair,
Or virtuous; I should so have lost all sense.
What can be then less in me than desire
To see thee and approach thee, whom I know
Declared the Son of God, to hear attent
Thy wisdom, and behold thy godlike deeds?
Men generally think me much a foe
To all mankind: why should I? they to me
Never did wrong or violence, by them
I lost not what I lost; rather by them        390
I gained what I have gained, and with them dwell
Copartner in these regions of the World,
If not disposer—lend them oft my aid,
Oft my advice by presages and signs,
And answers, oracles, portents, and dreams,
Whereby they may direct their future life.
Envy, they say, excites me, thus to gain
Companions of my misery and woe!
At first it may be: but, long since with woe
Nearer acquainted, now I feel by proof,        400
That fellowship in pain divides not smart,
Nor lightens aught each man's peculiar load;

Small consolation, then, were Man adjoined.
This wounds me most (what can it less?) that Man,
Man fall'n, shall be restored, I never more.'
    To whom our Saviour sternly thus replied:—
'Deservedly thou griev'st, composed of lies
From the beginning, and in lies wilt end,
Who boast'st release from Hell, and leave to come
Into the Heaven of Heavens. Thou com'st, indeed,          410
As a poor miserable captive thrall
Comes to the place where he before had sat
Among the prime in splendour, now deposed,
Ejected, emptied, gazed, unpitied, shunned,
A spectacle of ruin, or of scorn,
To all the host of Heaven; the happy place
Imparts to thee no happiness, no joy—
Rather inflames thy torment, representing
Lost bliss, to thee no more communicable;
So never more in Hell than when in Heaven.          420
But thou art serviceable to Heaven's King.
Wilt thou impute to obedience what thy fear
Extorts, or pleasure to do ill excites?
What but thy malice moved thee to misdeem
Of righteous Job, then cruelly to afflict him
With all inflictions? but his patience won.
The other service was thy chosen task,
To be a liar in four hundred mouths;
For lying is thy sustenance, thy food.
Yet thou pretend'st to truth; all oracles          430
By thee are given, and what confessed more true
Among the nations? that hath been thy craft,
By mixing somewhat true to vent more lies.
But what have been thy answers? what but dark,
Ambiguous, and with double sense deluding,
Which they who asked have seldom understood,
And, not well understood, as good not known?
Who ever, by consulting at thy shrine,
Returned the wiser, or the more instruct
To fly or follow what concerned him most,          440
And run not sooner to his fatal snare?
For God hath justly given the nations up
To thy delusions; justly, since they fell

Idolatrous, but, when his purpose is
Among them to declare his providence,
To the not known, whence hast thou then thy truth,
But from him, or his Angels president
In every province, who, themselves disdaining
T' approach thy temples, give thee in command
What, to the smallest tittle, thou shalt say            450
To thy adorers? Thou, with trembling fear,
Or like a fawning parasite, obey'st;
Then to thyself ascrib'st the truth foretold.
But this thy glory shall be soon retrenched;
No more shalt thou by oracling abuse
The Gentiles; henceforth oracles are ceased,
And thou no more with pomp and sacrifice
Shalt be inquired at Delphos or elsewhere—
At least in vain, for they shall find thee mute.
God hath now sent his living Oracle                      460
Into the world to teach his final will,
And sends his Spirit of Truth henceforth to dwell
In pious hearts, an inward oracle
To all truth requisite for men to know.'
    So spake our Saviour; but the subtle Fiend,
Though inly stung with anger and disdain,
Dissembled, and this answer smooth returned:—
'Sharply thou hast insisted on rebuke,
And urged me hard with doings which not will,
But misery, hath wrested from me.  Where            470
Easily canst thou find one miserable,
And not enforced oft-times to part from truth,
If it may stand him more in stead to lie,
Say and unsay, feign, flatter, or abjure?
But thou art placed above me: thou art Lord;
For thee I can, and must, submiss, endure
Check or reproof, and glad to scape so quit.
Hard are the ways of truth, and rough to walk,
Smooth on the tongue discoursed, pleasing to th' ear,
And tunable as sylvan pipe or song;                      480
What wonder, then, if I delight to hear
Her dictates from thy mouth? most men admire
Virtue who follow not her lore: permit me
To hear thee when I come (since no man comes),

And talk at least, though I despair to attain.
Thy Father, who is holy, wise and pure,
Suffers the hypocrite or atheous priest
To tread his sacred courts, and minister
About his altar, handling holy things,
Praying or vowing, and vouchsafed his voice          490
To Balaam reprobate, a prophet yet
Inspired: disdain not such access to me.'
   To whom our Saviour, with unaltered brow:—
'Thy coming hither, though I know thy scope,
I bid not, or forbid; do as thou find'st
Permission from above; thou canst not more.'
   He added not; and Satan, bowing low
His grey dissimulation, disappeared,
Into thin air diffused: for now began
Night with her sullen wing to double-shade          500
The desert; fowls in their clay nests were couched;
And now wild beasts came forth the woods to roam.

*The End of the First Book.*

# PARADISE REGAINED

## THE SECOND BOOK

MEANWHILE the new-baptized, who yet remained
At Jordan with the Baptist, and had seen
Him whom they heard so late expressly called
Jesus Messiah, Son of God declared,
And on that high authority had believed,
And with him talked, and with him lodged—I mean
Andrew and Simon, famous after known,
With others, though in Holy Writ not named—
Now missing him, their joy so lately found,
So lately found and so abruptly gone,                    10
Began to doubt, and doubted many days,
And, as the days increased, increased their doubt:
Sometimes they thought he might be only shown,
And for a time caught up to God, as once
Moses was in the Mount and missing long,
And the great Tishbite, who on fiery wheels
Rode up to Heaven, yet once again to come.
Therefore, as those young prophets then with care
Sought lost Elijah, so in each place these
Nigh to Bethabara—in Jericho                             20
The city of palms, Ænon, and Salem old,
Machærus, and each town or city walled
On this side the broad lake Gennesaret,
Or in Peræa—but returned in vain.
Then on the bank of Jordan, by a creek,
Where winds with reeds and osiers whisp'ring play,
Plain fishermen (no greater men them call),
Close in a cottage low together got,
Their unexpected loss and plaints outbreathed:—

    'Alas, from what high hope to what relapse           30
Unlooked for are we fallen! our eyes beheld
Messiah certainly now come, so long
Expected of our fathers; we have heard
His words, his wisdom full of grace and truth:

"Now, now, for sure, deliverance is at hand;
The kingdom shall to Israel be restored:"
Thus we rejoiced, but soon our joy is turned
Into perplexity and new amaze.
For whither is he gone? what accident
Hath rapt him from us? will he now retire                    40
After appearance, and again prolong
Our expectation? God of Israel,
Send thy Messiah forth; the time is come;
Behold the kings of the earth, how they oppress
Thy chosen, to what height their power unjust
They have exalted, and behind them cast
All fear of thee; arise, and vindicate
Thy glory; free thy people from their yoke!
But let us wait; thus far he hath performed—
Sent his Anointed, and to us revealed him,                   50
By his great Prophet pointed at and shown
In public, and with him we have conversed.
Let us be glad of this, and all our fears
Lay on his providence; he will not fail,
Nor will withdraw him now, nor will recall—
Mock us with his blest sight, then snatch him hence:
Soon we shall see our hope, our joy, return.'
    Thus they out of their plaints new hope resume
To find whom at the first they found unsought.
But to his mother Mary, when she saw                         60
Others returned from baptism, not her Son,
Nor left at Jordan, tidings of him none,
Within her breast though calm, her breast though pure,
Motherly cares and fears got head, and raised
Some troubled thoughts, which she in sighs thus clad:—
    'Oh, what avails me now that honour high,
To have conceived of God, or that salute,
"Hail, highly favoured, among women blest!"
While I to sorrows am no less advanced,
And fears as eminent above the lot                           70
Of other women, by the birth I bore:
In such a season born, when scarce a shed
Could be obtained to shelter him or me
From the bleak air? A stable was our warmth,
A manger his; yet soon enforced to fly

Thence into Egypt, till the murd'rous king
Were dead, who sought his life, and, missing, filled
With infant blood the streets of Bethlehem.
From Egypt home returned, in Nazareth
Hath been our dwelling many years; his life            80
Private, unactive, calm, contemplative,
Little suspicious to any king; but now,
Full grown to man, acknowledged, as I hear,
By John the Baptist, and in public shown,
Son owned from Heaven by his Father's voice,
I looked for some great change; to honour? no;
But trouble, as old Simeon plain foretold,
That to the fall and rising he should be
Of many in Israel, and to a sign
Spoken against—that through my very soul               90
A sword shall pierce, this is my favoured lot,
My exaltation to afflictions high!
Afflicted I may be, it seems, and blest!
I will not argue that, nor will repine.
But where delays he now? some great intent
Conceals him: when twelve years he scarce had seen
I lost him, but so found, as well I saw
He could not lose himself, but went about
His Father's business; what he meant I mused—
Since understand; much more his absence now           100
Thus long to some great purpose he obscures.
But I to wait with patience am inured;
My heart hath been a storehouse long of things
And sayings laid up, portending strange events.'
    Thus Mary, pondering oft, and oft to mind
Recalling what remarkably had passed
Since first her salutation heard, with thoughts
Meekly composed awaited the fulfilling:
The while her Son, tracing the desert wild,
Sole, but with holiest meditations fed,               110
Into himself descended, and at once
All his great work to come before him set—
How to begin, how to accomplish best
His end of being on Earth, and mission high:
For Satan, with sly preface to return,
Had left him vacant, and with speed was gone

Up to the middle region of thick air,
Where all his Potentates in council sat;
There, without sign of boast, or sign of joy,
Solicitous and blank, he thus began:—                                    120
   'Princes, Heaven's ancient Sons, Ethereal Thrones,
Demonian Spirits now, from the element
Each of his reign allotted, rightlier called
Powers of Fire, Air, Water, and Earth beneath
(So may we hold our place and these mild seats
Without new trouble!)—such an enemy
Is risen to invade us, who no less
Threatens than our expulsion down to Hell;
I, as I undertook, and with the vote
Consenting in full frequence was empowered,                              130
Have found him, viewed him, tasted him; but find
Far other labour to be undergone
Than when I dealt with Adam, first of men,
Though Adam by his wife's allurement fell,
However to this Man inferior far—
If he be Man by mother's side at least,
With more than human gifts from Heaven adorned,
Perfections absolute, graces divine,
And amplitude of mind to greatest deeds.
Therefore I am returned, lest confidence                                 140
Of my success with Eve in Paradise
Deceive ye to persuasion over-sure
Of like succeeding here; I summon all
Rather to be in readiness with hand
Or counsel to assist, lest I, who erst
Thought none my equal, now be overmatched.'
   So spake the old Serpent, doubting, and from all
With clamour was assured their utmost aid
At his command; when from amidst them rose
Belial, the dissolutest Spirit that fell,                                150
The sensualest, and, after Asmodai,
The fleshliest incubus, and thus advised:—
   'Set women in his eye and in his walk,
Among daughters of men the fairest found;
Many are in each region passing fair
As the noon sky, more like to goddesses
Than mortal creatures, graceful and discreet,

Expert in amorous arts, enchanting tongues
Persuasive, virgin majesty with mild
And sweet allayed, yet terrible to approach,          160
Skilled to retire, and in retiring draw
Hearts after them tangled in amorous nets.
Such object hath the power to soften and tame
Severest temper, smooth the rugged'st brow,
Enerve, and with voluptuous hope dissolve,
Draw out with credulous desire, and lead
At will the manliest, resolutest breast,
As the magnetic hardest iron draws.
Women, when nothing else, beguiled the heart
Of wisest Solomon, and made him build,                170
And made him bow, to the gods of his wives.'
    To whom quick answer Satan thus returned:—
'Belial, in much uneven scale thou weigh'st
All others by thyself; because of old
Thou thyself doat'st on womankind, admiring
Their shape, their colour, and attractive grace,
None are, thou think'st, but taken with such toys.
Before the Flood, thou, with thy lusty crew,
False titled Sons of God, roaming the Earth,
Cast wanton eyes on the daughters of men,             180
And coupled with them, and begot a race.
Have we not seen, or by relation heard,
In courts and regal chambers how thou lurk'st,
In wood or grove, by mossy fountain-side,
In valley or green meadow, to waylay
Some beauty rare, Calisto, Clymene,
Daphne, or Semele, Antiopa,
Or Amymone, Syrinx, many more
Too long, then lay'st thy scapes on names adored,
Apollo, Neptune, Jupiter, or Pan,                     190
Satyr, or Faun, or Sylvan? But these haunts
Delight not all; among the sons of men
How many have with a smile made small account
Of Beauty and her lures, easily scorned
All her assaults, on worthier things intent!
Remember that Pellean conqueror,
A youth, how all the beauties of the East
He slightly viewed, and slightly overpassed;

How he surnamed of Africa dismissed,
In his prime youth, the fair Iberian maid.          200
For Solomon, he lived at ease, and, full
Of honour, wealth, high fare, aimed not beyond
Higher design than to enjoy his state;
Thence to the bait of women lay exposed;
But he whom we attempt is wiser far
Than Solomon, of more exalted mind,
Made and set wholly on the accomplishment
Of greatest things. What woman will you find,
Though of this age the wonder and the fame,
On whom his leisure will vouchsafe an eye          210
Of fond desire? Or should she, confident,
As sitting queen adored on Beauty's throne,
Descend with all her winning charms begirt
To enamour, as the zone of Venus once
Wrought that effect on Jove (so fables tell),
How would one look from his majestic brow,
Seated as on the top of Virtue's hill,
Discount'nance her despised, and put to rout
All her array, her female pride deject,
Or turn to reverent awe! For Beauty stands          220
In the admiration only of weak minds
Led captive; cease to admire, and all her plumes
Fall flat, and shrink into a trivial toy,
At every sudden slighting quite abashed.
Therefore with manlier objects we must try
His constancy, with such as have more show
Of worth, of honour, glory, and popular praise
(Rocks whereon greatest men have oftest wrecked);
Or that which only seems to satisfy
Lawful desires of nature, not beyond;          230
And now I know he hungers, where no food
Is to be found, in the wide Wilderness:
The rest commit to me; I shall let pass
No advantage, and his strength as oft assay.'
    He ceased, and heard their grant in loud acclaim;
Then forthwith to him takes a chosen band
Of Spirits likest to himself in guile,
To be at hand, and at his beck appear,
If cause were to unfold some active scene

Of various persons, each to know his part;                    240
Then to the desert takes with these his flight,
Where still, from shade to shade, the Son of God,
After forty days' fasting, had remained,
Now hung'ring first, and to himself thus said:—
    'Where will this end?  Four times ten days I have
        passed
Wandering this woody maze, and human food
Nor tasted, nor had appetite: that fast
To virtue I impute not, or count part
Of what I suffer here; if nature need not,
Or God support nature without repast,                    250
Though needing, what praise is it to endure?
But now I feel I hunger; which declares
Nature hath need of what she asks; yet God
Can satisfy that need some other way,
Though hunger still remain: so it remain
Without this body's wasting, I content me,
And from the sting of famine fear no harm;
Nor mind it, fed with better thoughts, that feed
Me hung'ring more to do my Father's will.'
    It was the hour of night, when thus the Son                    260
Communed in silent walk, then laid him down
Under the hospitable covert nigh
Of trees thick interwoven; there he slept,
And dreamed, as appetite is wont to dream,
Of meats and drinks, nature's refreshment sweet.
Him thought he by the brook of Cherith stood,
And saw the ravens with their horny beaks
Food to Elijah bringing even and morn—
Though ravenous, taught to abstain from what they
        brought;
He saw the Prophet also, how he fled                    270
Into the desert, and how there he slept
Under a juniper; then how, awaked,
He found his supper on the coals prepared,
And by the Angel was bid rise and eat,
And eat the second time after repose,
The strength whereof sufficed him forty days:
Sometimes that with Elijah he partook,
Or as a guest with Daniel at his pulse.

Thus wore out night; and now the herald lark
Left his ground-nest, high towering to descry            280
The Morn's approach, and greet her with his song.
As lightly from his grassy couch uprose
Our Saviour, and found all was but a dream;
Fasting he went to sleep, and fasting waked.
Up to a hill anon his steps he reared,
From whose high top to ken the prospect round,
If cottage were in view, sheep-cote, or herd;
But cottage, herd, or sheep-cote, none he saw—
Only in a bottom saw a pleasant grove,
With chant of tuneful birds resounding loud;            290
Thither he bent his way, determined there
To rest at noon, and entered soon the shade
High-roofed, and walks beneath, and alleys brown,
That opened in the midst a woody scene;
Nature's own work it seemed (Nature taught Art),
And, to a superstitious eye, the haunt
Of wood-gods and wood-nymphs; he viewed it round;
When suddenly a man before him stood,
Not rustic as before, but seemlier clad,
As one in city or court or palace bred,            300
And with fair speech these words to him addressed:—
    'With granted leave officious I return,
But much more wonder that the Son of God
In this wild solitude so long should bide,
Of all things destitute, and, well I know,
Not without hunger. Others of some note,
As story tells, have trod this wilderness:
The fugitive bond-woman, with her son,
Outcast Nebaioth, yet found here relief
By a providing Angel; all the race            310
Of Israel here had famished, had not God
Rained from heaven manna; and that Prophet bold
Native of Thebez, wandering here, was fed
Twice, by a voice inviting him to eat.
Of thee these forty days none hath regard,
Forty and more deserted here indeed.'
    To whom thus Jesus:—'What conclud'st thou hence?
They all had need; I, as thou seest, have none.'
    'How hast thou hunger then?' Satan replied.

Both table and provision vanished quite,
With sound of harpies' wings and talons heard;
Only th' importune Tempter still remained,
And with these words his temptation pursued:—

  'By hunger, that each other creature tames,
Thou art not to be harmed, therefore not moved;
Thy temperance, invincible besides,
For no allurement yields to appetite;
And all thy heart is set on high designs,          410
High actions: but wherewith to be achieved?
Great acts require great means of enterprise;
Thou art unknown, unfriended, low of birth,
A carpenter thy father known, thyself
Bred up in poverty and straits at home;
Lost in a desert here, and hunger-bit.
Which way, or from what hope, dost thou aspire
To greatness? whence authority deriv'st?
What followers, what retinue canst thou gain,
Or at thy heels the dizzy multitude,          420
Longer than thou canst feed them on thy cost?
Money brings honour, friends, conquest, and realms;
What raised Antipater the Edomite,
And his son Herod placed on Judah's throne,
*Thy* throne, but gold, that got him puissant friends?
Therefore, if at great things thou wouldst arrive,
Get riches first, get wealth, and treasure heap—
Not difficult, if thou hearken to me.
Riches are mine, fortune is in my hand;
They whom I favour thrive in wealth amain,         430
While virtue, valour, wisdom, sit in want.'

    To whom thus Jesus patiently replied:—
'Yet wealth without these three is impotent
To gain dominion, or to keep it gained.
Witness those ancient empires of the earth,
In height of all their flowing wealth dissolved;
But men endued with these have oft attained,
In lowest poverty, to highest deeds—
Gideon, and Jephtha, and the shepherd lad
Whose offspring on the throne of Judah sat         440
So many ages, and shall yet regain
That seat, and reign in Israel without end.

Among the Heathen (for throughout the world
To me is not unknown what hath been done
Worthy of memorial) canst thou not remember
Quintius, Fabricius, Curius, Regulus?
For I esteem those names of men so poor,
Who could do mighty things, and could contemn
Riches, though offered from the hand of kings.
And what in me seems wanting but that I      450
May also in this poverty as soon
Accomplish what they did, perhaps and more?
Extol not riches, then, the toil of fools,
The wise man's cumbrance, if not snare; more apt
To slacken virtue and abate her edge
Than prompt her to do aught may merit praise.
What if with like aversion I reject
Riches and realms? yet not for that a crown,
Golden in show, is but a wreath of thorns,
Brings dangers, troubles, cares, and sleepless nights,      460
To him who wears the regal diadem,
When on his shoulders each man's burden lies;
For therein stands the office of a king,
His honour, virtue, merit, and chief praise,
That for the public all this weight he bears.
Yet he who reigns within himself, and rules
Passions, desires, and fears, is more a king—
Which every wise and virtuous man attains;
And who attains not ill aspires to rule
Cities of men, or headstrong multitudes,      470
Subject himself to anarchy within,
Or lawless passions in him, which he serves.
But to guide nations in the way of truth
By saving doctrine, and from error lead
To know, and, knowing, worship God aright,
Is yet more kingly, this attracts the soul,
Governs the inner man, the nobler part;
That other o'er the body only reigns,
And oft by force—which to a generous mind,
So reigning, can be no sincere delight.      480
Besides, to give a kingdom hath been thought
Greater and nobler done, and to lay down
Far more magnanimous, than to assume.

Riches are needless then, both for themselves,
And for thy reason why they should be sought—
To gain a sceptre, oftest better missed.'

*The End of the Second Book.*

# PARADISE REGAINED
## THE THIRD BOOK

So spake the Son of God; and Satan stood
A while as mute, confounded what to say,
What to reply, confuted and convinced
Of his weak arguing and fallacious drift;
At length, collecting all his serpent wiles,
With soothing words renewed, him thus accosts:—
'I see thou know'st what is of use to know,
What best to say canst say, to do canst do;
Thy actions to thy words accord; thy words
To thy large heart give utterance due; thy heart     10
Contains of good, wise, just, the perfect shape.
Should kings and nations from thy mouth consult,
Thy counsel would be as the oracle
Urim and Thummim, those oraculous gems
On Aaron's breast, or tongue of Seers old
Infallible; or, wert thou sought to deeds
That might require th' array of war, thy skill
Of conduct would be such that all the world
Could not sustain thy prowess, or subsist
In battle, though against thy few in arms.     20
These godlike virtues wherefore dost thou hide?
Affecting private life, or more obscure
In savage wilderness, wherefore deprive
All Earth her wonder at thy acts, thyself
The fame and glory—glory, the reward
That sole excites to high attempts the flame
Of most erected spirits, most tempered pure
Ethereal, who all pleasures else despise,
All treasures and all gain esteem as dross,
And dignities and powers, all but the highest?     30
Thy years are ripe, and over-ripe; the son
Of Macedonian Philip had ere these
Won Asia, and the throne of Cyrus held
At his dispose; young Scipio had brought down
The Carthaginian pride; young Pompey quelled

The Pontic king, and in triumph had rode.
Yet years, and to ripe years judgement mature,
Quench not the thirst of glory, but augment.
Great Julius, whom now all the world admires,
The more he grew in years, the more inflamed       40
With glory, wept that he had lived so long
Inglorious: but thou yet art not too late.'
    To whom our Saviour calmly thus replied:—
'Thou neither dost persuade me to seek wealth
For empire's sake, nor empire to affect
For glory's sake, by all thy argument.
For what is glory but the blaze of fame,
The people's praise, if always praise unmixed?
And what the people but a herd confused,
A miscellaneous rabble, who extol            50
Things vulgar, and, well weighed, scarce worth the praise?
They praise and they admire they know not what,
And know not whom, but as one leads the other;
And what delight to be by such extolled,
To live upon their tongues, and be their talk?
Of whom to be dispraised were no small praise—
His lot who dares be singularly good.
Th' intelligent among them and the wise
Are few, and glory scarce of few is raised.
This is true glory and renown—when God,        60
Looking on the Earth, with approbation marks
The just man, and divulges him through Heaven
To all his Angels, who with true applause
Recount his praises; thus he did to Job,
When, to extend his fame through Heaven and Earth,
As thou to thy reproach may'st well remember,
He asked thee, "Hast thou seen my servant Job?"
Famous he was in Heaven; on Earth less known,
Where glory is false glory, attributed
To things not glorious, men not worthy of fame.   70
They err who count it glorious to subdue
By conquest far and wide, to overrun
Large countries, and in field great battles win,
Great cities by assault: what do these worthies
But rob and spoil, burn, slaughter, and enslave
Peaceable nations, neighbouring or remote,

Made captive, yet deserving freedom more
Than those their conquerors, who leave behind
Nothing but ruin wheresoe'er they rove,
And all the flourishing works of peace destroy;          80
Then swell with pride, and must be titled Gods,
Great Benefactors of mankind, Deliverers,
Worshipped with temple, priest, and sacrifice.
One is the son of Jove, of Mars the other;
Till conqueror Death discover them scarce men,
Rolling in brutish vices, and deformed,
Violent or shameful death their due reward.
But if there be in glory aught of good,
It may by means far different be attained,
Without ambition, war, or violence;          90
By deeds of peace, by wisdom eminent,
By patience, temperance; I mention still
Him whom thy wrongs, with saintly patience borne,
Made famous in a land and times obscure;
Who names not now with honour patient Job?
Poor Socrates (who next more memorable?)
By what he taught and suffered for so doing,
For truth's sake suffering death unjust, lives now
Equal in fame to proudest conquerors.
Yet, if for fame and glory aught be done,          100
Aught suffered—if young African for fame
His wasted country freed from Punic rage—
The deed becomes unpraised, the man at least,
And loses, though but verbal, his reward.
Shall I seek glory, then, as vain men seek,
Oft not deserved? I seek not mine, but his
Who sent me, and thereby witness whence I am.'
   To whom the Tempter, murmuring, thus replied:—
'Think not so slight of glory, therein least
Resembling thy great Father: he seeks glory,          110
And for his glory all things made, all things
Orders and governs; nor content in Heaven,
By all his Angels glorified, requires
Glory from men, from all men, good or bad,
Wise or unwise, no difference, no exemption.
Above all sacrifice, or hallowed gift,
Glory he requires, and glory he receives,

Promiscuous from all nations, Jew, or Greek,
Or barbarous, nor exception hath declared;
From us, his foes pronounced, glory he exacts.'  120
   To whom our Saviour fervently replied:—
'And reason; since his Word all things produced,
Though chiefly not for glory as prime end,
But to show forth his goodness, and impart
His good communicable to every soul
Freely; of whom what could he less expect
Than glory and benediction—that is, thanks—
The slightest, easiest, readiest recompense
From them who could return him nothing else,
And, not returning that, would likeliest render  130
Contempt instead, dishonour, obloquy?
Hard recompense, unsuitable return
For so much good, so much beneficence!
But why should man seek glory, who of his own
Hath nothing, and to whom nothing belongs
But condemnation, ignominy, and shame?
Who, for so many benefits received,
Turned recreant to God, ingrate and false,
And so of all true good himself despoiled;
Yet, sacrilegious, to himself would take  140
That which to God alone of right belongs?
Yet so much bounty is in God, such grace,
That who advance his glory, not their own,
Them he himself to glory will advance.'
   So spake the Son of God; and here again
Satan had not to answer, but stood struck
With guilt of his own sin—for he himself,
insatiable of glory, had lost all;
Yet of another plea bethought him soon:—
   'Of glory, as thou wilt,' said he, 'so deem;  150
Worth or not worth the seeking, let it pass.
But to a kingdom thou art born—ordained
To sit upon thy father David's throne,
By mother's side thy father, though thy right
Be now in powerful hands, that will not part
Easily from possession won with arms;
Judæa now, and all the Promised Land,
Reduced a province under Roman yoke,

Obeys Tiberius, nor is always ruled
With temperate sway: oft have they violated        160
The Temple, oft the Law, with foul affronts,
Abominations rather, as did once
Antiochus: and think'st thou to regain
Thy right by sitting still, or thus retiring?
So did not Maccabeus: he indeed
Retired unto the desert, but with arms;
And o'er a mighty king so oft prevailed
That by strong hand his family obtained,
Though priests, the crown, and David's throne usurped,
With Modin and her suburbs once content.        170
If kingdom move thee not, let move thee zeal
And duty—zeal and duty are not slow,
But on Occasion's forelock watchful wait:
They themselves rather are occasion best—
Zeal of thy Father's house, duty to free
Thy country from her heathen servitude.
So shalt thou best fulfil, best verify,
The Prophets old, who sung thy endless reign—
The happier reign the sooner it begins:
Reign then; what canst thou better do the while?'
      To whom our Saviour answer thus returned:—        180
'All things are best fulfilled in their due time;
And time there is for all things, Truth hath said:
If of my reign Prophetic Writ hath told
That it shall never end, so, when begin
The Father in his purpose hath decreed—
He in whose hand all times and seasons roll.
What if he hath decreed that I shall first
Be tried in humble state, and things adverse,
By tribulations, injuries, insults,        190
Contempts, and scorns, and snares, and violence,
Suffering, abstaining, quietly expecting
Without distrust or doubt, that he may know
What I can suffer, how obey? Who best
Can suffer, best can do; best reign, who first
Well hath obeyed; just trial ere I merit
My exaltation without change or end.
But what concerns it thee when I begin
My everlasting Kingdom? Why art thou

Solicitous? What moves thy inquisition?                    200
Know'st thou not that my rising is thy fall,
And my promotion will be thy destruction?'
    To whom the Tempter, inly racked, replied:—
'Let that come when it comes; all hope is lost
Of my reception into grace; what worse?
For where no hope is left is left no fear;
If there be worse, the expectation more
Of worse torments me than the feeling can.
I would be at the worst; worst is my port,
My harbour, and my ultimate repose,                       210
The end I would attain, my final good.
My error was my error, and my crime
My crime; whatever for itself condemned,
And will alike be punished, whether thou
Reign or reign not—though to that gentle brow
Willingly I could fly, and hope thy reign,
From that placid aspect and meek regard,
Rather than aggravate my evil state,
Would stand between me and thy Father's ire
(Whose ire I dread more than the fire of Hell),          220
A shelter and a kind of shading cool
Interposition, as a summer's cloud.
If I, then, to the worst that can be haste,
Why move thy feet so slow to what is best?
Happiest, both to thyself and all the world,
That thou, who worthiest art, shouldst be their king!
Perhaps thou linger'st in deep thoughts detained
Of the enterprise so hazardous and high;
No wonder; for, though in thee be united
What of perfection can in Man be found,                    230
Or human nature can receive, consider
Thy life hath yet been private, most part spent
At home, scarce viewed the Galilean towns,
And once a year Jerusalem, few days'
Short sojourn; and what thence couldst thou observe?
The world thou hast not seen, much less her glory,
Empires, and monarchs, and their radiant courts,
Best school of best experience, quickest in sight
In all things that to greatest actions lead.
The wisest, unexperienced, will be ever                    240

Timorous, and loth, with novice modesty
(As he who, seeking asses, found a kingdom),
Irresolute, unhardy, unadventurous.
But I will bring thee where thou soon shalt quit
Those rudiments, and see before thine eyes
The monarchies of the Earth, their pomp and state—
Sufficient introduction to inform
Thee, of thyself so apt, in regal arts
And regal mysteries; that thou may'st know
How best their opposition to withstand.'            250
     With that (such power was given him then), he took
The Son of God up to a mountain high.
It was a mountain at whose verdant feet
A spacious plain outstretched in circuit wide
Lay pleasant; from his side two rivers flowed,
Th' one winding, the other straight, and left between
Fair champaign, with less rivers interveined,
Then meeting joined their tribute to the sea:
Fertile of corn the glebe, of oil, and wine;
With herds the pastures thronged, with flocks the hills;
Huge cities and high-towered, that well might seem    261
The seats of mightiest monarchs; and so large
The prospect was that here and there was room
For barren desert, fountainless and dry.
To this high mountain-top the Tempter brought
Our Saviour, and new train of words began:—
     'Well have we speeded, and o'er hill and dale,
Forest, and field, and flood, temples and towers,
Cut shorter many a league; here thou behold'st
Assyria, and her empire's ancient bounds,            270
Araxes and the Caspian lake; thence on
As far as Indus east, Euphrates west,
And oft beyond; to south the Persian bay,
And, inaccessible, the Arabian drouth:
Here, Nineveh, of length within her wall
Several days' journey, built by Ninus old,
Of that first golden monarchy the seat,
And seat of Salmanassar, whose success
Israel in long captivity still mourns;
There Babylon, the wonder of all tongues,            280
As ancient, but rebuilt by him who twice

Judah and all thy father David's house
Led captive, and Jerusalem laid waste,
Till Cyrus set them free; Persepolis,
His city, there thou seest, and Bactra there:
Ecbatana her structure vast there shows,
And Hecatompylos her hundred gates;
There Susa by Choaspes, amber stream,
The drink of none but kings; of later fame,
Built by Emathian or by Parthian hands,                    290
The great Seleucia, Nisibis, and there
Artaxata, Teredon, Ctesiphon,
Turning with easy eye, thou may'st behold.
All these the Parthian (now some ages past
By great Arsaces led, who founded first
That empire) under his dominion holds,
From the luxurious kings of Antioch won.
And just in time thou com'st to have a view
Of his great power; for now the Parthian king
In Ctesiphon hath gathered all his host                    300
Against the Scythian, whose incursions wild
Have wasted Sogdiana; to her aid
He marches now in haste: see, though from far,
His thousands, in what martial equipage
They issue forth, steel bows and shafts their arms,
Of equal dread in flight or in pursuit—
All horsemen, in which fight they most excel;
See how in warlike muster they appear,
In rhombs, and wedges, and half-moons, and wings.'
     He looked, and saw what numbers numberless           310
The city gates outpour'd, light-armed troops
In coats of mail and military pride.
In mail their horses clad, yet fleet and strong,
Prancing their riders bore, the flower and choice
Of many provinces from bound to bound—
From Arachosia, from Candaor east,
And Margiana, to the Hyrcanian cliffs
Of Caucasus, and dark Iberian dales;
From Atropatia, and the neighbouring plains
Of Adiabene, Media, and the south                          320
Of Susiana, to Balsara's hav'n.
He saw them in their forms of battle ranged,

How quick they wheeled, and flying behind them shot
Sharp sleet of arrowy showers against the face
Of their pursuers, and overcome by flight;
The field all iron cast a gleaming brown,
Nor wanted clouds of foot, nor, on each horn,
Cuirassiers all in steel for standing fight,
Chariots, or elephants indorsed with towers
Of archers; nor of labouring pioneers                          330
A multitude, with spades and axes armed,
To lay hills plain, fell woods, or valleys fill,
Or where plain was raise hill, or overlay
With bridges rivers proud, as with a yoke:
Mules after these, camels and dromedaries,
And waggons fraught with utensils of war.
Such forces met not, nor so wide a camp,
When Agrican, with all his northern powers,
Besieged Albracca, as romances tell,
The city of Gallaphrone, from thence to win         340
The fairest of her sex, Angelica,
His daughter, sought by many prowest knights,
Both Paynim and the peers of Charlemagne.
Such and so numerous was their chivalry;
At sight whereof the Fiend yet more presumed,
And to our Saviour thus his words renewed:—
    'That thou may'st know I seek not to engage
Thy virtue, and not every way secure
On no slight grounds thy safety; hear and mark
To what end I have brought thee hither, and shown  350
All this fair sight: thy kingdom, though foretold
By Prophet or by Angel, unless thou
Endeavour, as thy father David did,
Thou never shalt obtain: prediction still
In all things, and all men, supposes means;
Without means used, what it predicts revokes.
But say thou wert possessed of David's throne
By free consent of all, none opposite,
Samaritan or Jew; how couldst thou hope
Long to enjoy it quiet and secure                              360
Between two such enclosing enemies,
Roman and Parthian? Therefore one of these
Thou must make sure thy own: the Parthian first,

By my advice, as nearer, and of late
Found able by invasion to annoy
Thy country, and captive led away her kings,
Antigonus and old Hyrcanus, bound,
Maugre the Roman: it shall be my task
To render thee the Parthian at dispose;
Choose which thou wilt, by conquest or by league     370
By him thou shalt regain, without him not,
That which alone can truly reinstall thee
In David's royal seat, his true successor—
Deliverance of thy brethren, those Ten Tribes
Whose offspring in his territory yet serve
In Habor, and among the Medes dispersed:
Ten sons of Jacob, two of Joseph, lost
Thus long from Israel, serving, as of old
Their fathers in the land of Egypt served,
This offer sets before thee to deliver.     380
These if from servitude thou shalt restore
To their inheritance, then, nor till then,
Thou on the throne of David in full glory,
From Egypt to Euphrates and beyond,
Shalt reign, and Rome or Cæsar not need fear.'
    To whom our Saviour answered thus, unmoved:—
'Much ostentation vain of fleshly arm
And fragile arms, much instrument of war,
Long in preparing, soon to nothing brought,
Before mine eyes thou hast set, and in my ear     390
Vented much policy, and projects deep
Of enemies, of aids, battles, and leagues,
Plausible to the world, to me worth naught.
Means I must use, thou say'st; prediction else
Will unpredict, and fail me of the throne:
My time, I told thee (and that time for thee
Were better farthest off), is not yet come;
When that comes, think not thou to find me slack
On my part aught endeavouring, or to need
Thy politic maxims, or that cumbersome     400
Luggage of war there shown me—argument
Of human weakness rather than of strength.
My brethren, as thou call'st them, those Ten Tribes,
I must deliver, if I mean to reign

David's true heir, and his full sceptre sway
To just extent over all Israel's sons!
But whence to thee this zeal? Where was it then
For Israel, or for David, or his throne,
When thou stood'st up his tempter to the pride
Of numb'ring Israel—which cost the lives            410
Of threescore and ten thousand Israelites
By three days' pestilence? such was thy zeal
To Israel then, the same that now to me.
As for those captive tribes, themselves were they
Who wrought their own captivity, fell off
From God to worship calves, the deities
Of Egypt, Baal next and Ashtaroth,
And all the idolatries of heathen round,
Besides their other worse than heathenish crimes;
Nor in the land of their captivity            420
Humbled themselves, or penitent besought
The God of their forefathers; but so died
Impenitent, and left a race behind
Like to themselves, distinguishable scarce
From Gentiles, but by circumcision vain,
And God with idols in their worship joined.
Should I of these the liberty regard,
Who, freed, as to their ancient patrimony,
Unhumbled, unrepentant, unreformed,
Headlong would follow, and to their gods perhaps   430
Of Bethel and of Dan? No; let them serve
Their enemies who serve idols with God.
Yet he at length, time to himself best known,
Rememb'ring Abraham, by some wondrous call
May bring them back, repentant and sincere,
And at their passing cleave the Assyrian flood,
While to their native land with joy they haste,
As the Red Sea and Jordan once he cleft,
When to the Promised Land their fathers passed;
To his due time and providence I leave them.'       440
    So spake Israel's true King, and to the Fiend
Made answer meet, that made void all his wiles.
So fares it when with truth falsehood contends

*The End of the Third Book.*

# PARADISE REGAINED

## THE FOURTH BOOK

PERPLEXED and troubled at his bad success
The Tempter stood, nor had what to reply,
Discovered in his fraud, thrown from his hope
So oft, and the persuasive rhetoric
That sleeked his tongue, and won so much on Eve,
So little here, nay lost; but Eve was Eve;
This far his over-match, who, self-deceived
And rash, beforehand had no better weighed
The strength he was to cope with, or his own:
But as a man who had been matchless held          10
In cunning, over-reached where least he thought,
To salve his credit, and for very spite,
Still will be tempting him who foils him still,
And never cease, though to his shame the more;
Or as a swarm of flies in vintage-time,
About the wine-press where sweet must is poured,
Beat off, returns as oft with humming sound;
Or surging waves against a solid rock,
Though all to shivers dashed, the assault renew,
(Vain battery!) and in froth or bubbles end;      20
So Satan, whom repulse upon repulse
Met ever, and to shameful silence brought,
Yet gives not o'er, though desperate of success,
And his vain importunity pursues.
He brought our Saviour to the western side
Of that high mountain, whence he might behold
Another plain, long, but in breadth not wide,
Washed by the southern sea, and on the north
To equal length backed with a ridge of hills
That screened the fruits of the earth and seats of men  30
From cold Septentrion blasts; thence in the midst
Divided by a river, of whose banks
On each side an imperial city stood,
With towers and temples proudly elevate
On seven small hills, with palaces adorned,

Porches and theatres, baths, aqueducts,
Statues, and trophies, and triumphal arcs,
Gardens and groves, presented to his eyes
Above the height of mountains interposed.
By what strange parallax, or optic skill                          40
Of vision, multiplied through air, or glass
Of telescope, were curious to inquire:
And now the Tempter thus his silence broke:—
    'The city which thou seest no other deem
Than great and glorious Rome, queen of the earth
So far renowned, and with the spoils enriched
Of nations; there the Capitol thou seest,
Above the rest lifting his stately head
On the Tarpeian rock, her citadel
Impregnable; and there Mount Palatine,                           50
The imperial palace, compass huge, and high
The structure, skill of noblest architects,
With gilded battlements, conspicuous far,
Turrets, and terraces, and glittering spires.
Many a fair edifice besides, more like
Houses of gods, (so well I have disposed
My aery microscope) thou may'st behold
Outside and inside both, pillars and roofs,
Carved work, the hand of famed artificers
In cedar, marble, ivory, or gold.                                60
Thence to the gates cast round thine eye, and see
What conflux issuing forth, or entering in:
Prætors, proconsuls to their provinces
Hasting, or on return, in robes of state;
Lictors and rods, the ensigns of their power;
Legions and cohorts, turms of horse and wings;
Or embassies from regions far remote,
In various habits, on the Appian road,
Or on the Æmilian, some from farthest south,
Syene, and where the shadow both way falls,                      70
Meroë, Nilotic isle, and, more to west,
The realm of Bocchus to the Blackmoor sea;
From the Asian kings (and Parthian among these),
From India and the Golden Chersonese,
And utmost Indian isle Taprobane,
Dusk faces with white silken turbans wreathed;

From Gallia, Gades, and the British west;
Germans, and Scythians, and Sarmatians north
Beyond Danubius to the Tauric pool.
All nations now to Rome obedience pay—                      80
To Rome's great Emperor, whose wide domain,
In ample territory, wealth and power,
Civility of manners, arts, and arms,
And long renown, thou justly may'st prefer
Before the Parthian. These two thrones except,
The rest are barbarous, and scarce worth the sight,
Shared among petty kings too far removed;
These having shown thee, I have shown thee all
The kingdoms of the world, and all their glory.
This Emperor hath no son, and now is old,                   90
Old and lascivious, and from Rome retired
To Capreæ, an island small but strong
On the Campanian shore, with purpose there
His horrid lusts in private to enjoy;
Committing to a wicked favourite
All public cares, and yet of him suspicious;
Hated of all, and hating; with what ease,
Endued with regal virtues as thou art,
Appearing, and beginning noble deeds,
Might'st thou expel this monster from his throne,          100
Now made a sty, and, in his place ascending,
A victor-people free from servile yoke!
And with my help thou may'st; to me the power
Is given, and by that right I give it thee.
Aim, therefore, at no less than all the world;
Aim at the highest; without the highest attained
Will be for thee no sitting, or not long,
On David's throne, be prophesied what will.'
     To whom the Son of God, unmoved, replied:—
'Nor doth this grandeur and majestic show                   110
Of luxury, though called magnificence,
More than of arms before, allure mine eye,
Much less my mind; though thou should'st add to tell
Their sumptuous gluttonies, and gorgeous feasts
On citron tables or Atlantic stone
(For I have also heard, perhaps have read),
Their wines of Setia, Cales, and Falerne,

Chios and Crete, and how they quaff, in gold,
Crystal, and myrrhine cups, embossed with gems
And studs of pearl—to me should'st tell, who thirst    120
And hunger still: then embassies thou show'st
From nations far and nigh: what honour that,
But tedious waste of time, to sit and hear
So many hollow compliments and lies,
Outlandish flatteries? Then proceed'st to talk
Of the Emperor, how easily subdued,
How gloriously: I shall, thou say'st, expel
A brutish monster: what if I withal
Expel a Devil who first made him such?
Let his tormentor, Conscience, find him out;        130
For him I was not sent, nor yet to free
That people, victor once, now vile and base,
Deservedly made vassal—who, once just,
Frugal, and mild, and temperate, conquered well,
But govern ill the nations under yoke,
Peeling their provinces, exhausted all
By lust and rapine; first ambitious grown
Of triumph, that insulting vanity;
Then cruel, by their sports to blood inured
Of fighting beasts, and men to beasts exposed;        140
Luxurious by their wealth, and greedier still,
And from the daily scene effeminate.
What wise and valiant man would seek to free
These, thus degenerate, by themselves enslaved,
Or could of inward slaves make outward free?
Know, therefore, when my season comes to sit
On David's throne, it shall be like a tree,
Spreading and overshadowing all the earth,
Or as a stone that shall to pieces dash
All monarchies besides throughout the world;        150
And of my kingdom there shall be no end:
Means there shall be to this; but what the means
Is not for thee to know, nor me to tell.'
    To whom the Tempter, impudent, replied:—
'I see all offers made by me how slight
Thou valu'st, because offered, and reject'st:
Nothing will please the difficult and nice,
Or nothing more than still to contradict:

On the other side, know also thou that I
On what I offer set as high esteem,                          160
Nor what I part with mean to give for naught.
All these, which in a moment thou behold'st,
The kingdoms of the world to thee I give
(For, given to me, I give to whom I please),
No trifle; yet with this reserve, not else,
On this condition, if thou wilt fall down,
And worship me as thy superior lord,
Easily done, and hold them all of me;
For what can less so great a gift deserve?'
    Whom thus our Saviour answered with disdain:—
'I never liked thy talk, thy offers less;                    171
Now both abhor, since thou hast dared to utter
The abominable terms, impious condition;
But I endure the time, till which expired
Thou hast permission on me. It is written,
The first of all commandments, "Thou shalt worship
The Lord thy God, and only him shalt serve;"
And dar'st thou to the Son of God propound
To worship thee, accurs'd? now more accurs'd
For this attempt, bolder than that on Eve,                   180
And more blasphemous; which expect to rue.
The kingdoms of the world to thee were given!
Permitted rather, and by thee usurped;
Other donation none thou canst produce:
If given, by whom but by the King of kings,
God over all supreme? If given to thee,
By thee how fairly is the Giver now
Repaid! But gratitude in thee is lost
Long since. Wert thou so void of fear or shame
As offer them to me, the Son of God—                         190
To me my own, on such abhorred pact,
That I fall down and worship thee as God?
Get thee behind me; plain thou now appear'st
That Evil One, Satan for ever damned.'
    To whom the Fiend, with fear abashed, replied:—
'Be not so sore offended, Son of God—
Though Sons of God both Angels are and Men—
If I, to try whether in higher sort
Than these thou bear'st that title, have proposed

What both from Men and Angels I receive,          200
Tetrarchs of fire, air, flood, and on the Earth
Nations besides from all the quartered winds,
God of this World invoked, and World beneath;
Who then thou art, whose coming is foretold
To me so fatal, me it most concerns.
The trial hath endamaged thee no way,
Rather more honour left and more esteem:
Me naught advantaged, missing what I aimed.
Therefore let pass, as they are transitory,
The kingdoms of this world; I shall no more          210
Advise thee; gain them as thou canst, or not.
And thou thyself seem'st otherwise inclined
Than to a worldly crown, addicted more
To contemplation and profound dispute;
As by that early action may be judged,
When, slipping from thy mother's eye, thou went'st
Alone into the Temple; there wast found
Amongst the gravest Rabbis, disputant
On points and questions fitting Moses' chair,
Teaching, not taught.  The childhood shows the man,
As morning shows the day: be famous, then,          221
By wisdom; as thy empire must extend,
So let extend thy mind o'er all the world,
In knowledge, all things in it comprehend;
All knowledge is not couched in Moses' law,
The Pentateuch, or what the Prophets wrote;
The Gentiles also know, and write, and teach
To admiration, led by Nature's light;
And with the Gentiles much thou must converse,
Ruling them by persuasion, as thou mean'st.          230
Without their learning, how wilt thou with them,
Or they with thee, hold conversation meet?
How wilt thou reason with them, how refute
Their idolisms, traditions, paradoxes?
Error by his own arms is best evinced.
Look once more, ere we leave this specular mount,
Westward, much nearer by south-west; behold
Where on th' Ægean shore a city stands,
Built nobly, pure the air and light the soil—
Athens, the eye of Greece, mother of arts          240

And eloquence, native to famous wits
Or hospitable, in her sweet recess,
City or suburban studious walks and shades;
See there the olive-grove of Academe,
Plato's retirement, where the Attic bird
Trills her thick-warbled notes the summer long;
There, flow'ry hill, Hymettus, with the sound
Of bees' industrious murmur, oft invites
To studious musing; there Ilissus rolls
His whispering stream; within the walls then view          250
The schools of ancient sages—his who bred
Great Alexander to subdue the world,
Lyceum there; and painted Stoa next:
There thou shalt hear and learn the secret power
Of harmony, in tones and numbers hit
By voice or hand, and various-measured verse,
Æolian charms and Dorian lyric odes,
And his who gave them breath, but higher sung,
Blind Melesigenes, thence Homer called,
Whose poem Phœbus challenged for his own.                  260
Thence what the lofty grave Tragedians taught
In chorus or iambic, teachers best
Of moral prudence, with delight received
In brief sententious precepts, while they treat
Of fate, and chance, and change in human life,
High actions and high passions best describing:
Thence to the famous Orators repair,
Those ancient, whose resistless eloquence
Wielded at will that fierce democracy,
Shook the Arsenal, and fulmin'd over Greece                270
To Macedon and Artaxerxes' throne;
To sage Philosophy next lend thine ear,
From Heaven descended to the low-roofed house
Of Socrates—see there his tenement—
Whom, well inspired, the oracle pronounced
Wisest of men; from whose mouth issued forth
Mellifluous streams, that watered all the schools
Of Academics old and new, with those
Surnamed Peripatetics, and the sect
Epicurean, and the Stoic severe;                           280
These here revolve, or, as thou lik'st, at home,

Till time mature thee to a kingdom's weight;
These rules will render thee a king complete
Within thyself, much more with empire joined.'
    To whom our Saviour sagely thus replied:—
'Think not but that I know these things; or think
I know them not, not therefore am I short
Of knowing what I ought: he who receives
Light from above, from the Fountain of Light,
No other doctrine needs, though granted true;                    290
But these are false, or little else but dreams,
Conjectures, fancies, built on nothing firm.
The first and wisest of them all professed
To know this only, that he nothing knew;
The next to fabling fell and smooth conceits;
A third sort doubted all things, though plain sense;
Others in virtue placed felicity,
But virtue joined with riches and long life;
In corporal pleasure he, and careless ease;
The Stoic last in philosophic pride,                             300
By him called virtue, and his virtuous man,
Wise, perfect in himself, and all possessing,
Equal to God, oft shames not to prefer,
As fearing God nor man, contemning all
Wealth, pleasure, pain or torment, death and life—
Which, when he lists, he leaves, or boasts he can;
For all his tedious talk is but vain boast,
Or subtle shifts conviction to evade.
Alas! what can they teach, and not mislead,
Ignorant of themselves, of God much more,                        310
And how the World began, and how Man fell,
Degraded by himself, on grace depending?
Much of the Soul they talk, but all awry;
And in themselves seek virtue; and to themselves
All glory arrogate, to God give none;
Rather accuse him under usual names,
Fortune and Fate, as one regardless quite
Of mortal things. Who, therefore, seeks in these
True wisdom finds her not, or, by delusion
Far worse, her false resemblance only meets,                     320
An empty cloud. However, many books,
Wise men have said, are wearisome; who reads

Incessantly, and to his reading brings not
A spirit and judgement equal or superior
(And what he brings what needs he elsewhere seek?),
Uncertain and unsettled still remains,
Deep-versed in books and shallow in himself,
Crude or intoxicate, collecting toys
And trifles for choice matters, worth a sponge,
As children gathering pebbles on the shore.          330
Or, if I would delight my private hours
With music or with poem, where so soon
As in our native language can I find
That solace? All our Law and Story strewed
With hymns, our Psalms with artful terms inscribed,
Our Hebrew songs and harps, in Babylon
That pleased so well our victor's ear, declare
That rather Greece from us these arts derived—
Ill imitated while they loudest sing
The vices of their deities, and their own,          340
In fable, hymn, or song, so personating
Their gods ridiculous, and themselves past shame.
Remove their swelling epithets, thick-laid
As varnish on a harlot's cheek, the rest,
Thin-sown with aught of profit or delight,
Will far be found unworthy to compare
With Sion's songs, to all true tastes excelling,
Where God is praised aright and godlike men,
The Holiest of Holies and his Saints
(Such are from God inspired, not such from thee);    350
Unless where moral virtue is expressed
By light of Nature, not in all quite lost.
Their orators thou then extoll'st as those
The top of eloquence—statists indeed,
And lovers of their country, as may seem;
But herein to our Prophets far beneath,
As men divinely taught, and better teaching
The solid rules of civil government,
In their majestic, unaffected style,
Than all the oratory of Greece and Rome.            360
In them is plainest taught, and easiest learnt,
What makes a nation happy, and keeps it so,
What ruins kingdoms, and lays cities flat;

These only, with our Law, best form a king.'
   So spake the Son of God; but Satan, now
Quite at a loss (for all his darts were spent),
Thus to our Saviour, with stern brow, replied:—
   'Since neither wealth nor honour, arms nor arts,
Kingdom nor empire, pleases thee, nor aught
By me proposed in life contemplative                                    370
Or active, tended on by glory or fame,
What dost thou in this world? The Wilderness
For thee is fittest place: I found thee there,
And thither will return thee, yet remember
What I foretell thee, soon thou shalt have cause
To wish thou never hadst rejected, thus
Nicely or cautiously, my offered aid,
Which would have set thee in short time with ease
On David's throne, or throne of all the world,
Now at full age, fulness of time, thy season,                           380
When prophecies of thee are best fulfilled.
Now contrary, if I read aught in Heaven,
Or Heaven write aught of fate, by what the stars
Voluminous, or single characters
In their conjunction met, give me to spell,
Sorrows and labours, opposition, hate,
Attends thee; scorns, reproaches, injuries,
Violence and stripes, and, lastly, cruel death.
A kingdom they portend thee, but what kingdom,
Real or allegoric, I discern not;                                       390
Nor when: eternal sure, as without end,
Without beginning; for no date prefixed
Directs me in the starry rubric set.'
   So saying, he took (for still he knew his power
Not yet expired), and to the Wilderness
Brought back the Son of God, and left him there,
Feigning to disappear. Darkness now rose,
As daylight sunk, and brought in louring Night,
Her shadowy offspring, unsubstantial both,
Privation mere of light and absent day.                                 400
Our Saviour, meek, and with untroubled mind
After his aery jaunt, though hurried sore,
Hungry and cold, betook him to his rest,
Wherever, under some concourse of shades,

Whose branching arms thick intertwined might shield
From dews and damps of night his sheltered head;
But, sheltered, slept in vain; for at his head
The Tempter watched, and soon with ugly dreams
Disturbed his sleep; and either tropic now
'Gan thunder, and both ends of heaven; the clouds    410
From many a horrid rift abortive poured
Fierce rain with lightning mixed, water with fire
In ruin reconciled; nor slept the winds
Within their stony caves, but rushed abroad
From the four hinges of the world, and fell
On the vexed wilderness, whose tallest pines,
Though rooted deep as high, and sturdiest oaks,
Bowed their stiff necks, loaden with stormy blasts,
Or torn up sheer: ill wast thou shrouded then,
O patient Son of God, yet only stood'st    420
Unshaken; Nor yet stayed the terror there:
Infernal ghosts and hellish furies round
Environed thee; some howled, some yelled, some
     shrieked,
Some bent at thee their fiery darts, while thou
Sat'st unappalled in calm and sinless peace.
Thus passed the night so foul, till Morning fair
Came forth with pilgrim steps, in amice grey,
Who with her radiant finger stilled the roar
Of thunder, chased the clouds, and laid the winds
And grisly spectres, which the Fiend had raised    430
To tempt the Son of God with terrors dire.
And now the sun with more effectual beams
Had cheered the face of earth, and dried the wet
From drooping plant, or dropping tree; the birds,
Who all things now behold more fresh and green,
After a night of storm so ruinous,
Cleared up their choicest notes in bush and spray,
To gratulate the sweet return of morn;
Nor yet, amidst this joy and brightest morn,
Was absent, after all his mischief done,    440
The Prince of Darkness; glad would also seem
Of this fair change, and to our Saviour came;
Yet with no new device (they all were spent),
Rather by this his last affront resolved,

Desperate of better course, to vent his rage
And mad despite to be so oft repelled.
Him walking on a sunny hill he found,
Backed on the north and west by a thick wood;
Out of the wood he starts in wonted shape,
And in a careless mood thus to him said:—          450
'Fair morning yet betides thee, Son of God,
After a dismal night; I heard the wrack,
As earth and sky would mingle; but myself
Was distant; and these flaws, though mortals fear them,
As dangerous to the pillared frame of Heaven,
Or to the Earth's dark basis underneath,
Are to the main as inconsiderable
And harmless, if not wholesome, as a sneeze
To man's less universe, and soon are gone.
Yet, as being oft-times noxious where they light          460
On man, beast, plant, wasteful and turbulent,
Like turbulencies in the affairs of men,
Over whose heads they roar, and seem to point,
They oft fore-signify and threaten ill:
This tempest at this desert most was bent;
Of men at thee, for only thou here dwell'st.
Did I not tell thee, if thou didst reject
The perfect season offered with my aid
To win thy destined seat, but wilt prolong
All to the push of fate, pursue thy way          470
Of gaining David's throne no man knows when
(For both the when and how is nowhere told),
Thou shalt be what thou art ordained, no doubt;
For Angels have proclaimed it, but concealing
The time and means: each act is rightliest done,
Not when it must, but when it may be best,
If thou observe not this, be sure to find
What I foretold thee, many a hard assay
Of dangers, and adversities, and pains,
Ere thou of Israel's sceptre get fast hold;          480
Whereof this ominous night that closed thee round,
So many terrors, voices, prodigies,
May warn thee, as a sure foregoing sign.'
     So talked he, while the Son of God went on,
And stayed not, but in brief him answered thus:—

'Me worse than wet thou find'st not; other harm
Those terrors which thou speak'st of did me none.
I never feared they could, though noising loud
And threat'ning nigh: what they can do as signs
Betok'ning or ill-boding I contemn                                        490
As false portents, not sent from God, but thee;
Who, knowing I shall reign past thy preventing,
Obtrud'st thy offered aid, that I, accepting,
At least might seem to hold all power of thee,
Ambitious Spirit, and would'st be thought my God;
And storm'st, refused, thinking to terrify
Me to thy will; desist (thou art discerned,
And toil'st in vain), nor me in vain molest.'
    To whom the Fiend, now swoll'n with rage, replied:—
'Then hear, O Son of David, virgin-born!                                   500
For Son of God to me is yet in doubt;
Of the Messiah I have heard foretold
By all the Prophets; of thy birth, at length
Announced by Gabriel, with the first I knew,
And of the angelic song in Bethlehem field,
On thy birth-night, that sung thee Saviour born.
From that time seldom have I ceased to eye
Thy infancy, thy childhood, and thy youth,
Thy manhood last, though yet in private bred;
Till, at the ford of Jordan, whither all                                   510
Flocked to the Baptist, I among the rest
Though not to be baptized, by voice from Heaven
Heard thee pronounced the Son of God beloved.
Thenceforth I thought thee worth my nearer view
And narrower scrutiny, that I might learn
In what degree or meaning thou art called
The Son of God, which bears no single sense;
The Son of God I also am, or was;
And, if I was, I am; relation stands:
All men are sons of God; yet thee I thought                                520
In some respect far higher so declared.
Therefore I watched thy footsteps from that hour,
And followed thee still on to this waste wild,
Where, by all best conjectures, I collect
Thou art to be my fatal enemy.
Good reason, then, if I beforehand seek

To understand my adversary, who
And what he is; his wisdom, power, intent:
By parle or composition, truce or league,
To win him, or win from him what I can.          530
And opportunity I here have had
To try thee, sift thee, and confess have found thee
Proof against all temptation, as a rock
Of adamant and as a centre, firm
To the utmost of mere man both wise and good,
Not more; for honours, riches, kingdoms, glory,
Have been before contemned, and may again:
Therefore, to know what more thou art than man,
Worth naming Son of God by voice from Heaven,
Another method I must now begin.'          540
    So saying, he caught him up, and, without wing
Of hippogrif, bore through the air sublime,
Over the wilderness and o'er the plain,
Till underneath them fair Jerusalem,
The holy city, lifted high her towers,
And higher yet the glorious Temple reared
Her pile, far off appearing like a mount
Of alabaster, topped with golden spires:
There, on the highest pinnacle, he set
The Son of God, and added thus in scorn:—          550
    'There stand, if thou wilt stand; to stand upright
Will ask thee skill; I to thy Father's house
Have brought thee, and highest placed: highest is best:
Now show thy progeny; if not to stand,
Cast thyself down; safely, if Son of God;
For it is written, "He will give command
Concerning thee to his Angels; in their hands
They shall uplift thee, lest at any time
Thou chance to dash thy foot against a stone." '
    To whom thus Jesus: 'Also it is written,          560
"Tempt not the Lord thy God." ' He said, and stood;
But Satan, smitten with amazement, fell.
As when Earth's son, Antæus (to compare
Small things with greatest), in Irassa strove
With Jove's Alcides, and oft foiled, still rose,
Receiving from his mother Earth new strength,
Fresh from his fall, and fiercer grapple joined,

Throttled at length in th' air, expired and fell,
So, after many a foil, the Tempter proud,
Renewing fresh assaults, amidst his pride          570
Fell whence he stood to see his Victor fall.
And, as that Theban monster that proposed
Her riddle, and him who solved it not devoured,
That once found out and solved, for grief and spite
Cast herself headlong from th' Ismenian steep,
So, struck with dread and anguish, fell the Fiend,
And to his crew, that sat consulting, brought
Joyless triumphals of his hoped success,
Ruin, and desperation, and dismay,
Who durst so proudly tempt the Son of God.         580
So Satan fell; and straight a fiery globe
Of Angels on full sail of wing flew nigh,
Who on their plumy vans received him soft
From his uneasy station, and upbore,
As on a floating couch, through the blithe air;
Then, in a flow'ry valley, set him down
On a green bank, and set before him spread
A table of celestial food, divine,
Ambrosial, fruits fetched from the Tree of Life,
And from the Fount of Life ambrosial drink,        590
That soon refreshed him wearied, and repaired
What hunger, if aught hunger had impaired,
Or thirst; and, as he fed, angelic quires
Sung heavenly anthems of his victory
Over temptation and the Tempter proud:—
    'True Image of the Father, whether throned
In the bosom of bliss, and light of light
Conceiving, or remote from Heaven, enshrined
In fleshly tabernacle and human form,
Wand'ring the wilderness; whatever place,          600
Habit, or state, or motion, still expressing
The Son of God, with Godlike force endued
Against th' attempter of thy Father's throne
And thief of Paradise! Him long of old
Thou didst debel, and down from Heaven cast
With all his army; now thou hast avenged
Supplanted Adam, and, by vanquishing
Temptation, hast regained lost Paradise,

And frustrated the conquest fraudulent.
He never more henceforth will dare set foot          610
In Paradise to tempt; his snares are broke.
For, though that seat of earthly bliss be failed,
A fairer Paradise is founded now
For Adam and his chosen sons, whom thou,
A Saviour, art come down to reinstall;
Where they shall dwell secure, when time shall be,
Of tempter and temptation without fear.
But thou, Infernal Serpent, shalt not long
Rule in the clouds; like an autumnal star,
Or lightning, thou shalt fall from Heaven, trod down
Under his feet: for proof, ere this thou feel'st       621
Thy wound (yet not thy last and deadliest wound)
By this repulse received, and hold'st in Hell
No triumph; in all her gates Abaddon rues
Thy bold attempt; hereafter learn with awe
To dread the Son of God: he, all unarmed,
Shall chase thee, with the terror of his voice,
From thy demoniac holds, possession foul,
Thee and thy legions; yelling they shall fly,
And beg to hide them in a herd of swine,             630
Lest he command them down into the Deep,
Bound, and to torment sent before their time.
Hail, Son of the Most High, heir of both worlds,
Queller of Satan! on thy glorious work
Now enter, and begin to save mankind.'
     Thus they the Son of God, our Saviour meek,
Sung Victor, and, from heavenly feast refreshed,
Brought on his way with joy; he, unobserved,
Home to his mother's house private returned.


*The End.*

# SAMSON AGONISTES

## OF THAT SORT OF DRAMATIC POEM WHICH IS CALLED TRAGEDY

TRAGEDY, as it was anciently composed, hath been ever held the gravest, moralest, and most profitable of all other poems; therefore said by Aristotle to be of power, by raising pity and fear, or terror, to purge the mind of those and such-like passions; that is, to temper and reduce them to just measure with a kind of delight, stirred up by reading or seeing those passions well imitated. Nor is Nature wanting in her own effects to make good his assertion; for so, in physic, things of melancholic hue and quality are used against melancholy, sour against sour, salt to remove salt humours. Hence philosophers and other gravest writers, as Cicero, Plutarch, and others, frequently cite out of tragic poets, both to adorn and illustrate their discourse. The Apostle Paul himself thought it not unworthy to insert a verse of Euripides into the text of Holy Scripture, 1 Cor. xv. 33; and Paræus, commenting on the *Revelation*, divides the whole book, as a tragedy, into acts, distinguished each by a Chorus of heavenly harpings and song between. Heretofore men in highest dignity have laboured not a little to be thought able to compose a tragedy. Of that honour Dionysius the elder was no less ambitious than before of his attaining to the tyranny. Augustus Cæsar also had begun his *Ajax*, but, unable to please his own judgement with what he had begun, left it unfinished. Seneca the philosopher is by some thought the author of those tragedies (at least the best of them) that go under that name. Gregory Nazianzen, a Father of the Church, thought it not unbeseeming the sanctity of his person to write a tragedy, which he entitled *Christ Suffering*. This is mentioned to vindicate Tragedy from the small esteem, or rather infamy, which in the account of many it undergoes at this day, with other common interludes; happening through the poet's error of intermixing comic stuff with tragic sadness and gravity, or introducing trivial and vulgar persons: which by all judicious hath been counted absurd, and brought in without discretion, corruptly to gratify the people. And, though ancient Tragedy use no Prologue, yet using sometimes, in case of self-defence or explanation, that which Martial calls an Epistle; in behalf of this tragedy, coming forth after the ancient manner, much different from what among us passes for best, thus much beforehand may be *epistled*—that Chorus is here introduced after the Greek manner, not ancient only but modern, and still in use among the Italians. In the modelling therefore of this poem, with good reason, the Ancients and Italians are rather followed, as of much more authority and fame. The measure of verse used in the Chorus is of all sorts, called by the Greeks *Monostrophic*, or rather *Apolelymenon*, without regard had to Strophe, Antistrophe, or Epode; which were a kind of stanzas framed only for the music, then used with the Chorus that sung; not essential to the poem, and therefore not material; or, being divided into stanzas or pauses, they may be called *Allœostropha*. Division into act and scene, referring chiefly to the stage (to which this work never was intended), is here omitted.

It suffices if the whole drama be found not produced beyond the fifth Act. Of the style and uniformity, and that commonly called the plot, whether intricate or explicit—which is nothing indeed but such economy, or disposition of the fable, as may stand best with verisimilitude and decorum—they only will best judge who are not unacquainted with Æschylus, Sophocles, and Euripides, the three tragic poets unequalled yet by any, and the best rule to all who endeavour to write Tragedy. The circumscription of time, wherein the whole drama begins and ends, is, according to ancient rule and best example, within the space of twenty-four hours.

# THE ARGUMENT

*Samson, made captive, blind, and now in the prison at Gaza, there to labour as in a common workhouse, on a festival day, in the general cessation from labour, comes forth into the open air to a place nigh, somewhat retired, there to sit a while and bemoan his condition: where he happens at length to be visited by certain friends and equals of his tribe, which make the Chorus, who seek to comfort him what they can; then by his old father, Manoa, who endeavours the like, and withal tells him his purpose to procure his liberty by ransom; lastly, that this feast was proclaimed by the Philistines as a day of thanksgiving for their deliverance from the hands of Samson—which yet more troubles him. Manoa then departs to prosecute his endeavour with the Philistian lords for Samson's redemption: who, in the meanwhile, is visited by other persons, and, lastly, by a public officer to require his coming to the feast before the lords and people, to play or show his strength in their presence; he at first refuses, dismissing the public officer with absolute denial to come; at length, persuaded inwardly that this was from God, he yields to go along with him, who came now the second time with great threatenings to fetch him; the Chorus yet remaining on the place, Manoa returns full of joyful hope to procure ere long his son's deliverance; in the midst of which discourse an Hebrew comes in haste, confusedly at first, and afterwards more distinctly, relating the catastrophe, what Samson had done to the Philistines, and by accident to himself; wherewith the Tragedy ends.*

## THE PERSONS

SAMSON.

MANOA, the father of Samson.

DALILA, his wife.

HARAPHA of Gath.

Public Officer.

Messenger.

Chorus of Danites.

The Scene before the Prison in GAZA.

# SAMSON AGONISTES

*Sam.* A LITTLE onward lend thy guiding hand
To these dark steps, a little further on;
For yonder bank hath choice of sun or shade.
There I am wont to sit, when any chance
Relieves me from my task of servile toil,
Daily in the common prison else enjoined me,
Where I, a prisoner chained, scarce freely draw
The air, imprisoned also, close and damp,
Unwholesome draught: but here I feel amends—
The breath of Heaven fresh blowing, pure and sweet,  10
With day-spring born; here leave me to respire.
This day a solemn feast the people hold
To Dagon, their sea-idol, and forbid
Laborious works, unwillingly this rest
Their superstition yields me; hence, with leave
Retiring from the popular noise, I seek
This unfrequented place to find some ease,
Ease to the body some, none to the mind
From restless thoughts, that, like a deadly swarm
Of hornets armed, no sooner found alone,  20
But rush upon me thronging, and present
Times past, what once I was, and what am now.
Oh, wherefore was my birth from Heaven foretold
Twice by an Angel, who at last, in sight
Of both my parents, all in flames ascended
From off the altar where an offering burned,
As in a fiery column charioting
His godlike presence, and from some great act
Or benefit revealed to Abraham's race?
Why was my breeding ordered and prescribed  30
As of a person separate to God,
Designed for great exploits, if I must die
Betray'd, captiv'd, and both my eyes put out,
Made of my enemies the scorn and gaze,
To grind in brazen fetters under task
With this heaven-gifted strength? O glorious strength,

Put to the labour of a beast, debased
Lower than bond-slave! Promise was that I
Should Israel from Philistian yoke deliver;
Ask for this great deliverer now, and find him          40
Eyeless in Gaza at the mill with slaves,
Himself in bonds under Philistian yoke;
Yet stay, let me not rashly call in doubt
Divine prediction; what if all foretold
Had been fulfilled but through mine own default?
Whom have I to complain of but myself?
Who this high gift of strength committed to me,
In what part lodged, how easily bereft me,
Under the seal of silence could not keep,
But weakly to a woman must reveal it,                   50
O'ercome with importunity and tears.
O impotence of mind, in body strong!
But what is strength without a double share
Of wisdom? Vast, unwieldy, burdensome,
Proudly secure, yet liable to fall
By weakest subtleties; not made to rule,
But to subserve where wisdom bears command.
God, when he gave me strength, to show withal
How slight the gift was, hung it in my hair.
But peace! I must not quarrel with the will             60
Of highest dispensation, which herein
Haply had ends above my reach to know:
Suffices that to me strength is my bane,
And proves the source of all my miseries;
So many, and so huge, that each apart
Would ask a life to wail, but, chief of all,
O loss of sight, of thee I most complain!
Blind among enemies, O worse than chains,
Dungeon, or beggary, or decrepit age!
Light, the prime work of God, to me is extinct,         70
And all her various objects of delight
Annulled, which might in part my grief have eased,
Inferior to the vilest now become
Of man or worm, the vilest here excel me,
They creep, yet see; I, dark in light, exposed
To daily fraud, contempt, abuse, and wrong,
Within doors, or without, still as a fool,

In power of others, never in my own;
Scarce half I seem to live, dead more than half,
O dark, dark, dark, amid the blaze of noon, 80
Irrecoverably dark, total eclipse,
Without all hope of day!
O first-created beam, and thou great Word,
'Let there be light, and light was over all,'
Why am I thus bereaved thy prime decree?
The Sun to me is dark
And silent as the Moon,
When she deserts the night,
Hid in her vacant interlunar cave.
Since light so necessary is to life, 90
And almost life itself, if it be true
That light is in the soul,
She all in every part, why was the sight
To such a tender ball as th' eye confined,
So obvious and so easy to be quenched,
And not, as feeling, through all parts diffused,
That she might look at will through every pore?
Then had I not been thus exiled from light,
As in the land of darkness, yet in light,
To live a life half dead, a living death, 100
And buried; but, O yet more miserable!
Myself my sepulchre, a moving grave;
Buried, yet not exempt,
By privilege of death and burial,
From worst of other evils, pains, and wrongs
But made hereby obnoxious more
To all the miseries of life,
Life in captivity
Among inhuman foes.
But who are these? for with joint pace I hear 110
The tread of many feet steering this way;
Perhaps my enemies, who come to stare
At my affliction, and perhaps to insult,
Their daily practice to afflict me more.
    _Chor._ This, this is he; softly a while;
Let us not break in upon him.
O change beyond report, thought, or belief!
See how he lies at random, carelessly diffused,

With languished head unpropped,
As one past hope, abandoned,                                      120
And by himself given over,
In slavish habit, ill-fitted weeds
O'er-worn and soiled.
Or do my eyes misrepresent? Can this be he,
That heroic, that renowned,
Irresistible Samson? whom, unarmed,
No strength of man, or fiercest wild beast, could with-
    stand;
Who tore the lion as the lion tears the kid;
Ran on embattled armies clad in iron,
And, weaponless himself,                                          130
Made arms ridiculous, useless the forgery
Of brazen shield and spear, the hammered cuirass,
Chalybean-tempered steel, and frock of mail
Adamantean proof:
But safest he who stood aloof,
When insupportably his foot advanced,
In scorn of their proud arms and warlike tools,
Spurned them to death by troops. The bold Ascalonite
Fled from his lion ramp; old warriors turned
Their plated backs under his heel,                                140
Or grovelling soiled their crested helmets in the dust.
Then with what trivial weapon came to hand,
The jaw of a dead ass, his sword of bone,
A thousand foreskins fell, the flower of Palestine,
In Ramath-lechi, famous to this day:
Then by main force pulled up, and on his shoulders bore,
The gates of Azza, post and massy bar,
Up to the hill by Hebron, seat of giants old,
No journey of a sabbath-day, and loaded so;
Like whom the Gentiles feign to bear up Heaven.      150
Which shall I first bewail,
Thy bondage or lost sight,
Prison within prison
Inseparably dark?
Thou art become (O worst imprisonment!)
The dungeon of thyself; thy soul
(Which men enjoying sight oft without cause complain)
Imprisoned now indeed,

In real darkness of the body dwells,
Shut up from outward light                                    160
To incorporate with gloomy night;
For inward light, alas!
Puts forth no visual beam.
O mirror of our fickle state,
Since man on earth, unparalleled,
The rarer thy example stands,
By how much from the top of wondrous glory,
Strongest of mortal men,
To lowest pitch of abject fortune thou art fallen!
For him I reckon not in high estate                            170
Whom long descent of birth,
Or the sphere of fortune, raises;
But thee, whose strength, while virtue was her mate,
Might have subdued the Earth,
Universally crowned with highest praises.

    *Sam.* I hear the sound of words; their sense the air
Dissolves unjointed ere it reach my ear.

    *Chor.* He speaks: let us draw nigh. Matchless in
      might,
The glory late of Israel, now the grief!
We come, thy friends and neighbours not unknown,   180
From Eshtaol and Zora's fruitful vale,
To visit or bewail thee; or, if better,
Counsel or consolation we may bring,
Salve to thy sores: apt words have power to 'suage
The tumours of a troubled mind,
And are as balm to festered wounds.

    *Sam.* Your coming, friends, revives me; for I learn
Now of my own experience, not by talk,
How counterfeit a coin they are who 'friends'
Bear in their superscription (of the most         190
I would be understood); in prosperous days
They swarm, but in adverse withdraw their head,
Not to be found, though sought. Ye see, O friends,
How many evils have enclosed me round;
Yet that which was the worst now least afflicts me,
Blindness; for, had I sight, confused with shame,
How could I once look up, or heave the head,
Who, like a foolish pilot, have shipwrecked

My vessel trusted to me from above,
Gloriously rigged, and for a word, a tear,                      200
Fool! have divulged the secret gift of God
To a deceitful woman? Tell me, friends,
Am I not sung and proverbed for a fool
In every street? do they not say, 'How well
Are come upon him his deserts'? yet why?
Immeasurable strength they might behold
In me; of wisdom nothing more than mean.
This with the other should at least have paired;
These two, proportioned ill, drove me transverse.

   *Chor.* Tax not divine disposal. Wisest men          210
Have erred, and by bad women been deceived;
And shall again, pretend they ne'er so wise.
Deject not, then, so overmuch thyself,
Who hast of sorrow thy full load besides.
Yet, truth to say, I oft have heard men wonder
Why thou shouldst wed Philistian women rather
Than of thine own tribe fairer, or as fair,
At least of thy own nation, and as noble.

   *Sam.* The first I saw at Timna, and she pleased
Me, not my parents, that I sought to wed                        220
The daughter of an infidel: they knew not
That what I motioned was of God; I knew
From intimate impulse, and therefore urged
The marriage on, that, by occasion hence,
I might begin Israel's deliverance,
The work to which I was divinely called.
She proving false, the next I took to wife
(O that I never had! fond wish too late!)
Was in the vale of Sorec, Dalila,
That specious monster, my accomplished snare.                   230
I thought it lawful from my former act,
And the same end, still watching to oppress
Israel's oppressors: of what now I suffer
She was not the prime cause, but I myself,
Who, vanquished with a peal of words (O weakness!),
Gave up my fort of silence to a woman.

   *Chor.* In seeking just occasion to provoke
The Philistine, thy country's enemy,
Thou never wast remiss, I bear thee witness;

Yet Israel still serves with all his sons. 240

 *Sam.* That fault I take not on me, but transfer
On Israel's governors, and heads of tribes,
Who, seeing those great acts which God had done
Singly by me against their conquerors,
Acknowledged not, or not at all considered,
Deliverance offered: I, on th' other side,
Used no ambition to commend my deeds;
The deeds themselves, though mute, spoke loud the
  doer;
But they persisted deaf, and would not seem
To count them things worth notice, till at length 250
Their lords, the Philistines, with gathered powers,
Entered Judea seeking me, who then
Safe to the rock of Etham was retired—
Not flying, but forecasting in what place
To set upon them, what advantaged best;
Meanwhile the men of Judah, to prevent
The harass of their land, beset me round;
I willingly on some conditions came
Into their hands, and they as gladly yield me
To the uncircumcised a welcome prey, 260
Bound with two cords; but cords to me were threads
Touched with the flame: on their whole host I flew
Unarmed, and with a trivial weapon felled
Their choicest youth; they only lived who fled.
Had Judah that day joined, or one whole tribe,
They had by this possessed the towers of Gath,
And lorded over them whom now they serve;
But what more oft, in nations grown corrupt,
And by their vices brought to servitude,
Than to love bondage more than liberty, 270
Bondage with ease than strenuous liberty;
And to despise, or envy, or suspect,
Whom God hath of his special favour raised
As their deliverer; if he aught begin,
How frequent to desert him, and at last
To heap ingratitude on worthiest deeds?

 *Chor.* Thy words to my remembrance bring
How Succoth and the fort of Penuel
Their great deliverer contemned,

The matchless Gideon, in pursuit                    280
Of Madian, and her vanquished kings;
And how ingrateful Ephraim
Had dealt with Jephtha, who by argument,
Not worse than by his shield and spear,
Defended Israel from the Ammonite,
Had not his prowess quelled their pride
In that sore battle when so many died
Without reprieve adjudged to death,
For want of well pronouncing *Shibboleth*.

   *Sam.* Of such examples add me to the roll.        290
Me easily indeed mine may neglect,
But God's proposed deliverance not so.

   *Chor.* Just are the ways of God,
And justifiable to men,
Unless there be who think not God at all.
If any be, they walk obscure;
For of such doctrine never was there school,
But the heart of the fool,
And no man therein doctor but himself.

   Yet more there be who doubt his ways not just,    400
As to his own edicts found contradicting;
Then give the reins to wandering thought,
Regardless of his glory's diminution,
Till, by their own perplexities involved,
They ravel more, still less resolved,
But never find self-satisfying solution.

   As if they would confine th' interminable,
And tie him to his own prescript,
Who made our laws to bind us, not himself,
And hath full right to exempt                       810
Whom so it pleases him by choice
From national obstriction, without taint
Of sin, or legal debt;
For with his own laws he can best dispense.

   He would not else, who never wanted means,
Nor in respect of the enemy just cause,
To set his people free,
Have prompted this heroic Nazarite,
Against his vow of strictest purity,
To seek in marriage that fallacious bride,           820

Unclean, unchaste.
  Down, Reason, then; at least, vain reasonings down;
Though Reason here aver
That moral verdict quits her of unclean:
Unchaste was subsequent; her stain, not his.
  But see! here comes thy reverend sire,
With careful step, locks white as down,
Old Manoa: advise
Forthwith how thou ought'st to receive him.
  *Sam.* Ay me! another inward grief, awaked          330
With mention of that name, renews th' assault.
  *Man.* Brethren and men of Dan, for such ye seem,
Though in this uncouth place; if old respect,
As I suppose, towards your once gloried friend,
My son, now captive, hither hath informed
Your younger feet, while mine, cast back with age
Came lagging after; say if he be here.
  *Chor.* As signal now in low dejected state
As erst in highest, behold him where he lies.
  *Man.* O miserable change! is this the man,          340
That invincible Samson, far renowned,
The dread of Israel's foes, who with a strength
Equivalent to Angels' walked their streets,
None offering fight; who, single combatant,
Duelled their armies ranked in proud array,
Himself an army—now unequal match
To save himself against a coward armed
At one spear's length. O ever-failing trust
In mortal strength! and, oh, what not in man
Deceivable and vain? Nay, what thing good          350
Prayed for, but often proves our woe, our bane?
I prayed for children, and thought barrenness
In wedlock a reproach; I gained a son,
And such a son as all men hailed me happy:
Who would be now a father in my stead?
O wherefore did God grant me my request,
And as a blessing with such pomp adorned?
Why are his gifts desirable, to tempt
Our earnest prayers, then, given with solemn hand
As graces, draw a scorpion's tail behind?          360
For this did the Angel twice descend? for this

Ordained thy nurture holy, as of a plant;
Select and sacred? glorious for a while,
The miracle of men; then in an hour
Ensnared, assaulted, overcome, led bound,
Thy foes' derision, captive, poor, and blind,
Into a dungeon thrust, to work with slaves?
Alas! methinks whom God hath chosen once
To worthiest deeds, if he through frailty err,
He should not so o'erwhelm, and as a thrall        370
Subject him to so foul indignities,
Be it but for honour's sake of former deeds.

    *Sam.* Appoint not heavenly disposition, father.
Nothing of all these evils hath befall'n me
But justly; I myself have brought them on;
Sole author I, sole cause: if aught seem vile,
As vile hath been my folly, who have profaned
The mystery of God, given me under pledge
Of vow, and have betrayed it to a woman,
A Canaanite, my faithless enemy.        380
This well I knew, nor was at all surprised,
But warned by oft experience: did not she
Of Timna first betray me, and reveal
The secret wrested from me in her height
Of nuptial love professed, carrying it straight
To them who had corrupted her, my spies
And rivals? In this other was there found
More faith? who, also in her prime of love,
Spousal embraces, vitiated with gold,
Though offered only, by the scent conceived,        390
Her spurious first-born, treason against me?
Thrice she assayed, with flattering prayers and sighs,
And amorous reproaches, to win from me
My capital secret, in what part my strength
Lay stored, in what part summed, that she might know:
Thrice I deluded her, and turned to sport
Her importunity, each time perceiving
How openly and with what impudence
She purposed to betray me, and (which was worse
Than undissembled hate) with what contempt        400
She sought to make me traitor to myself;
Yet, the fourth time, when, mustering all her wiles,

With blandished parleys, feminine assaults,
Tongue-batteries, she surceased not day nor night
To storm me, over-watched and wearied out.
At times when men seek most repose and rest,
I yielded, and unlocked her all my heart,
Who, with a grain of manhood well resolved,
Might easily have shook off all her snares;
But foul effeminacy held me yoked                    410
Her bond-slave; O indignity, O blot
To honour and religion! servile mind
Rewarded well with servile punishment!
The base degree to which I now am fall'n,
These rags, this grinding, is not yet so base
As was my former servitude, ignoble,
Unmanly, ignominious, infamous,
True slavery; and that blindness worse than this,
That saw not how degenerately I served.
    *Man.* I cannot praise thy marriage-choices, son—   420
Rather approved them not; but thou didst plead
Divine impulsion prompting how thou might'st
Find some occasion to infest our foes.
I state not that; this I am sure, our foes
Found soon occasion thereby to make thee
Their captive, and their triumph; thou the sooner
Temptation found'st, or over-potent charms
To violate the sacred trust of silence
Deposited within thee; which to have kept
Tacit, was in thy power; true; and thou bear'st        430
Enough, and more, the burden of that fault;
Bitterly hast thou paid, and still art paying,
That rigid score. A worse thing yet remains:
This day the Philistines a popular feast
Here celebrate in Gaza, and proclaim
Great pomp, and sacrifice, and praises loud
To Dagon, as their god who hath delivered
Thee, Samson, bound and blind, into their hands;
Them out of thine, who slew'st them many a slain.
So Dagon shall be magnified, and God,                  440
Besides whom is no god, compared with idols,
Disglorified, blasphemed, and had in scorn
By th' idolatrous rout amidst their wine;

Which to have come to pass by means of thee,
Samson, of all thy sufferings think the heaviest,
Of all reproach the most with shame that ever
Could have befall'n thee and thy father's house.

   *Sam.* Father, I do acknowledge and confess
That I this honour, I this pomp, have brought
To Dagon, and advanced his praises high          450
Among the Heathen round; to God have brought
Dishonour, obloquy, and oped the mouths
Of idolists and atheists; have brought scandal
To Israel, diffidence of God, and doubt
In feeble hearts, propense enough before
To waver, or fall off and join with idols:
Which is my chief affliction, shame and sorrow,
The anguish of my soul, that suffers not
Mine eye to harbour sleep, or thoughts to rest.
This only hope relieves me, that the strife      460
With me hath end; all the contest is now
'Twixt God and Dagon; Dagon hath presumed,
Me overthrown, to enter lists with God,
His deity comparing and preferring
Before the God of Abraham. He, be sure,
Will not connive, or linger, thus provoked,
But will arise, and his great name assert:
Dagon must stoop, and shall ere long receive
Such a discomfit as shall quite despoil him
Of all these boasted trophies won on me,      470
And with confusion blank his worshippers.

   *Man.* With cause this hope relieves thee; and these words
I as a prophecy receive; for God,
Nothing more certain, will not long defer
To vindicate the glory of his name
Against all competition, nor will long
Endure it doubtful whether God be Lord,
Or Dagon. But for thee what shall be done?
Thou must not in the meanwhile, here forgot,
Lie in this miserable loathsome plight      480
Neglected. I already have made way
To some Philistian lords, with whom to treat
About thy ransom: well they may by this

Have satisfied their utmost of revenge,
By pains and slaveries, worse than death, inflicted
On thee, who now no more canst do them harm.

    *Sam.* Spare that proposal, father; spare the trouble
Of that solicitation; let me here,
As I deserve, pay on my punishment,
And expiate, if possible, my crime,     490
Shameful garrulity. To have revealed
Secrets of men, the secrets of a friend,
How heinous had the fact been, how deserving
Contempt and scorn of all—to be excluded
All friendship, and avoided as a blab,
The mark of fool set on his front!
But I God's counsel have not kept, his holy secret
Presumptuously have published, impiously,
Weakly at least and shamefully—a sin
That Gentiles in their parables condemn     500
To their abyss and horrid pains confined.

    *Man.* Be penitent, and for thy fault contrite;
But act not in thy own affliction, son.
Repent the sin, but if the punishment
Thou canst avoid, self-preservation bids;
Or th' execution leave to high disposal,
And let another hand, not thine, exact
Thy penal forfeit from thyself; perhaps
God will relent, and quit thee all his debt;
Who evermore approves and more accepts     510
(Best pleased with humble and filial submission)
Him who, imploring mercy, sues for life,
Than who, self-rigorous, chooses death as due;
Which argues over-just, and self-displeased
For self-offence more than for God offended.
Reject not, then, what offered means who knows
But God hath set before us to return thee
Home to thy country and his sacred house,
Where thou may'st bring thy offerings, to avert
His further ire, with prayers and vows renewed.     520

    *Sam.* His pardon I implore; but, as for life,
To what end should I seek it? when in strength
All mortals I excelled, and great in hopes,
With youthful courage, and magnanimous thoughts

Of birth from Heaven foretold and high exploits,
Full of divine instinct, after some proof
Of acts indeed heroic, far beyond
The sons of Anak, famous now and blazed,
Fearless of danger, like a petty god
I walked about, admired of all, and dreaded                    530
On hostile ground, none daring my affront.
Then, swoll'n with pride, into the snare I fell
Of fair fallacious looks, venereal trains,
Softened with pleasure and voluptuous life,
At length to lay my head and hallowed pledge
Of all my strength in the lascivious lap
Of a deceitful concubine, who shore me,
Like a tame wether, all my precious fleece,
Then turned me out ridiculous, despoiled,
Shaven, and disarmed among my enemies.                         540

   *Chor.* Desire of wine and all delicious drinks,
Which many a famous warrior overturns,
Thou couldst repress; nor did the dancing ruby,
Sparkling out-poured, the flavour, or the smell,
Or taste, that cheers the heart of gods and men,
Allure thee from the cool crystalline stream.

   *Sam.* Where ever fountain or fresh current flowed
Against the eastern ray, translucent, pure
With touch ethereal of Heaven's fiery rod,
I drank, from the clear milky juice allaying                    550
Thirst, and refreshed; nor envied them the grape
Whose heads that turbulent liquor fills with fumes.

   *Chor.* O madness! to think use of strongest wines
And strongest drinks our chief support of health,
When God with these forbidden made choice to rear
His mighty champion, strong above compare,
Whose drink was only from the liquid brook.

   *Sam.* But what availed this temperance, not complete
Against another object more enticing?
What boots it at one gate to make defence,                      560
And at another to let in the foe,
Effeminately vanquished? by which means,
Now blind, disheartened, shamed, dishonoured, quelled,
To what can I be useful? wherein serve

My nation, and the work from Heaven imposed,
But to sit idle on the household hearth,
A burdenous drone; to visitants a gaze,
Or pitied object; these redundant locks,
Robustious to no purpose, clustering down,
Vain monument of strength; till length of years      570
And sedentary numbness craze my limbs
To a contemptible old age obscure.
Here rather let me drudge, and earn my bread,
Till vermin, or the draff of servile food,
Consume me, and oft-invocated death
Hasten the welcome end of all my pains.

    *Man.* Wilt thou then serve the Philistines with that gift
Which was expressly given thee to annoy them?
Better at home lie bed-rid, not only idle,
Inglorious, unemployed, with age outworn.      580
But God, who caused a fountain at thy prayer
From the dry ground to spring, thy thirst to allay
After the brunt of battle, can as easy
Cause light again within thy eyes to spring,
Wherewith to serve him better than thou hast;
And I persuade me so; why else this strength
Miraculous yet remaining in those locks?
His might continues in thee not for naught,
Nor shall his wondrous gifts be frustrate thus.

    *Sam.* All otherwise to me my thoughts portend—      590
That these dark orbs no more shall treat with light,
Nor th' other light of life continue long,
But yield to double darkness nigh at hand;
So much I feel my genial spirits droop,
My hopes all flat: nature within me seems
In all her functions weary of herself;
My race of glory run, and race of shame,
And I shall shortly be with them that rest.

    *Man.* Believe not these suggestions, which proceed
From anguish of the mind and humours black,      600
That mingle with thy fancy. I, however,
Must not omit a father's timely care
To prosecute the means of thy deliverance
By ransom or how else: meanwhile be calm,

And healing words from these thy friends admit.
  *Sam.* O that torment should not be confined
To the body's wounds and sores
With maladies innumerable
In heart, head, breast, and reins,
But must secret passage find           610
To th' inmost mind,
There exercise all his fierce accidents,
And on her purest spirits prey,
As on entrails, joints, and limbs,
With answerable pains, but more intense,
Though void of corporal sense!
  My griefs not only pain me
As a lingering disease,
But, finding no redress, ferment and rage;
Nor less than wounds immedicable      620
Rankle, and fester, and gangrene,
To black mortification.
Thoughts, my tormentors, armed with deadly stings,
Mangle my apprehensive tenderest parts,
Exasperate, exulcerate, and raise
Dire inflammation, which no cooling herb
Or med'cinal liquor can assuage,
Nor breath of vernal air from snowy Alp.
Sleep hath forsook and given me o'er
To death's benumbing opium as my only cure;  630
Thence faintings, swoonings of despair,
And sense of Heaven's desertion.
  I was his nursling once and choice delight,
His destined from the womb,
Promised by heavenly message twice descending.
Under his special eye
Abstemious I grew up and thrived amain;
He led me on to mightiest deeds,
Above the nerve of mortal arm,
Against the uncircumcised, our enemies:    640
But now hath cast me off as never known,
And to those cruel enemies,
Whom I by his appointment had provoked,
Left me all helpless, with th' irreparable loss
Of sight, reserved alive to be repeated

The subject of their cruelty or scorn.
Nor am I in the list of them that hope;
Hopeless are all my evils, all remediless;
This one prayer yet remains, might I be heard,
No long petition—speedy death,                    650
The close of all my miseries and the balm.

   *Chor.*  Many are the sayings of the wise,
In ancient and in modern books enrolled,
Extolling patience as the truest fortitude,
And to the bearing well of all calamities,
All chances incident to man's frail life,
Consolatories writ
With studied argument, and much persuasion sought,
Lenient of grief and anxious thought,
But with th' afflicted in his pangs their sound   660
Little prevails, or rather seems a tune
Harsh and of dissonant mood from his complaint,
Unless he feel within
Some source of consolation from above,
Secret refreshings that repair his strength
And fainting spirits uphold.

   God of our fathers, what is Man!
That thou towards him with hand so various,
Or might I say contrarious,
Temper'st thy providence through his short course,  670
Not evenly, as thou rul'st
The angelic orders, and inferior creatures mute,
Irrational and brute.
Nor do I name of men the common rout,
That, wandering loose about,
Grow up and perish as the summer fly,
Heads without name, no more remember'd;
But such as thou hast solemnly elected,
With gifts and graces eminently adorned,
To some great work, thy glory,                    680
And people's safety, which in part they effect:
Yet toward these, thus dignified, thou oft,
Amidst their height of noon,
Changest thy countenance and thy hand, with no regard
Of highest favours past
From thee on them, or them to thee of service.

Nor only dost degrade them, or remit
To life obscured, which were a fair dismission,
But throw'st them lower than thou didst exalt them
    high;
Unseemly falls in human eye,                           690
Too grievous for the trespass or omission;
Oft leav'st them to the hostile sword
Of heathen and profane, their carcases
To dogs and fowls a prey, or else captiv'd;
Or to the unjust tribunals, under change of times,
And condemnation of the ingrateful multitude.
If these they scape, perhaps in poverty
With sickness and disease thou bow'st them down,
Painful diseases and deformed,
In crude old age;                                      700
Though not disordinate, yet causeless suffering
The punishment of dissolute days, in fine,
Just or unjust alike seem miserable,
For oft alike both come to evil end.
    So deal not with this once thy glorious champion,
The image of thy strength, and mighty minister.
What do I beg? how hast thou dealt already?
Behold him in this state calamitous, and turn
His labours, for thou canst, to peaceful end.
    But who is this, what thing of sea or land?       710
Female of sex it seems,
That, so bedecked, ornate, and gay,
Comes this way sailing,
Like a stately ship
Of Tarsus, bound for th' isles
Of Javan or Gadire,
With all her bravery on, and tackle trim,
Sails filled, and streamers waving,
Courted by all the winds that hold them play;
An amber scent of odorous perfume                      720
Her harbinger, a damsel train behind;
Some rich Philistian matron she may seem;
And now, at nearer view, no other certain
Than Dalila, thy wife.
    *Sam.* My wife, my traitress, let her not come near
    me.

*Chor.* Yet on she moves; now stands and eyes thee
    fixed,
About t' have spoke; but now, with head declined,
Like a fair flower surcharged with dew, she weeps,
And words addressed seem into tears dissolved,
Wetting the borders of her silken veil:     730
But now again she makes address to speak.

    *Dal.* With doubtful feet and wavering resolution
I came, still dreading thy displeasure, Samson;
Which to have merited, without excuse,
I cannot but acknowledge; yet, if tears
May expiate (though the fact more evil drew
In the perverse event than I foresaw),
My penance hath not slackened, though my pardon
No way assured. But conjugal affection,
Prevailing over fear and timorous doubt,     740
Hath led me on, desirous to behold
Once more thy face, and know of thy estate,
If aught in my ability may serve
To lighten what thou suffer'st, and appease
Thy mind with what amends is in my power,
Though late, yet in some part to recompense
My rash but more unfortunate misdeed.

    *Sam.* Out, out, hyæna! These are thy wonted arts,
And arts of every woman false like thee,
To break all faith, all vows, deceive, betray;     750
Then, as repentant, to submit, beseech,
And reconcilement move with feigned remorse,
Confess, and promise wonders in her change;
Not truly penitent, but chief to try
Her husband, how far urged his patience bears,
His virtue or weakness which way to assail:
Then, with more cautious and instructed skill,
Again transgresses, and again submits;
That wisest and best men, full oft beguiled,
With goodness principled not to reject     760
The penitent, but ever to forgive,
Are drawn to wear out miserable days,
Entangled with a pois'nous bosom snake,
If not by quick destruction soon cut off,
As I by thee, to ages an example.

*Dal.* Yet hear me, Samson; not that I endeavour
To lessen or extenuate my offence,
But that, on th' other side, if it be weighed
By itself, with aggravations not surcharged,
Or else with just allowance counterpoised,                    770
I may, if possible, thy pardon find
The easier towards me, or thy hatred less.
First granting, as I do, it was a weakness
In me, but incident to all our sex,
Curiosity, inquisitive, importune
Of secrets, then with like infirmity
To publish them, both common female faults;
Was it not weakness also to make known
For importunity, that is for naught,
Wherein consisted all thy strength and safety?               780
To what I did thou show'dst me first the way.
But I to enemies revealed, and should not!
Nor shouldst thou have trusted that to woman's frailty:
Ere I to thee, thou to thyself wast cruel.
Let weakness, then, with weakness come to parle,
So near related, or the same of kind;
Thine forgive mine, that men may censure thine
The gentler, if severely thou exact not
More strength from me than in thyself was found.
And what if love, which thou interpret'st hate,              790
The jealousy of love, powerful of sway
In human hearts, nor less in mine towards thee,
Caused what I did? I saw thee mutable
Of fancy; feared lest one day thou wouldst leave me
As her at Timna; sought by all means, therefore,
How to endear, and hold thee to me firmest:
No better way I saw than by importuning
To learn thy secrets, get into my power
Thy key of strength and safety: thou wilt say,
'Why, then, revealed?' I was assured by those               800
Who tempted me that nothing was designed
Against thee but safe custody and hold.
That made for me; I knew that liberty
Would draw thee forth to perilous enterprises,
While I at home sat full of cares and fears,
Wailing thy absence in my widowed bed;

Here I should still enjoy thee, day and night,
Mine and love's prisoner, not the Philistines',
Whole to myself, unhazarded abroad,
Fearless at home of partners in my love.          810
These reasons in Love's law have passed for good,
Though fond and reasonless to some perhaps;
And love hath oft, well meaning, wrought much woe,
Yet always pity or pardon hath obtained.
Be not unlike all others, not austere
As thou art strong, inflexible as steel.
If thou in strength all mortals dost exceed,
In uncompassionate anger do not so.
    *Sam.* How cunningly the sorceress displays
Her own transgressions, to upbraid me mine!          820
That malice, not repentance, brought thee hither
By this appears: I gave, thou say'st, th' example,
I led the way—bitter reproach, but true;
I to myself was false ere thou to me.
Such pardon, therefore, as I give my folly
Take to thy wicked deed; which when thou seest
Impartial, self-severe, inexorable,
Thou wilt renounce thy seeking, and much rather
Confess it feigned; weakness is thy excuse,
And I believe it; weakness to resist          830
Philistian gold. If weakness may excuse,
What murderer, what traitor, parricide,
Incestuous, sacrilegious, but may plead it?
All wickedness is weakness; that plea, therefore,
With God or man will gain thee no remission.
But love constrained thee; call it furious rage
To satisfy thy lust: Love seeks to have love;
My love how couldst thou hope, who took'st the way
To raise in me inexpiable hate,
Knowing, as needs I must, by thee betrayed?          840
In vain thou striv'st to cover shame with shame,
Or by evasions thy crime uncover'st more.
    *Dal.* Since thou determin'st weakness for no plea
In man or woman, though to thy own condemning,
Hear what assaults I had, what snares besides,
What sieges girt me round, ere I consented;
Which might have awed the best-resolved of men,

The constantest, to have yielded without blame.
It was not gold, as to my charge thou lay'st,
That wrought with me: thou know'st the magistrates
And princes of my country came in person,      851
Solicited, commanded, threatened, urged,
Adjured by all the bonds of civil duty
And of religion—pressed how just it was,
How honourable, how glorious to entrap
A common enemy, who had destroyed
Such numbers of our nation: and the priest
Was not behind, but ever at my ear,
Preaching how meritorious with the gods
It would be to ensnare an irreligious      860
Dishonourer of Dagon: what had I
To oppose against such powerful arguments?
Only my love of thee held long debate,
And combated in silence all these reasons
With hard contest. At length, that grounded maxim,
So rife and celebrated in the mouths
Of wisest men, that to the public good
Private respects must yield, with grave authority
Took full possession of me, and prevailed;
Virtue, as I thought, truth, duty, so enjoining.      870
     *Sam.* I thought where all thy circling wiles would end:
In feigned religion, smooth hypocrisy:
But, had thy love, still odiously pretended,
Been, as it ought, sincere, it would have taught thee
Far other reasonings, brought forth other deeds.
I, before all the daughters of my tribe
And of my nation, chose thee from among
My enemies, loved thee, as too well thou knew'st;
Too well! unbosomed all my secrets to thee,
Not out of levity, but overpowered      880
By thy request, who could deny thee nothing;
Yet now am judged an enemy. Why, then,
Didst thou at first receive me for thy husband?
Then, as since then, thy country's foe professed:
Being once a wife, for me thou wast to leave
Parents and country; nor was I their subject,
Nor under their protection, but my own;
Thou mine, not theirs: if aught against my life

Thy country sought of thee, it sought unjustly,
Against the law of nature, law of nations;          890
No more thy country, but an impious crew
Of men conspiring to uphold their state
By worse than hostile deeds, violating the ends
For which our country is a name so dear;
Not therefore to be obeyed. But zeal moved thee;
To please thy gods thou didst it; gods unable
To acquit themselves and prosecute their foes
But by ungodly deeds, the contradiction
Of their own deity, gods cannot be:
Less therefore to be pleased, obeyed, or feared.      900
These false pretexts and varnished colours failing,
Bare in thy guilt, how foul must thou appear!

   *Dal.* In argument with men a woman ever
Goes by the worse, whatever be her cause.

   *Sam.* For want of words, no doubt, or lack of breath!
Witness when I was worried with thy peals.

   *Dal.* I was a fool, too rash, and quite mistaken
In what I thought would have succeeded best.
Let me obtain forgiveness of thee, Samson;
Afford me place to show what recompense          910
Towards thee I intend for what I have misdone,
Misguided: only what remains past cure
Bear not too sensibly, nor still insist
To afflict thyself in vain: though sight be lost
Life yet hath many solaces, enjoyed
Where other senses want not their delights,
At home, in leisure and domestic ease,
Exempt from many a care and chance to which
Eyesight exposes, daily, men abroad.
I to the lords will intercede, not doubting          920
Their favourable ear, that I may fetch thee
From forth this loathsome prison-house, to abide
With me, where my redoubled love and care,
With nursing diligence, to me glad office,
May ever tend about thee to old age
With all things grateful cheered, and so supplied
That what by me thou hast lost thou least shalt miss.

   *Sam.* No, no! of my condition take no care;
It fits not; thou and I long since are twain;

Nor think me so unwary or accursed                              930
To bring my feet again into the snare
Where once I have been caught; I know thy trains,
Though dearly to my cost, thy gins, and toils;
Thy fair enchanted cup, and warbling charms,
No more on me have power; their force is nulled;
So much of adder's wisdom I have learnt
To fence my ear against thy sorceries.
If in my flower of youth and strength, when all men
Loved, honoured, feared me, thou alone could hate me,
Thy husband, slight me, sell me, and forgo me,           940
How wouldst thou use me now, blind, and thereby
Deceivable, in most things as a child
Helpless, thence easily contemned and scorned,
And last neglected? How wouldst thou insult,
When I must live uxorious to thy will
In perfect thraldom! how again betray me,
Bearing my words and doings to the lords
To gloss upon, and, censuring, frown or smile?
This jail I count the house of liberty
To thine, whose doors my feet shall never enter.         950
    *Dal.*  Let me approach at least, and touch thy hand.
    *Sam.*  Not for thy life, lest fierce remembrance wake
My sudden rage to tear thee joint by joint.
At distance I forgive thee; go with that;
Bewail thy falsehood, and the pious works
It hath brought forth to make thee memorable
Among illustrious women, faithful wives;
Cherish thy hastened widowhood with the gold
Of matrimonial treason: so farewell.
    *Dal.*  I see thou art implacable, more deaf          960
To prayers than winds and seas; yet winds to seas
Are reconciled at length, and sea to shore:
Thy anger, unappeasable, still rages,
Eternal tempest never to be calmed.
Why do I humble thus myself, and, suing
For peace, reap nothing but repulse and hate?
Bid go with evil omen, and the brand
Of infamy upon my name denounced?
To mix with thy concernments I desist
Henceforth, nor too much disapprove my own.              970

Fame, if not double-faced, is double-mouthed,
And with contrary blast proclaims most deeds;
On both his wings, one black, th' other white,
Bears greatest names in his wild aery flight,
My name, perhaps, among the circumcised
In Dan, in Judah, and the bordering tribes,
To all posterity may stand defamed,
With malediction mentioned, and the blot
Of falsehood most unconjugal traduced.
But in my country, where I most desire,                      980
In Ecron, Gaza, Asdod, and in Gath,
I shall be named among the famousest
Of women, sung at solemn festivals,
Living and dead recorded, who, to save
Her country from a fierce destroyer, chose
Above the faith of wedlock-bands; my tomb
With odours visited and annual flowers.
Not less renowned than in Mount Ephraim
Jael, who, with inhospitable guile,
Smote Sisera sleeping, through the temples nailed.     990
Nor shall I count it heinous to enjoy
The public marks of honour and reward
Conferred upon me for the piety
Which to my country I was judged to have shown.
At this whoever envies or repines,
I leave him to his lot, and like my own.
    *Chor.* She's gone—a manifest serpent by her sting
Discovered in the end, till now concealed.
    *Sam.* So let her go; God sent her to debase me,
And aggravate my folly, who committed                       1000
To such a viper his most sacred trust
Of secrecy, my safety, and my life.
    *Chor.* Yet beauty, though injurious, hath strange
        power,
After offence returning, to regain
Love once possessed, nor can be easily
Repulsed, without much inward passion felt,
And secret sting of amorous remorse.
    *Sam.* Love-quarrels oft in pleasing concord end;
Not wedlock-treachery endangering life.
    *Chor.* It is not virtue, wisdom, valour, wit,          1010

Strength, comeliness of shape, or amplest merit,
That woman's love can win, or long inherit;
But what it is, hard is to say,
Harder to hit
(Which way soever men refer it),
Much like thy riddle, Samson, in one day
Or seven though one should musing sit:
    If any of these, or all, the Timnian bride
Had not so soon preferred
Thy paranymph, worthless to thee compared,          1020
Successor in thy bed,
Nor both so loosely disallied
Their nuptials, nor this last so treacherously
Had shorn the fatal harvest of thy head.
Is it for that such outward ornament
Was lavished on their sex, that inward gifts
Were left for haste unfinished, judgement scant,
Capacity not raised to apprehend
Or value what is best,
In choice, but oftest to affect the wrong?          1030
Or was too much of self-love mixed,
Of constancy no root infixed,
That either they love nothing, or not long?
    Whate'er it be, to wisest men and best,
Seeming at first all heavenly under virgin veil,
Soft, modest, meek, demure,
Once joined, the contrary she proves—a thorn
Intestine, far within defensive arms
A cleaving mischief, in his way to virtue
Adverse and turbulent; or by her charms          1040
Draws him awry, enslaved
With dotage, and his sense depraved
To folly and shameful deeds, which ruin ends.
What pilot so expert but needs must wreck,
Embarked with such a steers-mate at the helm?
    Favoured of Heaven who finds
One virtuous, rarely found,
That in domestic good combines:
Happy that house! his way to peace is smooth:
But virtue which breaks through all opposition,          1050
And all temptation can remove,

Most shines and most is acceptable above.
　Therefore God's universal law
Gave to the man despotic power
Over his female in due awe,
Nor from that right to part an hour,
Smile she or lour:
So shall he least confusion draw
On his whole life, not swayed
By female usurpation, nor dismayed. 1060
　But had we best retire? I see a storm.
　*Sam.* Fair days have oft contracted wind and rain.
　*Chor.* But this another kind of tempest brings.
　*Sam.* Be less abstruse; my riddling days are past.
　*Chor.* Look now for no enchanting voice, nor fear
The bait of honeyed words; a rougher tongue
Draws hitherward; I know him by his stride,
The giant Harapha of Gath, his look
Haughty, as is his pile high-built and proud.
Comes he in peace? what wind hath blown him hither
I less conjecture than when first I saw 1071
The sumptuous Dalila floating this way:
His habit carries peace, his brow defiance.
　*Sam.* Or peace or not, alike to me he comes.
　*Chor.* His fraught we soon shall know: he now
　　arrives.
　*Har.* I come not, Samson, to condole thy chance,
As these perhaps, yet wish it had not been,
Though for no friendly intent. I am of Gath;
Men call me Harapha, of stock renowned
As Og, or Anak, and the Emims old 1080
That Kiriathaim held; thou know'st me now,
If thou at all art known. Much I have heard
Of thy prodigious might and feats performed,
Incredible to me, in this displeased,
That I was never present on the place
Of those encounters, where we might have tried
Each other's force in camp or listed field;
And now am come to see of whom such noise
Hath walked about, and each limb to survey,
If thy appearance answer loud report. 1090
　*Sam.* The way to know were not to see, but taste

*Har.* Dost thou already single me; I thought
Gyves and the mill had tamed thee? O that fortune
Had brought me to the field where thou art famed
To have wrought such wonders with an ass's jaw;
I should have forced thee soon with other arms,
Or left thy carcase where the ass lay thrown;
So had the glory of prowess been recovered
To Palestine, won by a Philistine                1099
From the unforeskinned race, of whom thou bear'st
The highest name for valiant acts; that honour,
Certain to have won by mortal duel from thee,
I lose, prevented by thy eyes put out.

   *Sam.* Boast not of what thou wouldst have done, but do
What then thou wouldst; thou seest it in thy hand.

   *Har.* To combat with a blind man I disdain,
And thou hast need much washing to be touched.

   *Sam.* Such usage as your honourable lords
Afford me, assassinated and betrayed;
Who durst not with their whole united powers        1110
In fight withstand me single and unarmed,
Nor in the house with chamber ambushes
Close-banded durst attack me, no, not sleeping,
Till they had hired a woman with their gold,
Breaking her marriage faith, to circumvent me.
Therefore, without feigned shifts, let be assigned
Some narrow place enclosed, where sight may give thee,
Or rather flight, no great advantage on me;
Then put on all thy gorgeous arms, thy helmet
And brigandine of brass, thy broad habergeon,       1120
Vant-brass and greaves and gauntlet; add thy spear,
A weaver's beam, and seven-times-folded shield:
I only with an oaken staff will meet thee,
And raise such outcries on thy clattered iron,
Which long shall not withhold me from thy head,
That in a little time, while breath remains thee,
Thou oft shalt wish thyself at Gath, to boast
Again in safety what thou wouldst have done
To Samson, but shalt never see Gath more.

   *Har.* Thou durst not thus disparage glorious arms
Which greatest heroes have in battle worn,          1131

Their ornament and safety, had not spells
And black enchantments, some magician's art,
Armed thee or charmed thee strong, which thou from
    Heaven
Feign'dst at thy birth was given thee in thy hair,
Where strength can least abide, though all thy hairs
Were bristles ranged like those that ridge the back
Of chafed wild boars or ruffled porcupines.
    *Sam.* I know no spells, use no forbidden arts;
My trust is in the Living God who gave me,    1140
At my nativity, this strength, diffused
No less through all my sinews, joints, and bones,
Than thine, while I preserved these locks unshorn,
The pledge of my unviolated vow.
For proof hereof, if Dagon be thy god,
Go to his temple, invocate his aid
With solemnest devotion, spread before him
How highly it concerns his glory now
To frustrate and dissolve these magic spells,
Which I to be the power of Israel's God    1150
Avow, and challenge Dagon to the test,
Offering to combat thee, his champion bold,
With the utmost of his godhead seconded:
Then thou shalt see, or rather to thy sorrow
Soon feel, whose God is strongest, thine or mine.
    *Har.* Presume not on thy God; whate'er he be,
Thee he regards not, owns not, hath cut off
Quite from his people, and delivered up
Into thy enemies' hand; permitted them
To put out both thine eyes, and fettered send thee    1160
Into the common prison, there to grind
Among the slaves and asses, thy comrades,
As good for nothing else, no better service
With those thy boisterous locks; no worthy match
For valour to assail, nor by the sword
Of noble warrior, so to stain his honour,
But by the barber's razor best subdued.
    *Sam.* All these indignities, for such they are
From thine, these evils I deserve and more,
Acknowledge them from God inflicted on me    1170
Justly, yet despair not of his final pardon,

Whose ear is ever open, and his eye
Gracious to readmit the suppliant;
In confidence whereof I once again
Defy thee to the trial of mortal fight,
By combat to decide whose god is God,
Thine, or whom I with Israel's sons adore.

    *Har.* Fair honour that thou dost thy God, in trusting
He will accept thee to defend his cause,
A murderer, a revolter, and a robber.                    1180

    *Sam.* Tongue-doughty giant, how dost thou prove
        me these?

    *Har.* Is not thy nation subject to our lords?
Their magistrates confessed it, when they took thee
As a league-breaker, and delivered bound
Into our hands; for hadst thou not committed
Notorious murder on those thirty men
At Ascalon, who never did thee harm,
Then, like a robber, stripp'dst them of their robes?
The Philistines, when thou hadst broke the league,
Went up with armed powers thee only seeking,                    1190
To others did no violence nor spoil.

    *Sam.* Among the daughters of the Philistines
I chose a wife, which argued me no foe,
And in your city held my nuptial feast;
But your ill-meaning politician lords,
Under pretence of bridal friends and guests,
Appointed to await me thirty spies,
Who, threatening cruel death, constrained the bride
To wring from me, and tell to them, my secret,
That solved the riddle which I had proposed.                    1200
When I perceived all set on enmity,
As on my enemies, where ever chanced,
I used hostility, and took their spoil
To pay my underminers in their coin.
My nation was subjected to your lords.
It was the force of conquest; force with force
Is well ejected when the conquered can.
But I, a private person, whom my country
As a league-breaker gave up bound, presumed
Single rebellion, and did hostile acts!                    1210
I was no private, but a person raised,

With strength sufficient, and command from Heaven,
To free my country; if their servile minds
Me, their deliverer sent, would not receive,
But to their masters gave me up for nought,
Th' unworthier they; whence to this day they serve.
I was to do my part from Heaven assigned,
And had performed it if my known offence
Had not disabled me, not all your force:
These shifts refuted, answer thy appellant,          1220
Though by his blindness maimed for high attempts,
Who now defies thee thrice to single fight,
As a petty enterprise of small enforce.

   *Har.* With thee, a man condemned, a slave enrolled,
Due by the law to capital punishment?
To fight with thee no man of arms will deign.

   *Sam.* Cam'st thou for this, vain boaster, to survey
      me,
To descant on my strength, and give thy verdict?
Come nearer; part not hence so slight informed;
But take good heed my hand survey not thee.          1230

   *Har.* O Baal-zebub! can my ears unused
Hear these dishonours, and not render death?

   *Sam.* No man withholds thee; nothing from thy hand
Fear I incurable; bring up thy van;
My heels are fettered, but my fist is free.

   *Har.* This insolence other kind of answer fits.

   *Sam.* Go, baffled coward, lest I run upon thee,
Though in these chains, bulk without spirit vast,
And with one buffet lay thy structure low,
Or swing thee in the air, then dash thee down          1240
To the hazard of thy brains and shattered sides.

   *Har.* By Astaroth, ere long thou shalt lament
These braveries, in irons loaden on thee.

   *Chor.* His giantship is gone somewhat crestfall'n,
Stalking with less unconscionable strides,
And lower looks, but in a sultry chafe.

   *Sam.* I dread him not, nor all his giant-brood,
Though fame divulge him father of five sons,
All of gigantic size, Goliah chief.

   *Chor.* He will directly to the lords, I fear,          1250
And with malicious counsel stir them up

Some way or other yet further to afflict thee.

   *Sam.* He must allege some cause, and offered fight
Will not dare mention, lest a question rise
Whether he durst accept the offer or not;
And that he durst not plain enough appeared.
Much more affliction than already felt
They cannot well impose, nor I sustain,
If they intend advantage of my labours,
The work of many hands, which earns my keeping,   1260
With no small profit daily to my owners.
But come what will; my deadliest foe will prove
My speediest friend, by death to rid me hence;
The worst that he can give, to me the best.
Yet so it may fall out, because their end
Is hate, not help to me, it may with mine
Draw their own ruin who attempt the deed.

   *Chor.* O how comely it is, and how reviving
To the spirits of just men long opprest,
When God into the hands of their deliverer   1270
Puts invincible might,
To quell the mighty of the earth, th' oppressor,
The brute and boist'rous force of violent men,
Hardy and industrious to support
Tyrannic power, but raging to pursue
The righteous, and all such as honour Truth!
He all their ammunition
And feats of war defeats
With plain heroic magnitude of mind
And celestial vigour armed;   1280
Their armouries and magazines contemns,
Renders them useless, while
With winged expedition
Swift as the lightning glance he executes
His errand on the wicked, who, surprised,
Lose their defence, distracted and amazed.
   But patience is more oft the exercise
Of saints, the trial of their fortitude,
Making them each his own deliverer,
And victor over all   1290
That tyranny or fortune can inflict.
Either of these is in thy lot,

Samson, with might endued
Above the sons of men; but sight bereaved
May chance to number thee with those
Whom patience finally must crown.

    This Idol's day hath been to thee no day of rest,
Labouring thy mind
More than the working day thy hands;
And yet, perhaps, more trouble is behind.      1300
For I descry this way
Some other tending; in his hand
A sceptre or quaint staff he bears,
Comes on amain, speed in his look.
By his habit I discern him now
A public officer, and now at hand.
His message will be short and voluble.

    *Off.* Hebrews, the pris'ner Samson here I seek.
    *Chor.* His manacles remark him; there he sits.
    *Off.* Samson, to thee our lords thus bid me say:   1310
This day to Dagon is a solemn feast,
With sacrifices, triumph, pomp, and games;
Thy strength they know surpassing human rate,
And now some public proof thereof require
To honour this great feast, and great assembly;
Rise, therefore, with all speed, and come along,
Where I will see thee heartened and fresh clad,
To appear as fits before th' illustrious lords.

    *Sam.* Thou know'st I am an Hebrew; therefore tell them
Our law forbids at their religious rites      1320
My presence; for that cause I cannot come.

    *Off.* This answer, be assured, will not content them.
    *Sam.* Have they not sword-players, and every sort
Of gymnic artists, wrestlers, riders, runners,
Jugglers and dancers, antics, mummers, mimics,
But they must pick me out, with shackles tired,
And over-laboured at their public mill,
To make them sport with blind activity?
Do they not seek occasion of new quarrels,
On my refusal, to distress me more,      1330
Or make a game of my calamities?
Return the way thou cam'st; I will not come.

*Off.* Regard thyself; this will offend them highly.

*Sam.* Myself? my conscience, and internal peace.
Can they think me so broken, so debased
With corporal servitude, that my mind ever
Will condescend to such absurd commands?
Although their drudge, to be their fool or jester,
And, in my midst of sorrow and heart-grief,
To show them feats, and play before their god—     1340
The worst of all indignities, yet on me
Joined with extreme contempt? I will not come.

*Off.* My message was imposed on me with speed,
Brooks no delay: is this thy resolution?

*Sam.* So take it with what speed thy message needs.

*Off.* I am sorry what this stoutness will produce.

*Sam.* Perhaps thou shalt have cause to sorrow
indeed.

*Chor.* Consider, Samson; matters now are strained
Up to the height, whether to hold or break.
He's gone, and who knows how he may report     1350
Thy words by adding fuel to the flame?
Expect another message, more imperious,
More lordly thund'ring than thou well wilt bear.

*Sam.* Shall I abuse this consecrated gift
Of strength, again returning with my hair
After my great transgression—so requite
Favour renewed, and add a greater sin
By prostituting holy things to idols,
A Nazarite, in place abominable,
Vaunting my strength in honour to their Dagon?     1360
Besides, how vile, contemptible, ridiculous,
What act more execrably unclean, profane?

*Chor.* Yet with this strength thou serv'st the Philistines,
Idolatrous, uncircumcised, unclean.

*Sam.* Not in their idol-worship, but by labour
Honest and lawful to deserve my food
Of those who have me in their civil power.

*Chor.* Where the heart joins not, outward acts defile
not.

*Sam.* Where outward force constrains, the sentence
holds:

But who constrains me to the temple of Dagon,     1370
Not dragging? the Philistian lords command.
Commands are no constraints. If I obey them,
I do it freely, venturing to displease
God for the fear of man, and man prefer,
Set God behind; which, in his jealousy,
Shall never, unrepented, find forgiveness.
Yet that he may dispense with me or thee,
Present in temples at idolatrous rites
For some important cause, thou need'st not doubt.
 *Chor.* How thou wilt here come off surmounts my
  reach.     1380
 *Sam.* Be of good courage; I begin to feel
Some rousing motions in me, which dispose
To something extraordinary my thoughts.
I with this messenger will go along,
Nothing to do, be sure, that may dishonour
Our Law, or stain my vow of Nazarite.
If there be aught of presage in the mind,
This day will be remarkable in my life
By some great act, or of my days the last.     1389
 *Chor.* In time thou hast resolved: the man returns.
 *Off.* Samson, this second message from our lords
To thee I am bid say. Art thou our slave,
Our captive, at the public mill our drudge,
And dar'st thou, at our sending and command,
Dispute thy coming? come without delay;
Or we shall find such engines to assail
And hamper thee, as thou shalt come of force,
Though thou wert firmlier fastened than a rock.
 *Sam.* I could be well content to try their art,
Which to no few of them would prove pernicious.     1400
Yet, knowing their advantages too many,
Because they shall not trail me through their streets
Like a wild beast, I am content to go.
Masters' commands come with a power resistless
To such as owe them absolute subjection;
And for a life who will not change his purpose?
(So mutable are all the ways of men)
Yet this be sure, in nothing to comply
Scandalous or forbidden in our Law.

*Off.* I praise thy resolution; doff these links:          1410
By this compliance thou wilt win the lords
To favour, and perhaps to set thee free.

   *Sam.* Brethren, farewell; your company along
I will not wish, lest it perhaps offend them
To see me girt with friends; and how the sight
Of me, as of a common enemy,
So dreaded once, may now exasperate them
I know not. Lords are lordliest in their wine;
And the well-feasted priest then soonest fired
With zeal, if aught religion seem concerned;          1420
No less the people, on their holy-days,
Impetuous, insolent, unquenchable;
Happen what may, of me expect to hear
Nothing dishonourable, impure, unworthy
Our God, our Law, my nation, or myself;
The last of me or no, I cannot warrant.

   *Chor.* Go, and the Holy One
Of Israel be thy guide
To what may serve his glory best, and spread his name
Great among the Heathen round;          1430
Send thee the Angel of thy birth, to stand
Fast by thy side, who from thy father's field
Rode up in flames after his message told
Of thy conception, and be now a shield
Of fire; that Spirit that first rushed on thee
In the camp of Dan,
Be efficacious in thee now at need.
For never was from Heaven imparted
Measure of strength so great to mortal seed,
As in thy wondrous actions hath been seen.          1440
But wherefore comes old Manoa in such haste
With youthful steps? much livelier than erewhile
He seems: supposing here to find his son,
Or of him bringing to us some glad news?

   *Man.* Peace with you, brethren; my inducement
     hither
Was not at present here to find my son,
By order of the lords new parted hence
To come and play before them at their feast.
I heard all as I came; the city rings,

And numbers thither flock: I had no will, 1450
Lest I should see him forced to things unseemly.
But that which moved my coming now was chiefly
To give ye part with me what hope I have
With good success to work his liberty.

  *Chor.* That hope would much rejoice us to partake
With thee; say, reverend sire; we thirst to hear.

  *Man.* I have attempted, one by one, the lords,
Either at home, or through the high street passing,
With supplication prone and father's tears,
To accept of ransom for my son, their pris'ner; 1460
Some much averse I found, and wondrous harsh,
Contemptuous, proud, set on revenge and spite:
That part most reverenced Dagon and his priests:
Others more moderate seeming, but their aim
Private reward, for which both God and State
They easily would set to sale: a third
More generous far and civil, who confessed
They had enough revenged, having reduced
Their foe to misery beneath their fears;
The rest was magnanimity to remit, 1470
If some convenient ransom were proposed.
What noise or shout was that? it tore the sky.

  *Chor.* Doubtless the people shouting to behold
Their once great dread, captive and blind before them,
Or at some proof of strength before them shown.

  *Man.* His ransom, if my whole inheritance
May compass it, shall willingly be paid
And numbered down: much rather I shall choose
To live the poorest in my tribe, than richest,
And he in that calamitous prison left. 1480
No, I am fixed not to part hence without him.
For his redemption all my patrimony,
If need be, I am ready to forgo
And quit: not wanting him, I shall want nothing.

  *Chor.* Fathers are wont to lay up for their sons;
Thou for thy son art bent to lay out all:
Sons wont to nurse their parents in old age;
Thou in old age car'st how to nurse thy son,
Made older than thy age through eyesight lost.

  *Man.* It shall be my delight to tend his eyes, 1490

And view him sitting in the house, ennobled
With all those high exploits by him achieved,
And on his shoulders waving down those locks
That of a nation armed the strength contained:
And I persuade me God had not permitted
His strength again to grow up with his hair
Garrisoned round about him like a camp
Of faithful soldiery, were not his purpose
To use him further yet in some great service—
Not to sit idle with so great a gift            1500
Useless, and thence ridiculous, about him.
And, since his strength with eyesight was not lost,
God will restore him eyesight to his strength.

    *Chor.* Thy hopes are not ill founded, nor seem vain,
Of his delivery, and thy joy thereon
Conceived, agreeable to a father's love;
In both which we, as next, participate.

    *Man.* I know your friendly minds, and—O, what
noise!
Mercy of Heaven! what hideous noise was that?
Horribly loud, unlike the former shout.          1510

    *Chor.* Noise call you it, or universal groan,
As if the whole inhabitation perished!
Blood, death, and deathful deeds, are in that noise,
Ruin, destruction at the utmost point.

    *Man.* Of ruin indeed methought I heard the noise.
Oh! it continues; they have slain my son.

    *Chor.* Thy son is rather slaying them: that outcry
From slaughter of one foe could not ascend.

    *Man.* Some dismal accident it needs must be;
What shall we do—stay here, or run and see?      1520

    *Chor.* Best keep together here, lest, running thither,
We unawares run into danger's mouth.
This evil on the Philistines is fall'n:
From whom could else a general cry be heard?
The sufferers, then, will scarce molest us here:
From other hands we need not much to fear.
What if his eyesight (for to Israel's God
Nothing is hard) by miracle restored,
He now be dealing dole among his foes,
And over heaps of slaughtered walk his way?      1530

*Man.* That were a joy presumptuous to be thought.

*Chor.* Yet God hath wrought things as incredible
For his people of old; what hinders now?

*Man.* He can, I know, but doubt to think he will:
Yet hope would fain subscribe, and tempts belief.
A little stay will bring some notice hither.

*Chor.* Of good or bad so great, of bad the sooner;
For evil news rides post, while good news baits.
And to our wish I see one hither speeding—
A Hebrew, as I guess, and of our tribe.            1540

*Messenger.* O, whither shall I run, or which way fly
The sight of this so horrid spectacle
Which erst my eyes beheld, and yet behold?
For dire imagination still pursues me.
But providence or instinct of nature seems,
Or reason, though disturbed and scarce consulted,
To have guided me aright, I know not how,
To thee first, reverend Manoa, and to these
My countrymen, whom here I knew remaining,
As at some distance from the place of horror,      1550
So in the sad event too much concerned.

*Man.* The accident was loud, and here before thee
With rueful cry; yet what it was we hear not.
No preface needs; thou seest we long to know.

*Mess.* It would burst forth; but I recover breath,
And sense distract, to know well what I utter.

*Man.* Tell us the sum; the circumstance defer.

*Mess.* Gaza yet stands; but all her sons are fall'n,
All in a moment overwhelmed and fall'n.

*Man.* Sad, but    thou    know'st    to    Israelites    not
    saddest                                            1560
The desolation of a hostile city.

*Mess.* Feed on that first, there may in grief be surfeit.

*Man.* Relate by whom.

*Mess.*                    By Samson.

*Man.*                                That still lessens
The sorrow, and converts it nigh to joy.

*Mess.* Ah! Manoa, I refrain too suddenly
To utter what will come at last too soon,
Lest evil tidings, with too rude irruption
Hitting thy aged ear, should pierce too deep.

*Man.* Suspense in news is torture; speak them out.

*Mess.* Then take the worst in brief: Samson is
dead.                                                    1570

*Man.* The worst indeed! O, all my hope's defeated
To free him hence! but Death, who sets all free,
Hath paid his ransom now and full discharge.
What windy joy this day had I conceived,
Hopeful of his delivery, which now proves
Abortive as the first-born bloom of spring
Nipped with the lagging rear of winter's frost.
Yet, ere I give the reins to grief, say first
How died he? death to life is crown or shame.
All by him fell, thou say'st; by whom fell he,        1580
What glorious hand gave Samson his death's wound?

*Mess.* Unwounded of his enemies he fell.

*Man.* Wearied with slaughter, then, or how? explain.

*Mess.* By his own hands.

*Man.*                    Self-violence? what cause
Brought him so soon at variance with himself
Among his foes?

*Mess.*            Inevitable cause
At once both to destroy and be destroyed;
The edifice, where all were met to see him,
Upon their heads and on his own he pulled.

*Man.* O lastly over-strong against thyself!        1590
A dreadful way thou took'st to thy revenge.
More than enough we know; but, while things yet
Are in confusion, give us, if thou canst,
Eye-witness of what first or last was done,
Relation more particular and distinct.

*Mess.* Occasions drew me early to this city;
And, as the gates I entered with sun-rise,
The morning trumpets festival proclaimed
Through each high street: little I had dispatched,
When all abroad was rumoured that this day        1600
Samson should be brought forth, to show the people
Proof of his mighty strength in feats and games;
I sorrowed at his captive state, but minded
Not to be absent at that spectacle.
The building was a spacious theatre,
Half round on two main pillars vaulted high,

With seats where all the lords, and each degree
Of sort, might sit in order to behold;
The other side was open, where the throng
On banks and scaffolds under sky might stand:    1610
I among these aloof obscurely stood.
The feast and noon grew high, and sacrifice
Had filled their hearts with mirth, high cheer, and wine,
When to their sports they turned. Immediately
Was Samson as a public servant brought,
In their state livery clad: before him pipes
And timbrels; on each side went armed guards;
Both horse and foot before him and behind,
Archers, and slingers, cataphracts and spears.
At sight of him the people with a shout    1620
Rifted the air, clamouring their god with praise,
Who had made their dreadful enemy their thrall.
He patient, but undaunted, where they led him,
Came to the place; and what was set before him,
Which without help of eye might be assayed,
To heave, pull, draw, or break, he still performed
All with incredible, stupendious force,
None daring to appear antagonist.
At length, for intermission sake, they led him
Between the pillars; he his guide requested    1630
(For so from such as nearer stood we heard),
As over-tired, to let him lean a while
With both his arms on those two massy pillars,
That to the arched roof gave main support.
He unsuspicious led him; which when Samson
Felt in his arms, with head a while inclined,
And eyes fast fixed, he stood, as one who prayed,
Or some great matter in his mind revolved.
At last, with head erect, thus cried aloud:—
'Hitherto, Lords, what your commands imposed    1640
I have performed, as reason was, obeying,
Not without wonder or delight beheld.
Now, of my own accord, such other trial
I mean to show you of my strength, yet greater;
As with amaze shall strike all who behold.'
This uttered, straining all his nerves, he bowed;
As with the force of winds and waters pent,

When mountains tremble, those two massy pillars
With horrible convulsion to and fro
He tugged, he shook, till down they came, and drew
The whole roof after them with burst of thunder        1651
Upon the heads of all who sat beneath,
Lords, ladies, captains, counsellors, or priests,
Their choice nobility and flower, not only
Of this, but each Philistian city round,
Met from all parts to solemnize this feast.
Samson, with these immixed, inevitably
Pulled down the same destruction on himself;
The vulgar only scaped, who stood without.

    *Chor.* O dearly-bought revenge, yet glorious!        1660
Living or dying thou hast fulfilled
The work for which thou wast foretold
To Israel, and now ly'st victorious
Among thy slain self-killed
Not willingly, but tangled in the fold
Of dire Necessity, whose law in death conjoined
Thee with thy slaughtered foes, in number more
Than all thy life had slain before.

    *Semichor.* While their hearts were jocund and sub-
      lime,
Drunk with idolatry, drunk with wine        1670
And fat regorged of bulls and goats,
Chanting their idol, and preferring
Before our living Dread, who dwells
In Silo, his bright sanctuary:
Among them he a spirit of frenzy sent,
Who hurt their minds,
And urged them on with mad desire
To call in haste for their destroyer;
They, only set on sport and play,
Unweetingly importuned        1680
Their own destruction to come speedy upon them.
So fond are mortal men,
Fallen into wrath divine,
As their own ruin on themselves to invite,
Insensate left, or to sense reprobate,
And with blindness internal struck.

    *Semichor.* But he, though blind of sight,

Despised, and thought extinguished quite,
With inward eyes illuminated,
His fiery virtue roused                              1690
From under ashes into sudden flame,
And as an evening dragon came,
Assailant on the perched roosts
And nests in order ranged
Of tame villatic fowl, but as an eagle
His cloudless thunder bolted on their heads.
So Virtue, given for lost,
Depressed and overthrown, as seemed,
Like that self-begotten bird
In the Arabian woods embost,                         1700
That no second knows nor third,
And lay erewhile a holocaust,
From out her ashy womb now teemed,
Revives, reflourishes, then vigorous most
When most inactive deemed;
And, though her body die, her fame survives,
A secular bird, ages of lives.

    *Man.* Come, come; no time for lamentation now,
Nor much more cause; Samson hath quit himself
Like Samson, and heroicly hath finished           1710
A life heroic, on his enemies
Fully revenged—hath left them years of mourning,
And lamentation to the sons of Caphtor
Through all Philistian bounds. To Israel
Honour hath left and freedom, let but them
Find courage to lay hold on this occasion;
To himself and father's house eternal fame;
And, which is best and happiest yet, all this
With God not parted from him, as was feared,
But favouring and assisting to the end.            1720
Nothing is here for tears, nothing to wail
Or knock the breast; no weakness, no contempt,
Dispraise, or blame; nothing but well and fair,
And what may quiet us in a death so noble.
Let us go find the body where it lies
Soaked in his enemies' blood, and from the stream
With lavers pure, and cleansing herbs, wash off
The clotted gore. I, with what speed the while

(Gaza is not in plight to say us nay),
Will send for all my kindred, all my friends,                    1730
To fetch him hence, and solemnly attend,
With silent obsequy and funeral train,
Home to his father's house: there will I build him
A monument, and plant it round with shade
Of laurel ever green and branching palm,
With all his trophies hung, and acts enrolled
In copious legend, or sweet lyric song.
Thither shall all the valiant youth resort,
And from his memory inflame their breasts
To matchless valour and adventures high;                        1740
The virgins also shall, on feastful days,
Visit his tomb with flowers, only bewailing
His lot unfortunate in nuptial choice,
From whence captivity and loss of eyes.
     *Chor.* All is best, though we oft doubt
What th' unsearchable dispose
Of Highest Wisdom brings about,
And ever best found in the close.
Oft he seems to hide his face,
But unexpectedly returns,                                        1750
And to his faithful champion hath in place
Bore witness gloriously; whence Gaza mourns,
And all that band them to resist
His uncontrollable intent:
His servants he, with new acquist
Of true experience from this great event,
With peace and consolation hath dismissed,
And calm of mind, all passion spent.


*The End.*

# A READER'S GUIDE TO MILTON

*Compiled by*

**WALTER SKEAT, M.A.**

*Sometime Scholar of Christ's College, Cambridge.*

# NOTE TO THE READER'S GUIDE

OWING to the universal element in Milton's knowledge (extending to the utmost limits of the erudition of his time), no really exhaustive glossary to his poems is possible within the limits of the space here available. Every effort, therefore, has been made in the present guide to concentrate mainly upon obscurer words and passages. Only, in 'border-line' cases it has been thought better to include rather than omit.

To meet the difficulties arising from a different arrangement of the Sonnets in modern editions, the references to them include, in each case, the opening words.

The abbreviations are meant to be, so far as possible, self-explanatory.

W. S.

## LIST OF ABBREVIATED TITLES HERE EMPLOYED

| | |
|---|---|
| On the Morning of Christ's Nativity | Nat. Od. |
| The Passion | Pass. |
| On Time | Time. |
| Upon the Circumcision | Circ. |
| At a Solemn Music | Mus. |
| An Epitaph on the Marchioness of Winchester | March. Win. |
| On May morning | May morn. |
| On Shakespeare | Shaks. |
| On the University Carrier | Univ. Carr. |
| L'Allegro | L'All. |
| Il Penseroso | Il Pens. |
| Sonnets | Sonn. |
| Arcades | Arc. |
| Lycidas | Lyc. |
| A Mask (Comus) | Com. |
| On the Death of a fair Infant | D.F.I. |
| At a Vacation Exercise | Vac. Ex. |
| Translation (Horace) | Trans. Hor. |
| On the new forcers of Conscience, etc. | Forc. Consc. |
| Passages translated by M., etc. | Trans.* (with name of author) |

| | |
|---|---|
| PARADISE LOST | P.L. i to xii |
| PARADISE REGAINED | P.R. i to iv |
| SAMSON AGONISTES | S.Ag. |

[* References to the translations made by Joseph Washington in 1692, which Mr. John Gawsworth has recently shown to have been included in Mitford's edition by inadvertence, have here been omitted.]

# A READER'S GUIDE TO MILTON

ABADDON: the Pit of Hell (strictly the name of its angel, Rev. ix. 11); P.R. iv. 624.

ABARIM: the Mts. of Moab (E. of Jordan), including Nebo and Pisgah; P.L. i. 408.

ABASSIN: Abyssinian or Ethiopian (the Abyssinians still call their country Itiopia); P.L. iv. 280. See also AMARA.

ABBANA: Abana, 'r. of Damascus' (2 Kings v. 12); P.L. i. 469.

ABDIEL (lit. 'Servant of God'): a seraph, who rebukes Satan's seditious speech, and (later) brings him to his knees in battle; P.L. v. 802, 896, vi. 111, 171, 369.

ACADEME: Plato's 'Academy', the site of which was recently rediscovered. (*Journ. Hellenic Studies*, liii, liv); P.R. iv. 244, 278.

ACCARON (Vulgate reading): Ekron (now Akir in Wadi Surar, 5 m. SE. of Ramleh), one of the five chief Philistine cities; P.L. i. 466; Ecron, in S.Ag. 981.

ACHERON: (*a*) a river of Hades; P.L. ii. 578. Two rivers in Greece and one in S. Italy (Bruttium), so called, were held to be connected with Hades.
(*b*) Hades itself; Com. 604.

ACQUIST, sb.: acquisition; S.Ag. 1755.

ADAMANT: P.L. ii. 436, vi. 110, 255, x. 318; P.R. iv. 534. See DIAMOND.

ADDREST, prepared; S.Ag. 729; cp. 731.

ADES (i.e. Hades): P.L. ii. 964.

ADIABENE: the district of Mosul or Mossul (which is the modern city replacing Nineveh) in Assyria proper, formerly part of ancient Parthia; P.R. iii. 320.

ADMIRE, vb. to wonder; P.L. ii. 677 and numerous other passages.

ADMIT, vb. to approve (Newton): P.L. viii. 637.

ADONIS: (*a*) the youthful hunter beloved of Venus; Com. 999; P.L. ix. 440.
(*b*) the river; P.L. i. 450.

ADRAMELEK: a rebel angel named from the god of Sepharvaim on the Euphrates; P.L. vi. 365.

ADRIA (Hadria): the Adriatic; P.L. i. 520.

ADUST: burnt up, reduced by fire; P.L. xii. 635.

ÆMILIAN ('Way'): this Roman Road, built by M. Æmilius Lepidus, was part of the Flaminian Way, and was continued by Æ. to Placentia (Piacenza). It led to the North, the Appian to the South; P.R. iv. 67-9.

ÆOLIAN charms: songs of Alcaeus and Sappho; P.R. iv. 257.

ÆQUINOCTIAL winds: trade winds; P.L. ii. 637.

AFER (the 'African'): WSW. wind; P.L. x. 702.

AFFRONT (= 'confront'): encounter; P.L. i. 391; S.Ag. 531.

AFRICAN, the: (a) Hannibal; Sonn. to Sir H. Vane (Vane, young in yeares), 4.

(b) Scipio Africanus ('hee sirnam'd of *Africa*'; the ref. here is to his chivalry towards a lady betrothed to a Spaniard (Aluccius)—Livy, xxvi. 50); P.R. ii. 199, iii. 34, 101;

AGONISTES: combatant.　　　　　　　　　　　　　　　[P.L. ix. 510.

AGRICAN, K. of Tartary: famous for his (alleged) army of 2,000,000 men and his siege of Albracca in Cathay, undertaken to capture Angelica, d. of Gallaphrone, K. of Cathay; the story is taken from Boiardo's romance of *Orlando Innamorato*, bk. i.; P.R. iii. 338-9; cp. Ariosto, *Orlando Furioso*, 3rd ed. (1634), xxxiv. 72, ll. 58, 79. ll. 5-8 Sir J. Harington's translation.

AIALON: Ajalon (now *Yalo*); P.L. xii. 266.

AIR, MIDDLE: see 'MIDDLE AIR'.

ALADULE: greater Armenia—named from Aladules, the last K. of A., slain by the Turks under Selim I; P.L. x. 435.

ALBRACCA: a city in Cathay; P.L. iii. 339; see AGRICAN and CATHAIAN COAST.

ALCAIRO ('Cairo'): used by M. for Memphis. 'Cairo' is an abbreviation of El- or Al-cairo = AL-KAHIRA, the 'victorious' (city) or 'Conqueress' (= Lat. *Augusta*) because built in 968 A.D., when the planet Mars (Ar. *Kahir*) was in the ascendant, by the general of the first Fatimite Sultan of Egypt; P.L. i. 718.

ALCESTIS: d. of Pelias, who died to redeem her husband Admetus from death, and was brought back from Hades by Heracles; Sonn. xix. (Methought I saw) 2.

ALCHYMIE ('the sounding'): a trumpet, made of an amalgam of the alchemists called 'alchemy gold' or 'alchemy'; P.L. ii. 517.

ALCIDES: Hercules, as being s. of Amphitryon, and grandson of Alcæus; P.L. ii. 542; P.R. iv. 565.

ALCINOUS: K. of the Phæacians, famous in Homer (Od. vii); Vac. Ex. 48-52; P.L. v. 341, ix. 441.

ALEIAN FIELD (expld. as the 'Field of Wandering' from Gk. ἄλη): a tract in Cilicia E. of the r. Sarus in A.M., not far from Tarsus, where Bellerophon is supposed to have fallen from the winged steed. Pegasus—see Hom. Il. vi. 201; P.L. vii. 19.

ALEXANDER: (Pellean Conquerour) P.R. ii. 196; (s. of Philip) P.R. iii. 32; (s. of Olympias and Ammonian Jove); P.L. ix. 509; P.R. iii. 84, iv. 252, etc.

ALGARSIFE: eldest s. of Cambuscan, (q.v.); Il Pens. 111.

ALGIERS: one of the five Barbary states in N. Africa; P.L. xi. 404.

ALLARM'D: prepared for battle (It. '*all' arme*', 'to arms') as in P.L. iv. 985.

ALLEY: an embowered path or walk in a wood; Com. 311, 990; P.L. iv. 626; PR. ii. 203.

**Almansor**: acc. to Masson the famous second Abbasid Caliph of Bagdad (754-5 A.D.) conqueror of N. Africa; P.L. xi. 403.

**Alp**: used for any high mountains; P.L. ii. 620; S.A. 628.

**Alpheus**: the chief r. of Peloponnesus, rising in SE. Arcadia, sinks underground more than once in the limestone country, and, rising again, falls into the Ionian sea. Hence the story of his reappearing in Sicily in the fountain of Arethusa, and the symbol of pastoral verse; Lycidas, 132; Arc. 30.

**Alt** (M.'s spelling): It. *far alto*, to halt (mil.); P.L. xi. 210.

**Amalthea**: (a) Nurse of infant Zeus; P.R. ii. 356.
(b) one of the names of the m. of Bacchus; P.L. iv. 278; see NYSEIAN ISLE.

**Amara** (Amhara): (whence 'Amharic') Mt. range in Abyssinia, the retreat where the Emperors of Abyssinia educated their sons (cp. Johnson's *Rasselas*); P.L. iv. 281.

**Amarant** (i.e. AMARANTH): lit. 'unfading'; the 'immortal' flower of Paradise; P.L. iii. 352; cp. P.L. xi. 78.

**Ambient**: surrounding; P.L. vi. 481, vii. 89.

**Ambition**: lit. 'going round' to collect votes or get favour (as in Lat.), soliciting or canvassing; S.A. 247.

**Amerce**: to deprive; P.L. i. 609.

**American**: American Indian; P.L. ix. 1116.

**Amice**: the cape and hood worn by Religious Orders; it was lined with (or made of) grey fur—hence M.'s 'amice gray' of Morning; P.R. iv. 427; Cp. Com. 189 (of Evening).

**Ammiral**: Flagship; P.L. i. 294.

**Ammon**: (a) the god, see HAMMON.
(b) the Ammonites (collectively); Ps. lxxxiii. 25.

**Amphisbaena**: traditionally, a double snake with head at each end (really a lizard with indistinguishable head and tail); in M. a snake; P.L. x. 524

**Amphitrite**: wife of Poseidon, hence queen of the sea; Com. 921.

**Amymone**: d. of Danaus, beloved of Poseidon; P.R. ii. 188.

**Anchises**: f. of Æneas: Com. 923; see BRUTUS.

**Andromeda**: the constellation; P.L. iii. 559; see ETHIOPE (QUEEN).

**Angelica**: d. of Gallaphrone, q.v.

**Angola** (cap. St. Paul): Loanda, Portuguese E. Africa; P.L. xi. 401.

**Antæus**: P.R. iv. 563; see IRASSA.

**Antic**: (a) sb. a performer of 'antics', a clown or buffoon; S.Ag. 1325.
(b) antick, adj., app. 'antique', Il. Pens. 158.

**Antigonus**: K. of Judea; *not* supported by the R. and captured by the Parthians, as suggested by M.; the Parthians supported him against his uncle, Hyrcanus (he was eventually captured, and executed, 37 B.C., by the Romans); P.R. iii. 367.

**Antiochus**: i.e. A. Epiphanes, K. of Syria, 168 B.C.; P.R. iii. 163.

**ANTIOPA**: a princess of Thebes, beloved of Zeus, and m. of Amphion; P.R. ii. 187.

**ANTIPATER**: f. of Herod the Great, the wealthy noble of Edom, who became procurator of Judea (47 B.C.) and died by poison, 43 B.C.; P.R. ii. 423.

**ANUBIS** (in Eg. hieroglyphs 𓀀𓏤𓃣 *INPU* or *ANUP*): the Jackal-god, s. of Set; local deity of the Necropolis at Abydos; represented by Gks. and R. as dog-headed. He was guardian of the Scale at the *Psychostasia* or weighing of the heart in Eg. funerary ritual. For the 'dog Anubis' see Nat. Od. 212.

**AONIAN MOUNT**: i.e. Mount Helicon: one of the chief haunts of the Muses; P.L. i. 15.

**APPAID**: satisfied; P.L. xii. 401.

**APPELLANT**: challenger; S.Ag. 1220.

**APPIAN** ('Way'): the Roman road built by Appius Claudius leading S. to Brundusium; P.R. iv. 68.

**AQUILO** (Gk. Boreas): the N. Wind; D.F.I. 8.

**ARACHOSIA**: extreme E. of Parthia (now extending roughly from the N.E. part of Baluchistan into Afghanistan); P.R. iii. 316.

**ARAXES**: now *Eraskh*, or *Aras*, a r. of Armenia, entering the Caspian; P.R. iii. 271.

**ARBORETS**: shrubs or saplings forming underwood or 'bush'; P.L. ix. 437.

**ARCADY, STAR OF**: the Great Bear. The nymph of *Arcady*, Kallisto, beloved by Jupiter, was turned into a she-bear by him to deceive Juno. But she was slain by Juno and set among the stars as Arctos by Jupiter, her son Arcas becoming the lesser Bear; Com. 341. See CALISTO.

**ARCH-CHIMIC SUN**: i.e. arch-chemist, or supreme alchemist; metaph. of the sun, whose influence was held to create gems underground; see P.L. iii. 609–12.

**ARCHIMEDES**, the celebrated mathematician and engineer of Syracuse (287–212 B.C.). Sonn. xviii. 7 (Cyriack, whose Grandsire).

**ARETHUSE**: (i.e. the fountain or spring of Arethusa in the I. of Ortygia at Syracuse, for which see ALPHEUS. Here it suggests Sicily, typifying Greek pastoral verse: Arc. 31; Lyc. 85.

**ARGESTES**: prob. here the NW. wind (WSW., Vitruvius, or WNW., Pliny); P.L. x. 699.

**ARGOB**: a city and district in Bashan, E. of Jordan, the country of Og; later = Trachonitis; P.L. i. 398.

**ARGUS**: cruel hundred-eyed guardian of the heifer Io (=Isis): P.L. xi. 131.

**ARIEL** (lit. 'Lion of God'): a rebel angel; P.L. vi. 371 (perhaps from Isaiah xxix. 1; of Jerusalem), cp. Ezra viii. 16.

**ARIES**: the constellation; P.L. x. 329; cp. P.L. iii. 558.

**ARIMASPIAN**: traditional one-eyed race of Scythia, E. of the Volga, who stole the gold of the Ural mountains from its guardians, the gryphons, to make ornaments for their hair; P.L. ii. 945.

ARIOC (perhaps from Dan. ii. 14): a rebel angel; P.L. vi. 371.

ARMORIC: adj. of Armorica or Brittany; P.L. i.581.

ARNON: r. on N. boundary of Moab, entering the Dead Sea; P.L. i. 399.

AROER: t. on N. side of the Arnon; P.L. i. 407-11.

ARREEDE, vb. to advise; P.L. iv. 962.

ARSACES (i.e. Arsâces): he revolted against the Seleucids, and founded the Parthian Empire, with a capital at Ctesiphon, about 256 B.C.; P.R. iii. 295. See CTESIPHON.

ARSENAL, SHOOK THE: M. is paraphrasing Aristoph. *Acharn.* 530-1 and 539; ἐντεῦθεν ὀργῇ Περικλέης οὑλύμπιος | ἤστραπτ' ἐβρόντα ξυνεκύκα τὴν Ἑλλάδα | . . . κἀντεῦθεν ἤδη πάταγος ἦν τῶν ἀσπίδων. App. he is generalizing too (as usual) and is thinking of the entire course of these wars; 'resistless eloquence' referring to Athenian oratory as a whole (with special recollection of Pericles, 'thundering and lightening', and Demosthenes. The defeats of Artaxerxes by the Greeks took place in the latter half of the 5th c. B.C., the speeches of Demosthenes against Philip belong to the latter part of the 4th. I have to thank Mr. A. J. Hughes for pointing out that the ἐκκλησία was sometimes held in the Piraeus (in the theatre on the NW. slope of Munichia; Dem. *de fals. Leg.* 67 ἠκκλησιάζετε . . . ἐν τῷ Πειραεῖ. 'Shook the Arsenal' is a paraphrase of l. 539; M. must certainly have read of the famous *armamentarium* in the Piraeus, built by the architect Philo, where '1000 ships could lie', though this was not built till the last quarter of that century; P.R. iv. 267-71.

ARTAXATA: ancient capital of Armenia, on the Araxes; P.R. iii. 292.

ARTFUL: artistic, skilful, beautiful; Com. 494 (artfull); Sonn. xvii. (Lawrence, etc.) artful; cp. P.R. iv. 33.

ARTHUR, K. (UTHER'S SON, M.'s proposed subject for Epic): see P.L. i. 580; cp. P.R. ii. 360; Pr. Wks. *Hist. of Brit.*, etc.

ARTIST ('the Tuscan'): Galileo (q.v.); P.L. i. 288.

'A.S.': see STEUART, ADAM.

ASCALONITE: inhabitant of Ascalon (Ashkelon, Askelon); S.Ag. 138.

ASHTAROTH: (*a*) the Hebrew equivalent of ASTARTE, the Phœnician Moon-goddess (q.v.); Nat. Od. 200; P.R. iii. 417.         i. 438.
(*b*) spelt Astoreth, identified with the rebel angels; P.L.

ASMODEUS: (*a*) a lustful angel of the Incubus type mentioned in the Bk. of Tobit, iii. 8, 17. After destroying seven husbands of Sarah, d. of Raguel, was driven off by Tobias, s. of Tobit, who by advice of Raphael burnt the heart and liver of a fish to expel him, and drove him to Egypt; P.L. iv. 168.
(*b*) identified by M. with one of the fallen angels; Asmodai, P.R. ii. 151; or Asmadai, P.L. vi. 365.

ASP, etc., P.L. x. 524; cp. Lucan's List (bk. ix).

ASPECTS (astrol.). See Trine, Square, Sextile, Conjunction, Opposition, and Synod.

**Asphaltick Pool**: the Dead Sea; P.L. i. 411; cp. x. 562.

**Asphaltus**: pitch; P.L. i. 729.

**Aspramont**: a t. 6 m. N. of Nice, famous in medieval romances; P.L. i. 583.

**Assassinate**, vb.: to wound by treachery; S.Ag. 1109.

**Assyrian**, ad.: (a) Assyrian Mount, i.e. Niphates (q.v.); P.L. iv. 126.
(b) A. Flood, the Euphrates river; P.R. iii. 436.
(c) A. Queen, Ishtar, the Assyrian Venus; Com. 1002.
(d) A. Garden, i.e. Eden (q.v.); P.L. iv. 285.

**Astarte, Astoreth**: Ishtar, the great Love-goddess of Mesopotamia and Phoenicia, goddess of the Moon and Evening Star, identified with Aphrodite or Venus: P.L. i. 438, 439, etc.

**Astracan** (Astrakhan): t. of Russia (at mouth of Volga); P.L. x. 432.

**Atabalipa** (the Spanish form of Atahualpa): last Inca Emperor of Peru, famed for his wealth; P.L. xi. 409.

**Athenian Damsel**: Oreithyia, a princess of Athens, d. of K. Erectheus; straying beyond the Ilissus she was carried off by *Boreas*, who came from his cave in Thrace; D.F.I. 9.

**Atlantean** ('shoulders'): powerful as those of Atlas, supporter of the firmament; P.L. ii. 306.

**Atlantick**: (a) 'sisters'; the seven daughters of Atlas, who, raised to heaven, became the Pleiads; P.L. x. 674; cp. Pleiades, P.L. vii. 374.
(b) Atl. Stone: called *giallo antico*; Numidian marble quarried near Mt. Atlas; P.R. iv. 115. See Blakeney (notes).

**Atropatia** (or **Atropatene**): N. Media, extending to the Caspian, and S. of the Araxes; P.R. iii. 319.

**Atropos**: One of the three Fates who bore the shears, and cut the thread of life (March. Win. 28); cp. Lyc. 75.

**Attick Boy**: Cephalus, beloved of Eos (Aurora), who gave him the unerring spear with which he unwittingly slew his wife Procris; Il Pens. 124.

**Attrite** (of the air): converted or reduced to fire by friction; P.L. x. 1073.

**Auran**: (Hauran) part of Bashan, on the E. frontier of Palestine; P.L. iv. 211.

**Ausonian**: Italian (poet. for Italy); P.L. i. 739.

**Autumnal Stars**: Stars such as Sirius, in the autumn, were believed to bring much mischief to men; P.R. iv. 619.

**Azazel**: the name of one of the rebel angels, app. from Levit. xvi. 8 (A.V. marg.). Acc. to A.V. 'the scapegoat', but acc. to Newton 'brave in retreat' (either sense would suit M.'s purpose as an ironical name for Satan's Standard-bearer); P.L. i. 534.

**Azotus**: Ashdod (now *Esdud*): anciently the chief seat of the worship of Dagon P.L. i. 464. Ashdod also occurs; S.Ag. 981.

**Azza**: Gaza (now *Azzah*), once the capital city of Philistia; S.Ag. 147; (Gaza) S.Ag. 98.

BAALIM: the collective title for all the rebel angels named after those Mesopotamian and Palestinian gods who were copied from the chief Babylonian (Semitic) god Belu (lit. Lord) the god of Babylon. His female counterpart was Ishtar, whence Astarte or Ashtaroth (a collective name as well); P.L. i. 422. See BABEL.

BAAL-ZEBUB: the name under which Baal was worshipped by the Philistines (at Ecron), S.Ag. 1231. For Bëëlzebub see P.L. i. 81, 271, ii. 299, 378.

BABEL ('Tower of'): early Semitic name of the Great Tower of Babylon, the city whose name in the Babylonian tongue meant the 'Gate of God' (*Bab ili = Bab El*) being named after the chief Bab. god, *Marduk*, whose title was *Belu* or *Bel*. A modern excavator (Koldewey) has discovered the foundations of the tower and has shown that the tower was 'no dream', but an amazingly lofty and solid rectangular tower of brick compacted with bitumen in several successive terraces of respectively diminishing proportions; the total height of these should apparently have reached an altitude of approximately 300 ft. Such towers, called ZIKKURAT (or 'ZIGGURAT') i.e. mountain peaks, were built on (to their chief Temples only) by the early Sumerian conquerors or settlers in Babylon, app. in substitution for the actual mountain tops on which they held, their chief gods should in preference be worshipped. From these, through the Arab minaret, was derived the 'Spire'. A second Tower stood, and still stands, more than 150 ft. high near Babylon at Borsippa, left incomplete by the king who began it; it was completed by Neb. II. Some, like that at Ur, also had cultivated plants or trees on their terraces, recalling Nebuchadnezzar's 'Hanging Gardens' at Babylon which became one of the Seven Wonders of the World; P.L. i. 694. Cp. P.L. iii. 466, 468.

BACTRA (now *Balkh*) in Afghan Turkistan: a great city of Bactria, or Bactriana, and part of the Persian Empire. It was destroyed by Ghengis Khan in A.D. 1220; P.L. x. 433; P.R. iii. 285.

BANKS, benches: S.Ag. 1610.

BATES ('at noone'): if we may judge by S.Ag. 1538, M. certainly meant 'baits', i.e. 'takes refreshment', the allusion being explained by his just having reached the opening line of the *Twelfth Book*; this then would be the inward significance of the line: 'As one who in his journey, bates at noon': (i.e. Twelve o'clock); P.L. xii. 1.

BALSARA: Bassora, or Basra, on the Pers. Gulf; P.R. iii. 321.

BARCA: an inland town of Cyrenaica, founded by a Graeco-Libyan colony, mostly seceders from Cyrene, c. 554 B.C. Destroyed by the Persian satrap of Egypt, Aryandes, in 510 B.C.; P.L. ii. 904.

BARRICADO, vb.: to barricade or bar off; P.L. viii. 241.

BASE: a short skirt or 'jupon', worn by a knights on horseback; P.L. ix. 36.

BATTEL: army; P.L. vi. 202.

BAUK (i.e. BAULK) your eares: to miss, or spare; this line, when first drafted, had a reference to the lawyer Prynne, whose ears were cropped by order of the Star-Chamber. Forc. Consc. 17.

BAYONA'S HOLD: a stronghold on the Galician Coast of Spain; Lyc. 162.

BEAR: to outwatch the Bear meant to sit up all night, since the Bear never sets. Il Pens. 87. See CYNOSURE and CALISTO.

BEARTH: what the Earth *bears*, or yields; i.e. her produce (often misprinted *birth*): I have not, however, found this form in the *Oxford Dictionary*. P.L. ix. 624.

BEËLZEBUB. See BAAL-ZEBUB.

BELIAL: the rebel angel who 'came last' (P.L. i. 490), was one of the chiefest among the rebel angels; it was not a personal name, but indicated the principle of evil (utter worthlessness); almost equiv. to Antichrist (2 Cor. vi. 15).

BELLEROPHON: v. ALEIAN FIELD.

BELLERUS: see FABLE OF BELLERUS.

BELLMAN: the watchman whose task it formerly was to cry the hours of the night, state of the weather, and call for blessings on sleepers. Il Pens. 83.

BELLONA: Roman war-goddess; P.L. ii. 922.

BELUS (i.e. Bel or Baal): chief god of Babylon, whence *Bab-ilu* ('Gate of the god') = Babylon. His early Babylonian title was BELU, 'Lord', since he was held to be 'Lord' of all the gods; P.L. i. 720; see BABEL.

BISERTA: a city of Tunis well known in medieval romance; P.L. i. 585.

BIZANCE: Byzantium, the name of Constantinople before Constantine made it his capital, and called it after his name; P.L. xi. 395.

BLACK-MOOR SEA: The Moorish or Morocco Sea; P.R. iv. 72.

BLEAR: blurring the sight; Com. 155.

BOCCHUS: K. of Gaetulia in N. Africa (Mauretania); he was father-in-law of Jugurtha; P.R. iv. 72.

BOLT: vb. tr. either (*a*) (metaph.) = 'boult', to sift or refine to subtlety, Com. 760, or (*b*) to shoot forth as an arrow; S.Ag. 1696.

BONNET: a cap such as was at one time worn by men; Lyc. 104.

BOSKY: bushy, Com. 313; cp. imbos[k]t in S.Ag. 1700.

BOTCH, sb.: a boil; P.L. xii. 180.

BOUT, sb.: a 'run' of notes in music; L'All. 139.

BOY, ATTICK: see ATTICK.

BRIARIOS: the Titan, was the 3rd s. of Uranus (Heaven), of whom Homer (Il. i. 403) says that men called him Ægæon, but the blessed gods called him Briareus. A giant with 50 heads and 100 arms, in older trad. he fought for Zeus against the Titans; P.L. i. 199.

BRIGANDINE: a coat of mail; S.Ag. 1120.

BRINDED: more or less broadly striped; Com. 443; P.L. vii. 466.

BRITAIN, BRITISH: P.L. i. 581; P.R. iv. 77; Sonn. xviii. 2 (Cyriack, whose grandsire); cp. Com. 27-9. See also ENGLAND, ENGLISH, and under TROY and BRUTUS.

'BROWN'. M. uses 'brown' for 'dusky' shades, esp. those of evening; cp. Il Pens. 134 ('shadows brown'); cp. P.L. ix. 1087-8 (umbrage . . . 'brown as evening'); P.R. ii. 293 ('alleys brown').

BRUTUS (in M.'s projected Epic of Britain): great-grandson of Æneas of Troy, legendary ancestor of the Britons; cp. the lines from Hist. Brit., 7. See also under BRITAIN.

BUDGE, adj.: used of the lambskin or goatskin fur of 'doctors'' hoods, hence—Fur-hooded doctors of the Stoic sect; Com. 707.

BULLION DROSS: scum thrown up in founding by the (impure) boiling metal; P.L. i. 704.

BUSIRIS: acc. to Gk. tradition, a K. of Egypt notorious for persecuting foreigners; taken by Raleigh (Hist. of the World) for the first oppressor of the Israelites; but M. uses it of the Pharaoh who chased (but was not drowned in chasing) the Israelites. Busiris is also the name of a town in the Delta, now Abousir; P.L. i. 307.

BUSKIN: (a) a high boot (silver buskind); Arc. 33.
(b) the high thick-soled boot of Gk. tragedians; Il Pens. 102.

BUXOM: (a) yielding (of the air); P.L. ii. 842, v. 270.
(b) (bucksom) lithe and lively; L'All. 24.

CAECIAS: the NE. wind (strictly NE. by E.); P.L. x. 699.

CALABRIA: Calabria is the SW. projection of Italy, app. by extension made to include Bruttium, once famous (acc. to Ovid and others) for the copper mines of Témésè; P.L. ii. 661.

CALES (in Campania): famous for its wines; P.R. iv. 117.

CALISTO (Callisto): an Arcadian nymph, d. of Lycaon, huntress in Artemis' train, beloved by Zeus, who changed her into a she-bear to deceive Hera, and then into the Great Bear, her s. Arcas becoming the little Bear; P.R. ii. 186. See ARCADY, STAR OF.

CAMBALL: (a) the younger s. of CAMBUSCAN, q.v.
(b) app. a second person of the same name, in love with, and ultimately married to, Canace; Il. Pens. 111-12.

CAMBALU (properly Can-baluc or 'City of the Khan'): the former capital of Cathay and residence of the Mongol Emperors; now Pekin, but supposed in M.'s time to be a different city; P.L. xi. 388; see CATHAIAN COAST and PAQUIN.

CAMBRIDGE: Univ. Carr. i. 8; Sonn. xi. (A book was writ); see also CAME or CAMUS, HELICON.

CAMBUSCAN: (better Cámbŭscán, i.e. Chingis, Jinghis, Genghis, or Ghengis Khan; all = the 'Great' Khan), who had two sons, Camball and Algarsife, and was the subject of Chaucer's Squire's Tale (note that in all the Chaucer MSS. the name is given as Cambynskan); Il Pens. 110.

CAME: the Cam (March. Winch. 59); also CAMUS (Lyc. 103).

CAN (i.e. the Khan, or 'Cham'): title of the Mongol Emperors of China; P.L. xi. 388. See also CAMBALU.

CANACE: d. of Cambuscan, eventually wedded to Camball, not the s. of Cambuscan, but another of the same name; Il Pens. 112. See CAMBALL.

CANDAOR (Candahar or Kandahar): A city of N. Parthia, now capital of the Province of K. in Afghanistan, 318 m. SW. of Cabul; P.R. iii. 316.

CANIE, adj.: made of 'cane' (so-called), but really of bamboo; P.L. iii. 439.

CANON LAWS: used by M. in irony as an eccles. term; Com. 808.

CANOPIE: the shadow of the earth cast by the sun from day to day; P.L. iii. 556.

CAPARISON: a rich cloth covering (for saddle or harness); P.L. ix. 35.

CAPHTOR, sons of: i.e. the Philistines; S.Ag. 1713.

CAPITOL: the temple, not the Hill; P.R. iv. 47.

CAPITOLINE JOVE: trad. f. of Scipio Africanus; P.L. ix. 508.

CARNAGE: a heap of dead bodies, P.L. x. 268.

'CARPATHIAN WISARD': Proteus, the infallible seer, who dwelt in the I. of Carpáthus, between Crete and Rhodes; Com. 872.

CASBEEN (Casveen or Kasvin), a city in the Elburz Mts., NW. of Teheran, in what was once greater Media; P.L. x. 436.

CASELLA: an old musician friend of Dante, whom D. describes (Purg. ii. 10) as singing at his request, in Purgatory, the second Canzone of his Convito; Sonn. xiii. (Harry, whose tuneful) 12-14.

CASIUS, Mt.: (now Elkas, or Katieh) the summit of a lofty range of sandstone hills on the NE. border of Egypt, just S. of the 'SERBONIAN' L. q.v. On its W. flank was the Tomb of Pompey. P.L. ii. 593.

CASTALIAN SPRING: the Spring near Apollo's Grove at Daphne near Antioch (where in the time of Seleucus I the tree into which 'root-bound' Daphne was transformed was still actually shown) P.L. iv. 274.

CATAPHRACT (Gk. κατάφρακτος): 'all-armed', horse and man; S.Ag. 1619.

CATHAIAN COAST: (Areopagitica, Cataio) correctly explained as China. But in M.'s time often supposed to be a separate country N. of China (in NE. Siberia?), with Cambaluc as its capital, and Pekin as the capital of China proper. Actually, however, Cambaluc (q.v.) was Pekin; cp. P.L. x. 293, xi. 388 (Paquin), 390. From Russ. Kitai (= China).

CAUSEY: causeway; P.L. x. 415.

CERASTES (Gk. κεράστης): a horned serpent; P.L. x. 525.

CERBERUS: see EREBUS.

CERES' FIELDS: cornfields; cp. P.L. iv. 981 ('a field of Ceres').

CHAERONEA: a city in Boeotia, where the liberties of Greece were destroyed by the victory of Philip of Macedon over the Gk. states in 338 B.C.; Sonn. x. 7 (Daughter to that good Earl).

CHALYBEAN TEMPER'D: the Chalybes were famous iron-workers of Scythia; S.Ag. 133.

CHAM (i.e. HAM): identified by M. with the 'Lybian Jove' (Ammon) as well as with the Gk. Zeus (Ζεὺς Ἄμμων), the Roman 'Jupiter Ammon', and Egyptian 'Amun' or 'Amun-Ra'; P.L. iv. 276, ix. 508. See NYSEIAN ISLE and cp. Lybic Hammon; Nat. Od. 203.

CHAMPAIN: flat, level country; P.L. iv. 134, vi. 2; P.R. iii. 257.

CHARLEMAIN: P.L. i. 586; Charlemane P.R. iii. 343. See FONTARABBIA.

CHARM: Song (esp. used of the songs of birds); P.L. iv. 642, 651.

CHARYBDIS: the Sicilian Whirlpool; Com. 259; P.L. ii. 1020.

CHAUMP (i.e. CHAMP), vb.: P.L. iv. 859.

CHEBAR FLOOD (now the Khabur): a tributary of the Euphrates. Pass. 37. For 'the Prophet' see ELIAH.

CHEEK, Sir John: first Professor of Greek at Camb. Univ.; Sonn. xi. (A Book was writ).

CHEMOS (i.e. CHEMOSH): see PEOR.

CHERSONESE 'the golden' (P.L. xi. 392); or CHERSONESS (P.R. iv. 74): the Peninsula of Malacca or Malay Peninsula; see OPHIR.

CHERUBIM: the names of the Cherubs, as given by M., are usually of Biblical origin though not the actual names of Cherubs in the Bible; in several cases the names are chosen with reference to the tasks they have to perform; see ZEPHON, ITHURIEL, ZOPHIEL. M. uses Cherub in the Biblical sense, characteristic of the order being fullness of Knowledge, and Contemplation; Il Pens. 54.

CHIMERA: (a) the three-fold monster, compounded of lion, goat, and serpent, slain by Bellerophon mounted on Pegasus; see ALEIAN FIELD.
(b) other such compound monsters; Com. 517; P.L. ii. 628.

CHIOS: C. wine was one of the costliest Gk. wines, as the Caecuban (not here given) of the Roman; P.R. iv. 118.

CHOASPES (now the Kherkah): a r. of the ancient prov. of Susiana, rising in the Luristan Mts. and flowing, after passing Susa, into the Tigris; the 'drink of none but Kings' was an idea perhaps from Athenæus; Herod. (i. 188) only says, the K. 'drank no other'. P.R. iii. 288.

CIMMERIAN: of a distant race mentioned in the Odyssey as living 'beyond the ocean-stream, unblest by the rays of Helios'. Though they were later identified with a race of the Black Sea Region (whence 'Crimea') the original legend persisted, as of a people living in perpetual darkness; L'All. 10.

CIPRES (lawn): Il Pens. 35; also CIPRESS (bud) March. Winch. 22, see CYPRESS.

CIRCE: Com. 50, 153, 253, 522; P.L. ix. 522. Called (a) Persean priestess of Phoebus in M.'s Lat. Poems, as being d. of Phoebus and Perseis; also (b) according to post-Homeric tradition, mother of Telegonus.

CITTRON ('tables'): tables of citron wood from Mount Atlas (where such trees are still grown); it was considered as valuable as gold by the Romans, and cost fabulous sums; P.R. iv. 115; cp. Rev. xviii. 12.

CLASSIC: the Presb. 'classis' = 'parish'. Forc. Consc. 7.

'CLEAVING MISCHIEF': Dalila is so called because she 'cleaves' to Samson, as the poisoned shirt of Nessus (under his armour and next to his skin) to Hercules; S.Ag. 1039.

CLEOMBROTUS: a young student of philosophy, from Ambracia in Epirus. On reading Plato's discourse in the *Phaedo*, on the immortality of the soul, he leapt into the sea, to enjoy the delights of Elysium; P.L. iii. 473.

CLOYSTERS PALE: see PALE.

CLYMENE: beloved by Helios or Apollo, and m. of Phaethon; P.R. ii. 186.

COARSE: sb. a dead body; D.F.I. 30. See also CORPS.

COCYTUS: the 'r. of lamentation', one of the rivers of Hades; P.L. ii. 579.

COLD-KIND ('embrace'): a close embrace in which the cold-ness of ice took the place of warmth; D.F.I. 20.

COLKITTO: see MACDONNELL.

COLUMBUS: P.L. ix. 1116.

COLURES: two great imaginary circles drawn from the poles intersecting at right-angles on the celestial sphere, and passing through the solstitial and equinoctial points (of the ecliptic); P.L. ix. 66.

COMMERCE, vb.: to hold intercourse with; Il Pens. 39.

COMUS: (Gk. κῶμος) 'revelry'; the name of the wicked Magician in M.'s 'Mask', which was later called after him.

CONCENT: concord; variant reading of 2nd ed. and MSS.; Mus. 6.

CONCLAVE: used by M. in irony, as an ecclesiastical term; P.L. i. 795.

CONGLOBE, vb.: to gather into a sphere; P.L. vii. 239.

CONJUR'D: sworn to act together (as conspirators); P.L. ii. 693.

CONNATURAL: innate, sharing the same nature; P.L. x. 246, xi. 526.

CONNIVE, vb.: to 'wink at' or shut the eyes to what is hap-pening; S.Ag. 466.

CONSISTORY: here used ironically by M. as an ecclesiastical term; P.R. i. 42.

CONVINCE, vb. to convict; P.R. iii. 3.

CORPS: here used of a quasi-living body; P.L. x. 601.

CORSE: see COARSE.

COTYTTO (or Cotys): a Thracian goddess of the Phrygian (highly secret licentious) type, worshipped with nocturnal rites; Com. 129.

COUCH'D ('well-couch'd'): well-hidden, or ready and waiting to spring (metaph.); P.R. i. 97.

CRANK: a fantastic phrase; L'All. 27.

'CREMONA'S TRUMP': the *Christiad*, a Latin poem, on the life of Christ, by Marco Girolamo Vida, of Cremona; Pass. 26.

CRONIAN SEA: a name given to the Arctic Ocean (usually called *Mare Concretum*, or Frozen Sea) by Pliny; P.L. x. 290. Here Sin and Death, flying into Chaos and driving all before them 'in shoals' to Hell-mouth, are compared to two opposite winds from North and South, choking the NE. passage with icebergs.

CROW-TOE ('the tufted'): either a wild hyacinth or, as usually supposed, the 'crow-flower'; Lyc. 143.

CTESIPHON (or TESIPHON): nr. Seleucia, a winter-palace of the Parthian Kings, but sacked by Saracens A.D. 637; the spelling is Tesiphon in P.R. iii. 292; Ctesiphon, P.R. iii. 300.

'CUBIC' phalanx (mil.): usually taken as in 'square' formation, but may also be cubical, as the Saints are marching aloft in air; P.L. vi. 399.

CUPID'S SHAFTS: (a) golden, to kindle love, and (b) leaden to repel or divert it. For (a) see P.L. iv. 763.

CURIUS (DENTATUS): Roman Consul, who refused the Samnite bribes, and kept no booty for himself in the R. wars; P.R. ii. 446.

CUSCO (i.e. CUZCO): a town in the Peruvian Andes, ancient capital of the Inca Empire; P.L. xi. 408.

CYBELE (= Rhea): great Mother goddess of A. Minor (Phrygia) usually represented with a high turretted headdress; Arc. 21.

CYCLADES: it should be noted that Samos was not one of the Cyclades; probably M. used the name for the Gk. Islands generally; P.L. v. 264.

CYCLE: a celestial sphere; P.L. viii. 84; see SPHEAR.

CYLLENE: a lofty Mt. in NE. Arcadia, traditionally famous as the birthplace of Hermes; Arc. 98.

CYNOSURE (lit. Hound's-tail): (a) the Gk. name for the Lesser Bear (with the Polestar); the Greeks steered by the Great Bear (star of Arcady), the Phœnicians by the Lesser Bear; hence the phrase 'Tyrian (i.e. Phœnician) Cynosure'; Com. 342. See ARCADY, STAR OF.
(b) an object of universal attraction; L'All. 80.

CYPRESS: of Cyprus; (a) Cypress lawn (a black gauze or 'crape'); Il Pens. 35.
(b) cypress bud (an emblem of mourning); March.Winch. 22.

CYRENE: see BARCA.

CYRIACK SKINNER: M.'s pupil and lawyer friend and (at one time) neighbour and amanuensis; Sonn. xviii. 1 (Cyriack, whose grandsire). Sonn. to Mr. C. S. upon his blindness (Cyriack, this three years).

CYTHEREA: a name of Venus, probably from the I. of Cythera (now *Cerigo*), near the spot where she was said to have risen from the sea-foam, and where one of her chief shrines existed; P.L. ix. 19.

DAGON: (a) god of Ashdod (Azotus), P.L. i. 463; (b) used by M. for the name of a rebel angel; P.L. i. 457.

DAMSEL, ATHENIAN: see ATHENIAN DAMSEL.

DAPHNE ('grove of, by Orontes'): see CASTALIAN SPRING (b).

DARDANIAN (i.e. Trojan) SHIPS: see TROY.

DARWEN, r. in Lancs. (entering the Ribble near Preston): scene of the three days' battle of Preston at which Cromwell routed the invading army of Scots under the Duke of Hamilton, in 1648 (Cromwell's letter to Speaker Lenthall describes the battle for 'the Darwen bridge'); Sonn. xvi. 7 (Cromwell our cheif).

DAY-STAR: here the Sun; Lyc. 168.

DEBEL, vb.: to conquer; P.R. iv. 605.

DEE, the r. of Chester: see DEVA, and WISARD.

DEFEND: forbid; P.L. xi. 86, xii. 207; P.R. ii. 370.

DELOS: one of the Cyclades in the Ægæan; P.L. v. 265; birthplace of Apollo; P.L. x. 296.

DELPHOS: M's name for Delphi. D. was s. of Poseidon and Melanthō (some say, of Apollo and Celæno); he founded Delphi (hence 'Steep of Delphos'); Nat. Od. 168; P.R. i. 458.

DEMODOCUS: famous blind Bard at the Court of King Alcinous, who sang of the gods while Ulysses feasted (Od. viii); Vac. Ex. 48.

DEMOGORGON: a formless Shape of Horror, or Power of Evil, not worshipped, but invoked as the climax of Terror. As ruler of the Fates he is jointly enthroned, with the Ruler of Chaos; P.L. ii. 965.

DEPRAVE, vb.: depreciate; P.L. vi. 174.

DERIVE: to turn aside; P.L. x. 77.

DESCRY: to reveal; Com. 171.

DETERMIN'D: p.p. terminated, brought to an end; P.L. ii. 330; determine, P.L. vi. 318, xi. 227; S.Ag. 843.

DEVA: the Dee, the r. of Chester; Vac. Ex. 98; Lyc. 55. See also WISARD.

DIAMOND, ROCK OF: some think 'diamond' here = 'adamant'; P.L. vi. 364; but taken in the usual sense of the gem, the vigour of the conception is worthier of M. And cp. P.L. v. 759; Com. 881.

DICTAEAN: CRETAN (from Mt. Dicte in Crete, birthplace of Zeus); P.L. x. 584.

DIMENTIONLESS: non-material (lacking the 'dimensions' of matter); P.L. xi. 17.

DIPSAS: a snake whose bite caused an unendurable agony of mortal thirst; P.L. x. 526.

DIRE-LOOKING (in active sense): shedding evil influence; Arc. 52.

DIS: the Rom. god of Hades = Gk. Pluto, who aided his brothers Jupiter and Neptune against Saturn and the Titans; P.L. iv. 270.

DISASTROUS: 'foreboding' used as in astrology; 'ill-starred'; P.L. i. 597.

DISMAL: in its astrological sense of 'unlucky day', as applied to events; Vac. Ex. 68; P.L. ii. 572; P.R. i. 101; S.Ag. 1519; Nat. Od. 210 (dismall).

DISPLODE, vb.: explode; P.L. vi. 605.

DIVAN: a Council of Oriental, or Turkish, sort, used here ironically; P.L. x. 457; cp. P.L. i. 764 (champions . . . at the Soldan's chair).

DIVIDUAL: (a) separable, or rather separated from others; P.L. xii. 85. (b) shared with others; P.L. vii. 382.

DIVINE ('of something ill'): foreboding; P.L. ix. 845; cp. Hor. C. III. xxvii. 10.

DIVULGE, vb.: proclaim; P.R. iii. 62.

DODONA: the oracle of Zeus in Epirus; P.L. i. 518.

DORIC: pastoral; Lyc. 189; cp. Dorian, P.R. iv. 257.

DOTHAN (still called *Dothan*), c. 4 m. SW. of Jenin and 10 m. N. of Samaria, scene of the vision of the chariots of fire about Elisha when he was threatened by the Syrians (2 Kings vi. 17); P.L. xi. 217.

DOUBLE-FOUNTED: the r. Jordan had two chief sources, the Leddan and the Banias; P.L. xii. 144.

DOUBLE-SHADE: P.R. i. 500; cp. Virg. Cul. 204.

DOWNIE GOLD: i.e. Golden Down; P.L. v. 282.

DRAFF: dregs, or refuse; P.L. x. 630; S.Ag. 574.

DRIFT: intention; P.R. iii. 4; Sonn. to Sir H. V. (Vane, young in yeares), 6.

DROP SERENE (Lat. *gutta serena*): amaurosis, given by M. as a possible cause of his blindness, alternatively with 'dim diffusion' (i.e. cataract). But it was more probably glaucoma. For this passage see P.L. iii. 25.

DROWSIE FRIGHTED: the Cambridge MSS. read 'drowsy-flighted'; but the reading 'drowsie-frighted' follows the 1645 and 1673 edns.; Com. 553.                          [Lyc. 53.

DRUIDS: the priests, prophets, and instructors of the Britons;

DRYOPES: a primitive people of Greece, at first settled in the neighbourhood of Mt. Œta. Their king, Theiodamas, was traditionally the father of HYLAS, q.v.

DUN: the river Don (Yorks.); Vac. Ex. 92.

DUNBAR FIELD: the 'Roundhead' victory of 3 Sept. 1650; Sonn. to Cromwell, 8 (Cromwell, our cheif).

EARL: (a) 'an Earl's heir'; i.e. of Thomas Darcy, Earl Rivers; March. Winch. 3.
        (b) 'that good Earl': James Ley, Lord High Treasurer, 1624, first Earl of Marlboro', 1626; Lord President of the Council, 1628. Sonn. x. 1 (Daughter to that good Earl).

ECBATAN (P.L. xi. 393): Ecbatana (P.R. iii. 286): a capital c. of ancient Media, and summer residence of the Persian kings; captured by Cyrus.

EDEN: the name is not that of the Garden (as often popularly supposed), but of the Land of Eden where the Garden was planted 'Eastward in Eden' (Gen. ii. 8). This Land, part of the great Mesopotamian plain, was called 'Edin' by the early Sumerian settlers, in whose language 'Edin' actually meant 'the plain'. Of unexampled fertility, its grain was described by ancient writers as producing 100 to 300 seeds for each grain sown, with several crops within the year. As part of the 'Fertile Crescent' it also produced palms or fruit-trees that grew wild (cp. Gen. ii. 9); aboriginal wheat still grows wild on Mt. Hermon near Damascus. See esp. P.L. iv. 132, 210–14, etc.

EDWARD: K. Edward VI; Sonn. xi. 14 ('A Book was writ').

EDWARDS (Rev. Thomas): M.'s 'shallow Edwards'; a well-known Presbyterian preacher and author of *Gangræna* (1645), in which M.'s Divorce pamphlets were attacked. Forc. of Consc. 12.

EGLANTINE: not, as sometimes explained, sweet-briar (mentioned already in the preceding line), but prob. a kind of 'dog-rose'; called by some *rosa eglanteria*; others think woodbine or honeysuckle (because 'twisted'), but 'eglantine' is named from its thorns; L'All. 48.

EL DORADO: supposed, in M.'s time, to be a city (Ralegh's legendary 'golden city of Manoa'), but the Spanish phrase 'el dorado' (sc. *hombre*) shows that it really was the *Inca* (Peruvian Emperor), who once a year sprinkled himself all over with gold dust, app. to represent the sun god, and bathed in one of the sacred Lakes (e.g. Titicaca or Guatabita); jars for such gold dust from these lakes being in the Brit. Museum; P.L. xi. 411.

ELEALE (or *Elealeh*, now *El-aal* or *El 'Al*): a t. of the Reubenites, 1 m. from Heshbon, in Moab; P.L. i. 411.

ELECTRA'S POET: Euripides, author of the Tragedy so called; Sonn. viii. 13 (Captain or Colonel).

ELEMENTS: in addition to the four usually reckoned, Plato and Aristotle suggest a fifth (the 'quintessence', ether) from which, it was thought, the stars and heavens were made; P.L. iii. 716.

ELIAH, the Prophet (P.R. i. 353, ii. 19): Elijah (P.R. ii. 268, 277). And see 2 Kings ii. 11, the scene of which M. places on the Chebar; Pass. 36.

ELIXIR (Ar. *al ikthîr*): the Philosophers' Stone; an essence thought to turn baser metals into gold and to prolong life; P.L. iii. 607.

ELLOPS (Gk. ἔλλοψ, 'mute' or 'dumb'): orig. used of fishes, then of serpents—in M. a serpent; P.L. x. 525.

ELOQUENT: see OLD MAN ELOQUENT.

EMATHIA: Macedonian, from part of Macedonia, so called; P.R. iii. 290; Sonn. viii. 10 (Captain or Colonel).

EMBOST (for Emboskt): surrounded with woods; S.Ag. 1700; cp. bosky, Com. 313.

EMIMS (double pl., from EMIM): a giant race of Moab; S.Ag. 1080.

EMPEDOCLES: b. at Agrigentum in Sicily in the fifth century B.C. Was the poet, physician, and philosopher who established the four elements; his throwing himself into the crater of Etna is traditional; P.L. iii. 471–2.

EMPYREAL: heavenly, celestial; P.L. ii. 430, *et pass.*

EMPYREAN: heaven; P.L. ii. 771 *et pass.*

ENDORST: loaded on the back (of elephants); P.R. iii. 329.

ENFOLDED: enclosed one with the other; Arc. 64. See SPHEAR.

ENGIN, TWO-HANDED: there are two main divisions of opinion
in regard to this crucial passage: (a) that it refers to a
sword, and (b) that it is an axe. For the first view it is
held that the 'engin' may be the two-handed sword of
Christ such as that described in Rev. i. 16; cp. ch. ii. 12
and ii. 16. Even the words 'at the door' might be an un-
conscious echo of Christ's words as given in Rev. iii. 20,
'Behold I stand at the door', etc.; for the general threat
to false teachers see 2 Pet. ii. Alternatively the sword is
believed to be that of the archangel Michael; for sup-
porting passages see P.L. ii. 294–5, and vi. 250–3, and
especially vi. 317–18: 'one stroke . . . That might determine and not need repeat': the exact equivalent of
'Stands ready to strike once, and strike no more'. Those
who believe that an axe is intended point to the subsequent execution of Laud, though Laud was not in fact
beheaded till eight years after the writing of *Lycidas*.
Mr. Tillyard suggests (*Milton* 385) that the 'engin' may
be 'the iron rod of Christ's anger', quoting Milton's pamphlet *Of Reformation in England* (Bohn ii. 412). But
Mr. Visiak has pointed out to me that a passage in the
very same pamphlet does in fact actually mention the
axe in this connexion; the relevant part is here given from
Mitford's edition. Milton is asking whether 'mischiefe'
can ever be 'neerer hand' than when '*Bishops* shall openly
affirme that, No *Bishop*, no King? a trimme Paradox, and
that yee may know where they have beene a begging for
it, I will fetch you the Twin-brother to it out of the
Jesuites Cell; they feeling the Axe of Gods reformation
hewing at the old and hollow trunk of Papacie, and finding
the Spaniard their surest friend . . . have invented this
super-politick Aphorisme, as one termes it, One Pope,
and one King.' A third view, that the instrument of which
M. was thinking may have been a battery engine, is based
upon the passage in Ezekiel xxvi. 9: 'he shall set engines
of war against thy walls, and with his axes he shall break
down thy towers.' But this view does not seem to be
widely supported (and even here the axe is mentioned),
and Sir Thos. Smith's (1549) 'This day made new
Duke, Marquis, Earl or Baron, Yet maie the ax stand
next the dore' have recently been shown to be the source
of this Lycidas passage—see *N. & Q.* 1, ix. 38.

ENGLAND, ENGLISH: Sonn. x. 2 (Daughter to that); Sonn.
xiii. 2 (Harry whose tuneful). See also THAMES, BRUTUS,
BRITAIN, TROY.

ENORMOUS: beyond all knowledge or experience; P.L. v. 297.

EPEIROT, THE FEIRCE: Pyrrhus, K. of Epirus; Sonn. to
Sr. H. V. the younger (Vane young in yeares) 4.

EPICYCLE: a small circle revolving round a centre on the
circumference of a great circle or 'cycle'; P.L. viii. 84.

EPIDAURUS: (the 'God in Ep.' i.e. Æsculapius) of whose cult
Ep. on the Saronic gulf, in Argolis (now *Pidavro*), was the
chief centre; P.L. ix. 507.

EQUINOCTIAL: (a) applied by M. to the terrestrial equator;
P.L. ix. 64; cp. Æquinoctial ii. 637.
  (b) the celestial equator; (Equinoctial Rode) P.L. x. 672.

ERCOCO (now *Arkoko* or *Arkeeko*): northern port of Abyssinia, on the Red Sea; P.L. xi. 398.

ERE, compar. adv.: = before; P.L. iv. 10: 'erst' is the superlative.

EREBUS: in classic myth. husband of Night (but M. substitutes Cerberus in L'All. 2). Com. 804; P.L. ii. 883.

ERECTED: high-souled, exalted, sublime; P.L. i. 679; P.R. iii. 27.

EREMITE, GLORIOUS: i.e. Jesus Christ; P.R. i. 8.

ERRONEOUS: wandering, straying; P.L. vii. 20.

ERUPTION: the escape of the rebel Angels from Hell; P.L. i. 656, viii. 235.

ERYMANTH (i.e. Erymanthus): a lofty range on the borders of Arcadia, Achaia, and Elis; Arc. 100.

ESHTAOL: a c. of Judah, allotted to Dan, near which Samson (b. at Zora) was buried; S.Ag. 181.

ESTOTILAND: in seventeenth century, a vast tract of country between Baffin's and Hudson's Bays, in N. America; P.L. x. 686.

ETHAM (or ETAM, now *Beit 'Atub*): an isolated rock-mass beside which was Samson's 'retirement'; S.Ag. 253.

ETHIOPE (QUEEN): Cassiopeia, who boasted of the beauty of her d. Andromeda. (M. says of her own); Il Pens. 19.

ETHIOPIAN (Sea): M. here means the Indian Ocean (as in classical usage), though in his day it also often meant the Sea off W. and SW. Africa (the South Atlantic); P.L. ii. 641.

EUBOIC ('Sea'): between the I. of Euboea and the Gk. mainland; P.L. ii. 546.

EUPHRASIE: formerly much used as an eye specific (bearing, according to the doctrine of signatures, an eye-like mark); P.L. xi. 414.

EUPHRATES: P.L. i. 420, xii. 114; P.R. iii. 272, 384.

EUPHROSYNE: one of the three Graces 'with two sister graces more', viz. Aglaia and Thalia; L'All. 12.

EUROTAS: chief r. of Laconia, also, acc. to some accounts, the name of the father of Hyacinthus; D.F.I. 25.

EURYNOME ('Wide-ruling'): wife of Ophion, one of the oldest of the Titans, with whom she ruled Olympus, till they were conquered by Kronos and Rhea; P.L. x. 581.

EVINCE, vb. tr.: conquer; P.R. iv. 235.

EXORBITANT: 'out of orbit' (astron.); hence 'extravagant, irregular'; P.L. iii. 177.

EXPATIATE, vb. intr.: to walk abroad, 'take the air'; P.L. i. 774.

EXPLODE: to hoot or 'hiss off' (the stage); to chase away; P.L. xi. 665.

EXTENUATE, vb.: to make less (Lat. *tenuis*), 'make light of', underrate, disparage; P.L. x. 645; S.Ag. 767.

FABLE OF BELLERUS: i.e. 'fabled Bellerus'; the name being taken by M. from Bellerium (Belerium in Diodorus), i.e. the 'Land's End', Bellerus suggesting one of the Cornish giants; Lyc. 160.

FABRICIUS: the heroic antagonist of Pyrrhus; P.R. v. 446.

FADOM: M.'s spelling of fathom; P.L. ii. 934.

FAIRFAX: Thomas, third Lord Fairfax (1612–71), contemporary of M.'s at Cambridge (at St. John's), later Commander-in-Chief of the forces of the Parlt. in the Civil War; Sonn. On the Lord Gen. F. 1 (Fairfax whose name).

FAME: personified; Arc. 8, 41; Sonn. to H. Lawes (Harry whose tuneful) 12 (of Dante); Lyc. 70–84.

FAUN: one of a class of semi-divine beings haunting the countryside; Lyc. 34.

FAUNUS (P.L. iv. 708); or FAWN (P.R. ii. 191): the god of the countryside (esp. of shepherds and farms).

FAVONIUS: Sonn. xvii. (Lawrence of vertuous) 6.

FAVOURITE, the (of Tiberius): i.e. Sejanus; P.R. iv. 95.

FEATURE: 'a shape'; cp. Dante Par. c. ix. (*fatture empie*): P.L. x. 279.

FENCE: skill in 'parrying' questions; Com. 791.

FENEL (i.e. FENNEL): attractive to serpents, as helping them to shed their skins and to clear their sight; P.L. ix. 581.

FET: fetched; P.R. ii. 401.

FEZ: one of the five Barbary States in N. Africa; P.L. xi. 403.

FIERY ROD, HEAV'NS: the sun's rays; S.Ag. 549.

FIGTREE ('not that . . . for Fruit renown'd): Pliny (Nat. Hist. xi. 5), followed by Gerard, confuses the banyan-tree of India (*ficus indica*), whose leaves are quite small, with the banana (*Musa Paradaisica*), whose leaves are quite as large as here described. It may be added that (perhaps owing to some such confusion) small bananas are still called 'figs' by Barbadians in the B.W.I.; note that the phrase 'broad as Amazonian targe' exactly translates Pliny's phrase; P.L. ix. 1101.

FIRST MOV'D, THAT: the *Primum Mobile*. See SPHEAR.

FLAMIN: one of the orders of R. priests, each serving one special god (e.g. Jupiter, Mars, Quirinus; hence 'each peculiar power'); Nat. Od. 194.

FLEDGE, adj.: fledged or full-feathered; P.L. vii. 420; cp. P.L. iii. 627

FLEECIE STARR: Aries; P.L. iii. 558.                    [off; Lyc. 79.

FOIL: a leaf of metal placed at the back of a gem to set it

FONTARABBIA (now Fuentarabbia): a frontier fortress of Spain, S. of Biarritz on the B. of Biscay. F. is about 40 miles from Roncesvalles, the scene of the defeat of the rearguard of Charlemagne's army when the Gascons or Basques joined the Saracens in attacking the Franks in A.D. 778. Charles himself was not slain, as this passage suggests, but d. and was buried at Aix in 814; P.L. i. 587.

FORGERY: fabrication; S.Ag. 131.

FREAKT WITH JEAT (or 'jet'): because broadly splashed with black as pansies are (a finely imaginative phrase), not merely spotted or 'freckled', as sometimes inadequately explained; Lyc. 144.

FREQUENT: thronged or crowded; P.L. i. 797, *et pass.*

**FRET**, sb.: (*a*) a small crosspiece of wood or other material, set transversely on the finger-board of a guitar or lute, to guide the fingering; P.L. vii. 597.
(*b*) fretted; i.e. adorned with 'fret-work' designs or rather traceries; P.L. i. 717.

**FRIAR'S LANTHORN**: Will o' the Wisp; a sardonic phrase invented by M. to disparage the Friars. L'All. 104.

**FRIARS** ('White, Black, and Grey'); P.L. iii. 474–5.
(*a*) the White Friars were the Carmelites (so called from Mt. Carmel, where they were first established); they wear a white garb.
(*b*) the Black Friars (so called from their black garb) were the Dominicans; they were founded by St. Dominic of Spain.
(*c*) the Grey Friars (who are garbed in grey) are the Franciscans, and were founded by St. Francis of Assisi.
(*d*) The fourth order, Augustinians, or 'Austin' Friars, is omitted by M.

**FRIZL'D**: curled or 'crisped' (of foliage); P.L. vii. 323.

**FRONTISPIECE**: the principal front or pediment of a building designed in the classical tradition; P.L. iii. 506.

**FRORE**: frozen; P.L. ii. 595.

**FROUNC'T**: with crimped or 'fluffed' hair; Il P. 123.

**FULGENT**: shining, gleaming; P.L. x. 449.

**FULMIN'D**, vb.: thundered (metaph.); this refers to Demosthenes and Pericles; P.R. iv. 270. See ARSENAL.

**FURNITURE**: tilting equipment; P.L. ix. 34.

**FURY, BLIND**: really Atropos, one of the Fates. Lyc. 75.

**FUSIL**: molten, or cast in moulds; P.L. xi. 573.

**GABRIEL**: 'hero of God', one of the chief warrior angels, though inferior to Michael, q.v.; P.L. iv. 549, *et pass.*

**GADEZ**: see GADIRE.

**GADIRE** (1st ed. GADIER from Gk. Γάδειρα—in the orig. Phœnician *Gadir*) = L. *castrum* (S.Ag. 716) or Gadez (P.R. iv. 77); Cadiz in Spain.

**GALASP**: app. (George) Gillespie, a Scottish Presbyterian representative at Westminster; Sonn. xi. 9 (A Book was writ).

**GALAXIE**: Galileo hoped that with a sufficiently powerful telescope the stars of the Galaxy might be resolved; P.L. vii. 579. See next entry.

**GALILEO**: G. (P.L. i. 288, v. 262) taking the *idea* of a telescope from Lippershey, the Dutch optician, re-invented it for himself, and in 1609 applied it to astronomy, discovering the spotted and uneven surface of the moon (P.L. v. 262, 419, viii. 145; and esp. P.L. i. 291); the 'moons' or satellites of Jupiter and Saturn (P.L. viii. 149); the crescent form of Venus in or near conjunction (P.L. vii. 366); and the stars of the Galaxy (that 'Milkie way: . . . pouderd with stars'; P.L. vii. 579–81). These passages are clearly among the fruits of M.'s friendship with G. See GALAXIE.

**GALLAPHRONE**, K. of Cathay, and father of Angelica. See AGRICAN; P.R. iii. 340.

GELONI: a race of Asiatic Sarmatia E. of the Don (Tanais).

GERYON'S SONS: Spaniards (named ironically from Geryon, an early but monstrous, perhaps deformed, K. of Erythia, usually identified with Cadiz in Spain); P.L. xi. 410.

GINN: short for ENGIN: a snare; S.Ag. 933.

GIVES: i.e. gyves, here ankle-fetters; S.Ag. 1093.

GLAUCUS SPELL: this Glaucus was a fisherman of Anthedon in Boeotia, who became immortal through eating part of the divine herb sown by Kronos; a clever diver, he became a sea deity; Com. 874.

GLIBB'D, vb. tr.: made glib or fluent; P.R. i. 375.

GOBLIN, DRUDGING: Robin Goodfellow; L'All. 105.

GOD IN EPIDAURUS: see EPIDAURUS.

GORDIAN: this famous 'knot' was the 'inextricable' fastening of tree-bark fibre, used by Gordius, the Phrygian K., for binding the yoke of his chariot to the chariot-pole when he dedicated it to the gods in their temple; Richardson (Remarks 160) says it was his *plough*; Vac. Ex. 90; P.L. iv. 348.

GORDON: either (a) George, Lord Gordon, e. s. of the Marquis of Huntley, or (b) his brother, Charles Gordon, Viscount Aboyne; both of whom were among the chief supporters of Montrose; Sonn. xi. 8 (A Book was writ).

GOSHEN, SOJOURNERS OF: the Israelites; P.L. i. 309.

GRAIN: scarlet dye; P.L. v. 285; xi. 242.

GRAND, THE: grandees; P.L. x. 427.

GRANDSIRE: Sir E. Coke, the famous judge (1551–1634): see CYRIACK SKINNER.

GRAY-FLY: the trumpet-fly or 'breeze' (a great pest to cattle); Lyc. 28.

GREEK, THE: Ulysses; P.L. ix. 19.

'GREEN' CAPE: Cape Verde; P.L. viii. 631.

GRIDE: to cut with a grating sound; P.L. vi. 329.

GRINDE ('the air'): to reduce or convert the air by friction into fire; P.L. x. 1072.                                    [344.

GRIS-AMBER-STEAM'D: steamed with 'amber-gris'; P.R. ii.

GROTTESQUE: irregularly, or strangely and picturesquely shaped (like a grotto); whence 'grotesque'; P.L. iv. 136.

GRUNSEL (or 'grundsel', i.e. 'ground-sill') edge: the door-sill; P.L. i. 460.

GRYFON: a GRYPHON or GRIFFIN. These were eagle-headed winged lions, fabled guardians of the gold in the Rhipæan (or Ural) Mountains, the country lying between the lands of the Hyperboreans and the one-eyed Arimaspians, who had been first to discover how to steal this gold, with which they adorned their hair; P.L. ii. 943.

GUENDOLEN: here the daughter of Corinëus (the Cornish giant) and wife of Locrine, q.v.; Com. 830.

GURGE: a flood; P.L. xii. 41.

GYVES: see GIVES.

HABERGEON: a coat of chain-mail or plate worn as armour; S.Ag. 1120.

HABOR (now *Kabur*): trib. of the Euphrates ('in Habor' = in the land of H.); P.R. iii. 376.

HÆMONY: M.'s name for a magical plant, prob. so called from the ancient association of Hæmonia or Thessaly with magic; Com. 638.

HALF-MOON (mil.): an ancient battle-formation, in the shape of a crescent with backward-pointing horns; P.R. iii. 309.

HAMMON: identified by M. with Zeus Ammon in Gk., and with Jupiter Ammon in Latin; as worshipped especially in N. Africa—as well as with Cham and with the Ram-headed god Amun-Ra of Egypt (hence 'Libyc Hammon shrinks his horn', he being a ram-headed god himself). For identifications see Nat. Od. 203; P.L. iv. 276-7, cp. iv. 508-9.

HARAN (HARRAN or CHARRAN; Lat. CARRHÆ) (scene of the defeat of Crassus by the Parthians, 53 B.C.): the town at which Abraham settled on leaving Ur. In the cuneiform Assyrian inscriptions Harran or Harranu means the 'Road'; an Arab village in this district is still called *Harran*; P.L. xii. 130-1.

HARAPHA: the name was app. suggested to M. by 'Rapha' (f. of Goliath) in the O.T. (cp. for similar names 1 Chron. viii. 37; 2 Sam. xxi. 16, 18, 20, A.V. marg., etc.); S.Ag. 1068, 1079.

HARNEST: armoured; Nat. Od. 244; P.L. vi. 202.

HARPYIES (HARPIES): see PHINEUS. HARPY-FOOTED: with taloned feet like the Harpies; P.L. ii. 596; P.R. ii. 403.

HARRY (LAWES): the famous musician and friend of M., to whom M. owed the production of *Comus*; Sonn. xiii. (Harry whose tuneful).

HEAR, vb.: 'to be called' (as in Gk. and L.): P.L. iii. 7.

HEARS (March. Winch. 58), or HERSE (Lyc. 151): a tri-angular frame (L. *hirpex*, 'harrow'), for lights, esp. for the Tenebræ service (*hercia ad tenebras*) in Holy Week; the triangular framework cover for a bier, with lights at ends; hence the bier itself.

HEBRUS (now *Maritza*) the chief R. of Thrace, rising in Rhodope; Lyc. 63; cp. P.L. vii. 34-8.

HECAERGE: see DELOS.

HECAT' (abbr. of Hecatë): the Moon-goddess, called tri-form or 'triple', from her three phases ('crescent', 'full', and 'waning'). She was held (as in Shakesp. M.N.D.) to be a great enchantress; Com. 135, (Hecate) 535.

HECATOMPYLOS (city of the 'hundred gates' or 'pylons'): the capital c. of Elam, later of central Parthia, which became chief residence of the Parthian Kings under the Arsacidæ; P.R. iii. 287. [Other cities, e.g. Thebes in Upper Egypt, were similarly named—Thebes from the pylons of its temples.]

HELICON: here means 'our *new* Helicon', i.e. the University of Cambridge as a seat of the Muses; March. Winch. 56, 59; and see Tillyard, *Milt. Priv. Corr. and Prol.*, p. 123, etc.

HERARCHIE: i.e. hierarchies, referring to the nine celestial orders (three hierarchies each of three orders or 'quires'); P.L. i. 737; (Hierarchies) P.L. v. 591, vii. 192; cp. Forc. Consc. 7.

HERMES: (a) 'volatil', in sense of 'quicksilver' or 'Mercury'; P.L. iii. 603.
(b) HERMES, thrice-great, (the god): HERMES, identified by the Gks. with the Eg. god Tahuti (usually known as Thoth), who was the divine scribe of the Eg. gods (and hence the Eg. god of knowledge) came to be regarded as the composer of the forty-two 'Hermetic' books (so called); the work of philosophers of the Neo-platonic school in the third century A.D. Hence the books of Hermes 'thrice great' (Gk. τρισμέγιστος) came to be held as an encyclopaedic medieval authority on philosophy, alchemy, and the Black Art or Magic; I. Pens. 88. [Recently translated by the late Walter Scott and published as *Hermetica* (4 vols.), O.U.P. 1924–36.]

HERMIONE: Harmonia, wife of Cadmus; P.L. ix. 506.

HEROD: s. of Antipater, q.v. Appointed K. of Judea by Mark Antony; P.R. ii. 424.

HESEBON (Heshbon): P.L. i. 408.

HESPERIA: a name given by the Gks. to Italy (as being W. of Greece); and then by the Romans to Spain and Portugal (as being W. of Italy). See P.L. i. 520.

HESPERIAN GARDENS: i.e. of the Hesperides; P.L. iii. 568 (Hesperean), viii. 632; cp. (Hesperian) Com. 393; P.L. iv. 250; ('Hesperides') P.R. ii. 357.

HESPERUS: (a) the Evening Star; P.L. iv. 605, ix. 49. And see Galileo.
(b) father of the Hesperides, who guarded the golden apples; Com. 982.

HILL (of Scandal): see SCANDAL.

HILL (the Opprobrious): see OPPROBRIOUS.

HIMERA: Himēra or Hemēra: was the name of 'Prince Memnon's sister'; Il Pens. 18.

HINGES: cardinal points (L. *cardines*); P.R. iv. 415.

HIPPOGRIF: a creature with the forepart of a griffin, and the hindpart of a horse; taken by M. from Ariosto's *Orlando Furioso*; P.R. iv. 542.

HIPPOTADES: s. of Hippotas, i.e. Æolus, the god of the winds; Lyc. 96. For the caves in which the winds were bound see also P.R. iv. 414.

HISPAHAN (Ispahan or *Isfahan*, anciently *Aspadana*): c. on the r. Zayendeh; it became the capital city of Persia, the t. of Shah Abbas, flourishing still in the seventeenth century, though now decayed; P.L. xi. 394.

HOLOCAUST: a burnt-offering offered whole; S.Ag. 1702.

HOMER (MELESIGENES): so called from the Meles, a r. of Smyrna; P.R. iv. 259; also MAEONIDES, i.e. son of Mæon, or from Mæonia (Lydia); P.L. iii. 35.

HOOK: i.e. the shepherd's crook; Lyc. 120; Com. 872.

HOOKED CHARIOT: doubtless in ref. to the (reputed) scythed

chariot-wheels of the Britons, **a** view now questioned; Nat. Od. 56–7.

HORNED FLOUD: the flood with its main stream divided into two channels. So Ovid calls the Nile 'Seven-horned' (from its seven branches or mouths), and river gods were called by the Romans 'bull-horned' (*tauri-formis*), from their divided channels; P.L. xi. 827.

HORONAIM: a c. of Moab; P.L. i. 409.

HOSTING, sb.: a warlike encounter; P.L. vi. 93.

HUDDLING: hurrying; Com. 495.

HULL DOWN, vb.: to drift with all sails down, or without sails, as here; P.L. xi. 836.

HUMOURS (doctrine of the four): formerly held to be blood, choler, phlegm, and black bile (melancholy); S.Ag. 600.

HYACINTH (HYACINTHUS): the comely youth of the classical legend; D.F.I. 23–8.

HYALINE: the 'glassy sea' of Rev. iv. 6, xv. 2; see P.L. vii. 619.

HYDASPES (Sanskr. *Vitasta*), now the r. *Jhelum* or *Jelum*, one of the chief rivers of the Punjab; P.L. iii. 436.

HYDRA: the many-headed snake slain by Hercules at Lerna at the SW. end of the Argive plain; Com. 605; P.L. ii. 628; Sonn. On the Lord General Fairfax, 7.

HYDRUS: a sea-snake; P.L. x. 525.

HYLAS: s. of Theiodamas, k. of the Dryopes, famous for his comeliness; a companion of Hercules in the Argo, he was carried under water by a nymph in Asia Minor and drowned; P.R. ii. 353.

HYRCANIA: a prov. of Parthia, separated by the Oxus from Margiana and bounded on the N. by the Caspian; P.R. iii. 317.

HYRCANUS: i.e. H. II, the uncle of Antigonus and grandf. of Mariamne. He was High Priest (78 B.C.), a prince who was last but one of the royal House of the Maccabees, Asmonean dynasty. Though carried away by the Parthians, and mutilated, his ears being cropped by Antigonus, he returned to Jerusalem, and lived there under Herod till 40 B.C., when Herod executed him; P.R. iii. 367.

IBERIA: (a) Spain and Portugal; Com. 60; P.L. ii. 200. See also HESPERIA.
(b) a province of ancient Parthia, lying N. of Armenia, between the Black Sea and the Caspian, roughly equivalent to the modern Georgia, or Grusia (in Russia). Hence 'dark Iberian dales'; P.R. iii. 318.

IDA, MOUNT: (a) in Crete, trad. the birthplace of Zeus; Il Pens. 29; P.L. i. 515.
(b) in Mysia (Asia Minor) S. boundary of the Troad. Mt. Alexandria near Antandrus, which is part of the range of Ida, is mentioned by ancient writers (Strabo, etc.) as having been the actual scene of the judgement of Paris; P.L. v. 382.

IDOL: in special sense of 'mock image', 'simulacrum'; P.L. vi. 101.

IDOLISMS: personal prejudices; P.R. iv. 234.

IDOLIST: idolater; S.Ag. 453.

IMAUS, Mt.: (Sanskr. *Himara* 'snowy') the name of this system of mountain ranges in Central Asia was applied at first by the Gk. geographers to the Hindu Kush and Himalayas, and later employed app. for the Bolor Range between China and Turkistan (Ptolemy places it much too far to the East); P.L. iii. 431.

IMP: (a) sb. an evil spirit; P.L. ix. 89.
(b) impe. vb. to graft a sound feather in place of a broken one (hawking term); Sonn. On the Lord General F. (Fairfax whose name), 8.

IMPALE: to surround, enclose (as with a palisade); P.L. ii· 647, vi. 553.

IMPERTINENCE: irrelevance; P.L. viii. 195.

IMPERVIOUS: impenetrable; P.L. x. 254.

IMPLICIT (of bushes): entangled, interwoven (as in Lat.); P.L. vii. 323.

IMPRESES, sb. pl. (Ital. *impresa*): devices on shields; P.L. ix. 35.

INCENTIVE (reed): reed for 'kindling' (used of the 'match' for firing cannon); P.L. vi. 519.

INCOMPOS'D: discomposed; P.L. ii. 989.

INCORPORATE: dwelling together in one body (cp. Rom. vii. 20); P.L. x. 816; cp. S.A. 161.

INCUBUS: see ASMODEUS.

INDECENT: ungraceful, unbecoming; P.L. vi. 601.

INDENTED: with short sharp curves or turns (of the banks of a river or the track of a serpent, etc.); Vac. Ex. 94; P.L. ix. 496.

INDITE: to describe in writing; P.L. ix. 27.

INDIVIDUAL: indivisible, inseparable, distinctive. Time, 12; P.L. iv. 486, etc.

INDUCE: to bring on; P.L. vi. 407.

INDULGENCE: formal remission of penalty for sin, after absolution; P.L. iii. 492.

INDUSTRIOUS: zealous (for a particular object); P.L. ii. 116.

INFAM'D, INFAMOUS: defam'd, notorious; P.L. ix. 707.

INFANTRY: of a body of foot-soldiers, e.g. of the Dwarfs ('that small infantry') in their war with the Cranes (prob. with play on the word 'infantry'); P.L. i. 575.

INFINITE, sb. (a) Illimitable; P.L. iii. 273 (of God).
(b) void and formless, of Chaos; P.L. ii. 405.

INFLUENCE: the good or evil force believed to emanate from the stars, as 'cosmic rays' from space; Nat. Od. 71; L'All. 122; Com. 336; P.L. ii. 1034, etc.

INFRINGE, vb. tr.: to break up or shatter; P.R. i. 62.

INLAND: the interior of Hell; P.L. x. 423.

INSCRIB'D WITH WOE: The sedge of the Cam, when dry, shows

markings like a palm-leaf MS. (or like the traditional marks of the hyacinth); Lyc. 105.

INSENSATE: devoid of understanding; P.L. vi. 787; S.Ag. 1885.

INSINUATE: to progress sinuously or in curves (of a serpent, etc.); P.L. iv. 348.

INSIST: persist; S.Ag. 913.

INSPHEAR: to 'translate' or raise to a celestial sphere; Com. 3; cp. unsphear, Il Pens. 88. And see SPHEAR.

INSTILL'D: poured in drop by drop; P.L. xi. 416.

INSTINCT, p.p.: impelled; P.L. ii. 937, vi. 752.

INSTRUCT, p.p.: instructed, taught; P.R. i. 439; cp. Pass. 48; S.Ag. 757.

INSUPPORTABLY: irresistibly; S.Ag. 136.

INTEND: to occupy one's-self; P.L. ii. 457.

INTENSE, p.p.: strained to the uttermost, taut (opposed to 'remiss', i.e. slackened, as of a violin string); P.L. viii. 387.

INTERLUNAR CAVE: M. imagines the Moon to retire into a cavern during the intervals between the Old Moon and the New; S.Ag. 89.

INTERMINABLE: the 'Illimitable' or 'Infinite', i.e. God; S.Ag. 307.

INTERNAL: mental, spiritual; S.Ag. 1334, 1686.

INTERVEIND: (of a country, intersected by rivers, like the veinings of a leaf); P.R. iii. 257.

INTERVOLV'D: with linked, or interlocked, revolutions; P.L. v. 623.

INVERT: to reverse the purpose (e.g. of a deed); Com. 632.

INVEST: to clothe as with a garment (e.g. night 'invests' the sea); P.L. i. 208.

INVIOLABLE: (a) inviolate; P.L. iv. 843.
(b) unyielding, hence safe (from violence); P.L. vi. 398.

INVISIBLE: 'the invisible glory of Him that made them' app. means (by hypallage) the 'glory of the Invisible' (i.e. God); P.L. i. 369.

INVOLVE: (a) to entwine or entangle; P.L. vii. 483.
(b) to envelop; P.R. i. 41, etc.

IRASSA: t. and district of N. Africa (in Lybia not far from Cyrene); acc. to M. the scene of the conflict between Hercules and Antæus, described by Pindar. But Pindar tells how Alexidamus won the d. of a *later* Antæus in marriage. M. has 'confused the two'—Blakeney, notes (more probably, *more suo*, was 'fusing' them); P.R. iv. 564. [The name 'Irassa' is from Pindar, *Pyth.* ix. 106, but should be spelt *Irasa*.]

IRIS: (a) the rainbow goddess; Com. 83, 992; P.L. xi. 244.
(b) the plant; P.L. iv. 698.

IRRESOLUTE: undecided, 'irr. of thoughts revolv'd', unable to decide between all the plans considered; P.L. ix. 87.

IRRIGUOUS: well-watered; P.L. iv. 255.

ISIS: the Eg. goddess, wife of Osiris; P.L. i. 478; Nat. Od. 212.

**ISMENIAN** (i.e. 'Theban') steep: the Theban acropolis overlooking the r. Ismenus; called the Hill or Rock of the Sphinx (Mt. Phicium), as being the Rock from which she flung herself when her riddle was guessed by Œdipus; P.R. iv. 575.

**ITHURIEL** (lit. 'Search of God'): the cherub who, finding Satan disguised in Eden 'squat like a Toad, close at the eare of Eve', pricks him with his spear, forcing him to return to his own shape; P.L. iv. 788, 810–14.

**JACULATION**: the act of throwing or hurling; P.L. vi. 605.

**JANUS**: the R. god with two faces, looking opposite ways; hence a 'double Janus' would have four faces; P.L. xi. 129.

**JAPHET**: identified by M. with Iapetus, the Titan, f. of Prometheus and ancestor, acc. to the Gks., of mankind; P.L. iv. 717.

**JAUNT**: a short journey; P.R. iv. 402.

**JAVAN**: s. of Japhet; rightly identified by M. with Ion, ancestor of the Ionians, and hence of the Greek race; P.L. i. 508; S.Ag. 716.

**JESUS**: (a) the Gk. septuagint form of Joshua as a type of Christ; P.L. xii. 310.
(b) elsewhere, Christ himself.

**JOCOND**: blithe and gay; L'All. 94.

**JONSON, BEN**: L'All. 132.

**JOVE**: identified by M. (a) with Heb. Jehovah.
(b) with N. African or Lybian Ammon (or Cham).
(c) with Zeus Ammon, Jupiter Ammon, and Eg. Amun-Ra. See HAMMON.

**JUBILY**: joyful acclaim; Mus. 9; P.L. iv. 348 (Jubilee), vi. 884 (Jubilie); cp. vii. 564.

**JULEP** (from Pers. word for 'rose water'): a sweet drink or potion; Com. 672.

**JULIUS** (CÆSAR): weeps at Alexander's tomb; P.R. iii. 41.

**JUNKET**: Ital. cream cheese in rush basket; L'All. 102.

**JUSTLING ROCKS**: the Symplegades, at the mouth of the Black Sea. The Argo and her crew, by the advice of Phineus the sage, and Hera's aid, passed through in safety, and thenceforth they were fixed and motionless; P.L. ii. 1018.

**KEYES** (of St. Peter): Lyc. 110; Com. 13; P.L. iii. 484–5.

**KIRIATHAIM**: a c. in Moab; S.Ag. 1081.

**KNEW NOT EATING DEATH**: a Grecism; cp. Oppian, Halieut. ii. 106 οὐδ᾽ ἐνόησαν | σπεύδοντες ὄλεθρον.

**KSAR** (abbn. of Kaisar, i.e. 'Czar' or 'Tsar'): see 'the Russian Ksar In Mosco'; P.L. xi. 394.

[Arcad. 97.
**LADON**: a Gk. r. in Arcadia, flowing into the Alpheus;

**LANCELOT** (the knight of Arthur): P.R. ii. 361. See also ARTHUR, KING.

**LANTSKIP** (M.'s usual spelling): landscape. M. is said to have borrowed the word from the great Dutch landscape painters; L'All. 70.

LAPLAND: one of the chief reputed homes of witchcraft and sorcery; P.L. ii. 665.

LAPSE (in sense of a flowing current): P.L. viii. 263.

LARS: household (tutelary) ancestral spirits worshipped in ancient Rome; Nat. Od. 191.

LATONA: m. of Apollo and Artemis; Arc. 20; Sonn. (I did but prompt).

LAUREAT: adorned or furnished with laurels; Lyc. 151; Sonn. to Cromwell, 9 (Cromwell, our cheif).

LAVER: a vessel for bathing; Com. 838; cp. S.Ag. 1727.

LAVINIA: d. of Latinus, betrothed to Turnus, but later perfidiously married to Æneas (the cause of that war); P.L. ix. 17.

LAWES, H.: see HARRY (Lawes).

LAWN (cipres): black gauze or crape—'cypress' (named from 'Cyprus') cloth and 'lawn' (named from Laon), usually distinguished, are here identified; Il Pens. 35.

LAWN: a cleared space in the woods, a glade; also used of pasture land; Nat. Od. 85; L'All. 71; Lyc. 25; Com. 568, 965; P.L. iv. 252.

LAWRENCE: s. of Henry Lawrence, Lord President of Cromwell's State Council; Sonn. xvii. 1 (Lawrence of virtuous).

LAXE ('inhabit laxe'): dwell at ease, or 'at large'; P.L. vii. 162.

LAZAR-HOUSE: leper-house; P.L. xi. 479.

LEMURES: spectres of the departed in ancient Rome, spirits of evil; Nat. Od. 191.

LEUCOTHEA: (a) identified with Ino, wife of Athamas, who became a sea-goddess when drowned; Com. 875.
(b) id. with the Roman goddess Matuta or goddess of Dawn; P.L. xi. 135.

LEVANT, LEVANTINE: the Rising, or 'Dawn' wind; P.L. x. 704. See PONENT.

LEWDLY-PAMPER'D: basely indulged; Com. 770.

LIBBARD: used in sixteenth century for leopard; P.L. vii. 467.

LIBECCHIO: the SW. wind; P.L. x. 706.

LIBRA: the Constellation (lit. the 'Scales'); P.L. iii. 558, iv. 887.

LICHAS: the attendant of Hercules who brought him the poisoned robe, was thrown into the sea by H.; he was changed into the *Lichadian Islands*; P.L. ii. 545.

LICKERISH: seductive; Com. 700.

LIGEA: a sea-nymph (as in Georg. iv. 336); Com. 880. (Lewis and Short give Ligea as a wood-nymph, or Dryad.) See SIRENS.

LIMBEC: an alembic (Ar. *al anbiq*); P.L. iii. 605.

LIMBER FANS: pliant wings; P.L. vii. 476.

LIMBO (*limbus fatuorum*): Milton's idea of this region as one of the extra-mundane regions to which all vain and foolish persons and things were consigned, pending the Last Day's arrival, seems to partake of the popular ideas; acc. to the Schoolmen it was a definite region next to Hell, to which the souls of unbaptized infants went; P.L. iii. 495.

# A READER'S GUIDE 517

LIMITARIE CHERUBE: app. ch. of the frontiersmen or of the 'marches' (and of nothing else, as in the Tennysonian 'Lords of waste marches'; cp. Lat. *milites limitanei*). Satan's mocking allusion to the 'hallow'd limits' mentioned in the speech of Gabriel; P.L. iv. 971.

LINEAMENTS: outlines (not merely of the countenance but of the body also); the limbs, P.L. v. 278.

LIQUID: clear (*not* flowing); S.Ag. 557.

LISTED: (*a*) broadly striped; P.L. xi. 862.
(*b*) used of an enclosed space, roped off like a ring, or enclosed with 'lists', as for a tournament; S.Ag. 1087.

LITTER: a horse-litter, suspended between two horses at front and back, such as that used for Qu. Henrietta Maria, wife of Charles I, at her entry into London; cp. Com. 554.

LOCRINE: son of BRUTUS, Com. 827, 922; v. BRUTUS and ANCHISES.

LODGE: a shelter of boughs; cp. P.L. iv. 720, v. 377; the small rustic cottage of the keeper of the wood; Com. 346.

LOFTS: the middle stratum of the atmosphere, Vac. Ex. 42; see 'MIDDLE AIR'.

LOGRES: the Midlands, or main part of England E. of the Severn (called Loegria in M.'s P. Wks.); as dist. from Lyones or Cornwall; P.R. ii. 360.

LUCIFER: (*a*) Satan, as in Isa. xiv. 12; P.L. v. 757, vii. 131, x. 425; cp. P.L. v. 655 ('his former name'); P.R. iv. 57.
(*b*) the Morning Star; Nat. Od. 74. Note—that when W. of the Sun, Venus rises as the Morning Star, or Lucifer; when E. of the Sun, as Vesper or Hesperus. cp. P.R. i. 294, our 'Morning Star' (Christ).

LUCRINE BAY: now the Gulf of Pozzuoli, near Naples, famous for oysters; P.R. ii. 347.

LUZ ('Hazel-trees'): the older name of the settlement at Bethel; P.L. iii. 513.

LYCÆUS (now *Dioforti*): a range of Mts. in SW. Arcadia, the resort of Pan and the Nymphs; Arc. 98.

LYCEUM: the schools where Aristotle taught, outside Athens —not inside the walls, as here; P.R. iv. 253.

LYCID, LYCIDAS: Edw. King, of Chr. Coll., and friend of M., drowned at sea, 1637.

LYNX: the OUNCE, q.v.

LYONES: in Camden, a tract of land now lost in the sea, between the Scillies and Cornwall, perhaps here put for Cornwall, but alternatively held to be Brittany, or Armorica, whence Sir Tristram came; P.R. ii. 360.

MAB: the Fairy Queen; L'All. 102.

MACDONNEL (or Macdonald): prob. Alexander Macdonald the younger, one of the chief officers on the royal side under Montrose; the members of this family being called MacCollkittok or 'descendants of Colin the Lame'; Sonn. xi. 9 (A Book was writ).

MACHABEUS: Judas Maccabeus; P.R. iii. 165.

MACHÆRUS: a stronghold of the Kings of Ar. Petraea in the

time of Herod, situated in S. Peraea, E. of the Dead Sea—
the Baptist's prison. It was reckoned by Pliny as second
in strength after Jerusalem; P.R. ii. 22.

MADIAN (as Vulgate): Midian; S.Ag. 281.

MÆNALUS: a Mt. of Arcadia, especially sacred to Pan (the
god of Mænalus); he was often trad. heard here playing
on his pipes; Arc. 102.

MÆONIDES: one of the names given to Homer, either because
he was said to be Mæonian (i.e. Lydian) by birth, or
because Mæon was said to be his father's name; P.L. iii.
35. See HOMER.

MÆOTIS, THE POOLE: Sea of Azov; P.L. ix. 78. See TAURIC
POOL.

MAGNETIC: sb., P.R. ii. 168, the loadstone; adj., P.L. iii. 583.

MAHANAIM: E. of Jordan, S. of the Jabbok, on the bounda-
ries of Gad and Manasseh; P.L. xi. 214.

MAIA: d. of Atlas, and m. of Hermes; P.L. v. 285.

MAIN, THE: the universe; P.R. iv. 457.

MAMMON: ('Wealth', in Syriac) the name of one of the chief
rebel angels; P.L. i. 678, ii. 228, 291.

MANACLES: in special sense of ankle-fetters; S.Ag. 1309; cp.
GIVES.

MANTLE, HAIRY: perhaps referring to the 'river-sponge' of
the Cam; Lyc. 104.

MANTLING: raising both wings to meet each other, cloak-
wise (of a swan); P.L. vii. 439; cp. P.L. v. 279.

MANURING (i.e. 'manœuvring'); in older use of 'manual
labour'; P.L. iv. 628, xi. 28.

MARASMUS: consumption (the 'wasting' sickness); P.L. xi.
487.

MARBLE: transparent, pure, glistening (of the air); P.L. iii.
564.

MARGARET ('honour'd'): Lady M. Ley, d. of James Ley; see
EARL (b) Sonn. x. 14 (Daughter to that good Earl).

MARGIANA (now roughly Khorassan): named from its chief
river Margus (now the Murg Roab or Murgav), in Merv
district of Russ. Cent. Asia; P.R. iii. 317.

MARLE: soil; perhaps attributed by M. to Hell because of
its frequently rich brown and consequently 'burnt' appearance; P.L. i. 296.

MAROCCO (Arab. *Marrakush*): one of the five Barbary states
in N. Africa; P.L. i. 584, xi. 404.

MARSHAL'D, p.p.: at a medieval feast the Marshal superin-
tended the seating and serving of the guests; hence
'marshal' = 'master of the ceremonies'; P.L. ix. 37.

MASSY PROOF: the general sense is of *tried* stability; Il Pens.
158.

MAUGRE: notwithstanding. P.L. iii. 255, ix. 56; P.R. iii. 368.

MEANDER (i.e. Mæander, now the r. Mendereh), which rises
near Celænæ in Phrygia; it was famed for its windings,
and is much haunted by wild swans; Com. 232.

MEATH: mead; P.L. v. 345.

MEDAL: metal; P.L. iii. 592.

MEGÆRA: 'snakie locks that curld'; one of the grim Eume-
nides, or Furies, whose 'snakie locks' (P.L. x. 560) are
described by Æschylus.

MELANCHOLY: see HUMOURS.

MELESIGENES: see HOMER.

MELIBÆAN: Melibæa in Thessaly was famed for its purple
dyes; P.L. xi. 242.

MELIND (Melinda): a seaport and t. in the N. prov. of Zanzibar; P.L. x. 399.

MEMNON: Prince of Ethiopia; the comely s. of Tithonus (the
founder of Susa) and Eos, and brother of the beautiful
Himera or Hemera. He was famed as the builder of Susa's
citadel, and was said to have been slain at Troy; Il Pens.
18; P.L. x. 308. See HIMERA.

MEMPHIS: referred to as great Alcairo; P.L. i. 718. See
ALCAIRO.

MERIDIAN TOWRE: noonday height (of the Sun); P.L. iv.
30; (n. hour) 58.

MEROE ('Nilotic Isle'): in upper Nubia, or Ethiopia, far
south of Syene and under the equator. Though described
as an island by old geographers, it was really an irregular
space between confluent rivers; P.R. iv. 70–71.

MESSAGE: messenger; S.Ag. 635.

MICHAEL: the archangel; leader-in-chief of the warrior
angels; P.L. ii. 294, and numerous other passages.

MICROSCOPE (AERIE): Satan is using the air as the means for
refracting and magnifying the distant view, and implies
that he has given the air these special properties; P.R.
iv. 57.

MIDDLE AIR: this was the 'middle region' of the atmosphere
in late medieval theory; indescribably cold, and full of
vapours, where rain and hail and snow were born; D.F.I.
16; Nat. Od. 164; P.L. i. 516; P.R. i. 39, ii. 117; Vac.
Ex. 41–2; cp. P.L. ii. 718, vi. 314, 536; P.R. i. 39; P.L.
iv. 940.

MILKIE WAY: see GALAXIE.

MIMICS (misprinted mimirs in 1st ed.): players, actors; S.Ag.
1325.

MINCING, adj.: daintily-stepping; Com. 964.

MINCIUS (now Mincio): a tributary of the r. Po, which it
joins near Mantua. As Virgil dwelt on its banks, it here
typifies Roman pastoral verse; Lyc. 86.

MINIMS (from the Lat.): minute humans, pygmies, or dwarfs
—perhaps survivors of some primitive race (the word is
said to be still used in Cornwall); P.L. vii. 482.

MISSIVE: missile; P.L. vi. 519.

MITER'D (i.e. mitred). Masson noted that M. allowed to the
Apostle what he ridiculed in English bishops. But it was
spiritual wickedness, not spiritual goodness, in high places
that M. attacked. He had no hatred of kings qua kings,
but as tyrants (Blakeney, P.R. ii. 463 n.), and he had a
strong friend among the Roman cardinals; Lyc. 112.

MODIN ('and her suburbs'): the original home of the Maccabees near Bethhoron; P.R. iii. 170.

MOGUL, 'great': this title, which means 'Great Mongol', came to be used of the Mongol Empire in India, established by Akbar at Agra (the court being afterwards transferred to Lahore); P.L. xi. 391.

MOLOCH: (a) the chief god of the Ammonites (from Malik = King): Nat. Od. 205.
(b) one of the rebel angels: P.L. i. 392, 417, etc.).

MOLY: the magical herb of Homer (Od. iv. 219–29); Com. 636.

MOMBAZA (Mombasa): Island and t. N. of Zanzibar; P.L. xi. 399.

MONTALBAN: a castle in Quercu, a subdivision of Guienne in Languedoc (France), famous in romance for the deeds of its owner, the Knight Renaud, or Rinaldo; P.L. i. 583.

MOONS, ATTENDANT: satellites (app. a reference to the discovery by Galileo of the satellites of Jupiter and Saturn); P.L. viii. 149.

MOREH ('PLAINE OF'): near Shechem; P.L. xii. 137; cp. 'oak of', Gen. xii. 6, R.V.

MOROCCO: see MAROCCO.

MORRICE: i.e. Morris or Moorish; hence 'morris-dance'; also called the 'Morisco'; (metaph.) Com. 116.

MOSCO: v. KSAR.

MOTEZUME (also in 1st ed.): nearer to the native Aztec form of the name (Moteuczoma, Verity) than the Spanish Montezuma: the famous Emperor of Mexico conquered by Cortez; P.L. xi. 407.

MOULD: in M. means (a) soil; P.L. vi. 473.
(b) substance or essence; Nat. Od. 138; Arc. 73; Com. 17, 244, etc.

MOUNTAIN, TH'OFFENSIVE: the S. summit of Olivet, profaned by Solomon, who built 'high places' there for the gods of his many wives; P.L. i. 443; cp. i. 403; i. 416.

MOUST, sb.: must; unfermented grape-juice; P.L. v. 345; P.R. iv. 16.

MOZAMBIC (Mozambique): a Portuguese Prov. in E. Africa, opp. Madagascar; P.L. iv. 161.

MULCIBER: P.L. i. 740; see VULCAN.

MUSÆUS: trad. a great early Gk. poet, contemporary with Orpheus; Il Pens. 104.

MYRRHINE: cups or vases made of murra, either some kind of mined stone, as in Pliny—Blakeney suggests 'fluorspar'—or glass imitations of it such as the Polychrome Roman glass of which specimens found in Britain are in the B.M. (millefiori glass is also suggested; but myrrhine does not appear to be millefiori, and identification is still uncertain). Cp. Stuart Jones, Compan. Rom. Hist., O.U.P., 1912, p. 442; P.R. iv. 119.

MYSTERIOUSLY, symbolically: 'each stair mysteriously was meant', i.e. had a mystic meaning; cp. Dante's account of the three steps in Purgatory (white, burnt black, and 'porphyry'; Purg. c. ix. 68–92; P.L. iii. 516.

NAIADES: nymphs of rivers or springs; Com. 254; P.R. ii. 355.

NAMANCOS: a stronghold of Spain, in Galicia, near Cape Finisterre; Lyc. 162.

NAPHTHA: fluid asphaltus (mineral or 'rock'-oil); P.L. i. 729.

NARCISSUS (legend of); Com. 237.

NAVIL: central point; Com. 520.

NEBAIOTH: Ishmael's first-born s., but put here for Ishmael himself; his descendants settled in Mt. Seir and Petra (the 'rose-red city') and later became allies of the Jews; P.R. ii. 309.

NECESSITY: i.e. Destiny (or Fate) personified; Arc. 69; cp. P.L. vii. 172; S.Ag. 1666.

NECTAR: a divine liquid of which (a) heavenly beings drink, and (b) in which they bathe. (a) See Vac. Ex. 39; P.L. iv. 240, v. 428, 633, ix. 838; (b) D.F.I. 49; Lyc. 175; Com. 838, etc.

NEGUS: lit. 'King', the Emperor of Abyssinia; P.L. xi. 397.

NEPENTHES: the magical, care-dispelling drink in Homer (Od. iv. 219–21, etc.); Com. 675.

NICE: over-particular or fastidious; Com. 139.

NIGHTINGALE: see Com. 234 (metaph.), 566; P.L. iv. 602, 771, v. 40 (Nightingal), vii. 435; Sonn. 1 (O Nightingale).

NIGHT-RAVEN (νυκτικόραξ): a raven in poetic usage only, neither ravens nor crows being night-birds. It is now identified (see Sir D'Arcy Thompson, Gloss. of Gk. Birds, new ed. s.v., and Liddell and Scott, 1936) as the long-eared owl; L'All. 7.

NIGHT-STEEDS: prob. the steeds of Night's car; others say night-hags (or night-mares?); Nat. Od. 236; cp. P.L. ii. 662.

NIMROD: the 'mighty hunter' but not, as in M., the builder of Babel; P.L. xii. 44.

NINEVEE: Nineveh, confused by M. at first with Susa. See NINUS. M. takes Jonah iii. 3 to mean the compass of the city 'within her wall', but the passage only says 'an exceedingly great city of three days' journey', probably including all her suburbs—cp. 'greater than Babylon' (Strabo); of 60 m. circumference (Diodorus); P.R. iii. 275.

NINUS: trad. founder of Nineveh, the city of Ninus (but the Assyrian name, Ninuwa, or Ninua, is more probably connected with the word for 'Fish' as it is written in cuneiform, with the 'fish' character); P.R. iii. 275.

NIPHATES: 'the Assyrian Mount' (Niphates—10,000 ft.—is explained as meaning 'Snow' mountain). Part of the Taurus range in Armenia, W. of Lake Van, on the Assyrian border; P.L. iii. 742; formerly supposed near Eden.

NISIBIS (now Nisibin): a famous t. of NE. Mesopotamia on the Tigris, flourishing down to the Parthian Period, when it was taken, lost, and retaken by Rome; P.R. iii. 291.

NISROC: one of the chief rebel angels; the name is taken from 2 Kings xix. 37. P.L. vi. 447.

NITRE: saltpetre. Hence nitrous powder: gunpowder; P.L. iv. 815, vi. 512; cp. P.L. ii. 937.

NOCENT: harmful; P.L. ix. 186.

NORUMBEGA: in seventeenth-century maps a tract of S. and
SE. Canada, at that time including the states of N. York
and Maine; P.L. x. 696.

NOTUS: the SW. wind; P.L. x. 702.

NYSEIAN ISLE: this island of *Nysa* (whence the name *Dionysus*) is described as 'girt by the river Triton', and was
situate off the coast of Lybia, near Tunis; in tradition it
was the island where Amalthea's 'florid son' (Bacchus)
grew up, being hidden by Hammon (or Ammon), the
'Lybian Jove', from the jealous eyes of Rhea. This
account, which explains the whole passage, is from Diodorus Siculus, iii. 67; P.L. iv. 275. See also HAMMON
(AMMON).


OB: the r. Obi in W. Siberia; P.L. ix. 78.

OBLIGE: to make liable to penalty; to 'render guilty'; P.L.
ix. 980.

OBNOXIOUS: liable, exposed to harm or injury; S.Ag. 106;
P.L. ix. 170, 1094.

OBSEQUIOUS: (a) complaisant, but perhaps with root sense
of following in the train, as night after day; P.L. vi. 10;
cp. vi. 783; S.Ag. 1732.
(b) compliant; P.L. viii. 509.

OBSTRICTION: obligation; S.Ag. 312.

OBVIOUS: lying or being in the way (as in Lat.); P.L. vi. 69.

OCCASION: personified; P.R. iii. 173.

ŒALIA (1st ed. reading for OECHALIA): a t. in Thessaly;
P.L. ii. 542.

ŒTA, Mt. (now *Katavothra*): mountain-range in Central
Greece between Ætolia and Thessaly, the t. of Trachis
being situated on part of it; P.L. ii. 545.

OFFENSIVE MOUNTAIN: see MOUNTAIN, OFFENSIVE.

OFFICIATE: to supply; P.L. viii. 22.

OFFICIOUS: ministering, obliging; P.L. ii. 102.

OLD MAN ELOQUENT: Isocrates (the orator), said to have
expired on hearing of Philip's victory over the Athenians
(338 B.C.); Sonn. x. (title in Camb. MSS., To Lady M. Ley)
7–8 (Daughter to that good Earl).

OLIVE, the (as a symbol of peace): Nat. Od. 47; P.L. xi. 856.

OLIVE-GROVE of Academe: see ACADEME.

OLYMPIAS: wife of Philip II of Macedon., and m. of Alexander
(traditionally by Zeus); P.L. ix. 509.

OMNIFIC: all-creating; P.L. vii. 217.

OOSE: prob. the Northamptonshire Ouse, flowing ultimately
into the Wash; Vac. Ex. 92.

OPHION: one of the oldest of the Titans, the first, with
Eurynome, to rule Olympus, before the time of Kronos
(Saturn); P.L. x. 581.

OPHIR: one of the chief trad. sites of Mt. Ophir was the
mountain near Malacca in the Malay Peninsula (anciently
called the 'Golden Chersonese'). M. evidently had doubts,

since he speaks of 'Sofala thought Ophir' (the southern-most prov. of Zanzibar). There can be little doubt, how-ever, that Solomon's Ophir was really in Southern Arabia; P.L. xi. 392, 400; P.R. iv. 74.

OPHIUCHUS (in Gk. lit. 'Serpent-holder'): a constellation next to, but quite distinct from, Serpens; P.L. ii. 708.

OPHIUSA: the 'I. of Serpents' (the 'Colubraria' of the Romans) now Formentera, one of the Balearic Isles; or Iviza; P.L. x. 528.

OPPORTUNE: liable or exposed (to injury or harm); P.L. ix. 481.

OPPOSITE: two planets are said to be in opposition (or 'opposite') when separated by 180° (or half the zodiac), a fatal omen (astrol.); P.L. vi. 314, x. 659, etc. And cp. P.L. ii. 803.

OPPROBRIOUS HILL: (the Mt. of Olives, because of the temple to Moloch built there by Solomon); P.L. i. 403. Also called 'Hill of Scandal' and 'Offensive Mountain', q.v.

OPS: wife of Cronos (Saturn); id. with Rhea or Cybele; P.L. x. 584; id. with R. goddess of Plenty; P.L. x. 584.

ORBICULAR: spherical; P.L. x. 381, cp. iii. 718.

ORC: a grampus or whale? P.L. xi. 835.

ORCUS: the god of the lower world = Pluto; P.L. ii. 964.

ORE: in sense of 'gold'; Lyc. 170.

OREAD: a mountain nymph; P.L. ix. 387.

ORGAN (M.'s favourite instrument); Nat. Od. 130; Il Pens. 161; P.L. i. 708, vii. 596, xi. 556.

ORIENT: in earlier sense of 'rising'; P.L. ii. 399, iv. 644, vi. 524.

ORIGINALS (adj. for sub.): originators; P.L. ii. 375.

ORION: the constellation; P.L. i. 305.

ORMUS (or HORMUZ): formerly ARMUZA, a great mart for pearls and gems (on an island near the opening of the Persian Gulf). Taken by D'Albuquerque in 1507, it flourished greatly till taken by Shah Abbas, 1662; P.L. ii. 2.

ORONTES (now *Nahr el 'Asi*): the frontier stream of N. Syria, emptying itself into the Gulf of Issus; P.L., iv. 273, ix. 80.

ORPHEUS: one of M.'s favourite Bards; L'All. 145; Il Pens. 105; Lyc. 58; P.L. iii. 17.

ORUS (properly HORUS from Eg. *Her* or *Hor*): (a) the falcon-headed sun-god of Egypt, s. of Osiris and Isis; Nat. Od. 212. (b) the name used by M. for one of the rebel angels; P.L. i. 478.

OSIRIS: (a) husband of Isis and f. of Horus (Orus). Trad. the earliest introducer of agriculture and viticulture into Egypt. Became chief agricultural god, and hence chief god of the Dead, Eg. mummies being moulded in his image. The Bull Apis (Eg. Hapi) was one of his manifesta-tions, or theophanies; (Nat. Od. 213) different bull-theophanies (Apis, Mnevis, Bouchis) appearing in different Eg. cities.
(b) Osiris, Isis, Orus, and their train, names used by M. for rebel angels; P.L. i. 478.

OUGHLY-HEADED ('monsters'): understood to be a fanciful
spelling of ugly-headed, and commonly so corrected by
modern editors; is it possible that M. may have followed
some variant spelling of 'ouphe', which is found in use
with oaf, auf, or alf for 'Elf' (in which case it would signify
'oaf-headed' or 'elf-headed')? It seems best in any case
to keep the spelling 'oughly' as here; Com. 695.

OUNCE, the lynx; Com. 71; P.L. iv. 344, vii. 466.

OUSE. See OOSE.

OUTFLEW: 'shot forth', i.e. were flourished; P.L. i. 663.

OUTLANDISH: foreign, hence extravagant (of flatteries);
P.R. iv. 125.

OUTLAST, vb. to outlive; D.F.I. 3.

OUTLIVE: to survive; Pass. 7; P.L. xi. 538.

OUTRAGEOUS: excessively violent, with unrestrained fury;
P.L. ii. 485, v. 587, vii. 212, x. 232.

OVERBUILD: to build over, to span; P.L. x. 416.

OVER-EXQUISITE: over-particular, over-careful; Com. 359.

OVERPLY: to exhaust the strength by excessive effort. Sonn.
to C. Skinner (Cyrack, this three), 10.

OXUS: the great r. of Central Asia (now called the *Jihoun* or
*Amou*), flowing into the sea of Aral. But 'Samarchand by
Oxus', as M. calls it, is about 100 m. from the river; P.L.
xi. 389.

PACKING: trickeries; Forc. of Consc. 14.

PALE (studious Cloysters): if 'pale' is here a noun = an
'enclosed place', like 'cloisters', it is surely redundant.
And M.'s habit of placing a noun between two adjectives
seems to show it should be adjectival; if so, he is thinking
of his beloved 'shadows', as in P.R. iv. 243, studious walks
and *shades*; Il Pens. 156.

PALES: protecting god (or goddess?) of farms and flocks;
(treated by M. as goddess); P.L. ix. 393.

PALMER: strictly a pilgrim who brought a palm-leaf home
with him; Com. 189. For palm-leaves as emblems of victory,
see S.Ag. 1735; Mus. 14.

PALPABLE OBSCURE: darkness that may be felt; P.L. ii. 406;
cp. P.L. xii. 188.

PAN: (*a*) As a type of Christ; Nat. Od. 89.
(*b*) For the god himself; Arc. 106; Com. 176, 268; P.L.
iv. 266, 707; P.R. ii. 190.

PANDÆMONIUM: the name of Satan's capital; P.L. i. 756,
x. 424.

PANDORA: trad. the first woman, created by Hephaistos at
the bidding of Zeus, to avenge the theft of fire by Prometheus; P.L. iv. 714.

PANEAS (Banias): the Gk. name of Dan, named from the
cave of Pan at Cæsarea Philippi, near the fountains of
Jordan; P.L. iii. 535.

PANIM (P.L. i. 765), paynim (P.R. iii. 343): Pagan.

PANOPE: a sea-nymph, one of the fifty beautiful daughters
of Nereus; Lyc. 99.

PAQUIN (for Pekin, now Peiping): the recent capital of China, before the establishment of a more inland capital. P.L. xi. 390. See also CAMBALU.

PARAGOND, p.pt.: paralleled or compared with another person or object; P.L. x. 426.

PARALLAX: apparent displacement or change of position of an object seen from different-angled view points; P.R. iv. 40.

PARAMOUNT, sb.: supreme chief (a law term for the head of an estate); P.L. ii. 508.

PARANYMPH; 'Friend of the Bridegroom' (the Gk. word used in St. John iii. 29); corresponding to our own phrase 'best-man'; S.Ag. 1020.

PARLIAMENT: Sonn. x. 5 (Daughter to that good Earl); ('Parliament') Forc. of Consc. 15.

PARTHENOPE: one of the Sirens, trad. d. of Achelous, whose 'tomb' was said to have been at Naples, and after whom N. was sometimes called; Com. 879.

PARTIAL: prejudiced in their own favour; P.L. ii. 552.

PARTICULAR: circumstantial, S.Ag. 1595.

PARTITION: in sense of compartment, P.L. viii. 105.

PASSENGER: a wayfarer, Com. 39.

PAYNIM: see PANIM.

PEAL: to assail, or 'din' the ears; P.L. ii. 920; cp. S.Ag. 235, 906.

PECHORA: see PETSORA.

PECULIAR (adj. for sb.): exclusive property; P.L. vii. 368.

PEEL, vb.: to plunder or pillage; P.R. iv. 136.

PEER: one of the Twelve Peers of France, P.R. iii. 343.

PEGASEAN (of the Winged Horse of the Muses): hence 'P. Wing' means in M. the vehicle of poetic inspiration; P.L. vii. 4.

PELLEAN CONQUEROR: Alexander (named from his birthplace at Pella, Macedonia); P.R. ii. 196.

PELLEAS, PELLENORE: knights of Arthur's 'Round Table'; P.R. ii. 361.

PELOPS: Il Pens. 99. F. of Atreus, and grandf. of Agamemnon.

PELORUS (now Capo di Faro): the NE. cape of Sicily; P.L. i. 232.

PENANCE: penitence; S.Ag. 738.

PENDANT WORLD: not the Earth, but the Universe; P.L. ii. 1052.

PENDULOUS: suspended (of the Earth); P.L. iv. 1000.

PENNON: a pinion or wing; P.L. ii. 933, vii. 441.

PENNS (i.e. 'pens' or feathers): see SUMM'D.

PENSIONERS: personal attendants or 'body-guard' of a king (mostly old pensioned soldiers), like the bodyguard of Henry VIII and that of Queen Elizabeth; Il Pens. 10.

PENURIOUS: miserly, parsimonious; Com. 726,

**PEOR** (more fully Baal-Peor): a god held by some to be identical with Chemosh, the god of licentiousness worshipped by the Moabites; Nat. Od. 197; ('Chemos') P.L. i. 406–12.

**PEREA** (Perœa): the Gk. name given by the Romans to Transjordania, esp. Moab and Gilead; P.R. ii. 24.

**PERIPATETICS**: the School of Philosophy founded by Aristotle; P.R. iv. 279.

**PERNICIOUS** ('with one touch to fire'): baleful or ruinous (here perhaps with some sense of swiftness); P.L. vi. 520.

**PERSEIS, PRIESTESS OF PHŒBUS**: Circe (whose m. was the ocean-nymph Perse). v. CIRCE.

**PERSEPHONE** (Gk.): = the Roman PROSERPINA, q.v.

**PERSEPOLIS**: the Gk. name of the great city that succeeded Pasargadæ as the Persian capital. Later, in the Middle Ages, it was called *Istakhar*, now *Takht-i-Jamshid* (or *Chihal-Minar*); i.e. Throne of Jamshid, or the Forty Pillars, no doubt from the surviving pillars of the Palace; P.R. iii. 284.

**PEST, PESTILENCE**: the Plague; (metaph. of Death) P.L. ii. 735; cp. ('pestilence') D.F.I. 68; P.L. ii. 711; P.R. iii. 412.

**PETRIFIC**: petrifying; P.L. x. 294.

**PETSORA: PECHORA** (Petzora, in M.'s *History of Mosco*): a r. flowing into a gulf of the same name on the Arctic Ocean, in the extreme NE. of Russia; P.L. x. 292.

**PHARAOH'S DAUGHTER**: see 1 Kings iii. 1. She was the Egyptian princess (cp. Song of Sol. vii. 1) whom Solomon married; P.L. ix. 442.

**PHILOSOPHER**: in sense of alchemist; P.L. iii. 601.

**PHINEUS**: the king of Thrace, old, blind, and a seer, who was tormented by the Harpies; P.L. iii. 36.

**PHLEGETON**: one of the rs. of Hades; P.L. ii. 580.

**PHLEGRA** (now Kassándra): former name of the Isthmus of Pallene (the westernmost of three headlands) in Macedonia, where the ancient conflict between the giants and the gods is said to have taken place; P.L. i. 577.

**PHŒNIX**: the beautiful solitary Arabian bird that was believed, after completing each fifth century, to immolate itself and rise from its own ashes—being, acc. to the Rabbis, the only bird that did not eat of the forbidden fruit, and therefore remained immortal; P.L. v. 272; S.Ag. 1699–1707.

**PIEMONT, ON THE LATE MASSACHER IN**: this massacre, by the Duke of Savoy, took place in 1655; Sonn. xv. (Avenge O Lord).

**PIGMEAN RACE**: i.e. the Pygmies or race of African Dwarfs; P.L. i. 780.

**PINACLE**: (of the Temple) not what is now so called, but the crowning point of the lofty columnar 'Porch' overlooking the Tyropœon Valley, reminiscent of its Mesopotamian origin, in form between the square ramps of the Babel Tower and the minaret; P.R. iv. 549.

**PINDARUS** (PINDAR): Sonn. viii. 11 (Captain or Colonel); cp. P.R. iv. 257 ('Dorian lyric odes').

PIN-FOLD: a pound, for confining or impounding 'strays', here metaph. of the world; Com. 7.

PIONER: pioneer; P.L. i. 676; P.R. iii. 330.

PLANTER, THE SOVRAN: in reference to God; P.L. iv. 691.

PLATAN: a plane-tree; P.L. iv. 478.

PLATO: Il Pens. 89; P.L. iii. 472; P.R. iv. 245.

PLAUSIBLE: genuinely deserving of applause; P.R. iii. 393.

PLEIADES: the group of stars into which the daughters of Atlas were said to have been changed (hence called the 'Atlantick Sisters')—to be found in the constellation Taurus; P.L. vii. 374; cp. P.L. x. 674.

PLUTO, or Hades: god of the Infernal Regions (the name means 'wealth'); for his various names see L'All. 149; Il Pens. 107; P.L. x. 444. [Acc. to Plato, Hades was called Pluto 'for euphony'.]

PLY: (a) to hasten; P.L. ii. 642, 954.
  (b) to apply oneself; Com. 750; P.L. ix. 201.

POISE: (a) give weight to; P.L. ii. 905.
  (b) balance; Com. 410; P.L. v. 579.

POLITIC, POLITICIAN: intriguing; P.R. iii. 400; S.Ag. 1195.

POLLUTE, p.p.: polluted; Nat. Od. 41.

POMONA: goddess of fruit; P.L. v. 378; ix. 393, 394.

POMP: a magnificent procession or train; P.L. vii. 564.

POMPEY, YOUNG: but P. beat Mithradates when forty-four; P.R. iii. 35.

PONENT: wind of the sunset; opp. to Levant; P.L. x. 704.

PONTIFICAL: bridge-building, with veiled religious allusion; P.L. x. 313.

PONTIFICE: a bridge; P.L. x. 348.

PORT: (a) 'Ivorie Port', i.e. gate; P.L. iv. 778.
  (b) to port arms: to carry aslope in both hands, pointing across the left shoulder (mil.); P.L. iv. 980 (with ported spears).

POURLIEU (P.L. ii. 833), purlieu (P.L. iv. 404): the precincts or outskirts of a palace, a forest, etc.

PREAMBLE: prelude; P.L. iii. 367.

PRECINCTS: confines (of light); P.L. iii. 88.

PRESBYTER: see PRIEST.

PRETENDED: stretched, spread before screen-wise (as Lat.); P.L. x. 872.

PRETOR: a civil officer, equivalent to Mayor or Magistrate, at Rome; P.R. iv. 63.

PREVENIENT: forestalling; P.L. xi. 3.

PREVENT: to forestall; Nat. Od. 24.

PRIEST: abbreviation of Presbyter (Gk. πρεσβύτερος); Forc. Consc. 20.

PRIME WHEEL OF CREATION: see SPHEAR.

PRINCIPALITIES: the seventh order of heavenly beings, here of the rebel angels; P.L. vi. 447; x. 186.

PROCINCT: in p., i.e. in prompt readiness; P.L. vi. 19 (cp. SUCCINCT, q.v.).

PRODIGIOUS: monstrous, unnatural; P.L. ii. 625, xii. 683.

PROEM: preface; P.L. ix. 549.

PROLIFIC: fertilizing, generative; P.L. vii. 280.

PROSERPIN, PROSERPINA: P.L. iv. 269, ix. 396, etc.

PROSPECTIVE GLASS: glass by which the future can be fore-cast; Vac. Ex. 71.

PROWEST: most valiant; P.R. iii. 342.

PSYCHE (the soul): beloved and wedded to Eros. (M. uses Plato's story to suggest that there is love in Heaven—i.e. spiritual love); Com. 1003–11.

PUNCTUAL SPOT: a spot the size of a mere point in com-parison; P.L. viii. 23.

PUNIE (lit. later-born, Fr. *puis-ne*, hence inferior); P.L. ii. 367.

PURCHASE: (*a*) prey or quarry (hunting term); P.L. x. 579; Com. 607.
 (*b*) to gain; P.L. x. 500.

PURFL'D: decorated with a coloured border (e.g. with blue and white, gold and pearl, etc.); fig. of the rainbow; Com. 995.

PURPOSE: conversation; P.L. iv. 337, viii. 337.

PYRAMIDS: P.L. v. 755; On Shaks. 4.

PYTHON: the famous serpent slain by the sun-god, whence Apollo's name of 'Pythian'; P.L. x. 530, 531.

QUADRATE: in 'square' formation; P.L. vi. 62.

QUADRATURE: M. describes the territory of heaven as being of four-square shape (like the Heavenly Jerusalem of Rev. xxi. 16); P.L. x. 351. Earlier (P.L. ii. 1048) he had declared its shape to be uncertain ('undetermin'd square or round').

QUAFF: vb. to drink in (met.) immortality and joy; P.L. v. 638 (added in 1674 edn.).

QUAINT: exquisite, pretty; Lyc. 139; strange, Nat. Od. 194.

QUARRY: (*a*) a squared stone block (as in Latin, cp. Pliny's *saxum quadratum*); hence, a stone meant to bear an in-scription; Pass. 46.
 (*b*) a place for quarrying stone; P.L. v. 756.

QUARRY: object of pursuit, or chace; P.L. x. 281.

QUATERNION: 'in quat.' i.e. in fourfold combination; (of the elements, Air, Earth, Water, Fire); P.L. v. 131.

QUILL: a pipe or tube used as a musical instrument; Lyc. 188.

QUILOA: (or *Kilwa*) Island and t. off E. Africa, a province of Zanzibar; P.L. xi. 399.

QUINTESSENCE: a fifth 'essence' apart from (or supplemen-tary to) the four elements (in Plato and Aristotle); P.L. iii. 716, vii. 244.

QUINTILIAN: M. Fabius, b. in Spain, A.D. 40, the most cele-brated of Roman rhetoricians. Sonn. xi. (A Book was writ), 11.

QUINTIUS: L. Qu. Cincinnatus, the Dictator; P.R. ii. 446.

QIRE: M.'s spelling of 'choir' (as in the Prayer-book rubrics —'in quires and places where they sing'); Nat. Od. 27, 115; Il Pens. 162; (of birds) P.L. iv. 264, etc.

RABBA: the capital of the Ammonite country; P.L. i. 397.

RAMATH-LECHI: S.Ag. 145.

RAMIEL: ('Exaltation of God') one of the rebel angels (M.'s authority for this name is unknown); P.L. vi. 372.

RAMOTH (in Gilead): P.R. i. 373.

RATHE: old positive form of 'rather' (in the sense of 'soon' or 'early'); Lyc. 142.

REALTIE: reality; P.L. vi. 115 (perhaps an error for 'fealtie').

REBECK (Ar. *rĕbab*): a fiddle; it reached Spain through the Moors; L'All. 94.

REBUFF: repulsion; P.L. ii. 936.

RECORDER: a kind of flageolet, with a pitch an octave above the flute, and very soft in tone; P.L. i. 551.

RECREANT: renegade, apostate; P.R. iii. 138.

RECURE, vb. to recover; P.L. xii. 393.

REDOUBLE: (a) to re-echo; Sonn. xv. (Avenge, O Lord).
  (b) to repeat; P.L. ix. 562.
  (c) to make twice as great; S.Ag. 923.

REDOUND: (a) to be superfluous or excessive; P.L. v. 438; cp. ii. 889.
  (b) to return or rebound upon; P.L. iii. 85, vii. 57, x. 739.

RED SEA: v. SERBONIAN BOG.

REGION: the upper air, P.L. vii. 425; also in the phrase the 'airy region'; Nat. Od. 103.

REGORGE: to gorge to surfeit; S.Ag. 167.

REGULUS: M. Atilius R., the heroic R., prisoner of the 1st Punic War. P.R. ii. 446.

REINS: the kidneys; P.L. vi. 346; S.Ag. 609.

RELIQUE: P.L. v. 273, On Shaks., 3; cp. P.L. iii. 491.

RELUCTANT: forcing violent way through (of flames); P.L. vi. 58.

REMARK, vb.: to distinguish; S.Ag. 1309.

REMEDILES: irreparable Circ. 17; ('remediless') P.L. ix. 919, S.Ag. 648.

REPROBATE (Gk. ἀδόκιμος): used especially in metallurgy of an alloy that will not endure the trial, but shows itself to be adulterate when tested. So in Jer. vi. 30 (A.V.) of 'reprobate silver'); cp. the description *of the metal workers* in Hell; P.L. i. 697; and cp. P.R. i. 491; S.Ag. 1685.

RESONANT: repeating or re-echoing the same notes from part to part (as in a fugue); P.L. xi. 559.

RESPIRATION: a refreshing; P.L. xii. 540.

RETORTED: flung back; P.L. v. 906, x. 751.

RHEA: (a) wife of Saturn, and m. of Jove; P.L. i. 513.
  (b) wife of the Libyan 'Jupiter Ammon'; P.L. iv. 279.

RHENE: the Rhine; P.L. i. 353.

RHEUM: rheumatism; P.L. xi. 485.

RHODOPE, Mt.: the W. continuation of the Hæmus range, between Thrace and Macedonia and the source of the Hebrus; P.L. vii. 35.

RHOMB: (a) an infantry formation in the shape of a diamond (or acute-angled parallelogram); P.R. iii. 309 (mil.). (b) wheel-like revolution of the heavens (from Gk. ῥόμβος, wheel); P.L. viii. 134.

RIDGES: ranks; P.L. vi. 236.

RIN'D: spelt by M. as if pp. from a vb. 'rine' = rinded (i.e. furnished with a rind or husk); P.L. v. 342. See also RINDE.

RINDE: a thick outer coat or skin; Com. 664, etc.; cp. RIN'D.

RINGLET: the curled foliage of trees; Arc. 47.

RIMMON: the storm god, worshipped in Damascus, whose name was taken by M. for one of his rebel angels; P.L. i. 467.

RIVER-DRAGON: a crocodile, used fig. of Pharaoh; P.L. xii. 191.

RIVER-HORSE: hippopotamus; P.L. vii. 474.

RIVERS: probably in allusion to the sons of Sir John Rivers; Vac. Ex. 91.

ROBUSTIOUS: superlatively vigorous; S.Ag. 569.

ROD: a sunbeam (Heaven's fiery rod); S.Ag. 549.

ROMULUS: in this passage the 's. of Mars . . . violent death'. M. seems to allude to the tradition that R. was murdered by the senators (Liv. i. 16); the death of Alexander (the reputed s. of Jove) of fever brought on by drink took place in 323 B.C. at Babylon; P.R. iii. 84.

RUBRIC, THE STARRY: fig. of the directions, or prognostications, to be read in the stars; like the law-headings in red ochre (rubrica) of ancient Rome; P.R. iv. 393.

RUTHERFORD (1673 ed. ROTHERFORD): Samuel Rutherford, a prominent Divine of M.'s time, Professor of Divinity at St. Andrews and one of the eight Scottish members of the Westminster Assembly; Forc. Consc. 8.

SABEAN (i.e. SABÆAN): of the land of Saba or Sheba in SW. Arabia ('Araby the blest'); P.L. iv. 162; cp. P.R. ii. 363.

SABRINA, trad. d. of Locrine, q.v.; Com. 826, 859, 922.

SAFFRON: the colour of the marriage robe in ancient Rome; L'All. 126.    [P.L. x. 281.

SAGACIOUS: keen-scented (hunting term, used of hounds);

SAINT, LATE ESPOUSED: M.'s 2nd wife, Cath. Woodcock, d. 1657; Sonn. (Methought I saw).

SALEM: (a) Salim, near the springs of Ænon on the Jordan— exact position unknown; P.R. ii. 21. (b) Jerusalem; Pass. 39.

SALMANASSAR: this means—not Shalmaneser IV, as is often stated, but Shalmaneser V, who besieged, but did not take, Samaria. The city was taken in 722 B.C. by Shar-ukin or Sargon (Is. xx), an Assyrian general, who thereupon seized the throne and reigned as Sargon II (721 B.C.), and became the f. of Sennacherib; P.R. iii. 278.

SALVE: to redeem or save: e.g. 'salve his credit'; P.R. iv. 12.

SAMARCHAND ('by Oxus'): earlier called Maracanda, a great city of what was once called Sogdiana (q.v.); in the thirteenth century it became the capital of Timur i Leng, commonly called Tamurlane, who was buried there. But it is at least 100 m. from Oxus. Now in Russian Turkestan; P.L. xi. 389.

SAMOED SHOAR: NE. of Siberia; P.L. x. 696.

SAMOS: the Island. (Note that Samos is not one of the Cyclades, but M. may be referring to the Gk. islands generally); P.L. v. 265.

SANGUINE: blood-red, e.g. that sanguine flower (of the Hyacinth); Lyc. 106.

SARMATIANS: the S. of Europe, including a number of vague nomad ethnic groups between the Vistula and the Volga, the Asiatic groups extending to the Caucasus, Astrakhan, Kazan, etc.; P.R. iv. 78.

SARRA: one of the old names of Tyre; hence used of the Tyrian purple dye; P.L. xi. 243.

SCALES OF FATE, THE: P.L. iv. 997, 1014 (with ref. to Libra, the constellation; P.L. x. 676).

SCANDAL, HILL OF: the S. crest of Olivet; P.L. i. 416; see also OPPROBRIOUS HILL, and MOUNTAIN, OFFENSIVE.

SCIPIO: P.L. ix. 510; P.R. iii. 34; see AFRICAN.

SCORPION: the constellation; P.L. iv. 998, x. 328.

'SCOTCH WHAT D'YE CALL': this was the Rev. Robt. Baillie, Prof. of Divinity at Glasgow, and afterwards Principal, a strong critic of M.'s 'Divorce Pamphlets'; Forc. Consc. 12.

SCRANNEL: shrivelled and thin, harsh, rasping, 'screeching' (still used in northern Eng. dialects; cp. scrawny, scranky, etc.); Lyc. 124.

SCULLES: shoals of fish; in some southern Eng. dialects, 'shoals' of herrings are 'sculls'; cp. also the sailor's 'Schools' of fish; P.L. vii. 402.

SCYLLA: a beautiful maiden beloved by Glaucus; changed by Circe (who in jealousy of her threw magic herbs into the water where she bathed) into a monster from the waist downwards, ending in the tail of a fish, encircled by barking dogs; Com. 257, hence metaph. of Sin; P.L. ii. 660, 795.

SDEIND: disdained (cp. Spenser's 'Sdeigne'); P.L. iv. 50.

SEA-IDOL: Dagon, the fish-god ('upward man and downward fish'); P.L. i. 462; S.Ag. 13.

SEAVENTIMES-WEDDED MAID: Sara, in the Book of Tobit; P.L. v. 223. See ASMODEUS.

SECHEM (i.e. Shechem): a c. in central Palestine, between Ebal and Gerizim; P.L. xii. 136.

SECULAR: age-old; in sense of living for 'ages' (of the Phoenix); S.Ag. 1707.

SECURE: care-free; L'All. 91, etc.

SELEUCIA (the 'Great'): the magnificent city built by Seleucus I (Nicator, d. 280 B.C.) on the W. bank of the Tigris,

20 m. SE. of Baghdad; he ruled it from Antioch, and it was later eclipsed by Ctesiphon, q.v.; P.L. iv. 212; P.R. iii. 291.

SEMELE: d. of Cadmus, k. of Thebes, and m. of Bacchus. Beloved of Zeus, she was slain when he visited her as Thunder-god, but her child Dionysus (or Bacchus) was saved by Z. She was also called Thyóně; P.R. ii. 187.

SENATE: (a) of Rome; Sonn. to Sir H. V. the younger, 2 (Vane, young in yeares).    (b) the Seventy Elders; P.L. xii. 225.

SENESHAL: house-steward; P.L. ii. 38.

SENIR: properly an ancient Amorite name of Mt. Hermon, but M. app. means some south-easterly range; P.L. xii. 146.

SENNAAR: the Plain of Shinar; P.L. iii. 467.

SENT: (It.) M.'s spelling = scent, P.L. x. 267.

SENTERY: sentry; P.L. ii. 412.

SEPTENTRION (i.e. northern) constellation, the Plough; P.R. iv. 31; the 7 stars near the N. Pole were called 'septentriones'.

SERAPIS (L. Sĕrăpis = Gk. Serăpis): the Eg. Usir-Hāpi was the Osirified or 'Underworld' form of the Bull god Hāpi, whose cult, Hellenized by Ptolemy I, spread over the Gk. world; the most famous Serapeum (T. of Sĕrăpis) being at Alexandria, the lesser at Memphis (Wilcken, *Urkunden der Ptolemäerzeit* ii. 82, 85); P.L. i. 720.

SERBONIAN BOG (Hebr. *Yam Suf*): on the coast of Lower Egypt, separated from the sea by a strip of sand (Herod. iii. 5). The idea of the loss of whole armies here is from D. Siculus (i. 30); Darius II (Nothus) lost *part* of his army there on his invasion of Egypt; P.L. ii. 592. See BUSIRIS. (Note that the words 'Red Sea' do not occur in the Hebrew but in the Gk. LXX translation.)

SERICANA: a vaguely described country, lying WSW. of China; P.L. iii. 438.

SERRALIONA: W. Afr. (mountainous) colony, with 6 months' rainy season; P.L. x. 703.

SETIA: an ancient (originally Volscian) city of Latium, which became a Roman colony, and later provided some of the best wine in Italy; P.R. iv. 117.

SEWER: the Head-servant in charge of the Dishes at a medieval feast; P.L. ix. 38.

SEXTILE: in astrology the influences of stars or planets were said to be benign or favourable whenever they were 'in trine', or 'in sextile', i.e. when their rays met indirectly instead of being in direct opposition. Here 'Sextile' means at a distance of 60° (or a sixth of the zodiac) from each other; P.L. x 659.

SHAKSPEAR: with M.'s lines On S., compare L'All. 133.

SHINAR: see SENNAAR.

SHOALE (of fish): see SCULLE.                                    [147.

SHROUD, sb.: shelter or concealment; Nat. Od. 218; Com.

SIBMA (or Sibmah): a valley in Transjordania, once famous for its vineyards (Isa. xvi. 8); P.L. i. 410.

SIBYL: see SYBIL.

SIDEBORD (STATELY): evidently in the earlier (medieval) sense of a shelf or shelves for drinking cups at the side of the hall; a sideboard of state is a court 'cup-board', or shelves, for royal plate. Court cupboards of five shelves (built in tiers) being a privilege reserved for kings, it was thus a royal compliment to Christ ('stately', here meaning royal); P.R. ii. 350.

SIDING: defending or protecting; Com. 212.

SILENT (of the moon): dark, not shining (at end of month); S. Ag. 87, as in Latin, cp. Columella, i (Loeb).

SILLY: in old sense of innocent, simple, harmless; Nat. Od. 92.

SILO (SHILOH): t. in Ephraim where the ark was kept, down to the time of Samuel; S.Ag. 1674. Silo as in Vulg.

SILOA'S BROOK: the stream that formed the Pool of Siloam; [P.L. i. 11.

SILVAN, SILVANUS: see SYLVAN.

SINÆAN (KINGS): i.e. Emperors of China; P.L. xi. 390.

SIRENS: acc. to one account there were three, Parthenope, Ligea, and Leucosia, and three small rocky islets off Cape Misenum in Campania were named as their abode (Æn. v. 864); Com. 253, 878; Arc. 63; Mus. 1. See SPHEAR.

SIROCCO (from Ar. 'Shark' or 'Sharq'): the E. or SE. wind; P.L. x. 706. [P.L. i. 413.

SITTIM (i.e. *Abel-Sittim* or *Shittim*) in the plains of Moab;

SKIE ROBES: i.e. robes dyed with the hues of the rainbow, perhaps also with some suggestion of their fitness to be worn in heaven; Com. 83; cp. P.L. v. 285.

SKINNER: see CYRIACK.

SOCK: the light shoe worn by actors in R. Comedy; L'All. 132.

SODOM: P.L. i. 503; x. 562.

SOFALA ('thought Ophir'): properly pronounced Sofâla, the Saphara of Ptolemy, a district of Mozambique in Portuguese E. Africa; P.L. xi. 400.

SOGDIANA (now roughly Turkestan and Bokhara) still called Sogd, the northernmost prov. of Parthia, between the Oxus and Jaxartes; P.R. iii. 302.

SOLSTICES: the two points in the apparent path of the sun when it is furthest (N. or S.) from the Equator; Pass. 6; P.L. x. 656.

'SONS OF GOD': in Christ's teaching confined to those who are willing to accept His Kingdom. Not so SATAN (see Blakeney); P.R. iv. 520.

SOPHI, the Bactrian: i.e. the 'Sâfi' (pron. broadly Sofi), i.e. the 'Elect' Rulers of Persia, a title used during the *Sufawi* dynasty; P.L. x. 433.

SORD: sward; P.L. xi. 433.

SOREC: thought to be Surar, in the neighbourhood of Ekron, the (Philistine) city of Delilah; S.Ag. 229.

SPAN, vb.: app. to 'space out' words in reading, giving full unforced natural stress and value to each syllable; Sonn. xiii. 2 (Harry whose tuneful).

SPARTAN TWINS: Castor and Pollux; P.L. x. 674.

SPEAKABLE OF MUTE: able to speak, from dumb; P.L. ix. 564.

SPECKL'D: spotted as with plague-spots; Nat. Od. 136.

SPECT: (i.e. SPECKED) marked with spots; P.L. ix. 429.

SPECULAR MOUNT: point of observation or 'Look-out' Hill; P.R. iv. 236; cp. P.L. xii. 588.

SPET, vb. tr.: to eject from the mouth; Com. 132.

SPHEAR: the older astronomers, down to Milton's time, still held the theories of Ptolemy, the geographer. The universe consisted of a succession or set of eight hollow globes or 'spheres', revolving round a common centre, and, according to M.'s understanding of Plato, bearing round with them as they revolved the heavenly bodies, affixed to their surface. The view was, however, post-Platonic. The outermost sphere, of some opaque material, was the Prime Mover or Primum Mobile, which gave motion to all the rest. Two more spheres, making ten in all, were added to this system by Alphonsus; D.F.I. 30; etc. It was, indeed, further imagined (by Plato) that nine 'sirens' sat, one in each of the planetary orbits, and that as they all sang together, they provided the 'harmony' or 'music' of the spheres of which so many poets have written; Arc. 64. Aristotle (De Caelo II. ix. 290) denies this, declaring that there is no such 'harmony' and that the 'sphere music' has never been heard. The Diurnal Sphere is the one to which, in later theory, the 'astronomical Universe' or system was attached, and which was believed to rotate around the earth itself once in every twenty-four hours; the ninth or 'crystalline' sphere being sometimes identified with the waters that were above the firmament; P.L. iii. 482, *et pass.*

SPIRES: (i) coils, P.L. ix. 402: (ii) steeples, P.R. iv. 54. Blakeney points out this anachronism, the 'spire' being medieval. But see PINACLE (the form out of which the spire grew).

SPRING: (e.g. of roses) a thicket; P.L. iv. 219.

SPUNGE (sponge), 'worth a spunge': i.e. worth the effort of obliteration (and no more!); P.R. iv. 329.

SQUARE: when two planets are separated by 90° (a quarter of the zodiac), they are said to be 'in square'; P.L. x. 659.

SQUINT, adj.: looking askance; Com. 413.

STABL'D WOLVES: either wild, in their native dens, or wolves that have been captured, and imprisoned in cages; Com. 534.

STAKES (to 'fall on iron s.': the advice is merely cautionary). It is possible that M. may have been thinking of the thin wooden or iron spikes planted at the bottom of medieval pitfalls by trappers, to kill the wild beasts that fell into them. But in any case, the phrase is used figuratively of the swords; Com. 491.

STARR'D: translated to the stars; Il Pens. 19.

STARVE: to become numb, or die with cold; P.L. iv. 769.

STAR-YPOINTING: pointing to the stars. On Shaks. 4. [An irregularly formed compound, the 'y' being properly the prefix of the past part.]

STATE: canopy; hence (a) chair or throne of state, a chair with a canopy or 'dais' (in the older sense); P.L. x. 445; Arc. 81. (b) a royal *levée*; L'All. 60.

STATELY: adj. royal. See SIDEBORD.

STATIST: stateman; P.R. iv. 354.

STEAD, sb.: service, assistance; Com. 611; P.R. i. 473.

STEAR (i.e. steer): Satan 'steering his zenith' directed the highest part of his flight towards the opening at the top of the 'sphear' through which he had entered; P.L. x. 328.

STEUART, ADAM: was the 'mere A.S.' of M.'s sonnet because of his pamphlets published in 1644 with those initials only: a conspicuous Presbyterian; Forc. of Consc. 8.

STOA (from Gk. στοά, a Porch): especially the 'Painted Porch' (or Stoa) of Athens, really a marble colonnade, famous for its wall-paintings by Polygnotus, and as the School where Zeno taught his 'Stoic' philosophy; P.R. iv. 253.

STOLE: in M. usually a veil (as in Spenser); Il Pens. 35.

STOOP, vb.: to swoop down upon the quarry (hawking term); P.L. xi. 185.

STOPS: the small ventages, or windholes, in a flute by means of which the notes are produced; Com. 345; P.L. xi. 557; Lyc. 188; P.L. vii. 596. [But in Com. 552 'stop' refers to the cessation of the dance.]

STORIED: adorned with scenes from sacred story, or church history; Il Pens. 159.

STUB: stump; P.R. i. 339.

STUPENDIOUS: in M.'s time this was the form used in the London dialect—and M. was a Londoner! see P.L. x. 351; S.A. 1627.

SUBDUCT: to take away; P.L. viii. 536.

SUBLUNAR VAULT: the open expanse of heaven below the moon; P.L. iv. 777.

SUBMISS: i.e. submissive; P.L. v. 359, viii. 316, ix. 377; P.R. i. 476.

SUBORN: to incite or tempt to evil; P.L. ix. 361.

SUBURBAN: N. = Lat. *suburbanum*, a country estate or settlement, P.R. iv. 243.

SUCCESS: the issue or 'result' of an enterprise; hence in some cases it even comes to mean ill-fortune or non-success (e.g. in P.L. ii. 9, 123, iv. 932, vi. 161; P.R. iv. 1—elsewhere in a good sense).

SUCCINCT: i.e. girt up; P.L. iii. 643.

SUCCOTH: site near Jordan, not far s. of the confluence of the Jabbok; S.Ag. 278.

SUFFUSION: see DROP SERENE.

SULPHUROUS FIRE: gunpowder; P.L. xi. 654; cp. P.L. vi. 512 (and see NITRE).

SUMLESS: incalculable; P.L. viii. 36.

SUMM'D THIR PENNS: completed the full growth of all their feathers (a hawking term); P.L. vii. 421; cp. P.R. i. 14.

SUPPLANT, vb.: to trip up by the heels, an 'athletic' term; P.L. x. 513.

SURCEASE: to come to a dead stop; P.L. vi. 258; S.Ag. 404.

SUS: (*a*) a prov. of Morocco (now Tunis); one of the five Barbary States in N. Africa; P.L. xi. 403.  (*b*) see SUSA.

SUSA (i.e. 'Shushan the Palace', of the Bks. of Esther and Daniel), capital of Susiana; winter residence and Treasury of the Old Persian Kings, situate on the Choaspes (or Eulæus), their 'only Drink'; Herod. i. 88. Founded traditionally by Tithonus, f. of Memnon, Memnon himself building the Acropolis. The site is now identified as that of the modern *Sus*; P.L. x. 308; P.R. iii. 288. See MEMNON.

SUSIANA: see SUSA.

SWEDE (the 'Swede'): the allusion is to Chas. X, then at war with Russia and Poland; Sonn. xviii. 8 (Cyriack, whose Grandsire).

SWILL'D: drunken; Com. 178.

SWINDGE, vb.: to lash; Nat. Od. 172.

SWINK'T, p.p.: worn out with toil; Com. 293.

SYBIL: i.e. Sibyl; Vac. Ex. 69.

SYENE: Aswan or Assouan, long the southernmost outpost of the R. Empire. The midday sun at Syene being vertical, casts no shadow—Pliny (*N.H.*) says that at Meroe (S. of Syene) the sun twice a year 'casts no shadow'; P.R. iv. 70.

SYLVAN: the god Sylvanus, the deity of fields and forests (and also of flocks); Il Pens. 134; (Silvan) Com. 268; cp. P.R. ii. 191; P.L. iv. 707 (Silvanus).

SYMPHONIOUS: harmonious; P.L. vii. 559.

SYNOD: (*a*) assembly; P.L. ii. 391, vi. 150, xi. 67. (*b*) conjunction of planets; P.L. x. 661.

SYRTIS: name of two gulfs on the N. African coast, called the Greater and the Lesser; now called *Cabes* and *Sidra* respectively. Notorious for their quicksands. Hence here, a quicksand; P.L. ii. 939.

TAINT-WORM: the 'harvester' pest, Lyc. 46; identified (N. & Q. 18 Feb. '39) by Sir J. Graham Kerr.

TAMMUZ: see THAMUZ.

TAPROBANE: the form. name of Ceylon (to which isl. the Roms. sent an embassy in the reign of Claudius); P.R. iv. 75.

TAPSTRY: (i.e. 'tapestried') Halls; Com. 324.

TARPEIAN ROCK: the southern summit of the Capitoline Hill P.R. iv. 49.

TARSUS (Ship of): Tarsus is here (since Aesch. and Pindar both describe Typhoeus—here called Typhon—as pent in a Cilician cave) the capital of Cilicia; it had a great harbour, 12 miles from the city, and a great commerce; P.L. 200; S.Ag. 715.

TARTAR, adj. of Tartary, the chief country of Central Asia; Il Pens. 115; P.L. iii. 432, x. 431.

TARTARUS: (placed in Homer below Hades) identified by M. with Hell; P.L. ii. 858, vi. 54.

TARTESSUS: identified as Tarshish on the Atlantic coast of Spain (now *El Rocadillo*), W. of Gibraltar. See Comus 97, where M. actually printed 'Tartessus' for 'Atlantick' in his ed. of 1673.

TAURIC, adj.: (of Taurica, now the Crimea): e.g. Tauric Pool (L. Mæotis); the sea of Azov; P.R. iv. 79. See also MÆOTIS.

TAURIS: Tabriz, the chief t. of Azerbaijan, the N.W. prov. of Persia; P.L. x. 436.

TEAR, sb.: sometimes taken in the sense of a poetical lament or Elegy; Lyc. 14. [But the simpler sense seems more suitable here.]

TEDDED (of grass): spread out to dry after mowing; P.L. ix. 450.

TELASSAR (Thelassar): a district of Western Mesopotamia, where the 'sons of Eden' once dwelt; P.L. iv. 214.

TEMESÆAN BRONZE. See CALABRIA.

TEMIR: i.e. Timur ('the Tartar'), commonly called Tamerlane (the *Lame* Timur); the Mongul conqueror; P.L. xi. 389.

TEREDON (Diridotis, now *Dorah*?): a great city in ancient Babylonia. The site is now identified as Jebel Sanam (on the Euphrates) considerably north of the present mouth of the Euphrates and the Persian Gulf; P.L. iii. 292.

TERF: turf; Lyc. 140; Com. 280; P.L. v. 391; (terfe) P.L. xi. 324.

TERNATE: Island of the Moluccas, the native region of the clove-tree; visited by Drake, 1579; P.L. ii. 639.

TERRENE: ground, i.e. earth (F. *terrain*); P.L. vi. 78.

TETHYS: wife of Oceanus and m. of the ocean-nymphs; Com. 870.

TETRACHORDON: lit. 'Four-stringed' (as of a musical instrument, from Gk. τετράχορδος), the title given by M. to his pamphlet on the 'Four chief places in Scripture' dealing with marriage and its dissolution; pubd. in 1645; Sonn. xi. 1 (A Book was writ).

TETRARCH: the R. Governor of the fourth part of a province (Gk. τετράρχης), hence a sub-governor, given as a title to the four rebel angels represented by M. as governors of the 'four Elements', Fire, Air, Flood, Earth; P.R. iv. 201.

THAME (or Thames): Vac. Ex. 100.

THAMUZ (THAMMUZ or TAMMUZ): A Semitic form of the original Sumerian 'Dumuzi'. From the Babylonian Semites the legend of Tammuz passed to the Phœnicians, the Israelites, and the Greeks: the latter, however, substituted for Tammuz the name Adonis, the Babylonian Semitic goddess Ishtar (Astarte of the Phœnicians and Ashtoreth of the Israelites) being identified with Aphrodite and (by the Romans) with Venus. For Thamuz, see Nat. Od. 204; elsewhere his name is used for that of one of the rebel angels; (Thammuz) P.L. i. 446, 452. See also ADONIS.

THAMYRIS: a Thracian seer blinded for challenging the Nine Muses to surpass him in song; P.L. iii. 35.

THEBAN MONSTER: the Sphinx (of Thebes); P.R. iv. 572.

THEBEZ: a t. in Ephraim, app. taken by M. for Tisbeh or Thesbeh (1 Kings, xvii. 1), a village in Gilead; (some, however, read the Jabeshite, 'of Jabesh'); the birthplace of Elijah; P.R. ii. 16, 313; iv. 97–100. [Note:—M. may well have avoided the 'sh' in such names in following the Vulgate (Blakeney, note, p. 111), but Lowell's argument from P.L. vi. 340 fails since it misses the intentional harshness of that line.] See ELIAH.

THEB'S: (a) (for Thebes in Egypt) Egyptian; P.L. v. 274. (b) THEBS (for Thebes in Greece); Il Pens. 99; also Theb's in P.L. i. 578.

THISBITE: (Gk. Θεσβίτης); cp. P.R. ii. 16. See also THEBEZ.

THONE: k. of the c. of Thone at Egypt (Strabo); the incident of Polydamna, his wife, is from Homer (Od. iv. 219-29); Com. 675. (See Strabo, xvii. 800.)

THRACIAN BARD: Orpheus; P.L. vii. 34. See ORPHEUS.

THRASCIAS: the NNW. wind (or N. by NW. ?): P.L. x. 700.

THUNDERER, the: i.e. Zeus or Jove, identified by M. with Jehovah; P.L. ii. 28, vi. 491.

THWART: thwarting, i.e. transverse or crosswise; hence, injurious. Arc. 51.

THYESTEAN BANQUET: the feast at which Atreus served up the murdered bodies of his brother Thyestes' children— a crime against nature so revolting that M. represents the sun in the heavens as shrinking sympathetically backwards to avoid the sight of Eve's crime (and travelling from W. to E. for a whole day); P.L. x. 688.

TIAR: tiara; P.L. iii. 625.

TIBER: P.R. iv. 32.

TIDORE (i.e. TIDOR): one of the islands of the Malayan Archipelago in the Moluccas close to TERNATE, q.v.; P.L. ii. 639.

TIGRIS: P.L. ix. 71.

TILTH: land that is tilled, P.L. xi. 430.

TIMELESSLY: unseasonably, D.F.I. 2.

TIMELY-HAPPY: successful in early life (i.e. in season); Sonn. vii. (How soon hath Time), 8.

TIMNA: i.e. Timnath, a Philistine c. of the N. frontier of Judah; S.Ag. 219, 383, 795; cp. 1018.

TINCTURE: absorption (e.g. of the sun's rays); P.L. vii. 367.

TINE (whence 'tinder'): to kindle; P.L. x. 1075.

TINE: the river Tyne; Vac. Ex. 98.

TINSEL: an exceedingly fine gauze tissue interwoven with gold or silver threads; P.L. ix. 36; cp. Com. 877.

TIRESIAS: the blind soothsayer of Thebes; P.L. iii. 36.

TISHBITE: see THISBITE.

TISSUE: an exceedingly fine cloth enwrought with gold or silver; P.L. v. 592; cp. Nat. Od. 146.

TITAN: the eldest of the Titans, Oceanus; here identified with one of the rebel angels; P.L. i. 510.

TITULAR: merely nominal; P.L. v. 774.

TOBIAS: son of Tobit; P.L. v. 222.

TOBIT: see ASMODEUS.

TOPHET: a site in the Valley of Hinnom, defiled by Moloch-worship, hence abominable; P.L. i. 404. Also called Gehenna; P.L. i. 405.

TOUR (i.e. 'tower': a mounting or 'soaring' flight; (hawking term) P.L. xi. 185; cp. ii. 635.

TOWR'D: furnished with towers, turreted (of the headdress of Cybele, etc.); Arc. 21.

TRAGEDY (personified): Il Pens. 97.

TRAINS, sb.: tricks or wiles; Com. 151; S.Ag. 533, 932 (traines); P.L. xi. 620.

TRANSVERSE: = THWART, q.v.

TRAVELL'D (steps): It. *travagliato* (= travailed, toilsome); P.L. iii. 501.

TREBISOND: a great port of the R. Empire on the coast of Pontus, formerly called Trapezus. Surrendered to Muhammad II in 1460, it has been ever since a Turkish town. Once very celebrated in medieval romances; P.L. i. 584.

TREMISEN: t. and province, one of the five N. African ('Barbary') states; corresponding to Algiers; P.L. xi. 404.

TRENT, THE COUNCIL OF: 1545-63, where the R. Catholic members controlled the assembly; Forc. of Consc. 14.

TRENT, the r.: Vac. Ex. 93.

TREPIDATION: the theory of the oscillations of the 'Starry Sphere' under the Ptolemaic system; P.L. iii. 483. See SPHEAR.

TRINACRIAN: Sicilian (from Trinacria, an old name of Sicily); P.L. ii. 661.

TRINE, in: the aspect of two planets, 120° (or one-third of the Zodiac) apart, and therefore a 'benign' aspect; P.L. x. 659. See SEXTILE.

TRIPLE TYRANT: an allusion to the Triple Crown of the Papacy; Sonn. xv. 12 (Avenge O Lord).

TRITON, the River: see NYSEIAN ISLE.

TRIUMPHALS: trophies; P.R. iv. 578.                    [x. 675.

TROPIC: (*a*) the tropic Crab, i.e. the tropic of Cancer; P.L. (*b*) either tropic; the arctic and antarctic (i.e. Northern and Southern) regions of the sky; P.R. iv. 409.

TROULE, vb. tr.: to 'roll' the tongue, i.e. to speak glibly; P.L. xi. 616.

TROY: in M.'s proposed 'Epic of Britain', Troy, as the mother city of the Britons (descendants of the Trojan Brutus), was to have taken a great place. Hence the many refs. See Il Pens. 100; P.L. ix. 16; Lines from the *Hist. of Brit.* 12, etc.

TRUMP ('Cremona's'): the *Christiad*, a poem on Christ by M. G. Vida, a poet of Cremona; Pass. 26.

TRUMPETER (= HERALD) OF THE SEA: i.e. Triton; Lyc. 89; cp. Com. 873; (M.'s usual spelling is 'Harald').

TUB ('the Cynick'): i.e. the 'tub' in which the cynic Diogenes is said to have lived; Com. 708.

TUBE (glaz'd optic): a telescope; P.L. iii. 590.

TURBANT: turban; P.R. iv. 76.

TURCHESTAN: Turkestan; P.L. xi. 396.

TURKIS: turquoise; Com. 894.

TURME: a Roman military expression for a troop of horse, upwards of thirty in number; P.R. iv. 66.

TURNEY: tournament; Il Pens. 118.

TURNUS: K. of Rutulians, who fought against Æneas, because K. Latinus, f. of Lavinia, to whom Turnus was first betrothed, bestowed her upon Æneas instead; P.L. ix. 17.

TUSCAN ARTIST: see Galileo.

TWEED: (the r.) Vac. Ex. 92.

TWIN-BORN PROGENY (Latona's): i.e. Apollo and Artemis, Sonn. xii (I did but prompt).

TWINS, THE SPARTAN: the constellation named after Castor and Pollux, sons of Tyndareus, k. of Sparta; P.L. x. 674.

TWO-HANDED ENGIN: see ENGIN.

TYNE. See TINE.

TYPHON, TYPHŒUS: comparison of the Eng. with the Latin poems shows that M. did distinguish between them just as Hesiod does. Typhœus, a hundred-headed giant, who lived in a cave in Cilicia, was slain by Zeus with a thunderbolt, and buried under Mt. Etna; Typhaon, a fearful monster, was his son. But Typhaon, or rather Typhon, was later identified, as by M., with Set, the Eg. god of evil. For Typhon, see Nat. Od. 226; P.L. i. 199; cp. P.L. ii. 539.

TYRIAN: Phœnician (esp. of purple dyes); Nat. Od. 204. See also SARRA.

TYRIAN CYNOSURE: see ARCADY, STAR OF.

TYRRHENE SHORE: i.e. the coast of the Tyrrhene (Etruscan) Sea; Com. 49.

ULISSES: Vac. Ex. 50; (Ulysses) Com. 637; P.L. ii. 1019.

UMBRAGE: shade or foliage; P.L. ix. 1087; cp. P.L. iv. 257.

UNARGU'D: unquestioningly; P.L. iv. 636.

UNCESSANT: The MS. reading is incessant, but uncessant was printed both in the 1645 and 1673 edns,, and is therefore kept here; Lyc. 64.

UNCIRCUMSCRIB'D: unrestricted; P.L. vii. 170.

UNCOLOURD SKIE: of the dull leaden uniform morning heavens, not yet diversified with the many-hued clouds of sunrise; P.L. v. 189.

UNCOMPOUNDED: elemental; P.L. i. 425.

UNCONFORM: dissimilar; P.L. v. 259.

UNCOUTH: unknown; P.L. viii. 230.

UNCREATE, vb.: to reverse the act of creation, hence to annihilate; P.L. v. 892; ix. 943.

UNCTION: anointing with consecrated oil; P.L. vi. 709.

UNCTUOUS: oily; P.L. ix. 635.

UNESSENTIAL: lacking real essence, uncreated; P.L. ii. 439.

UNEXEMPT: admitting no exception; Com. 685.

UNEXPRESSIVE: unutterable; Lyc. 176.

UNFOUNDED: bottomless, foundationless; P.L. ii. 829.

UNFUM'D: undistill'd; P.L. v. 349.

UNHARBOUR'D: shelterless; Com. 423.

UNHIDE-BOUND: 'undistended' (not enlarged, as is usual after food)—Death being gaunt with famine; P.L. x. 601.

UNISON: sung by a single voice, a solo; P.L. vii. 599.

UNIVERSE, MANS LESS: because man himself is a microcosm; [P.R. iv. 459.

UNJOINTED: disconnected; S.Ag. 177.

UNLAID: unexorcised; Com. 434.

UNLIGHTSOM: devoid of light; P.L. vii. 355.

UNMINDED: unnoticed; P.L. x. 352.

UNOBNOXIOUS: unliable or unexposed (to); P.L. vi. 404.

UNORIGINAL (used of Night): without origin or beginning; hence existent from the first—pre-existent; P.L. x. 477.

UNPREDICT: to revoke (or reverse) a prediction; P.R. iii. 395.

UNPREVENTED: unanticipated; P.L. iii. 231.

UNPRINCIPL'D: ungrounded in principles; Com. 367.

UNREPROV'D: without fear of blame, blameless; P.L. iv. 493; cp. unreproved pleasures; L'All. 40.

UNSHOWR'D (grass): unwatered (because of the absence of rain in Egypt); Nat. Od. 215.

UNSPHEAR: Il Pens. 88. See INSPHEAR.

UNSUCCEEDED: without successor; P.L. v. 818.

UNVALU'D: i.e. inestimable. On Shaks., 11.

UNVOYAGEABLE: impassable, P.L. x. 366.

UNWEETING: i.e. unwitting; D.F.I. 28, et pass.

UP-LIFT: p.pt., P.L. i. 193; (elsewhere 'uplifted').

UR ('of the Chaldees'): formerly considered to be Urfa on the Upper Euphrates (about 400 miles from its true position); now proved by excavation to have been one of the earliest great capital Sumerian cities in Southern Babylonia (the scene of the epoch-making discoveries of Sir L. Woolley); when built, it stood on the Euphrates, but is now a few miles off in the desert; P.L. xii. 130.

URANIA: not the ancient Gk. muse of Astronomy, but of divine inspiration; the heavenly Muse; P.L. i. 6–16, vii. 1–31.

URCHIN: adj. elvish, mischievous; Com. 845.

URIEL: the archangel (as Regent of the Sun; P.L. iii. 690, ix. 60); see P.L. iii. 648.

UTENSILS: (implements of war); P.R. iii. 335.

UTHER (Pendragon): P.L. i. 580, cp. ARTHUR, and see also TROY.

UZZEAN JOB: Job of the land of Uz; the latter was probably part of the wide tract of open country extending eastward between Jordan and the Arabian desert—Blakeney; P.R. i. 369.

UZZIEL: 'Strength of God', one of the cherubim named by M.; P.L. iv. 782. See CHERUBIM.                    [vi. 614.

VAGARIES: wild or extravagant actions or attitudes; P.L.

VALDARNO (i.e. Val d'Arno): the valley of the Arno at Florence; P.L. i. 290.

**VALLOMBROSA** (the Leafy Vale): sit. about 18 m. E. of Florence; visited by M., who is said to have played the organ at the monastery; P.L. i. 303.

**VANE, Sir H.** (the 'younger'): b. 1612, he became Governor of Massachusetts in 1636-7, and Treasurer of the Navy under Charles I. Later he became one of the leaders of the Independents and Republicans (M.'s party), who were implacably opposed to King Charles, and one of the prominent members of the Long Parlt. He was executed at the Restoration in 1662; Sonn. to Sir H. V. (Vane, young in yeares).

**VANNES:** wings; P.L. ii. 927; (vans) P.R. iv. 583.

**VANT-BRASS** (i.e. 'Vambrace'): armour for the fore-arm; S.Ag. 1121.

**VARIOUS-MEASUR'D:** with a variety of metres; P.R. iv. 256.

**VARNISH:** 'make-up'; P.R. iv. 344; cp. P.L. ii. 485; S.Ag. 901.

**VENUS:** L'All. 14; Com. 124; P.R. ii. 214.

**VERDIT:** verdict; S.Ag. 324, 1228.

**VERMEIL-TINCTURED:** vermilion-tinted; Com. 752.

**VERNANT:** i.e. verdant, vernal; P.L. x. 679.

**VERTUMNUS:** lover of Pomona, and god of the Change of Seasons and of the Development of flower and fruit; P.L. ix. 395.

**VESTA,** the R. Hearth-Goddess: M. makes her m. of Melancholy by Saturn; Il Pens. 23.

**VILLATIC:** 'Farmyard' (used of fowls, Pliny, N. Hist. xxiii. 17); S.Ag. 1695.

**VINTAGE TIME:** P.R. iv. 15.

**VIOL:** a six-stringed somewhat large instrument of the violin type played with a bow. Now disused; the name serves as a general term in phrases such as 'tenor-viol', 'bass-viol', etc. Pass. 28.

**VIRGIL:** see Mincius, Lyc. 86.

**VISCOUNT SAVAGE:** March. Winch. 3.

**VISOR'D** (FALSHOOD): masked deceit; Com. 698.

**VOLANT** (lit. 'flying'): of light, quick, nimble touch; P.L. xi. 557.

**VOLATIL:** winged, hence passing off or evaporating into air, used of Hermes or Mercury, with play on the word, Hermes being the winged God; P.L. iii. 603.

**VOLUBIL:** rolling, revolving; P.L. iv. 594.

**VOLUMINOUS, THE STARS:** i.e. reading of the stars, by volumes or single characters; P.R. iv. 384; Starry rubric, ib. 393.

**VOTARIST:** votary; Com. 189.

**VOUTSAFE:** M.'s spelling of vouchsafe (prob. to avoid the awkward sound 'chs'; but still said to be sometimes pronounced as M. spelt it); P.L. xi. 170, *et pass.*

**VULCAN** (or MULCIBER): Com. 655; P.L. i. 740.

**WARDROP** (i.e. wardrobe): fig. of the 'attire' of flowers; Lyc. 47; cp. WARDROPE, fig. of the 'trimings' of words and phrases; Vac. Ex. 18.

WARRANTED: safeguarded; Com. 327.

WAY (MILKIE): see GALAXIE.

WEDGE (mil.): a troop-formation of infantry in the shape of half a rhomb (q.v.)—hence an acute-angled triangle, with the angle in front; cp. P.R. iii. 309.

WHILEARE: a little while since; Circ. 10.

WHILOME: once on a time, formerly; D.F.I 24.

WHIST: hushed; Nat. Od. 64.

WHITE THORN: the hawthorn; Lyc. 48.

WICKET: a small side-gate; P.L. iii. 484.

WIDE-ENCROACHING: i.e. trespassing, used of Eve—probably to 'set off' the description of Eurynome ('wide-governing'); P.L. x. 581.

WINCHESTER: Marquis of: i.e. J Paulet, fifth Marquis; March. Win. 2.

WINDS, CAVE OF THE: see HIPPOTADES.

WINE-PRESS: P.R. iv. 16.

WINNOW: to beat the air with wings; P.L. v. 270.

WISARD (used of the Dee): because it was thought to foretell the future by its encroachments now on English, now on Welsh territory; Lyc. 55.

WISARD, a 'Wise Man': (a) of the Magi (Star-led Wisards); Nat. Od. 23.
(b) of Proteus; Com. 872.
(c) the chief magician in Comus; Com. 571.

WITCHES (of Lapland); P.L. ii. 655.

WOLVES (used of false clergy); Lyc. 128; P.L. xii. 508; Sonn. to Cromwell, 14 (Cromwell our cheif).

WONNS, vb.: i.e. dwells; P.L. vii. 457.

WOODS (the 'Arabian woods'): strictly, there was but one solitary tree wherein the Phœnix nested; S.Ag. 1700.

WORM: the Serpent; P.L. ix. 1068.

WORSTER (battle of) in 1651 (Worsters laureat wreath); Sonn. to Cromwell, 9 (Cromwell our cheif).

WRENCH, vb.: to pervert, or wrest (the law); Sonn. xviii. 4 (Cyriack whose Grandsire).

XERXES: k. of Persia (scourges the Hellespont); P.L. x. 311.

YOUNGEST TEEMED STAR: latest-appearing (of the Star of Bethlehem); Nat. Od. 240.

ZEPHON (lit. 'Searcher'); name of one of the cherubim; P.L. iv. 781, etc.

ZOPHIEL (lit. 'Spy' or 'Scout' of God): a cherub; P.L. vi. 535.

ZORA: a town situated a little s. of ESHTAOL, q.v.

# APPENDIX

HESPERUS, GARDENS FAIR OF: (Com. 393, 982, etc.): The
source of the idea that these gardens were 'up in the
broad fields of the sky' is the Basle edn. of Hesiod (*Scholia
Basiliensia*, 1542; repr. Heinsius, 1603), the reference being
to Hes. *Theogony*, v. 215. The golden apples of the Hesperides
are thus explained as the stars in the sky, with Herakles
as the rising sun, plucking them as he makes them disappear. This *Scholion Basiliense* runs … ὅτι παρερχομένου τοῦ
Ἡλίου οὐκ ἔτι φαίνονται τὰ ἄστρα ὅ ἐστι τὸ τρυγῆσαι τὸν Ἡρακλέα τὰ
μῆλα—Robert Eisler in *Times Lit. Supplt.* of 22 Sept. 1945.
See also Pindar, *Ol.* ii. 62–88.

[See also the helpful letter by Mr. C. S. Lewis in *T.L.S.*
of 14 Sept. 1945, with regard to 'the Spirit'.]

PRINTED IN GREAT BRITAIN BY
MERRITT AND HATCHER, LTD., LONDON, S.E.10.

CONSTITUTION AND LAWS

CONSTITUTION AND LAW

# THE
# CONSTITUTION AND LAWS

OF THE

## Grand Lodge of Antient Free and Accepted Masons of Scotland

EDINBURGH:

PUBLISHED BY AUTHORITY OF GRAND LODGE
BY GRAND SECRETARY

1944

*First Impression,* 1940
*Reprinted (with Amendments to Laws* 92 *and* 241), 1943
*Reprinted (with Amendments to Laws* 230 *and* 233), 1944

GEO. STEWART AND CO. LTD.
PRINTERS
92 GEORGE STREET, EDINBURGH

# SANCTION

GRAND LODGE having at its Quarterly Communication on 1st February 1940, authorised the publication of an edition of the Constitution and Laws, embracing the additions and alterations confirmed by Grand Lodge on that date,

Therefore WE, The Right Honourable VISCOUNT TRAPRAIN, Grand Master Mason of Scotland; Brigadier-General Sir NORMAN A. ORR EWING, Bart., D.S.O., A.D.C., V.L., Past Grand Master; Captain J. C. STEWART, D.L., J.P., Depute Grand Master; JAMES S. M. GRIEVE, J.P., Substitute Grand Master; The Right Honourable THE EARL OF GALLOWAY, L.L., J.P., Senior Grand Warden; The Right Honourable THE EARL OF LAUDERDALE, D.L., Junior Grand Warden; and remanent Office-Bearers, and Members of Grand Lodge, do hereby promulgate the same as authority to all Free and Accepted Masons, and Lodges holding of the Grand Lodge of Antient Free and Accepted Masons of Scotland;—And we enjoin all Members of

Grand Lodge, as well as Subordinate Lodges, and the Brethren at large, immediately to provide themselves with copies of this Revised Edition of the Constitution and Laws, and give due obedience thereto in all points.

Given at Freemasons' Hall, in the City of Edinburgh, this First day of August, in the year of our Lord 1940, and of Light 5944.

TRAPRAIN,
*Grand Master Mason.*

NORMAN A. ORR EWING,
*Past Grand Master.*

J. C. STEWART,
*Depute Grand Master.*

JAMES S. M. GRIEVE,
*Substitute Grand Master.*

GALLOWAY,
*Senior Grand Warden.*

LAUDERDALE,
*Junior Grand Warden.*

T. G. WINNING, *Grand Secretary*

# NOTE

---

By appointment of GRAND LODGE, the Special Committee appointed to assist Grand Secretary in superintending the publication of this Edition of the Constitution and Laws, consisted of the following Brethren :—

> W. STEVENSON COCHRAN,
> JAMES SIME WATERSTON,
> PETER SMELLIE,
> GEORGE J. MILLER,
> JAMES S. M. GRIEVE,
> JOHN B. PEDEN,
> JAMES MURRAY,
> ALEXANDER PLANT, *Convener*.

*[signature]*
*Grand Secretary*

FREEMASONS' HALL,
EDINBURGH, 1st *August* 1940.

# CHANGE OF LAWS

*The following motions were approved at the Quarterly Communication of Grand Lodge on Thursday, 1st February 1945 :—*

That the following Law be substituted for Law 35 :—

"**35.** Every notice of motion must be in writing and signed by the proposer and seconder, who must be qualified members of Grand Lodge. It may be either (*a*) given in Grand Lodge by the proposer personally, read by him (unless this formality be dispensed with by the Grand Master Mason or other brother in the Chair), and delivered to Grand Secretary, before the close of the Communication at which notice is given, or (*b*) sent to Grand Secretary by registered post. All notices of motions shall be referred forthwith to the Laws and Rulings Committee."

That the following Law be substituted for Law 36 :—

"**36.** Every notice of motion given in Grand Lodge or received by Grand Secretary and the report thereon of the Laws and Rulings Committee shall be submitted to Grand Committee for its decision whether the notice (which expression in this Law includes the motion incorporated therein) is competent and regular and can be accepted. This shall be done at the first Ordinary Meeting of Grand Committee occurring not earlier than the fourteenth day after the date on which such notice was given or received, unless the report of the Laws and Rulings Committee is not ready, in which event consideration shall be deferred until the next Ordinary Meeting. Grand Secretary shall inform the proposer and seconder of the notice of the meeting of Grand Committee at which it is to be submitted, and of any adjournment thereof, and these members, if in attendance, shall be heard on any point raised at the consideration of the notice. The merits of the motion shall neither be discussed nor decided upon. Grand Committee in its discretion may permit the notice to be amended. If the notice be accepted by Grand Committee, without or with amendment, it shall thereupon be circulated in accordance with Law 37; if it be not accepted, the members concerned may appeal to Grand Lodge direct. The terms of a notice not accepted by Grand Lodge or Grand Committee shall not be minuted. A statement in the minutes to the effect that a notice of motion by Brothers (naming them) was, or was not, accepted, shall be a sufficient record of the matter.''

That the following sentences be added to Law 37, at the end thereof :—

''A notice of motion sent to Grand Secretary and accepted by Grand Committee shall be inserted in the circular intimating the next Quarterly Communication, and this shall be deemed to be compliance with the requirements of the preceding sentence of this Law. The notice of motion shall be repeated in the circular intimating the following Quarterly Communication for consideration at that Communication.''

That the following Law be substituted for Law 40 :—

"**40.** Notice of a motion for altering or abrogating an existing Law, or for enacting a new one, if given at a Quarterly Communication, cannot be discussed in Grand Lodge before the next Quarterly Communication. If it be sent to Grand Secretary by registered post, as provided in Law 35, it cannot be discussed in Grand Lodge before the second Quarterly Communication following the date of its consideration by Grand Committee."

That Law 91 be amended as follows :—

(1) That the words "not less than" be inserted immediately before the word "seven" in the first paragraph.

(2) That the second sentence of paragraph (c) be deleted.

(3) That the following new paragraphs be added to said Law, at the end thereof :—

"(h) A Laws and Rulings Committee, whose duties shall be to prepare rulings and opinions on questions relating to Masonic law or practice put to Grand Lodge, Grand Committee or Grand Secretary ; to examine all notices of motions given in Grand Lodge or sent to Grand Secretary or given in Grand Committee ; to take up all remits from Grand Lodge or Grand Committee (not falling within the duties of or referred specially to another Committee) relating to these Laws or to any regulations made or to be made thereunder, or to the preparation, alteration or revision of these Laws or such regulations ; and to consider and make suggestions for the improvement of these Laws or of such regulations. The Chairman of the Bye-Laws

iii.

Committee shall be a member of this Committee, *ex officio*. In his absence, another member of and appointed by the Bye-Laws Committee may attend meetings of this Committee."

"(i) A Special Purposes Committee, whose duties shall be to take up such matters as may be remitted to it by Grand Committee."

"Each member of Grand Committee, if he so desires, shall be appointed a member of a standing Committee. Grand Committee shall have power to make regulations with reference to such appointments. The provisions of this paragraph shall not apply to the Metropolitan District Committee."

"Grand Committee at any time may reduce or increase the number of members on a Standing Committee, subject to the limitations in the first paragraph of this Law, and at the request of a Standing Committee may transfer temporarily any of the duties of that Committee to another Committee. Grand Committee may, on cause shown, suspend its Standing Orders and Regulations, as also the operation of the restriction contained in Law 92 with reference to the period of tenure of the Chair of a Standing Committee, provided at least two-thirds of the qualified members of Grand Committee present vote in favour of the suspension."

# THE
# CONSTITUTION AND LAWS.

---

## GRAND LODGE.

**1.** THE GRAND LODGE OF ANTIENT FREE AND ACCEPTED MASONS OF SCOTLAND is composed of the Grand Office-Bearers (except Grand Tyler), all qualified Past Grand Masters, Provincial and District Grand Masters, Past Provincial and District Grand Masters, and Proxy District Grand Masters, and the Master and Wardens, or in their absence the Proxy Master and Proxy Wardens, of each Daughter Lodge in good standing with Grand Lodge.

*Constitution of Grand Lodge.*

**2.** Every Member of Grand Lodge must be a qualified brother thereof as defined in Law 272. The absence of any requisite qualification, or failure to pay by 31st January annually the dues of membership or appropriate fees of honour as set forth in the First Schedule to these Laws, shall disqualify for membership of Grand Lodge.

*Qualification for membership.*

A

**3.** The Office-Bearers of Grand Lodge are :—

> The Grand Master Mason,
> Immediate Past Grand Master,
> Depute Grand Master,
> Substitute Grand Master,
> Senior Grand Warden,
> Junior Grand Warden,
> Grand Secretary,
> Grand Treasurer,
> Grand Almoner,
> Senior Grand Chaplain,
> Junior Grand Chaplain,
> Senior Grand Deacon,
> Junior Grand Deacon,
> Grand Director of Ceremonies,
> Grand Architect,
> Grand Jeweller,
> Grand Bible-Bearer,
> Grand Bard,
> Grand Sword-Bearer,
> Grand Director of Music,
> Grand Organist,
> Grand Piper,
> Grand Marshal,
> Grand Inner Guard,
> President of Grand Stewards,
> Grand Tyler.

Style and title
of the Grand
Master Mason.

**4.** The style and title of "MOST WORSHIP-FUL" and "GRAND MASTER MASON" belong only to the Grand Master Mason.

**5.** The style of "Right Worshipful" is accorded to all Past Grand Masters, the Depute Grand Master, the Substitute Grand Master, the Grand Wardens, Grand Secretary, Grand Treasurer, and Grand Almoner. The style of "Very Worshipful" is given to the Grand Chaplains, Grand Deacons, Grand Director of Ceremonies, Grand Architect, Grand Jeweller, and Grand Bible-Bearer; and the style of "Worshipful" to the Grand Bard, Grand Sword-Bearer, Grand Director of Music, Grand Organist, Grand Piper, Grand Marshal, Grand Inner Guard, and President of Grand Stewards.

*Style of other Grand Office-Bearers.*

**6.** The Grand Office-Bearers, other than the four hereinafter mentioned, shall be elected annually. The Depute Grand Master and the Substitute Grand Master shall be appointed annually by the Grand Master Mason on the day of his installation. Grand Secretary and Grand Treasurer shall not be subject to annual election, but the appointment of each of them shall be terminable on Saint Andrew's Day annually, on three months prior notice being given by resolution of Grand Lodge to terminate his engagement.

*Grand Office-Bearers elected or appointed annually.*

*Exceptions.*

**7.** At the Quarterly Meeting of Grand Lodge immediately preceding Saint Andrew's Day the Grand Office-Bearers for the ensuing year

*Date of nomination and election.*

shall, subject as hereinbefore provided, be nominated and elected. All Meetings of Grand Lodge are hereafter referred to in these Laws as " Communications."

**Nomination in absence.**

8. It shall not be competent to nominate an absent brother for office in Grand Lodge unless his consent has been previously obtained and is vouched for by a Member of Grand Lodge.

**Vote, how taken.**

9. When more candidates than one have been nominated for any office in Grand Lodge, the voting shall be by show of hands, and if there be more than two candidates for the office, the voting shall be repeated, if necessary, until the brother to be elected shall have a majority of those voting in the last vote. If more than one office be contested, these must be voted on separately and in order of seniority, and the voting on one office must be completed and the result declared before the vote on the office next in order is taken.

**Date of installation.**

**Festival of Saint Andrew (see also Law 52).**

10. The brethren elected or appointed annually as Grand Office-Bearers shall be installed on Saint Andrew's Day (30th November) prior to the celebration of the Festival of Saint Andrew. In the event of Saint

Andrew's Day occurring on a Saturday or a Sunday, the installation and Festival shall take place on the Friday preceding. Any Office-Bearer unable to attend shall be installed at the first Communication thereafter at which he is present.

**11.** An elective Grand Office-Bearer (the Grand Master Mason, Grand Secretary, Grand Treasurer, Grand Almoner, Grand Director of Ceremonies, Grand Organist, Grand Piper, and Grand Tyler excepted) shall not hold the same office longer than two years consecutively. *Tenure of office.*

**12.** On the death, resignation, or disqualification, of any elective Grand Office-Bearer, Grand Lodge at the first Quarterly Communication following, or at a *pro re nata* Communication, may elect a qualified brother to fill the vacancy. *Vacancies, how filled.*

**13.** Any Past Grand Office-Bearer, Past Provincial or District Grand Office-Bearer, member of Grand Committee, and Grand Steward, on payment to Grand Lodge of the fee set forth in the First Schedule, Part I., Item 13, shall be entitled to receive from Grand Secretary a Certificate of his having held such office or appointment. *Certificate of past service.* *Fee.*

The Grand Master Mason a member of every subordinate Lodge.

**14.** The Grand Master Mason shall be *ex officio* a member of every Daughter Lodge, and of each Provincial or District Grand Lodge, but, as such, shall not be liable in payment of any contribution to such Lodge.

Grand Secretary.

To have superintendence of Grand Lodge affairs.

Custodier of records, etc.

To attend meetings, prepare Minutes, keep Roll and Registers, etc.

To circulate Minutes and Abstract of Accounts.

**15.** Grand Secretary shall have the charge and superintendence of all the affairs of Grand Lodge, and shall have full control and direction of the staff of Grand Lodge. All communications shall be addressed to him. He shall be custodier of the Records, Deeds, Seal, and other moveable property of Grand Lodge. He shall attend all Communications of Grand Lodge and meetings of Grand Committee, prepare Minutes, keep the Roll of Members, enrol the names of Intrants, Affiliates, and Founder Members, keep Registers of Installed Masters and Mark Masters, prepare and despatch all Charters, Commissions, Diplomas, etc., issued by Grand Lodge; shall furnish quarterly to each Daughter Lodge, Provincial and District Grand Secretary, and Member of Grand Lodge, in the form to be submitted to the ensuing Communication, a printed copy of Minutes of Grand Lodge, Grand Committee, the Committee of Benevolence, and the Annuity Board, with a statement of the sums which have been received on behalf of Grand Lodge during the preceding three months; and shall also furnish to them annually an Abstract of Grand Lodge Accounts, as certified by the Auditor. He shall send copies of the Proceedings of Grand Lodge to the Grand Secretaries of Sister Grand Lodges; and to any Freemason who applies for a copy and who pays, annually, in advance, the sum set forth in the First Schedule, Part I., Item 18. He shall summon the Office-Bearers and Members of Grand Lodge to its Communications, and shall call all meetings of Grand Committee by circular, containing a statement of the business to be brought before such Communications and meetings so far as ascertained by him. He shall be *ex officio* Secretary to all Committees, and shall call meetings thereof. He shall cause stock books of Diplomas, Charters, Demits, Volumes of the Constitution and Laws, and such like property to be kept and balanced annually. He shall also carry out all instructions of Grand Lodge and Grand Committee.

*Copies of Proceedings.*

*Cost.*

*To convene meetings.*

*Secretary to all Committees.*

*Stock books.*

**16.** Grand Secretary shall devote his whole time to the duties of his office and shall find security for his intromissions to the extent of One thousand pounds, the premium on the Guarantee Policy being paid by Grand Lodge. He shall be paid such salary as shall from time to time be fixed by Grand Lodge.

*To devote whole time to duties.*

*Security for intromissions.*

*Salary.*

Assistance.

Any assistance required by him and authorised by Grand Committee, shall be paid for by Grand Lodge.    In his absence his duties shall be attended to by Grand Treasurer.

Duties in
absence.

Grand
Treasurer.

To keep
correct
Accounts

Remittances—
how made
payable.

Receipts.

Cash in hand.

Deposit of
moneys.

Payments.

**17.** Grand Treasurer shall keep regular and correct Accounts, according to forms approved by Grand Committee, of all moneys received and disbursed by him in connection with the funds of Grand Lodge.    Remittances shall be made payable to Grand Lodge of Scotland, and Grand Treasurer shall receive from Grand Secretary daily all remittances or sums which come into his hands, and shall check the entries of same in a Remittance Book.    He shall transmit without delay, through Grand Secretary, to the persons or Lodges sending remittances, the proper receipts or vouchers for the same. Receipts given by him for dues, payable to Grand Lodge by or in respect of intrants, affiliates, mark masters, and founder members, shall bear the names of the intrants and others so paid for.    He shall at no time retain in his hands more than Fifty pounds of the Funds of Grand Lodge.    Any sum in excess thereof shall be paid into the appropriate Bank account of Grand Lodge.    No accounts shall be paid by him except such as have been previously authorised by the Finance

Committee, and then only by cheque. At the end of each financial year (the last Thursday in November) he shall prepare a complete Abstract of the Accounts, to be submitted, along with the books and vouchers, to the Auditor. He shall keep in a separate book the Roll of Lettings of the Halls and other parts of Grand Lodge premises.

*To prepare Abstract of Accounts.*

*Audit.*

*Hall lets.*

**18.** Grand Treasurer shall receive and pay all moneys connected with the Benevolent Fund and Annuity Funds, and keep the Accounts thereof. There shall be allocated against each of these Funds, as the expense of managing the Fund, a sum equal to seven and one-half per cent. of the gross annual income from its invested funds, and of the surplus rents of any heritable properties. The sums so allocated shall be credited to the General Fund on the last day of each financial year.

*Accounts of the Benevolent and Annuity Funds.*

*Expense of management.*

**19.** Grand Treasurer shall devote his whole time to the duties of his office, and shall find security for his intromissions to the extent of One thousand pounds, the premium on the guarantee policy being paid by Grand Lodge. He shall be paid such salary as shall from time to time be fixed by Grand Lodge. In his absence his duties shall be attended to by Grand Secretary.

*Grand Treasurer to devote whole time to duties.*

*Security for intromissions.*

*Salary.*

*Duties in absence.*

**Expenses**

**20.** Expenses incurred shall be allowed to Grand Secretary and Grand Treasurer when their attendance is required on Grand Lodge business.

**Grand Almoner.**

**21.** Grand Almoner shall promote the interests of the Benevolent Fund and Annuity Funds of Grand Lodge; shall see that the Daughter Lodges fulfil their obligations to these Funds, and shall call the attention of Grand Committee to any Lodges which fail to do so; and, subject to the approval of Grand Committee, he shall make such appeals to Lodges and brethren as the circumstances of the Funds may from time to time require.

**Grand Chaplains.**

**22.** Grand Chaplains shall attend the Communications, and there offer solemn prayer suitable to the occasion, according to ancient usage among the Fraternity.

**Grand Director of Ceremonies.**

**23.** Grand Director of Ceremonies shall take sole charge of arranging the Office-Bearers and other Members of Grand Lodge according to precedence, and superintend the details of all ceremonies of Grand Lodge, within any building where it may meet.

**Grand Marshal.**

**24.** Grand Marshal shall form and superintend outdoor processions of Grand Lodge.

Daughter Lodges and others forming part of
the procession shall be under the direction
of the Grand Marshal.

**25.** Grand Tyler shall attend all Com-    Grand Tyler.
munications, assist in the arrangements, and
see that only brethren properly qualified
obtain admission.    He shall be paid such    Salary.
salary as shall from time to time be fixed
by Grand Lodge.    He shall have no vote in
Grand Lodge.

**26.** At the Quarterly Communication in    Auditor.
November, Grand Lodge shall appoint an    Appointed
Auditor for the ensuing year.    The person    annually.
so appointed must be a professional Account-    Qualifications.
ant or Auditor, and a qualified member of a
Daughter Lodge in good standing.    The    Duties.
Auditor shall examine the Accounts of all
the Funds of Grand Lodge and report thereon
in writing, quarterly and annually.    He shall
also furnish such interim reports and other
information regarding the Funds as may be
desired by Grand Lodge and its Committees.
For his services the Auditor shall be paid    Remuneration.
such remuneration as shall from time to time
be fixed by Grand Lodge.    In the event of    Vacancy, how
the office becoming vacant from any cause    filled.
during a financial year, Grand Committee
may appoint a qualified person to fill the

vacancy for the remainder of the year, subject to confirmation thereof by Grand Lodge at the first Quarterly Communication following such appointment.

**Board of Grand Stewards.**
**Appointed annually.**

**27.** Grand Lodge shall appoint annually, at the Quarterly Communication in November, not more than fifty qualified members of Grand Lodge, to act as a Board of Grand Stewards, to which, under the direction of Grand Committee, the management of the Festival of Saint Andrew, and other Festivals, shall be entrusted. The Grand Stewards, in their proper clothing, and with their rods of office, shall accompany all processions of Grand Lodge. Every brother on appointment and before acting as a Grand Steward, shall pay the appropriate fee of honour set forth in the First Schedule, Part I., Item 22.

**Duties.**

**Fee of honour.**

**Election of Vice-President.**

**28.** The Board of Grand Stewards, within seven days of its appointment, shall elect from its number its Vice-President, who shall hold the appointment for one year only. He shall pay, on appointment and before acting as Vice-President, the appropriate fee of honour set forth in the First Schedule, Part I., Item 22.

**Fee of honour.**

**29**. Grand Lodge shall hold four Quarterly Communications annually—viz., on the first Thursday of February, May, August, and November, at Three o'clock afternoon, or at such hour as Grand Lodge or Grand Committee may hereafter appoint. Twenty-one qualified members shall form a quorum. These Communications may be adjourned to a future day or days. The business of Grand Lodge shall be transacted in the Third Degree.

*Quarterly Communications.*
*Quorum.*
*Adjournment.*
*Business.*

**30**. A special Communication may be called at any time by the Grand Master Mason, or, in his absence, by the Immediate Past Grand Master, the Depute Grand Master, or the Substitute Grand Master, or upon an order by Grand Committee. It shall also be competent for twenty-one qualified members of Grand Lodge to present a requisition, signed by them, requiring that a special Communication be called, the purpose of which must be clearly stated in the requisition. On receipt of an order or requisition in due form, Grand Secretary shall immediately call a Communication to be held within fourteen days of the date on which he receives the order or requisition. The circular calling the Communication shall state the purpose for which the Communication is called, and no other business shall be discussed thereat. A

*Special Communications.*
*By whom called.*
*On requisition.*
*Business.*

Adjournment.

Special Communication may be adjourned to a future day or days.

Admission to Communications.

**31.** Grand Secretary shall issue tickets of admission to all members of Grand Lodge, annually, on payment of their fees. Such tickets shall be exhibited before admission to the Hall, and shall not be transferable under pain of forfeiture. Only members of Grand Lodge shall be admitted to the floor of the Hall.

Tickets not transferable.

Disqualified members to return tickets.

**32.** Members of Grand Lodge, on resigning or otherwise becoming disqualified during the year for which their fees have been paid, shall return to Grand Secretary their tickets of admission.

Throne—by whom filled in absence of Grand Master Mason.

**33.** In the absence of the Grand Master Mason, Grand Lodge shall be presided over as follows:—By the Immediate or any other Past Grand Master; Depute Grand Master; Substitute Grand Master; a Past Depute Grand Master; a Past Substitute Grand Master; a Provincial or District Grand Master; Senior Grand Warden; Junior Grand Warden; Senior Grand Deacon; or Junior Grand Deacon; whom all failing by any other Grand Office-Bearer present at the meeting in the order of their precedence.

**34**. Confirmation of Minutes of Grand Lodge implies that the proceedings of a previous Communication have been correctly recorded. No business or question disposed of at such former Communication can be raised or discussed when the minutes are submitted for confirmation.

Confirmation of Minutes—interpretation of.

**35**. Notices of motions must be given personally and in writing, signed by the proposer and seconder, who must be qualified members of Grand Lodge, and such notices shall be read by the proposer, and delivered to Grand Secretary, before the close of the Communication at which notice is given.

Notices of motions—how given.

**36**. If any motion of which notice has been given should appear to the Grand Master Mason or other brother in the Chair to be irregular, or not within the cognisance or jurisdiction of Grand Lodge, the matter shall be submitted to Grand Committee for its judgment. Grand Secretary shall inform the members of Grand Lodge who have given the notice of such motion, of the meeting of Grand Committee at which a decision is to be given thereon, and these members, if present at such meeting, shall be heard upon the point of order. If such notice of motion be accepted by Grand Com-

Competency of notices of motions.

mittee it shall thereupon be circulated in accordance with Law 37; if it be not accepted, the members concerned may appeal to Grand Lodge direct. A notice of motion not accepted by Grand Lodge or Grand Committee shall not be minuted.

**Circulation of notices of motions.**

**37.** Copies of notices of motions given in Grand Lodge and accepted shall be sent to the Secretary of each Provincial and District Grand Lodge, and to the Secretary of each Daughter Lodge, with instructions to bring the same before the brethren at a meeting of their respective Lodges.

**Proposal of motions.**

**38.** The brethren giving notice of a motion, which has been accepted and circulated, should be present to bring it forward at the Quarterly Communication immediately following the one at which it has been intimated. If, however, the proposer be absent, it shall be competent for the seconder to take up the motion as proposer on its coming before Grand Lodge, provided a seconder be obtained. Should the seconder only be absent, it shall be competent for any member to second the motion. If both proposer and seconder be absent, the motion shall fall.

**Absence of proposer.**

**Absence of seconder.**

**Absence of both —motion falls.**

**39**. When a competent motion shall have been regularly moved and seconded, it shall not be permissible for the Grand Master Mason or the brother in the Chair to refuse to put the same to the vote. A motion put on the Agenda for Grand Lodge cannot be postponed without cause shown. For its more convenient disposal, a motion may be divided and each part discussed and voted on separately.

*Chairman cannot refuse to put competent motion.*

*Postponement of motion.*

*Division of motion.*

**40**. A motion for altering or abrogating an existing law, or for enacting a new one, shall be made only at a Quarterly Communication; and such motion cannot be discussed in Grand Lodge before the next Quarterly Communication.

*Alteration of Laws.*

**41**. A motion, the substance of which Grand Lodge has already decided upon, shall not be brought forward again or be otherwise discussed until after the lapse of twelve months from the date of such decision.

*Time limit for renewal of motion.*

**42**. Laws enacted and resolutions adopted at Communications shall not be cancelled or altered within a shorter period than twelve months after the date of such enactment or adoption. If any doubt shall arise as to the interpretation of a Law, the power of

*Period within which Laws and resolutions may not be altered.*

*Interpretation of Laws vested in Grand Lodge.*

B

deciding the same shall be vested in Grand Lodge and not in the Chair.

**Standing Orders may be suspended.**

**43**. Grand Lodge may, on cause shown, suspend its Standing Orders, provided at least two-thirds of the qualified members present vote in favour of the suspension.

**Vote on question.**

**Casting vote.**

**44**. After a question has been discussed, the majority of the qualified members voting shall determine the point at issue. In case of an equality of votes, the Grand Master Mason, or the brother in the Chair, shall have a casting vote as well as a deliberative vote.

**Who may speak and vote.**

**No member shall speak twice.**

**Proposer's right of reply.**

**45**. Only qualified members of Grand Lodge have a right to speak and vote upon any question. A member shall not be entitled to speak more than once on any question, except strictly in explanation, and only the proposer of a motion shall have the right of reply.

**Members to vote as they think fit.**

**46**. Members of Grand Lodge shall give their votes on any matter brought before Grand Lodge in accordance with what they conceive to be the best interests of the Craft. It is not in the power of Provincial or District Grand Lodges or Daughter Lodges to instruct their representatives to vote in any particular manner, but they may inform their representatives of their views.

**47.** A Visiting Brother shall not be admitted to any Communication until he has been examined by three of the Grand Stewards, appointed for that purpose by their President or Vice-President, or has been duly vouched for otherwise.

*Visitors, how admitted (see also Law 31, last sentence).*

**48.** A brother shall not leave a Communication until the same has been closed, without permission asked and obtained from the Grand Master Mason, or the brother in the Chair.

*Permission to leave Grand Lodge.*

**49.** When the Grand Master Mason, any Past Grand Master, the Depute Grand Master, Substitute Grand Master, any Past Depute or Past Substitute Grand Master, or a Grand Warden, with other Grand Office-Bearers, visit officially any Provincial or District Grand Lodge or Daughter Lodge, the Master, Wardens, and other Office-Bearers of that Lodge shall offer to vacate their respective Chairs in favour of the corresponding Office-Bearers of Grand Lodge. In the event of the Grand Master Mason, or Office-Bearer heading the Visitation, exercising his right to

*Grand visitations (official).*

take the Chair, the Master of the Lodge shall sit at his right hand.

**Notice of visitations.**

**50.** Previous to the Visitation, Grand Secretary shall send notice thereof to the Lodge to be visited, and to the Provincial or District Grand Lodge in which the Lodge is situated. If the visit be to a Provincial or District Grand Lodge, notice shall be sent to the Provincial or District Grand Secretary, who shall send notices to the Daughter Lodges in the Province or District.

**Visitations for business.**

**51.** When Visitations are purely of a business character, and made for the purpose of inquiring into the mode of conducting a Lodge, examining the books, etc., no notice of such visits requires to be sent to the other Daughter Lodges in the Province or District.

**Festival of Saint Andrew (see also Law 10).**

**Is open to every brother.**

**52.** The Festival of Saint Andrew shall be celebrated in open Lodge in the First Degree, and may be attended by any brother of the Craft who provides himself with a ticket for that purpose. The price of the ticket shall be fixed by Grand Committee, subject to the approval of Grand Lodge at the Quarterly Communication immediately preceding Saint Andrew's Day. The Festival shall be so conducted as to ensure that the expenses thereof

**Expenses.**

(excepting always a reasonable allowance for music, and other incidental outlays, to be fixed by Grand Committee), shall be covered by the moneys to be drawn from the brethren attending.

**53.** In all cases when the Grand Master Mason is requested to officiate at the laying of foundation-stones, application must be made through Grand Secretary, who shall submit the same to Grand Committee. If the application is approved, Grand Committee shall have power to take steps to carry the same into effect.

*Application for Grand Master Mason to lay foundation-stones.*

**54.** Where foundation-stones are to be laid in the Provinces, at which ceremonies Grand Lodge may not find it convenient or may not have been invited to attend, the Provincial Grand Master shall make all necessary arrangements. The ceremony shall be presided over by the Provincial Grand Master, or in his absence by the Immediate or any other Past Provincial Grand Master, or the Depute or the Substitute Provincial Grand Master, or the Senior or the Junior Provincial Grand Warden, whom failing, by the Master of the Senior Daughter Lodge of the Province represented by its reigning Master. In the event of the Provincial Grand Lodge being

*Laying of foundation-stones when Grand Lodge not present.*

*Who shall preside.*

dormant, Grand Lodge or Grand Committee shall appoint a qualified brother to preside, and he may select the other Office-Bearers for the occasion.

Lodge laying foundation-stone.

Sanction required.

**55**. A Daughter Lodge shall not conduct the ceremony of laying a foundation-stone without sanction being first obtained from Grand Lodge or Grand Committee in the case of the Metropolitan District, and from the Provincial or District Grand Master in the case of a Province or District.

Use of consecration vessels.

**56**. When the use of Grand Lodge Consecration Vessels is required by Provincial Grand Lodges for the ceremony of laying foundation-stones, or other Masonic ceremonials, application must be made through Grand Secretary. All expenses connected with the transmission of the vessels, etc., shall be defrayed by the persons applying.

Precedence in Grand Lodge.

Past rank.

Honorary rank.

**57**. At all Communications, at public processions, and at all other Grand Lodge functions, precedence in Grand Lodge shall be regulated as follows—past rank being given to all Past Grand Office-Bearers and Past Provincial and District Grand Masters who are qualified members of Grand Lodge, and Honorary Grand Office-Bearers being regarded as next in order of precedence to Grand Office-Bearers of corresponding rank:—

The Grand Master Mason,
Past Grand Masters,
Depute Grand Master,
Past Depute Grand Masters,
Substitute Grand Master,
Past Substitute Grand Masters,
Provincial and District Grand Masters,
Past Provincial and District Grand Masters,
Proxy District Grand Masters,
Representatives of Sister Grand Lodges,
Grand Wardens,
Past Grand Wardens,
Grand Secretary,
Past Grand Secretaries,
Grand Treasurer,
Past Grand Treasurers,
Grand Almoner,
Past Grand Almoners,
Grand Chaplains,
Past Grand Chaplains,
Grand Deacons,
Past Grand Deacons,
Grand Director of Ceremonies,
Past Grand Directors of Ceremonies,
Grand Architect,
Past Grand Architects,
Grand Jeweller,

Past Grand Jewellers,
Grand Bible-Bearer,
Past Grand Bible-Bearers,
Grand Bard,
Past Grand Bards,
Grand Sword-Bearer,
Past Grand Sword-Bearers,
Grand Director of Music,
Past Grand Directors of Music,
Members of Grand Committee,
Grand Organist,
Past Grand Organists,
Grand Piper,
Past Grand Pipers,
Grand Marshal,
Past Grand Marshals,
Grand Inner Guard,
Past Grand Inner Guards,
President of Grand Stewards,
Past Presidents of Grand Stewards,
Grand Stewards,
Grand Tyler.

Precedence of other members of Grand Lodge. **58.** The other members of Grand Lodge shall be entitled to rank immediately after the Grand Office-Bearers, Past Grand Office-Bearers, Provincial and District Grand Masters, and others mentioned in Law 57, according to the seniority of their respective Lodges on the Roll of Grand Lodge.

**59.** Daughter Lodges shall take precedence according to their seniority on the Roll of Grand Lodge, and the Office-Bearers thereof shall take precedence according to their respective offices.

**60.** In all processions in the Metropolitan District, the Senior Member out of office of the Lodge of Journeymen Masons, No. 8, shall be entitled to carry the mallet, and Apprentices of the same Lodge shall carry the working tools. On all other occasions where Grand Lodge is officiating in laying foundation-stones, similar members of the Senior Daughter Lodge of the Province or District shall be entitled to do so. The other paraphernalia shall on all occasions be carried by Office-Bearers of Grand Lodge.

**61.** Processions or other public appearances of the Craft in Masonic regalia are prohibited unless by permission of the Grand Master Mason, or of the Provincial or District Grand Master, or in his absence, the Depute or the Substitute Provincial or District Grand Master, or, in the Metropolitan District, of the Chairman of the Metropolitan District Committee.

**62.** Masters and Wardens of Daughter Lodges intending to represent their respective

Lodges in Grand Lodge personally, shall, through the Secretaries of their Lodges, give notice of such intention to Grand Secretary, immediately after their installation, and in no case later than the 15th of January following.

Intimation
thereof.

**63**. Any Daughter Lodge which is not to be represented in Grand Lodge by its Master in terms of the immediately preceding Law may appoint a qualified Master Mason to represent it as its Proxy Master, and he shall have power if necessary to appoint Proxy Wardens.

Representation
by Proxies.

**64**. Proxy Commissions by Daughter Lodges shall be granted and dated on the day of the Annual Election of Office-Bearers of such Lodges. All Proxy Commissions, except those which may be granted by Daughter Lodges abroad, must be lodged with Grand Secretary before the 15th day of January. Proxy Commissions by Daughter Lodges abroad may be received at any time. In the event of any Lodge not appointing a Proxy Master, or of any Proxy Master not appointing Proxy Wardens, it shall be in the power of Grand Committee to do so, and a proxy representative so appointed shall have the same powers and privileges and be subject to the same regulations as if he had

Proxy
Commissions.

Granting of.

Lodging of.

Appointment
of Proxies by
Grand Com-
mittee.

been duly appointed in terms of Law 63 or
Law 67.

**65.** A Daughter Lodge for which a Proxy
Master has been appointed under Law 63,
Law 64, or Law 67 shall not be entitled to
be represented in Grand Lodge by its Master
unless the Proxy appointment be recalled as
provided in Law 66.

*Position of Daughter Lodge for which Proxy Master appointed.*

**66.** A Daughter Lodge represented by proxy
in Grand Lodge shall not cancel or recall a
Proxy appointment except on the day of the
Lodge's Annual Election of Office-Bearers. A
Proxy Commission shall not be held as cancelled or recalled unless intimation thereof be
sent by registered letter to Grand Secretary
and to the Proxy Master holding the cancelled appointment, within fourteen days
after the date on which it was cancelled or
recalled.

*Cancelling of Proxy Commission.*

*Notice thereof.*

**67.** In the event of the death, resignation,
or disqualification of a Proxy Master, the
Daughter Lodge for which he was appointed
may meet immediately thereafter to elect
another Proxy Master, but the Proxy Wardens formerly appointed shall continue as
such until the day of the next Annual
Election of the Lodge.

*Death or disqualification of Proxy Master.*

*Does not disqualify Proxy Wardens.*

**Change of Proxy Wardens.**

**68.** A Proxy Master shall not change either of his Proxy Wardens during the year for which their fees have been paid, except in the case of death, disqualification, or resignation.

**Disqualification of Proxy Commissions.**

**69.** Proxy Commissions from Lodges in arrear of Grand Lodge dues cannot be received, and if a Lodge be one year in arrear, or be suspended, or become dormant, its Proxy Commission immediately lapses.

**Commissions to be registered and reported to Grand Lodge.**

**Fee.**

**70.** If Grand Secretary be satisfied that the Commission in favour of a Proxy Master is in order, the same shall be registered in the Roll of Grand Lodge and reported at the following Communication. For recording each Proxy Commission or appointment there shall be paid to Grand Lodge the appropriate fee set forth in the First Schedule, Part I., Item 7.

**Proxy District Grand Masters.**

**71.** It shall be competent for any District Grand Lodge to nominate and appoint a qualified member of any Daughter Lodge in good standing as its Proxy District Grand Master, who may vote and act in Grand Lodge.

**Restriction on Proxy Representation.**

**72.** A brother cannot represent as a proxy more than one District Grand Lodge or Daughter Lodge at a time.

**73.** A brother shall not introduce or assist in the introduction of any person, not being a qualified member of Grand Lodge, to act or vote in Grand Lodge, on pain of suspension from all Masonic privileges during the pleasure of Grand Lodge, and any person so introduced, if a member of the Scottish Craft, shall be subject to the same penalty.

*Fraudulent introduction of voters.*

**74.** As a test of membership, there shall be payable to Grand Lodge, annually, by each qualified member of Grand Lodge other than the representatives of Daughter Lodges, the sum set forth in the First Schedule, Part I., Item 1. Members' fees must be paid on enrolment, at whatever period in the course of each year they may be enrolled.

*Test of membership*

*Fee.*

*Payment on enrolment.*

**75.** The Roll of Members constituting Grand Lodge shall be made up as at the first day of February in each year, and shall consist of all brethren who are qualified members of Grand Lodge on that day; and only the members on the Roll so made up shall be qualified to vote in Grand Lodge at any Communication held previous to the Quarterly Communication in February of the following year, except in the cases following, viz. :—(1) The places of members dying, resigning or becoming disqualified may be filled up at any

*Roll of Members —when and how made up.*

*Filling up vacancies.*

*Deaths, etc.*

Lodges abroad.

Lodges which
instal in June.

Copy of Roll
to be sent to
members.

time; (2) Representatives of Daughter Lodges abroad may be put on the Roll at any time; (3) Representatives of Daughter Lodges which appoint their Office-Bearers on St John's Day in June, may be put on the Roll not later than the first Monday of August following appointment. A copy of the Roll so made up, and containing an appendix of unqualified and unrepresented Lodges, shall be sent to every member of Grand Lodge prior to the Quarterly Communication in May.

Fees for Annual
Certificate and
representation
—when payable
(*see* also Law
154).

**76.** Each Daughter Lodge shall pay the fees exigible for its Annual Certificate and representation in Grand Lodge not later than 1st January annually.

Members and
brethren to
provide them-
selves with
copies of these
Laws (*see* also
Law 165).

**77.** All Members of Grand Lodge, all Lodges, and the brethren generally, are enjoined to provide themselves with copies of the latest edition of these Laws as printed and published by authority of Grand Lodge. The cost of such copies shall be fixed by Grand Committee.

Honorary
Members.

**78.** It shall be in the power of the Grand Master Mason to nominate distinguished Brethren for Honorary Membership of Grand Lodge. Such nominations shall be subject to confirmation by Grand Lodge.

**79.** Honorary Members have no vote in Grand Lodge.

*Have no vote.*

**80.** The badge of Honorary Members shall be worn on the breast.

*Their badge.*

**81.** Representatives to Sister Grand Lodges may be appointed by Grand Lodge at any Quarterly Communication. Representatives from Sister Grand Lodges, who must be qualified Members of Grand Lodge, may, on presentation of their commissions, be received at any Quarterly Communication, and shall thereafter take rank as such representatives.

*Representatives to and from Sister Grand Lodges.*

*Their rank (see Law 59).*

**82.** Representative Members to Sister Grand Lodges may wear clothing (viz., apron, sash, and ribbon with badge) similar to the clothing of Grand Office-Bearers. Badges provided by Grand Lodge shall remain its property, and shall be handed over to each new Representative to a Sister Grand Lodge, on his appointment.

*Their clothing, etc. (see Laws 259, 260, 261, 265, and 267).*

**83.** Brethren of eminence and outstanding ability who have rendered service to the Craft may, by appointment of the Grand Master Mason, have conferred on them such Honorary rank of Office-Bearers of Grand Lodge as may be thought proper.

*Honorary rank.*

Degrees of
Masonry.

**84.** The Degrees of Freemasonry authorised and governed by Grand Lodge are those of Entered Apprentice, Fellow-of-Craft (including the Mark), and Master Mason, and no other.

Ceremonial of
Installed
Master.

**85.** Grand Lodge recognises a Ceremonial of Installed Master. That Ceremonial shall be communicated only to the Grand Master Mason, Provincial and District Grand Masters, Masters of Daughter Lodges at their installation or during their occupancy of the Chair, or any Past Master who for the term of one year has occupied the Chair of a Daughter Lodge as a duly elected Master. It can be communicated only when three or more Installed Masters are present. In the event of any Lodge not having a sufficient number of Installed Masters present, the Master of that Lodge, or any Past Master, may have the Ceremonial communicated to him in any other Lodge having three Installed Masters present, provided he produce evidence to the satisfaction of these Installed Masters that he is *bona fide* Master of a Lodge, or has served as such for the period before stated. In Lodges abroad, the Ceremonial may be communicated by one or more Installed Masters, on obtaining a dispensation from the District Grand Master, or,

where there is no District Grand Master, from
Grand Committee. To entitle a Master to
an Installed Master's Diploma from Grand
Lodge, the following Certificates must be sent
to Grand Secretary by the Secretary of the
Lodge:—(1) A Certificate signed by three
Installed Masters registered as such in Grand
Lodge (or in the case of Lodges abroad by
one or more Installed Masters so registered)
that the brother named therein has passed
through the Ceremonial; and (2) a Certificate
signed by the Secretary of the Lodge that
the brother has filled the Chair of the Lodge
for one year as Master. For such Diploma
and for registration there shall be payable to
Grand Lodge the fee set forth in the First
Schedule, Part I., Item 12.

*Installed Master's diploma.*

*Fee.*

**86.** The power of granting Diplomas in
connection with the Scottish Craft is vested
solely in Grand Lodge. In the event of
a brother's Diploma being lost or destroyed,
a duplicate may be issued by Grand Lodge,
but only on the recommendation of applicant's Lodge, and on receipt by Grand
Secretary of a Declaration satisfactory to
Grand Committee (made by the applicant
before a Magistrate, Justice of the Peace,
Notary Public, or British Consul, certifying
the circumstances of the loss or destruction

*Grand Lodge diplomas.*

*Duplicate diplomas.*

*Declaration as to loss.*

c

Fee.

of the original), accompanied by the fee set forth in the First Schedule, Part I., Item 15.

Amended diplomas. Fee.

The like fee shall be payable to Grand Lodge for each amended Diploma.

Dispensations by Grand Master Mason.

**87.** The Grand Master Mason, or his Depute or Substitute, in his name and on his behalf, has power to grant such Dispensations as may be expedient, although the subject matter of any such Dispensation may not be specially provided for in these Laws. For

Fee.

each Dispensation granted there shall be payable to Grand Lodge the fee set forth in the First Schedule, Part I., Item 16.

## GRAND COMMITTEE.

Grand Committee—how constituted.

**88.** Grand Committee consists of the Grand Master Mason, Past Grand Masters, Depute Grand Master, Substitute Grand Master, Provincial Grand Masters, Senior Grand Warden, Junior Grand Warden, and Grand Almoner all *ex officiis*, forty-eight elective members (who must be qualified members of Grand Lodge), and the Law Agent, who shall be a member *ex officio*, but without a

Quorum.

vote. Nine shall be a quorum. Depute Grand Masters, Substitute Grand Masters or Grand Wardens, finally demitting office in November of any year, shall continue members of Committee until the period of election in February following.

**89.** Sixteen of the elective members of Grand Committee shall retire at the Quarterly Communication in February in each year, but they shall be eligible for re-election at that Communication. Those who retire shall be the sixteen members whose names stand at the top of the official list of Grand Committee. Grand Secretary shall intimate by circular, annually, between 10th and 15th December, to the members of Grand Committee who retire in February following, the fact of their having so to retire, and that should they desire to become candidates for re-election, their nomination papers, signed by two qualified members of Grand Lodge, must be lodged with Grand Secretary not later than 15th January.

*Sixteen members retire annually.*

*Intimation of retiral.*

**90.** The manner of nomination and election of Grand Committee shall be as follows:— In the circular intimating the Quarterly Communication for November annually, a paragraph shall be inserted reminding members of Grand Lodge that the election of members of Grand Committee in room of those who retire shall take place at the Quarterly Com-

*Nomination and election.*

Date for lodging nominations.

munication in February. It shall be further stated that any qualified members of Grand Lodge wishing to nominate a brother for election shall lodge with Grand Secretary a written nomination on or before the 15th day of January. Such brother must be a qualified member of Grand Lodge, and the nomination paper shall state his full name, the name and number of a Daughter Lodge of which he is a qualified member and the name and number of his Mother Lodge, his Masonic rank in these Lodges, the name and number of the Daughter Lodge which he represents in Grand Lodge, or his qualification otherwise as a member of Grand Lodge, and his representative rank; also the names and designations of his proposer and seconder. Grand Secretary shall thereafter make up a list of qualified brethren who have been duly nominated, and issue it with the circular calling the Quarterly Communication for February. The voting shall be by ballot. A Voting Card, in a form approved by Grand Committee, shall be given out, under the supervision of Grand Secretary, to each qualified member on entering Grand Lodge at the February Communication. The Voting Cards shall be completed by the members receiving them, and thereafter collected by Tellers appointed for that purpose, who shall

Qualification.
Particulars required in nominations.

Vote—how taken.

forthwith deliver them to Grand Secretary. Grand Secretary shall act as Returning Officer, deposit the Voting Cards in the Ballot Box, seal the same in the presence of Grand Lodge, and thereafter count the votes and declare the results not later than the day following said Communication, all in accordance with instructions laid down by Grand Committee. *Declaration of results.*

In the event of a tie, the Grand Master Mason, or, in his absence, the Depute Grand Master, whom failing, the Substitute Grand Master, shall have a casting vote. *Casting vote.*

**91.** Grand Committee shall annually, at its February meeting, appoint from its own members the following Standing Committees, each to consist of seven members, except the Metropolitan District Committee, which shall consist of not less than twelve nor more than twenty members, of whom three shall be a quorum in each case, who shall meet monthly or as required and shall report their proceedings to Grand Committee for approval, viz. :— *Standing Committees.* *Quorum.*

(*a*) A Finance Committee, not more than two members of which shall come from the same Province or from the Metropolitan District. The whole of the funds of Grand Lodge shall come under the direct supervision of the Finance Committee. Subject *Finance.* *Supervision of funds.*

to the approval of Grand Committee, it shall be responsible for the investment of all the funds of Grand Lodge, and for the expenditure of the income of its General Fund. The Cash Book of Grand Lodge, regularly and correctly entered up and balanced monthly by Grand Treasurer, together with the Auditor's report thereon, shall be submitted to the Committee at each meeting. All cheques and orders drawn upon any of the Grand Lodge Bank Accounts must be signed by the Chairman of the Finance Committee, or, in his absence, by another member of that Committee authorised by Grand Committee, and countersigned by Grand Treasurer, or in his absence by Grand Secretary. Deposit Receipts shall be similarly endorsed when uplifted.

*Cash book to be balanced monthly.*

*Signing of cheques, etc.*

(*b*) A Hall and Buildings Committee, whose duty shall be to see that all contracts for work have been duly executed, and to attend to the letting and upkeep and generally take the care and management of the whole buildings occupied by Grand Lodge, and the furnishings thereof.

*Hall and Buildings.*

(*c*) A Bye-Laws Committee, whose duty shall be to revise all Bye-Laws or alterations thereon sent to Grand Secretary for approval, previous to their being submitted to Grand

*Bye-Laws.*

Committee. It shall also prepare rulings on questions relating to Masonic law or practice put by Lodges or brethren to Grand Lodge or Grand Committee.

*Rulings on questions.*

(*d*) A Foreign and Colonial Committee, to which questions affecting the interest of the Scottish Craft in Foreign countries and the British Dominions and Colonies shall be referred for investigation.

*Foreign and Colonial.*

(*e*) A Petitions, Complaints, and Appeals Committee, which shall investigate cases of dispute or difference arising in the Craft; petitions, complaints or appeals made to Grand Lodge or to Grand Committee; judgments of Provincial or District Grand Lodges or of Daughter Lodges; and cases of breach of Grand Lodge Laws.

*Petitions, Complaints, and Appeals.*

(*f*) The Metropolitan District Committee, the members of which must be Masters or Past Masters of Daughter Lodges, whose duty shall be to supervise, guide and control, on behalf of Grand Lodge, the Lodges in the Metropolitan District, to visit these Lodges annually, examine their books, inquire into their mode of working, and administer the sums collected in terms of Law 140 other than the Benevolent Fund of the District.

*Metropolitan District.*

(*g*) A Museum and Library Committee, which shall supervise the Museum and

*Museum and Library.*

Library and the catalogue thereof, and enact Regulations for the use of the Library. A book shall be kept in which the names and addresses of borrowers, dates of lending and returning of books borrowed, shall be entered.

**Chairmen of Committees— how appointed.**

**92.** The Chairman of each Standing Committee shall be appointed annually by Grand Committee, but no member shall hold the Chairmanship of any Standing Committee for a longer period than three years.

**Vacancies— how filled.**

**93.** The election of qualified members to fill vacancies caused by death, resignation, or disqualification, between the dates of election by Grand Lodge, shall lie with the remaining members of Grand Committee. Such interim appointments shall continue to the date of next annual election of Grand Committee. The interim members so appointed shall be eligible for re-election.

**Chairman of Grand Committee.**

**94.** The Grand Master Mason is *ex officio* Chairman of Grand Committee. In his absence the following Grand Office-Bearers shall preside :—Past Grand Masters in their order; Depute Grand Master; Substitute Grand Master; Senior Grand Warden; Junior Grand Warden. In the event of the absence of all those Grand Office-Bearers, the meeting shall appoint its own Chairman.

**Grand Committee.**

**95.** Grand Committee is the ordinary judicial tribunal for Grand Lodge. It shall have full power to investigate and judge all cases of complaint, dispute, or difference arising in the Craft; appeals against judgments of Provincial or District Grand Lodges or of Daughter Lodges; and any breach of Grand Lodge Laws. If in its opinion any judgment pronounced, whether appealed against or not, is inadequate or too severe, it shall have power to vary the same, subject to a right of appeal to Grand Lodge by the parties concerned. It shall have power to call for written pleadings and answers, with copies thereof and productions, fix the time within which these must be lodged, summon parties and witnesses to attend, take evidence, hear the parties concerned, and adopt such other measures and proceedings as it may deem necessary and advisable; and all or any of these powers may be exercised on its behalf by the Petitions, Complaints, and Appeals Committee, or other Committee appointed by Grand Committee for the purpose. All transactions of Grand Committee shall, after the Minutes thereof have been approved by Grand Committee, be reported for the consideration of Grand Lodge at its next Quarterly Communication, and be subject to its approval or disapproval, but the minutes of the meetings of Grand Committee as correct records of the business

*Powers and duties.*

*To deal with complaints, etc.*

*To review judgments.*

*To delegate powers.*

*Approval of transactions.*

*Minutes not subject to alteration by Grand Lodge.*

done, and its judgments if not timeously appealed against in accordance with Law 109, shall not be subject to alteration by Grand Lodge. All remits from Grand Lodge shall be taken up by Grand Committee at its first ordinary meeting after each remit.

*Remits.*

**96.** The Ordinary Meetings of Grand Committee shall be held on the second last Thursday of every month. Meetings shall also be held on the first Thursday of February, May, August, and November, prior to the Quarterly Communications on these days, to approve of the Minutes of the previous Ordinary Meetings of Grand Committee the transactions of which fall to be reported at such Quarterly Communications. Grand Committee may dispense with or alter the date of any of its statutory meetings.

*Ordinary Meetings.*

*Additional Meetings.*

**97.** Grand Secretary shall, upon the requisition of five qualified members of Grand Committee, call a meeting thereof, to be held within ten days after receipt of such requisition. The circular calling the meeting shall state the purpose for which the meeting is called and no other business shall be discussed thereat.

*Special Meetings.*

**98.** All business to be considered by Grand Committee shall be notified in the circular

*Business to be notified.*

calling the meeting, except such as may be received by Grand Secretary subsequent to the printing of the Agenda, and may require immediate attention.

**99.** A meeting of Grand Committee shall be held at least one month previous to the Quarterly Communication in November, to take measures for the recommendation of candidates to fill up the offices in Grand Lodge for the ensuing year. Such recommendation shall, however, be subject to the ultimate decision of Grand Lodge in the election of its Office-Bearers.

Recommendation of candidates for offices in Grand Lodge.

**100.** At the meeting of Grand Committee in January annually, a report shall be made by Grand Secretary of all Lodges which have failed to obtain their Annual Certificate.

Annual report of Lodges without Certificates.

**101.** An inventory and valuation of the moveable property belonging to Grand Lodge, together with a rental and valuation of the heritable property, shall be made up by Grand Secretary and Grand Treasurer annually, and laid before Grand Committee at its meeting in December. These shall be docqueted by the Chairman, and a reference thereto inserted in the Minutes.

Inventory and valuation of property.

**102.** All heritable property and other investments belonging to Grand Lodge shall be vested in the following Grand Office-Bearers as Trustees *ex officiis*, viz., the Grand Master Mason, the Immediate Past Grand Master, the Grand Wardens, and Grand Secretary, and their successors from time to time in these offices; but it shall be competent for Grand Committee to resolve that investments other than heritable property may be placed in the name of Grand Lodge Bankers, or Bank-Nominees, in trust for Grand Lodge and subject to the control of Grand Committee. All investments shall be such as are sanctioned by the Trusts (Scotland) Acts only, and all interest and dividends thereon shall be paid direct to Grand Lodge Bankers on account of Grand Lodge. No property or investments shall be purchased or sold and no Funds shall be disposed of without the consent and authority of Grand Committee.

**103.** Estimates shall be taken preferably from persons connected with the Craft for all work to be executed for Grand Lodge, the expense of which Grand Committee shall have reason to believe may exceed five pounds sterling. Unless with the special permission of Grand Committee, members of Grand Committee shall not offer or be accepted to

*Marginal notes:*

Holding of property and investments.

Trustees.

Investments may be in name of Bankers or their Nominees.

Application of Trusts Acts.

Interest, etc,, to be paid direct to Bank.

Purchase or sale of property, etc. —sanction required.

Estimates to be taken for work.

Position of members of Grand Committee.

execute work for Grand Lodge. This prohibition shall not apply to the Law Agent,
nor to the Grand Architect, and Grand
Jeweller, should they be members.

**104.** In the event of complaints, disputes, *Procedure in cases of complaints, etc.*
or differences arising, the brethren or Lodges
involved may lay the same before Grand
Committee by a written petition or complaint, duly signed, stating distinctly the
matter at issue.

**105.** Such petition or complaint, and eight *Papers to be served and lodged.*
copies thereof, together with a certificate by
the petitioner or complainer that a copy
thereof has been served on the other party
by registered letter, shall be lodged with
Grand Secretary, and the proper fees paid
therewith. If these requirements have been
complied with, Grand Secretary shall lay the *To be laid before Petitions, Complaints, and Appeals Committee.*
petition or complaint before the first meeting
of the Petitions, Complaints, and Appeals
Committee, which, after investigating the
matter, shall report the ascertained facts to *Report to Grand Committee.*
Grand Committee and suggest a judgment
for its consideration and disposal.

**106.** Contending parties and witnesses, *Appearance of parties and witnesses.*
when duly summoned, shall appear before
Grand Committee, or the Petitions, Com-

plaints, and Appeals Committee, or as the case may be. It shall be competent for any contending party to have the assistance of an agent or mandatory at any diet of appearance, but such agent or mandatory must be a qualified member of a Daughter Lodge in good standing, and intimation of his appointment must be given to Grand Secretary and to the other contending parties or their declared agents or mandatories at least seven days prior to such diet of appearance.

*Agents and Mandatories.*

**107.** There shall be payable to Grand Lodge at the time of lodging a petition, complaint or appeal, at the time of lodging answers or other pleadings, at each borrowing and return of the process or productions, and for all extracts or copies of papers or proceedings, the appropriate fees set forth in the First Schedule, Part I., Item 19.

*Fees with papers.*

**108.** The judgments of Grand Committee shall be intimated in writing by Grand Secretary by registered letter, to the parties to the petition, complaint, or appeal, who shall therein be apprised that the same shall become final unless appealed to Grand Lodge, as provided by Law 109, within twenty-eight days of the date of posting said intimation by Grand Secretary, or within

*Intimation of judgments.*

*Time limit for appeal.*

such extended period as in special circumstances Grand Committee may decide.  If not so appealed, the judgments shall be final.

*Judgments final if not so appealed.*

**109.** It shall be in the power of any of the contending parties who may feel themselves aggrieved by the judgment of Grand Committee in the matter of a dispute or complaint, to appeal the same to Grand Lodge, by Note of Appeal lodged with Grand Secretary along with eight copies thereof.   In such case the party appealing must, if called upon, forthwith deposit with Grand Secretary a sum equal to the amount of the reasonable expenses already incurred by the other party, which sum Grand Secretary is hereby empowered to fix, and the same or any part thereof may, in the discretion of Grand Committee, be forfeited and be paid to the other party if Grand Lodge shall affirm the judgment of Grand Committee.   If the judgment be reversed, or if Grand Lodge shall so order, the deposit shall be returned.

*Appeal to Grand Lodge— procedure.*

*Deposit of expenses.*

*Disposal thereof.*

**110.** In all cases of petition, complaint, or appeal, Grand Secretary shall mark on the back of each paper the date when the same was lodged.

*Marking of date of lodging papers.*

Pleadings on appeal.

**111.** In cases of appeal it shall be competent for Grand Lodge to call for further productions, pleadings, or evidence and to hear parties or their agents or mandatories.

Appeal competent on merits only.

In no case shall an appeal be competent except upon the merits of the cause, and after the deliberate judgment of Grand Committee thereupon.

Grand Lodge judgments final.

**112.** The judgments of Grand Lodge shall be final and not reviewable by any

Penalty for non-implement.

tribunal whatever. Any party challenging, or refusing to submit to or implement the same or any judgments of Grand Committee which have become final, shall be liable to expulsion from the Craft, suspension from Masonic privileges, or such other judgment as Grand Lodge may see proper to pronounce.

## PROVINCIAL AND DISTRICT GRAND LODGES.

Erection of Provinces and Districts.

**113.** For the more efficient government and control of Daughter Lodges and members of the Scottish Craft, outwith the Metropolitan District, Grand Lodge may divide Scotland, the British Dominions and Colonies, and Foreign parts into Provinces or Districts for Masonic purposes, each having a Provincial or District Grand Lodge with local jurisdiction, on behalf of Grand Lodge, over the Daughter Lodges and Assemblies and the members of the Scottish Craft in such Province or District. Provinces or Districts may be defined, enlarged, restricted, combined, divided, or altered by Grand Lodge, at any time. The precedence of Provincial and District Grand Lodges shall be regulated by the dates of their original formation.

*Precedence.*

**114.** Each Province or District shall have a Provincial or District Grand Master appointed by Commission from Grand Lodge. Prior to the appointment Grand Secretary shall invite the Daughter Lodges in the Province or District to recommend by a specified date a suitable brother for appointment, and shall submit to Grand Committee, for its consideration and recommendation, such replies as are received, but the right of appointment is vested in Grand Lodge alone, except in the case of the Province of Ayrshire, which appointment is provided for in the agreement entered into between Grand Lodge and Mother Kilwinning Lodge in the year 1807. Every Provincial and District Grand Master must be or become a qualified member of a Daughter Lodge in good standing in his Province or District. For his Commission, there shall be payable to

*Appointment of Provincial or District Grand Masters.*

*Procedure.*

*Qualification.*

*Fee.*

D

Grand Lodge by each Provincial or District Grand Master the fee set forth in the First Schedule, Part I., Item 2.

Duration of Commission.

May be renewed.

Renewal fee.

**115.** Commissions to Provincial and District Grand Masters shall lapse at the expiry of five years from date of issue. Provincial and District Grand Masters shall be eligible for reappointment. There shall be payable to Grand Lodge, on each renewal of Commission, the fee set forth in the First Schedule, Part I., Item 3.

Constitution of Provincial or District Grand Lodges.

**116.** Each Provincial or District Grand Lodge shall be composed of the following brethren provided they are duly qualified members thereof as defined in Law 272, viz., the Provincial or District Grand Master, Past Provincial or District Grand Masters, all the Provincial or District Grand Office-Bearers (excepting the Provincial or District Grand Tyler), all Past Masters who have filled the Chair for one year as Master of a Daughter Lodge in the Province or District, and the Masters, Immediate Past Masters, and Wardens of the several Daughter Lodges in the Province or District which are in good

Disqualification for office, etc.

standing; but a member of a Daughter Lodge who holds office in or is a member of Committee of a Lodge under any other Masonic Constitution, shall not be entitled to hold office or be a member of Committee, or to vote, in any District Grand Lodge, or Daughter Lodge abroad, unless under Dispensation granted by the District Grand Master. In the case of a Daughter Lodge abroad under the direct supervision of Grand Lodge, any Dispensation required must be obtained from the Grand Master Mason.

117. Each Provincial or District Grand Master shall be entitled to choose and appoint by Commission, from time to time, a Depute Master, a Substitute Master, a Secretary and a Chaplain or Chaplains. The other Provincial or District Grand Office-Bearers (except the Immediate Past Provincial or District Grand Master), viz., Senior Warden, Junior Warden, Treasurer or Treasurers, Almoner, Senior Deacon, Junior Deacon, Director of Ceremonies, Bible - Bearer, Sword - Bearer, Organist, Marshal, Inner Guard, President of Stewards, and Tyler, shall be elected annually by Provincial and District Grand Lodges. A Provincial or District Grand Lodge may have other Office-Bearers provided these are sanctioned by Grand Lodge. In the case of Provincial Grand Lodges having the supervision of more than twenty Daughter Lodges, the Provincial Grand Master shall have power to appoint additional Substitute Provincial

*Office-Bearers—commissioned and elective.*

*Additional Substitute Provincial Grand Masters.*

Grand Masters provided that the number so appointed shall not exceed one for each additional seven Lodges, which Substitutes shall take precedence according to the dates of their Commissions.

**Provincial or District Grand Committee.** A Provincial or District Grand Lodge may appoint a Provincial or District Grand Committee of such number and composition as the Lodge shall determine and whose powers and duties shall *mutatis mutandis* be of a nature similar to those of Grand Committee with such modifications as the Provincial or District Grand Lodge may think proper: provided that all judgments of the Committee shall be subject to confirmation by the Lodge.

**Board of Provincial or District Grand Stewards.** A Provincial or District Grand Lodge may appoint annually from its qualified members a Board of Provincial or District Grand Stewards, whose duties within the Province or District shall be similar to those of the Board of Grand Stewards.

**Residential Qualification.** All Provincial and District Grand Office-Bearers (other than the Provincial or District Grand Master, his Depute or Substitute) and all Stewards and members of Committee must have a residence within or in the neighbourhood of the Province or District.

**District Grand Masters may appoint Superintendents.** **118.** In District Grand Lodges embracing large territory, it shall be competent for District Grand Masters to appoint Superintendents over outlying districts of such territory, whose duty shall be to superintend the working of the Daughter Lodges in the localities assigned to them, subject to the control and direction of their District Grand Masters, to whom they shall report from time to time. It shall be in the power of a District Grand Master to confer on a Superintendent and on brethren who have rendered good service to Scottish Freemasonry in the District, such District Grand Rank as he may in the circumstances deem fitting.

*Can confer District Grand Rank.*

**119.** For the purpose of the supervision of Daughter Lodges abroad where there is no District Grand Lodge, Grand Lodge may, in its discretion, appoint Superintendents, whose duty shall be to supervise, on behalf of Grand Lodge, the Daughter Lodges in the localities assigned to them, to visit these Lodges, examine their books, and enquire into their mode of working, and to report from time to time to Grand Lodge.

*Appointment of Superintendents by Grand Lodge.*

**120.** Provincial and District Grand Masters and Superintendents shall be styled " Right Worshipful." Other Office-Bearers, the Tyler excepted, shall be styled " Worshipful."

*Style of Provincial and District Grand Masters and Office-Bearers.*

Tenure of office.

**121.** Law 11, which prohibits the holding of the same office in Grand Lodge longer than two years consecutively, shall apply also to the elective Office-Bearers of Provincial or District Grand Lodges, and with the same exceptions.

Filling Chair in absence of Provincial or District Grand Master.

**122.** In the absence of the Provincial or District Grand Master the Chair shall be taken by the Provincial or District Grand Office-Bearers in the following order:—The Immediate Past or, in his absence, any Past Provincial or District Grand Master of the Province or District, the Depute Provincial or District Grand Master, the Substitute Provincial or District Grand Master, Past Depute Provincial or District Grand Masters, Past Substitute Provincial or District Grand Masters, the Provincial or District Senior Grand Warden, the Provincial or District Junior Grand Warden, whom all failing by any other Provincial or District Grand Office-Bearer present at the meeting in the order of precedence.

Rank and precedence.

Past rank.

**123.** At all meetings of a Provincial or District Grand Lodge, precedence and past rank shall be regulated by the practice of Grand Lodge. Installed Office-Bearers, on the expiry of their periods of office, shall be entitled to the past rank of their respective offices.

**124.** The Office-Bearers of a Provincial or District Grand Lodge (with the exception of the Provincial or District Grand Master and Past Provincial or District Grand Masters) do not take rank out of their Province or District; they are, however, entitled to wear their clothing as Provincial or District Grand Office-Bearers at all Masonic meetings.

Office-Bearers do not rank out-with Province or District.

May wear their clothing.

**125.** Each Provincial or District Grand Master, either personally or through the Depute or the Substitute Provincial or District Grand Master, shall visit annually every Daughter Lodge under his charge; call special meetings of the Provincial or District Grand Lodge at such places and times as he shall think fit; examine into the state of Freemasonry in his Province or District, correct any faults, omissions, or wrongful actings; give such directions as he may think necessary; pronounce any admonition which in his opinion may have been incurred; and report from time to time to Grand Lodge.

Provincial or District Grand Masters to visit Lodges annually.

**126.** When a Provincial or District Grand Master, or a Depute or Substitute Provincial or District Grand Master, or the Provincial or District Grand Wardens, with other Provincial

Official visitations.

or District Grand Office-Bearers, or the Metropolitan District Committee, shall visit officially a Daughter Lodge, the Master and Wardens of that Lodge shall offer to vacate their respective Chairs in favour of the brethren holding or filling for the time the corresponding offices in Provincial or District Grand Lodge, or to three members of the Metropolitan District Committee. In the event of the Provincial or District Grand Master, or the Office-Bearer or Brother heading the Visitation, exercising his right to take the Chair, the Master of the Lodge **How received.** shall sit at his right hand. A Provincial or District Grand Master, or his Depute or Substitute, or the Metropolitan District Committee, shall be received in the Third Degree unless otherwise ordered by him or them.

**Consecration of new Lodges.**
**In Provinces and Districts.**

**127.** The Provincial or District Grand Master, the Past Provincial or District Grand Masters, the Depute or the Substitute Provincial or District Grand Master, shall consecrate all new Daughter Lodges chartered in their respective Provinces or Districts, and shall also, in the absence of the Grand Office-Bearers, preside at all Masonic ceremonials within their respective **In Metropolitan District.** Provinces or Districts. In the Metropolitan District new Daughter Lodges shall be

consecrated by the Grand Master Mason,
or, in his absence, by the Chairman of the
Metropolitan District Committee, whom failing, by such other qualified brother as the
Grand Master Mason may nominate.

**128.** A Provincial or District Grand Lodge
shall hear and determine all subjects of
Masonic complaint, dispute or difference initiated before or appealed or remitted to it
respecting Daughter Lodges or brethren of
the Scottish Craft within the Province or
District, and may admonish, or pronounce a
sentence of suspension, and, in the case of a
Lodge, may suspend its Charter. The procedure
in all such subjects of complaint, dispute, or
difference shall be regulated *mutatis mutandis*
by Laws 104 to 111 inclusive, but admonitions by Provincial or District Grand Lodges
or Provincial or District Grand Masters or
their Deputes or Substitutes, cannot be
appealed against, although they may be
reviewed by Grand Committee in virtue of
Law 95. Provincial or District Grand Secretaries shall notify all sentences to Grand
Committee. On a sentence becoming final,
Grand Secretary shall so inform the Provincial or District Grand Secretary concerned,
who shall thereupon notify the Daughter
Lodges in the Province or District.

*(marginal notes:)*
Provincial and District Grand Lodges to hear and determine complaints, etc.

Procedure.

Admonitions not appealable.

May be reviewed by Grand Committee.

Sentences to be notified.

Additional powers to District Grand Masters.

**129.** Grand Lodge delegates to its District Grand Masters, in addition to the powers herein given, the power of investigating, regulating, and deciding all matters relative to Lodges and brethren of the Scottish Craft within their respective Districts. This power they may exercise either of themselves, or by a Committee of their District Grand Lodge, reserving to those concerned the right of appeal to Grand Lodge against any judgment (other than an admonition) that may be pronounced in the matter.

Application of Laws affecting Lodges abroad.

**130.** In questions affecting Daughter Lodges abroad, or District Grand Lodges, Grand Committee shall have power, through Grand Secretary, to decide on the reasonable application or effect of any enactments of these Laws, the literal interpretation of which may be inadvisable in the circumstances or conditions of such Lodges or District Grand Lodges.

Fees with papers.

**131.** The fees exigible by Provincial or District Grand Lodges for papers in process before Provincial or District Grand Lodges, shall be one-half of those payable to Grand Lodge, set forth in the First Schedule, Part I., Item 19.

**132.** Provincial and District Grand Masters are forbidden to recognise any organisation, purporting to be Masonic, which does not hold of Grand Lodge or of a Sister Grand Lodge or other Masonic Grand Body, or to allow any brother under their jurisdiction to join, visit, or countenance the same, or to allow any member of such unrecognised organisation to attend any Masonic meeting or ceremonial held within their Province or District.

*Irregular organisations not to be recognised.*

**133.** Each Provincial and District Grand Lodge shall hold Quarterly Communications on such convenient days as shall be fixed by the Provincial or District Grand Master, or in his absence, by his Depute or Substitute. Meetings may be adjourned from time to time, but no business shall be taken up or dealt with at any such adjourned meeting, except that carried forward from the previous meeting.   All business shall be transacted in the Third Degree.   The meetings of a Provincial or District Grand Lodge shall not be interrupted by the death, or retirement, or disqualification of a Provincial or District Grand Master.

*Communications to be held quarterly.*

*Adjournment.*

*Business*

**134.** A Provincial or District Grand Lodge which has not assembled for the space of two

*Failure to assemble for two years.*

years becomes dormant, and shall have no power to meet until authorised by Grand Lodge.

**135.** When a Provincial or District Grand Lodge becomes dormant, or fails to comply with the requirements of these Laws, the Daughter Lodges in the Province or District shall come under the immediate superintendence of Grand Lodge, and all the books, papers, funds and paraphernalia belonging to the dormant Province or District shall become the property of Grand Lodge and be forthwith handed over to it.

**136.** Grand Lodge or Grand Committee has full power at any time to convene a Provincial or District Grand Lodge, independently of the Provincial or District Grand Master, who shall be notified thereof.

**137.** A Provincial or District Grand Master shall, on appointment, convene the Provincial or District Grand Lodge, and lay before it his Commission, within six months of its date, otherwise it shall be null and void, unless on cause shown to the satisfaction of Grand Committee.

**138.** An Office-Bearer of a Provincial or District Grand Lodge is not entitled to act as such until he has been installed into office.

*Dormant or defaulting Provincial or District Grand Lodges come under control of Grand Lodge.*

*Grand Lodge or Committee may convene a Provincial or District Grand Lodge.*

*Provincial or District Grand Master to present Commission.*

*Office-Bearers to be installed.*

**139.** Bye-Laws of a Provincial or District Grand Lodge must be in accordance with these Laws and shall not be valid until approved by Grand Committee. *Bye-Laws.*

**140.** Every Provincial or District Grand Lodge shall fix a sum to be paid to it annually by each Daughter Lodge in the Province or District of not less than the sum set forth in the First Schedule, Part II., Item I. (*a*) (1), and in addition may fix a sum, not exceeding the sum set forth in the First Schedule, Part II., Item I. (*a*)(2), to be paid to it by such Lodge for each initiate or brother affiliated thereto. These sums shall be for necessary purposes. A further sum, not exceeding the sum set forth in the First Schedule, Part II., Item I. (*b*), shall be fixed and paid as aforesaid for each candidate initiated or affiliated as aforesaid, which last mentioned sum shall form a Benevolent Fund, and be kept separate from the ordinary income of the Provincial or District Grand Lodge, and after deduction of any expenses incidental to management shall be devoted solely to purposes of Masonic benevolence. The above provisions shall apply also to the Metropolitan District, and the sums exigible from the Daughter Lodges therein shall be fixed from time to time by, and be payable to, Grand

*Annual payments from Lodges.*

*General Fund.*

*Benevolent Fund.*

*Metropolitan Lodges.*

Committee.   The funds of a Provincial or District Grand Lodge shall be administered by it
or by Committees constituted in terms of Law
117 and of its Bye-Laws.   The Benevolent
Fund of the Metropolitan District shall, in
terms of its Constitution, be distributed by a
Committee consisting of the Metropolitan
District Committee and the Masters of the
Daughter Lodges in good standing in the
District; the other Funds of the District shall
be administered by the Metropolitan District

Committee.   A Lodge in arrear of such annual
contribution or other sums foresaid shall
have no right to be represented in Provincial
or District Grand Lodge, or in the Benevolent
Fund Committee of the Metropolitan District,
or in Grand Lodge, and shall also be liable
to suspension, or to have its Charter recalled.

The provisions in the preceding paragraph
so far as relating to Benevolent Funds shall
apply *mutatis mutandis* to every Annuity
Fund and Fund for Special Masonic Benevolent purposes which has been or may be
established by a Provincial or District Grand
Lodge or the Metropolitan District.

**141.** Every Provincial or District Grand
Lodge shall levy annually from its Office-
Bearers and Stewards fees of honour, and from
its members fees of membership, the amount of

which may be determined by each Provincial or District Grand Lodge. Such fees of **Commutation.** membership may, in the case of Provincial or District Grand Masters, qualified Past Provincial or District Grand Masters, and qualified Masters and Past Masters of Daughter Lodges in a Province or District, be commuted by a single payment, the amount of which shall **Amount.** be determined by the Provincial or District Grand Lodge, but shall not be less than the minimum commutation fee set forth in **Minimum.** the First Schedule, Part II., Item 3. All sums received in commutation of fees of membership shall be dealt with as provided in said Item 3. Every Provincial and **Certified list of Past Provincial** District Grand Lodge shall, before 15th **and District Grand Masters** January annually, transmit to Grand Sec- **annually.** retary a certified list of the Past Provincial and District Grand Masters of the Province or District who are qualified members of the Provincial or District Grand Lodge.

**142.** In addition to the sums authorised **District Grand Lodges—addi-** by Laws 140 and 141, a District Grand **tional powers of** Lodge may levy, in respect of every qualified **levy.** member of the Daughter Lodges under its jurisdiction, an annual sum in the case of each contributing member and a single sum in the case of each member whose contributions to his Lodge shall have been commuted—both of such amounts as the District Grand Lodge shall determine. It may also levy such other sums as it may fix for District Grand Office-Bearers' certificates, Dispensations, revision of Bye-Laws, and other administrative acts.

**Proxies admissible to District Grand Lodges.**

**143.** It shall be competent for Daughter Lodges abroad in good standing to nominate any three qualified brethren to represent their Master and Wardens at all meetings of the District Grand Lodge of which the Master and Wardens of such Daughter Lodges are qualified members, with all their powers.

## DAUGHTER LODGES.

**Application for a Charter.**

**144.** Any number, not fewer than seven, of Master Masons in good standing, who are desirous of establishing a new Daughter Lodge, may apply by petition, setting forth the reasons why such new Lodge is craved to be erected, and praying Grand Lodge to constitute them a regular Lodge, and to grant them a Charter accordingly.

**Recommendation of petition.**

**145.** Petitioners for a new Lodge must along with the petition, produce a recommendation signed with consent of their Lodges

by the Master and Wardens of at least two **By two Lodges.**
Daughter Lodges in the Province or District
in which it is proposed to erect the new Lodge.
Such petition must be recommended by the **By Provincial or District Grand Lodge, etc.**
Provincial or District Grand Lodge, or, if in
the Metropolitan District, by the Metropolitan District Committee. In the event of
a petition being received for a Lodge in a place,
outwith the Metropolitan District, where there **Where no Provincial or District Grand Lodge.**
is no Provincial or District Grand Lodge, such
petition must be accompanied by a recommendation signed with consent of their Lodges
by the Master and Wardens of two Lodges
near the place of proposed erection.

**146**. All Charters shall bear date from the **Precedence of Lodges.**
day of granting the same, and the Daughter
Lodges shall take precedence accordingly.
All Charters shall be duly recorded by Grand
Secretary in the Chartulary of Grand Lodge.

**147**. The fee payable to Grand Lodge for **Fee for Charter.**
a Charter shall be the sum set forth in the
First Schedule, Part I., Item 4, and that
sum shall be lodged in the hands of Grand
Secretary at the time of presenting the peti-
tion. Qualified brethren petitioning for a **Founder Members' fees**
Charter, which is granted, shall pay to
Grand Lodge the appropriate fees set forth
in the First Schedule, Part I., Item 5.

E

**148.** It shall be the special duty of the Master of a Lodge to see to the safe custody of its Charter. In the event of the Charter of any Lodge being lost, destroyed, or unlawfully taken possession of, the issue of a Duplicate Charter may be authorised by Grand Committee, for which there shall be payable the fee set forth in the First Schedule, Part I., Item 14. Such Duplicate Charter shall be signed by the Grand Master Mason and Grand Secretary, and shall have the same force and validity as the original Charter. The application for a Duplicate Charter must be in writing, and must be accompanied by a Statutory Declaration, stating the fact and probable cause of the loss, destruction, or detention of the Charter. Such Declaration shall be made by the Master and Wardens, or, in case of the death or absence of such Office-Bearers, by five brethren authorised for that purpose by the Lodge, and shall be made before a Magistrate, Justice of the Peace, Notary Public, or British Consul.

*Custody of Charter.*

*Charter lost or withheld.*

*Duplicate may be issued.*

*Fee.*

*Statutory declaration as to loss.*

**149.** A Lodge must be consecrated before it can act under its Charter. When a Charter for the erection of a Lodge is granted in a district where there is no Provincial or District Grand Lodge, Grand Lodge shall at the same

*A Lodge must be consecrated.*

time appoint a qualified brother to consecrate the Lodge.

**150.** The Charter of a Lodge must be in the Lodge-Room throughout every meeting, in view of, and open to the inspection of the brethren. If the Charter is not in the Lodge-Room the meeting cannot be constituted.

*Charter to be open for inspection.*

The Charter, books, papers, jewels, clothing, and paraphernalia of a Lodge shall be inalienable. Should the majority of any Lodge retire from it, the power of carrying on the work remains with the minority, but if the number of qualified brethren be fewer than seven, the Lodge may be declared dormant, in which event the Charter, books, papers, jewels, clothing, paraphernalia, and funds (including Benevolent and Annuity Funds) shall become the property of Grand Lodge for corresponding Masonic purposes, and shall forthwith be transferred and delivered to Grand Lodge. In the event of the Charter, books, papers, jewels, clothing, paraphernalia, and funds being withheld by a member or members of the Scottish Craft, he or they shall be subject to suspension or expulsion. Grand Secretary, or the Provincial or District Grand Secretary, or any of the remaining members of the dormant Lodge so authorised, may apply on behalf

*Charter and property inalienable.*

*Right of minority.*

*Dormant Lodge.*

*Illegal retention of Charter and property.*

of Grand Lodge to the Civil Courts for a warrant for the delivery of the foresaid articles, and for payment of said funds, to Grand Lodge. A dormant Lodge may be resuscitated by Grand Lodge, or by the Provincial or District Grand Lodge, on the application of not fewer than seven qualified brethren, resident in the Province or District, or (if there be no Provincial or District Grand Lodge) resident in or near the proposed meeting place of the Lodge, acting in conjunction with one or more members of the Lodge.

**Dormant Lodges may be resuscitated.**

**151.** Every Daughter Lodge must have a fixed place or places of meeting, approved as provided by Law 161, which cannot be changed without similar approval.

**Fixed place of meeting.**

**152.** If circumstances shall render it expedient, a Provincial or District Grand Lodge, or, in the Metropolitan District, the Metropolitan District Committee, or in localities where there is no Provincial or District Grand Lodge, Grand Committee, may authorise a Lodge to hold a meeting or meetings in another meeting place in the same town or locality, under such conditions and restrictions as the Authority granting the permission may impose.

**Occasional change of place of meeting.**

**153**. Lodges are prohibited from holding meetings of any kind on a Sunday except for the purposes of Divine or Memorial Services or the Funeral of a brother.

*No meetings on Sundays.*

**154**. Every Daughter Lodge shall annually, on or before 1st January, apply for and obtain a certificate from Grand Lodge; which certificate shall renew and continue to such Lodge for the twelve months ending 31st December following the privilege of holding Masonic meetings under the sanction and authority of Grand Lodge. The said certificate shall be subscribed by Grand Secretary and sealed with the Seal of Grand Lodge. For such certificate there shall be paid to Grand Lodge by each Daughter Lodge, not later than 1st January annually, the sum set forth in the First Schedule, Part I., Item 6, which shall include the fees of Representation in Grand Lodge and a copy of Grand Lodge Proceedings for the Lodge and for each Representative or Proxy Representative in Grand Lodge.

*Annual Certificate.*

*Right of renewal to meet.*

*Fee.*

**155**. In order to entitle a Lodge to the benefit of the foresaid Annual Certificate, there shall be sent to Grand Secretary an affirmation by the Master and Secretary, or, in the event of their absence, by two other Office-Bearers

*Declaration on applying for Certificate.*

authorised by the Lodge, declaring, on their honour as Freemasons, that the Lodge is really held under the denomination of a Lodge of Freemasons, and in strict conformity with these Laws; that the terms of the Charter granted by Grand Lodge have been duly observed; and that these Laws have been fully complied with.

**Demits.**

**156.** Daughter Lodges may grant Demits to qualified members in the form prescribed **Cost to Lodge.** and supplied by Grand Lodge, the charge for which against the Lodge shall be the sum set forth in the First Schedule, Part I., Item 17. Demits shall be signed by the Master and Secretary of the Lodge granting the same, **Must be counter-** and be countersigned by Grand Secretary, **signed by Grand** **Secretary.** and shall be retained by the Lodge to which **Limit of** the brother affiliates. A Demit shall be valid **validity.** for twelve months from its date. If a Demit be not given up within that period on application for membership of another Lodge, the brother's full membership will revive, and he will be held to be in arrear of his annual contribution.

**Degrees to** **157.** Daughter Lodges are strictly pro-
**which Lodges** **are restricted.** hibited from practising any degrees other than those of Entered Apprentice, Fellow-of-Craft (including the Mark), and Master

Mason, and the Ceremonial of Installed Master; and from giving countenance to any organisation purporting to be Masonic, not recognised by Grand Lodge or any other Masonic Grand Body.

*Prohibition against recognising irregular organisations.*

**158.** A brother of any Daughter Lodge shall not take part in or be concerned with the working or promulgation in any manner of way of any Degree, Rite, or Order, purporting to be Masonic, which is not authorised by Grand Lodge, or by another Masonic Grand Body, nor join, visit or countenance any organisation, purporting to be Masonic, not recognised as such by Grand Lodge or another Masonic Grand Body. Any brother acting in breach hereof shall be liable to suspension or expulsion.

*Brethren forbidden to take part in unauthorised degrees or organisations.*

*Penalty for breach.*

**159.** The Mark shall be conferred only on Master Masons whose names have been registered in the books of Grand Lodge. The Mark shall not be conferred upon any brother belonging to another Constitution until he has been recorded as an Affiliate in the books of Grand Lodge, but it shall be competent for a Daughter Lodge, as a favour, without affiliation, to confer the Mark on a member of another Daughter Lodge. This shall be done only on a written request, signed by

*The Mark—on whom conferred.*

*Conferring Mark as a favour.*

*Written request.*

the Master and Wardens of the Lodge
requesting the favour, which request must
be entered in the Minutes of both Lodges.

**Fees for the Mark.**
**Special Bye-Laws.**
**Minimum.**

**160.** A Daughter Lodge may by its special
Bye-Laws enact a fee for the Mark not exceeding the sum set forth in the First Schedule,
Part III., Item 3 (*a*).   If no fee be so enacted,
there shall be charged the fee set forth in
said Schedule, Part III., Item 3 (*b*).   Every
brother before receiving the Mark shall pay
to his own Lodge the fee exigible.   The
**Fee to Grand Lodge.** Lodge shall remit to Grand Lodge the fee
set forth in the First Schedule, Part I., Item
10, for the registration and Diploma of
each brother who has received the Mark.

**Lodge Bye-Laws.**

**161.** With the exception of such Laws as
relate exclusively to Grand Lodge, Grand
Committee, and Provincial and District Grand
Lodges, and cannot be made applicable to
Daughter Lodges, these Laws *mutatis mut-
andis* shall regulate the affairs of every
Daughter Lodge.   In its application to
Daughter Lodges the expression "Quarterly
Communication" shall mean "Regular Meet-
**Position of existing Bye-Laws.** ing."   All existing Bye-Laws shall cease
to have effect so far as inconsistent with
**General Bye-Laws.** these Laws and the General Bye-Laws set
forth in the Second Schedule, which shall

be applicable to all Daughter Lodges. It shall not be necessary for any Lodge to have special Bye-Laws except to the extent and effect of fixing its place or places of meeting, the method of convening meetings, the dates and hours of its regular meetings (including its nomination, election and installation meetings), its office-bearers, committees, and auditors, and their appointment, the remuneration of officials, the management of its various funds, the holding and disposal of heritable or real property and other investments, its initiation and other fees, the amount of its members' annual contributions and the sum (if any) to be accepted in commutation of such contributions, and any other matters which in the opinion of Grand Committee require to be specially provided for. Those Bye-Laws, and alterations of or additions to them, shall in the first place be submitted to the Provincial or District Grand Lodge, or, in the Metropolitan District, to the Metropolitan District Committee, for revision. After being so revised they shall be forwarded to Grand Committee for approval. In places where there are no Provincial or District Grand Lodges, Bye-Laws shall be submitted direct to Grand Committee for revision and approval. When approved, two printed copies of

*Special Bye-Laws—how far necessary.*

*Revision and approval of Special Bye-Laws.*

Copies to be furnished.

all Bye-Laws must be sent to Grand Lodge, and also to the Provincial or District Grand Lodge (if any) or to the Metropolitan District Committee, as the case may be.

Emergency Meetings.

**162.** The Master of a Lodge, or, in his absence, the Immediate Past Master or the Depute or Substitute Master, shall have power to authorise and hold emergency or special meetings of the Lodge for any purpose which may be competent.

Lodge Books.

**163.** There shall be a set of books kept by Daughter Lodges, including (1) an Application Book or Books, each having an index thereto; (2) a Minute Book; (3) a Roll Book; (4) an Attendance Book; (5) a Receipt Book; (6) Treasurer's Books. Patterns of these shall be kept by Grand Secretary for the guidance of Lodges.

Annual examination of books.

**164.** The books of Daughter Lodges shall be examined annually on behalf of Grand Lodge by the Provincial or District Grand Master, or by brethren appointed by him, and in the Metropolitan District by the Metropolitan District Committee. Any faults, omissions, or wrongful actings found to exist shall be corrected.

**165.** Every Daughter Lodge shall be bound to have a printed copy of the latest published edition of these Laws, which shall be open for inspection to the members of such Lodge at all reasonable times, when required. Each candidate on initiation or on affiliation from another Constitution shall receive a copy of an abridged edition of these Laws, which shall be prepared under the direction of Grand Committee, and supplied to Daughter Lodges at such price as shall be fixed by Grand Committee. Such edition shall contain in full the First and Second Schedules.

*Lodges must possess latest edition of these Laws.*

*Candidates to receive abridged edition.*

**166.** Every Daughter Lodge shall hold a meeting annually for the election of Office-Bearers at which (unless in the case of Lodges abroad by Dispensation from the Grand Master Mason or the District Grand Master) at least seven qualified members of the Lodge must be present. Such election (and the election of all Committees for purely Masonic purposes) must be conducted in the Third Degree, and only qualified members can take part and vote thereat or be elected or appointed to office or committee. The election must be completed at one meeting and cannot be adjourned. During the election a copy of these Laws shall be laid on the table, and that fact must be minuted.

*Annual election meeting.*

*To take place in Third Degree.*

*Cannot be adjourned.*

*These Laws to be laid on the table.*

Vacancies
during year.

The provisions of this Law shall apply to
the filling of vacancies occurring during the
year.    If a Lodge should hold separate meet-

Interval
between
Nomination
and Election
Meetings.

ings for nomination and election of Office-
Bearers, the interval between the meetings
must be at least six days, exclusive of the
dates of both meetings.

Qualification
for Affiliates
to vote.

**167.** Affiliated members of Lodges require
to have been admitted at a regularly convened meeting at least fourteen days prior
to the nomination of Office-Bearers, before
they can vote at an election or be elected or
appointed to office or committee.

Office-Bearers
of Lodges.

**168.** Each Daughter Lodge must have the
following Office-Bearers viz., the Master,
Depute Master, Substitute Master, Senior
Warden, Junior Warden, Secretary, Treasurer,
Senior Deacon, Junior Deacon, Inner Guard,
and Tyler.  The Immediate Past Master shall
be an Office-Bearer *ex officio*.  A Lodge may
have other offices, provided such offices are
in accordance with its custom or traditions,

Lodges cannot
elect Mark
Office-Bearers.

and not contrary to these Laws.  Unless
otherwise determined by its Charter, it shall
not be competent for any Lodge to elect a
Mark Master or other Office-Bearers for the
Mark Degree, the working of that Degree
being the duty of the Master of the Lodge

or brethren chosen by him for the time and acting under his authority.

**169.** Any qualified member of a Lodge may be nominated for and elected to any elective office in that Lodge. Unless by Dispensation from Grand Committee, or, if in a District abroad, from the District Grand Master, a brother cannot be Master of more than one Lodge at the same time, nor hold two offices in the same Lodge, nor be an Office-Bearer in two Lodges in the same Province or District at the same time, but none of these disabilities shall apply to the office of Tyler, nor to membership of Committees in two Daughter Lodges.

*Qualification for election to office.*

*Must not be Master of more than one Lodge at same time, nor hold two offices in same Lodge; nor office in two Lodges in same Province or District.*

*Exceptions.*

**170.** All Daughter Lodges shall have a fixed day for the annual installation of Office-Bearers, at which meeting (unless in the case of Lodges abroad by Dispensation from the Grand Master Mason or the District Grand Master) at least seven qualified members of the Lodge must be present. A brother elected or appointed as an Office-Bearer is not entitled to act as such until he has been installed.

*Installation on a fixed day annually.*

*Office-Bearers to be installed.*

**171.** Every Daughter Lodge, on the occasion of its Annual Installation, shall take a collection for the Annuity Funds of Grand Lodge.

*Annual collection for Annuity Funds.*

Prior to the collection being taken, the Master shall make a statement recommending those Funds to the benevolence of the brethren. The whole proceeds of the collection shall be remitted forthwith to Grand Lodge by the Treasurer of the Lodge and shall be allocated as set forth in the First Schedule, Part I., Item 23. A list of Lodges and of their contributions shall be published in the Proceedings of Grand Lodge in May of each year.

*Allocation.*

**172.** The Secretary of each Daughter Lodge shall, within one month after the annual election of Office-Bearers, transmit to Grand Secretary the names and addresses of the Master, Wardens, Secretary, and Treasurer, otherwise no representative of the Lodge shall be permitted to attend and vote at meetings of Grand Lodge in his official capacity.

*Annual return of Office-Bearers.*

**173.** Masters of Daughter Lodges shall be styled " Right Worshipful," and the Wardens " Worshipful."

*Style of Masters and Wardens.*

**174.** In the absence of the Master and the Immediate Past Master of a Daughter Lodge, any Past Master thereof in order of precedence from the Immediate Past Master (*i.e.*, the nearest to the Chair in date of holding

*Filling the Chair in absence.*

office), shall officiate. In the absence of all these, the Depute or Substitute Master shall occupy the Chair. No other Office-Bearer or brother of the Lodge can occupy the Chair. In the conferring of degrees, the Master or presiding brother may permit other Office-Bearers or brethren to give portions of the ritual usually given by the Master, but, in every case, the obligation must be administered by the Master, a Past Master, the Depute or Substitute Master, or the Senior or Junior Warden of the Lodge, or by an Installed Master of another Daughter Lodge under Grand Lodge or a Sister Grand Lodge.

*Who may administer obligation.*

**175**. Every candidate for initiation or affiliation must present an application to a Daughter Lodge, giving his name, occupation, date and place of birth, nationality, and residence, and declaring, (1) whether he has ever made application for admission to a Lodge, under Grand Lodge or any Sister Grand Lodge, and, if so, when and to which Lodge or Lodges, and (2) whether he has been refused admission, and, if so, when and by which Lodge or Lodges. If application has been made to any Lodge and subsequently withdrawn, that fact, and the reason for withdrawal, must also be declared. Every application shall be subscribed by the

*Applications for admission.*

*Particulars required.*

*By whom subscribed.*

candidate and by two qualified members of the Daughter Lodge, as his proposer and seconder.

*Affiliations—productions required.*

In the case of a candidate for affiliation there must be produced the Diploma or Certificate of Membership issued to him by Grand Lodge or a Sister Grand Lodge, together with (*a*) a valid Demit in regular form, or (*b*) if he intends to retain his membership of his Lodge, a Certificate, signed by the Master and Secretary thereof, that he is in good standing.

*Disqualifications.*

An application for initiation shall not be received from a person who is totally blind, or who is a deaf mute, or whose application for admission to another Lodge has not been disposed of, but Lodges may exercise their discretion as to the initiation of candidates who are mutilated in, or minus, a limb.

*When fresh application necessary.*

Any candidate who does not present himself for initiation or affiliation within twelve months after he has passed the ballot, must make a fresh application, which shall be dealt with in all respects as if it were an original application.

*Applications by residents within English or Irish jurisdiction.*

**176.** A Daughter Lodge shall not consider an application for initiation by any candidate whose place of residence is in England or Ireland, or in any place where the United Grand Lodge of England or the Grand Lodge of Ireland has exclusive Masonic jurisdiction, without first obtaining a Dispensation from the Grand Master Mason, the fee for which shall be payable by the candidate in addition to his initiation fee. This Law shall not apply to members of His Majesty's Forces on the active list, or to applicants for admission to any University, College, or School Lodge.

*Dispensation necessary.*
*Fee (First Sched., Part I., Item 16).*
*Exceptions.*

**177**. Every Daughter Lodge shall have a Committee of Enquiry consisting of the Master, the Immediate Past Master, the Wardens, the Secretary, the Treasurer, and not fewer than two other qualified members, to be appointed at the annual election or installation meeting. Four shall be a quorum. All applications for initiation or affiliation shall be read to the Lodge at a regular meeting, and forthwith remitted to the Committee of Enquiry.

*Committee of Enquiry.*
*Applications to be read and remitted.*

**178**. The duties of the Committee of Enquiry shall be to make full enquiry into the character and qualifications of every candidate; to interview his proposer and seconder, and to ascertain from them how long they have known him and what opportunities they have had of judging of his character and fitness for membership; to communicate with any Lodge which may have refused his application for membership,

*Duties of Committee of Enquiry.*
*To interview proposer and seconder.*
*To communicate with other Lodges.*

F

and with any Lodge to which application may have been made and subsequently withdrawn; to interview the candidate himself; and, in the case of a candidate for initiation who has not resided or carried on business or been employed within or in the neighbourhood of the Province or District for at least three years immediately prior to the date of application, to ask a report from a Lodge in the locality in which he had such residence or business or employment, or from such other source as may be approved by Grand Committee or by Grand Secretary on its behalf; to keep Minutes of its own proceedings; and to report to the Lodge the result of its enquiries.   An application shall not be considered by a Lodge until its Committee of Enquiry has reported, which report must be made within twelve months.   As regards Daughter Lodges abroad, the regulation in this Law as to residence, or carrying on business or employment for three years, shall not apply; but District Grand Lodges (or Grand Committee in cases where there is no District Grand Lodge) shall have power to lay down such rules for enquiry as may seem to them right.

**179.** When the report of its Committee of Enquiry has been handed to the Secretary

*To interview candidate.*

*Report necessary when candidate from another Province or District.*

*Minutes.*

*Report to Lodge.*

*Application of Rules to Lodges abroad.*

*Procedure after enquiry.*

of a Daughter Lodge, due intimation of the application shall be made to the members of the Lodge. If this be done by circular or notice, it must be delivered or posted to every qualified member at least five days prior to the meeting at which the application is to be considered, and must set forth the name, occupation, date and place of birth, nationality, and residence, of each candidate, and the names of his proposer and seconder. In the case of a Lodge which convenes its meetings by advertisement, the insertion of the word "Ballot" in the advertisement of any meeting shall be sufficient notice to its members. A Lodge which does not issue circulars or notices or publish advertisements as aforesaid, shall have the application read at a regular meeting (*see* Law 177) and considered at a subsequent regular meeting, held not earlier than fourteen days thereafter, and in the event of the report of the Committee of Enquiry being delayed for any cause, due intimation shall be made to the Lodge at a regular meeting that said application shall be considered at the next regular meeting.

*Intimation of Applications to Members.*

*By circular.*

*By advertisement.*

*Other cases.*

**180.** At the meeting at which an application is to be considered, the report of the Committee of Enquiry shall be read and a ballot shall then be taken on the application.

*Reading of Committee's Report.*

*Ballot*

All applications which have been submitted to the Committee of Enquiry, unless withdrawn by leave of the Lodge, must be reported on and put to the ballot. If the result of the ballot be favourable, the applicant may be admitted forthwith. If the result of the ballot be unfavourable, the decision of the Lodge shall be communicated to the candidate in writing by the Secretary of the Lodge.

Black balls. Three black balls shall exclude a candidate. Daughter Lodges abroad may enact by their Bye-Laws that two black balls shall exclude. In case of doubt the ballot may be taken

Who may vote. a second time if done forthwith. Only qualified members of the Lodge shall be entitled to vote. Prior to initiation or affiliation every candidate and his proposer and seconder shall sign the appropriate Lodge Petition Book.

Age of candidates. **181.** Every candidate shall be at least twenty-one years of age at the date of his application, with the exception of sons of Master Masons under Grand Lodge, who may apply at any time after attaining eighteen years of age.

Candidates pledged to Grand Lodge. **182.** At the time of initiation, or of affiliation from a Sister Grand Lodge, each candidate shall pledge himself to support and maintain these Laws and to obey the Bye-Laws of the Daughter Lodge.

**183.** An initiate shall not be admitted for a smaller fee than that set forth in the First Schedule, Part III., Item 1, which shall entitle him to receive the degrees of Entered Apprentice, Fellow-of-Craft (including the Mark subject to payment of the additional fee authorised by Law 160), and Master Mason. The whole fee first mentioned shall be paid prior to initiation, and no part thereof shall be remitted or deferred for any reason. The minimum fee payable for affiliation to a Daughter Lodge shall be the sum set forth in the First Schedule, Part III., Item 2, in addition to which (if a Lodge by its special Bye-Laws so enacts) each candidate shall pay the amount by which its initiation fee may at the date of his application for affiliation exceed the initiation fee of any Lodge of which he is a qualified member or from which he holds a valid Demit in regular form. *Lodge Fees. Initiation.*  *Affiliation.*

**184.** Gratuitous initiation into the Craft, and gratuitous affiliation into Lodges, are prohibited. *Gratuitous admission prohibited.*

**185.** Every Daughter Lodge shall pay to Grand Lodge for each candidate initiated, the appropriate sums set forth in the First *Fees payable to Grand Lodge by Lodges.* *For Initiates.*

For Affiliates.

Schedule, Part I., Item 8, and, for each candidate affiliated, the appropriate sums set forth in said Schedule, Part I., Item 9. These sums shall be remitted to Grand Lodge by the Treasurer of the Lodge within one month of the initiation or affiliation in respect of which they are exigible, along with the Return required by the first paragraph of Law 192.

Individual contribution to Grand Lodge by Initiates, and by Affiliates from other Constitutions.

Each candidate initiated, and each affiliate from another Constitution, shall pay at initiation and affiliation respectively, the sum set forth in the First Schedule, Part I., Item 11., as a direct individual contribution to the General Fund of Grand Lodge and not as an addition to the fee due to the Daughter Lodge. The said individual contribution shall be collected by the Daughter Lodge on behalf of Grand Lodge and remitted along with the dues exigible from the Daughter Lodge.

Diplomas.

When issued.

**186**. The Diplomas of members admitted to a Daughter Lodge shall be issued by Grand Lodge alone. Diplomas of initiates shall be issued only after they shall have become Master Masons, and those of affiliates, Founder Members, and Mark Master Masons, only after their names have been registered in Grand Lodge books as such.

**187.** Every Daughter Lodge shall be bound to levy from its members (Apprentices and Fellows-of-Craft excepted, as having neither voice nor vote), an annual contribution of not less than the sum set forth in the First Schedule, Part III., Item 4, which contribution, unless otherwise provided in the special Bye-Laws of the Lodge, shall be payable in advance prior to the Annual Meeting for the nomination of Office-Bearers. A Lodge may by its special Bye-Laws exempt from further contributions qualified members who have paid their annual contributions for twenty-one consecutive years. From each annual contribution levied, a sum of not less than the sum set forth in the First Schedule, Part III., Item 6, shall be paid into the Benevolent Fund of the Lodge. The remainder shall be paid into the General Fund of the Lodge.

*Every Lodge must levy an annual contribution.*

*Minimum sum.*

*When payable.*

*Exemption.*

*Allocation between Benevolent and General Funds.*

**188.** When a Lodge has or resolves to have a commutation fee, qualified members may commute their annual contributions by a single payment, the amount of which shall be determined by the Lodge and set forth in its special Bye-Laws, but shall not be less than the minimum commutation fee set forth in the First Schedule, Part III., Item 5. The sums thus received shall be kept as a separate

*Commutation fee.*

*Minimum sum.*

*To form separate fund.*

Withdrawals.

fund, and such part of that fund as the Lodge by its special Bye-Laws shall enact (being not more than the proportion specified in the First Schedule, Part III., Item 5, of the amount of the fund at the close of each financial year) shall be withdrawn therefrom annually and added to and dealt with as part of the annual contributions of the year.

Benevolent Fund.

**189.** The Benevolent Fund of every Daughter Lodge shall consist of the proportion of the annual contributions payable to that Fund, as provided in Law 187; a corresponding proportion of the sum withdrawn annually from the Commutation Fees Fund referred to in Law 188; all sums that may from time to time be transferred to the Benevolent Fund from the General Fund of the Lodge, and all donations or legacies to the Benevolent Fund from any source whatsoever.

Purposes.

The Benevolent Fund shall not be liable or be used for the expenses or debts of the Lodge but shall be held in trust, kept separate from all other funds of the Lodge, and administered as the Lodge may determine but solely for the purposes of Masonic Benevolence.

Investment.

The Fund shall be invested only in the manner sanctioned by the Trusts (Scotland) Acts, and all investments shall be taken in the names of the Master and Secretary of the Lodge, and the Treasurer or Almoner of the Fund, and their successors in these offices, as Trustees of the Fund, but it shall be competent for the Lodge to resolve that investments may be placed in name of any Bank approved by Grand Committee, or of such Bank's nominees, in trust for the Lodge. A separate bank account shall be kept for the Benevolent Fund.

Separate Bank Account.

The provisions of the preceding paragraph shall apply *mutatis mutandis* to every Annuity Fund and Fund for special Masonic Benevolent purposes which has been or may be established by a Daughter Lodge.

Annuity and Special Benevolent Funds.

**190.** All bank accounts of a Lodge, and Deposit Receipts of a Lodge, shall be in name of the Lodge. Cheques and drafts on the accounts must be signed by any two of the following Office-Bearers viz.—the Master, the Secretary, and the Treasurer or Almoner of the Fund. Deposit receipts shall be endorsed in the same manner.

Banking transactions.

Signing of cheques, etc.

**191.** Any brother in arrear of the annual contribution levied in accordance with Law 187, shall not be entitled to receive notices calling meetings, nor be eligible as an Office-Bearer or a member of Committee, nor

Arrears of annual contribution a disqualification.

be entitled to intromit with, or have any vote in the disbursement of, any of the Lodge Funds, nor be permitted to speak or vote on any matter brought before the **Payment of arrears.** Lodge. Arrears shall in no case be chargeable for more than five years, and it shall not be competent to abate arrears. Nonpayment of his annual contribution shall not deprive a brother of the Masonic privilege of attending his own Lodge, but he shall not be entitled to attend meetings of other **Lodges abroad may make distinction between annual contributions of members within and beyond defined radius.** Lodges. A Daughter Lodge abroad, by its special Bye-Laws, may make a distinction between the annual contributions of members living within and beyond a defined radius, subject always to the minimum annual contribution fixed by Law 187.

**Registration of Intrants and Affiliates in Grand Lodge.**

**Within one month.**

**Returns and particulars required.**

192. Every intrant or affiliate to a Daughter Lodge must be registered in the books of Grand Lodge. All Daughter Lodges must, within one month of each initiation or affiliation, send to Grand Lodge a Return which shall contain the name, occupation, and age of each intrant and affiliate, with the date on which the degree or affiliation was conferred, and shall specify the amount charged for initiation, or affiliation, and, in addition, in the case of an affiliate, shall give the date of registration, the name and number of

his Mother Lodge, and the date of Diploma. Every Lodge shall within one month of the passing or raising of a member, or of his receiving the Mark, send intimation of the same to Grand Lodge.

*Intimation of passings, raisings, and Mark.*

Every Daughter Lodge shall furnish to Grand Lodge, within three months from the date of the request being made by Grand Secretary, a list, in a form to be approved by Grand Committee, of all qualified members of the Lodge; and shall also furnish, annually thereafter, a statement, in a form to be approved as aforesaid, of all alterations which have taken place during the twelve months from the date of the last statement.

*List of qualified members to be furnished on request.*

*Statement of alterations annually thereafter.*

**193**. In the event of a Lodge failing to return the name and pay the Grand Lodge dues of any member, the said member, on producing evidence to Grand Secretary of his having paid his fees in full to the Lodge, shall be entitled to be registered, and the Lodge shall forthwith pay the necessary fees.

*Omission by Lodge to make return. Rectification by Grand Secretary.*

**194**. A Daughter Lodge one year in arrear of returns or dues to Grand Lodge shall, *ipso facto*, forfeit the privilege of being represented in Grand Lodge until these returns are made and arrears are paid. A Lodge two years in arrear of Grand Lodge

*Penalty for neglecting returns or dues.*

*Lodges considered dormant if two years in arrears.*

dues, shall be considered dormant, but may be reponed upon such terms and conditions as Grand Lodge shall appoint.

**Penalty for failure to make returns, etc.**

**195**. A Daughter Lodge failing to make returns, or pay dues, or making incomplete or fraudulent returns, or failing to implement its other financial obligations, shall be liable to have its Charter recalled and cancelled ; or to suspension from Masonic privileges ; or to such other judgment as Grand Lodge may pronounce.

**Limit on number of candidates in one day.**

**Intervals between degrees.**

**Exceptions by Dispensation.**

**196**. A Daughter Lodge shall not initiate more than seven candidates on the same day, nor pass to the Second Degree or raise to the Third Degree more than seven brethren in either of said degrees on any one day. An Entered Apprentice shall not be passed to Fellow-of-Craft, and a Fellow-of-Craft shall not be raised to the degree of Master Mason, unless at least fourteen days shall have elapsed since he received the previous degree. Grand Committee may confer on District Grand Masters, and on Masters of Daughter Lodges abroad where there is no District Grand Master, a power of Dispensation, in case of emergency, for brethren to be advanced to a higher degree at an interval of not less than seven days instead of fourteen days, and such power of Dispensation shall remain in force during the pleasure of Grand Committee.

**197**. A brother about to be passed or raised must, previous to the ceremonial, if not already a member of the Daughter Lodge officiating, be affiliated as a member, but it shall be competent for any Daughter Lodge, as a favour, without affiliation, and always in conformity with Law 196, to pass or raise an Entered Apprentice or Fellow-of-Craft of another Daughter Lodge or of a Lodge on the Roll of any Sister Grand Lodge which, by arrangement with Grand Lodge, extends a reciprocal privilege to members of Daughter Lodges under the Scottish Constitution, but such passing and raising can only be done on a written request signed by the Master and Wardens of the Lodge requesting the favour, which request must be entered in the Minutes of both Lodges and—in the case of a brother of a Lodge under a Sister Grand Lodge — transmitted through the Grand Secretaries of the two Grand Lodges concerned. Such passing or raising as a favour shall have the same effect as if the brother had been passed or raised in his own Lodge.

*Affiliation of Entered Apprentices and Fellows of Craft.*

*Passing or raising as a favour.*

*Procedure.*

*Effect.*

**198**. Every Daughter Lodge shall be entitled to try any member accused of any offence.

*Trial of offences.*

**Complaint in writing served.**

A complaint, in writing, shall be served on the accused brother, by registered letter posted to his last known address, specifying **Time for Answers.** the offence of which he is charged, which he shall be entitled to answer in writing within fourteen days of the date of posting of the complaint, or within such longer time as may be specified in the complaint **Consideration of Complaint.** On the answer being lodged, or on the expiry of the time for doing so, the matter of the complaint shall be brought before the Lodge for consideration and judgment, either at a special meeting called for that purpose, **How meeting called.** or at a regular meeting of the Lodge. The meeting at which it is to be considered must be called by circular sent by the Secretary, which shall state the fact that the complaint, and answer, if any, are to be brought before the Lodge for consideration and judgment. In the case of a Lodge which does not convene its meetings by Circular, the meeting shall be called in such manner as may be ordered by Grand Committee, or by Grand Secretary **Notice of meeting to be sent to accused.** on its behalf. Notice of the meeting shall be sent to the accused brother by registered letter posted to his last known address at least fourteen clear days prior to the day of the meeting and that whether he has lodged **Accused entitled to appear.** a written answer or not, and he shall be entitled to appear at the meeting and any adjournment thereof and state his defence. After the case has been considered, the Lodge shall give its decision. Such decision shall be by the votes of a majority of the qualified members voting thereon, and only those present throughout the hearing of the case shall be entitled to vote. If the complaint be sustained, the Lodge shall pronounce such admonition or sentence as shall be decided by the majority of votes as aforesaid. The judgment pronounced shall be intimated forthwith in writing by registered letter to the said brother, who shall therein be apprised that it shall be final unless appealed against to the Provincial or District Grand Lodge, or to Grand Lodge in the case of a Daughter Lodge not within the jurisdiction of a Province or District, within one month after the date of posting the said intimation. In special circumstances, Grand Committee, through Grand Secretary, may extend the period within which an appeal may be made.

*Decision by Lodge.*

*Judgment by Lodge.*

*Intimation thereof.*

*Right of appeal.*

*Time for appeals.*

**199.** A sentence shall not be acted on or published until it becomes final; but power is reserved to the Daughter Lodge in the interval to exclude from its meetings a suspended member should the Lodge consider this desirable in the interests of peace and harmony.

*Interim exclusion.*

Notice of sentences to be sent to Grand Secretary, etc.

**200**. Notice of all sentences pronounced in terms of Law 198 shall be forwarded forthwith by the Secretary of the Daughter Lodge to Grand Secretary, and to Provincial or District Grand Secretary. The notice shall contain a certificate that the sentence pronounced has been intimated in writing to the brother concerned in accordance with Law 198 and shall also specify the date of the posting of such intimation.

Appeals.

To whom made.

Procedure.

Law 128.
Laws 95 and 104 to 111.

**201**. A brother thinking himself aggrieved by any judgment of a Daughter Lodge pronounced against him may appeal against the same within the period allowed under Law 198, to the Provincial or District Grand Lodge, or to Grand Lodge, as the case may be. The procedure in any such appeal shall be regulated *mutatis mutandis* by the enactments in these Laws concerning processes before a Provincial or District Grand Lodge, Grand Committee, or Grand Lodge, as the case may be.

Neglect to appeal.

Sentence becomes final.

**202**. A sentence pronounced upon any brother who does not appeal timeously against the same and which has not been varied by Grand Committee in virtue of Law 95, shall *ipso facto* become final, and that brother shall be deemed to have lost his Masonic privileges, and shall not be permitted to appear in Grand Lodge, or in any Provincial or District Grand Lodge, or in any Daughter Lodge, until such sentence has expired or been recalled.

**203.** Sentences of suspension *sine die*, which have become final, can be recalled only by Grand Lodge.

Recall of sentences.

**204.** Daughter Lodges, and brethren individually or collectively, are prohibited from issuing for publication in newspapers or to Lodges or members of the Craft, circulars, reports or other communications relative to proceedings before Grand Lodge or Grand Committee, without having previously obtained the sanction of Grand Committee, which shall not be unreasonably withheld.

Prohibition against issue for publication of circulars, etc., relative to proceedings before Grand Lodge, etc., without sanction.

**205.** Brethren are strictly forbidden to use or exhibit any of the emblems of Freemasonry on business premises; or in connection with any business; or in any advertisement which does not relate exclusively to Masonic intimations or the sale of Masonic publications, regalia or furnishings. They are also forbidden to use in connection with or as part of a trade or business name, any word which, in the opinion of Grand Lodge or Grand

Prohibition against use for business purposes of Craft emblems, etc.

And against use in business name of word associated with Freemasonry.

G

Committee, may suggest or imply an association with Freemasonry.

**Applications for contributions—sanction necessary.**

**206.** Applications for contributions to aid the funds of a Daughter Lodge shall not be made or issued, to persons or bodies other than the members of the Lodge concerned, save under the sanction of Grand Committee, and must have the approval in writing of the Provincial or District Grand Master or of the Metropolitan District Committee, as the case may be.

**Penalties for disrespect and for disobedience to and non-observance of instructions, etc.**

**207.** Daughter Lodges, and members of Daughter Lodges, acting in a disrespectful manner towards the Grand Master Mason, a Provincial or District Grand Master, or anyone acting on behalf of any of them, or towards Grand Lodge, or Grand Committee, or a Provincial or District Grand Lodge, or the Metropolitan District Committee, or disobeying their instructions or judgments, or failing to observe any of these Laws, shall be liable, in the case of Lodges, to suspension or forfeiture of their Charters, and in the case of individuals, to suspension.

**Disqualification of members of suspended Lodges, etc.**

**208.** A brother of a Lodge which has been suspended or has had its Charter forfeited shall not be eligible as a member of Grand

Lodge or of a Provincial or District Grand
Lodge or of another Daughter Lodge until
he shall have expressed, in writing, his dis-
approbation of the conduct which led to
such suspension or forfeiture, and his dis-
claimer has been accepted by Grand Committee.

**209.** It shall not be competent for Daughter
Lodges having benefit societies connected
therewith to make membership of such
societies a condition of Lodge membership
or a necessary qualification for the holding
of any office in the Lodge.   Lodges having
benefit societies must keep the funds of the
Lodge separate and distinct from those of
the Society.

*Benefit Societies
in connection
with Lodges.*

## ACCOUNTS.

**210.** Accounts shall be kept in respect of
the different Funds of, or administered from
time to time by, Grand Lodge, including,
without prejudice to the said generality, a
General Fund, a Fund of Scottish Masonic
Benevolence, a General Annuity Fund, and an
Orphan Annuity Fund.   All such Accounts
and all Abstracts thereof shall be in the
form approved by the Finance Committee,
Grand Committee, and Grand Lodge.   The

*Accounts.*

*Form.*

Separate
Accounts for
each Fund.

Date of annual
balance.

Accounts of each Fund shall be kept separate from those of all other Funds and shall distinguish between capital, income, and sinking fund if any. The Accounts of all the Funds shall be balanced as at the last Thursday in November yearly, and shall be published simultaneously.

## SINKING FUNDS.

Sinking Funds.

**211.** There shall be established for each of the four Funds of Grand Lodge specified in Law 210, a Sinking Fund for the purpose of covering any depreciation of the investments belonging to such Funds. There may also be established, for the like purpose, a Sinking Fund in connection with any other Fund of or administered at any time by Grand Lodge. The amounts to be transferred to the credit of all such Sinking Funds respectively and the investment thereof shall be determined from time to time by the Finance Committee, subject to the approval of Grand Committee.

Transfers to
Sinking Funds
and investment
thereof.

## THE GENERAL FUND.

General Fund.

**212.** A Fund called " The General Fund " (in this part of these Laws referred to as " The Fund ") shall be maintained for the purpose of meeting all expenditure and charges of every kind, of or connected with Grand Lodge, which are not chargeable against any other Fund of or administered by Grand Lodge. It shall be in the power of the Finance Committee, subject to the approval of Grand Committee, to determine the expenditure and charges to be debited to Capital and Income respectively.

*Purpose.*

*Allocation of expenditure to Capital and Income.*

213. The capital of the Fund shall consist of the property and assets, heritable and moveable, at present belonging to the capital of the Fund; all moneys and investments which from time to time may be transferred thereto from the Income Account of the Fund or from any other source; and all donations and legacies to Grand Lodge not expressly given or bequeathed to the income of the Fund or to the capital or income of any other Fund of, or administered by, Grand Lodge.

*Capital.*

214. The income of the Fund shall consist of the rents, interest, dividends and other revenue derived from its property and assets; the fees and other sums set forth in the First Schedule, so far as payable to the Fund; and any donations or legacies expressly made or bequeathed to the income of the Fund.

*Income.*

Disposal of surplus income.

**215**. In the event of a surplus of accumulated income over expenditure remaining in the Income Account of the Fund at the end of any financial year, such portion (if any) of that surplus as the Finance Committee, with the approval of Grand Committee, may determine, shall be transferred to the Capital Account of the Fund and shall become and be thereafter treated as capital, with right, however, to resort to the capital of the Fund in any future year or years in the event contemplated by Law 216; and the remainder of such surplus shall be retained in the Income Account of the Fund and carried forward to the following year.

Deficiency of income may be taken from capital.

**216**. If in any year there shall be a balance at debit of the Income Account of the Fund, the deficiency may be taken from the capital of the Fund so that the income and expenditure may be balanced.

## THE FUND OF SCOTTISH MASONIC BENEVOLENCE.

Fund of Scottish Masonic Benevolence.

**217**. The name of the Fund shall be "The Fund of Scottish Masonic Benevolence." It is referred to in this part of these Laws as "the Fund."

**218.** The capital of the Fund shall consist Capital. of the investments and moneys at present belonging to the capital of the Fund; all moneys which may from time to time be transferred thereto from the income of the Fund or from any other sources; the fees and other sums which, by the First Schedule, Part I., are or may be allocated to the capital of the Fund; and all donations or legacies to the Fund, not expressly made or bequeathed to the income of the Fund.

**219.** The income of the Fund shall consist Income. of the interest, dividends and other revenue derived from its invested funds; the fees and other sums which, by the First Schedule, Part I., are or may be allocated to the income of the Fund; and any donations and legacies expressly made or bequeathed to the income of the Fund.

**220.** The capital of the Fund shall be Investments. invested in terms of Law 102, and income not immediately required may be similarly invested.

**221.** The income of the Fund and the dis- Distribution of income. posal and distribution thereof shall be under the control of the Committee of Benevolence Committee of Benevolence. (in this part of these Laws referred to as

" the Committee "), which shall consist of the members of Grand Committee. Nine members shall form a quorum. The Committee shall appoint annually a Sub-Committee of its number to investigate the cases of applicants and to report thereon to the Committee. Grand Almoner, *ex officio*, shall be the Convener of the Sub-Committee. In cases of pressing emergency when the time necessary for lodging a formal Petition and carrying through the ordinary procedure would cause distress to an applicant, it shall be in the power of the Sub-Committee, after enquiry, to make such grant to any eligible person as it may consider necessary, and to report the same to the Committee at its next meeting. The Committee shall meet on the second last Thursday of every month; but, when it sees fit, it may dispense with or alter the date of any statutory meeting. Grand Secretary shall send to each member of the Committee, prior to each meeting, a list of the applications to be considered at such meeting, setting forth the names, designations, and places of residence of the applicants, and the grounds upon which their applications are based.

*Quorum.*

*Sub-Committee.*

*Convener thereof.*

*Emergency grants by Sub-Committee.*

*Meetings.*

*List of applications to be circulated.*

*Funds to be lodged in bank.*

    **222.** All moneys received by Grand Treasurer on account of the Fund shall be paid

orthwith into bank, to an account or accounts
ept in name of Grand Lodge and ear-marked
o the Fund. These accounts and any Deposit
Receipts belonging to the Fund shall be
perated on as provided in Law 91 (*a*).

*Operations on Bank Accounts. (Applies also to Annuity Funds.)*

223. The income of the Fund (after deduc-
ion of the expenses of management as
rovided in Law 18, and also of any sums
ransferred to the Sinking Fund by virtue
f Law 211) shall be devoted, so far as may
e required, to the relief of any poor and
istressed brother (or the indigent parent,
vife, widow, sister, or child of a brother)
vhose name has been registered in the books
f Grand Lodge for at least five years, and
vho has been a qualified member of a
Daughter Lodge during the five years im-
nediately preceding the date of the application for benevolence, or who (if deceased at
that date) had been so qualified during the
five years immediately preceding the date of
his death. Should the neglect to register
a brother's name be the fault of his Lodge,
the applicant's petition may be considered if
in other respects in form. Notwithstanding the
foregoing conditions of registration and membership, necessitous cases arising from circumstances of special hardship may be considered
and relieved in the discretion of the Com-

*Application of income.*

*Recipients.*

*Qualifications.*

*Neglect to register a brother.*

*Necessitous cases.*

mittee, provided three-fourths of the member
present agree.

**Assistance to members, etc., of Sister Grand Lodges.**

224. The Committee may, in cases of ex
traordinary distress, afford relief to brethre
of Sister Grand Lodges, or their indigen
parents, wives, widows, sisters, or childrer
on the production of valid certificates o
registration and of good standing from thei
respective Lodges, and on proof of th
identity and distress of the applicants.

**Applications to be made through a Lodge.**

**Certificate by Lodge.**

**Supply of forms.**

225. All applications for benevolence sha
be considered by and made through any Lodg
of which the brother referred to in th
petition is, or was, a member. It shall be th
duty of that Lodge to certify as to whethe
or not the said brother is or was a qualifie
member for the period specified in Law 223
Grand Secretary shall supply forms o
petition through the Lodge, but when
Lodge has become dormant, or declines t
supply a form of petition, Grand Secretar
may supply the same to an applicant direct

**Time of lodging petitions.**

**Certification by Grand Secretary.**

226. All petitions must be lodged with
Grand Secretary at least thirty days prio
to consideration by the Committee. Gran
Secretary shall examine each petition, and
shall certify to the Sub-Committee and the
Committee as to whether or not the

applicant or, in the event of the petition being from a parent, wife, widow, sister, or child, the son, husband, brother, or father of the applicant has been registered in the books of Grand Lodge for the period specified in Law 223. Grand Secretary shall send intimation in writing to the Lodge concerned of the day and hour of the meeting of the Committee at which the petition is to be considered, in order that the Lodge may be represented at such meeting if it shall think fit. The Committee, after hearing the report of the Sub-Committee, and the Lodge representative if present, shall decide on the application. On presentation of petitions by relatives of brethren, evidence of relationship may be required.

*Intimation to Lodge.*

*Hearing and decision.*

*Evidence of relationship.*

**227.** Grand Secretary shall enter in a book the number of each petition, the name of the applicant, and any sum granted. The Chairman shall sign or initial, upon each application, the deliverance of the Committee. Grand Treasurer shall keep account of all sums received and disbursed in connection with the Fund.

*Records to be kept.*

*Accounts.*

**228.** It shall be competent for Grand Secretary to authorise Grand Treasurer to give such poor brethren as may appear

*Grants by Grand Secretary.*

Limit.

worthy of relief, a sum not exceeding twenty shillings in each case, if the exigency of the circumstances should not admit of the delay necessary to lay the case before the Sub Committee.

Record of these.

Each sum so paid shall be regularly entered in a book kept for the purpose, together with the name of the individual relieved and the name and number of the Lodge of which he is a member.

Repeated applications discouraged.

**229.** The Committee shall not allow applicants to become pensioners on the Fund; and repeated applications from the same person are to be discouraged.

Limitation of expenditure.

**230.** The sums to be distributed in each year by the Committee shall not exceed the income of the Fund for that year, under deduction as aforesaid of the expenses of management and of any sums transferred to

No grants in anticipation of income.

the Sinking Fund. It shall not be competent to make grants in anticipation of income. Any surplus shall be carried forward; but if

Capitalisation and allocation of surplus income.

at the end of any financial year there shall be at the credit of the Income Account of the Fund an accumulated balance of unapplied income exceeding £500, the excess over that sum, or such part of said excess as may be determined by the Committe, shall be transferred to the Capital of the Fund.

**231.** The Committee, with the approval of Grand Lodge, may make regulations for the more efficient management and administration of the Fund.

*Power to make regulations. (Applies also to Annuity Funds.)*

## THE GENERAL ANNUITY FUND.

**232.** The name of the Fund shall be "The General Annuity Fund." It is referred to in this part of these Laws as "the Fund."

*General Annuity Fund.*

**233.** The capital of the Fund shall consist of the investments and moneys at present belonging to the capital of the Fund; all moneys which may from time to time be transferred thereto from the income of the Fund, and from any other sources; the fees and other sums which, by the First Schedule, Part I., are or may be allocated to the capital of the Fund; and all donations and legacies to the Fund, not expressly made or bequeathed to the income of the Fund.

*Capital.*

**234.** The income of the Fund shall consist of the interest, dividends, and other revenue derived from its invested funds; the fees and other sums which, by the First Schedule, Part I., are or may be allocated

*Income.*

to the income of the Fund; and any donations and legacies expressly made or bequeathed to the income of the Fund.

Investments.
(Applies also to
Orphan Fund.)

**235**. The capital of the Fund shall be
invested in terms of Law 102, and income
not immediately required may be similarly
invested.

Application
of income.

**236**. Subject always to Law 241, the income of the Fund (after deduction of the
expenses of management, as provided in Law
18, and of any sums transferred to the Sinking Fund by virtue of Law 211), shall, so
far as may be required, be distributed in
annuities. It shall not be competent to
make grants in anticipation of income. Any
surplus shall be carried forward; but if at
the end of any financial year there shall
be at the credit of the income account
of the Fund an accumulated balance of
unapplied income exceeding £2500, the excess
over that sum, or such part of said excess
as may be determined by the Board, shall
be transferred to the capital of the Fund.

No grants in
anticipation of
income.

Disposal of
surplus income.

Distribution of
income.
(Applies also to
Orphan Fund.)

Annuity Board.

**237**. The income of the Fund and the
disposal and distribution thereof shall be
under the control of the Annuity Board
(in this part and the next part of these Laws
referred to as "the Board"), which shall

onsist of the members of Grand Committee.
Nine members shall form a quorum of the *Quorum.*
Board.   The Board shall appoint annually a
sub-Committee of its number to investigate *Sub-Committee.*
all cases of applicants and to report thereon
to the Board.   Grand Almoner *ex officio* shall *Convener*
be the Convener of the Sub-Committee. *thereof.*

238.  The Board shall meet in April of each *Meetings.*
year for the election of annuitants, and at *(Applies also to Orphan Fund.)*
such other times as may be necessary.   It
shall meet in October for the revision of the
existing list of annuitants.

239.  Grand Secretary shall keep a register of *Grand*
applications, with the particulars thereof, and *Secretary's duties.*
record the result of the same.   He shall send *(Applies also to Orphan Fund.)*
to the members of the Board, at least seven *Notice of*
days prior to the meeting in April, intimation *amount available.*
of the probable amount of money which will
then be available for disposal; a list of the *Lists of revised*
annuitants as revised at the previous October *annuitants and new applicants*
meeting; and a list of the applicants for *to be circulated.*
election as annuitants, setting forth their
names, designations, and places of residence,
and the grounds on which their applications
are based.

240.  Grand Treasurer shall keep account *Accounts.*
of all sums received and disbursed in con- *(Applies also to Orphan Fund.)*
nection with the Fund.

Number and
value of
annuities.

**241.** The Board shall have power in th
exercise of its discretion to continue annuitie
and grant new annuities up to a cumul
amount not exceeding in any year nine-tenth
of the income of the Fund for the previou
financial year remaining after deduction a
aforesaid of the expenses of management o
that year and any sums transferred to th
Sinking Fund in that year, the number an
value of which annuities shall be based o
the following scale, viz. :—out of each complet
One Thousand Pounds of free income avai
able, there shall be not more than one annuit
of £50, one of £45, two of £40, three of £3
four of £30, and four of £25, and the re
mainder may be granted in annuities of £2
or such smaller sum as the Board may con
sider sufficient in the circumstances of an
applicant. If three-fourths of its member
present so agree, the Board may vary th
foregoing scale as regards the number o
annuities of £25 and upwards, but the tota
value of such annuities shall at no tim
exceed one-half of the free income available

To be reported
to Grand Lodge.

The number and amount of annuities grante
at the preceding meeting of the Board sha
be reported to the Quarterly Communicatio
of Grand Lodge in May.

Payment of
annuities.
(Applies also to
Orphan Fund.)

**242.** Annuities shall be payable by Gran
Treasurer in equal half-yearly sums in Ma
and November yearly, but the Board sha
have power to appoint annuities to be pai
or applied at other times, by other insta
ments or in one sum, and in such way an
manner, all as the Board in its discretio

may determine as best suited to each individual case.

**243**. Every indigent brother registered and qualified as set forth in Law 223, and whose Lodge (if not dormant) has contributed to the Annuity Funds in terms of Law 171; and every indigent parent, wife, widow, sister, or child of a brother so registered and qualified and whose Lodge (if not dormant) has contributed as aforesaid, shall be eligible to be placed on the roll of annuitants; but it shall not be competent to have on the roll at the same time more than one annuity in favour of persons deriving right through the same brother. The provisions of Law 223 with regard to necessitous cases shall apply *mutatis mutandis* to applications for annuities from the Fund.

*Qualification of applicants.*

*Necessitous cases.*

**244**. All grants shall be made and continued at and during the pleasure of the Board, and any grant may be withdrawn or varied in amount at their discretion.

*Grants made during pleasure of Board. (Applies also to Orphan Fund.)*

**245**. Every application for an annuity shall be in duplicate on a form approved by the Board, and must, along with any relative recommendations, be forwarded duly completed in every respect, not later than 1st January, to Grand Secretary by a Daughter

*Applications for annuities. (Applies also to Orphan Fund.)*

*Time of lodging.*

H

*To be made through a Lodge.*

Lodge of which the brother applying is a member, or, in the case of a parent, wife, widow, sister, or child, by a Daughter Lodge of which the brother in virtue of whom they apply, is or was a member, or, where such Lodge is dormant, by any other Daughter Lodge in the same Province or District.

*Lodge dormant, etc.*

When a Lodge is dormant or declines to supply a form of application, Grand Secretary may supply the same to an applicant direct.

*Visits and reports by Lodge. (Applies also to Orphan Fund.)*

**246.** It shall be the duty of every Daughter Lodge through which an annuity has been granted to arrange for a visit to the recipient at least once every half-year, and to report to Grand Secretary, on a form provided for that purpose, on the circumstances of the annuitant.

*Visits and reports by Provincial and District Grand Lodges and Metropolitan District Committee. (Applies also to Orphan Fund.)*

**247.** Grand Secretary shall send annually before 1st February the duplicate applications of all petitioners for and recipients of annuities in each Province or District to the Provincial or District Grand Lodge, or the Metropolitan District Committee, as the case may be, and these shall be returnable by them along with their reports. All Provincial and District Grand Lodges, and the Metropolitan District Committee, shall undertake the supervision of all recipients of annuities residing within their respective Provinces and Districts. It shall be their duty to make arrangements for the visitation of all such annuitants by such visitor or visitors as they may choose (not necessarily members of Provincial or District Grand Lodge or of the Metropolitan District Committee) at least once every year. Such visitation shall be for the purpose of ascertaining whether, in the opinion of the visitors, the grants are being well and usefully applied and the recipients continue to be deserving, and in the case of children, whether they are comfortably provided for and suitably educated and maintained. Provincial or District Grand Lodges, or the Metropolitan District Committee, as the case may be, shall submit to the Board, on or before 1st March annually, special reports based on the information received by them from such visitors, and on such other enquiries as they in their discretion may from time to time think proper to make. It is recommended that, as far as possible, visitors to be appointed as aforesaid should not be members of a Daughter Lodge on whose recommendation an annuity has been granted.

**248.** Laws 222 and 231 shall apply *mutatis mutandis* to The General Annuity Fund, and are here held as repeated *brevitatis causa*.

Laws in common with Benevolent Fund.

## THE ORPHAN ANNUITY FUND.

**Orphan Annuity Fund.**

**249.** The name of the Fund shall be "The Orphan Annuity Fund." It is referred to in this part of these Laws as "the Fund."

**Capital.**

**250.** The capital of the Fund shall consist of the investments and moneys at present belonging to the capital of the Fund; all moneys which may from time to time be transferred thereto from the income of the Fund and from any other source; the fees and other sums which, by the First Schedule, Part I., are or may be allocated to the capital of the Fund; and all donations and legacies to the Fund, not expressly made or bequeathed to the income of the Fund.

**Income.**

**251.** The income of the Fund shall consist of the interest, dividends, and other revenue derived from its invested funds; the fees and other sums which, by the First Schedule, Part I., are or may be allocated to the income of the Fund; and any donations and legacies expressly made or bequeathed to the income of the Fund.

**Application of income.**

**252.** The income of the Fund (after deduction of the expenses of management as provided in Law 18 and of any sums transferred to the Sinking Fund by virtue of Law 211) shall be available for distribution in annuities to indigent children of deceased brethren who were registered and qualified as set forth in Law 223, and whose Lodges (if not dormant) have contributed to the Annuity Funds in terms of Law 171. The provisions of Law 223 with regard to necessitous cases shall apply *mutatis mutandis* to applications for annuities and other grants from the Fund. It shall not be competent to make grants in anticipation of income.

Qualification of applicants.

Necessitous cases.

No grants in anticipation of income.

**253.** Any surplus income remaining at the end of each financial year shall be carried forward; but if at the end of any financial year there shall be at the credit of the income account of the Fund an accumulated balance of unapplied income exceeding £2500, the excess over that sum, or such part of said excess as may be determined by the Board, shall be transferred to the capital of the Fund.

Disposal of surplus income.

**254.** Subject to Law 252 the Board shall have power to grant out of the income of the Fund, annuities for the maintenance of a child or children of a deceased brother, of amounts not exceeding £20 where there is only one child, and not exceeding £15 for each child

Granting of annuities.

Amount of annuities.

where there are two or more children; and
if, in their opinion, the circumstances merit
special treatment, the Board shall have power
to grant an annuity of £25, of £30, or of £40,
for any child, but the number of such
annuities of £25, £30, and £40 payable at
any one time shall not exceed twenty, ten, and

five respectively.   All annuities permitted by
this Law shall be available only for children
under seventeen years of age; but the
Board shall not be precluded from granting
from The General Annuity Fund to children
of any age an annuity under Law 241.

255. For the purpose of aiding Orphans
who are or have been on the Roll of the
Fund and are desirous of entering on special
training for a profession or skilled occupation,
or require aid to enter upon and complete a
regular indenture of apprenticeship to a
skilled occupation or profession, the Board
shall have power to grant or to expend, out
of the income of the Fund, such annual or
other sum or sums as it may think proper in
payment in whole or in part of the fee for
such indenture and of the cost of necessary
tools, instruments, books, or others required
in connection with the selected profession or
occupation and of the expenses (including
maintenance expenses) of education or tech-

nical training of such Orphans who have given promise of ability to profit by such indenture, further education or training—

1. At a technical school, college, or workshop;

2. At evening classes for higher education or technical instruction;

3. At a secondary school, higher-grade school, central institution or University; or

4. At such other educational institution, or in such other manner for technical, professional, or practical training, as may be approved from time to time by the Board.

Such payments shall be made only in respect of Orphans not under fifteen years of age who submit proof, by head master's certificate or otherwise, that they have completed a satisfactory course of education, and that they are capable of taking the course of study, training, or work to which they intend to apply themselves. *Qualification for grants.*

**256.** Every Applicant for a grant under Law 255 shall apply on a form approved by the Board, which shall be issued by Grand Secretary, when requested, to any Daughter Lodge of which the appli- *Applications for special grants.*

cant's father was a member, and the statements entered therein shall be verified and vouched for by the Master and Secretary of that Lodge, and those Office-Bearers shall at the same time state whether they recommend the applicant as eligible and deserving. Such application must be lodged with Grand Secretary before the first day of September. When a Lodge is dormant or declines to supply a form of application, Grand Secretary may supply the same to an applicant direct.

The Board shall annually, by reports from Heads of educational institutions, professors, employers, or otherwise, satisfy itself as to the regularity of attendance, progress, and good conduct of students, apprentices, or others in receipt of grants under Law 255, and the said grants may be discontinued in the case of recipients concerning whom such reports shall not be considered by the Board to be satisfactory. It shall be the duty of the Daughter Lodge through which an application originally came (1) to obtain and forward these reports to Grand Secretary by the first day of September in each year, and (2) to visit the recipient twice yearly, by an Office-Bearer or proxy, to ascertain if by his or her behaviour and diligence the donee continues to merit the grant.

*Margin notes:*

Certification and recommendation by Lodges.

Time of lodging applications.

Lodge dormant, etc.

Annual reports on progress, etc., of recipients.

Duty of Lodges to obtain reports and to visit recipients.

**257.** A recipient of a grant under Law 255 shall not have a legal right to insist on payment of an annual grant to the end of the term of years for which it was originally donated if in the opinion of the Board the payments ought to be discontinued.

*Grants made during pleasure of Board.*

**258.** Laws 222, 231, 235, 237, 238, 239, 240, 242, 244, 245, 246, and 247 shall apply *mutatis mutandis* to The Orphan Annuity Fund, and are here held as repeated *brevitatis causa.*

*Laws in common with Benevolent Fund and General Annuity Fund.*

## CLOTHING AND REGALIA.

**259.** Full Masonic costume consists of evening dress, white tie, white gloves, and the appropriate regalia; but at Quarterly Communications of Grand Lodge, at meetings of Provincial and District Grand Lodges and Daughter Lodges, and at laying of foundation-stones, and other functions out of doors, brethren may wear dark clothes and black ties. Present and Past Grand Office-Bearers, Members of Grand Committee and Grand Stewards at Quarterly Communications should wear white gloves.

*Masonic costume.*

*At outdoor functions.*

**260.** Only Regalia appertaining to Craft Masonry shall be worn in Grand Lodge, or in any Subordinate Lodge.

*Only Craft regalia to be worn.*

Jewels of Grand
Office-Bearers.

**261.** The following are the Jewels authorised by Grand Lodge—

### The Grand Master Mason.

Pendant from the upper band of the collar,
a star set with brilliants, having in the centre
a field azure charged with the figure of Saint
Andrew on his Cross, gold; pendant from the
lower band, the compasses extended, with the
square, and an arc of 90°, the points of the
compasses resting on the arc, and in the
centre, the sun in his splendour.

### Past Grand Master.

A similar but smaller jewel, without the sun.

### Depute Grand Master.

The compasses and square united.

### Substitute Grand Master.

A square. In the angle the All-seeing eye.
On each blade of the square an Ionic column.

| | |
|---|---|
| *Senior Grand Warden* . | A level charged with a Doric column, above which is an irradiated sun declining to the west. |
| *Junior Grand Warden* . | A plumb-rule charged with a Corinthian column, above which is the sun, in his meridian glory. |
| *Grand Secretary* | A chased key and a pen. |
| *Grand Treasurer* | A chased key. |

| | |
|---|---|
| *Grand Almoner* | A level with compasses extended thereon. |
| *Grand Chaplains* | A triangle charged with an irradiated eye. |
| *Senior Grand Deacon* | A mason's mell. |
| *Junior Grand Deacon* | A trowel. |
| *Grand Director of Ceremonies* | Two batons in saltire with tie. |
| *Grand Architect* | A Corinthian column standing on an arc of 90°. |
| *Grand Jeweller* | A goldsmith's hammer. |
| *Grand Bible-Bearer* | An open Bible laid on two palm branches in saltire. |
| *Grand Bard* | A clarsach between the compasses and square. |
| *Grand Sword-Bearer* | Two swords in saltire with tie. |
| *Grand Director of Music* | Two trumpets in saltire. |
| *Grand Organist* | A Grecian lyre. |
| *Grand Piper* | A bagpipe between the compasses and square. |
| *Grand Marshal* | A baton and a sword in saltire with tie. |
| *Grand Inner Guard* | Two swords in saltire |
| *Grand Tyler* | A sword. |
| *Members of Grand Committee* | An irradiated Cross of Saint Andrew, charged with the figure of Saint Andrew and his Cross on a field enamelled azure. |
| *President of Grand Stewards* | A cornucopia and a cup in saltire, within a wreath of vine leaves and wheat ears, crossed behind by Grand Master's rods. |

| Vice - President of Grand Stewards | A cornucopia and a cup in saltire, within a wreath of vine leaves and wheat ears. |
|---|---|
| Grand Stewards | A breast jewel, being a Cornucopia laid on two rods in saltire, suspended from a thistle green ribbon one inch broad and a bar bearing the initials "GS: GLS." On the ribbon is the figure of Saint Andrew and his Cross in gold. |

### Representatives to a Sister Grand Lodge.

On a field azure, the figure of Saint Andrew and his Cross, surrounded by an oval inscribed "Representative from the Grand Lodge of Scotland," with a thistle and two leaves at the base, suspended from a collar of thistle green ribbon, one and a half inches broad.

### Honorary Grand Office-Bearers.

The jewel of their rank laid upon a wreath of oak leaves. When not wearing Grand Lodge Regalia, the jewel is worn suspended from a collar of thistle green ribbon, one and a half inches broad.

### Past Grand Office-Bearers.

The jewel of the office which they held, laid upon a wreath of laurel leaves.

*Provincial or District Grand Master or Proxy District Grand Master.*

The compasses and square united, with an arc of 90° containing a five-pointed star.

*District Superintendent.*

The compasses and square united, containing a five-pointed star.

*Depute Provincial or District Grand Master.*

The compasses and square united.

*Provincial or District Substitute Grand Master.*

A square.

*Provincial or District Grand Secretary.*

Two pens in saltire.

*All other Office-Bearers of Provincial or District Grand Lodges . .* Jewels of the same description as those worn by the Office-Bearers of Grand Lodge.

**262.** Past Provincial or District Grand Office-Bearers may wear the jewel of the office which they held, laid upon a wreath of laurel leaves.

**263.** The collar of the Grand Master Mason is of gold and enamel. It consists of an upper and a lower band. Each of these is made up of the Royal Arms of Scotland, with supporters and thistles alternately. From the upper band depends the jewel of Saint Andrew, and from the lower, the jewel of the Grand Master.

**Collars of other Grand Office-Bearers, etc.**

**264.** The collars of the other Grand Office-Bearers and of Provincial and District Grand Office-Bearers are of thistle green ribbon, four inches wide, bound at the lower edges by gold braid, half-inch wide, and a gold fringe, half-inch deep. The collars of Grand Lodge Office-Bearers to whose office the title "Right Worshipful" is accorded, have thistle embroidery, and are bound all round with gold braid, half-inch wide, with a torse of gold braid on each end.

Provincial and District Grand Masters, and Proxy District Grand Masters, may wear chains of metal gilt instead of collars.

**Sashes of Grand Office-Bearers, etc.**

**265.** The Office-Bearers of Grand Lodge, Provincial and District Grand Office-Bearers, Members of Grand Committee, and Grand Stewards wear, over the right shoulder and under the left arm, sashes of thistle green ribbon four inches broad, on which, in the case of Grand Office-Bearers, Members of Grand Committee and Grand Stewards, is

**Badge of Grand Lodge.**

embroidered the badge of Grand Lodge, which

is, on a field gules, the figure of Saint Andrew and his Cross, proper, surrounded by a circle of green on which is embroidered in gold "The Grand Lodge of Scotland," and edged with gold.   Provincial and District Grand Office-Bearers wear a sash with the same device as above, or the name of the Province or District, or its own distinctive device or badge.   The sashes of those Office-Bearers to whom is accorded the prefix "Right Worshipful" have an edging of gold braid similar to that on their collars.

Badge of Provincial or District Grand Lodges.

**266.** The apron of the Grand Master Mason is edged with two-inch acorn-pattern gold lace, and has embroidered in gold, on the semi-circular green satin lap, the compasses and square between the sun in his splendour, on the left side, and the moon surrounded by seven stars, on the right.   From each upper corner of the apron is suspended a gold tassel. Below the compasses and square there are, on the left side, a mallet, and on the right, the letter **G** within an equilateral triangle. At the bottom a Scots thistle is embroidered, and at each side from underneath the lap depends a gold tassel of seven chains.

Apron of Grand Master Mason.

**267.** The aprons of the other Grand Office-Bearers are trimmed with green, and have green laps, on which are embroidered in

Aprons of other Grand Office-Bearers, etc.

gold the emblems of their respective offices, and thistle ornamentation. The aprons of Members of Grand Committee and of the Grand Stewards are trimmed with green, and have green satin laps, on which are embroidered the badge of Grand Lodge. Aprons shall be fastened under the coat.

**Gauntlets.**

**268.** The Grand Master Mason, Past Grand Masters, all Grand Office-Bearers to whom is accorded the prefix of "Right Worshipful," Provincial and District Grand Masters, Past Provincial and District Grand Masters, Proxy District Grand Masters, Provincial and District Depute and Substitute Grand Masters, and Provincial and District Grand Wardens, wear gauntlets of green with gold edging, embroidered in gold with the appropriate emblem of their office, and thistle ornamentation.

**Jewels of Office-Bearers of Daughter Lodges.**

**269.** The jewels of the following Office-Bearers of Daughter Lodges are as under :—

| | |
|---|---|
| *Master* . . | The compasses and square united, with an arc of 90°, containing the sun in his splendour. |
| *Past Master* . | The compasses, square, and arc of 90°. |
| *Depute Master* . | The compasses and square. |
| *Substitute Master* | A square. |
| *Senior Warden* . | A level. |

| | |
|---|---|
| *Junior Warden* . | A plumb rule. |
| *Secretary* . | Two pens in saltire. |
| *Treasurer* . | A key. |
| *Almoner* . | A level with compasses extended thereon. |
| *Chaplain* . | An equilateral triangle containing an irradiated eye. |
| *Senior Deacon* . | A mason's mell. |
| *Junior Deacon* . | A trowel. |
| *Director of Ceremonies* . | Two batons in saltire with tie. |
| *Architect* . | A Corinthian column standing on an arc of 90°. |
| *Jeweller* . | A goldsmith's hammer. |
| *Bible-Bearer* . | An open Bible. |
| *Sword-Bearer* . | Two swords in saltire with tie. |
| *Director of Music* | Two trumpets in saltire. |
| *Marshal* . | A baton and a sword in saltire with tie. |
| *Steward* . | A cornucopia and a cup in saltire. |
| *Inner Guard* . | Two swords in saltire. |
| *Tyler* . | A sword. |

These jewels are worn pendant from a collar not exceeding two inches wide, of the colour adopted by the Lodge, or from a metal chain.

*How worn.*

**270.** The Office-Bearers of a Lodge may wear sashes of the colour adopted by the Lodge, not exceeding four inches broad, and in front may have embroidered, or otherwise distinctly marked thereon, the name and number or the badge of the Lodge, but no other device, edging, or ornamentation.  The

*Sashes of Office-Bearers of Daughter Lodges.*

I

Gauntlets.

Master, Past Masters, and Wardens, may wear gauntlets of the Lodge colour with the emblems of their respective offices embroidered thereon.

Aprons of Daughter Lodges.

**271.** The following patterns of aprons shall be used in Daughter Lodges and these shall be fastened under the coat:—

*Apprentice.*—A plain white lambskin, 16 inches wide and 14 inches deep; square at bottom; with semicircular lap without ornament.

*Fellow-of-Craft.*—Same as above, with the addition of two rosettes, of the colour worn by the Lodge, near the lower corners.

*Master Mason.*—Same as above, edged with the colour of the Lodge, and an additional rosette on the lap. It is permissible to substitute on full dress aprons the square and compasses and the letter "G" instead of the rosette on the lap.

*Masters, Past Masters, and Office-Bearers* wear emblems of their respective offices embroidered on the lap of the apron. Tassels suspended from ribbons of the Lodge colour are worn on each side, appearing from underneath the lap. In the case of Masters and Past Masters, levels take the place of rosettes.

MOURNING.—Lodge jewels, tassels, rosettes, and levels on aprons of Office-Bearers and other members shall be covered with black crape.

*Mourning.*

## INTERPRETATION.

272. In construing these Laws and the Schedules annexed or to be annexed hereto and any alterations of or additions to these Laws and said Schedules, the following words and expressions shall have the several meanings hereby assigned to them, unless there be something in the subject or context repugnant to such construction; that is to say :—

*Interpretation of words and expressions.*

"*Admonition*" includes censure.

"*Annuity Board*" means the Committee for the administration of the Annuity Funds of Grand Lodge, constituted as provided in Laws 237 and 258.

"*Annuity Funds*" means—

  1. As regards Grand Lodge—the Funds constituted for the purposes respectively set forth in those parts of these Laws under the headings of "The General Annuity Fund," and "The Orphan Annuity Fund," and

any other Funds which may be constituted for similar purposes subsequent to Saint Andrew's Day 1939;

2. As regards a Provincial or District
   Grand Lodge, the Metropolitan District, or a Daughter Lodge—any
   Fund which has been or may be
   constituted by any of them for the
   provision of annuities.

"*Benevolent Fund*" means—

1. As regards Grand Lodge—the Fund
   constituted for the purposes set forth
   in that part of these Laws under the
   heading of "The Fund of Scottish
   Masonic Benevolence";

2. As regards a Provincial or District
   Grand Lodge, or the Metropolitan
   District—its Benevolent Fund, constituted as provided in Law 140 and
   its Bye-Laws, if any;

3. As regards a Daughter Lodge—its
   Benevolent Fund constituted as pro-
   vided by Law 189 and its special
   Bye-Laws.

"*Bye-Laws*" means the General Bye-Laws
set forth in the Second Schedule to these
Laws and all Bye-Laws regularly enacted,
revised and approved as provided by Law 161.

*"Committee of Benevolence"* means the Committee for the administration of The Fund of Scottish Masonic Benevolence of Grand Lodge, constituted as provided in Law 221.

*Computation of time—*

1. "Clear days' notice" excludes the day on which the notice is dispatched or published and the day for which notice is given.

2. "Days' notice" excludes the day on which the notice is dispatched or published, but includes the day for which notice is given.

3. "One month" means at least 28 days.

4. "Three months" means at least 89 days, but as regards Grand Lodge includes the period of time intervening between any two Quarterly Communications.

5. "Twelve months" means 365 days, or 366 days in a Leap Year.

*"Daughter Lodge"* or *"Lodge"* means any Lodge now or hereafter holding of Grand Lodge.

*"District Grand Lodge"* means any District Grand Lodge, now or hereafter holding of

Grand Lodge, entrusted with the supervision, guidance and control, on behalf of Grand Lodge, of a Masonic District erected or to be erected by Grand Lodge.

*"Good Standing"* means, both as regards Lodges and Members, clear of all dues and fees payable to Grand Lodge, Grand Committee, Provincial and District Grand Lodges, the Metropolitan District, and Daughter Lodges, or as the case may be, and free from Masonic sentence.

*"Grand Committee"* means the Committee constituted as provided in Law 88 for the management of the affairs entrusted to it by these Laws or delegated to it by Grand Lodge.

*"Grand Lodge"* means The Grand Lodge of Antient Free and Accepted Masons of Scotland.

*"Judgment"* includes finding, decision, sentence, and admonition.

*"Masonic Grand Body"* means a Sister Grand Lodge and any other Grand Body from time to time officially recognised as Masonic by, and in amity with, Grand Lodge.

"*Masonic Sentence*" includes suspension, expulsion, and recall or forfeiture of Charter.

"*Metropolitan District Committee*" means the Committee entrusted with the supervision, guidance and control, on behalf of Grand Lodge, of the Lodges in the Metropolitan District.

"*Provincial Grand Lodge*" means any Provincial Grand Lodge, now or hereafter holding of Grand Lodge, entrusted with the supervision, guidance and control, on behalf of Grand Lodge, of a Masonic Province in Scotland, erected or to be erected by Grand Lodge.

"*Qualified Brother*" or "*Qualified Member*" does not include Honorary Member, as such. It means—

1. As regards a Daughter Lodge—a Master Mason of such Lodge (or a Master Mason affiliated thereto for at least fourteen days) in good standing, and who has been registered as a Master Mason in the Books of Grand Lodge.

2. As regards a Provincial or District Grand Lodge—a member thereof, as constituted by Law 116, who is a qualified member of a Daughter

Lodge in good standing in such Province or District, and who is in good standing with such Provincial or District Grand Lodge;

3. As regards Grand Lodge—a member thereof, as constituted by Law 1, who is a qualified member of a Daughter Lodge in good standing with Grand Lodge (and—if a Provincial or District Grand Master, or a Past Provincial or District Grand Master—is also a qualified member of his Provincial or District Grand Lodge), and who is in good standing with Grand Lodge.

"*Scottish Craft*" means The Antient Free and Accepted Masons of Scotland.

"*Sentence*" (see "*Masonic Sentence*").

"*Sister Grand Lodge*" means any other Grand Lodge of Freemasons from time to time officially recognised as such by, and in amity with, Grand Lodge.

"*Standing Orders*" means such of these Laws and such Bye-Laws as relate to the manner in which business is to be conducted.

"*These Laws*" means The Constitution and Laws of Grand Lodge, and relative Schedules, as enacted by Grand Lodge from time to time. A reference in these Laws to a Law or a Schedule, followed or preceded by a cardinal or an ordinal number, shall be a sufficient reference to the Law or Schedule in question.

*Words* used in the singular include the plural, and *vice versa*.

———————

# FIRST SCHEDULE.

## FEES AND OTHER SUMS ENACTED
## OR AUTHORISED BY THE FOREGOING LAWS.

*Notes.*—(1) All sums in Part I. of this Schedule are payable to
the Income of the General Fund unless otherwise
stated. They are payable in British Sterling
currency.

(2) Abbreviations used in Part I. of this Schedule.—
Gen. Fd. = General Fund; Ben. Fd. = Fund of
Scottish Masonic Benevolence; G. A. Fd. = General
Annuity Fund; O. A. Fd. = Orphan Annuity
Fund; cap. = capital; inc. = income.

## PART I.—SUMS PAYABLE TO GRAND LODGE.

ITEM.

**Test of Membership** (payable annually).

1    (Law 74)    Each Member of Grand Lodge
other than representatives of
Daughter Lodges (including
copy of Printed Proceedings
of Grand Lodge) . . . £0    5    0

**Provincial and District Grand Masters.**

2    (Law 114) Commission . . . 10 10    0
3    (Law 115) Each Renewal of Commission 2    2    0

**New Lodges.**

4    (Law 147) Charter . . . 10 10    0
5    (Law 147) Each Founder Member—
(a) If Member of a Daughter
Lodge—for registration
and Diploma . . 0    5    0

| ITEM. | | | | |
|---|---|---|---|---|
| 5 *(continued)* | (b) If Member of another Constitution . . . | | 1 10 | 0 |

To be allocated as follows—
(1) For registration and Diplomas £1 0 6
(2) Ben. Fd. (inc.) 0 4 6
(3) O.A. Fd. (cap.) 0 2 6
(4) O.A. Fd. (inc.) 0 2 6

£1 10 0

**6    Daughter Lodges.**

(Law 154) Annual Dues for Certificate, Representation Fees, and four copies of Printed Proceedings      1 10 0

To be allocated as follows—
(1) Gen. Fd. (inc.) £1 0 0
(2) Ben. Fd. (inc.) 0 10 0

£1 10 0

7    (Law 70) If represented by Proxy—additional Fee for recording Commission or Appointment of
(1) Each Proxy Master .      0 2 6
(2) Each Proxy Warden .      0 1 0

8    (Law 185) For each Intrant (Lodge No. 0, 1/– less) . . .      0 15 0

To be allocated as follows—
(1) For Diploma . £0 5 0
(2) For registration (Lodge No. 0, 1/– less) . 0 5 6
(2) Ben. Fd. (inc.) 0 4 6

£0 15 0

and

| ITEM. | | | | | |
|---|---|---|---|---|---|
| 8 *(continued)* | | By Lodges in Scotland—<br>1/- per £ (or per £1, 1/-) of Admission Fee of each Intrant, payable to O. A. Fd. and divisible equally between cap. and inc. thereof. | | | | |
| 9 | (Law 185) | For each Affiliate—<br>(a) If already registered in Grand Lodge Books—<br>For registration and Diploma | o | 5 | o |
| | | (b) If not so registered—<br>The like sums to those payable for each Intrant, set forth at Item 8, above. | | | |
| 10 | (Law 160) | Registration of each Mark Master, including Diploma | o | 2 | 6 |

**New Members of Daughter Lodges.**

| 11 | (Law 185) | Contribution payable by each Intrant, and by each Affiliate from another Constitution | o | 5 | o |
|---|---|---|---|---|---|

**Installed Masters.**

| 12 | (Law 85) | Registration and Diploma | o | 2 | 6 |
|---|---|---|---|---|---|

**Past Grand Office-Bearers, etc.**

| 13 | (Law 13) | Certificate of Service | o | 5 | o |
|---|---|---|---|---|---|

**General.**

| 14 | (Law 148) | Duplicate Charter | 2 | 2 | o |
|---|---|---|---|---|---|
| 15 | (Law 86) | Duplicate or Amended Diploma | o | 5 | o |
| 16 | (Law 87) | Dispensation by Grand Master Mason | 1 | 1 | o |
| 17 | (Law 156) | Book of 12 Demits | o | 2 | 6 |

| Item. | | | | | |
|---|---|---|---|---|---|
| 18 | (Law 15) | Copies of Printed Proceedings of Grand Lodge, per annum, each . . . . . | 0 | 5 | 0 |

Note.—The above Proceedings are available to any Freemason at the sum specified above.

## Papers in Process.

| 19 | (Law 107) | Lodging Petitions, Complaints, Answers, Appeals, or other Pleadings, each . . . | 0 | 5 | 0 |
|---|---|---|---|---|---|
| | | Each borrowing of process or productions . . . . | 0 | 1 | 0 |
| | | Each return of process or productions . . . . | 0 | 1 | 0 |
| | | Extracts or copies of papers or proceedings— | | | |
| | | (a) First sheet of 250 words or less . . . . | 0 | 2 | 6 |
| | | (b) Each subsequent sheet of 250 words or less . . | 0 | 1 | 6 |

## Constitution and Laws.

| 20 | (Law 77) | Complete Edition. |
|---|---|---|
| 21 | (Law 165) | Abridged Edition. |

(Both as may be fixed by Grand Committee.)

**Fees of Honour** (payable annually to the Ben. Fd. and in addition to Test of Membership payable to Gen. Fd.).

| 22 | (Law 2) | Grand Master Mason . | .£10 | 10 | 0 |
|---|---|---|---|---|---|
| | | Past Grand Masters . . | 5 | 5 | 0 |
| | | Depute Grand Master . | 5 | 5 | 0 |
| | | Substitute Grand Master . | 5 | 5 | 0 |
| | | Senior Grand Warden . . | 3 | 3 | 0 |
| | | Junior Grand Warden . . | 3 | 3 | 0 |
| | | Provincial or District Grand Master . . . | 3 | 3 | |

ITEM.
22
(*continued*)

|  |  |  |  |  |
|---|---|---|---|---|
| | Past Provincial or District Grand Master | . | . | . | 2 | 2 | 0 |
| | Proxy District Grand Master | . | 3 | 3 | 0 |
| | Grand Almoner . | . | . | 2 | 2 | 0 |
| | Senior Grand Chaplain . | . | 1 | 1 | 0 |
| | Junior Grand Chaplain . | . | 1 | 1 | 0 |
| | Senior Grand Deacon | . | . | 2 | 2 | 0 |
| | Junior Grand Deacon | . | . | 2 | 2 | 0 |
| | Grand Director of Ceremonies | 1 | 1 | 0 |
| | Grand Architect . | . | . | 1 | 1 | 0 |
| (Law 2) | Grand Jeweller . | . | . | 1 | 1 | 0 |
| | Grand Bible-Bearer | . | . | 1 | 1 | 0 |
| | Grand Bard . | . | . | 1 | 1 | 0 |
| | Grand Sword-Bearer | . | . | 1 | 1 | 0 |
| | Grand Director of Music | . | 1 | 1 | 0 |
| | Grand Marshal . | . | . | 1 | 1 | 0 |
| | Grand Inner Guard | . | . | 1 | 1 | 0 |
| | President of Grand Stewards (in addition to Fee as Grand Steward) . | . | . | 0 | 10 | 6 |

| (Law 28) | Vice-President of Grand Stewards (in addition to Fee as Grand Steward) . | . | 0 | 10 | 6 |
|---|---|---|---|---|---|
| (Law 27) | Each Grand Steward . | . | 0 | 12 | 6 |

**Other Sums.**

23      (Law 171) Collections for Annuity Funds—
                    To be allocated as follows—
                    G. A. Fd. (cap.) . . .          50 %
                    O. A. Fd. (cap.) . . .          25 %
                    O. A. Fd. (inc.) . . .          25 %

PART II.—Sums exigible by Provincial
and District Grand Lodges and in
the Metropolitan District.

ITEM.

## A. By all Provinces and Districts, including Metropolitan District.

**From Daughter Lodges.**

1    (Law 140) (a) For necessary purposes—
     (1) Minimum annual sum . £1 0 0
     (2) In respect of each Initiate
     or Affiliate, maximum
     sum . . . 0 5 0
     (b) For Benevolent Fund—
     In respect of each Initiate or
     Affiliate, maximum sum 0 5 0

## B. By Provincial and District Grand Lodges only.

**Test of Membership** (payable annually).

2    (Law 141) As may be fixed by each Provincial or
District Grand Lodge.

**Commutation Fee** (optional).

3    (Law 141) Minimum sum :—10 times amount of
annual fee. To be kept as a separate
Fund. Not more than 10 % of sum at
credit of that Fund at end of each
financial year may be withdrawn to form
part of membership fees for that year.

**Fees of Honour.**

(Law 141) As may be fixed by each Provincial or
District Grand Lodge.

ITEM. **Papers in Process.**

5  (Law 131) One half of fees specified in Part I., Item 19, of this Schedule.

## C. By District Grand Lodges only.

### From Daughter Lodges.

6  (Law 142) Annual sum for each contributing Member;

Single sum for each Member whose annual contributions are commuted;

Dispensations;

Revision of Bye-Laws;

Other administrative acts;

(all as may be fixed by District Grand Lodge).

### District Grand Office-Bearers' Certificates.

7  (Law 142) As may be fixed by District Grand Lodge.

## PART III.—SUMS EXIGIBLE BY DAUGHTER LODGES.

| ITEM. | | |
|---|---|---|
| | **Initiation Fee.** | |
| 1 | (Law 183) Minimum Fee . . . £5 5 0 | |
| | **Affiliation Fee.** | |
| 2 | (Law 183) Minimum Fee . . . 2 2 0 | |
| | **Mark.** | |
| 3 | (Law 160) (a) Maximum fee under special Bye-Laws . . . 0 10 6 | |

or

(b) For Registration and Diploma, if no special fee . 0 2 6

**Annual Contribution (Test Fee).**

4   (Law 187) Minimum . . . . 0 2 6

**Commutation Fee** (optional).

5   (Law 188) Minimum sum;—10 times amount of annual contribution. To be kept as separate Fund. Not more than 10 % of sum at credit of that Fund at end of each financial year may be withdrawn to form part of membership fees for that year.

**Benevolent Fund.**

6   (Laws 187 Not less than 1/- from each annual contribution, and 189) tribution, and corresponding proportion of sum withdrawn annually from Commutation Fees Fund.

**Dispensation by Grand Master Mason.**

7   (Law 87) The fee payable to Grand Lodge, specified in Part I., Item 16, of this Schedule.

**Other Sums.**

8   (Law 161) As may be fixed by special Bye-Laws.

K

* See Laws 161,
  165, and 272.

# *SECOND SCHEDULE.

## INTRODUCTION.

In terms of Grand Lodge Law, No. 161, the Laws of Grand Lodge, the General Bye-Laws set forth herein, and any special Bye-Laws which may be enacted by any Lodge, shall be its Bye-Laws. For reference, the various sections of this Schedule are indexed with the general index to the Constitution and Laws under the heading of "Daughter Lodges."

## I. MEETINGS.

**Emergency and Special Meetings.**—An Emergency Meeting for conferring Degrees may be called at any time by the Master; or, in his absence, by the Immediate Past Master, the Depute Master, or the Substitute Master. A Special Meeting for any other purpose may be called in the same manner, or on a requisition, stating the purpose of the Meeting, signed by seven or more qualified members, addressed to the Secretary, who shall immediately communicate the same to the Master. A Special

Meeting must be convened by Circular stating or Advertisement indicating the particular business for which it is called, and no other business shall be entered upon.

## II. OFFICE-BEARERS.

1. Any recommendation of Office-Bearers made by a Committee shall not prejudice the right of the members of the Lodge to nominate any brother for any elective office. No brother may be nominated in his absence, unless his consent has been previously obtained and vouched for by a qualified brother.

2. At the Election of Office-Bearers and Committees for purely Masonic purposes, the vote may be taken by ballot or by a show of hands, as the Lodge shall decide.

3. **Vacancies in Office.**—In the event of the death, resignation, or disqualification, of the Master, the duties of the office shall devolve upon the Immediate Past Master; and in the like event with regard to any other elected Office-Bearer, the Lodge may, at the next, or any subsequent Regular Meeting, elect a brother to fill the vacant office till next Annual Election, due notice being given to all qualified members.

**4. Absence of Office-Bearers.**—Any Office-Bearer, the Master excepted, absenting himself from three Regular Meetings of the Lodge consecutively shall be communicated with by the Secretary, and should no reason for his absence satisfactory to the Lodge be given, the Lodge may declare the office vacant, and elect another brother to it, as provided for in the foregoing Sub-section 3.

**5. The Master.**—The Master shall preside over every Meeting of the Lodge and Committees thereof. In all divisions he shall have a deliberative vote, and in case of equality a casting vote also. In his absence, the Chair shall be occupied as prescribed in Grand Lodge Law, No. 174. At Committee Meetings the same order of precedence shall be followed except in cases of Special Committees when another brother shall have been appointed to preside in the Master's absence.

**6. The Secretary.**—It shall be the duty of the Secretary to issue the Notices calling all Meetings of the Lodge and Committees thereof, attend all such Meetings, keep regular and distinct records of the proceedings, engross them in the Minute Book, read the Minutes at the next Regular Meeting of the Lodge, and make due returns to Grand Lodge and

Provincial or District Grand Lodge. He shall be custodier of all Books and Documents belonging to the Lodge, except the Charter (which is the Master's special care) and the Treasurer's Cash and other Books and Vouchers, and shall keep an inventory of the same.

7. **The Treasurer.**—The Treasurer shall collect, and shall be custodier of, all monies belonging to the Lodge. He shall be provided with Books, wherein he shall keep a correct account of his whole intromissions with the funds of the Lodge. He shall keep a Bank Account for each Fund in the name of the Lodge, to be operated upon by the Master and Secretary, and the Treasurer for the time being of the Fund, or any two of them, one of whom should be the Treasurer, if available. Deposit receipts shall be similarly endorsed when uplifted. The Treasurer shall not retain in his hands at any time more than Five Pounds of the Lodge Funds. He shall pay all Grand Lodge and Provincial or District Grand Lodge dues, irrespective of any order from the Lodge or the Committee thereof, and all other claims after being sanctioned by the Lodge and initialled by the Master or the brother who presides in his absence. He may be called upon at

any time by the Committee for an account of his intromissions. At the end of each financial year, he shall close his books and prepare an Abstract Statement of Receipts and Expenditure and a Balance Sheet, for submission to the Auditors. On being docquetted or certified by them, the Abstract Statement of Accounts, with the Balance Sheet, shall be published and submitted to the qualified members in accordance with the provisions of the Special Bye-Laws of the Lodge. This Sub-Section shall also apply to any Benevolent Fund Treasurer or Almoner.

## III. COMMITTEES.

1. **General Committee.**—A General Committee for the management of the affairs of the Lodge shall be elected annually at the Election Meeting, and shall consist of such Office-Bearers and members as the Lodge may determine by its Special Bye-Laws, with power to delegate to sub-committees of their own number. The election must be completed at that Meeting and cannot be adjourned.

2. **Special Committees.**—Special Committees may be appointed from time to time as occasion may require.

3. Four shall form a quorum at Meetings of the General Committee and the Committee of Enquiry; and the quorum of other Committees shall be fixed by the Lodge.

4. The transactions of all Committees shall be reported at the next regular meeting of the Lodge for the information and approval of the brethren.

## IV. ORDER OF BUSINESS.

1. At each Regular Meeting of the Lodge, including the Annual Meeting, the Minutes of the previous Regular Meeting and of all subsequent Emergency and Special Meetings shall be read and, after confirmation, shall be signed by the presiding brother and the Secretary. Reports from Committees shall then be considered, and thereafter the other business as stated in the Circular or Advertisement calling the Meeting or otherwise competent shall be proceeded with.

2. Any brother desirous of speaking shall rise and remain standing during his speech, addressing himself to the Master or other presiding brother, and observing due order and decorum. No brother shall speak more than once on the same subject without permission

from the presiding brother, unless in explanation, or, as mover of a proposition, in reply.

3. All questions shall be decided by a majority of the qualified members present who vote, taken by a show of hands or by ballot if the Lodge should so decide, with the exception of the disposal of the Lodge Funds, or an alteration of the Special Bye-Laws of the Lodge, which are specially provided for.

4. All business shall be transacted in the Entered Apprentice Degree, with the exception of the Election of Office-Bearers and Committees for purely Masonic purposes.

5. The Master, or other presiding brother, shall decide all points of order not provided for in these Bye-Laws, but the power of deciding as to the interpretation of a Law or Bye-Law shall be vested in the Meeting and not in the Chair.

## V. PROPERTY AND FUNDS.

1. The whole Property of the Lodge, heritable and moveable, of whatever description, except cash in Bank, shall be vested in such Office-Bearers and members as the Lodge may from time to time determine, and their

successors in office, in trust for and subject to the directions and control of the Lodge. The Trustees shall insure the property of the Lodge against loss or damage by fire and/or burglary for such sums as they may consider necessary.

2. The Ordinary Funds shall be applied in defraying the necessary expenses of the Lodge and providing and maintaining the Clothing and Jewels of the Lodge.

3. A motion for disposing of any part of the Lodge Property or Funds for extraordinary purposes shall not be made unless a notice of such motion shall have been tabled at a Meeting at least one month previously. A copy of the motion shall appear in the Circular or a distinct reference to it shall appear in the Advertisement calling the Meeting at which it falls to be considered, and it must be approved by at least two-thirds of the qualified members present before it can be adopted.

4. A motion, the substance of which the Lodge has already considered and decided upon, shall not be again brought forward or otherwise discussed until after the lapse of twelve months from the date of such decision.

## VI. ANNUAL CONTRIBUTION.

1. Any brother in arrear with his Annual Contribution shall not be entitled to receive Notices calling the Meetings.

## VII. ADMISSION OF MEMBERS.

1. Any applicant excluded upon a ballot shall not be eligible to be proposed again until after the expiry of one year from the date of the ballot. A member or visiting brother shall not attempt to discover what brother or brothers oppose the admission of any applicant.

2. Brethren of other Lodges who are distinguished for their zeal in Freemasonry may be admitted Honorary Members of the Lodge on being duly proposed by the Master and accepted at any Regular Meeting. Honorary Members shall be entitled to all the privileges of Ordinary Members, except those of holding office or of speaking or voting on Lodge business.

## VIII. DEMEANOUR IN LODGE.

1. On the Master or other presiding brother calling to order, there shall be immediate silence. All brethren shall keep their places, except those Office-Bearers who require to

move about in discharge of their duties. No brother shall enter, or retire from, the Lodge without paying due respect to the Chair.

2. Should any brother behave in such a manner as to disturb the harmony of the Lodge and persist in such conduct after being admonished from the Chair, the Master or other presiding brother may order him to retire, and that order shall be obeyed forthwith.

## IX. VISITORS.

A brother shall not be introduced into the Lodge as a visitor unless he has been regularly vouched for by a Master Mason known to an Office-Bearer of the Lodge: or until he has produced his Grand Lodge Diploma, or other evidence of membership in writing signed by the Secretary or the Treasurer of his Lodge, and has been examined by two brethren appointed by the Master, or other presiding brother, for the purpose, and they submit a favourable report and recommend his admission.

## X. ALTERATIONS.

A motion for the abrogation or alteration of any of the Special Bye-Laws of the Lodge, or for any addition thereto, shall not be

considered unless at least one month's previous
notice of such motion be given at a Regular
Meeting of the Lodge, and the Circular calling
the Meeting at which it falls to be considered
contains a copy of it, or the Advertisement
calling the Meeting, contains a distinct reference to it.   If the proposed alteration be
approved by at least two-thirds of the
qualified members present who vote, and
afterwards be confirmed by the Provincial
or District Grand Lodge (if any) and by
Grand Committee, it shall come into full
force and operation.

## XI. GENERAL.

In any case for which the foregoing Lodge
Bye-Laws or the Special Bye-Laws do not
provide, the Laws of Grand Lodge shall be
binding on all concerned.

# APPENDIX

AIMS AND RELATIONSHIPS OF THE CRAFT.

From time to time the Grand Lodge of Scotland has deemed it desirable to set forth in precise form the aims of Freemasonry as consistently practised under its jurisdiction since it came into being as an organised body in 1736, and also to define the principles governing its relations with those other Grand Lodges with which it is in fraternal accord.

In view of representations which have been received, and of statements recently issued which have distorted or obscured the true objects of Freemasonry, it is once again considered necessary to emphasise certain fundamental principles of the Order.

The first condition of admission into, and membership of, the Order is a belief in the Supreme Being. This is essential and admits of no compromise.

The Bible, referred to by Freemasons as the Volume of the Sacred Law, is always

open in the Lodges. Every candidate is
required to take his obligation on that Book
or on the Volume which is held by his
particular Creed to impart sanctity to an
oath or promise taken upon it.

Everyone who enters Freemasonry is, at
the outset, strictly forbidden to countenance
any act which may have a tendency to
subvert the peace and good order of society;
he must pay due obedience to the law of
any State in which he resides or which may
afford him protection, and he must never be
remiss in the allegiance due to the Sovereign
of his native land.

While Scottish Freemasonry thus incul-
cates in each of its members the duties of
loyalty and citizenship, it reserves to the
individual the right to hold his own opinion
with regard to public affairs. But neither in
any Lodge nor at any time in his capacity
as a Freemason is he permitted to discuss
or to advance his views on theological or
political questions.

The Grand Lodge has always consistently
refused to express any opinion on questions
of foreign or domestic state policy either at
home or abroad, and it will not allow its
name to be associated with any action, how-

ever humanitarian it may appear to be, which infringes its unalterable policy of standing aloof from every question affecting the relations between one Government and another, or between political parties, or questions as to rival theories of government.

The Grand Lodge is aware that there do exist bodies styling themselves Freemasons, which do not adhere to these principles, and while that attitude exists the Grand Lodge of Scotland refuses absolutely to have any relations with such bodies or to regard them as Freemasons.

The Grand Lodge of Scotland is a sovereign and independent body practising Freemasonry only within the three Degrees and only within the limits defined in its Constitution. It does not recognise or admit the existence of any superior Masonic authority however styled.

On more than one occasion the Grand Lodge has refused, and it will continue to refuse, to participate in conferences with so-called International Associations claiming to represent Freemasonry, which admit to membership bodies failing to conform strictly to the principles upon which the Grand Lodge of Scotland is founded. The Grand Lodge does not admit any such claim, nor can its views be represented by any such Association.

There is no secret with regard to any of the basic principles of Freemasonry some of which have been stated above. The Grand Lodge will always consider the recognition of those Grand Lodges which profess and practise, and can show that they have consistently professed and practised, those established and unaltered principles, but in no circumstances will it enter into discussion with a view to any new or varied interpretation of them. They must be accepted and practised whole-heartedly and in their entirety by those who desire to be recognised as Freemasons by the Grand Lodge of Scotland.

---

# CHARGES READ AT INSTALLATION

The Charges read at the Installation of the Master of a Lodge:—

"1. You agree to be a good man and true, and strictly to obey the moral law.

"2. You agree to be a peaceable subject, and to conform to the laws of the country in which you reside.

"3. You promise not to be concerned in plots or conspiracies against the Government, but to submit patiently to the decisions of the Supreme Legislature.

"4. You agree to pay a proper respect to the Civil Magistrate, to work diligently, live creditably, and act honourably towards all men.

"5. You agree to hold in veneration the original Rulers and Patrons of the Order of Freemasonry, and their regular successors, supreme and subordinate, according to their stations, and to submit to the awards and resolutions of your brethren in Grand Lodge assembled, in every case consistent with the Constitutions of the Order; and that you will not practise or recognise in connection with Lodges any Degrees except those of Apprentice, Fellow-Craft (including the Mark), and Master Mason, and the ceremony of Installed Master.

"6. You agree to avoid private quarrels, and to guard against all intemperance and excess.

"7. You agree to be cautious in your behaviour, courteous to your brethren, and faithful to your Lodge.

L

"8. You promise to respect true and faithful brethren, and to discountenance all Imposters and Dissenters from the original plan of the Institution.

"9. You agree to promote the general good of Society, to cultivate the social virtues, and to propagate the knowledge of the art of Freemasonry, so far as your influence and ability can extend.

"10. You admit that it is not in the power of any man, or body of men, to make alteration or innovation in Freemasonry.

"11. You promise to submit to the Most Worshipful the Grand Master Mason, for the time being, and to his Office-Bearers, when duly installed; and strictly to conform to every regulation of Grand Lodge that is not subversive of the principles of Freemasonry.

"12. You admit that no Lodge can be constituted without a Charter from a Grand Lodge, or other supreme body with similar powers, and that no countenance be given to an Irregular Lodge, or to any person clandestinely initiated therein; and that no Procession, Consecration, or other Ceremonial of Freemasons, clothed with the badges of the Order, can take place without the special permission of Grand Lodge, or of the Provincial or District Grand Master of the Province or District, or, in his absence, of his Depute or his Substitute.

"13. You admit that no person can be regularly made a Freemason or admitted a member of any Lodge, without previous notice, and due inquiry into his character.

"14. You promise that no Visitors shall be received into your Lodge without due examination, or producing proper vouchers of initiation in a regular Lodge."

# INDEX

NOTE.—The references are to the *numbers* of the "Laws," except where "p." is prefixed to figures. In the latter case the references are to pages of the Schedules.